El Paso and West Texas........ **362**
El Paso......................... 367
Guadalupe Mountains National Park.. 384
Midland and Odessa.............. 388

Big Bend Region **397**
Big Bend National Park and Vicinity... 401
Marfa and Vicinity 418

Panhandle Plains.............. **433**
Lubbock 438
Amarillo and Vicinity.............. 446
Abilene 458
San Angelo 465

Background **47**
The Landscape 470
Plants and Animals 473
Climate 477

History........................... 479
Government and Economy......... 482
People and Culture 484

Essentials **492**
Transportation................... 492
Sports and Recreation............ 495
Food 498
Travel Tips 500
Health and Safety 501
Information and Services 502

.... **503**
.... 503
.... 505

.... **506**

.... **520**

T0204482

Although every effort was made to make sure the information in this book was accurate when going to press, research was impacted by the COVID-19 pandemic. Some things may have changed during this crisis and the recovery that followed. Be sure to confirm specific details when making your travel plans.

TEXAS

ANDY RHODES

Contents

Discover Texas **6**
    10 Top Experiences 10
    Planning Your Trip 18
    The Best of Texas 23
    • Barbecue as a Way of Life 25
    Remember the Alamo! 27
    Family Fun 28
    • Best Scenic Drives 30

Dallas and Fort Worth **31**
    Dallas 36
    Vicinity of Dallas 60
    Fort Worth 68
    Vicinity of Fort Worth 89
    Wichita Falls 94

Austin and the Hill Country ... **97**
    Austin 102
    Vicinity of Austin 135
    Waco 145
    The Hill Country 151

**San Antonio and
    South Texas** **167**
    San Antonio and Vicinity 172
    Del Rio 208
    Laredo 214
    Rio Grande Valley 222

Houston and East Texas **234**
    Houston 239
    Vicinity of Houston 275
    Piney Woods 279

The Gulf Coast **303**
    Galveston 308
    Brazosport Area 326
    Corpus Christi 330
    Mustang Island 343
    Kingsville 348
    South Padre Island 352

DISCOVER

Texas

Y ou can't talk about Texas without mentioning size. It's enormous. It's colossal. It's just a big ol' place. And it's not just flat and dry—Texas is geographically diverse, with mountains, tropics, pine forests, beaches, and prairies within its borders. Toss in an eclectic mix of regional cuisine, national parks, and real-life cowboys and you'll find a rich experience representative of Texas's distinct character.

Texas has an unmatched independent spirit. Its people, like its landscapes, are rugged, captivating, and endearing. The one element that ropes them all together is an immense Texas pride. The Lone Star State's mystique is enormous, and for good reason—Texas is practically a country unto itself.

The proud residents of this vibrant state manage to reflect and defy the stereotypes associated with them. For every good ol' boy who's set in his ways, there's a progressive genius building her Web-based empire. For every brash oilman making millions, there's a humble educator affecting lives. Like anywhere else, people in Texas have their differences, but there's one thing that transcends obstacles that is wholly unique to this state—the common bond of being Texan.

Clockwise from top left: the Texas State Capitol in Austin; tacos in Brownsville; M. L. Leddy's Boots & Saddlery in Fort Worth; the stockyards in Fort Worth; a chapel in South Texas; Willie Nelson performing in Amarillo

This spirit is evident in the Panhandle plains, where chicken-fried steak is served at diners along old Route 66, and in the Hill Country, where Texas troubadours play beer-soaked blues guitar on the Luckenbach stage, and all over the Rio Grande Valley, where Lone Star flags are as abundant as the bountiful groves of grapefruit trees.

Friday Night Lights, barbecued beef ribs, Austin City Limits, Chisholm Trail cowboys—you can't swing a piñata stick in Texas without encountering a cultural icon, and there's plenty more to discover: Excavated shipwrecks, Spanish missions, majestic courthouses, cattle drives, oil booms, and JFK's assassination all occurred under the state's legendary six flags.

You could spend a year exploring the natural and cultural wonders of Texas and still find yourself with dozens of destinations remaining on your must-see list—all certain to become unforgettable memories.

Clockwise from top left: Denton County Courthouse near Dallas; the Texas Gulf Coast; traditional Tex-Mex on San Antonio's River Walk; historic Brownsville Museum

10 TOP EXPERIENCES

1 **Follow the Rio Grande:** Everything about **Big Bend National Park** is vast—the sky, the views, the mountains, the canyons, and especially the sense of wonder (page 401).

> ˄
> ˄ ˄
> ˄ ˄
> **2** **See the Sea:** Get away to the longest remaining undeveloped stretch of barrier island in the world at **Padre Island National Seashore** (page 343).

3 **Take in Historic Views:** Enjoy the stunning panorama from atop the 570-foot-tall monument that commemorates the **San Jacinto Battleground,** a triumphant battle site where Texas earned its independence (page 254).

4 **Listen to Live Music:** Austin, the "Live Music Capital of the World," delivers the goods nightly. Catch a scruffy troubadour in a dive bar, a soulful blues guitarist at a historic club, or a global legend at festivals like South by Southwest and Austin City Limits (page 117).

5 **Experience Cowboy Culture:** Hear the distinctive clip-clop of longhorn hooves on **Fort Worth**'s brick streets (page 70), or watch a genuine cowboy herd cattle at the iconic **King Ranch** (page 349).

6 **Taste Texas Cuisine:** Texas's holy trinity of cuisine—barbecue (page 25), Tex-Mex (page 192), and Southern (page 283)—provide a culinary journey. Why choose between smoky beef brisket, spicy chile dishes, and chicken-fried steak when you can try them all?

7 **Explore Space:** Feel your goosebumps rise as you gaze upon the awe-inspiring original Mission Control Center at the **NASA Space Center** (page 252).

8 **Hike a Colorful Canyon:** The stratified colors of America's second-largest canyon are stunning. Sheer cliffs and rock towers display hues of red, yellow, and orange at **Palo Duro Canyon State Park** (page 456).

9 **Celebrate Presidential Legacies:** Downtown Dallas's **Sixth Floor Museum** brings JFK's powerful political career into focus (page 39). **Lyndon B. Johnson National Historic Park** offers insight about the humble Hill Country roots of the 36th president (page 160).

>>>

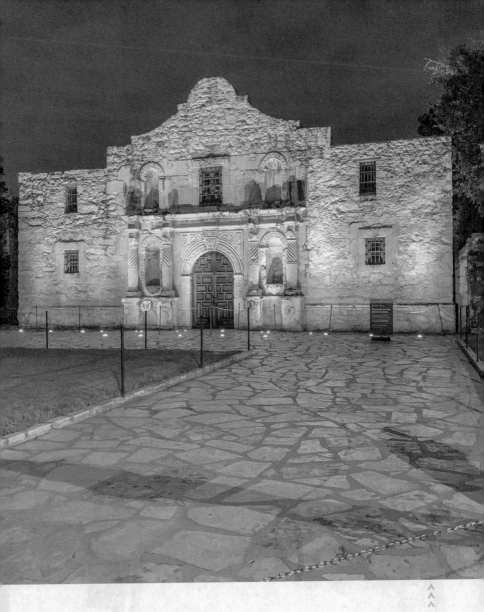

10 **Remember the Alamo:** Inside the Shrine of Texas Liberty's hallowed halls, you'll learn the meaning of Texas pride (page 175).

Planning Your Trip

Where to Go

Dallas and Fort Worth

The towering twin cities of Dallas and Fort Worth are only separated by 35 miles (56 km), but their cultural differences are extensive, offering travelers the best of both worlds—**glitz and grit,** the Big D and Cowtown, the Old South and the Wild West. Though dominated by the Metroplex, North Texas is also home to a large concentration of **rivers, lakes,** and **charming small towns.**

Austin and the Hill Country

Dubbed the **"Live Music Capital of the World,"** Austin is Texas's mecca for music. Home to the **University of Texas at Austin,** the city is a hotbed for creative thinkers. With a decade-plus atop the nation's fastest-growing population lists, Austin boasts countless new entrepreneurial endeavors, especially culinary destinations. Geographically, this region is marked by a convergence of the cotton-rich **Blackland Prairie** and the granite outcroppings of the **Hill Country;** culturally, it's known for its **German heritage,** honky-tonks, and **Magnolia,** based in Waco.

San Antonio and South Texas

Most of South Texas is defined and unified by its **Tejano heritage.** The majority of the region's culture is tied to Mexico, including the legendary **Alamo,** constructed with four other San Antonio missions in the early 1700s to expand Spain's control of the New World. Tejano heritage is concentrated in **South Texas,** where the border towns of **Laredo, Del Rio,** and **Brownsville** offer a taste of Mexico with a uniquely Texan twist.

San Antonio's Mission San José

Houston and East Texas

With historic **oil boomtowns,** five **national forests,** and the megalopolis of Houston, this enormous region is an ideal place to experience the legacy of the Lone Star State. East Texas has a distinct **Southern bayou** influence, reflected in the food, heritage, and even the accents. Standing apart is Houston, the fourth-largest city in the country and home to **NASA,** oil-related industries, and some of the most preeminent restaurants, museums, and humidity in the nation.

The Gulf Coast

Stretching 350 miles (560 km) along the Gulf of Mexico, this region's **moderate beaches and waves** draw casual beachcombers, salty anglers, and frolicking families. The biggest city on the gulf, **Corpus Christi,** offers plenty of recreational activities to accommodate a quick weekend getaway and the ubiquitous Winter Texans. Once a year, students from across the country invade **South Padre Island** for a rollicking spring break, but otherwise, the region remains as **low-key** as the gulf's lightly lapping waves.

El Paso and West Texas

This region is what most people envision when they hear the word *Texas*—hot and dry with an occasional cactus or cow skull. The **Wild West spirit** thrives in sunbaked cities like **El Paso** and **Midland,** and the **Guadalupe Mountains National Park** offers stunning views of colorful canyon walls and rugged outcroppings. Local cuisine reflects the personality of the region,

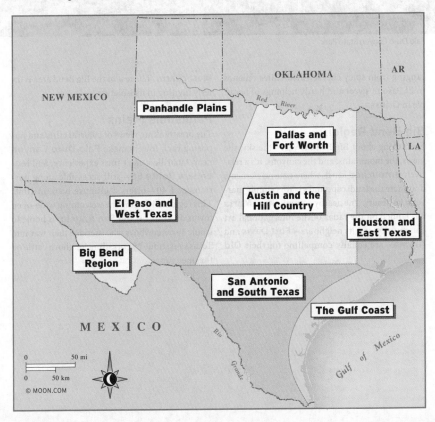

Palo Duro Canyon State Park

ranging from spicy cheese-filled chiles rellenos in El Paso to sweet and hardy helpings of pecan pie in **Odessa.**

Big Bend Region

Everything about Big Bend is vast—the sky, the views, the mountains, and the canyons. It's a relatively **untouched land,** where natural elements dominate the landscape and visitors simply marvel at its beauty. The nearby community of **Marfa** has landed on the radar of the international art community, and its neighbors—**Fort Davis** and **Alpine**—are equally compelling for their **Old West charm.** The rest of the Big Bend area is utterly inviting in its isolation.

Panhandle Plains

The breathtaking views of colorful cliffs and imposing rock towers make **Palo Duro Canyon** near Amarillo a can't-miss experience, and **legendary Route 66**—still accessible along portions of I-40—offers a glimpse back in time. This region, including the welcoming wide-open towns of **Abilene** and **San Angelo,** is home to iconic Texas cowboys who branded their way into Texas's mystique by corralling longhorn cattle on the open range.

Know Before You Go

When to Go

Texans like to joke about their two distinct seasons: hot and less hot. **Summer** can indeed be brutal, with long stretches of 100°F-plus (38°C) temperatures, and the humidity is usually also a factor. Austin and San Antonio are mildly comfortable in the summer, but arid West Texas offers a "cool" respite thanks to the low humidity.

Many Texans take summer vacations at the Gulf Coast, but travelers prefer **spring** in Texas. One of the state's venerable springtime activities is viewing **wildflowers** throughout the state's midsection. Bluebonnets, daisies, and Indian paintbrushes turn pastures and highway medians into colossal canvases of vivid color, a compelling counterpart to northern states' fall colors.

Spring is an **optimal time to visit Texas parks.** Big Bend, the Guadalupe Mountains, and the Rio Grande Valley come alive in March-April, with migrating birds and butterflies dotting the landscape as they feed on fresh foliage. This is also a good time of the year to explore the East Texas Piney Woods—humidity isn't as oppressive as the summer months, and lakes and creeks are brimming with cool, clear water.

Fall can be variable—it often reaches 90°F (32°C) as late as November—and **winters** are surprisingly chilly, with ice storms and snow in the Panhandle and northern plains. That being said, the tropical environs of the Rio Grande Valley are a major draw for Winter Texans arriving from the chilly Midwest, who revel in the comparatively balmy 70°F (21°C) temperatures while golfing or birding.

Transportation

Texas is far removed from the transportation hubs on the East and West Coasts, but it's easily accessible by plane and relatively accessible by car. Air travel is the best option: Houston is a hub for

bluebonnets in the Hill Country

the River Road in Big Bend Ranch State Park

United Airlines, and Dallas is a hub for American Airlines. It's wise to reserve a rental car before arriving, and to specify a fuel-efficient vehicle, since you'll likely be driving a lot. If you wait to rent a vehicle on arrival, there's a good chance you'll have to choose from the remaining fleet—typically an SUV or a minivan.

In a state this big, **a vehicle is virtually a necessity,** despite some recent advances in metropolitan public transportation systems. Fortunately, the interstate highway system is impressive—you can drive between major cities (excluding El Paso) in a few hours.

The Best of Texas

Since Texas is such an enormous state, many travelers opt to focus on a manageable region to maximize their time (it can take 12 hours to drive from Houston to El Paso). Instead of scraping the surface by visiting several major cities in different areas, it's more rewarding to delve into one part of the state and soak up the local culture via regional restaurants, historic sites, and recreational activities.

The following itineraries represent an overview of Texas's most-visited regions. The accompanying sights represent the best of each region. Travelers can expect to accomplish most of the activities listed in these regional itineraries within a few days. With extra time, consider exploring another region—the first three are within a three-hour drive of each other. The Big Bend area, however, is a slightly longer detour. It's an eight-hour drive to this part of West Texas from Dallas, Austin, or San Antonio.

San Antonio, Austin, and the Hill Country

This part of the state is a magnet for those seeking a laid-back getaway. Austin and San Antonio are navigable and comfortably sized, and the equally welcoming Hill Country offers low-key recreational destinations surrounded by rolling landscapes and panoramic skies.

DAY 1

Start in **San Antonio** by visiting Texas's most famous attraction: the **Alamo.** Next, head to the nearby **River Walk** for some local scenery and a classic Tex-Mex lunch at **Casa Rio.** Afterward, visit the Alamo's historic siblings, the four other 18th-century structures that make up the **Missions National Historical Park,** or search for tempting Mexican imports and dinner in the **King William Historic District.**

a tour boat on the River Walk in San Antonio

DAY 2

Head north for 1.5 hours on I-35 to **Austin** for a day and night in Texas's creative hotbed. Visit the **State Capitol**, take a stroll down trendy **South Congress Avenue**, watch a million bats emerge from under a downtown bridge, and experience the "Live Music Capital of the World" at a hip **East Side** club.

DAYS 3-4

Plan to spend a weekend exploring the **Hill Country**, which offers all kinds of compelling options. Choose from dude ranches in **Bandera**, the **Lyndon B. Johnson National Historical Park** near Fredericksburg, or paddling or tubing on the **Frio River**.

Dallas and Fort Worth

DAY 1

Begin in **Fort Worth**, even if your hotel is in Dallas, in which case the 40-minute drive west on I-30 is still worth the effort. Go directly to the **Fort Worth Stockyards** and immerse yourself in Texas's cattle-driving heritage.

Spend the afternoon at the internationally acclaimed **Kimbell Art Museum** and **Modern Art Museum of Fort Worth** before devoting the evening to eating and nightlife at **Sundance Square**.

DAY 2

One of **Dallas's** lasting legacies is its association with President John F. Kennedy's assassination, and the **Sixth Floor Museum** deftly documents its political and cultural implications. After lunch in the **West End District** and shopping at the original **Neiman Marcus**, visit the fascinating **Perot Museum of Nature and Science** or **Fair Park**, where several museums tell the story of Texas's rich past. For dinner and drinks, be sure to visit the **Greenville Avenue** entertainment district.

Houston and the Gulf Coast

DAY 1

Head to **Houston** for an out-of-this-world experience at the **NASA Space Center**. Visit the **Museum District** to choose from 19 world-class

the Texas Capitol in Austin

downtown Dallas

Barbecue as a Way of Life

Barbecue is an art form and a lifestyle in Texas. In other places, the term *barbecue* is used informally as a general reference to tossing meat on a grill. In Texas, barbecue is a verb referencing the calculated effort of smoking specific meats with the right kind of wood for the optimal amount of time. Several different styles of barbecue are said to be the most authentic, depending on where you are. Why not try all of them and decide for yourself?

LOCKHART

Purists consider Lockhart the holy land of Texas barbecue. Hard-core aficionados insist the ideal experience is at **Kreuz Market,** where the meat is so perfectly smoked—particularly the pork chop—it would be insulting to slather it with sauce, which isn't even available. Just down the road is the amazing **Black's Barbecue,** which doesn't frown on sauce with its succulent meats. You can't go wrong with **Smitty's** or **Chisholm Trail BBQ,** which offer more traditional, equally tempting fare.

AUSTIN AND ENVIRONS

Several joints in Austin's outlying areas are nationally known for venerable and authentic 'cue (**Cooper's** in Llano, **Louie Mueller's** in Taylor, and **Southside Market** in Elgin), and the Capital City boasts its own acclaimed restaurants. Most notable is **Franklin Barbecue,** where diners regularly wait at least three hours to experience the succulent beef brisket, tender pork ribs, and flavorful sausage. **La Barbecue's** perfect pulled pork is legendary—the brisket is stellar too—and the sauce is among the best in town: a perfect combination of vinegary tang and peppery bite.

a traditional plate of Texas barbecue

WEST TEXAS

Not as acclaimed as other approaches, West Texas's open-pit cowboy-style barbecue is worth sampling. One of the best examples is at **Jack Jordan's Bar-B-Q** in Odessa, where the beef ribs reign supreme and the fiery disposition of the locals is represented in the restaurant's ample supply of jalapeños and Tabasco. While you're out roaming the range, stop by **Western Sky** in San Angelo for a tasty cowboy-style rib plate.

facilities, or for something completely distinctive, check out the bizarre folk art of **The Orange Show.**

DAYS 2-3

For a beach fix, head three hours southwest to **Corpus Christi** for a weekend of wave-based recreation, seafood, and cultural attractions (the **Texas State Aquarium,** in particular). If you're short on time, **Galveston** offers distinctive historical destinations and prime beachcombing just an hour southeast of Houston.

Big Bend Area

West Texas is quite a jaunt but worth it. The wide-open spaces and enormous sky in Marfa and the natural wonders of Big Bend National Park give travelers a true sense of the Texas mystique.

Big Bend National Park

DAY 1

Begin your journey in **Marfa** with the fascinating **Chinati Foundation,** which features contemporary art in a historic Army base. Later, head to nearby **Fort Davis** for a quick visit to **McDonald Observatory** or to **Alpine** for the **Museum of the Big Bend.** After sundown, be sure to look for the mysterious **Marfa Lights.**

DAYS 2-3

Head an hour south to **Big Bend National Park** for a couple of days of camping and hiking in the Chisos Mountains (**Santa Elena Canyon** is a must-see). A side trip to the abandoned mining town of **Terlingua,** an hour away, is also a worthy option. Spend the night in a tent or the **Chisos Mountains Lodge.**

The *Elissa* in Galveston

Cadillac Ranch

Remember the Alamo!

The Lone Star State's rich heritage is displayed throughout Texas, but several attractions outside the big cities offer authentic windows to the past. For a chronological perspective, start with the San Antonio missions, from the early 1700s, which tell the story of Spain's role in early Texas history when priests attempted to assimilate Native Americans by converting them to Catholicism. In the latter part of the 1800s, Texas's cowboy legacy came to life along the Chisholm Trail, where millions of longhorns and other cattle were herded northward from the King Ranch near Corpus Christi. In the 1940s, legendary Route 66 blazed a different kind of trail through the Texas Panhandle, allowing motorists to hit the road in search of adventure and new horizons.

San Antonio

You can spend an entire day or two along a 5-mile (8-km) stretch of Texas's living history at the **San Antonio Missions National Historical Park.** Each of these historic stone structures—Mission Concepción, Mission San José, Mission San Juan, Mission Espada, and the famous Mission San Antonio de Valero, a.k.a. the **Alamo**—offers a different perspective on the Spanish influence in Texas. For an added dose of Spanish colonial history, visit the **Spanish Governor's Palace,** built in 1749, and the stately **San Fernando Cathedral** (1755).

Austin and the Hill Country

Austin's most-impressive historic building is the 1888 **State Capitol**—it's worth spending a few hours exploring the architectural magnificence of this significant structure.

If you become inspired by Texas's larger-than-life political heritage, consider a trip to the Hill Country for a day of fascinating stories and structures at the **Lyndon B. Johnson National Historical Park.**

Houston

Just east of Houston lies the sacred ground of **San Jacinto Battleground Historic Site.** With its remarkable 570-foot-tall (175-m) monument, 15 feet (4.6 m) taller than the Washington Monument, honoring Texas's victory in its fight for independence, this 1,200-acre site commemorates the legendary battleground where Texas Army troops defeated the Mexican Army with rallying cries of "Remember the Alamo!" under General Sam Houston in 1836.

The Gulf Coast

Cattle made their way to the Chisholm Trail from Texas's southern tip, with many originating from the legendary **King Ranch** near Corpus Christi. Spend a day touring the historic ranching facilities. For maritime history, head to Galveston and step aboard the 1877 *Elissa,* one of the only ships of its kind in the world restored to full sailing capacity.

Panhandle Plains

"The Mother Road" beckons along legendary **Route 66** in Texas's Panhandle. Though it was displaced by I-40 in the 1960s, there are still magnificent stretches of the original road offering travelers comfort and nostalgia in a dozen small towns along the way. Visit **Cadillac Ranch** and **The Big Texan** in Amarillo, the **Texas Old Route 66 and Devil's Rope Museums** in McLean, the **U-Drop Inn and Conoco Station** in Shamrock, and the **MidPoint Café** in Adrian.

Family Fun

With its mild climate, Texas is a year-round family-friendly travel destination. The warm weather allows for outdoor recreational fun. Families will find that many cities have kid-related destinations, including new or expanded children's museums, clustered in one part of town, allowing for easy walking, even with strollers, between attractions, and plenty of nearby parkland.

Dallas and Fort Worth

Fort Worth is more kid-oriented than Dallas, so families should plan to spend a day or two exploring the **Fort Worth Stockyards** (be sure to catch the daily cattle drive), the **National Cowgirl Museum and Hall of Fame,** and the **Fort Worth Zoo** (considered the best in Texas).

In **Dallas,** families should prioritize a visit to the **Perot Museum of Nature and Science** and the museums at historic **Fair Park.**

Many Texas families spend a weekend each summer in suburban **Arlington,** the "Midway of the Metroplex." Attractions include **Six Flags Over Texas** and its companion water park **Six Flags Hurricane Harbor,** professional sports venues for the **Texas Rangers** and **Dallas Cowboys,** and . . . the **International Bowling Museum and Hall of Fame.**

San Antonio

Since it's one of the most-visited cities in the country, San Antonio knows how to accommodate traveling families. Wee ones may not remember the **Alamo,** but families with older children should take the lively guided tour. **SeaWorld** and the **Six Flags Fiesta Texas** amusement park are must-sees for families, and a trip to the **Mexican rodeo** is an especially unique experience.

Austin and the Hill Country

Families can plan to spend a full afternoon on **Congress Avenue** in downtown Austin. Start

Fort Worth Stockyards

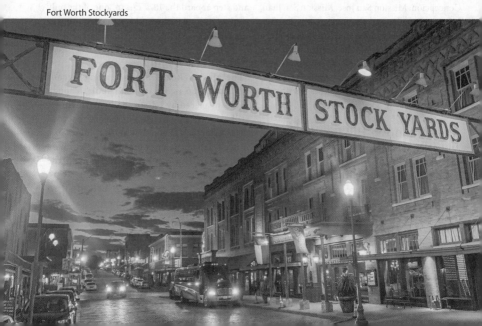

with the fun and engaging **Bullock Texas State History Museum,** continue with a quick walk to the remarkable **State Capitol** (be sure to roll down the hills on the expansive South Lawn), and wrap up the day with a sunset viewing of the one million **bats** emerging from beneath the Congress Avenue Bridge.

For a fun family excursion, consider taking the **Hill Country Flyer steam train** from Austin to the pleasant Hill Country community of Burnet.

Houston

Start things off in Houston at the fascinating **Museum of Natural Science,** then experience the interactive exhibits at the nearby **Children's Museum.** Another option is to head southeast of town for a day of family fun at the legendary **NASA Space Center** or amusement park atmosphere of **Kemah Boardwalk.** If you have the time, stick around for an animal-oriented day at the **Houston Zoo** and **Downtown Aquarium** (the Shark Voyage train ride is a must).

The Gulf Coast

For water-based fun, head to **Galveston,** one of the most popular getaways for local families. In addition to beach and recreational activities at **Galveston Island State Park,** visitors can spend a day or two riding roller coasters and rides at **Pleasure Pier** or strolling among rainforest and marine creatures in the glass pyramids at **Moody Gardens.** For a completely different kind of aquatic adventure, spend the day on the water rides at **Schlitterbahn Waterpark.**

It's worth making the trip to **Corpus Christi** (a 3.5-hour drive from Houston) just to play on **Mustang Island.** The **Texas State Aquarium** features a dolphin habitat and otter slides, and one of the region's best restaurants awaits at **Water Street Seafood Co.,** which serves everything tasty in the region—fresh seafood, Mexican influences, Cajun flavors, and Southern cooking.

SeaWorld in San Antonio

Texas has no shortage of scenic vistas to enjoy on a classic road trip, and the diverse topography allows for mountainous views, forested drives, and dramatic canyon descents. Whatever your destination, these journeys will provide plenty of oohs, aahs, and Instagram-worthy photo ops.

BIG BEND AREA

A couple drives in and around Big Bend offer spectacular unmatched views. Starting in the western portion of Big Bend National Park, **Ross Maxwell Scenic Drive** (30 mi/48 km, plan at least 2 hours with stops at historic sites and viewpoints) features vast vistas transforming into striking views of volcanic rock formations reminiscent of a *Star Trek* episode.

Just west of the national park is Big Bend Ranch State Park, featuring magnificent mountain views around each turn, the **River Road** (50 mi/80 km, plan for 2.5 hours) has compelling immediacy to the Rio Grande, just a few feet away.

For those with an adventurous spirit and a high-clearance vehicle, head farther west to the tiny village of Ruidosa, where a century-old adobe church marks the beginning and end of the extremely rugged **Pinto Canyon Road** (50 mi/80 km, plan for 3 hours) to Marfa. The Chinati Mountains serve as a picturesque backdrop, and the road is so rural you may lose track of its route. Talk about a road trip.

THE HILL COUNTRY

A pleasant drive through the bucolic Hill Country provides visitors with sweeping views of rolling hills and sheer canyon walls lining the rivers that carve through limestone bluffs. The scenery isn't as stunning as the Big Bend area, but there's a pleasant appeal to the outstretched topography.

Start the **Hill Country journey** (66 mi/106 km, plan at least 2 hours) in Bandera, a.k.a. the "Cowboy Capital of the World," with gentle pastures and scenic ranches. Head west on **Highway 16 and FM 337,** where you'll be treated to inviting scenery along the lazy Medina River. Things start to change as you get farther west and closer to the Frio River, which runs north-south along **Highway 83.** Take a few hours to check out a

U-Drop Inn and Conoco Station along old Route 66

swimming hole on the Frio, or spend the night at a classic Hill Country cabin in a charming river community like Leakey or Concan.

ROUTE 66

Travelers can get their kicks along Texas's entire stretch of Route 66, **along I-40 in the Panhandle between Oklahoma and New Mexico** (95 mi/153 km, plan on over 2 hours), but the best collection of roadside attractions is between Amarillo and Shamrock. This eastern portion of the Panhandle is flat, but the compelling attractions—art deco motor courts, service stations, and diners—make the drive worthwhile. Amarillo is home to the famous Cadillac Ranch and Sixth Street's historic storefronts, while tiny McLean and Shamrock offer iconic structures from the golden era of automobile travel. These small-town highlights include one of the country's first Phillips 66 gas stations, and the amazing U-Drop-Inn tower, which offered food, gas, and lodging to weary Route 66 travelers.

Dallas and Fort Worth

The Dallas-Fort Worth Metroplex packs a powerful one-two punch. These two heavyweight cities embody two sides of Texas: the Southern-fried glitzy lifestyle and the Wild West cattle-driving culture.

This perfect combination of uniquely Texas elements makes the Metroplex an ideal place to kick off a journey to the Lone Star State. Visitors can immerse themselves in all things Texas and have themselves a good ol' time in the process. Stop by the Stockyards. Do the *Dallas* TV show museum. Buy those boots, hats, and belt buckles. And be sure to load up on the trinity of Texas cuisine—barbecue, Tex-Mex, and down-home Southern cookin'—at any of the dozens of top-notch restaurants throughout Dallas and Fort Worth. After soaking up the

Dallas 36
Vicinity of Dallas 60
Fort Worth 68
Vicinity of Fort Worth . . 89
Wichita Falls 94

Highlights

Look for ★ to find recommended sights, activities, dining, and lodging.

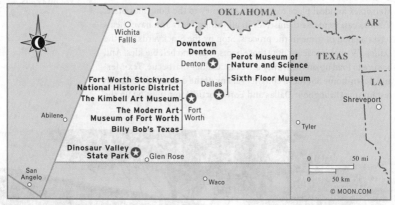

★ **Learn the story of JFK,** his political career, and his family's version of Camelot at the **Sixth Floor Museum** (page 39).

★ **Learn something new** via state-of-the-art learning kiosks and hands-on scientific displays at the **Perot Museum of Nature and Science** (page 39).

★ **Cheer at a championship rodeo.** You can also wander historical museums, saloons, and boutiques—and even see some genuine livestock activity at the **Fort Worth Stockyards National Historic District** (page 70).

★ **Admire masterpieces.** Works from Monet, Cezanne, and Matisse are on display at the **Kimbell Art Museum** (page 71).

★ **Appreciate cutting-edge artwork.**

The visual delights at **The Modern Art Museum of Fort Worth** include the remarkable building (page 73).

★ **Hit "the world's largest honky-tonk."** At least that's what **Billy Bob's Texas** claims to be. It's hard to argue, considering its 32 individual drink stations and even a live bull riding ring in its three acres of interior space (page 78).

★ **Stroll through courthouse square,** the centerpiece of **Downtown Denton.** From here you can browse the antique shops and art galleries or grab a bite a trendy café (page 89).

★ **Follow in dinosaurs' footsteps.** Their tracks were set in limestone riverbeds 100 million years ago at **Dinosaur Valley State Park** (page 92).

Metroplex, discover the genuine charm of the area's outlying communities. Magnificent courthouses anchor downtown squares that offer distinct Texas antiques, refurbished historic theaters, and perfect pecan pies.

Daily weather reports remind North Texans they're still firmly planted on the southern edge of the Great Plains. Summertime highs regularly reach triple digits, and winters often bring subfreezing temperatures and snowstorms. Diversions from the weather include world-class art museums, professional sports teams, rodeos, and shopping Side trips to charming nearby towns such as Waxahachie and Denton reveal the community spirit that migrated to the area with its proud pioneers. The region's 30-plus lakes offer additional sources of entertainment and respite, an inviting option on a hot summer day.

Separated by only 35 miles (56 km), Dallas is the financial hub of the South, and Fort Worth is an agricultural center of the West, offering travelers the best of both worlds: glitz and grit, The Big D and Cowtown, the Old South and the Wild West.

PLANNING YOUR TIME

To get a true sense of the differences between Dallas and Fort Worth, plan to spend three or four days in the Metroplex; add another couple of days for side trips to nearby communities.

Downtown Dallas is a good place to start. Spend the morning in the busy historic commercial district—check out the art deco skyscrapers and the original Neiman Marcus store—and use the afternoon to soak up local history in the West End district, including the essential Sixth Floor Museum. Afterward, drop by the Greenville entertainment district for dinner, clubbing, or live music.

Spend the following day absorbing Dallas culture at Fair Park, just a few minutes east of downtown, home to several museums and the enormous State Fair of Texas in October, and

the Dallas Arts District, which features the must-see Dallas Museum of Art and several other notable cultural attractions.

If you have kids or are just playful by nature, spend a day between Dallas and Fort Worth in Arlington, home to several amusement parks (the legendary Six Flags Over Texas and Six Flags Hurricane Harbor), Cowboys Stadium, and the Rangers' Globe Life Field in Arlington.

The Fort Worth Stockyards National Historic District is an essential stop for any Texas traveler. Spend half a day absorbing the sights, sounds, and smells of the Livestock Exchange, Cowtown Coliseum, and Stockyards Museum. Plan to spend an entire day in the Fort Worth Cultural District, which includes the world-class Kimbell Art Museum as well as other essential attractions, such as the Amon Carter Museum, The Modern Art Museum of Fort Worth, and the National Cowgirl Museum and Hall of Fame. If you still have time, visit the impressive Fort Worth Zoo.

INFORMATION AND SERVICES

There are plenty of resources available to help make a trip to the Metroplex area hassle-free. It may seem daunting to tackle the country's ninth-largest city, but Dallas has several excellent information centers nearby where visitors can inquire about directions, equipment rental, and other travel-related assistance. Likewise, the region's outlying smaller communities have visitors centers offering maps and advice for navigating rural areas.

A handy service is **Travelers Aid Dallas/ Fort Worth** (972/973-4420, http://tarrant. tx.networkofcare.org): Rather than providing tips about where to go and how to get there, this service offers specific information about travel-related issues such as foreign-language translation, car-seat rental, military assistance, crisis counseling, and emergency travel

---

Previous: the daily cattle drive in the Stockyards; the famous ferris wheel at the State Fair of Texas; Sundance Square in downtown Fort Worth.

Dallas and Fort Worth

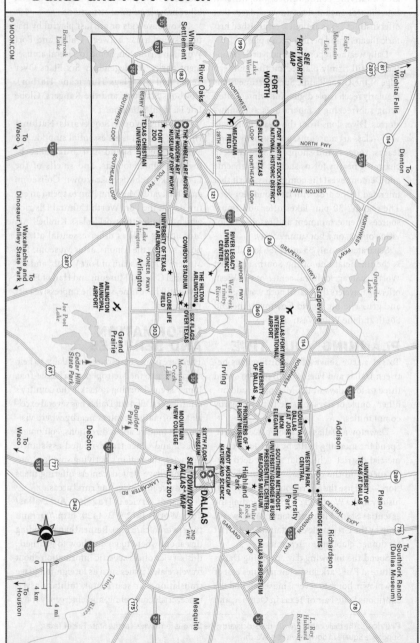

© MOON.COM

SEE "FORT WORTH" MAP

FORT WORTH

To Wichita Falls

To Denton

White Settlement

River Oaks

★ MEACHAM FIELD

★ BILLY BOB'S TEXAS
★ FORT WORTH STOCKYARDS
NATIONAL HISTORIC DISTRICT

NORTH FWY

DENTON HWY

★ FORT WORTH ZOO
★ THE MODERN ART MUSEUM OF FORT WORTH
★ THE KIMBELL ART MUSEUM
★ TEXAS CHRISTIAN UNIVERSITY

To Waco

Benbrook Lake

SOUTHWEST LOOP

BERRY ST

POLY FWY

SOUTHEAST LOOP

UNIVERSITY OF TEXAS AT ARLINGTON

To Waxahachie and Dinosaur Valley State Park

Arlington

Lake Arlington

Pioneer Pkwy

COWBOYS STADIUM

RIVER LEGACY LIVING SCIENCE CENTER

THE HILTON ARLINGTON

West Fork Trinity River

AIRPORT FWY

Grapevine

GRAPEVINE HWY

Grapevine Lake

★ ARLINGTON MUNICIPAL AIRPORT

★ GLOBE LIFE FIELD
★ SIX FLAGS OVER TEXAS

Joe Pool Lake

Grand Prairie

Mountain Creek Lake

Irving

★ DALLAS/FORT WORTH INTERNATIONAL AIRPORT

UNIVERSITY OF DALLAS

Addison

Cedar Hill State Park

Boulder Park

MOUNTAIN VIEW COLLEGE

FRONTIERS OF FLIGHT MUSEUM

THE COURTYARD DALLAS LBJ AT JOSEY
MCM ELEGANTE

WESTIN PARK CENTRAL

University Park

UNIVERSITY OF TEXAS AT DALLAS

Plano

DeSoto

SIXTH FLOOR MUSEUM

SEE "DOWNTOWN DALLAS" MAP

DALLAS ZOO

★★ DALLAS

LANCASTER RD

SOUTHERN METHODIST UNIVERSITY/GEORGE W BUSH PRESIDENTIAL CENTER/ MEADOWS MUSEUM

Highland Park

PEROT MUSEUM OF NATURE AND SCIENCE

White Rock Lake

DALLAS ARBORETUM

STAYBRIDGE SUITES

CENTRAL EXPY

Richardson

To Southfork Ranch (Dallas Museum)

2ND AVE

GARLAND RD

L. Roy Hubbard Reservoir

Mesquite

To Houston

0   4 km
0   4 mi

Trinity River

assistance. If you're arriving by air, **DFW Airport Visitor Information** (972/574-3694, www.dfwairport.com) outlines transportation options from the airport and directions to Metroplex-area accommodations and attractions. For international travelers, the DFW Airport has a useful 24-hour foreign-exchange machine (972/574-4754) that handles 20 different currencies. Also, the **Texas Department of Transportation** (800/452-9292, www.txdot.gov) provides emergency road condition information and suggested road-trip routing.

To speak with someone face-to-face, there are several visitors centers throughout North Texas offering detailed maps, brochures, and local know-how about specific travel services in the area. Two of the most comprehensive services for travel in North Texas are located in small surrounding communities. They are the **Dallas/Fort Worth Area Tourism Council** (3703, 1090 Texan Trail, Suite 199, Grapevine, 817/329-2438, www.visitdfw.com) and the Texas Historical Commission's **Lakes Trail Region** office (116 W. Bridge St., Granbury, 817/573-1114, www.texaslakestrail.com).

Other North Texas travel centers focusing on specific cities include the **Dallas Tourism Information Center** (325 North St. Paul St., Dallas, 800/232-5527, www.tourtexas.com/dallas) and the **Fort Worth Visitors Center** (508 Main St., Sundance Square, Fort Worth, 817/698-3300, www.fortworth.com).

GETTING THERE AND AROUND

Texas is the land of wide-open spaces, so cars are the primary mode of transport. Traveling to the Metroplex by auto from Houston, I-45 is the only major path. It's a 250-mile (400-km) drive, which takes about 3.5 hours on weekends. The drive up I-35 from Austin is 200 miles (320 km), about 3 hours on weekends.

Add another 90 miles (145 km) and 90 minutes for San Antonio.

During the week, drivers should factor up to an hour extra for commuter traffic. Dallas has a somewhat incomplete loop road: I-635 to the north and east, which morphs into I-20 to the south. Westward traffic to Fort Worth uses I-30 or I-20. The other major freeways in Dallas are I-35 (north-south) and Central Expressway (U.S. 75), which whizzes commuters north, occasionally via subterranean methods, to the sprawling suburbs of Plano and Richardson.

Dallas/Fort Worth International Airport (DFW, 972/973-3112, www.dfwairport.com) is the world's fourth-busiest passenger airport and serves 158,000 passengers daily to 200 worldwide destinations. The city's old airport now houses Southwest Airlines' **Love Field Airport** (DAL, 214/670-6080, www.dallas-lovefield.com). It's not nearly as overwhelming as DFW, but its smaller size also means fewer flight options. The **Wichita Falls Municipal Airport** (SPS, 940/855-3621, www.flywichitafalls.net), a joint military-civilian facility, has four flights daily to DFW airport on American Eagle.

Since the Metroplex is so spread out, renting a car is usually the best option to maximize flexibility while traveling. However, Dallas and Fort Worth both have surprisingly popular and well-designed public transportation systems. The **Dallas Area Rapid Transit** system (214/979-1111, www.dart.org) runs in 13 area communities with rail, bus, and rideshare services. DART has a line to the DFW airport and also to Fort Worth via Trinity Metro. Single-ride tickets are about $5. The **Fort Worth Transportation Authority** (817/215-8600, www.ridetrinitymetro.org) provides buses to the Stockyards and the Cultural District, with access to Dallas via Trinity Metro.

Two Days in Dallas

DAY 1

Consider making Main Street your home base. Although a historic business district doesn't sound like a happening place to anchor your visit, Dallas's downtown is a comfortable urban environment offering a surprising range of hotel and restaurant options—from the affordable and trendy **Hotel Indigo** to the opulent and semi-affordable **Adolphus Hotel.**

Walk down to the West End District for a dose of history at the JFK-based **Sixth Floor Museum** and **Old Red Museum of Dallas County History and Culture.** Have a crab cake sandwich or *charro* tacos and a local craft beer at the comfy and stylish **Woolworth,** then take a selfie in front of the giant eyeball (you'll see). Stop by the original **Neiman Marcus** on Main Street to get a sense of Dallas's cosmopolitan style. Spend the afternoon in the Dallas Arts District, just a few blocks north. Explore the **Dallas Museum of Art's** impressive international collections and visit the **Nasher Sculpture Center.** Head back downtown for dinner, with options that include the casual and flavorful Tex-Mex at **Wild Salsa** or the upscale **Dakota's,** offering creative and tasty Texas comfort food. Top off the evening with a cocktail or a draft beer at **City Tavern.**

DAY 2

Start the day with a hearty breakfast at the West End's **Ellen's Southern Kitchen** (the biscuits and gravy are phenomenal), then head out for a day of museums that can only be experienced in the Big D. The compelling **Perot Museum of Nature and Science** offers five floors with 11 permanent exhibit halls featuring local dinosaur fossils, physics (with Legos), and the solar system. Have a sandwich or salad on hip Greenville Avenue at the independent **Libertine,** then visit the nearby **George W. Bush Presidential Center,** dedicated to the 43rd president's time in office. When you're done, head on over to **Southfork Ranch,** a.k.a. the *Dallas* museum. The hit 1970s TV show takes the spotlight at its original filming location, where you can relive the drama. Afterward, you might be craving a complementary dining environment, so get back downtown for dinner at **YO Ranch Steakhouse,** which has all the basic cuts of meat without the stuffy atmosphere (the bone-in rib eye is delectable).

Dallas

Dallas (population 1,345,047) prospered and declined at different times compared to most other major U.S. cities, and its downtown buildings reflect these fluctuations. In the course of a single city block you'll find everything from late-19th-century commercial structures to Classical Revival buildings to art deco office towers to 1950s modern architecture. Many of Dallas's significant historical events occurred in the mid-20th century, evident in the locales associated with John F. Kennedy's assassination and in Fair Park's stunning edifices.

Downtown Dallas's first transformation occurred in the late 1800s, when the city became an increasingly important financial center. Intersecting railroads brought business, and Dallas's cotton exchange and agricultural equipment manufacturers added to the city's growth. The city's distinctive historic architecture is displayed in its buildings from the 1936 Texas Centennial Exposition, which brought more than 50 new art deco structures to Fair Park as well as world-renowned science exhibits, music, and attractions for millions of visitors to experience. Dallas also has the distinction of introducing the convenience store to suburban America, with the Oak Cliff area south of downtown spawning the 7-Eleven chain (it offered milk

Downtown Dallas

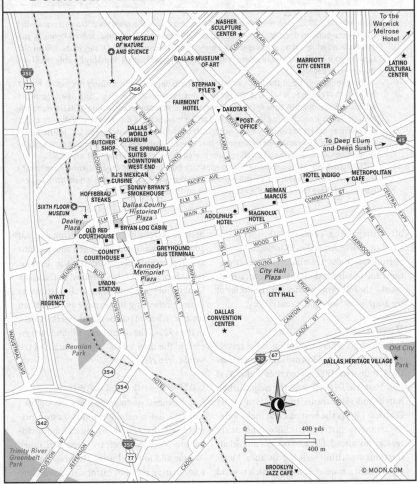

Map labels: To the Warwick Melrose Hotel, NASHER SCULPTURE CENTER ★, PEROT MUSEUM OF NATURE AND SCIENCE, DALLAS MUSEUM OF ART ★, MARRIOTT CITY CENTER, LATINO CULTURAL CENTER ★, STEPHAN PYLE'S ▼, FAIRMONT HOTEL, DAKOTA'S ▼, POST OFFICE, THE BUTCHER SHOP, DALLAS WORLD AQUARIUM ★, THE SPRINGHILL SUITES DOWNTOWN/WEST END, To Deep Ellum and Deep Sushi, RJ'S MEXICAN CUISINE, HOFBBRAU STEAKS, SONNY BRYAN'S SMOKEHOUSE, HOTEL INDIGO, METROPOLITAN CAFE ▼, NEIMAN MARCUS, SIXTH FLOOR MUSEUM ★, Dealey Plaza, Dallas County Historical Plaza, OLD RED COURTHOUSE, BRYAN LOG CABIN, ADOLPHUS HOTEL, MAGNOLIA HOTEL, COUNTY COURTHOUSE, GREYHOUND BUS TERMINAL, Kennedy Memorial Plaza, City Hall Plaza, UNION STATION, HYATT REGENCY, CITY HALL, DALLAS CONVENTION CENTER ★, Reunion Park, Old City Park, DALLAS HERITAGE VILLAGE ★, Trinity River Greenbelt Park, BROOKLYN JAZZ CAFE ▼, 0 400 yds, 0 400 m, © MOON.COM

and eggs on Sundays and evenings, when most grocery stores were closed).

The city is still often remembered as the site of John F. Kennedy's shocking assassination on November 22, 1963, when shots were fired at the president's motorcade in Dealey Plaza. The ramifications of the fatal gunshots would last for decades, as politicians and citizens deliberated over details while forming and debunking countless assassination conspiracy theories. Add to that the Dallas Cowboys and all the hoopla surrounding home games and the famous *Dallas* TV show, and the result is a fascinatingly diverse Southern city that Texas is proud to call its own.

DALLAS ORIENTATION

Dallas's sprawl has more in common with California cities than it does with Texas metro areas like Houston. The outer-ring suburbs like Plano, Frisco, and Grand Prairie have become large cities themselves, with populations

JFK's Assassination

November 22, 1963, is so momentous that it's the basis of the question, "Do you remember where you were on the day . . . ?" At 12:30pm that afternoon, Texas time, John F. Kennedy was assassinated while riding in a presidential motorcade through Dallas's Dealey Plaza. Ask an old-timer in your family or at work where they were that day, and they'll probably be able to tell you their precise details.

You can literally be at the place where everything happened by visiting the **Sixth Floor Museum** (411 Elm St., 214/747-6660, www.jfk.org, Mon. noon-6pm, Tues.-Sun. 10am-6pm, $18 adults, $16 seniors, $14 ages 6-18). Stand next to the infamous "sniper's nest." Gaze upon the famous Grassy Knoll. See the video clips and artifacts associated with that fateful day.

The issue still hadn't entirely been put to rest by the late 1970s, when the U.S. House Select Committee on Assassinations determined that Oswald likely was involved in a conspiracy. The subject was again debated when Oliver Stone released his controversial 1991 movie *JFK*.

The Sixth Floor Museum in the book depository building details the best-known conspiracy theories and includes an eerie exhibit preserving the spot by the window where investigators later found three spent shells, the assassination perch, and a rifle.

often surpassing Texas's established mid-sized cities like Amarillo, Waco, and Laredo. Fortunately, most of Dallas's cultural attractions and notable restaurants are centrally located—the following entries outline the lay of the land for exploring the central city.

Downtown

Downtown is where the action is for travelers during the day. Downtown encompasses the arts district, JFK-related sites in the West End Historic District, and the major urban hotels and restaurants in the Main Street District. This is the best place to make lodging arrangements, since the historic hotels are reasonably affordable, and many cultural attractions are within walking distance. Much of downtown is quiet at night, which is good news for those who want to get a peaceful night of sleep or are traveling with children. If you're looking to do some pub-crawling, however, the West End offers plenty of nightlife options.

Deep Ellum

Just east of downtown, Deep Ellum has undergone several changes in recent years. After having been an ultra-trendy hipster district in the 1990s, most of its notable live music venues closed in the mid-2000s. The district

became sketchy before experiencing a recent small resurgence in reopened music clubs and restaurants. Regardless of the destination, there's definitely an appeal in the area's local history, evident in the architecture and signage reflecting its heritage as an African American hub of business and entertainment in the 1920s. The name Deep Ellum is attributed to the then-locals' pronunciation of the words *deep elm*.

Uptown and Oak Lawn

Just northeast of downtown are the Uptown and Oak Lawn neighborhoods, known primarily for their eclectic art galleries and architecture. Vintage streetcars along McKinney Avenue add to the charm. The area features a fascinating blend of historic mansions and ultramodern high-rise condos. Shopping and nightlife are big draws in Uptown's West Village, and the Oak Lawn area is known for its scenic views along Turtle Creek, trendy gay bars, and chic restaurants.

Greenville Avenue

One of Dallas's most popular destinations for nightlife is Greenville Avenue, paralleling Central Expressway (U.S. 75). Just north of downtown and east of the Southern Methodist University campus, the district is referred to by locals as Upper Greenville and Lower Greenville; Mockingbird Lane is the dividing line.

Park Cities

Known for its high-end homes and residents, the Park Cities area (Highland Park and University Park) in north Dallas is the most exclusive part of town. Opulence exudes from the mansions and luxury hotels, making it an interesting destination for those who like to ogle the elite lifestyle through car windows. The tony Southern Methodist University to the east is home to George W. Bush's presidential museum and library.

SIGHTS

TOP EXPERIENCE

★ Sixth Floor Museum

Among the most-visited attractions in North Texas is the **Sixth Floor Museum** (411 Elm St., 214/747-6660, www.jfk.org, Mon. noon-6pm, Tues.-Sun. 10am-6pm, $18 adults, $16 seniors, $14 ages 6-18). The museum is dedicated to the life, death, and legacy of John F. Kennedy, the 35th president of the United States. Summarizing the museum's mission is a dramatic quote from JFK: "History, after all, is the memory of a nation."

The museum's exhibits, artifacts, and films provide a slice of American life in the early 1960s and the subsequent impact of JFK's assassination. The most intense and sobering area of the museum is the spot near the 6th-floor window where the fatal shots were allegedly fired. The area remains in its original setting as the school book depository, and its Plexiglas enclosure provides a somewhat creepy window to the afternoon of November 22, 1963. By the time most visitors leave, they've come away with a sense of how the world was affected that day, and hopefully have captured the spirit of Kennedy's life to use in a positive way. Note: The museum offers an advance ticket entry option, so consider reserving a spot online to avoid the occasional long lines.

George W. Bush Presidential Center

One of the most popular sites for political and cultural junkies is the impressive **George W. Bush Presidential Center** (2943 SMU Blvd., 214/200-4303, www.bushcenter.org, Mon.-Sat. 9am-5pm, Sun. noon-5pm, $16 adults, $14 ages 13-17, $10 military and ages 5-11) on the eastern edge of the Southern Methodist University campus. Opened in 2013, the center, sometimes referred to as the Bush Library, is dedicated to W's life and presidency. The museum is recommended mostly for fans of the 43rd president, but it's still worth visiting as a cultural attraction.

The innovative and effective use of video is notable—the ubiquitous coverage of the events of his presidency on 24-hour news channels at the time provides compelling footage. The 9/11-related exhibits are powerful and emotional, and little details will put smiles on even the most cynical faces, such as a spirited written exchange between Bush and Bono, and a video montage of "the lighter moments of a presidency" hosted by the First Daughters. Other highlights include a full-scale Oval Office replica with a desk that visitors can pose behind for a photo, a giant-screen theater, and artifacts such as the gun that was found on Saddam Hussein when he was captured.

Visitors are also encouraged to experience the challenges Bush faced as "the decider" by participating in an interactive activity called Decision Points, where they can use a sliding scale to indicate how much they agree with the expert advice being offered to the president. It's an interesting and engaging way to consider the many disparate choices a president faces on a daily basis.

★ Perot Museum of Nature and Science

Another of Dallas's newer cultural attractions is the compelling **Perot Museum of Nature and Science** (2201 N. Field St., 214/428-5555, www.perotmuseum.org, Mon.-Sat. 10am-7pm, Sun. noon-5pm, $19 adults, $13 seniors, $12 ages 2-17, parking $10, additional fees for special exhibits and movies). The first thing visitors notice about the Perot is its stunning architectural design, a thoroughly modern structure with several jarring features (a glass rectangle affixed to the exterior wall, undulating wavelike patterns in the concrete exterior). The bold architecture is the work of Thom Mayne, who also designed a 54-foot (16-m) continuous-flow escalator with a dramatic window extending outside the building.

The facility has five floors with 11 permanent exhibit halls. The museum's collection includes state-of-the-art learning kiosks and hands-on activities, and there are regular traveling exhibits offering hands-on ways to learn about scientific evidence, mathematical concepts, and natural history. The museum demands repeated visits due to the overwhelming number of exhibits and features, so don't try to experience everything in an afternoon. Instead, choose a couple areas of interest and focus your time there. For example, the natural science floor offers dinosaur fossils and fascinating exhibits dedicated to birds, including a flying game and a hawk's-eye view. The science section provides areas for learning about physics via Legos, sound waves via musical instruments, and electricity via a circuit board. Consider devoting some extra time to the displays about the solar system and universe, and the exhibits dedicated to playing with light.

Fair Park

Fair Park (www.fairpark.org) makes things easy for visitors by concentrating its diverse mix of museums, exhibit halls, parks, plazas, sports facilities, theaters, parking lots, and livestock facilities in one 300-acre complex. Fair Park was the site of the grand 1936 Texas Centennial Exposition, and it's best known for its 100-plus years as the site of the gigantic State Fair of Texas each October. For those visiting Dallas any other time of the year, Fair Park still has plenty of entertaining attractions. The park's centerpiece is the stunning **Hall of State** (3939 Grand Ave., 214/421-4500, Tues.-Sat.

10am-5pm, Sun. 1pm-5pm, free), a National Historic Landmark building offering Texas history exhibits along with tours and stage performances providing additional insight into this remarkable art deco structure. Also on the grounds is the 1930 Cotton Bowl, the legendary stadium that served as the first home of the Dallas Cowboys and currently hosts the Cotton Bowl Classic and highly anticipated "Red River Rivalry"— the traditional University of exas versus University of Oklahoma football game each October (unless Dallas Cowboys owner Jerry Jones lures it to his team's stadium). Of the museums in the Fair Park complex, the following are most notable.

Children's Aquarium at Fair Park (1462 1st Ave., 469/554-7340, www. oceansofadventure.org, daily 9am-4:30pm, $8 adults, $6 seniors and ages 3-11) houses thousands of aquatic animals selected with kids in mind, including marine and freshwater fish, amphibians, reptiles, and invertebrates, in its original art deco building from the Texas Centennial. The aquarium features a good sampling of some of the world's more bizarre aquatic animals, such as the "fishing" anglerfish, poisonous stonefish, albino alligators, and species from popular movies and books. Kids and adults will also enjoy the daily fish feedings at Stingray Bay, where they can interact with rays and small sharks.

Texas Discovery Gardens (3601 Martin Luther King Jr. Blvd., 214/428-7476, www. texasdiscoverygardens.org, daily 10am-5pm, $10 adults, $8 seniors, $5 ages 3-11) strives to teach ways to conserve nature in urban environments with a focus on sustainable and organic gardening. The site's 7.5 acres includes the Rosine Smith Sammons Butterfly House and Insectarium, where guests can meander down a canopy walkway

---

1: Sixth Floor Museum 2: The Perot Museum of Nature and Science 3: The Hall of State at Dallas's Fair Park 4: Old Red Museum of Dallas County History and Culture

1

2

3

4

as they view hundreds of free-flying tropical butterflies and plants.

The African American Museum (3536 Grand Ave., 214/565-9026, www.aamdallas.org, daily 10am-7pm, free) showcases African American artistic, cultural, and historical materials and features one of the largest African American folk-art collections in the United States. The 38,000-square-foot structure is made of stone and built in the shape of a cross. To evoke preindustrial cultures of the African continent, the museum uses natural materials and design motifs throughout the building. Four galleries feature the cultural heritage of African American art and history along with a research library, a theater, a studio arts area, and classrooms. The museum's permanent collections include African art, African American fine art, and historical and political archives.

Just a block from the Texas Discovery Gardens on the edge of Fair Park is the **South Dallas Cultural Center** (3400 S. Fitzhugh Ave., 214/671-0727, group tours 214/671-0058, Tues.-Fri. 1pm-9pm, Sat. 9am-5pm, free). The 18,000-square-foot center bills itself as "an Afro-centric venue that provides instruction and enrichment in the performing, literary, media, and visual arts." Its programs and facilities showcase African culture through a visual arts gallery, a 100-seat black box theater, studios for dance, arts, and photography, a digital recording studio, and a video production studio. Public tours of the South Dallas Cultural Center are available to small groups with advance appointment. The tours are free, and donations are encouraged.

Dallas County Historical Plaza

Bounded by Elm, Market, Commerce, and Houston Streets, this area is divided into two separate parts: **Founders Plaza** and the **Kennedy Memorial Plaza.** Founders Plaza contains an open area with several historical monuments and a reconstruction of Dallas founder John Neely Bryan's original log cabin. The Kennedy Memorial Plaza houses an unusual concrete structure surrounding a small JFK monument. Dallas residents tend to have a love-hate relationship with the structure, and each viewer interprets its meaning and value differently.

One of Dallas's most beloved buildings stands on the western end of the Kennedy plaza: "Old Red," the 70,580-square-foot 1892 Romanesque-style Dallas County Courthouse. The enormous stately building served a variety of public functions throughout the 1900s, but efficiency concerns resulted in several remodelings. Old Red has been undergoing restoration for many years and reopened as the **Old Red Museum of Dallas County History and Culture** (100 S. Houston St., 214/757-1914, www.oldred.org, daily 9am-5pm, $10 adults, $8 students and seniors, $7 ages 3-16). Its mission is to "inspire and educate visitors about the rich and varied cultural, economic, political and social history of the Dallas County area."

Dallas Museum of Art

The city's crown jewel of cultural museums is the **Dallas Museum of Art** (1717 N. Harwood St., 214/922-1200, www.dma.org, Tues.-Wed. and Fri.-Sun. 11am-5pm, Thurs. 11am-9pm, free), containing more than 24,000 works of world-class international art from ancient to modern times. Anchoring the city's arts district, the museum covers prehistoric Latin American ceramics and sculpture to contemporary artists such as Jackson Pollock and Tatsuo Miyajima.

The highlight is the remarkable collection of European and impressionist art by Renoir, Van Gogh, Cézanne, and Monet. Also of note is the facility's impressive artwork from Africa, Asia, and the ancient Mediterranean, as well as the outdoor sculpture garden with water walls and contemporary benches. Make a point of visiting the museum's Decorative Arts Wing, which features a recreated Mediterranean villa with lavish furniture and silver furnishings sharing space with masterpieces by Cézanne and Van Gogh. The museum also contains the Center for Creative Connections, an interactive space

To experience the State Fair of Texas's sacred trinity, you'll need to (1) eat a corny dog while (2) watching the University of Texas versus University of Oklahoma football game in the shadow of (3) Big Tex. Throw in some fried Twinkies and the country's tallest Ferris wheel, and you have a cultural legacy befitting the Lone Star State.

This venerable autumn event—held the first three weeks of October at the historic Fair Park campus—has been a Texas tradition since 1886, and during that time, it has experienced as many ups and downs as the old Comet roller coaster.

One of the highest peaks was in 1936, when Fair Park served as the site of Texas's mammoth state centennial celebration, featuring science exhibits with items made from a crazy new product called "plastic." The event's edible fare is another custom, with bizarre fried items like cookies, candy bars, and even ice cream drawing people to brazenly sample the newest concoction.

Big Tex

For many, Big Tex is the ultimate representative of the State Fair of Texas. Brought on board in 1952, the big fella is a 52-foot-tall (16-m) mechanical cowboy figure at the entrance of Fair Park who welcomes visitors with a huge "Howdy, folks!" Big Tex was originally a Santa Claus in Kerens, Texas, and was purchased for $750. After being outfitted with size 70 boots and a 75-gallon hat, Big Tex was transformed into the beloved Texas-size ambassador for the State Fair of Texas. In 2012, Big Tex caught fire (the dramatic photos are easy to find online), but he was replaced with a bigger, better fire-resistant version.

For the past decade or so, the fair has become best known for its featured fried food. Each year, vendors try to top previous experiments by introducing something even more outrageous than before. The additions have included fried Snickers, fried bacon, fried cola, and fried beer. Yum!

that engages visitors in the creative process by experiencing works of art in a more direct way.

Nasher Sculpture Center

Providing a downtown urban oasis of art and nature in the arts district is the impressive **Nasher Sculpture Center** (2001 Flora St., 214/242-5100, www.nashersculpturecenter. org, Tues.-Sun. 11am-5pm, $10 adults, $7 seniors, $5 students, free 1st Sat. and under age 5). Directly across from the Dallas Museum of Art, the facility includes an elegant 54,000-square-foot building by architect Renzo Piano (known for designing Paris's Pompidou Center) featuring the contemporary art collection of philanthropist and collector Raymond Nasher. It's worth making the trip to experience the stunning two-acre sculpture garden, created by landscape architect Peter Walker. The open-air environment offers a distinctive museum experience featuring internationally acclaimed artwork. The Nasher Collection is considered one of the primary collections of contemporary 20th-century sculpture in the world and comprises hundreds of works by internationally acclaimed artists. The facility is particularly proud of the depth of perspective it provides for prominent artists such as Henri Matisse, Pablo Picasso, Raymond Duchamp-Villon, and Joan Miró.

Southfork Ranch (*Dallas* Museum)

The hit TV show *Dallas*, which became a

The *Dallas* Phenomenon

In the spring of 1980, *Dallas* was on everyone's mind. And the question on everyone's lips was "Who Shot J. R.?" The country was captivated by the mysterious intruder who fired at bullish oil magnate J. R. Ewing. With more than a dozen potential candidates, speculation ran rampant—people even placed Vegas bets on the outcome.

Decades later, most Americans don't remember or even care who pulled the trigger (incidentally, it was Kristin, J. R.'s recent romantic interest), but anyone who watched TV in the early 1980s likely recalls tuning in on Friday nights to keep up with the Ewing clan's latest dramatic adventures. Even if you were born a decade or two later, you can still experience the intrigue (and 1970s styles) at Southfork Ranch (3700 Hogge Rd., Parker, 972/442-7800, www.southforkranch.com).

The Texas mystique played a big role in the show's success, serving as an intriguing backdrop along with the stereotypical big oil, big money, and everything's-bigger-in-Texas sensibilities. The Ewing family's home base was Southfork Ranch, a fittingly sprawling kingdom that, along with the cowboy posturing, came to represent Texas excess to viewers around the globe.

The show itself, which aired 1978-1991, is considered one of TV's most significant prime-time dramas, launching countless other series dedicated to shady business dealings, romantic trysts, dysfunctional families, thrilling season finale cliffhangers, and incredibly puffy hair.

worldwide phenomenon in the late 1970s and early 1980s, spawned an equally popular spectacle when tours opened at the show's filming location, the mythical **Southfork Ranch** (3700 Hogge Rd., Parker, 972/442-7800, www.southforkranch.com, daily 9am-5pm, $16 adults, $14 seniors, $9 ages 5-12). Thanks to international syndication, *Dallas* became synonymous with Texas for millions of people around the globe. Whether this did more to help or hurt Texas's reputation remains a topic of debate, but there's no underestimating the pop culture marvel the show became. Therefore, it shouldn't be surprising that hordes of fans descend on Southfork annually to tour the famous Ewing Mansion and view memorabilia such as the gun that shot J. R., Lucy's wedding dress, and Jock Ewing's Lincoln Continental. From U.S. 75 north, take exit 30 and drive east on FM 2514 (Parker Rd.) for 6 miles (9.7 km); turn right onto FM 2551 (Hogge Rd.) and look for the sign on the left.

Dallas Heritage Village

On the southern edge of downtown, **Dallas Heritage Village** (1515 S. Harwood St., 214/421-5141, www.dallasheritagevillage. org, Tues.-Sat. 10am-4pm, Sun. noon-4pm, $10 adults, $8 seniors, $6 ages 4-12) is

an outdoor museum devoted to the turn-of-the-20th-century's architectural and cultural history. The heritage village is a living-history museum, meaning visitors will encounter employees dressed in period costume discussing the significance of the structures or the time period they represent. Through these interpreters and by soaking up the surrounding scenery, visitors learn about North Texas life 1840-1910. The museum features 38 restored historic structures, including Victorian homes, an antebellum mansion, a train depot, a barbershop, a school, a church, and several commercial buildings. The village sits on 13 wooded acres, which feel eerily uninhabited on slow days, and hosts events for children (summer camps, blacksmithing, theatrical performances, animal visits). There are also picnic areas and walking trails.

Meadows Museum

The **Meadows Museum** (Southern Methodist University campus, 5900 Bishop Blvd., 214/768-2516, www. meadowsmuseumdallas.org, Tues.-Sat. 10am-5pm, Sun. 1pm-5pm, $12 adults, $10 seniors, $4 students, free Thurs. 5pm-8pm) is best known for its enormous and impressive collection of Spanish art. The artwork and galleries were a gift to SMU from prominent Dallas businessman Algur Meadows, founder of the General American Oil Company of Texas. The museum includes work from the 15th-20th centuries by some of the foremost Spanish painters, including El Greco, Velázquez, Goya, Miró, and Picasso. The vast number of works by Goya is particularly noteworthy, as is the museum's collection of 20th-century sculpture.

Dallas Zoo

Although the **Dallas Zoo** (650 S. R. L. Thornton Freeway/I-35E, 469/554-7500, www.dallaszoo.com, daily 9am-5pm Mar.-Oct., daily 9am-4pm Nov.-Feb., $17 adults, $14 seniors and ages 3-11, parking $10) doesn't have the same top-notch reputation as the Fort Worth Zoo, it's still worth visiting. Beginning with the enormous giraffe sculpture at the front gate, it's clear the zoo's focus is on African animals, and they do a good job bringing the continent to life in the *Giants of the Savanna* and *Wilds of Africa* exhibits. Divided by geographical habitat, the Africa area features forests of monkeys and gorillas (be sure to check out the gorilla conservation center). A monorail ride through woodland, river, and desert regions of the continent provides glimpses of wildebeests, gazelles, and many bird species. Other areas of the zoo offer up-close views of big cats, elephants, kangaroos, and reptiles, and there's a special treat for those who've always wanted to ride a camel—camel rides! The children's zoo is worth visiting if you have little ones in tow.

Dallas World Aquarium

Not to be confused with the Dallas Aquarium in Fair Park, the **Dallas World Aquarium** (1801 N. Griffin St., 214/720-2224, www.dwazoo.com, daily 10am-5pm, $23 adults, $21 seniors, $17 ages 2-12) is a combination aquarium and zoo, with monkeys scurrying overhead and sharks lurking nearby. Exotic plants and creatures from around the world add to the sense of being transported to another habitat, especially in the *Orinoco—Secrets of the River* rainforest exhibit, with birds, bats, and reptiles in the company of a 40-foot (12-m) waterfall. The aquarium's highlight is a 22,000-gallon tunnel with a panoramic view of underwater reef life from the Continental Shelf. Be sure to attend a feeding event (schedules available at admission).

Dallas Arboretum

Overlooking scenic White Rock Lake, the **Dallas Arboretum** (8525 Garland Rd., 214/515-6500, www.dallasarboretum.org, daily 9am-5pm, $17 adults, $14 seniors, $12 ages 3-12) offers 66 acres of scenic grounds containing floral, herbal, and vegetable gardens. It's particularly fetching March-May when the grounds have an iridescent green glow peppered by floral bursts of red, yellow, and white. Although spring is the best time of year for the vegetation, any season is a good time to escape the hustle, bustle, and concrete of urban life for the arboretum's oasis of nature and peace. Also on-site are the Spanish colonial-style DeGolyer mansion and museum as well as the Camp Estate, both of which feature 17th- and 18th-century art and furniture.

Latino Cultural Center

Designed by noted architect Ricardo Legorreta, the **Latino Cultural Center** (2600 Live Oak, 214/671-0045, www.lcc.dallasculture.org, Tues.-Sat. 10am-5pm, admission for some events) is worth visiting for the building itself. The 27,000-square-foot facility doesn't offer large-scale exhibits, but it includes a gallery dedicated to Latino art and a courtyard featuring sculptures. The center has a 300-seat theater that hosts occasional cultural performances. Check the website for event listings.

Frontiers of Flight Museum

Located at Dallas Love Field, the **Frontiers of Flight Museum** (6911 Lemmon Ave., 214/350-3600, www.flightmuseum.com,

America's Team

Roger Staubach. Troy Aikman. Emmitt Smith. All are football legends. All were **Dallas Cowboys.** The Cowboys are a love-'em-or-hate-'em kind of team. With their dominant success in much of the 1970s and 1990s, the Cowboys garnered their share of bandwagon fans—earning them the nickname "America's Team"—which also had the polarizing effect of creating hordes of Cowboy haters.

Regardless of your feeling about the team, it's worth checking out their impressive home base via a stadium tour (www.attstadium.com). The self-guided tour ($22) is worth it to see the locker rooms and toss a football around on the field. For $10 more, you can see the luxury suites and press boxes with a knowledgeable and entertaining guide.

Legendary Yards

The team came to prominence under the helm of legendary coach Tom Landry, the fedora-donning head honcho who shaped and guided the team from its inception in 1960 until 1989. During that time, the Cowboys posted 20 consecutive winning seasons, won 13 division championships, and appeared in Super Bowls V, VI, X, XII, and XIII, winning VI and XII. Overall, they've appeared in eight Super Bowls and won five of them.

Any discussion about the Dallas Cowboys would be incomplete without mentioning their famous cheerleaders. The name alone conjures up images of feathered hair, short white shorts, and, of course, spirited cheers guiding the team to victory. Although they came to prominence during the *Charlie's Angels*-era 1970s, the cheerleaders continue to serve as worldwide ambassadors for America's Team.

The enormous AT&T Stadium, nicknamed "Jerry World" in reference to team owner Jerry Jones, includes a 60-yard-wide high-definition screen inside the world's largest domed stadium.

Regardless of the Cowboys' rank in their division, Texans and other Americans will faithfully follow the team every Sunday during football season. And whatever the final score is, you can bet fans across the Lone Star State will be cheering (or muttering) "How 'bout them Cowboys!"

Mon.-Sat. 10am-5pm, Sun. 1pm-5pm, $10 adults, $8 ages 3-17) features aircraft from the past 100 years. The museum covers everything from early aircraft of the 1920s to jets and rockets of the first decade of the new millennium. Of particular interest is the *Lighter than Air* exhibit, which pays homage to the zeppelins and giant blimps of the past.

RECREATION

Since it's the sixth-largest city in the country, Dallas has a remarkable selection of spectator sports to keep fans entertained. All the major professional sporting leagues are represented—football, baseball, basketball, and hockey—and several urban and suburban parks offer visitors a chance to get outside for sporting activities of their own. It's the rodeo, however, that sets Dallas's sports apart from other metropolitan areas in the United States.

Mesquite Championship Rodeo

The **Mesquite Championship Rodeo** (1818 Rodeo Dr., 972/285-8777, www.mesquiterodeo.com, $15-45) is the real deal. In the suburb of Mesquite—roughly a 20-minute drive east of downtown Dallas—this is a big-time professional rodeo featuring the sport's top riders, with broadcasts on the Nashville Network. The arena packs thousands of fans and families in a football-like environment every Friday and Saturday night early April-late September.

It's well worth making a visit to experience this Western cultural tradition. Witness time-honored events such as bareback riding, bull riding, cowgirl barrel racing, team roping, saddle bronco riding, and steer wrestling, along with rodeo clowns and plenty of cowboy activity. The arena is on I-635, just off the Military Parkway exit.

Professional Sports

FOOTBALL

The Dallas Cowboys, known by football fans as "America's Team," play August-December at the fancy $1 billion AT&T Stadium in Arlington (1 AT&T Way, 817/892-4000, www.dallascowboys.com). Texas-worthy amenities include seating capacity for 80,000 fans, a 60-yard-wide high-definition screen inside the column-free interior of the world's largest domed stadium. The Dallas Cowboy Cheerleaders are still there, along with their skimpy outfits and big hair. Loyal fans pack the stadium on Sunday, with hopes that the Cowboys will find a way to get back to regular playoff contention like in the good ol' glory days. With new coach Mike McCarthy at the helm, those dreams are potentially closer to becoming a reality.

BASEBALL

The Texas Rangers play April-October about 20 minutes west of town at the Globe Life Field (I-30 and Hwy. 157, Arlington, 817/273-5100, www.texasrangers.com), one of Major League Baseball's most pleasant and aesthetically enjoyable stadiums. The Rangers have come tantalizingly close to winning it all in the past decade, and their potent lineup and pitching staff give fans hope that the team will be competitive for years to come.

BASKETBALL

The Dallas Mavericks, one of the National Basketball Association's consistently compelling teams, play November-April (and often even longer if they manage to make it to the playoffs) at American Airlines Center (Victory Ave., off I-35E, 214/665-4797, www.mavs.com), just north of downtown.

HOCKEY

Despite its warm climate, Dallas has a respected hockey team that takes to the ice October-mid-April. The Dallas Stars play at the American Airlines Center (Victory Ave., off I-35E, 214/467-8277, www.dallasstars.com), just north of downtown.

SOCCER

Major League Soccer has a devoted fan base in the Metroplex, and FC Dallas (9200 World Cup Way, Frisco, 214/705-6700, www.fcdallas.com) is the city's popular franchise, playing 30 miles (48 km) north of downtown. The season for FC Dallas (the FC stands for Football Club) lasts April-October.

Nature Trails

Dallas isn't known for its abundance of green space, but the city boasts several nature and walking trails to help urban dwellers and visitors get a taste of the great outdoors. Most outlying communities have suburban parks, but the following sites offer hiking trails in relatively remote natural surroundings near downtown for jogging, biking, strolling, or people-watching.

Boulder Park (3200 W. Redbird Lane, 214/670-4100) includes more than 6 miles (9.7 km) of trails through trees and hilly terrain along Five Mile Creek, southwest of downtown. Most of the trails have been created for bike use, with sections for beginners and others for advanced riders, but there is a soft-surface hiking trail for nature lovers. Maintained by the Dallas Off-Road Bicycle Association, this park is conveniently located near I-20 and Highway 67.

The L. B. Houston Nature Trail (between Dallas and Irving at Wildwood and California Crossing Rd., 214/670-6244) is a good place to spot wildlife among native plants and trees. The 300-acre area offers four unpaved hiking trails in a dense wilderness area along the Elm Fork of the Trinity River. The trails are in slightly flatter terrain than the hike and bike trails, but the natural surfaces render them virtually impassable after heavy rainfall.

White Rock Creek Greenbelt (Hillcrest Rd. and Valley View Lane, 214/670-8895), northeast of downtown, is one of Dallas's natural gems. A 7-mile (11.3-km) paved hiking, bicycling, and jogging trail connects to a similar 9-mile (14.5-km) trail that circles picturesque White Rock Lake.

ENTERTAINMENT AND EVENTS

Performing Arts

The **Morton H. Meyerson Symphony Center** (2301 Flora St., 214/670-3600, www.dallassymphony.com) in the Dallas Arts District is the city's premier venue for the performing arts. In addition to housing the prestigious **Dallas Symphony Orchestra**, the impressive facility, with an auditorium designed by world-renowned architect I. M. Pei, also hosts touring shows for the cultured crowd, including a pops concert series and adult contemporary artists.

Another of the city's highly respected performing arts organizations is the **Dallas Opera** (2403 Flora St., 214/443-1043, www.dallasopera.org), which performs its work at the AT&T Performing Arts Center. Several annual high-profile operas have included international stars in their American debuts, including Joan Sutherland and Plácido Domingo.

The ornate **Majestic Theatre** (1925 Elm St., 214/670-3687, www.liveatthemajestic.com) is a 1921 vaudeville-era gem near the heart of downtown. The 1,700-seat Majestic stages national and local musical productions, dramatic plays, comedy, and concerts.

Bars and Clubs

Nightlife in Dallas is a big ol' happenin' scene, and there are plenty of bars, dance clubs, and live music venues for any crowd, from Texas chic to student hangouts to gay bars. Nightlife is far superior in Dallas than in Fort Worth. Like most happening entertainment centers, the bars and clubs in Dallas switch names and ownership quicker than a socialite changes trendy sunglasses, so consult a trusty website like the city's alternative weekly *Dallas Observer* (or pick up a print copy, published every Thursday) to keep up to speed on the latest developments in club names and trends.

UPPER AND LOWER GREENVILLE

One of the city's consistently reliable nightlife areas is along Greenville Avenue, paralleling Central Expressway (U.S. 75). Just north of downtown near the Southern Methodist University campus, the district is referred to by locals as Upper Greenville and Lower Greenville; Mockingbird Lane is the dividing line. Both have essentially the same offerings, though Lower Greenville has a slightly more concentrated area of taverns, making it a better choice for facilitated barhopping.

Lower Greenville is anchored by the **Granada Theater** (3524 Greenville Ave., 214/824-9933, www.granadatheater.com), a 1930s movie venue featuring live music, better-than-average food, and occasional special events projected on the big screen. Other options include grabbing a pint and some steak fries down the road at the **Libertine Bar** (2101 Greenville Ave., 214/824-7900, www.libertinebar.com) or comfy nearby pub **Dubliner** (2818 Greenville Ave., 214/818-0911, www.dallasdubliner.com).

Upper Greenville (north of Mockingbird Lane to I-635/LBJ Freeway) is also worth checking out, especially if you're up for grabbing a beer in a comfortable environment where college kids tend to gravitate. The best of the bunch are just off Greenville Avenue on Yale and Dyer Streets. **Milo Butterfinger's** (5645 Yale Blvd., 214/363-0660, www.milobutterfingers.com) features an impressive selection of draft brews, and the **Ozona Bar & Grille** (4615 Greenville Ave., 214/265-9105, www.ozonagrill.com) offers a comfy beer garden to kick back in and enjoy a cold one.

DEEP ELLUM

Although Deep Ellum was ultra-trendy in the 1990s—a hipster district teeming with alternative-music venues and edgy nightclubs—the area has undergone changes in recent years. After most of the notable live music venues closed in the mid-2000s, the district became sketchy before experiencing a recent resurgence in reopened music clubs.

For live music, Deep Ellum's stalwart **Sons of Hermann Hall** (3414 Elm St., 214/747-4422, www.sonsofhermann.com, Wed.-Sat.), a remarkable historic building that oozes character, is where Texas artists perform roots and country music.

The biggest news to hit Deep Ellum in the past decade was the reopening of former legendary nightclub **Trees** (2709 Elm St., 214/741-1122, www.treesdallas.com). Adding randomness to the story is the person behind the reopening: former Vanilla Ice drummer Clint Barlow. Trees, named for the venue's arboresque decor, opened in the same location and continues the same vibe as its previous existence: an alternative rock live-music venue that thrived in the mid-late 1990s. Trees holds only 500 people and hosts a range of musical performances, from indie touring acts like Cat Power to local rockers like the Toadies.

Another Deep Ellum institution is **Double Wide** (3510 Commerce St., 214/887-6510, www.double-wide.com), a rural-themed bar with a big ol' silver tornado sculpture on the roof, offering bluesy and rough-around-the-edges rock bands and appropriately cheap beer in cans. Or check out the venerable **Anvil Pub** (2638 Elm St., 972/707-0217), a hip Irish pub with crazy-strong bloody Marys and tasty food.

COUNTRY AND WESTERN DANCING

Visitors looking for a true taste of Texas should definitely check out the legendary local branch of Houston's "Urban Cowboy" locale, **Gilley's Dallas** (1135 S. Lamar St., 214/421-2021, www.gilleysdallas.com). It's the ultimate country-and-western honky-tonk to test your skills on the dance floor or the mechanical bull. Also worth checking out is the enormous and enormously entertaining **Cowboys Red River Dancehall** (10310 Technology Blvd. W., 214/352-1796, www.cowboysdancehall.com/dallas), near Arlington, and the modest and genuinely lowdown **Adair's Saloon** in Deep Ellum (2624 Commerce St., 214/939-9900, www.adairssaloon.com).

DANCE CLUBS

If you'd rather shake your hips than scoot your boots, head to **Lizard Lounge** (2424 Swiss Ave., 214/826-4768, www.thelizardlounge.com), featuring nationally known DJs, electro, neo-Gothic, and plenty of party people. One of downtown's best retro dance clubs is **The Church** (2424 Swiss Ave., 214/826-4769, www.thechurchdallas.com), featuring 1980s goth and industrial music; dress accordingly.

GAY BARS

Many of the city's gay bars are in the same block on Cedar Springs Road, northwest of downtown. The **Round-up Saloon** (3912 Cedar Springs Rd., 214/522-9611, www.roundupsaloon.com) features gay country-and-western dancing. **JR's Bar & Grill** (3923 Cedar Springs Rd., 214/528-1004, www.jrsdallas.com) and **Sue Ellen's** (3903 Cedar Springs Rd., 214/559-0707, www.sueellensdallas.com) are popular gay and lesbian bars with Dallas flavor.

Events

SPRING

A spicy-food festival typically held in early spring, **ZestFest** (972/252-7476, www.zestfest.net) is in suburban Irving. It offers plenty of spice for flavor-seeking food enthusiasts. The festival features cooking demos by celebrity chefs, live music, and food samples.

The **Cinco de Mayo** (214/650-8381) event in suburban Oak Cliff celebrates Mexico's victory over France in 1862 and features "the Big parade," carnival rides, food, and entertainment.

SUMMER

Each August, **Taste of Dallas** (www.tasteofdallas.org) features restaurants, retail booths, Kids' Taste Town, and multiple music stages at historic Fair Park.

FALL

The legendary **State Fair of Texas** (214/565-9931, www.bigtex.com), held at Fair Park for more than 70 years, runs late September-early October and is an absolute must-see if you're in the city. Experience fried Twinkies, Big Tex, corny dogs, livestock shows, and the tallest Ferris wheel in the western hemisphere.

WINTER

The popular **Trains at NorthPark** (www. thetrainsatnorthpark.com) runs November-January at the **NorthPark Center** (1030 NorthPark Center). The event, completely redesigned with new trains and landscapes, features 35 toy trains and has been a holiday tradition delighting children and toy train lovers since 1987.

The **Children's Health Holiday Parade** (214/456-0113, www.dallasholidayparade.com) features floats, marching bands, and Santa himself. This annual event, complete with reserved bleacher seating, is a Dallas holiday tradition.

SHOPPING

Dallas takes its shopping very seriously. Although it doesn't have many well-kept little secrets offering bargain leather goods or Mexican imports like some other Texas cities, it's brimming with trendy boutiques and big-name department stores. In fact, Dallas claims to have more shopping centers per capita than anywhere else in the United States. Regardless, there are several alternatives to the generic shops found in most American cities.

Fashion and Department Stores

The mecca for serious shoppers is the original **Neiman Marcus** store in downtown Dallas (1618 Main St., 214/741-6911, www.neimanmarcus.com). Although it offers the same standard high-quality Neiman Marcus fare as others across the country, the items are housed inside the original department store building, and walking out of its doors onto the hustle and bustle of a busy downtown street is a rare New York City-style experience for shoppers in the South.

The **Galleria** (13350 Dallas Pkwy., 972/702-7100, www.galleriadallas.com) is impressive for its mammoth size and shopping options. A multilevel center with a hotel attached, the Galleria includes four-star restaurants, a year-round ice rink in the center, a five-theater cinema, and 200 stores,

including Saks Fifth Avenue, Tiffany & Co., Gucci, and Nordstrom.

High-end stores are also the featured attraction at **NorthPark Center** (8687 N. Central Expressway, 214/363-7441, www.northparkcenter.com), one of the country's first upscale indoor malls, completed in 1965. NorthPark Center still continues this tradition, offering a mix of luxury retail and fine dining with spacious courtyards and lush landscaping.

Western Wear

Not surprisingly, Dallas has many stores offering Western wear, and the following locations provide plenty of options for a night out at a local honky-tonk. Although some of the city's larger chains have closed, there are several smaller shops worth exploring for authentic cowboy gear. Chuck Norris endorses **Wild Bill's Western** (311 N. Market St., 214/954-1050, www.wildbillswestern.com). On the upper end of the scale is the glitzy and high-quality **Cowboy Cool** (3699 McKinney Ave., 214/521-4500, www.cowboycool.com). Also worth visiting for affordable yet well-made cowboy gear—brand-name boots, shirts, hats, and jeans—is **Cavender's Boot City** (2833 LBJ Freeway, 972/239-1375, www.cavenders.com).

FOOD

Dallas has some of the finest restaurants in the Southwest, featuring an eclectic mix of cuisines. From regional fare like barbecue and Tex-Mex to fancier spots serving sushi, French, and Italian, there's no shortage of good eats in Big D.

Downtown

MEXICAN AND LATIN AMERICAN

If you're staying downtown (or even if you're in the area), make a point to eat a meal at **Wild Salsa** (1800 Main St., 214/741-9453, www.wildsalsarestaurant.com, Mon.-Thurs.

1: Wild Salsa in downtown Dallas **2:** The Woolworth **3:** The Granada Theater

11am-10pm, Fri.-Sat. 11am-11pm, $11-25). This contemporary Mexican spot draws diners with its savory smells and cool vibe. Another bonus: The salsa placed on the table upon arrival is indeed wild (in a good way), with tangy tomatillo and spicy jalapeño blending perfectly with the crispy-fresh tortilla chips. Enhance the craziness with a Wild Rita, an extremely flavorful cocktail with roasted pineapple juice and jalapeño-infused tequila. The food is amazing, with highlights ranging from hearty chicken-thigh enchiladas to Mexican street-vendor taqueria-style tacos (the steak and *al pastor* pork are highly recommended).

One of Deep Ellum's most popular Mexican restaurants is **Maracas Cocina Mexicana** (2914 Main St., 214/748-7140, www.maracascm.com, Tues.-Thurs. 11am-10pm, Fri.-Sat. 11am-11pm, Sun. 11am-9pm, Mon. 11am-2pm, $11-22). Live Latin music is on the menu at Maracas, and the food is just as commendable. Tacos are the specialty here, especially Jose's combo (pulled pork, purple onions, pineapple, and cilantro). The savory brisket enchiladas are another flavorful favorite. Be forewarned: Maracas can get extremely loud, especially on weekend nights.

Noteworthy for its convenient West End location, **RJ's Mexican Cuisine** (1701 N. Market St., 214/744-1420, http://rjmexicancuisine.com, Sun.-Thurs. 11am-10pm, Fri.-Sat. 11am-11pm, $8-20) offers a slightly different take on standard Mexican-style food by adding spicy peppers and fresh vegetables to spruce up the tacos and quesadillas. There are even some unconventional Mexican options, such as barbecued ribs and tuna.

A favorite among locals is ★ **Gloria's** (3223 Lemmon Ave., 214/303-1166, www.gloriascusine.com, Mon.-Thurs. 11am-10pm, Fri.-Sat. 11am-11pm, Sun. 11am-9pm, $10-19), known throughout the city for its delectable Salvadoran and Mexican specialties. Start with the signature black bean dip (with tortilla chips) and continue with Latin American favorites like cheese *pupusas,* fried plantains, *yuca,* and empanadas. Top it all off with a horchata, a sweet Mexican cocktail that can double as a dessert.

AMERICAN AND SOUTHWESTERN

After spending a morning or afternoon working up a hearty appetite visiting Dallas's downtown cultural sites, head directly to ★ **Ellen's Southern Kitchen** (1718 N. Market St., 469/206-3339, www.gritsrule.com, Mon.-Sat. 7am-9pm, Sun. 7am-2pm, $14-32). Ellen's is an ideal place to sample quality comfort food in a comfortable environment. The menu's down-home options are tantalizing, including the delectable Cajun shrimp and grits (a savory blend of seasoned grilled shrimp and crumbled bacon atop cheesy, buttery grits) and the hearty meatloaf (topped with flavorful gravy and onions). Pair anything on the menu with a local beer or strong house-blend coffee. Bonus: Ellen's serves breakfast all day, so order a stack of big ol' buttermilk pancakes.

For those willing to spend a little extra money, consider **Dakota's** (600 N. Akard St., 214/740-4001, www.dakotasrestaurant.com, Mon.-Fri. 11am-2:30pm and 5:30pm-10pm, Sat. 5pm-10:30pm, $19-48), a romantic spot featuring New American cuisine and steaks. The wild game mixed grill is a signature dish, and the cuts of beef are dazzling—particularly the bone-in rib eye. For a more affordable option, consider the fixed-price lunch or dinner menu, consisting of an appetizer, a choice of three entrées, and dessert. Reservations are recommended.

If you're staying on Main Street and looking for a quality affordable meal, head directly to **The Woolworth** (1520 Elm St., 214/814-0588, thewoolworthdallas.com, Mon. 11am-2pm, Tues.-Thurs. 11am-midnight, Fri.-Sat. 10am-2am, $12-30). The Woolworth's vibe and food are trendy without being pretentious, a refreshing change from some of the nearby stuffy high-end eateries. Kick things off with a handcrafted cocktail like the gin-based Tom Cat or a local pale ale. Snack on some truffle fries while waiting for one of the Woolworth's flavorful entrées, including *charro* tacos, Southern-fried chicken, or caramelized salmon. Pro tip: If the weather's nice, ask for a patio seat so you can gaze at the nearby giant eyeball sculpture (or vice versa).

For those seeking something even more casual—think shorts and beers—head directly to **City Tavern** (1402 Main St., 214/745-1402, www.citytaverndowntown.com, Mon.-Sat. 11am-2am, Sun. 11am-midnight, $9-25). Pub grub is the specialty, so order a cheeseburger, chicken strips doused in a flavorful buffalo sauce, and a big ol' plate of fries. One of the Tavern's specialties is fried pickles—prepared with a perfect ratio of crispy batter and pickle nugget.

LUNCH

If you're in the mood for sushi, the best option downtown is Deep Ellum's venerable ★ **Deep Sushi** (2624 Elm St., 214/651-1177, www.deepsushi.com, Mon.-Thurs. 11am-10pm, Fri. 11am-midnight, Sat. 5pm-midnight, Sun. 5pm-10pm, $9-23). The fresh tuna and spicy volcano roll are highly recommended, and even standard items like avocado-based rolls are bursting with flavor. Weekends are the best time to go, when you'll get bonus enjoyment from the patio's live music and lively pedestrian traffic.

Another good lunch option is Deep Ellum's **Murray Street Coffee Shop** (103 Murray St., 214/655-2808, www.murraystreetcoffee.com, Mon.-Fri. 7am-4pm, Sat. 8am-4pm, $6-13). Although the premium coffees are the main draw, Murray Street's tasty sandwiches and hummus are also nice ways to escape the hustle and bustle of downtown Dallas.

For a down-home experience, check out the laid-back **Metropolitan Cafe** (2030 Main St., 214/741-2233, Mon.-Fri. 8am-3pm, $9-28). This family-run operation (the owner is usually behind the register and serving food while his wife and mother run the kitchen) offers a genuine home-style experience, complete with legendary crab cakes (Wed.), hearty breakfasts, high-piled sandwiches, savory soups, and, best of all, cookies, cakes, and treats.

STEAK

In the upscale range without being too high-end is **YO Ranch Steakhouse** (702 Ross Ave., 214/744-3287, www.yoranchsteakhouse.com, Mon.-Thurs. 11am-10pm, Fri.-Sat. 11am-11pm, Sun. 11am-9pm, $14-38). In the busy West End district, the YO has all the basic cuts of meat without the stuffy atmosphere of other steak restaurants. The buffalo filet mignon and bone-in rib-eye are the most popular items on the menu for good reason—they're delectable.

A commendable uptown steak house is **Perry's Steakhouse & Grille** (2000 McKinney Ave., 214/855-5151, www.perryssteakhouse.com, Mon.-Fri. 4pm-10pm, Sat. 4pm-11pm, Sun. 4pm-9pm, $15-39). All cuts of meat here are above average, but the filet mignon and pork chop are especially tasty. Perry's pays close attention to the edible details (bread, sides, and especially the crab cakes), which make it recommendable.

Oak Lawn Area
AMERICAN AND SOUTHWESTERN

Since Oak Lawn is one of the tony parts of Dallas, it should come as no surprise that this is where some of the city's most exquisite restaurants are located. For years, the über-exclusive **Mansion on Turtle Creek** (2821 Turtle Creek, 214/559-2100, Mon.-Sat. 6:30am-10pm, Sun. 7am-9:30pm, $23-51) represented the height of luxury as Texas's only five-star, five-diamond hotel and five-diamond restaurant. Times have changed, and the Mansion is loosening up its black tie: Jackets are no longer required to partake of the restaurant's famous Southwestern gourmet offerings; in fact, even (gulp) jeans are allowed in the main dining room. Of the many top-notch options, several are supremely spectacular: the filet of tenderloin au poivre, porcini-crusted filet mignon, and Niman Ranch lamb. This meal will set you back a pretty penny to dine among the elite. Reservations are recommended.

LUNCH

Technically just north of Oak Lawn in the Park Cities area, the legendary ★ **Sonny Bryan's Smokehouse** (2202 Inwood Rd., 214/357-7120, www.sonnybryans.com, 24 hours daily, $11-21) is a must for authentic Texas-style barbecue. Traditional meats are the way to go—try the triple crown of brisket, pork ribs, and sausage—and the sauce offers the perfect tangy topping that ties it all together. If that weren't enough, the building itself provides an ideal atmosphere, with its smoke-drenched walls and old wooden school desks and picnic tables. There aren't too many places like this outside the Lone Star State, and judging by the long lines of locals clamoring to get in for lunch each day, there aren't many others quite as good in Dallas.

You'll notice the brightly colored **Cosmic Café** (2912 Oak Lawn Ave., 214/521-6157, Mon.-Thurs. 11am-10:30pm, Fri.-Sat. 11am-11pm, Sun. noon-10pm, $9-18) from blocks away, and the punchy flavors waiting inside will also get your attention. This vegetarian landmark offers excellent traditional Middle Eastern staples such as falafel and hummus as well as samosas and flavorful sweet treats like brownies, homemade ice cream, and fruit smoothies.

For standard diner fare, check out **Lucky's** (3531 Oak Lawn Ave., 214/522-3500, www.luckysdallas.com, daily 7am-10pm, $9-19), with sandwiches and burgers along with its big draw: chicken-fried steak topped with peppery cream gravy. Pour some of it on a mound of nearby homemade mashed potatoes and you'll be feeling lucky (and sleepy) for the rest of the afternoon.

TEX-MEX

In the 1970s and 1980s, **Mia's Tex-Mex** (4322 Lemmon Ave., 214/526-1020, www.miastexmex.com, Tues.-Thurs. 11am-10pm, Fri.-Sat. 11am-10:30pm, Sun.-Mon. 11am-9pm, $8-17) drew huge crowds, including the cast of *Dallas*, along with legendary Dallas Cowboys coach Tom Landry and many of his players. Though it's since lost much of its star luster, Mia's still serves some of the city's most authentic and tasty Tex-Mex. Standard fare like enchiladas and chicken tacos are worthwhile, but make a point of trying the perfectly battered and seasoned chiles rellenos or the tender brisket tacos for a truly distinctive food experience.

One of Oak Lawn's most popular Mexican restaurants is **Herrera's Cafe** (3311 Sylvan Ave., 214/954-7180, Mon. and Wed.-Fri. 11am-9pm, Sat.-Sun. 9am-9pm, $8-13). Don't be dismayed by the outdated exterior—the food within is high-quality authentic goodness. The salsa is spicy and garlicky, the cheese is gooey and satisfying, and the beef and chicken are tender and perfectly seasoned.

Outlying Areas

BRUNCH

An ideal place to have a weekend morning brunch is **Dream Café** (2800 Routh St., 214/954-0486, www.thedreamcafe.com, daily 7am-3pm, $9-18), especially if you're with the family. Kids will love the enormous playground, the oatmeal, and the french toast, while adults will savor the huevos rancheros, cheese grits, and the kids' french toast leftovers. Healthy options abound at this comfortable location north of downtown.

Brunchers will also find home-style goodness in a casual environment at local chain **Bread Winners Cafe and Bakery** (3301 McKinney Ave., 214/754-4940, http://breadwinnerscafe.com, Mon. 7am-4pm, Tues.-Sun. 7am-9pm, $7-17), north of downtown. Snag a spot on the inviting brick courtyard patio and enjoy a cup of joe while you munch on a fresh pastry or wait for an inspired breakfast dish, like the popular smoked salmon scrambler and French ham benedict.

TEX-MEX

For a feast of the senses, drop by **El Ranchito** (610 W. Jefferson Blvd., 214/946-4238, Sun.-Thurs. 10am-10pm, Fri.-Sat. 11am-11:30pm, $10-19), in Oak Cliff, just south of downtown. From the colorful decor to brassy mariachi bands to the smells and tastes of savory Tex-Mex (emphasis on the Mex), you can't go wrong here. If you're feeling adventurous, try the house specialty of *cabrito* (goat), tender and flavorful meat that tastes surprisingly delicious paired with El Ranchito's buttery tortillas and hearty salsa. The *caldo de pollo* (chicken soup) is also a nice option for lunch or dinner.

Another worthy Tex-Mex spot is **Pepe's & Mito's Mexican Café** (2911 Elm St., 214/741-1901, www.pepesandmitos.com, Mon.-Tues. 11am-3pm, Wed.-Thurs. 11am-10pm, Fri.-Sat. 11am-11pm, Sun. 11am-5pm, $9-17), just east of downtown. This is a great place to stick with the classics—the chicken enchiladas in a tangy green tomatillo sauce, tacos with superbly seasoned beef, and pinto beans that are better than they have to be.

ACCOMMODATIONS

Like most big cities, Dallas has a wide range of hotels, from generic chains on uninspiring urban beltways to charmingly restored historic downtown gems. The Big D doesn't have a lot of options near the nightlife, but most of the best enchanting historic hotels in the heart of the city are a 10-minute cab ride from the city's hopping entertainment districts. Not surprisingly, the alternatives for those keeping a close eye on their wallets are farthest away from many of the city's main activities. Keep in mind, safe and affordable hotels in one of the nation's largest cities will cost at least $130 per night, but it beats getting stuck in an anonymous or ominous location.

$50-100
Hawthorn Suites (7880 Alpha Rd., 972/391-0000, www.staybridge.com, $65 d), offers a "well-equipped kitchen" in every suite, free Wi-Fi, and an outdoor pool and whirlpool. The hotel is near the suburb of Richardson, from which a ride-share to downtown Dallas is typically $30.

For a slight step up, consider the **Courtyard by Marriott Dallas Northwest** (2930 Forest Lane, 972/620-8000, www.

marriott.com, $79 d), a reliable motel 12 miles (19.3 km) north of downtown and 14 miles (22.5 km) from the airport. The Courtyard features free Wi-Fi, an outdoor pool, and a whirlpool, and its suites offer microwaves and mini fridges. The adjacent Courtyard Café serves a hot breakfast daily.

If you want to avoid the chains, book a room at the Texas-based **MCM Elegante** (2330 W. Northwest Hwy., 214/351-4477, www.mcmelegantedallas.com, $99 d), with complimentary shuttle service to and from both DFW and Love Field airports, an outdoor splash pool and spa tub, and free Wi-Fi.

$100-150
Just north of downtown is the **Holiday Inn North Dallas at Preston** (6055 Lyndon B Johnson Freeway, 214/404-4500, www.ihg.com, $100 d). The 300 rooms feature the chain's signature plush bedding along with included Wi-Fi. Other amenities include a nice indoor-outdoor heated pool and a fitness center.

The only bad thing about **Westin Park Central** (12720 Merit Dr., 972/385-3000, www.westindallasparkcentral.com, $103 d) is its isolated location. Despite being on a major freeway in a busy spot, the hotel itself is an urban island without walking access to restaurants or typical urban amenities. Once inside, however, you'll have everything you need in a reliably high-quality package, including top-notch bedding, a free continental breakfast, internet access, and a heated rooftop pool.

A surprisingly affordable and worthy option downtown is ★ **Hotel Indigo** (1933 Main St., 214/741-7700, www.ihg.com, $148 d), a 14-story National Historic Landmark that was the first Hilton property to carry the Hilton name. Now appealing to travelers who favor the boutique concept, the Indigo approach is refreshing, with seasonally updated color schemes and artwork. The hotel offers included Wi-Fi, a fitness center, and contemporary guest rooms with hardwood-style flooring, trendy photographs, and spa-style showers. A breakfast package is available for $10 per night. It's worth it for the delicious huevos rancheros alone.

One of the best weekend options for budget-minded travelers is **Hyatt House Dallas/Lincoln Park** (8221 N. Central Expressway, 214/696-1555, www.dallaslincolnpark.house. hyatt.com, $149 d). The 161 spacious rooms include kitchens, and the hotel offers a continental breakfast daily. In the heart of Dallas's tony Park Cities area, Hyatt House is only 10 minutes north of downtown and within walking distance of the upscale NorthPark Center.

$150-200

SpringHill Suites Downtown/West End (1907 N. Lamar St., 214/999-0500, www. marriott.com, $153 d) is in the heart of the historic West End and just blocks away from the city's arts district. This is a good place to stay among the bustle of the entertainment scene. The rooms are spacious and comfortable, and offer an ideal place to relax. Amenities include an outdoor pool and an included hot buffet breakfast or grab-and-go options.

The Fairmont Dallas (1717 N. Akard St., 866/540-4427, www.fairmont.com/dallas, $169 d) is a worthy downtown option. Near the business and arts districts, the Fairmont is somewhat slight on amenities (you have to pay for Wi-Fi access and breakfast), but its location is ideal for exploring Dallas on foot. The hotel itself is stylish, with a fitness center and an outdoor pool.

The Dallas Marriott Downtown (650 N. Pearl St., 214/979-9000, www.marriott.com, $179 d) is a nice downtown option in the arts district. Business is key here—the hotel is appealing in a corporate way, as opposed to family-friendly (you won't find a pool or buffet or even complimentary internet access). But it's located in a massive eye-catching late-modern skyscraper, listed on the National Register of Historic Places. Notable amenities include an impressive gym facility, maps with suggested jogging routes, and live music during happy hour.

Also notable is **La Quinta Inn & Suites**

Downtown (302 S. Houston St., 214/761-9090, www.laquintadallasdowntown.com, $189 d). In a historic 1920s building with a bold exterior paint scheme, this is an inviting option in the downtown business district, providing a charming mix of old and new. The rooms are small, but the amenities are impressive, including a complimentary breakfast buffet and Wi-Fi access. Parking is by valet only.

Don't count out the **Grand Hyatt DFW** (2337 S. International Pkwy., 972/973-1234, www.granddfw.hyatt.com, $199 d). Sometimes you have to get a hotel near the airport, or in this case, at the airport. Aside from the ultimate convenience to your flight (the hotel provides free transportation to all terminals via the airport's high-speed train system or an ordinary shuttle bus), the Hyatt features free Wi-Fi, upscale rooms with quality bedding, granite-top desks, minibars, robes, and a free fitness center with a heated pool.

$200-250

You can't go wrong at the classic ★ **Magnolia Hotel** (1401 Commerce St., 214/915-6500, www.magnoliahoteldallas.com, $200 d), with its rich history, ornate furnishings, optimal location, and old-fashioned charm. The Magnolia played a vital role in Dallas's history, and the legendary red-neon Pegasus atop the building is a treasured city landmark. The logo is from the once-dominant Magnolia Petroleum Company, headquartered in the hotel's remarkable 1922 Renaissance Revival building. The Magnolia's 330 guest rooms feature high ceilings, fine linens, oversize soaking tubs, fridges, and bathrobes. The hotel also provides some pretty amazing complimentary services, including breakfast at the Magnolia Court, afternoon cocktails and hors d'oeuvres, and even nighttime cookies and milk in the Magnolia Club's library.

★ **The Adolphus Hotel** (1321 Commerce

1: Hotel Indigo in downtown Dallas
2: The Adolphus Hotel 3: *Eye* on Main Street in Dallas. Sculpture by Tony Tasset.

St., 214/742-8200, www.hoteladolphus.com, $204 d) is one of the best ways to experience Dallas. This beautiful baroque-style 1912 architectural gem from beer magnate Adolphus Busch welcomes visitors with an opulent lobby area and excellent dining. This is an ideal way to experience upscale Dallas without spending like a socialite. Be sure to admire the hotel's exterior facade, which features faces carved in stone and intricate design work. Exquisite woodwork and attention to detail are around every corner. This quality is evident in the 432 guest rooms, which feature antique furnishings and separate sitting areas, as well as minibars and walk-in closets, upscale baths, and flat-screen TVs. Walls display European lithographs, and feather pillows, deep tubs, and brass-accented fixtures add to the hotel's luxurious feel. To top things off, tea is served in the stately Lobby Living Room while beautiful music emanates from an authentic 1893 Victorian Steinway grand piano, reportedly destined for the *Titanic*.

The Highland Dallas (5300 E. Mockingbird Lane, 214/520-7969, www. thehighlanddallas.com, $209 d) is pretty fancy but worth the extra cost for the memorable experience. From the time you enter the spacious and impressive lobby, it's evident this is a hotel that pays attention to details— color schemes, geometric patterns, and open space are prevalent themes throughout the building, including the 200 guest rooms, which offer minibars, marble vanities, and bathrobes. The hotel hosts complimentary evening wine hours and serves light fare in the lobby lounge; its restaurant, Knife, was once a famous Polynesian spot where celebs such as Bob Hope, Kirk Douglas, and Mickey Mantle sampled the bar's inventive cocktails.

Over $250

The swanky and über-urban **Hotel ZaZa** (2332 Leonard St., 214/468-8399, www. hotelzaza.com, $255 d) offers spacious, chic rooms with minibars, luxury bedding, and "sensual lighting." The ZaSpa provides body therapies and a tropical pool, and the

Dragonfly Restaurant features global cuisine. The hotel's "custom-designed concept suites" include free Wi-Fi access and daily coffee service. On weekends, the hotel shows classic movies on a large screen near its outdoor patio.

The Warwick Melrose Hotel (3015 Oak Lawn Ave., 214/521-5151, www. warwickmelrosedallas.com, $259 d) is a 1924 historic Dallas landmark in the city's fashionable Oak Lawn area north of downtown. The Melrose's clean comfort and style is apparent in each of its 184 distinct extra-large guest rooms featuring mahogany furnishings, minibars, marble baths, terry-cloth robes, and incredible views of the downtown skyline. The Melrose has attracted international celebrities for eight decades and has a reputation as one of the city's best hotels. Its award-winning Landmark Restaurant specializes in spectacular New American food, and its comfy Library Bar is a Dallas tradition offering 100 types of martinis along with live entertainment and late-night dining.

The Rosewood Mansion on Turtle Creek (2821 Turtle Creek Blvd., 214/559-2100, www.mansiononturtlecreek.com, $349 d) provides lavish accommodations and has a worldwide reputation for its luxury. Rooms feature European-style decor with original artwork, antiques, 480-thread-count linens, fresh-cut flowers, walk-in closets, marble baths, robes, and slippers, along with French doors opening onto private balconies. As expected with a luxury hotel, the Southwestern cuisine-themed restaurant is exquisite and consistently named one of the top hotel restaurants in the country. The bar offers casual dining surrounded by a hunting-themed decor, and the hotel's Promenade restaurant serves breakfast overlooking the lush landscaped grounds.

Camping

Just 10 miles (16 km) southwest of Dallas, **Cedar Hill State Park** (1570 FM 1382, Cedar Hill, 972/291-3900, www.tpwd.state.tx.us, $10-30) is a 1,826-acre urban nature preserve on the 7,500-acre Joe Pool Reservoir. The 355 rural wooded campsites have water and electricity, and the park's facilities include restrooms with showers, 4 miles (6.4 km) of hiking and backpacking trails, and 10 miles (16 km) of mountain bike trails.

Other nearby camping options include **Dallas Hi-Ho** (18 mi/29 km south of town in Glenn Heights, 877/619-3900, www.hihorvpark.com, $35), which offers full hookups for motor homes and spots for trailers, fifth wheels, campers, and tents. Additional considerations include **Dallas/Arlington KOA** (2715 S. Cooper, 817/277-6600, www.koa.com, $37), and **Dallas Northeast Campground** (903/527-3615, www.dallasnortheastcampground.com, $28) in Caddo Mills. Both offer RV hookups, cabins, and swimming.

INFORMATION AND SERVICES
Tourism Offices
The Dallas/Fort Worth International Airport has handy visitor information booths to help fresh arrivals get oriented, but it's worth stopping by the **Dallas Convention and Visitors Bureau** (800/232-5527, www.visitdallas.com) information centers to get personalized information and maps. The main info center is housed in the city's landmark downtown **"Old Red" Courthouse** (100 S. Houston St., 214/571-1301, daily 9am-5pm) and features internet terminals and touch-screen computer information kiosks.

Publications
Entertainment and events are covered in several Dallas publications. The metro daily *Dallas Morning News* is an esteemed newspaper and offers thorough coverage of local, state, national, and international news. The best bet for cultural events is the *Dallas Observer,* the city's weekly alternative paper, published every Thursday.

GETTING THERE AND AROUND
Air
Dallas is served by the enormous **Dallas/Fort Worth International Airport** (DFW, 972/973-3112, www.dfwairport.com) and the smaller **Dallas Love Field** (DAL, 214/670-6080, www.dallas-lovefield.com). Downtown Dallas is accessible from DFW via **DART** (Dallas Area Rapid Transit) and on the **Trinity Metro** train Monday-Saturday.

If you're not taking a ride-share service, cabs are still a reliable way to get from the airport to a Metroplex destination, but it will cost $35-40. Another more-affordable option (averaging around $25) is the **SuperShuttle** (817/329-2000, www.supershuttle.com), available from DFW at all hours but occasionally sluggish depending on the number of passengers along for the ride and their destinations. In addition, many airport-area hotels offer pickup and drop-off services.

Dallas Love Field is more centrally located but is limited in flight options since only Southwest Airlines and one regional airline currently serve it. Love Field is about 7 miles (11.3 km) northwest of downtown, and local transportation is offered by taxi (approximately $30 to downtown) and **SuperShuttle** (817/329-2000, www.supershuttle.com).

Bus
Dallas Area Rapid Transit (DART, 1401 Pacific Ave., 214/979-1111, www.dart.org) operates bus service throughout the city Monday-Friday 6am-8pm and Saturday-Sunday 8am-5pm. The basic single-ride fare for most local trips is $2.50, and all-day passes are available for $5. Maps and schedules can be found at DART transit centers, libraries, and city hall.

Dallas's intercity buses are at the **Greyhound Bus Terminal** (205 S. Lamar St., 214/849-6831) at Union Station, the main downtown train station. Union Station is also serviced by Amtrak's *Texas Eagle* and is connected to the DART system.

Rapid Transit

DART (214/979-1111, www.dart.org) offers public transportation in and among 13 Dallas-area communities with rail, bus, and ride-share services. In addition to its airport line, DART provides service to Fort Worth via Trinity Metro (817/215-8600, www. ridetrinitymetro.org).

Vicinity of Dallas

The perfect antidote to the hustle and bustle of the Big D is a trip to a small nearby community. Most of these outlying towns began as humble villages out in the country. Now that they're filled with commuters, they've taken on a suburban feel, but their downtowns retain the quaint appeal of their days as mercantile centers and seats of government. You won't find historic courthouses or antiques shops in all these communities, however. Arlington's big draw is amusement, with Cowboys Stadium, the Six Flags amusement park, and the Texas Rangers ballpark.

ARLINGTON

Arlington is all about thrills. Whether it's the fluttering sensation in the belly from a roller coaster at Six Flags or the rush of adrenaline that comes with a home run at the Rangers' ballpark, Arlington (population 398,112) is a great setting for fun and games. This supersize suburb, occasionally referred to as the "Midway of the Metroplex," is also home to a science center and country music revue, allowing visitors several days of family fun, with side trips to the Metroplex for big-city activities (Dallas and Fort Worth are both 15 mi/24 km away on I-30). There is no shortage of major roadways or hotels near these attractions.

Cowboys Stadium

Arlington is known throughout the football world as the home of the state-of-the-art AT&T Stadium (925 N. Collins St., 817/892-4161, http://stadium.dallascowboys. com). Constructed for a mere $1.2 billion, the 660,800-square-foot home of the Dallas Cowboys is the largest domed structure in the world. Cynically referred to as the Taj Mahal of stadiums (or a monument to Cowboys owner Jerry Jones's ego), the stadium is a marvel to behold. Looming on the horizon like a massive spaceship, it features a retractable roof, luxury suites, and, perhaps most impressive and garish of all, a 60-yard-wide video screen suspended over the field.

Tours (Mon.-Sat. 10am-6pm, Sun. 11am-5pm) are available for Cowboys (and fancy stadium) fans. The self-guided tour ($22) lets you see the locker rooms and toss a football around on the field. For $32, you can see the luxury suites and press boxes with a knowledgeable and entertaining guide.

Globe Life Field

The brand-new Texas Rangers' Globe Life Field (734 Stadium Dr., 817/273-5100, www. rangers.mlb.com) is on track to be open for the first pitch of the baseball season in April 2020. Plans call for its roof to be the first of its kind in baseball, with parts of it made of a transparent material. Unlike the Rangers' "old" ballpark, which opened in 1994 and was deemed outdated 25 years later, the new stadium will have a retractable roof, allowing fans to catch a ballgame in air-conditioned comfort instead of 110°F (43°C) discomfort.

Six Flags Over Texas

Named for the six national flags that have flown over Texas during its history, Six Flags Over Texas (I-30 at Hwy. 360, 817/530-6000, www.sixflags.com/overtexas, Mon.-Fri. 10:30am-9pm, Sat.-Sun. 10:30am-10pm, hours vary spring and fall, $84, parking $28) has been the king of Texas amusement parks since 1961, when oil tycoon Angus G. Wynne

Vicinity of Dallas and Fort Worth

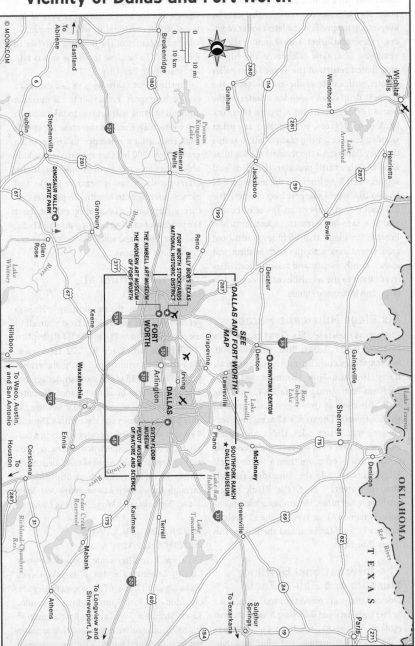

© MOON.COM

0   10 mi
0   10 km

To Abilene

To Waco, Austin,
and San Antonio

To Houston

To Longview and
Shreveport, LA

To Texarkana

Eastland

Dublin

Stephenville

Breckenridge

Possum
Kingdom
Lake

Mineral
Wells

Graham

Windthorst

Wichita
Falls

Lake
Arrowhead

Henrietta

Jacksboro

Bowie

Decatur

Denton

Gainesville

Sherman

Denison

OKLAHOMA

Red River

Lake Texoma

TEXAS

DINOSAUR VALLEY
STATE PARK

Granbury

Glen
Rose

Lake
Whitney

Brazos River

Reno

THE KIMBELL ART MUSEUM
THE MODERN ART MUSEUM
OF FORT WORTH
FORT WORTH STOCKYARDS
NATIONAL HISTORIC DISTRICT
BILLY BOB'S TEXAS

Keene

Hillsboro

Waxahachie

Ennis

Corsicana

Richland-Chambers
Res.

Cedar Creek
Reservoir

Mabank

Athens

Trinity River

FORT
WORTH

Arlington

Grapevine

Irving

DALLAS

Plano

McKinney

Greenville

Sulphur
Springs

Paris

Lake
Tawakoni

Kaufman

Terrell

Lake Ray
Hubbard

SIXTH FLOOR
MUSEUM
PEROT MUSEUM
OF NATURE AND SCIENCE
SOUTHFORK RANCH
DALLAS MUSEUM

"DALLAS AND FORT WORTH"
MAP

SEE

DOWNTOWN DENTON

Lewisville

Lake
Lewisville

Ray
Roberts
Lake

Jr. was so inspired by a visit to Disneyland he commissioned a similar park for the Lone Star State. Six Flags has evolved over the years by keeping up to speed on the latest roller coasters, rides, and other amusement park diversions. The park celebrated the highly anticipated return of the Texas Giant roller coaster, with a state-of-the-art steel track, the steepest drop of any wooden coaster in the world (79 degrees), and a record-breaking bank of 95 degrees, steeper than any other wooden coaster on the planet—all in trains that pay homage to the iconic 1961 Cadillac Deville. Other thrill-providers that elicit loud screams and long lines are the mammoth El Diablo (the world's largest loop coaster), the 315-foot (96-m) Superman Tower of Power, and the famous Batman, Joker, and Mr. Freeze. Six Flags also includes traditional amusement park activities such as theatrical shows, family events, and seasonal festivities in addition to the requisite cotton candy, hot dogs, and lemonade stands.

Six Flags Hurricane Harbor

Just across the street, **Six Flags Hurricane Harbor** (1800 E. Lamar Blvd., 817/640-8900, www.sixflags.com/hurricaneharbortexas, daily 10:30am-7pm summer, Sat.-Sun. 10:30am-7pm spring and fall, $42, parking $10) bills itself as the largest water park in the Southwest. The park's 47 acres are overflowing with water rides, slides, and pools. Millions of gallons of water propel, glide, and douse visitors on more than a dozen rides. Highlights include the Tornado's funnel-shaped waterfall ride, the Black Hole's gushing water tubes, the amusing and appropriately named Mega Wedgie, the 12 levels of activity in Surf Lagoon, and the Bubba Tub inner-tube ride.

The International Bowling Museum and Hall of Fame

One of Arlington's newest cultural attractions is The International **Bowling Museum and Hall of Fame** (621 Six Flags Dr., 817/385-8215, www.bowlingmuseum.com, Tues.-Sat.

9:30am-5pm, Sun. noon-6pm, $9.50 adults, $7.50 seniors and ages 4-18). The upscale 18,000-square-foot museum is part of the massive International Bowling Campus. So why is the center of the bowling universe in Arlington? To be close to all the sports fans and visitors in Fun City.

Bowling doesn't always get a fair shake as a competitive sport, but a visit to the museum and hall of fame will get you to take it much more seriously. Exhibits showcase the sport's past, including a reference to an Egyptian grave from 3200 BC that appeared to include objects for an early form of bowling. It also offers plenty of fun interactive kiosks and games, references to bowling in popular culture, a surprisingly fascinating exhibit about the process of making bowling pins and balls, and a fun mini-lane where visitors can knock down some real pins.

The Planetarium at UT Arlington

After a full day in the sun waiting in lines to get on rides and waterslides, treat yourself to the cool, dark **Planetarium at UT Arlington** (700 Planetarium Place, 817/272-1183, www.uta.edu/planetarium, open daily, showtimes vary, $7 adults, $5 seniors and under age 19). The planetarium boasts a 60-foot-diameter (18-m) dome and was upgraded to become the only planetarium in the state with a Digistar 4 system with DLP projectors, offering a surprisingly realistic experience of viewing stars as they appear in the night sky. Audiences are transported to various otherworldly locales through shows such as *Spacepark 360, Stars of the Pharaohs,* and *Wonders of the Universe.*

River Legacy Living Science Center

On a much smaller scale is **River Legacy Living Science Center** (703 NW Green Oaks Blvd., 817/860-6752, www.riverlegacy. org, Mon.-Sat. 9am-5pm, $5 adults, $4 seniors, $3 children), a popular family destination featuring interactive exhibits with a focus on regional flora and fauna. Visitors experience

Bowling for Dallas

The International Bowling Museum and Hall of Fame

When someone mentions bowling, do you immediately think of the Dallas suburbs? You should: The city of Arlington has become the center of the bowling universe. The **International Bowling Campus** (621 Six Flags Dr., 817/385-8215, www.bowlingmuseum.com)—the sport's educational, governing, and testing center—set up its pins in Fun City to be in proximity to high-profile destinations like Six Flags Over Texas, Cowboys Stadium, and Globe Life Field. This major move to the Lone Star State carried some controversy, however, since the sport's previous headquarters were located in traditional bowling hotbeds—the blue-collar beer-brewing cities of Milwaukee and St. Louis.

When the campus opened in 2010, representatives proudly announced that "for the first time in the 5,000-year history of the sport, the bowling industry is united under one roof." The massive complex includes a collection of organizations you probably never even knew existed: the International Bowling Museum and Hall of Fame, the International Training and Research Center, the National Headquarters for Bowling Proprietors' Association of America, and the United States Bowling Congress. This is where bowling's best and brightest minds gather to study scientific aspects of the sport, share knowledge with casual and die-hard fans, and test new equipment.

Perhaps most significantly, the campus is home to the new and expanded International Bowling Museum and Hall of Fame. The state-of-the-art museum offers interactive displays and exhibits along with distinctive items from bowling's various eras dating to 3200 BC.

According to the International Bowling Campus, there are more than 69 million bowlers in the United States alone. These facilities in Arlington are expected to draw many of them for bouts of bowling-related brainstorming.

the North Texas natural environment through the center's terrariums, aquariums, and a simulated raft ride on the Trinity River. Also on the grounds is a 950-acre nature park with educational and recreational activities and hiking and biking trails along the banks of the Trinity River. The park is home to a bizarre fungus known as the devil's cigar that breaks open with a hiss to issue "smoke" (a cloud of spores).

Food

TEX-MEX

Locals love North Arlington's **Mariano's Hacienda Arlington** (2614 Majesty Dr., 817/640-5118, www.marianosrestaurants.com, Sun.-Thurs. 11am-10pm, Fri.-Sat. 11am-11pm, $11-23), with its tender brisket tacos, spicy Texas Torpedos (stuffed jalapeños), and charmingly dated 1970s ambience. Even more impressive, however, is the restaurant owner's claim to fame as inventor of the world's first frozen margarita machine (inspired by a Slurpee machine at the local 7-Eleven store and now housed at the Smithsonian).

Closer to the theme parks is **Mercado Juarez Restaurant** (2222 Miller Rd., 817/649-0307, www.mercadojuarez.com, Sun.-Thurs. 11am-9:30pm, Fri.-Sat. 11am-10:30pm, $8-20), a local chain that's earned raves from Dallasites for decades. Known for its distinctive mesquite-fired grill, Mercado Juarez serves some of the Metroplex's best *carne guisada*. Wrap it up in a freshly made tortilla with the restaurant's signature warm salsa picante for a classic Tex-Mex flavor combo.

STEAK

The charming **Southern Recipes Grill** (2715 N. Collins St., 817/469-9878, Mon.-Fri. 11am-9pm, Sat. 8am-9pm, Sun. 8am-4pm, $11-28) is a great place to go if you're looking to unwind with a substantial meal after a day full of amusement. Waitstaff keep things casual here. If you've never tried a chicken-fried steak, this is a good place to start, and if you're already a CFS connoisseur, you won't be disappointed. Locals drop in for the black-eyed peas alone.

Accommodations

Arlington's best choice for moderate rates is **Days Inn & Suites** (2626 E. Randol Mill Rd., 817/649-0147, www.wyndhamhotels.com, $59 d), within a few miles of Hurricane Harbor, Six Flags Over Texas, and Globe Life Field. The hotel features complimentary breakfast, a pool, and rooms with fridges and microwaves.

A bit closer to Six Flags is the clean and comfortable **Residence Inn by Marriott** (1050 Brookhollow Plaza Dr., 817/649-7300, www.marriottn.com, $99 d), which offers big suites that are especially nice for families—kids can go to bed early in one room while mom and dad watch TV in the other. Other amenities include free breakfast, an outdoor pool, and free Wi-Fi.

If you're looking for a quality and affordable lodging option, head to **Lux Hotel and Spa** (117 S. Watson Rd., 800/896-1534, www.wyndhamhotels.com, $127 d). The boutique hotel's amenities include free Wi-Fi, a complimentary breakfast buffet, and rooms with fridges and microwaves.

The ★ **Hilton Arlington** (2401 E. Lamar Blvd., 817/640-3322, www.hilton.com, $129 d) offers a step up in the quality of amenities and service. The Hilton provides complimentary transportation to and from the airport and shuttle service within a 3-mile (4.8-km) radius of the hotel, which covers all the major attractions—Six Flags, Hurricane Harbor, Globe Life Field. The hotel's outdoor pool includes a splash area for kids and an outdoor lap section for adults.

Information and Services

The **Arlington Convention and Visitors Bureau's Visitor Information Center** (1905 E. Randol Mill Rd., 817/461-3888, www.arlington.org, Mon.-Sat. 9am-5pm) provides maps, brochures, and additional information about accommodations and restaurants in the area.

The Trolley (817/504-9744, www.arlingtontrolley.com) is a free shuttle service running among Arlington's major hotels and attractions. It occasionally runs a bit slow, but it's hard to complain when the service is free. Ride-shares and cabs are always an option for those who can't stand the idea of being on their feet another 20 or 30 minutes waiting for the trolley.

Getting There and Around

Arlington is geographically closer to Fort Worth, but it's often aligned with Dallas due to the Cowboys connection. To drive here from Dallas or Fort Worth, hop on I-30 or I-20 for the 30-minute drive, depending on the time of day. For those visiting from Houston, head north on I-45, and from Austin and San Antonio, on I-35, until you reach I-20. Take Highway 360 north to access all the sports facilities and theme parks.

WAXAHACHIE

In some ways, Waxahachie (population 36,807) is the opposite of Arlington. It's a quintessentially quaint town, known as the "Gingerbread Capital of Texas." As such, it is appropriately chock-full of rich history and charming heritage tourism attractions. About 30 miles (48 km) south of Dallas, Waxahachie's name originates from a Native American word meaning "cow" or "buffalo." Prosperity from the area's rich cotton farming industry in the early 1900s resulted in the construction of the attractive downtown buildings and the cotton barons' glamorous Victorian "gingerbread" homes. The city's crown jewel is the enormous and stunning 1897 Ellis County Courthouse, one of nearly 300 Waxahachie structures listed on the National Register of Historic Places. The town's true Texana appeal has resulted in numerous movies being filmed here, including *Bonnie and Clyde, Places in the Heart,* and *Tender Mercies.*

Ellis County Courthouse

The nine-story, red granite and sandstone **Ellis County Courthouse** (101 W. Main St., 972/825-5000, Mon.-Fri. 8am-5pm) is an architectural masterpiece worth making the 30-minute drive from Dallas to see. In the Romanesque Revival style, this 1897 building is a true sight to behold—ornate nooks and crannies give way to massive architectural features, and the entire castle-like element of the edifice is awe-inspiring. One of the fascinating pieces of folklore involves a face carved atop the sandstone columns. The face begins as an attractive homage to a woman, said to be the granddaughter of the stone carver's landlord,

but becomes progressively more grotesque, apparently reflecting the unrequited attraction she felt for him. The interior of the building is also a visual spectacle, with intricate detailing, historically accurate color schemes, and ornate woodwork.

Ellis County Museum

Across the street from the courthouse is the **Ellis County Museum** (201 S. College St., 972/937-0681, www.rootsweb.com/~txecm, Mon.-Sat. 10am-5pm, free). Housed in a historic 1889 Masonic temple, the museum contains exhibits depicting everyday life in the Waxahachie area from the mid-1880s to the early 1900s. The museum specializes in old commercial signage—it's interesting to see the variety of random local businesses (optometrists, printers, newspapers) and their methods of enticing customers at the turn of the 20th century.

Gingerbread Trail

Each June, Waxahachie's **Gingerbread Trail Tour of Homes** (972/937-0681) celebrates the city's architectural legacy by showcasing historic commercial and community sites. One of the featured attractions is the 1902 Chautauqua Auditorium, an octagonal 2,500-seat open-air pavilion built in conjunction with the late-1800s adult education movement in Chautauqua, New York. Other Gingerbread Trail events include an arts and crafts show, a street dance, and performances on the downtown square.

Food

After you've had your fill of heritage tourism on courthouse square, make a beeline for the deservedly popular ★ **Farm Luck Soda Fountain** (109 W. Franklin St., 214/903-8021, http://farmlucksodafountain.com, Mon.-Sat. 11am-9pm, Sun. 11am-3pm, $7-14). In a charming historic corner building with plenty of natural light on white ceramic tiles, Farm Luck offers down-home food with a welcoming small-town atmosphere. Stick with traditional favorites like the BLT, turkey club, or burger accompanied by a hot bowl of sublime tomato-basil soup.

Another popular place to dine in the historic downtown district is **The Dove's Nest** (105 W. Jefferson St., 972/938-3683, www.thedovesnestrestaurant.com, Mon.-Sat. 11am-2pm, $11-23). Fancy sandwiches are the specialty, from portabella veggie to ham and jam (as in smoked ham and peach habanero jam) to pulled pork barbecue. Locals have rewarded its efforts by making the restaurant a source of hometown pride.

A good spot to soak up local flavor is **Catfish Plantation** (814 Water St., 972/937-9468, www.catfishplantation.com, Fri. 5pm-9pm, Sat. 11am-9pm, Sun. 10am-8pm, $12-19). Located in one of the city's trademark Victorian gingerbread homes, the Catfish Plantation is perhaps known better as a haunted house than a restaurant. Although the Cajun specialties and cornmeal-battered catfish fillets are legendary, it's the three resident ghosts that supposedly slam doors, play pianos, and knock on walls that garner the most attention.

Accommodations

One of Waxahachie's least-expensive yet decent options is **La Quinta Inn** (311 Stadium Dr., 972/937-5525, www.laquintawaxahachie.com, $84 d), which includes free continental breakfast, free Wi-Fi, and an outdoor pool. Slightly more expensive and upscale is the **Hampton Inn & Suites** (2010 Civic Center Dr., 972/923-0666, www.hilton.com, $129 d), offering a free hot breakfast and studio suites. Even more expensive is **Holiday Inn Express** (984 U.S. 287 Bypass W., 972/938-3300, $140 d). This nice new hotel handles the basics effectively with above-average service and amenities, including free buffet breakfast and complimentary Wi-Fi.

Information and Services

The **Waxahachie Chamber of Commerce/Convention and Visitors Bureau** (102 YMCA Dr., 972/937-2390, www.waxahachiechamber.com) is a good place to drop by to speak with someone in person about area restaurants and attractions and to pick up maps and brochures.

Getting There and Around

Waxahachie is about 30 miles (48 km) and 30 minutes south of Dallas via I-35. Visitors should take the U.S. 287 Business exit (a.k.a. Main Street) and head east for a few miles to reach the historic downtown area. From

Ellis County Museum in downtown Waxahachie

Houston, take I-45 north for three hours, then take the U.S. 287 exit west to reach town (about 15 minutes).

MCKINNEY

Located 31 miles (50 km) north of Dallas off U.S. 75, this town of 191,645 residents was named for Collin McKinney, a signer of the Texas Declaration of Independence and author of a bill establishing North Texas's counties. For more than a century, McKinney primarily served as an agribusiness center (cattle, corn, horses, wheat), but by the mid-1980s it had become a commuter center for residents working in Dallas. It's currently home to nearly 300 businesses, including Collin County Community College, and is one of the fastest-growing cities of its size in Texas, largely due to its proximity to the Metroplex and outlying supersize suburbs like Plano, where many people commute from the comparatively appealing small-town atmosphere.

Historic Courthouse Square

McKinney's Historic Courthouse Square has more than 100 shops—primarily antiques stores, art galleries, restaurants, and specialty spots. The Old Collin County Courthouse, the centerpiece of this downtown historic district, was built in 1874 and remodeled nearly 50 years later to include its current neoclassical facade. Just off the square is the North Texas History Center (300 E. Virginia St., 972/542-9457, www.thenthc. org, Thurs.-Sat. 10am-4pm, free), offering occasional exhibits related to the pioneer settlers and agricultural heritage of the region. Housed in a remarkable 1911 U.S. post office made of limestone with Italianate detailing, the museum is known for its stunning 1934 Works Progress Administration-painted mural and hidden walkways and peepholes once used by postal inspectors.

Heard-Craig House Historic Center

The Heard-Craig House Historic Center

(205 W. Hunt St., 972/569-6909, www. heardcraig.org, Tues. and Thurs. 1pm, $10 for 2 plus tea) showcases the life of an affluent owner of a downtown mercantile store from the early 20th century. The Heard family's hospitality made this residence a center of social, business, art, and literary activities. Heard constructed the 7,000-square-foot mansion in 1900, and his family resided in the home for 70 years. Painstakingly restored, the grand home is now open for general visitation, guided tours, and private events. Tours are offered on Tuesday and Thursday at 1pm and by appointment.

Food

McKinney has several top-notch Mexican restaurants, and one of the city's finest is **El Juarez Mexican Restaurant** (311 E. Louisiana St., 972/548-9181, www.eljuarez. com, Tues.-Sun. 10am-8:30pm, $11-22). El Juarez has lured families, antiquers, and businesspeople to its cantina-esque location on the downtown square for several decades. Traditional Tex-Mex is the main draw—you can't go wrong with the chicken enchiladas, fajitas, or *carne guisada*.

Cristina's Fine Mexican Restaurant (216 E. Virginia St., 214/544-2800, www. cristinasmex.com, Sun.-Thurs. 11am-9pm, Fri.-Sat. 11am-10pm, $13-24) lives up to its name. The vibe at this regional suburban chain is semi-upscale, which can be a nice change of pace from the typically loud and distracting cantina-style restaurants. And the food is top-notch, with suggested items ranging from chicken flautas to chiles rellenos to the superb sopapillas.

Accommodations
BED-AND-BREAKFASTS

A bed-and-breakfast is an ideal place to spend the night in a historic spot like McKinney, and one of the town's best-regarded establishments is the **Chaska House** (716 W. Main St., 972/937-3390, www.chaskabb.com, $145-195). The 1900 Revival-style home is brimming with Southern historical charm, and its romantic ambience and quality amenities are extremely commendable.

HOTELS AND MOTELS

For budget-minded travelers, McKinney's **Super 8 Motel** (910 N. Central Expressway, 972/548-8880, www.super8.com, $60 d) is a decent option with a free continental breakfast. Also worth considering is **Best Western McKinney Inn & Suites** (480 Wilson Creek Blvd., 972/548-3000, www.bestwestern.com, $101 d), offering a complimentary deluxe breakfast and newspaper, an outdoor pool and indoor spa,

and free Wi-Fi. **Comfort Suites** (1590 N. Central Expressway, 972/548-9595, www. choicehotels.com, $119 d) has spacious suites with microwaves, fridges, free Wi-Fi, and free breakfast for a step up from the moderate-range options.

Information and Services

For information on McKinney's restaurants, accommodations, and events, drop by the city's **Convention and Visitors Bureau's Visitor Information Center** (1575 Heritage Dr., Suite 100, 888/649-8499, www. visitmckinney.com, Mon.-Fri. 8am-5pm).

Fort Worth

Fort Worth is the quintessential Texas city—it has a compelling heritage, dynamic culture, and true grit. With a comfortably sized population of 895,008, it's easy to get around, which is handy considering there are several days' worth of activities and attractions to experience.

A big part of the city's appeal is its rich history, which began in 1849 when it was established as a military post on the Texas frontier. By the 1860s, Fort Worth was the main destination for cattle drives, which originated on large South Texas ranches and moved along legendary routes like the Chisholm Trail. The city's historical heyday was during the late 1800s and early 1900s, when railroads transformed Fort Worth into a major cattle industry town with a railhead, extensive stockyards, and beef-packing facilities. Although the city would continue to grow as an agricultural center, the stockyards remained the most prominent feature of its cultural identity.

The area where most of the activity took place serves primarily as a tourism hub these days, but there's still some honest-to-goodness cowboy-related business in the Stockyards. Livestock auctions are held weekly, and there's a rodeo each weekend night at the legendary

Cowtown Coliseum. Culture of a completely different variety lies just a few miles down the road, where a collection of world-class museums (The Kimbell, The Modern, The Carter) showcase artwork from Texas and the rest of the world.

FORT WORTH ORIENTATION

Since Fort Worth is much smaller than Dallas, its noteworthy neighborhoods and travel-related districts are within several miles of each other in the downtown area. Its comfortable environs also mean there aren't any supersize suburbs looming on the outskirts of town. Visitors should consider getting a hotel near the Cultural District, since most of the city's major attractions are concentrated there. That being said, historic Stockyards lodging is far more unique to Fort Worth (albeit slightly removed from the other travel destinations).

Cultural District

It has this name for a reason—Fort Worth culture takes center stage in this west-end district, with prestigious, contemporary, Western, and family-friendly museums. Plan

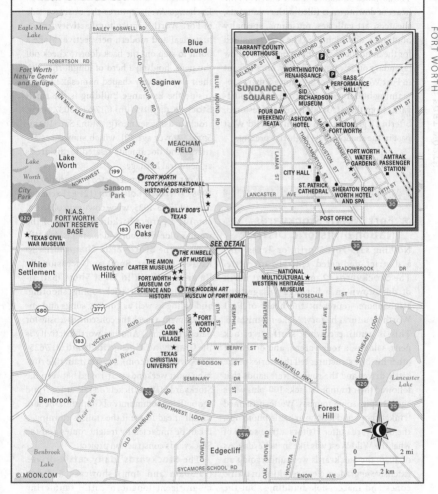

Fort Worth

to spend at least two days exploring this part of the city.

Camp Bowie

Just down the road from the Cultural District is Camp Bowie Boulevard, where visitors grab a bite to eat between museum explorations. This historic roadway features more than 30 blocks of redbrick streets leading to shopping boutiques and some of the city's most famous eateries, including Kincaid's Hamburgers and Blue Bonnet Bakery.

Stockyards District

A district dedicated entirely to cattle, the Stockyards, in a heritage village-type atmosphere, represent the heart of Fort Worth's cultural history and offer a true sense of what the Wild West was like in its heyday over a century ago.

Sundance Square

The 20-block Sundance Square district in the heart of downtown is filled with restaurants, theaters, art galleries, museums, specialty boutiques, and nightlife. The area is named for the Sundance Kid, who, along with fellow legendary outlaw Butch Cassidy, once hid out in Fort Worth. Most of Sundance Square's remaining buildings, brick streets, and courtyards from the late 1800s have been restored, offering a glimpse into the city's Wild West past in the shadow of its high-rise present.

SIGHTS

TOP EXPERIENCE

★ Fort Worth Stockyards National Historic District

Nothing says Fort Worth, or Texas, like a district dedicated entirely to cattle. The **Stockyards,** 2 miles (3.2 km) north of downtown in a heritage village-type atmosphere, represent the heart of Fort Worth's cultural history. Make no mistake: This is genuine cowboy stuff—livestock pens, saloons, a rodeo arena, and dozens of other historic structures tell the stories of the cattle drives and the rugged trail hands that followed their trampled tracks 100-plus years ago. Despite some touristy Western-themed trinket shops and longhorn cattle photo ops, the Stockyards offer visitors a true sense of what the Wild West was like in its heyday. As of 2020, the Stockyards were undergoing an extensive upgrade project, resulting in traffic cones and inaccessible buildings, but the main attractions, listed below, remain open to visitors.

A good place to start is the **Stockyards Visitor Center** (2501 Rodeo Plaza, 817/624-4741, www.fortworth.com, Mon.-Sat. 10am-5pm, Sun. 11am-5pm), just past the giant Fort Worth Stockyards sign that spans Exchange Avenue, just off Main Street. Friendly and helpful staffers will point out buildings and provide information about guided tours of the district.

Across the street, the stately 1902 **Livestock Exchange Building** (131 E. Exchange Ave.) captures the business side of Fort Worth's agricultural activity from a historical and modern perspective. Make a point to step out the back door to check out the pens, holding a herd of longhorns with their impressively shaped namesake horns. Inside the Exchange Building is the small **Stockyards Museum** (817/625-5087, www. stockyardsmuseum.org, Mon.-Sat. 10am-5pm, $2 over age 10), which showcases artifacts and documents related to the area's agricultural heritage.

Next door, the understated grandeur of the 1908 **Cowtown Coliseum** (121 E. Exchange Ave., 817/625-1025, www.cowtowncoliseum. com) is a perfect backdrop for one of the world's oldest indoor rodeo arenas. It's still home to the **Stockyards Championship Rodeo** (Fri.-Sat. 8pm) and occasionally **Pawnee Bill's Wild West Show** (Sat. afternoon), featuring trick roping, shooting, and riding as well as cowboy songs and entertainment. Check the coliseum's website for dates and times. Another worthy activity is the **Grapevine Vintage Railroad** (817/625-7245, www.gvrr.com), a rustic train ride running most weekends year-round between the Stockyard Station (tickets on sale at 1pm) and the outlying community of Grapevine. Be sure to call ahead to see if the train is running—it can be impacted by freight routes and the Stockyards construction project.

The **Stockyards' daily cattle drives** (11:30am and 4pm) showcase a dozen magnificent longhorn cattle sauntering and clip-clopping down the main drag accompanied by period-costumed drivers. The event offers a nice touch of living history, but don't feel compelled to plan your day around the five-minute occurrence.

To make the most of your trip to the Stockyards, visit on a weekend evening for a full slate of events: a stroll through Exchange Avenue's Western shops, a hearty meal at a steak house, a rodeo at the Coliseum, and top

Head 'Em Up!

longhorns in the Stockyards District

Although historians have debated aspects of the Chisholm Trail's storied past—including the exact route and even its name—none deny its significance in the settlement of the western United States.

Fort Worth visitors can get a glimpse of this heritage during the Stockyards' **daily cattle drives** (11:30am and 4pm), which showcase a dozen magnificent longhorn cattle sauntering and clip-clopping down the main drag accompanied by period-costumed drivers.

The trail was named for Jesse Chisholm, a trader who blazed a route through Kansas and Oklahoma that was eventually used by cowboys to drive Texas longhorns to the northern cattle markets. For roughly two decades—from the end of the Civil War until the mid-1880s—tens of thousands of cowboys rode trails from deep in the heart of Texas to the middle of Kansas, where railroads took millions of cattle east to meatpacking centers.

Not surprisingly, Texas is quite proud of its Chisholm Trail heritage. Cattle drives often started from legendary sites such as the 825,000-acre King Ranch near the state's southern tip and continued northwest to San Antonio. From there, cattle moved north through Austin and on to Fort Worth, dubbed "Cowtown," a nickname it still holds.

Although other cattle drive routes existed at the time, none penetrated the heart of popular imagination quite like the Chisholm Trail. Through songs, stories, and mythical tales, the Chisholm Trail has played an important role in developing Texas's Wild West mystique.

it all off with a whiskey or cold beer at the legendary White Elephant Saloon.

★ The Kimbell Art Museum

The cream of the crop in the Fort Worth Cultural District is **The Kimbell Art Museum** (3333 Camp Bowie Blvd., 817/332-8451, www.kimbellart.org, Tues.-Thurs. and Sat. 10am-5pm, Fri. noon-8pm, Sun. noon-5pm, free for permanent collection; varying fees for traveling exhibits), which regularly receives accolades for being one of the finest art museums of its kind in the country. Fort Worth entrepreneur Kay Kimbell donated his art collection and entire personal fortune to the Kimbell Art Foundation, which opened the museum in 1972.

Brimming with significant works of art, The Kimbell offers a rewarding visual experience that resonates with visitors long after

departing. The Louis I. Kahn-designed building enhances the experience by bathing the museum's concrete walls and artwork with indirect natural light from gently sloping overhead barrel-vault arches.

The works range from antiquity to the 20th century. The most memorable pieces are from Monet, Cézanne, Picasso, and Matisse. Though lacking in great number, the museum's collection of older European masters is also significant, including masterpieces from El Greco, Rubens, and Rembrandt, as well as an impressive collection of Asian art.

The Kimbell also regularly hosts world-class traveling exhibits highlighting masterworks of painting and sculpture from premier collections. In addition, the museum hosts arts-related lectures, seminars, films, and musical performances throughout the year.

The Kimbell recently opened a long-awaited expansion, allowing more of its permanent collection to be exhibited. Although it was considered a daunting task to compete with the museum's existing architectural brilliance, locals immediately praised the glass, concrete, and wood addition.

★ The Modern Art Museum of Fort Worth

Like the Kimbell, The **Modern Art Museum of Fort Worth** (3200 Darnell St., 817/738-9215, www.themodern.org, Tues.-Wed. and Fri.-Sun. 10am-5pm, Thurs. 10am-8pm, $16 ages 13-59, $12 seniors, $10 students) is in a stunning building, designed by renowned Japanese architect Tadao Ando, a remarkable structure that appears to float on a placid pond. Gazing upon the building's dramatic concrete and glass exterior—one of the best views is from the café's patio—reveals the intricate plan and attention to detail (notice how the pool reflects dancing splashes of gilded sunlight onto the underside of the museum's concrete roof).

1: The Modern Art Museum of Fort Worth 2: Fort Worth's Sundance Square 3: the coliseum in Fort Worth's Stockyards

The visual delights are equally amazing inside, with 2,600 significant works of international modern art, from compelling abstract expressionism to recognized pop art to abstract figurative sculpture. Andy Warhol's familiar silkscreens share space with Donald Judd's highly stylized artwork, and major traveling exhibits offer even more contemporary imagery.

Amon Carter Museum

Another of the city's world-class attractions is the **Amon Carter Museum** (3501 Camp Bowie Blvd., 817/738-1933, www.cartermuseum.org, Mon. noon-5pm, Tues.-Wed. and Fri.-Sat. 10am-5pm, Thurs. 10am-8pm, free). The museum received a cosmetic and collections update in 2019, resulting in some eye-catching large-scale works (check out the giant prism of colorful strings in the main stairwell) and an overall fresh feel. Although it's grounded in Western art, The Carter covers an impressive range of high-quality American art, from sculptures to paintings to photographs. Through his friendship with Will Rogers, Carter developed an interest in the work of legendary Western artists Frederic Remington and Charles M. Russell, and his extensive collection of their art is the basis for the museum.

The remainder of the collection is perhaps even more noteworthy. The photography, in particular, is stunning—the black-and-white images of American life are especially profound and gripping, and the paintings include the selections from Georgia O'Keeffe, Thomas Eakins, and Winslow Homer. The Carter has a reputation for having one of the foremost collections of American artwork.

Fort Worth Museum of Science and History

The most family-friendly destination in the Cultural District is the **Fort Worth Museum of Science and History** (1600 Gendy St., 817/255-9300, www.fwmuseum.org, Mon.-Sat. 10am-5pm, Sun. noon-5pm, $16 adults, $14 seniors, $13 ages 2-18). The bold, blocky, colorful museum building is an innovative work of architecture with Latin American design elements such as bright colors (deep red, yellow, bright pink), courtyards, and extensive use of glass.

The museum's collections and exhibits are equally compelling. Home to more than 175,000 historical and scientific objects with an emphasis on Texas and the Southwest, the museum showcases cultural heritage, botany, entomology, zoology, and paleontology. Popular attractions include the fascinating Cattle Raisers Museum, a dinosaur dig and laboratory, the Children's Museum, and IMAX movies.

National Cowgirl Museum and Hall of Fame

Make a point of visiting the **National Cowgirl Museum and Hall of Fame** (1720 Gendy St., 817/336-4475, www.cowgirl.net, Tues.-Sat. 10am-5pm, Sun. noon-5pm, $12 adults, $9 seniors and ages 4-12, $10 parking). Housed in a 33,000-square-foot building designed to mirror Fort Worth's historic Cowtown structures, the museum showcases the important role women played in the American West.

Its origins date to 1975 in the Panhandle community of Hereford, where the small National Cowgirl Hall of Fame honored pioneers, artists, writers, Native American leaders, social activists, and modern ranchers and rodeo cowgirls. These attributes became the basis for the current facility.

Visually stunning in its design and layout, the museum's interior is a dazzling spectacle of open spaces, bright colors, and a 45-foot-high (14-m) domed rotunda housing the impressive Hall of Fame honoree exhibits, which display changing images on glass screens. Although the museum makes a point of celebrating the heroines it honors, there's also a lot of fun to be had. Check out the media and fashion displays and be sure to stop by the simulated bronco-riding exhibit.

Will Rogers Memorial Center

The **Will Rogers Memorial Center** (3401 W. Lancaster Ave., 817/392-7469, www.fortworth. com, Mon.-Fri., equestrian events Sat.-Sun., free) presides over the Cultural District with its colossal art deco tower. Named by Fort Worth civic pioneer Amon Carter for his friend Will Rogers, the famous cowboy performer, the stately art deco buildings remain significant attractions in the district. The coliseum and auditorium appropriately represent Cowtown culture with livestock shows and theatrical events.

Be sure to note the magnificent architectural elements throughout the complex, including the coliseum's innovative girder support system allowing unobstructed views and the nearly 200-foot-tall (60-m) decorative tower. A bronze bust of Rogers in the facility's lobby is the subject of a popular local legend that claims rodeo cowboys have rubbed a dent into the statue's nose while attempting to bestow Rogers's good fortune on their performance. Although the nose bears a notable impression, it's really there from the statue being accidentally dropped during installation.

Fort Worth Zoo

Set aside an afternoon to experience the remarkable **Fort Worth Zoo** (1989 Colonial Pkwy., 817/759-7555, www.fortworthzoo. org, spring-fall daily 10am-5pm, winter daily 10am-4pm, $16 adults, $12 seniors and ages 3-12), considered one of the country's premier zoos, and for good reason. This sprawling eight-acre complex feels less like a zoo and more like a collection of habitats, with exotic African and Asian creatures (elephants, rhinos, monkeys, lions, tigers, giraffes, zebras, hippopotamuses) often lounging 100 feet (30 m) from visitors with only a pond separating you from them.

Bamboo and tropical trees are everywhere, giving the impression of walking through rainforest trails to hunt down the next attraction. Many exhibits, including the World of Primates, include large Plexiglas windows offering views so close that you can practically feel the beasts' breath. Kids will love seeing parakeets crawl onto their seed-on-a-stick treat (available for a few dollars), and adults will be fascinated with the prehistoric marvel and grace of exotic elephants, wrinkly rhinos, and hefty hippos. The Meerkat Mounds are popular, and the Texas Wild! exhibit is a good way to understand the impressive variety of creatures crawling around the Lone Star State.

Fort Worth Botanic Garden

Experience the sensory delight of the **Fort Worth Botanic Garden** (3220 Botanic Dr., 817/871-7686, www.fwbg.org, daily 8am-5pm, $12 adults, $10 seniors, $6 ages 6-15), with 2,500 species of native and exotic plants on display in 21 gardens throughout 109 acres of Trinity Park. Most of the garden has a tropical feel, with waterfalls, ponds, and lushly sur-rounded pathways offering visitors a welcome respite from the nearby urban environment. The Latin American tropics are highlighted in a 10,000-square-foot glass conservatory with more than 2,500 plants. Other areas worth meandering through are the sweetly scented Rose Garden and the artfully de-signed Japanese Garden. The garden center and conservatory are open at different times during the week and throughout the year, and various fees apply for different gardens; visit the website for specific information.

Sundance Square

The 35-block **Sundance Square Downtown Entertainment District** (817/255-5700, www.sundancesquare.com) is filled with restaurants, theaters, art galleries, museums, specialty boutiques, and nightlife. The area is named for the Sundance Kid, who, along with fellow legendary outlaw Butch Cassidy, reportedly conducted business in Fort Worth. In the late 1800s and early 1900s, Fort Worth's downtown was filled with saloons, gambling parlors, and dance halls, drawing a rough-and-tumble mix of cattlemen and outlaws. Many of Sundance Square's remaining buildings, brick streets,

and courtyards from that period have been restored, offering a glimpse into the city's Wild West past. Of particular note are the 1895 **Tarrant County Courthouse** (100 E. Weatherford St.), 1889 **Land Title Building** (111 E. 4th St.), the 1901 **Knights of Pythias Castle Hall** (315 Main St.), and the 1902 **Jett Building** (400 Main St.), featuring an enormous and legendary Chisholm Trail mural spanning the building's southern facade.

Grab a bite to eat at a quintessential Fort Worth spot like **Bird Cafe** (115 E. 4th St., 817/332-2473, Mon.-Thurs. 11am-2pm, Fri.-Sat. 11am-2am, Sun. 10am-10pm, $11-29). Created by noted regional restaurateur Shannon Wynne, Bird offers crafty cocktails and delicious shared plates, including a hearty rabbit pot pie and delectable Monte Cristo sandwich. Afterward, head to the adjacent **FunkyTown Donuts and Drafts** (132 E. 4th St., 817/862-7337, http://funkytowndonuts. com, Mon.-Thurs. 7am-8pm, Fri.-Sat. 7am-11pm, Sun. 7am-6pm, $4-10) for dessert or a nightcap. Pair a sprinkle doughnut with a chocolate stout—you (probably) won't regret it.

Fort Worth Water Gardens

If you're downtown, be sure to walk through the **Fort Worth Water Gardens** (1502 Commerce St., 817/392-7111), a remarkable urban park with water cascading, flowing, and bubbling in every direction. Designed by famed New York architect Philip Johnson, who also designed the Amon Carter Museum, the Water Gardens are a perfect oasis in a hot, dry Western town like Fort Worth. Visitors, residents, and nearby office employees gaze upon the pleasant fountains and flowing water as it channels throughout this architectural marvel, which opened in 1974. The open nature of the park has had its drawbacks, however: Over the years, several people have died at the Water Gardens, prompting a major renovation in 2007, with significant enhancements and changes such as interpretive plaques, additional railings,

Compelling County Courthouses

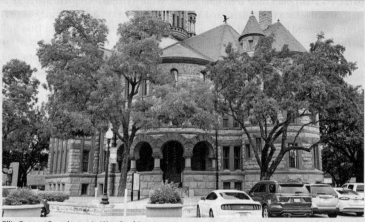

Ellis County Courthouse in Waxahachie

Texas isn't just bragging when it claims to have more historic courthouses than any other state. Incredibly, more than 225 courthouses still stand that are at least 50 years old, and nearly 80 of those were built before the turn of the 20th century. Because many of them have deteriorated due to abandonment or inadequate maintenance, the Texas Historical Commission developed a statewide program to preserve these majestic architectural gems.

Courthouses served as the centerpieces of most Texas communities, and they often brought striking sophistication to rural parts of the state. Elaborate architectural plans and a variety of styles—Romanesque Revival, beaux arts, Second Empire—contributed to the diversity of Texas's built environment. In addition to holding municipal records and offices, the courthouses also hosted community events and bolstered civic pride.

Several of the state's most impressive courthouses are in small communities just outside the Metroplex. The best examples of the restored dramatic grandeur are the **Ellis County Courthouse** in Waxahachie (south of Dallas), the **Denton County Courthouse** in Denton (north of Fort Worth), and the **Hopkins County Courthouse** in Sulphur Springs (northeast of Dallas).

warning signs, seats, and barriers around the pools.

Fort Worth Nature Center and Refuge

Ten miles (16 km) northwest of downtown, the **Fort Worth Nature Center and Refuge** (9601 Fossil Ridge Rd., 817/392-7410, www.fwnaturecenter.org, fall-spring daily 8am-5pm, summer daily 8am-7pm, $5 adults, $3 seniors, $2 ages 3-17) offers 3,600 acres of wilderness, primarily forests, prairies,

and wetlands. Residents and visitors can experience the natural side of North Texas through more than 20 miles (32 km) of hiking trails, an interpretive center, and occasional sightings of bison and white-tailed deer. The refuge is 2 miles (3.2 km) past the Lake Worth bridge on Jacksboro Highway (Hwy. 199).

Log Cabin Village

Families will enjoy the **Log Cabin Village** (2100 Log Cabin Village Lane, 817/392-5881, www.logcabinvillage.org, Tues.-Fri.

9am-4pm, Sat.-Sun. 1pm-5pm, $5.50 adults, $5 seniors and ages 4-17), featuring seven authentic pioneer homes built during the mid-19th century and moved to the current site in the 1950s. The site's exhibits include a water-powered gristmill, a one-room schoolhouse, and a blacksmith shop. Historical interpreters depict the lifestyle of the pioneers who settled in the area.

Texas Cowboy Hall of Fame

The **Texas Cowboy Hall of Fame** (2515 Rodeo Plaza, 817/626-7131, www.tchof.com, Mon.-Thurs. 10am-5pm, Fri.-Sat. 10am-7pm, Sun. 11am-5pm, $6 adults, $5 seniors and ages 13-17, $3 ages 5-12) is conveniently located in the Stockyards District. The museum features impressive exhibits with cowboy and Chisholm Trail memorabilia, an antique carriage collection, and a hall of fame honoring dozens of famous cowboys and cowgirls from Texas.

Sid Richardson Museum

In the historic Sundance Square District, the **Sid Richardson Museum** (309 Main St., 888/332-6554, www.sidrichardsonmuseum. org, Mon.-Thurs. 9am-5pm, Fri.-Sat. 9am-8pm, Sun. noon-5pm, free) offers free tours of its remarkable Western art collection. Highlights in the gallery-size space include paintings of the Old West by Frederic Remington, Charles M. Russell, and other artists in the collection of legendary Texas oilman and philanthropist Sid W. Richardson.

Western Currency Facility Tour and Visitor Center

If you've ever dreamed of making billions of dollars in mere minutes, visit "the money factory," a.k.a. the **Western Currency Facility Tour and Visitor Center** (9000 Blue Mound Rd., 817/231-4000, www. moneyfactory.gov, Tues.-Fri. 8:30am-5:30pm, free). This federal organization is affiliated with the U.S. Department of the Treasury. An elevated walkway over the production floor allows visitors to preside over millions of freshly printed bills as part of a 45-minute tour including interactive exhibits and an informative theater film. Tours are offered on a first-come, first-served basis, and be sure to allow 30 minutes for everyone to make it through the not surprisingly heavy security.

Texas Civil War Museum

The **Texas Civil War Museum** (760 Jim Wright Freeway N., 817/246-2323, www. texascivilwarmuseum.com, Tues.-Sat. 10am-5pm, $7 adults, $4 ages 7-12) is one of the largest Civil War museums in the country. Boasting 15,000 square feet of exhibits, the museum contains two major sections: a Civil War collection and a Victorian dress exhibit. Appropriately, the Union exhibits are displayed on the museum's north side, while the Confederate items are in the Southern part of the building. Incidentally, if you'd like to hear more than you ever wanted to know about the "War Between the States," be sure to ask the friendly docent.

National Multicultural Western Heritage Museum

The **National Multicultural Western Heritage Museum** (2029 N. Main St., 817/534-8801, www.cowboysofcolor.org, Wed.-Sat. noon-4pm, $10 adults, $8 over age 5) highlights the important contributions of the state's ethnically diverse cowboys and prominent African Americans. Featured exhibits showcase the frontier-era black servicemen known as Buffalo Soldiers, early African American flying pioneer Bessie Coleman, and significant achievements of Native Americans and Hispanics in Texas history.

Downtown Marker Program

Nearly two dozen bronze markers, known as the **Heritage Trails,** are scattered throughout downtown Fort Worth, offering a historical tour of the people and events that shaped the city's history. Notable markers include JFK, Gamblers & Gunfights, and Architectural

Diversity. For more information about the markers and a map of their locations, visit www.fortworthheritagetrails.com.

ENTERTAINMENT AND EVENTS

Nightlife in Fort Worth is generally separated into two hubs of activity: the Stockyards (historic locales) and Sundance Square (historic and hipper locales). Although the Stockyards' saloons are more touristy, you're more likely to have a memorable experience there—even if those memories are of saddle-shaped barstools, period-dressed waitstaff, and longhorns mounted on every wall. Sundance Square draws a younger professional crowd, and even though the bars are somewhat generic, they're more active and open later. For craft beer, fine food, and plenty of beards, head to the Near Southside district. If you're in search of higher culture, the magnificent Bass Performance Hall is a worthy destination even if you're not attending a show.

Performing Arts

For upscale entertainment, it doesn't get much classier than the remarkable **Bass Performance Hall** (525 Commerce St., 877/212-4280, www.basshall.com). Billed as the last great performance hall built in the 20th century, this stately facility is reminiscent of the classic European opera houses. Architectural features include two enormous 48-foot (15-m) angels sculpted from Texas limestone on the building's facade, and a colorfully painted 80-foot-diameter (24-m) "Great Dome" above the concert theater. Bass is home to the Fort Worth Symphony Orchestra, Texas Ballet Theater, Fort Worth Opera, and the Van Cliburn International Piano Competition. Visit the website for information about touring shows.

The improvisational comedy group **Four Day Weekend** (312 Houston St., 817/226-4329, www.fourdayweekend.com, shows Fri.-Sat. 7:30pm and 10pm, $25) traffics in interactive entertainment. The audience is invited to become part of the hilarity by submitting ideas for improv routines or by joining the cast on stage for short ad-lib routines. Video, music, and the cast's sharp skills enhance this unpredictable experience.

Bars and Clubs
★ **BILLY BOB'S TEXAS**
The most famous of Fort Worth's entertainment venues is **Billy Bob's Texas** (2520 Rodeo Plaza, 817/624-7117, www.billybobstexas.com, Mon.-Sat. 11am-2am, Sun. noon-2am, cover charge varies), billed as "the world's largest honky-tonk." Just a block north of the main drag in the Stockyards District, Billy Bob's has to be seen to be believed. From the outside, it looks like an enormous arena, and the three acres of interior space are reminiscent of a cavernous Las Vegas casino. There's a bull ring for live bull riding (no mechanical knockoffs here), an oversize Texas-worthy dance floor, a live music venue, arcade and casino games, dozens of good-times pool tables, and a monstrous gift shop. Concerts are held on most weekends, as are the bull-riding events. Check ahead to see if the semi-regular line-dancing lessons are taking place. Despite being a bit overboard on the over-the-top Texas atmosphere, Billy Bob's is worth visiting to enjoy a cold Lone Star draft and people-watching.

THE STOCKYARDS
This is a great place to spend a night on the town in Fort Worth. Several area saloons are legendary turn-of-the-20th-century watering holes, where cattlemen bellied up to the bar after a long day of trail driving.

Be sure to catch a glimpse of the boot-scootin' regulars as they two-step and waltz to traditional country-and-western swing music at notable Stockyards nightlife venues such as the **White Elephant Saloon** (106

1: Bass Concert Hall 2: Billy Bob's Texas in Fort Worth 3: Fort Worth's White Elephant Saloon 4: Cavender's Boot City in the Stockyards

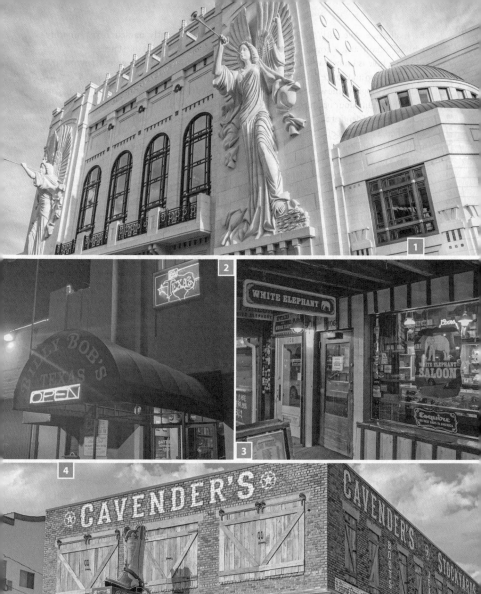

E. Exchange Ave., 817/624-8273, www.whiteelephantsaloon.com). This venerable watering hole is known as the district's most historic saloon and dance hall and features live music every night of the week. It's an ideal spot to catch a troubadour on stage while meeting your new best friend at the bar. Be sure to look up—there's a big ol' collection of Stetson hats up there on the ceiling. Also worth moseying into is the **Lil' Red's Longhorn Saloon** (121 W. Exchange Ave., 817-386-5962, www.longhornsaloonfortworth.com, Thurs.-Tues.), a genuine Western bar that's hosted legendary musicians like Hank Williams and Bob Wills. If you're staying at the Stockyards Hotel, or even if you aren't, saddle up (literally—the bar stools are saddles) to the downstairs bar at **H3 Ranch** (109 E. Exchange Ave., 817/624-1246, www.h3ranch.com) for a giant goblet of beer and prime people-watching.

NEAR SOUTHSIDE

As its name implies, Fort Worth's Near Southside district is just south of downtown. The district is anchored by Magnolia Street, with its charming homes and historic buildings from the early 1900s serving as restaurants, galleries, and studios. Recently the area has transformed from run-down and sketchy to a revitalized haven for artists and foodies. Along with this crowd comes craft brewers and the devotees who sample their evolving creations. In Fort Worth, Magnolia Street is an epicenter for the brewing scene, offering locals and visitors an ideal place to spend a night or three exploring the wares.

A good starting place is the **Bearded Lady** (1229 7th Ave., 817/349-9832), located in a comfy 100-year-old bungalow. There are beards aplenty on most of the men here, and they're accompanied by smiles of satisfaction due to the enviable beer selection (top-notch local breweries, regional favorites, and rare national varieties) and incredible food. Order a Steampipe Black IPA made by neighboring Hop Fusion Ale Works accompanied by the bar's famous Lust Burger, a poblano- and feta-stuffed masterpiece topped with fried leeks

that was recently named *Texas Monthly*'s third-best burger in the state.

Just down the street is **Brewed** (801 W. Magnolia Ave., 817/945-1545, www.brewedfw.com), offering a compelling combination of high-quality beers, coffees, and locally sourced food. Do it right by ordering a local Rahr & Sons brew on tap along with some duck-fat fries. Top it off with a rich cold-brewed coffee on tap.

SUNDANCE SQUARE

The Stockyards have the history, but Sundance Square has the downtown crowd. This comfortably sized 20-block area has an active nightlife scene with plenty of live music venues, dance clubs, and beer joints. Among the best is the **Red Goose Saloon** (306 Houston St., 817/332-4343), a gently worn club with two hopping areas inside. Downstairs is a traditional bar with reasonable prices and a welcoming atmosphere. Upstairs is the dance floor, with a rowdy crowd and fun beats. For an amazing beer selection, head directly to **Flying Saucer** (111 E. 3rd St., 817/336-7470, www.beerknurd.com), a laid-back place with more than 100 beers on tap, upper and lower beer gardens, and live local music a few nights a week.

Events
WINTER

The **Fort Worth Stock Show and Rodeo** (817/877-2400, www.fwssr.com) is one of the largest events of its kind in Texas. Dating to 1896, this annual 17-day event in January is highlighted by an "all-Western" parade (no motor vehicles) through downtown. Other events include nightly rodeos, cowboy competitions, commercial exhibits, and auctions; most events take place at **Dickies Arena** (1911 Montgomery St.) next to the Will Rogers Memorial Coliseum.

Held each February, the **Last Great Gunfight** (817/624-8273) is about as Wild West as it gets. In 1887, Luke Short, owner of the White Elephant Saloon, outdrew ex-Fort Worth marshal Jim "Longhair" Courtright on the street in front of the saloon. Deemed the town's last significant duel of its kind, the event is reenacted annually in front of the White Elephant.

SPRING
Mayfest (817/332-1055, www.mayfest.org), which actually begins in late April, is Fort Worth's annual celebration of spring, complete with arts, crafts, live music, sporting events, and food at Trinity Park near the Cultural District.

The **Van Cliburn International Piano Competition** (817/738-6536, www.cliburn. org) celebrates Fort Worth native Van Cliburn's victory at the first Tchaikovsky International Competition in Moscow in 1958. First held in 1962 and repeated every four years since, the Van Cliburn competition is considered one of the world's most prestigious classical piano contests.

SUMMER
Fort Worth's **Juneteenth Celebration** (214/353-4445), like others throughout the Lone Star State, celebrates the June 19, 1865, announcement of the Emancipation Proclamation, belatedly resulting in the freeing of 250,000 enslaved people in Texas. Fort Worth's annual event features daylong activities including a downtown parade along with hundreds of vendors lining the streets, as well as cultural activities, carnival rides, and live music.

FALL
The city's **Red Steagall Cowboy Gathering and Western Swing Festival** (800/433-5747, www.redsteagallcowboygathering. com) features three days of cowboy poetry, rodeos, campfire songs, children's events, and a chuck-wagon competition, all named for the venerable country-and-western entertainer.

The **National Cutting Horse Association** (817/244-6188, www. nchacutting.com) hosts an annual event where sports, music, and media icons ride horseback at Will Rogers Memorial Coliseum,

followed by an after-party concert, dinner, and silent auction.

SHOPPING
Not surprisingly, Fort Worth has an impressive collection of authentic Western wear and leather goods (boots, saddles, and more) in addition to several chic cowboy boutiques. Once again, the two main areas of activity are the Stockyards and Sundance Square.

The Stockyards
The Stockyards and Western wear fit together like leg and denim. A stroll through the district will take you past plenty of shops offering cowboy duds, but two of the most noteworthy are **Cavender's** (2601 N. Main St., 817/625-2391, www.cavenders.com) and **Maverick Western Wear** (100 E. Exchange Ave., 800/282-1315, www.maverickwesternwear. com). Both have authentic selections such as jeans, bolo ties, Western shirts, and vests.

For leather goods, including custom-made boots, saddles, hats, and tack, one of the best options in the entire city is **M. L. Leddy's Boots & Saddlery** (2455 N. Main St., 888/565-2668, www.leddys.com). Other leather and Western goods are available at **Ponder Boot Co.** (2358 N. Main St., 817/626-3523, www.ponderboot.com).

Sundance Square
In addition to its top-notch nightlife and restaurants, Sundance Square is a hot spot for shopping. Granted, you'll find some familiar stuff—trendy clothing shops and artsy boutiques—but there are several stores that are ambassadors of Fort Worth. One of the most popular is **Parts Unknown** (410 Houston St., 682/312-8292, www. partsunknown.com), offering fashions for cutting-edge cowgirls and cowboys plus an impressive assortment of jewelry and antiques. Another Cowtown-worthy venue is **Retro Cowboy** (406 Houston St., 817/338-1194), a retail outpost with Western clothing, gifts, and memorabilia. For real vintage gear, be sure to drop by **Peter Brothers Hats** (909

Houston St., 817/335-1715), an old-school haberdashery that's been in the same location since 1911.

Outlying Areas

Although most of Fort Worth's authentic and interesting Western shops are in the Stockyards, there are several other spots around town worth visiting for deals and different selections. Most notable is the **Justin Boot Co. Factory Outlet** (717 W. Vickery Blvd., 817/885-8089, www.justinboots.com), where bargains are the draw. Expect 30-40 percent off retail prices for cowboy boots, casual chukkas, steel-toed work boots, or classic lace-up ropers. Another popular destination for shoppers seeking treasures at affordable prices is **Cavender's Boot City** (857 W. Pipeline Rd., 817/589-2180), a large-scale Western-wear store with a special concentration on boots.

FOOD

Unless you're a vegetarian, eating a steak is often a high priority on a visit to Cowtown, and the city has plenty of fine options to choose from, particularly in the Stockyards. Once you've had your fill of steak, order more meat at a legendary barbecue joint or burger counter. If you're still hankering for a big plate of local goodness, drop by one of Fort Worth's fine Tex-Mex establishments for a beef taco. When in Cowtown . . .

The Stockyards
STEAK AND AMERICAN

Although the Stockyards have plenty of good steak restaurants to choose from, one of the best traditional options is ★ **Cattlemen's Steakhouse** (2458 N. Main St., 817/624-3945, www.cattlemenssteakhouse.com, Mon.-Thurs. 11am-10:30pm, Fri.-Sat. 11am-11pm, Sun. noon-9pm, $17-38). Immediately upon entering the weighty doors of this legendary establishment, there's no denying Cattlemen's is all about the beef. Enormous photos of stately bulls adorn the walls, and clanging steak knives presage the feast that awaits. The

popular Rose o' Texas tenderloin is a prime cut of savory charcoal-broiled beef, and the rib-eye steaks offer a joyful jolt of succulent flavor. Order the fresh sautéed mushrooms for a perfect flavorful accompaniment, and try to save room for blueberry cobbler.

Just down the street, **Lonesome Dove Western Bistro** (2406 N. Main St., 817/740-8810, www.lonesomedovebistro.com, Mon.-Sat. 11:30am-2:30pm and 5pm-11pm, $21-40) offers steaks and Southwestern fare with an eclectic twist. Esteemed chef (and native Texan) Tim Love focuses on steak and wild game, and the results are a true Texas original. It's the only place in the country where you can order huge cuts of Texas steer, grilled Texas quail quesadillas, or braised boar ribs seasoned with inventive rubs or sauces containing European influences. Even the buffalo burgers are exquisite. Food Network fans, take note: Love was one of the few competitors on *Iron Chef America* to defeat the esteemed Masaharu Morimoto in a chili competition. Reservations are recommended.

Around the corner in the shadow of the enormous Fort Worth Stockyards sign that spans Exchange Street is the legendary **Riscky's Steakhouse** (120 E. Exchange Ave., 817/624-4800, www.risckys.com, Sun.-Mon. 11am-9pm, Tues.-Thurs. 11am-10pm, Fri.-Sat. 11am-11pm, $13-49). A mainstay on the main drag since 1927, Riscky's is the quintessential steakhouse, with dark wood-paneled walls, professional waitstaff, and tempting selections. To go all out, select the prime cuts—rib-eye or bone-in filet. To spend less without sacrificing quality, the Stockyards Special is an acceptable option, although you may want to opt for the mushrooms and gravy on the side as opposed to the smothering approach. Regardless of what you order, you can sip on red wine, savor a quality cut of beef, enjoy a leisurely conversation with your companion, and savor the old-fashioned charm of dining in a traditional steakhouse in Cowtown.

Just a few blocks away is a legendary veteran of Texas barbecue: **Cooper's Old Time Pit**

Bar-B-Que (301 Stockyards Blvd., 817/626-6464, www.coopersbbqfortworth.com, Sun.-Thurs. 11am-8:30pm, Fri.-Sat. 11am-9:30pm, $12-42) an outpost of the original location in Llano, considered by aficionados to be among the best in Texas. The similarities to the Llano location are numerous, including the primary focus on quality meats as opposed to ambience. The signature "big chop" is a must—it's an enormously thick hunk of savory pork with a perfect mixture of flavors from the salt-and-pepper rub and slow-smoked pit. The tender brisket and beef ribs taste like prime rib, and there's even *cabrito* (goat) and ham on the menu.

TEX-MEX

One of the most famous Tex-Mex restaurants in the Metroplex is ★ Joe T. Garcia's (2201 N. Commerce St., 817/626-4356, www.joets.com, Mon.-Thurs. 11am-2:30pm and 5pm-10pm, Fri.-Sat. 11am-11pm, Sun. 11am-10pm, $9-20). Originally a small room with seating for 16, Joe's has evolved into a gigantic multi-winged facility that accommodates more than 1,000. There's still usually a line out the door, though it moves quickly. There are no menus for dinner, only a choice between two equally tasty options: the enchilada and taco plate combo or the equally satisfying fajitas. Lunch offers more to choose from, and it's all just as good, including chiles rellenos, tamales, and flautas. Make sure you don't fill up on the pre-meal tortillas and butter or thick chips, and be prepared to bring cash, since Joe T. still does not accept cards (although there's an ATM on-site).

Just across the street from Billy Bob's is Los Vaqueros (2629 N. Main St., 817/624-1511, www.losvaqueros.com, Mon.-Thurs. 11am-9pm, Fri.-Sat. 11am-10pm, Sun. 10:30am-9pm, $10-22), another enormous (yet less legendary) Fort Worth locale in a charming historic building. The food is standard Tex-Mex fare, with tacos and enchiladas among the best options. Complete your meal with an order of sopapillas, thin puffy pastries dusted with cinnamon and sugar and served with honey.

Downtown
AMERICAN AND SOUTHWESTERN

If you're looking for a fine steak dinner downtown, head to Del Frisco's Double Eagle Steak House (812 Main St., 817/877-3999, www.delfriscos.com, Mon.-Thurs. 11am-2:30pm and 5pm-10pm, Fri.-Sat. 5pm-11pm, Sun. 5pm-9pm, $25-41). Though it's not a Lone Star original, everything else about this place is pure Texas, from the huge cuts of succulent meat to the Wild West decor to the colossal chocolate cake. Reservations are recommended.

For those in search of something a bit more upscale, consider Grace (777 Main St., 817/877-3388, www.gracefortworth.com, Mon.-Thurs. 5pm-9:30pm, Fri.-Sat. 5pm-10pm, Sun. 4pm-9pm, $15-38). This is a great spot for drinks and appetizers, since Grace has developed a well-earned reputation for its quality cocktails and soups. The entrées are also top-notch, but sometimes an appealing dining experience consists of nothing more than an old-fashioned (or two), a mushroom and cognac soup, and a side of bacon-wrapped onions.

Southwestern cuisine is the main draw at ★ Reata (310 Houston St., 817/336-1009, www.reata.net, daily 11am-2:30pm and 5pm-10pm, $14-33). The Reata is a rare small-town import (the original is in the West Texas town of Alpine), but the food has become a Fort Worth tradition with cuisine inspired by regional cowboy cooking: Tenderloin tamales, barbecue shrimp enchiladas, and smoked jalapeño quail are signature dishes that don't appear on menus in most other cities. Reservations are recommended.

Another erstwhile Texas or American tradition is barbecue, and one of the city's favorite proprietors is Riscky's (300 Main St., 817/877-3306, www.risckys.com, Tues.-Thurs. 11am-10pm, Fri.-Sat. 11am-11pm, Sun.-Mon. 11am-9pm, $11-22). On historic Sundance Square, Riscky's offers traditional barbecue (brisket, sausage, chicken), but its biggest draw are the giant beef ribs smoked over a wood fire and rubbed with "Riscky's Dust," a concoction of nearly 20 spices.

Cultural District
BARBECUE

A few miles away from the Cultural District, **Angelo's Barbecue** (2533 White Settlement Rd., 817/332-0357, www.angelosbbq.com, Mon.-Wed. 11am-9pm, Thurs.-Sat. 11am-10pm, $12-22) is certainly worth the short drive. This no-frills joint appropriately focuses on the food, a rich, hickory-smoked Texas-style barbecue accompanied by a tangy sauce and savory rub. The brisket is especially tender, and traditional sides like potato salad and coleslaw balance the strong flavors with sweet undertones. Wash it all down with a signature (and gigantic) frosty mug of beer.

Similar yet less rustic is **Railhead Smokehouse** (2900 Montgomery St., 817/738-9808, www.railheadsmokehouse.com, Mon.-Sat. 11am-9pm, $11-24), where ribs and brisket are the top draws. Eschew the usual side dishes for Railhead's top-notch fries, and, if the weather's cooperating, enjoy your plate of smoked and fried goodness on the wholesome outdoor patio.

LUNCH

Long lines form early at ★ **Kincaid's** (4901 Camp Bowie Blvd., 817/732-2881, Mon.-Sat. 11am-8pm, Sun. 11am-3pm, $7-15), which, according to the surveys noted inside, serves the best burger in the country. That may be a stretch, but they certainly are juicy, flavorful, and immensely satisfying burgers worth waiting 20 minutes in line for. Kincaid's started as a grocery store in 1946, and it retains its old-school charm with produce shelves doubling as countertops and picnic tables near the street-side windows. Instead of fries or onion rings, consider ordering the homemade deviled eggs or jalapeño halves stuffed with pimento cheese.

For those in search of a big ol' burger and a craft draft within walking distance of the museums, mosey a half mile over to **Rodeo Goat** (2836 Bledsoe St., 817/877-4628, www.rodeogoat.com, Sun.-Thurs. 11am-10pm, Fri.-Sat. 11am-midnight, $9-20). Burgers are about the only thing on the menu (besides an impressive selection of local and national independent brews), but that's all you'll need. Keep it simple with a Blue Goat (a beef, chicken, veggie, or quinoa burger topped with bleu cheese crumbles, caramelized onions, and garlic mayo) or go nuts with toppings ranging from brisket chili to grilled peaches to green chili chutney.

Near the museums is the venerable **Paris Coffee Shop** (700 W. Magnolia Ave., 817/335-2041, www.pariscoffeeshop.net, Mon.-Fri. 6am-2:30pm, Sat. 6am-11am, $8-16). The historic building radiates old-urban charm, and the sandwiches are all above average. Locals make a point of stopping by for breakfast—especially the biscuits and gravy—and the Thursday lunch special (delectable home-style chicken and dumplings). Save room for the hearty fruit pies.

MEXICAN

For a down-home Tex-Mex experience, head to **La Familia** (841 Foch St., 817/870-2002, Tues.-Thurs. 11am-9pm, Sat. 9am-10pm, Sun. 9am-9pm, $11-25). Located in an unassuming strip mall just a few blocks east of the Cultural District's unofficial boundaries, La Familia welcomes guests with hearty handshakes and hellos. Be sure to check out the specials scribbled on pieces of butcher paper posted near the front door. The margaritas are highly recommended (they're served with a flaming sugar cube), and you can't go wrong with most of the entrées, though locals tend to gravitate toward the taco plates and beef enchiladas.

Magnolia Avenue

Just 1 mile (1.6 km) south of downtown is a stretch of fun and funky eateries in

1: Kincaid's 2: Cooper's Old Time Bar-B-Que
3: Texas White House bed-and-breakfast
4: Stockyards Hotel

century-old homes and office buildings that's well worth exploring. Local establishments offer everything from vegan to upscale urban fare to trendy tacos, and plenty of locally crafted beer. The following are among the most popular and highly regarded of the bunch.

Avoiding animal products in Cowtown is a hefty challenge, but vegans and vegetarians now have a habitat at the **Spiral Diner & Bakery** (1314 W. Magnolia Ave., 817/332-8834, www.spiraldiner.com, Sun.-Thurs. 7am-10pm, Fri.-Sat. 7am-11pm, $11-24). Spiral's is immediately welcoming (omnivores will also enjoy the flavorful options), and the '50s diner decor offers a fun experience. Instead of a standard veggie burger, opt for a McNut burger; enhance chips and salsa with a nacho dish using cashew "cheez" sauce; and spice up ordinary pasta by sampling the tasty curry noodles.

For a different twist on a typical Mexican meal in Fort Worth, head to **Yucatan Taco Stand** (909 W. Magnolia Ave., 817/924-8646, www.yucatantacostand.com, Sun.-Thurs. 11am-10pm, Fri. 11am-midnight, Sat. 10am-midnight, $11-26). Don't let the counter service fool you: This is quality fare from way south of the border. Start things off with a hefty margarita accompanied by lightly seasoned chips and salsa. Be sure to save room for a burrito bowl, filled with your choice of tasty pork, seafood, garlic, and peppers.

Authentic Italian meals aren't always easy to find in Texas, but if you're willing to endure a few quirks, you'll be duly rewarded by **Nonna Tata** (1400 W. Magnolia Ave., 817/332-0250, www.nonnatata.com, Tues.-Fri. 11am-2pm and 5:30pm-8:30pm, $15-36). First, come prepared with cash, wine, and a willingness to dine in a tiny establishment open only on weekdays. Also, you can expect at least a 30-minute wait; reservations are not accepted. Even with these limitations, Nonna Tata remains a popular and highly regarded restaurant thanks to its spectacular food. Start things off with the antipasti platter (an amazing board full of Italian meats and cheeses) and continue with one of the restaurant's seasonal specialties (pumpkin soup) or one of the tantalizing seafood dishes (calamari or shrimp—served with a homemade pasta and fresh pesto). If you still have room for dessert, be sure to order the terrific tiramisu.

ACCOMMODATIONS
$50-100

Offering the basics at a bargain price is **Microtel Inns & Suites** (3740 Tanacross Dr., 817/222-3740, www.fortworthmicrotel.com, $59 d). Amenities include a free continental breakfast, free Wi-Fi, and a fitness center. One of the best under-$100 deals in town is **Quality Inn & Suites** (2700 S. Cherry Lane, 817/560-4180, www.qualityinn.com, $59 d). Features include a free full hot breakfast, free Wi-Fi access, and an outdoor pool and sundeck.

Seven miles (11.3 km) from downtown, the **Fairfield Inn** (3701 NE Loop 820, 817/232-5700, www.fairfieldinn.com, $99 d) offers a complimentary breakfast and has an indoor pool and spa. The Fairfield includes an exercise room and mini suites with a private spa, a microwave, and a fridge.

$100-150

Just a few miles up the road from the Stockyards is **Hilton Garden Inn** (4400 North Freeway, 214/637-9000, www.hiltongardeninn.com, $100 d), a comfortable family-friendly option. Guests are greeted with warm cookies and cold fruit at the front desk, and the lobby area is stocked with board games. The indoor and outdoor pools and hot tub provide a relaxing way to wind down after a day of sightseeing. Amenities include free Wi-Fi and microwaves and fridges in all rooms.

Farther southwest of town is **Holiday Inn Express** (4609 Citylake Blvd. W., 817/292-4900, www.hiexpress.com, $111 d). Nothing too fancy here, but it's fairly new and offers reliable services such as free Wi-Fi, an outdoor pool and hot tub, a fitness center, and a free hot breakfast bar.

Though it's a few miles from the downtown

activity and on a strangely isolated parcel of land off the freeway, there's much to like about **Country Inn & Suites by Radisson** (2200 Mercado Dr., 817/831-9200, www.radisson. com, $112 d). Amenities in the standard rooms include a small sink, a fridge, a microwave, and a separate room with a couch (these are the, not an upgrade), as well as free high-speed internet access, complimentary breakfast, a heated outdoor pool and jetted tub, a fitness center, and pet-friendly rooms. The only other nearby establishment is Mercado Juarez Café, a Tex-Mex restaurant immediately adjacent to the hotel, which happens to be excellent.

$150-200

One of the best deals downtown is the ★ **Hilton Fort Worth** (815 Main St., 817/870-2100, www.hilton.com, $179 d). The Hilton is registered as a National Historic Landmark and has the distinction of being the place where President John F. Kennedy spent his final night (he was assassinated in Dallas the following morning). The hotel's large rooms offer all the standard amenities, with the small yet valued bonus of including two complimentary bottled waters daily.

Just a few miles from the Cultural District's attractions is **Residence Inn** (2500 Museum Way, 817/885-8250, www.residenceinn. com, $199 d), offering complimentary hot breakfasts, free drinks during "hospitality hour" (Mon.-Thurs.), an outdoor sports court and pool, and a whirlpool. The large suites feature separate living and sleeping areas and stocked kitchens.

A nice downtown option with easy access to most of the city's attractions is **Holiday Inn Express** (1111 W. Lancaster Ave., 817/698-9595, www.hiexpress.com, $199 d). Amenities include complimentary shuttle services anywhere within a 3-mile (4.8-km) radius of the hotel, an indoor pool and whirlpool, a fitness center, free Wi-Fi, and a free hot breakfast bar.

$200-250

Directly in the middle of all the Stockyards activity atop a small hill overlooking Exchange Avenue is **Hyatt Place Fort Worth Stockyards** (132 E. Exchange Ave., 817/626-6000, www.hyatt.com, $206 d). Amenities include a complimentary continental breakfast each morning, an outdoor heated pool, free Wi-Fi, and rooms with giant TVs.

For top-notch accommodations near the convention center, the remodeled **Sheraton Fort Worth Hotel and Spa** (1701 Commerce St., 817/335-7000, www.sheratonfortworth. com, $239 d) features rooms with HDTVs and Wi-Fi access, and the hotel's signature spa, including an indoor heated pool, a sauna, a whirlpool, and a fitness center.

One of Fort Worth's most elegant downtown options is the beautiful **Ashton Hotel** (610 Main St., 817/332-0100, www. theashtonhotel.com, $247 d). Renovated to its historic grandeur, the Ashton features designer bedding and furniture along with minibars, custom robes, and, perhaps most luxurious for parents, babysitting services. Reduced rates are available with 14-day advance purchases, and packages are available for parking and breakfast.

One of Fort Worth's newest downtown hotels is the stunning **Omni Fort Worth** (1300 Houston St., 817/535-6664, www. omnihotels.com, $249 d). Adjacent to the Fort Worth Convention Center, the Omni has a true Texas feel, with Lone Star-themed art and bedding (saddle-blanket throws and stitched pillows). Amenities include a full American breakfast, a fitness center, a full-service spa, and internet access.

Over $250

If you're planning to plunk down $300 for a night in the Stockyards, you may as well go whole hog and do it right at the historic 1907 **Stockyards Hotel** (109 E. Exchange Ave., 800/423-8471, www.stockyardshotel.com, $299 d), listed on the National Register of Historic Places. Once a hideout for notorious gangsters Bonnie and Clyde, the Stockyards Hotel is billed as "The Old West at its best," with different Western themes in each room.

Enjoy the plush leather details and luxury furnishings plus tasty snack baskets. If your room overlooks Exchange Avenue, you can even spend time in a leather rocking chair marveling at the revelers below (ear plugs, a.k.a. "cowboy silencers," are provided for the occasional weekend night as "the cure for loud cowboys"). The Wi-Fi is free, but you'll have to pay for breakfast at the café next door.

Another popular (yet extremely expensive) downtown option is the **Worthington Renaissance** (200 Main St., 817/870-1000, www.renaissancehotels.com, $339 d), which overlooks Sundance Square. It features an indoor pool, a spa tub, and a sauna, massage services, and rooms equipped with minibars.

Bed-and-Breakfasts

In a historic neighborhood south of downtown is the charming **Texas White House** (1417 8th Ave., 800/279-6491, www.texaswhitehouse. com, $169-250). The friendly folks offer three large rooms in the main house with full private baths and two suites in the carriage house with a fireplace, whirlpool tubs, and a sauna. On-site massage services are available, and a tasty breakfast (fancy egg dishes, homemade pastries, fresh fruit) at a time of your choosing starts the day off right. Additional services include early coffee service to your room, free soft drinks, afternoon snacks, and complimentary wine in the hallway. Bonus: The trendy Magnolia Street is just a few blocks away, offering amazing bar and restaurant options in cozy 100-year-old bungalows.

More historic hotel than typical bed-and-breakfast, **Miss Molly's** (109 W. Exchange Ave., 817/626-1522, www.missmollyshotel. com, $100-175) is one of the more colorful lodging options in the Stockyards. A former brothel, Miss Molly's was built nearly 100 years ago and reflects Fort Worth's colorful cowboy history in its seven rooms furnished with Old West antiques. Incidentally,

Miss Molly's has a reputation for hosting paranormal activity—which can either be fascinating or frightening, depending on your perspective—including ghost sightings and unexplained sounds.

Camping

Just 6 miles (9.7 km) southwest of town is **Benbrook Lake** (817/292-2400, www. recreation.gov, $14), where the U.S. Army Corps of Engineers administers six public campgrounds offering sites for utility hookups and primitive camping.

INFORMATION AND SERVICES

The **Fort Worth Convention and Visitors Bureau** (www.fortworth.com) operates several visitor information centers, including at the Stockyards (2501 Rodeo Ave., 817/624-4741) and Sundance Square (508 Main St., 817/698-3300). Friendly helpful staffers provide information and literature about attractions throughout the city. Pick up brochures and maps while viewing cowboy gear and historic Western artifacts.

GETTING THERE AND AROUND

Dallas/Fort Worth International Airport (DFW, 972/973-3112, www.dfwairport.com) is located between Dallas and Fort Worth, so Fort Worth visitors arriving by air can take a shuttle service or taxi to their destination for about $50. It's the world's fourth-busiest passenger airport with daily flights to more than 200 worldwide destinations. Visitors can move around Fort Worth, swiftly on the **Fort Worth Transportation Authority** (817/215-8600, www.ridetrinitymetro. org), which provides transportation to the Stockyards and the Cultural District, with access to Dallas via Trinity Metro.

Vicinity of Fort Worth

Unlike Dallas, Fort Worth's modest size doesn't prompt visitors to seek a respite from the busy metropolis. Regardless, outlying communities offer distinctive characteristics worthy of a day trip. Denton contains a compelling mix of student life and historical charm, and Glen Rose draws visitors from across the state in search of dinosaur tracks and exotic animals.

DENTON

Located 35 miles (56 km) north of the Metroplex, Denton (population 138,541) encompasses an intriguing combination of old and new. The charming historic downtown courthouse and surrounding Main Street district juxtapose the rollicking Texas Motor Speedway and the fresh faces at the University of North Texas and the Texas Woman's University. The universities play a major role in Denton's identity, with a sizable portion of the city's population consisting of college students. The University of North Texas has a national reputation for its communications and music programs, and Texas Woman's University is one of the country's largest universities primarily for women.

★ Downtown Denton

An impressive number of buildings in downtown Denton are listed in the National Register of Historic Places. Visitors flock to the courthouse square to browse the antiques shops, art galleries, gift boutiques, and restaurants. Presiding over all the activity is the majestic 1896 **Denton County Courthouse** (110 W. Hickory St.), featuring massive limestone walls and a prominent clock tower.

Over the past decade, the courthouse square has become a major destination for Dentonites, primarily due to the energetic mix of restaurants, bars, and shops in historic retail buildings surrounding the restored courthouse. Locals, students, and visitors gravitate to the courthouse square to play on the lush tree-lined grounds, eat at a trendy café, or enjoy a local craft beer from a balcony overlooking the enjoyable scene. Watch a movie on the courthouse lawn, then walk to a nearby candy store or snow-cone shop for a sweet nightcap.

During the day, visitors can step inside the courthouse to check out the **Denton County Courthouse-on-the-Square Museum** (110 West Hickory St., 940/349-2850, www. dentoncounty.com/chos, Mon.-Fri. 8am-5pm, free), recalling the town's history through exhibits showcasing historical pottery, pressed blue glass, weaponry, and dolls.

University of North Texas

One of Denton's most popular attractions is the **University of North Texas Sky Theatre Planetarium** (1704 W. Mulberry St., 940/369-8213, www.skytheater.unt.edu, Sat. 2pm and 8pm, $5 adults, $4 seniors, $3 under age 12). The 40-foot (12-m) domed theater features a projection system that reproduces the night sky with digital precision, and the planetarium's seating and technology make visitors feel like they're traveling to nearby stars on a celestial roller-coaster ride. The facility presents educational and entertainment-oriented features for UNT students and the public. While on campus, check out a completely different dramatic experience at the nearby **Campus Theatre** (214 W. Hickory St., 940/382-1915, www. campustheatre.com), a beautifully renovated 1940s art deco movie house staging live productions throughout the year.

Food

AMERICAN AND BARBECUE

For the ultimate downtown Denton experience, head directly to ★ **Barley & Board** (100 W. Oak St., 940/566-3900, www.barleyandboard.com, Sun.-Thurs. 11am-10pm, Fri. 11am-midnight, Sat. 10am-midnight, Sun. 10am-10pm, $12-23), in a prime spot overlooking the bustling courthouse square. The B&B burger is one of the most popular items—the hearty ground beef is topped with a perfect blend of grilled onions and sweet pickles. Other can't-miss items include the delectable curried shrimp and grits, perfectly prepared roasted stuffed quail, and hearty barbecue baby-back ribs. The toothpick fries are a nice change of pace, and the craft beer selection is extremely impressive.

If you have a hankering for a meat sandwich, head directly to **Rooster's Roadhouse** (113 Industrial St., 940/382-4227, www.roosters-roadhouse.com, Sun.-Tues. 11am-10pm, Wed.-Sat. 11am-11pm, $9-19). The burgers and sliced beef brisket sandwich are extremely satisfying, and the heaping helpings of side items (beans, coleslaw, potato salad) will have you gladly loosening your belt a notch afterward. Don't forget to order a fried pickle.

One of the highlights of a visit to Denton's downtown square is **Gnome Cones** (205 N. Elm St., 940/320-7772, www.gnomecones. com, Sun.-Thurs. noon-9pm, Fri.-Sat. noon-10pm, $4-8). This all-natural snow cone shop is the perfect place to cool off on a hot summer day or to top off an evening of exploring the downtown square. The shop looks like a mountain chalet, complete with arctic artwork and furnishings. Order a fruity Gnomesicle or standard snow cone (the goblinberry and lemon are sublime) and wait for your name to be called in a gnome-style high-pitched voice on the speaker.

TEX-MEX

Just southeast of downtown is the festive and fantastic **Fuzzy's Taco Shop** (115 Industrial St., 940/380-8226, www.fuzzystacoshop. com, Sun.-Tues. 6:30am-10pm, Wed.-Thurs. 6:30am-11pm, Fri.-Sat. 7am-2am, $7-16), a small statewide chain. Be sure to order one of Fuzzy's Baja tacos—the tempura fish and

shrimp are especially tasty—with feta and garlic sauce. The *queso* here is legendary, and the corn tortillas are *muy bien*.

Another downtown favorite is **Mi Casita** (110 N. Carroll Blvd., 940/891-1900, www. micasitafood.com, Mon.-Thurs. and Sat. 7am-4pm, Friday 7am-9pm, $8-17). College students line up for the bargain lunch specials of tacos, nachos, and burritos for a measly $4. The hearty breakfast tacos are also worth sampling, and there's no long lines of students in the morning.

Accommodations
MOTELS AND HOTELS

Since Denton is a college town, there are more hotel options than normal for a city of its size. Even the budget options are clean and dependable. **Days Inn** (4211 N. I-35, 940/383-1471, www.daysinn.com, $90 d) offers the basic amenities at an affordable price. For just a bit more, the **SpringHill Suites by Marriott** (1434 Centre Place Dr., 940/383-4100, www.marriott.com, $119 d) offers free Wi-Fi, free breakfast, and an indoor pool. At the slightly higher end of the chain is Denton's **Comfort Suites** (4050 Mesa Dr., 940/320-5150, www.choicehotels.com, $125 d), which offers an indoor heated pool, complimentary Wi-Fi access, and a free hot breakfast.

BED-AND-BREAKFASTS

Denton's tree-lined streets and collegiate atmosphere make it a good place to consider staying at a bed-and-breakfast, and one of the best choices available is the **Heritage Inns** (815 N. Locust St., 888/565-6414, www. theheritageinns.com, about $140). The Cluster consists of three separate houses, and each room features a queen bed and a private bath. Guests can have a full breakfast in the dining room or privately in bed. The B&B is just down the road from Denton's courthouse square.

1: the historic Campus Theatre 2: Gnome Cones on Denton's downtown square 3:the Denton County Courthouse

Information and Services

For information on lodging, dining, events, and points of interest, visit the **Denton Chamber of Commerce** (414 W. Parkway St., 888/381-1818, www.discoverdenton.com, Mon.-Fri. 8:30am-5pm).

Getting There and Around

For interstate nerds (is there even such a thing?), Denton represents the northern origin point of the split between I-35 West and I-35 East. So, if you're visiting from the Fort Worth area, head north on I-35W; if you're in Dallas, take I-35E. Denton is about 30 minutes from Fort Worth and 45 minutes from Dallas.

GLEN ROSE

About 60 miles (97 km) southwest of Fort Worth, Glen Rose (population 2,627) is a popular getaway for Metroplex residents. Community members joke that humans are latecomers to this region, since evidence of dinosaurs from 100 million years ago is pressed into the area's limestone riverbeds.

By the early 1900s, the town was known for its abundant mineral springs, which attracted doctors and healers. A modest population increase in the 1980s occurred with the construction of the Comanche Peak Nuclear Power Plant, which became the county's largest employer and main source of tax revenue. One of the community's biggest draws these days is its natural attractions—particularly a wildlife center, a fossil park, and camping.

Fossil Rim Wildlife Center

The Fossil Rim Wildlife Center (2155 County Rd. 2008, 254/897-2960, www.fossilrim.org, hours vary, guided tours $30-55, self-guided tours $20-30) features some of the planet's most endangered animals along with more than 60 other species on 2,700 acres of protected grasslands. The emphasis is on African animals such as the rhinoceros, giraffe, cheetah, gazelle, and zebra. Fossil Rim's 1,800 acres of open space allow visitors to get close-up experiences with the animals

through a self-guided 9.5-mile (15.3-km) driving tour.

Along the way are an education center, a restaurant, a petting pasture, a nature store, a playground, and picnic areas. The animals, with the exception of the carnivores, rhinos, and a few others, are free to roam across the hilly savannas. Fossil Rim also offers guided tours, mountain bike tours, and hiking tours, and guests can stay overnight at The Lodge or the Foothills Safari Camp. The center's hours of operation and admission fees vary throughout the year, so check the website to see what to expect.

★ Dinosaur Valley State Park

Thousands of visitors annually flock to **Dinosaur Valley State Park** (254/897-4588, www.tpwd.state.tx.us, daily 8am-5pm, $7 over age 12) to see the 100-million-year-old dinosaur tracks in its limestone riverbeds. This picturesque park along the Paluxy River contains some of the best-preserved dinosaur tracks in Texas. This is where the world's first tracks were found of the sauropod, a plant-eating reptile weighing 30 tons and measuring more than 60 feet (18 m) long.

Not as impressive in size yet still fascinating from a paleontological perspective are the tracks from two other creatures from the same era—the duckbilled dinosaurs (a mere 30 feet/9 m long) and the 12-foot-tall (3.7-m) meat-eating theropods. Dinosaur Valley also includes nature trails and areas for camping and picnicking. The park is 5 miles (8 km) west of Glen Rose via U.S. 67, FM 205, and Park Road 59.

Food
AMERICAN

A good spot filled with local flavor is **Hammond's BBQ** (1106 NE Big Bend Trail, 254/897-3008, www.hammondsbbq.com, Wed. and Sun. 11am-3pm, Thurs.-Sat. 11am-8pm, $9-21). Although Hammond's has had the misfortune of burning to the ground three times, locals have been fortunate to have it rebuilt each time. Demand is high for these perfectly smoked meats, including savory sausage and tender brisket.

For a fancier dining experience, consider **Riverhouse Grill** (210 SW Barnard St., 254/898-8914, Wed.-Sat. 11am-2pm and 5pm-9pm, Sun. 11am-2pm, $12-20). The restaurant in a historic home offers standard fare like steaks, fried catfish, and pasta.

Accommodations
HOTELS AND MOTELS
Glen Rose is a bed-and-breakfast kind of town, but for those who appreciate the familiarity of a standard hotel, try **Glen Rose Inn and Suites** (300 SW Big Bend Trail, 254/897-2940, $79 d) or **Americas Best Value Inn & Suites** (1614 NE Big Bend Trail, 254/897-2111, www.americasbestvalueinn.com, $89 d), featuring a pool, a fitness center, and free Wi-Fi.

BED-AND-BREAKFASTS
One of Glen Rose's most popular lodging options is **Country Woods Inn** (420 Grand Ave., 254/897-4586, www.countrywoodsinn.com, $175), which bucks the B&B trend with its kid-friendly approach. Barnyard animals, campfire circles, and walking trails share the 40 wooded acres with century-old guesthouses, charming cabins, a railroad car, and the main lodge. You haven't had this much fun since summer camp!

Another good choice is **The Hideaway Ranch and Retreat** (Private Rd. 1250, Bluff Dale, 254/823-6606, www.thehideawayranch.com, $150-180). Nestled among 155 acres of oak-laden countryside, The Hideaway offers secluded cabins with amenities such as private hot tubs, fully furnished kitchens, and outdoor grills. Activities on the property include horseback riding, swimming, hiking, and fishing.

For those willing to shell out the extra money, consider the beautiful **Inn on The River** (205 SW Barnard St., 254/897-2929, www.innontheriver.com, $159-179). Built in 1919, the site was originally part of a complex known as Dr. Snyder's Drugless Health Sanitarium, where "Doctor" Snyder, "the magnetic healer," treated patients with mineral water believed to have curative powers. Whatever the medical outcome, guests were pampered with luxurious accommodations and delectable meals. Those traditions continue at the meticulously restored current complex.

Information and Services
Contact the **Glen Rose Convention and Visitors Bureau** (1505 NE Big Bend Trail, 254/897-3081, www.glenrosetexas.net, Mon.-Fri. 9am-5pm) for printed and in-person information about local events, attractions, dining, and lodging.

Getting There and Around
Glen Rose isn't close to a major freeway, and that's part of its charm. To get there from Fort Worth, take I-35W south to Alvarado for about 30 minutes, then head west on U.S. 67 for another 30 minutes until you reach Glen Rose.

Wichita Falls

Wichita Falls (population 138,541) isn't really on the way to anywhere, but its history as a rough-and-tumble railroad and oil town make it a worthwhile place to visit if you're willing to undertake the two-hour drive from the Metroplex.

In 1882, the first railroad arrived in Wichita Falls, and the discovery of oil 20 years later established the town as a petroleum headquarters for this region of North Texas. The rugged nature of the agricultural and industrial base brought with it some unsavory characters, and their Wild West exploits in Wichita Falls's growing number of saloons earned the town the nickname "Whiskeytaw Falls." This legacy lives on in the "red draw," a dubious concoction consisting of beer and tomato juice, still available at many local watering holes. Oil and agriculture remain important elements of Wichita Falls's economy, as does Sheppard Air Force Base, which hosts the only NATO pilot training program in the world.

SIGHTS AND RECREATION

Wichita Falls Waterfall

Naturally, when visitors come to Wichita Falls, they ask, "Where are the falls?" For an entire century the answer was "Well . . . they're gone." Indeed, the town's namesake five-foot-high (1.5-m) waterfall on the Big Wichita River was washed away in a flood in 1886. A century later, the town compensated by constructing the 54-foot (16-m) multilevel cascading Wichita Falls Waterfall (940/716-5500) on the south bank of the river. Visitors to the falls, just north of town adjacent to I-44 south, can also experience the trails, a playground, a pool, and pavilions at the adjacent Lucy Park.

Pro Wrestling Hall of Fame and Museum

Believe it or not, Wichita Falls is home to the Pro Wrestling Hall of Fame and Museum (708 8th St., 940/264-8123, www.pwhf.org, Tues.-Sat. 10am-5pm, Sun. 1pm-5pm, $3 adults, $2 seniors and military). Located on the 1st floor of a big blue office tower (known locally as Big Blue), the museum showcases dozens of wrestling greats from across the country. The museum relocated from New York to Wichita Falls in late 2016 because, according to the museum's website, Texas has "tons of wrestling history," including Paul Boesch, The Funks, Stan Hansen, The Freebirds, and, of course, The Von Erichs. Step into the ring and check 'em all out!

Wichita Falls Railroad Museum

In the former downtown Union Station building, the Wichita Falls Railroad Museum (500 9th St., 940/723-2661, www.wfrrm.com, Sat. 11am-3pm, $2) is a showplace for railcars and memorabilia associated with "The Katy" (the Missouri, Kansas & Texas Railroad). The museum's vintage equipment includes a 100-year-old Fort Worth & Denver steam locomotive (one of only three in existence), a diesel switch engine, a baggage car, a post office car, two World War II troop sleepers, and several cabooses.

Wichita Falls Museum of Art at Midwestern State University

On the banks of Sikes Lake, the Wichita Falls Museum of Art at Midwestern State University (2 Eureka Circle, 940/397-8900, www.wfma.msutexas.edu, Tues.-Fri. 10am-5pm, Sat. 1pm-5pm, free) offers a combination of art, science, and regional history. Renovated in 2010, the facility features works of regional artists during the university's academic year, with an emphasis on student art May-July.

The museum also houses a planetarium and a hands-on science center for children.

River Bend Nature Center

On 15 acres in Lucy Park, the **River Bend Nature Center** (2200 3rd St., 940/767-0843, www.riverbendnaturecenter.org, Mon.-Fri. 9am-5pm, Sat. 10am-4pm, Sun. noon-4pm, $6 adults, $5 students) is an environmental education center featuring a remarkable butterfly conservatory (Thurs.-Sat. 10am-4pm, Sun. noon-4pm). Also on the grounds are a wetland pond habitat, a bird habitat, bird-watching opportunities, a weather station, and a 1-mile (1.6-km) interpretive nature trail.

Lake Arrowhead State Park

Approximately 14 miles (22.5 km) southeast of Wichita Falls, **Lake Arrowhead State Park** (229 Park Rd. 63, 940/528-2211, www.tpwd. state.tx.us, $3 over age 12) is on a reservoir on the Little Wichita River. On a former oil field, the lake literally reflects the site's past by retaining several of the oil derricks. Local anglers claim they're the best spots to catch crappie, perch, and bass. Built primarily as a water supply for the City of Wichita Falls, the lake is also a major recreational site for the North Central Plains. The park offers campsites, restrooms with showers, a boat ramp, an 18-hole disc golf course, fishing, swimming, and waterskiing.

ENTERTAINMENT AND EVENTS
Performing Arts

Wichita Falls residents are proud of their city's performing arts groups, including the **Wichita Falls Symphony Orchestra** (Wichita Falls Memorial Auditorium, 1300 7th St., 940/723-6202, www.wfso.org), which features more than 70 members who perform a full season of concerts each year. The group also offers a popular Children's Concert Series. Also noteworthy is the **Wichita Falls Ballet Theatre** (3412 Buchanan St., 940/322-2552, www.wichitafallsballettheatre.org),

performing traditional ballets such as *The Nutcracker* and hosting guest performers and school demonstrations. The **Wichita Theatre Performing Arts Centre** (919 Indiana Ave., at 10th St., 940/723-9037, www.wichitatheatre.com) is a 1908 historic landmark featuring family-friendly live concerts, touring shows, musical dramas, performing arts, and film events.

Bars and Clubs

Wichita Falls no longer revels in its former reputation as a hard-drinking town of rough characters, but there are still several worthy watering holes. For an authentic local experience, drop by the **Bar L Drive Inn** (908 13th St., 940/322-0003), a tiny downtown spot that claims to have invented the "red draw," a legendary local concoction consisting of beer and tomato juice.

Another favorite hangout for locals is the less charming but equally friendly **Iron Horse the Pub** (615 8th St., 940/767-9488), which features live music most weekends and serves cold beers along with darts and pool.

Events

The city's best-known event is the **Hotter 'n Hell One Hundred** (www.hh100.org), where bicycle racers and fitness-oriented endurance riders come to Wichita Falls each August from across the country to sweat, race, and sweat some more.

Each June, the city hosts professional circuit rodeo as part of the **Red River Rodeo** (940/592-2156). Held at the Wichita County Mounted Patrol Arena, the event draws nearly 10,000 people for the traditional rodeo attractions and a post-show dance.

FOOD
Mexican

Perhaps the most venerable of Wichita Falls's restaurants is ★ **Casa Manana** (609 8th St., 940/723-5661, Mon.-Sat. 11am-7:30pm, $9-18), a downtown institution that opened in 1947. The most popular item on the menu is the red soft taco, featuring a rich chili sauce that enhances the seasoned beef or chicken.

Steak and Barbecue

The McBride family is associated with good cooking in Wichita Falls, especially when it comes to preparing quality meats. One of the best places to get a steak in town is **Fat McBride's Steakhouse** (4537 Maplewood Ave., 940/696-0250, www. mcbridessteakhouse.net, Sun.-Fri. 11am-2pm and 5pm-9pm, Sat. 11am-10pm, $18-35). The saddle blanket sirloin (14 or 16 ounces) is a good choice, as are the ribs and brisket. Stick with the meat dishes, since the Mexican plates don't quite make the grade.

The other respected family eatery is **McBride Land and Cattle Co.** (501 Scott St., 940/322-2516, www.mcbrideslandandcattle. com, Mon.-Fri. 11am-1:30pm and 5pm-10pm, Sat.-Sun. 5pm-10pm, $17-33), where the food and atmosphere are truly Texan. Enjoy a hearty steak with all the fixings along with the mounted animal heads and an enormous fireplace.

For traditional Texas barbecue, locals line up downtown at the small yet satisfying **Branding Iron** (104 E. Scott Ave., 940/723-0338, Mon.-Thurs. 11am-3pm, Fri.-Sat. 11am-8pm, $9-20), where you can get a tasty lunch—the smoked turkey and spicy sausage are favorites—for under $10.

ACCOMMODATIONS

Motels and Hotels

Head to the **Fairfield Inn** (4414 Westgate Dr., 940/691-1066, www.marriott.com, $89 d), with an indoor pool and jetted tub, a free buffet breakfast, free Wi-Fi, and complimentary access to a nearby Gold's Gym.

South of Wichita Falls's center, **Lexington Suites** (1917 Elmwood Ave., 940/692-7900, www.lexingtonhotels.com, $89 d) offers various room options, ranging from basic (all rooms have a fridge, a microwave, and a sofa) to upscale (fireplaces and balconies). The hotel offers free breakfast and free Wi-Fi.

Homewood Suites (2675 Plaza Pkwy.,

940/691-4663, www.hilton.com, $119 d) is on a lake near Midwestern State University. All rooms have fully equipped kitchens (with full-size fridges) and free Wi-Fi, and the hotel features an indoor heated pool and a free hot breakfast.

Camping

The best place for camping in Wichita Falls is **Lake Arrowhead State Park** (229 Park Rd. 63, 940/528-2211, www.tpwd.state.tx.us, $4). Another option is the **Wichita Bend RV Park** (300 Central Freeway, 940/761-7490, $17), just a few miles northwest of downtown. The park is on the Wichita River adjacent to Lucy Park and offers 28 sites with hookups (no tents) along with a pool and nature trails.

INFORMATION AND SERVICES

Drop by the **Wichita Falls Convention and Visitors Bureau** (1000 5th St., 800/799-6732, www.wichitafalls.org) for basic information for travelers, even though it caters more to conventions than individuals. Visitors will find an abundance of helpful travel-related information—brochures, maps, personal suggestions—at the **Texas Travel Information Center** (900 Central Freeway/I-44, 940/723-7931).

GETTING THERE AND AROUND

It's possible to fly to Wichita Falls, but the vast majority of visitors travel here by car. From the Metroplex, take I-35W northbound from Fort Worth for about 10 miles (16 km) before heading westward on U.S. 287, which runs directly to Wichita Falls in about 90 minutes.

The **Wichita Falls Regional Airport** (SPS, 940/855-3621, www.flywichitafalls.net), a joint military-civilian endeavor, is served by American Eagle, with four daily flights to the DFW airport.

Austin and the Hill Country

People used to flock to Central Texas for the slow-rolling, low-key vibes. But things have shifted now that the region has spent a decade-plus atop the nation's list of fastest-growing cities. The growing pains haven't been all bad—Austin's good ol' laid-back lifestyle still exists in pockets around the city and in small towns. The positive part of the growth is a vast increase in entrepreneurial endeavors and cultural attractions, especially culinary destinations.

The Hill Country is rustic yet civil enough to have commendable camping and lodging facilities for a weekend escape. Things have always been pleasant in this part of the state, which attracted pioneers—mainly from Tennessee, Arkansas, and Missouri—for the same reasons Native Americans had inhabited the land for millennia: a temperate

Austin 102
Vicinity of Austin 135
Waco 145
The Hill Country 151

Highlights

Look for ★ to find recommended sights, activities, dining, and lodging.

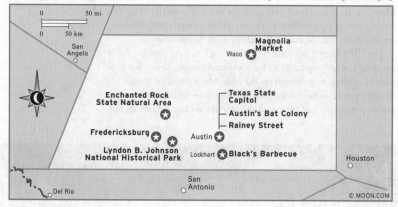

★ **Tour the Texas State Capitol.** This architectural and cultural wonder was designed in true Texas style—15 feet (4.6 m) taller than the U.S. Capitol (page 102).

★ **See the bats.** Each summer night, more than a million Mexican free-tailed bats emerge from beneath the downtown Congress Avenue Bridge, much to the delight of the hundreds of people who gather (page 106).

★ **Drink at Austin's coolest bars.** Historic bungalows have been carefully preserved and retrofitted as homey lounges offering top-notch local craft brews and food in the **Rainey Street District** (page 113).

★ **Get a taste of Texas** at a sacred spot. **Black's Barbecue** has smoked brisket and handmade sausage that shouldn't be missed (page 144).

★ **Shop for home decor** at Waco's famous **Magnolia Market,** popularized by HGTV's *Fixer Upper* show, which includes a retail store, a garden area, and an amazing bakery (page 146).

★ **Take a weekend trip** to one of Hill Country's most popular destinations. **Fredericksburg** is a favorite for its authentic German food, drink, and crafts, made just like they are in the Old Country (page 152).

★ **Learn the story of LBJ.** Tour the boyhood home of the native Texan who became the 36th president to get a fascinating perspective on his life and career at the **Lyndon B. Johnson National Historical Park** (page 160).

★ **Go stargazing.** The enormous pink granite dome at **Enchanted Rock State Natural Area** has been a natural beacon for more than 11,000 years (page 163).

climate and abundant natural resources. By the late 1800s, Germans were arriving in droves. Word got out in Germany that Texas was a land of opportunity, and so many people came that significant portions of Central Texas had a majority German population in the late 19th century. Evidence of their settlement remains in the form of sturdy barns, homes, and dance halls constructed more than 125 years ago. Czech immigrants settled along the Brazos River near Waco, and their cultural legacy is found in the remarkable churches (and *kolache* pastries) scattered throughout small communities on the fertile Blackland Prairie.

Austin has traditionally attracted another portion of the population not always found in rural parts of Texas: intellectuals. The University of Texas has been the main draw, but politicians and lawyers have proliferated since the city was named state capital in 1846. For the next century, government entities and the university raised Austin's profile by investing in infrastructure and academic projects (bridges, dams, laboratories, museums, stadiums) aimed at improving the city's quality of life. By the late 20th century, the city became a hotbed for creative thinkers, movers, and shakers, including computer guru Michael Dell, earning the tech-heavy business climate the nickname Silicon Hills while remaining a mecca for musicians and artists. The opening of a Formula 1 race track in 2012 brought Austin to an international stage.

Despite boasting a population of nearly 1 million, some Texans still consider Austin a college town due to the more than 50,000 students living here. University of Texas grads forced to flee Austin for big corporations and money in the Metroplex and Houston tend to have serious nostalgia for the "40 acres" (the UT campus), so they regularly return for football games or just to comment on how much the town has changed in the decades since they've been here. Austin isn't the only college town in this part of the state, as the 60,000 plus Aggies in College Station will remind you. Nearby San Marcos is also home to nearly 40,000 students at Texas State University.

Culturally, Central Texas is known for its barbecue, live music, and HGTV-based Magnolia empire. Geographically, the land is marked by a convergence of the cotton-rich Blackland Prairie and the granite outcroppings of the Hill Country. Communities near the Highland Lakes west of Austin and in small towns like Fredericksburg and Bandera draw hordes of visitors every weekend to experience the region's cooler temperatures, distinct history, and beautiful landscape.

PLANNING YOUR TIME

You could spend a couple of weeks in Central Texas and still have plenty of worthy places left to visit, but realistically you can experience everything the region has to offer in six or seven days. Plan to spend at least two or three days exploring Austin's cultural scene. Devote an entire day or two to the area just north of downtown, home to the State Capitol, Texas history museum, LBJ Library and Museum, and Blanton Museum of Art. You'll probably need two nights to take in the live music and club scene, and it's worth devoting an afternoon to a Lockhart day trip to experience Texas barbecue at its finest.

Set aside another two or three days to drive through the Hill Country, with suggested overnight stops at a bed-and-breakfast in Fredericksburg or a dude ranch in Bandera. Fredericksburg's German heritage offers a memorable getaway, and it's downright sacrilegious to be in Texas without experiencing Bandera, the "Cowboy Capital of the World."

Other worthy Central Texas side trips are Bryan-College Station for the George Bush Presidential Library and Museum and the whole Aggieland phenomena, San Marcos for floating on an inner tube down a river, and the Highland Lakes for more traditional water-based recreation.

Previous: Austin's skyline; sunset on the University of Texas campus; traditional Texas barbecue at Kreuz Market in Lockhart

Austin and the Hill Country

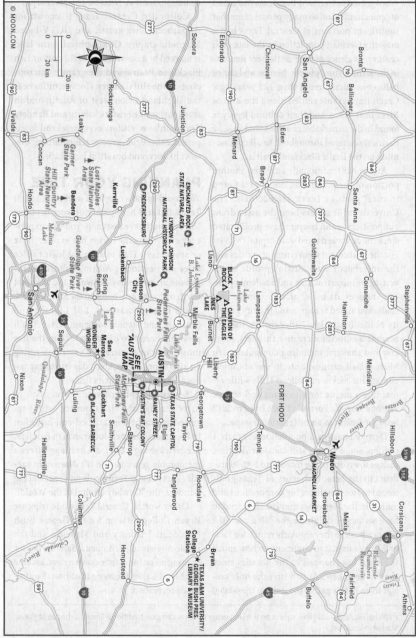

© MOON.COM

INFORMATION AND SERVICES

The best place to load up on travel information is the **Austin Visitor Center** (602 E. 4th St., 512/478-0098, www.austintexas.org, Mon.-Sat. 9am-5pm, Sun. 10am-5pm). Free maps and friendly staffers will help you find your way around town. The office also serves as the headquarters for two worthwhile tour services: **Austin Duck Adventures** (www.austinducks.com), conducted in an amphibious vehicle, and **Austin Overtours** (www.aotoursaustin.com), held in the comfort of a van. Official information about exploring the city is at the **Austin Convention and Visitors Bureau** (111 Congress Ave., Suite 700, 512/474-5171, www.austintexas.org, Mon.-Fri. 8am-5pm).

The **Capitol Visitors Center** (112 E. 11th St., 512/305-8400, daily 9am-5pm) is adjacent to the Capitol, housed in the restored 1856 General Land Office building, the oldest state office building in Texas. Within the visitors center is the Texas Department of Transportation's travel information counter (512/463-8563), with staffers offering free maps and literature on travel destinations throughout the state.

For an interesting and "witty" perspective on Austin and the Hill Country—including customized tours of the city's museums, parks, pubs, galleries, and gardens—contact veteran Austinite and self-proclaimed "Texpert" Howie Richey's **Texpert Tours** (512/383-8989, www.texperttours.com).

The **Waco Tourist Information Center** (106 Texas Ranger Trail, 800/922-6386, www.wacoheartoftexas.com, Mon.-Sat. 8am-5pm) offers free maps, visitors guides, and information about Waco area attractions.

GETTING THERE AND AROUND

Many travelers reach Austin by car. Freeways and speedy traffic allow travelers from Houston to arrive in 2.5 hours via I-10 west to Highway 71, and from the Metroplex, just over 3 hours straight south on I-35. From San Antonio, it's a quick 90-minute jaunt north on I-35.

Eight miles (12.9 km) southeast of downtown, **Austin-Bergstrom International Airport** (AUS, 512/530-2242, www.austintexas.gov/airport) is small and easily navigable, and noteworthy for its collection of exclusively local restaurants (where else can you eat a breakfast taco or brisket sandwich while waiting for a plane?). There's a stage with live music at the Hill Country Bar.

Although Austin is a progressive city, its public transportation systems are lacking, so you're better off taking a ride-share or renting a car than relying on buses or rail. For local ride-share alternatives to Uber and Lyft, download RideAustin. Otherwise, the city has three major cab companies: **American Yellow Checker Cab** (512/452-9999, www.yellowcabaustin.com), **Austin Express Cab** (512/666-4141), and **Lone Star Cab** (512/836-4900). Fares are around $30 from the airport to downtown. Another option is **Super Shuttle** (512/258-3826, www.supershuttle.com), which offers 24-hour shared-van service for $20-25 pp.

Waco Regional Airport (ACT, 254/750-8475, www.waco-texas.com/airport) is served by American Eagle. The airport received several upgrades after it became the main landing strip for President George W. Bush when he took refuge at his ranch in nearby Crawford. If you feel the need to fly to College Station, **Easterwood Airport** (CLL, 979/775-9900), owned and operated by Texas A&M University, offers daily service via American and United Airlines.

Austin

Austin (population 964,254) is often referred to in Texas as a blue island in the middle of a vast red sea. This progressive and dynamic city stands apart politically, culturally, and demographically. Austinites wouldn't have it any other way—they're proud of their comfortably sized, well-educated, fit, and socially conscious city.

Most people living in Austin are from someplace else—Dallas, Houston, California, the Midwest—which adds to the city's eclectic feel. The massive influx of people has watered down some of this college town's unassuming vibe, but Austin still retains a laid-back quality that out-of-towners find charming and appealing, particularly during the city's enormous annual South by Southwest and Austin City Limits music festivals, which draw bands and fans from around the globe.

ORIENTATION

During the past decade, Austin's population has exploded, resulting in a mix of sprawl to outer suburbs and a gaggle of new downtown high-rise condos. Although the metro area is now the 11th largest in the country, with a population beyond 1 million, Austin retains the feel of a small city, with most of its high-profile destinations clustered within a few miles in the downtown area. Fortunately, this allows exploration of much of the city on foot or by bike.

Downtown

For the 11th-largest city in the country, Austin has a minuscule downtown. Unlike other metropolises, downtown Austin is roughly one square mile, a 14-by-14-block area bordered by the grand State Capitol to the north and mighty Colorado River to the south. In between are towering skyscrapers along Congress Avenue and dozens of amazing restaurants, nightclubs, theaters, and heritage attractions.

South Austin

Once a desolate and sketchy stretch of road, South Congress Avenue is now one of Austin's most popular destinations for trendy shops and restaurants. Immediately south of the Colorado River, with picturesque views of the nearby State Capitol, this area, dubbed "SoCo" by some, offers a uniquely Austin twist on boutiques, eateries, and music venues. For a true local experience, book a room at the Austin Hotel and spend the day sampling inventive food and inspired fashion.

East Austin

During the past decade, East Austin (downtown, just east of I-35) has become a hip haven, where trendy clubs have replaced traditional Tejano bars. Even the music venues are decidedly more indie and divey, though to their credit, many have maintained the original decor and vibe of the previous tenants. Since hipsters tend to enjoy finely crafted beers and culinary delights, the options are endless for exploring and enjoying local culture mere minutes from downtown.

Campus Area

With its 50,000-plus students, the University of Texas has traditionally dominated Austin's identity; in fact, only recently has it ceased to be called a college town. UT still plays a major role in Austin—its high-level sports programs are the city's version of professional teams—and the vast number of creative and entrepreneurial students and graduates ensures the campus area is continually stocked with innovative museums, performing arts venues, and cultural destinations.

SIGHTS
★ Texas State Capitol

The **Texas State Capitol** (Congress Ave. and 11th St., 512/463-5495, www.tspb.state.tx.us, Mon.-Fri. 7am-10pm, Sat.-Sun. 9am-8pm, free

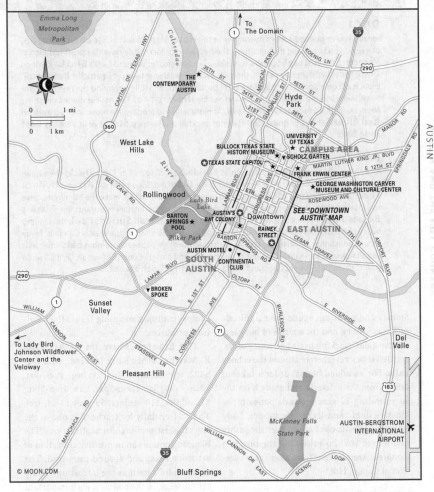

Austin

guided tours Mon.-Fri. 8:30am-4:30pm, Sat. 9:30am-3:30pm, Sun. noon-3:30pm) presides over the city and state with dignified grace. This magnificent 1888 Renaissance Revival edifice, with its captivating exterior of "sunset red" granite (actually a light pink hue), is nothing short of stunning. The capitol building truly represents Texas, from its legislative chambers to the tip of its dome—deliberately designed 15 feet (4.6 m) taller than the U.S. Capitol. Visitors from around the world flock to Austin to experience this National Historic Landmark for its significant contribution to American history.

The capitol's magnificent architectural features set it apart from its counterparts across the country. Notice the attention to detail, particularly inside the building. Upon close examination, themes and patterns emerge—stars, for instance—that tie all elements of the structure together: floor tiles, staircases, window frames, door fixtures, chandeliers.

Two Days in Austin

DAY 1

Ideally, you've booked a room downtown at the **Hotel Van Zandt** or **Stephen F. Austin**, or even if you're arriving mid-morning, the best way to start the day is with a breakfast taco at **Veracruz All Natural**. Spend a few leisurely hours strolling around **Lady Bird Lake** or on **Congress Avenue** downtown, then eat a hearty barbecue lunch at **Franklin Barbecue**. Work it off on a scooter or bike (or canoe or paddleboard) while exploring the rest of downtown, including the **State Capitol** and nearby **University of Texas**. For dinner, get some Mexican-inspired food at **La Condesa**. At night, enjoy legendary live music at **Mohawk** on **Red River Street** or grab a craft beer or cocktail on **Rainey Street** or at a trendy **East Side bar.**

DAY 2

Kick things off with a leisurely brunch at **Fonda San Miguel** or **Odd Duck,** then head to the **Museum District** to experience **The Blanton Museum of Art** and **Bullock Texas State History Museum.** If you're up for a little road trip, make the 30-minute drive to **Lockhart** for lunch at one of the original legendary barbecue restaurants like **Black's Barbecue.** Head back to town for a refreshing swim at **Barton Springs Pool,** then mosey over to **South Congress Avenue** for shopping, people-watching, and early cocktails. Enjoy an amazing dinner at **Uchi** or **Uchiko,** then head downtown to see the famous **bats** emerge at sunset followed by an upscale night at the theaters and bars on Congress Avenue. Or, if it's more your style, sample the shot bars and humanity on **"Dirty" 6th Street.**

Statues and paintings exude the magnitude of Texas history, and the sounds of busy legislative aides' clacking heels and tour guides' spirited shtick reverberate around the echoey halls. For an added bonus, order a takeout lunch from the cafeteria and enjoy it on the surrounding 22-acre grounds beneath the massive dome and its stately topper, Lady Liberty. Majestic oaks tower over the lushly manicured lawn, overlooking the bustling Congress Avenue scene from atop Texas's version of Capitol Hill.

The University of Texas

Not surprisingly, the University of Texas is enormous. With its 357-acre campus and student enrollment of 50,000, UT is a major entity in Austin, rivaling the state government for highest profile. Most of the attention is well deserved, since the university, thanks in part to its many affluent and loyal alumni, offers top-notch academic, athletic, and cultural services for students and the community. The public especially benefits from the following campus entities, showcasing Texas's finest cultural resources.

The Blanton Museum of Art (200 E. Martin Luther King Jr. Blvd., 512/471-5482, www.blantonmuseum.org, Tues.-Fri. 10am-5pm, Sat. 11am-5pm, Sun. 1pm-5pm, $12 adults, $10 seniors, $5 ages 13-21, free Thurs., free daily for teachers) is one of the city's highest-profile cultural attractions. The Blanton contains an impressive collection of art from Texas and around the world. The museum bills itself as the largest university art museum in the country, with important collections in Latin American art, American art, and European painting, prints, and drawings. It boasts 17,000 works of art, and its array of Latin American art is particularly notable, with works from more than 600 artists representing Mexico, the Caribbean, and South and Central America. In 2018, a major addition opened: Ellsworth Kelly's *Austin,* a "temple of light" featuring colored windows that bathe the building's interior in a prism of beauty.

Downtown Austin

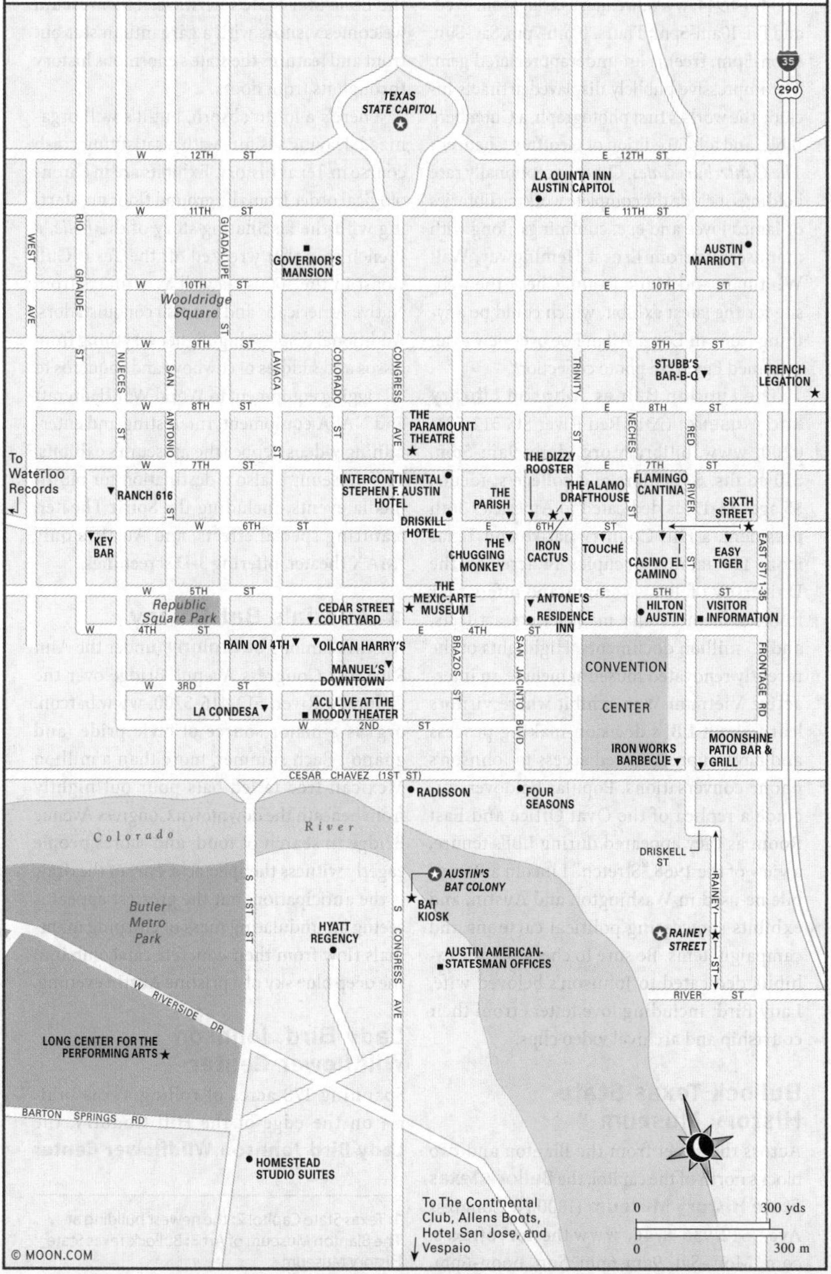

TEXAS STATE CAPITOL ✪

To Waterloo Records

To The Continental Club, Allens Boots, Hotel San Jose, and Vespaio

W 12TH ST — E 12TH ST
W 11TH ST — E 11TH ST
LA QUINTA INN AUSTIN CAPITOL ●

GOVERNOR'S MANSION ■
AUSTIN MARRIOTT ●
W 10TH ST — E 10TH ST

Wooldridge Square

W 9TH ST — E 9TH ST
STUBB'S BAR-B-Q ▼
FRENCH LEGATION ★

W 8TH ST — E 8TH ST

THE PARAMOUNT THEATRE ★

W 7TH ST — E 7TH ST
THE DIZZY ROOSTER
THE ALAMO DRAFTHOUSE ★
FLAMINGO CANTINA
SIXTH STREET
RANCH 616 ▼
INTERCONTINENTAL STEPHEN F. AUSTIN HOTEL ●
THE PARISH
DRISKILL HOTEL ■

W 6TH ST — E 6TH ST
KEY BAR ▼
THE CHUGGING MONKEY ▼
IRON CACTUS ▼
TOUCHÉ
CASINO EL CAMINO ▼
EASY TIGER

W 5TH ST — E 5TH ST
Republic Square Park
THE MEXIC-ARTE MUSEUM ■
ANTONE'S ★
HILTON AUSTIN ■
VISITOR INFORMATION
RESIDENCE INN ●

W 4TH ST — E 4TH ST
CEDAR STREET COURTYARD ▼

W 3RD ST — E 3RD ST
RAIN ON 4TH ▼
OILCAN HARRY'S ▼
MANUEL'S DOWNTOWN ▼
CONVENTION CENTER

LA CONDESA ▼
ACL LIVE AT THE MOODY THEATER ■
W 2ND ST
IRON WORKS BARBECUE ▼
MOONSHINE PATIO BAR & GRILL ▼

CESAR CHAVEZ (1ST ST)

RADISSON ●
FOUR SEASONS ●

Colorado   River

DRISKELL ST

Butler Metro Park

AUSTIN'S BAT COLONY ✪
BAT KIOSK ★
RAINEY STREET ★

HYATT REGENCY ●

AUSTIN AMERICAN-STATESMAN OFFICES ■

RAINEY ST
RIVER ST

W RIVERSIDE DR

LONG CENTER FOR THE PERFORMING ARTS ★

BARTON SPRINGS RD

HOMESTEAD STUDIO SUITES ●

0   300 yds
0   300 m

WEST AVE
RIO GRANDE ST
NUECES ST
SAN ANTONIO ST
GUADALUPE ST
LAVACA ST
COLORADO ST
CONGRESS AVE
BRAZOS ST
SAN JACINTO BLVD
TRINITY ST
NECHES ST
RED RIVER ST
EAST ST / I-35
FRONTAGE RD

S 1ST ST
S CONGRESS AVE

© MOON.COM

The **Harry Ransom Humanities Research Center** (21st St. and Guadalupe St., 512/471-8944, www.hrc.utexas.edu, Mon.-Wed. and Fri. 10am-5pm, Thurs. 10am-7pm, Sat.-Sun. noon-5pm, free) is an underappreciated gem. The impressive publicly displayed artifacts include the world's first photograph, a Gutenberg Bible, and a 1450 edition of Geoffrey Chaucer's *The Canterbury Tales.* Other exceptionally rare holdings include the complete working libraries of James Joyce and e. e. cummings along with manuscripts from Ernest Hemingway, Walt Whitman, and Mark Twain. Check the website for the latest exhibit, which could be anything from an Edgar Allan Poe overview to an esteemed Egyptian photo collection.

The **Lyndon Baines Johnson Library and Museum** (2313 Red River St., 512/721-0200, www.lbjlibrary.org, daily 9am-5pm, $10 adults, $7 seniors and college students, $5 ages 13-17) is dedicated to America's 36th president, a Hill Country native and Texas icon. The facility occupies 14 acres on the University of Texas campus and offers four floors of memorabilia, manuscripts, artifacts, and 45 million documents. Highlights of the recently renovated museum include an interactive Vietnam War exhibit where visitors learn about LBJ's decision-making process and have unprecedented access to Johnson's phone conversations. Popular holdovers include a replica of the Oval Office and East Room as they appeared during LBJ's tenure, a view of the 1968 "Stretch" Lincoln automobile he used in Washington and Austin, and exhibits showcasing political cartoons and campaign items. Be sure to check out the exhibits dedicated to Johnson's beloved wife, Lady Bird, including love letters from their courtship and archival video clips.

Bullock Texas State History Museum

Across the street from the Blanton and two blocks north of the capitol, the **Bullock Texas State History Museum** (1800 N. Congress Ave., 512/936-8746, www.thestoryoftexas.com, Mon.-Sat. 9am-6pm, Sun. noon-6pm, $13 adults, $11 seniors and college students, $9 ages 4-17, free 1st Sun. of month) showcases the Lone Star State's heritage. The museum welcomes visitors with a gargantuan star out front and features the state's enormous history through its front doors.

There's a lot to absorb, but it's well organized, leaving visitors with a satisfying crash course in Texas history. Exhibits are in chronological order from the ground floor up, starting with the fascinating story of the *Belle,* a French ship that wrecked off the Texas Gulf Coast in the 1600s, as well as artifacts from Native Americans and Spanish conquistadors. Additional displays highlight everything from lassos and saddles of cowboys and vaqueros to oil rigging equipment to World War II aircraft and NASA equipment. Interesting and entertaining videos pepper the museum's exhibits. The museum is also a destination for multimedia events, including the Spirit Theater, featuring special effects, and Austin's only IMAX theater, offering 3-D screenings.

★ Austin's Bat Colony

Austin's famous **bat colony** (under the Ann Richards Congress Avenue Bridge over the Colorado River, 512/416-5700, www.batcon. org) is a major source of civic pride (and guano). Each summer, more than a million Mexican free-tailed bats pour out nightly from beneath the downtown Congress Avenue Bridge in search of food, and scores people eagerly witness the spectacle. Part of the draw is the anticipation, but the greatest appeal is seeing an undulating mass of chirping mammals flow from their concrete catacomb into the deep blue sky of a pristine Austin evening.

Lady Bird Johnson Wildflower Center

Spanning 178 acres of rolling Texas prairie on the edge of the Hill Country, the **Lady Bird Johnson Wildflower Center**

1: Texas State Capitol **2:** the newest building at The Blanton Museum of Art **3:** Bullock Texas State History Museum

(4801 LaCrosse Ave., 512/232-0100, www.wildflower.org, daily 9am-5pm, $12 adults, $10 seniors, $6 ages 5-17) is well worth the 20-minute drive south of town. The Wildflower Center is a Central Texas treasure exploding with color, especially in the spring. Native flowers, bushes, trees, and grasses exhibit the region's natural beauty in numerous gardens and trails throughout a sprawling meadow, and an interpretive center and signage convey the passion Lady Bird (LBJ's wife) had for Texas's natural resources and educating people about the state's abundant botanical blessings.

Contemporary Austin

Austin's primary arts partnership is known as **Contemporary Austin,** a community art museum with two locations—a downtown exhibition facility and a West Austin art school. The downtown location is known as **Jones Center** (700 Congress Ave., 512/453-5312, www.thecontemporaryaustin.org, Tues.-Sat. 11am-7pm, Sun. noon-5pm, $10 adults, $5 seniors and students, free Tues.), housed in an inviting light-bathed building, offering a welcoming venue for viewing local and traveling art exhibits. It's a great place to pop in for an hour or two while downtown—check out a traveling exhibit before grabbing a cocktail or bite to eat on Congress Avenue. The Contemporary's art school is in West Austin's **Laguna Gloria** (3809 W. 35th St., 512/458-8191, Mon.-Wed. 8am–6pm, Thurs. 8am–9pm, Fri.–Sun. 8am–5pm), a gorgeous villa on Lake Austin featuring a 1916 Italianate mansion and lush grounds containing art exhibits and outdoor sculptures in a serene setting. The building is open only for special occasions, but the 14-acre grounds are well worth visiting due to the many art installations and outdoor exhibits.

Mexic-Arte Museum

The colorful **Mexic-Arte Museum** (419 Congress Ave., 512/480-9373, www.mexic-artemuseum.org, Mon.-Thurs. 10am-6pm, Fri.-Sat. 10am-5pm, Sun. noon-5pm, $7 adults, $4 seniors and students, $1 under age 12) provides cultural diversity in Austin's largely monochromatic downtown. More than a third of the city's population is Hispanic, but you wouldn't know it based on the Congress Avenue scene. The Mexic-Arte Museum, positioned on a prime piece of downtown real estate at 4th Street and Congress Avenue, features traditional and contemporary Latin American painting and sculpture, most of it focusing on social aspects of Latino life. The museum also includes a room dedicated to emerging local artists, who benefit from having a progressive venue for exhibiting their talent.

George Washington Carver Museum and Cultural Center

Just east of I-35 is the **George Washington Carver Museum and Cultural Center** (1165 Angelina St., 512/974-4926, www.austintexas.gov, Mon.-Thurs. 10am-6pm, Fri. 10am-5pm, Sat. 10am-4pm, free), another venue dedicated to one of Austin's underrepresented cultural groups. Education gets top billing here, evident in the museum's impressive galleries. The permanent exhibits showcase the significant contributions Austin's African American families have made to the city, including background information about the people behind the names of parks and streets. The Carver Museum also features a theater, a dance studio, an archive space, an artist's gallery, and a children's exhibit about African American scientists and inventors.

The Hill Country Flyer

Travel back in time on the slow-rolling, laid-back, completely relaxing trek through the scenic Hill Country and rural prairies on the **Hill Country Flyer** (trains depart at from 401 E. Whitestone Blvd., Cedar Park, 512/477-8468, www.austinsteamtrain.org, $30-50). Spring is the best time to go, for the added bonus of colorful wildflowers and ideal weather. The train's historic lounge cars are surprisingly comfortable, and the gentle clickety-clack of the rails and occasional

Mexican Free-Tailed Bats

So, you've seen (or are planning to see) the impressive mass of nearly one million bats emerge from under the **Ann Richards Congress Avenue Bridge** (http://www.batcon.org). But what exactly are these creatures?

Considered one of the smaller species of bats, Mexican free-tailed bats have a wingspan of 11-13 inches (28-33 cm). They're named free-tails because the lower half of their tail is free of a body-attached membrane. These little critters are typically dark to light brown.

Mexican free-tailed bats are found mostly in the western United States and Mexico, and it's estimated that 100 million of them arrive in Central Texas annually to raise their young. Nursing females require large quantities of high-fat insects, so they tend to feast upon egg-laden moths, including bollworm moths, cutworm moths, and other agricultural pests that migrate north from Mexico.

Free-tails usually emerge about 15 minutes after sunset, and the best time to see them in action is in the summer (July-Sept.). They leave the bridge (or, in most other locales, a cave) at speeds of up to 35 mph (56 km/h), and they can increase velocity up to 60 mph (97 km/h). A single bat pup is usually born in Junes-July, and the little ones take their first flight at five weeks old. The bats started gathering under the Congress Avenue Bridge in the early 1980s, when engineers designed the crevices that would ultimately become home to the now-famous colony of millions.

anecdotes from the seasoned volunteers make for a calm getaway on this peaceful train. After a two-hour ride, the train stops in the small towns of Brenham and Burnet (BUR-nit), where you can grab lunch at the **Dairy Bar** and **Trailblazer Grille,** respectively, both offering hearty and tasty cheeseburgers and sandwiches. You'll be back on the train by 2pm and in Cedar Park by 4pm.

RECREATION

The student athletes in burnt orange are perennial contenders for national titles in all sports (they've collectively won nearly 50 championship trophies), so the quality of action at the University of Texas is first-rate. Recreation-wise, Austin prides itself on its large amount of natural green space, and residents take full advantage of the city's hike and bike trails and waterways to keep fit and relax.

University of Texas Sports
FOOTBALL

College football is a religion in Texas, and the University of Texas's Royal Memorial Stadium is one of the houses of the holy. The atmosphere is exhilarating, especially at late-season games against nationally ranked division

rivals, and there's a good chance that many of the enormous players in will soon be playing in the NFL. The football program has won four national championships, most recently in 2005. The Horns' most-hyped game each year is against the University of Oklahoma, held in Dallas, an intense confrontation of strong, scrappy students battling for a year's worth of bragging rights.

BASKETBALL

No sport will displace football at the top of the food chain in Austin, but the UT men's basketball team always makes a valiant effort. The team has produced several highly touted NBA recruits, including Kevin Durant and LaMarcus Aldridge, and has made appearances in the NCAA tournament during the past decade. Although the team's home, the Frank Erwin Center, doesn't get as rollicking as Memorial Stadium, students and residents still fill the seats and provide the energy found in college basketball arenas in other parts of the country.

Also a formidable force on the Erwin Center court is the women's basketball team, still occasionally referred to as the Lady Longhorns. A longtime powerhouse in women's collegiate basketball, these Longhorns include some of the best athletes in the sport.

BASEBALL

UT's baseball program doesn't get the recognition it deserves. Despite taking a backseat to the football and basketball programs, baseball has a long tradition of championship teams. Many of the players, most notably Roger Clemens, have gone on to successful careers in Major League Baseball. The Horns' home base, Disch-Falk Field, recently received a much-needed upgrade, although the sight of artificial turf and sound of aluminum bats still makes baseball purists cringe.

Professional Sports

Austin did not have a major-league professional sports franchise until a soccer team, **FC Austin,** announced plans to kick off in 2021. A new stadium is in the works near the Domain shopping area. Keep an eye on www. austinfc.com for news about opening dates and upcoming matches.

The **Round Rock Express** (Dell Diamond, 3400 E. Palm Valley Blvd., 512/255-2255, www.roundrockexpress.com) is a minor-league affiliate of baseball's Houston Astros. Since the team is AAA, just below the major leagues, fans are treated to quality baseball with impressive hustle from burgeoning stars. Dell Diamond is a charming and comfy place to watch a game, with the amusing high jinks of minor league games (kids running the base paths, fans dancing on the dugout, races on the field).

Also just a step below the majors are the **Texas Stars** (512/467-8277, www.texasstars. com), the minor league outfit for the Dallas Stars ice hockey team. Games are played in the suburb of Cedar Park. Locals are also warming up to the **Austin Spurs** (512/236-8333, www.austinleague.nba.com), the NBA Development League minor league basketball team affiliated with the San Antonio Spurs. The Toros play at the Cedar Park Center November-April.

City Parks

Long considered Austin's crown jewel, **Barton Springs Pool** (2201 Barton Springs Rd., 512/476-9044, www.austintexas.gov, daily 5am-10pm, $2-4) in Zilker Metropolitan Park is the city's ultimate recreational experience. A source of cool refreshment for nearly a century, the 1,000-foot-long (300-m) pool is constantly replenished by 68°F (20°C) spring

University of Texas Longhorns football game

water, a necessary remedy for Austin's triple-digit summer temperatures. The remainder of 350-acre Zilker Park is a sprawling urban oasis, with soccer fields, a hillside theater, sand volleyball courts, a massive playground, a disc golf course, and picnic sites. Family-friendly activities include the serene and stunning **Zilker Botanical Gardens**, featuring the otherworldly Taniguchi Oriental Garden, and the Austin Nature and Science Center, a wonderful destination for children, offering glimpses at Texas wildlife (bobcats, owls, reptiles, raccoons), a dinosaur digging pit, science exhibits, and nature trails.

About 1 mile (1.6 km) east is **Town Lake Metropolitan Park,** spanning the shores of the downtown portion of the Colorado River formerly known as Town Lake (now Lady Bird Lake in honor of LBJ's wife, Lady Bird Johnson). The park contains an extremely popular 10-mile (16-km) shoreline trail and fields for baseball, football, soccer and rugby, and volleyball. The section of the park east of I-35 is a favorite spot for gatherings and events at Fiesta Gardens and Festival Beach. The parkland on the south side of Lady Bird Lake is known as Auditorium Shores, where numerous concerts are staged throughout the year; most are free public events. Standing in the shadows of the large stage erected for these shows is a statue of Austin's beloved guitarist Stevie Ray Vaughan, who died in a tragic 1990 helicopter accident. Fans pay homage to the legendary bluesman by leaving flowers and memorabilia at the base of the statue.

One of the city's overlooked recreational gems is **Emma Long Metropolitan Park** (1600 City Park Rd., 512/346-1831, www.austintexas.gov, daily 7am-10pm, $5-10). Named for an early member of the Austin City Council, the park is a massive expanse of natural Hill Country beauty, highlighted by a 350-foot-long (110-m) sandy beach on the north bank of the Colorado River. Visitors bask in the sun or play beach volleyball while Jet Skis zoom by. Emma Long is one of the few parks offering respite on a scorching summer day thanks to the breeze from the water and plentiful shade from the cypress trees along the riverbank. Incidentally, you'll find some of the tastiest burgers in town and a full bar with live music on weekends at the adjacent **Ski Shores Cafe** (2905 Pearce Rd., 512/394-7511, www.skishoresaustin.com).

Hiking and Biking
THE TRAIL AT LADY BIRD LAKE

This is the most popular place for Austinites to exercise and flirt in an outdoor setting. The 10-mile-long (16-km) crunchy and well-worn path offers an ideal representation of the city's physically fit population—healthy hikers, buff bikers, and strolling slackers. The hike and bike trail is a healthy place to meet people, and you can paddle Lady Bird Lake to soak up the surrounding greenery and clear blue sky. Rent a canoe or kayak at **Zilker Park Boat Rentals** (east of Barton Springs Pool, 512/478-3852, www.zilkerboats.com, daily 10am-dark, $10 per hour, $40 per day).

BARTON CREEK GREENBELT

It's hard to believe you're merely minutes from downtown once you've entered a trail and are surrounded by juniper trees, running water, and limestone cliffs. **The Barton Creek Greenbelt** (512/974-6700, www.austintexas.gov), an 8-mile (12.9-km) stretch of preserved space along Barton Creek, draws scores of nature-loving urbanites to its rugged trails, sheer cliff walls, and swimming holes. Two of the most popular and lively access points are Twin Falls near Loop 360 and MoPac (Loop 1) and Campbell's Hole at the end of Spyglass Drive.

THE VELOWAY

Tucked away in southwest Austin, **The Veloway** (4900 LaCrosse Ave., 512/974-6700, daily 5am-10pm) is a 3-mile (4.8-km) loop dedicated to cyclists and in-line skaters. A sign at the front gate provides a blunt reminder that joggers and walkers are not welcome here, which is fine, since bipeds have access to the rest of the city. The rolling Hill Country offers a welcoming backdrop to the

Wildflower Roots

For decades, Central Texas's highway medians have served as an unlikely springtime photo op for people with children and dogs. In March and April, these rural grassy knolls are bursting with bluebonnets and brightly blossoming Indian paintbrushes, black-eyed Susans, winecups, goldenrods, and Indian blankets. It's a Texas tradition to dress the kids and pets in their Sunday best and place them within the vibrant natural color palette for a picture.

For 130 million years, Texas's wildflowers have thrived in different soils—azaleas grow in acidic East Texas soil, for example, but struggle in the chalky Central Texas earth. Central Texans are fortunate since they're in the middle of several overlapping eco-regions. This biodiversity results in a plethora of 400 varieties of springtime wildflowers, most of them native species.

Not surprisingly, the best-known wildflower in Texas—the iconic bluebonnet—inspires the largest number of stories. A popular tale involves Lady Bird Johnson, wife of President Lyndon B. Johnson. An active naturalist, she

Lady Bird Johnson Wildflower Center

described the phenomenon of a bluebonnet's white flowers turning progressively redder as "blushing." She claimed the color change happened after a bee had pollinated the flower, sending a natural signal to other bees to seek out the virginal white blossoms. Lady Bird's legacy endures at the **Lady Bird Johnson Wildflower Center** (4801 LaCrosse Ave., Austin, 512/232-0100, www.wildflower.org, daily 9am-5pm, $12 adults, $10 seniors, $6 ages 5-17), where an impressive collection of gardens, trails, meadows, and a gallery offer a glimpse of Texas's diverse native species.

surrounding 100-acre park, and the Veloway's proximity to Lady Bird Johnson Wildflower Center makes this a pleasantly natural way to get a workout.

ENTERTAINMENT AND EVENTS

For the most part, the "Live Music Capital of the World" lives up to its billing. On any given night you can catch blues, reggae, country, and punk. Red River Street has a core of steady live-music venues, 6th Street retains its distinction as a mini Bourbon Street, the Warehouse District offers folks in their 30s a place to gather without screaming to be heard, and East Austin is the hipster hot spot.

Performing Arts
PARAMOUNT THEATRE

The beautiful historic **Paramount Theatre** (713 Congress Ave., 512/472-5470, www.austintheatre.org) is the city's crown jewel for performing arts events. The magnificent 1915 venue is just four blocks south of the capitol and originally served as a vaudeville theater and variety house. It continues to stage a wide variety of live shows and films under a faux sky ceiling and glamorous balconies. The Paramount also operates the adjacent **State Theatre** (719 Congress Ave.) as Stateside at the Paramount. The State is a remarkable art deco theater with 300 seats, allowing it to host more intimate comedy, live music, and film festivals.

UNIVERSITY OF TEXAS PERFORMING ARTS CENTER

The university's primary venue is the **Bass Concert Hall** (2350 Robert Dedman Dr., 512/471-2787, www.texasperformingarts.org), which brings an eclectic mix of internationally acclaimed performers to the UT campus. Pop legends, dance performances, chamber orchestras, alternative rockers, and world music superstars take the stage throughout the year to the benefit of students and residents. Superior acoustics and comfortable seating make this an especially inviting venue to experience a show.

LONG CENTER FOR THE PERFORMING ARTS

The architecturally stunning **Long Center for the Performing Arts** (701 W. Riverside Dr., 512/457-5100, www.thelongcenter.org) is the city's most prominent performing arts venue. Home to the Austin Symphony Orchestra, Austin Lyric Opera, and Ballet Austin, the Long Center is truly a center stage for Austin's fine arts. With multiple stages and an eclectic mix of performers, the venue represents Austin's diverse cultural scene. Bonus: The lakeside veranda offers incredible views of the Austin skyline, an ideal photo op.

Bars and Clubs
★ RAINEY STREET

How often is the city's coolest collection of laid-back bars and food trailers located near a corporate-minded convention center? It wasn't necessarily planned that way in Austin, but a collection of historic bungalows in a formerly run-down neighborhood has been repurposed as the **Rainey Street District** (www.raineystbars.com). More than a dozen historic houses have been carefully preserved and retrofitted as homey lounges offering top-notch local craft brews and food.

Rainey Street is an ideal place to plan a night of pub crawling and exploring. Several spots are worth prioritizing due to their longevity and charm. Start with the funky and fun **Container Bar** (90 Rainey St., www.

austincontainerbar.com), a unique space made entirely of recycled shipping containers. Snag a spot on the spacious back patio, where you can grab a local pint and soak up the attractive scenery. Across the street is a traditional down-home **Clive Bar** (609 Davis St., 512/494-4120, www.clivebar.com). Candles, friendly bartenders, and strong cocktails make this a comfy spot to relax and enjoy a mellow evening.

For an extensive local craft beer selection, head to **Craft Pride** (61 Rainey St., 512/428-5571, www.craftprideaustin.com). More than 20 breweries are represented in the 50-plus taps. Some local favorites are Austin Beerworks, Real Ale, and Hops & Grain. Grab a draft or a can, sit on the dog-friendly patio, and save some room for Detroit-style pizza at the Via 313 food trailer out back.

If cuisine is a priority, head directly to **Banger's Sausage House and Beer Garden** (79 Rainey St., 512/386-1656, www.bangersaustin.com). As its name implies, it celebrates the best German beer and sausages. Order a fancy bratwurst on a pretzel bun with spicy mustard, pair it with a hoppy local beer (like Fire Eagle IPA), and revel in the perfection.

6TH STREET

Most of the hopping bar activity on 6th Street is happening just west of the behemoth I-35 freeway, but the scene isn't for everyone. In fact, 6th Street can be divided into three distinct areas—trendy East of I-35, rowdy East of Congress Avenue, and low-key West of Congress.

East of I-35: During the past decade, hipsters have taken over a formerly mellow stretch of Hispanic nightclubs on East 6th Street. These bars are much more laid-back than the raucous shot bars just a half mile away, and they cater to a slightly older crowd. But make no mistake—people are still dressed to impress. A good starting point is the welcoming **Shangri-La** (1016 E. 6th St., 512/524-4291, www.shangrilaaustin.com). Known for its spacious courtyard and impressive beer

selection, Shangri-La is an ideal place to spend a cool spring evening or warm summer night. Just a few blocks away is the welcoming **The Liberty** (1618 E. 6th St., 512/600-4791, www.thelibertyaustin.com), with a spacious patio and plenty of local brews on tap. Be sure to grab some tantalizing Japanese street food at the on-site food truck **East Side King.**

East of Congress is Austin's party central. Shot bars, dance clubs, beer joints, and more shot bars are the featured attractions, and thousands of students and 20-somethings revel in the debauchery each weekend. The streets are closed to cars on most weekends, allowing revelers to stumble between bars and jabber with their brand-new best friends. A word of warning: This area has earned the nickname Dirty 6th, so don't be surprised if you encounter some dubious characters amid the craziness.

One of the premier spots for soaking up the whole scene is the rooftop patio at **Iron Cactus** (606 Trinity St., 512/472-9240, www.ironcactus.com). Its spectacular top-shelf margaritas taste even better on the balcony on a perfect spring evening. For a genuine sense of the 6th Street party atmosphere, check out **Touché** (417 E. 6th St., 512/472-9841), known for its laid-back vibe and literally hot bartenders: The specialty of the house is Flaming Dr Peppers, a Southern tradition involving shots of Amaretto and Everclear set ablaze, then dropped in a glass of beer. The kids claim it tastes exactly like a Dr Pepper soda.

If you insist on doing a body shot, stagger to the zoos known as **The Chuggin' Monkey** (219 E. 6th St., 512/476-5015, www.thechugginmonkey.com) and **The Dizzy Rooster** (306 E. 6th St., 512/236-1667, www.dizzyrooster.com). Those looking for a comparatively mellower 6th Street venue are still in luck. Several bars cater to Austin's laid-back alternative clientele, content to kick back on a patio with tequila on the rocks or a pale ale

while the jukebox cranks out Johnny Cash and St. Vincent.

Drawing an eclectic crowd is **Casino el Camino** (517 E. 6th St., 512/469-9330, www.casinoelcamino.net). Don't be too frightened by the graphic scenes painted on the wall or the dungeon decor—even goths occasionally like to whoop it up. Be sure to sample one of Casino's enormous and immensely flavorful burgers (split one with a pal and expect a 20-minute wait) while vintage Clash tunes from the jukebox drown out a Stanley Kubrick movie.

Just down the street is a welcome alternative to the craziness known as **Easy Tiger** (709 E. 6th St., 512/614-4972, www.easytigeraustin.com). A traditional bakery scene immediately greets guests, where they can buy a fresh-baked pretzel, baguette, or pastry. Head downstairs for an impressive selection of local and national craft brews on tap, and enjoy them on the back patio while playing table tennis alongside Waller Creek.

West of Congress: Like the nearby Warehouse District, this (much smaller) area draws an older crowd that prefers a neat pour of Scotch over a dollar shot of Jäger. Twenty years ago, this depressing part of downtown was filled with used car lots and auto repair shops; now it's in the shadow of condo towers and company headquarters. Check out the lively scene at **Concrete Cowboy** (719 W. 6th St., 512/987-0860, www.concretecowboybar.com). It can get loud, but you can always escape to the rooftop patio. Just down the street is the hip yet relaxed **Key Bar** (617 W. 6th St., 512/236-9389, www.keybaraustin.com), located in a former locksmith shop. The outdoor lounge is a cool place to enjoy a cold beer or a signature cocktail with a juice Popsicle garnish.

WAREHOUSE DISTRICT

Compared to 6th Street, the Warehouse District is downright civil. You won't find too many UT coeds at these bars, but that doesn't mean it's a subdued scene. Instead of angry punk bands, you'll often hear jazz

---

1: Stubb's Bar-B-Q **2:** Paramount Theatre **3:** Broken Spoke honky-tonk

Austin City Limits

Paul McCartney at the Austin City Limits festival

These days, the words *Austin City Limits* are associated more with the annual music festival than a revered public television program, but the roots of this world-renowned entity run deep in the city's musical heritage. Willie Nelson was an early regular guest, and each season continued the tradition of showcasing worthy country, blues, folk, rock and roll, bluegrass, and zydeco artists that weren't getting the radio airplay they deserved.

The show was inspired by Austin's burgeoning live music scene in the early 1970s, and it has since featured more than 500 regional and internationally acclaimed artists on its stage. Memorable performances include such diverse acts as B. B. King, the Pixies, Wilco, Ray Charles, Foo Fighters, and Kendrick Lamar.

Staging History

For 25 years, the show was taped in a studio on the University of Texas campus, with a stage containing fake trees and a backdrop of the city skyline. Not surprisingly, many viewers assumed the show was taped outside and were surprised to learn the stage was on the 6th floor of UT's communications building. The skyline set debuted in 1982 and has remained the series' backdrop ever since.

The ACL studio and stage moved from the UT campus to downtown Austin in 2011, placing it in a more prominent and accessible location with a larger capacity. Show tapings accommodate 800 (an increase from 320), and the venue holds 2,750 at its concert venue called Austin City Limits Live at Moody Theater. Appropriately, the ACL stage opened its new venture with a Willie Nelson concert.

For **tickets,** visit www.acltv.com or call 512/475-9077.

trios. Women order cosmopolitans rather than mind erasers. Food options include tapas instead of hot dogs from a cart. And if your fourth glass of cabernet makes your feet restless, there are several nearby clubs with crafty DJs playing hopping dance music. Rowdier 6th Street is a mere 20-minute walk away.

Catch some live music and spot the scenesters at **Cedar Street Courtyard** (208 W. 4th St., 512/495-9669, www. cedarstreetaustin.com). One of the district's first successful establishments, Cedar Street features a sunken courtyard with live music and some of the city's stiffest drinks. Martinis are the specialty, and the friendly bartenders will gladly help you find your favorite blend. The vibe is laid-back and welcoming at **Lavaca Street Bar** (405 Lavaca St., 512/469-0106, www.lavacastreet.com). It features an impressive beer selection and a tasty selection of pub grub.

GAY BARS

Austin doesn't have a large downtown area exclusively devoted to gay bars, but several are in the Warehouse District. One of the city's stalwarts is **Oilcan Harry's** (211 W. 4th St., 512/320-8823, www.oilcanharrys.com), known for its dance scene and bartenders. The crowd here is mostly gay, but straight folks are welcome. The other venerable gay venue in town is right next door. **Rain** (217 W. 4th St., 512/494-1150, www.rainon4th.com) features strong drinks and a lively dance floor. A few blocks away is **The Iron Bear** (301 W. 6th St., 512/482-8993, www.theironbear.com), a cozy unpretentious den.

TOP EXPERIENCE

Live Music

Musicians have been drawn to Austin for decades to take advantage of the city's abundant stages, open-minded atmosphere, and formerly cheap rent. Several notable artists persevered beyond free meals and tip-jar paychecks, including Janis Joplin and Stevie Ray Vaughan, and, more recently, acts such as Spoon and Gary Clark Jr. have seen their names ascend from the bottoms of flyers to the tops of marquees. Drop by any of the 100-plus venues in town that host live music, and you just might be lucky enough to discover the next Black Angels or Black Pumas.

EAST AUSTIN

Now that the hipsters have taken over East Austin from the traditional Tejano bars, the music venues are decidedly more indie and divey, although to their credit, many have maintained the original decor and vibe of the previous tenants. One of the best examples of this assimilation is the **Scoot Inn** (1308 E. 4th St., 512/478-6200, www.scootinnaustin.com). Recently upgraded yet still retaining its historic charm, Scoot Inn is an ideal atmosphere to watch a band play on the outdoor stage while sipping a can of PBR or a local craft beer. Bands range from up-and-coming indie acts to occasional touring shows.

The coolest spot to catch a show is the similarly comfy **White Horse Tavern** (500 Comal St., 512/553-6756, www.thewhitehorseaustin.com). The two best words to describe the vibe here are "honky-tonk" and "hipster," both in the most accommodating way. Cowboy and porkpie hats easily coexist, and everyone can agree on the music (Americana) and the beer (Lone Star).

Legendary punk club **Emo's** (2015 E. Riverside Dr., 512/477-3667, www.emosaustin.com) moved to East Austin from its iconic downtown location a decade ago, but people still attend shows in the cavernous room, which stages local and touring bands ranging from indie to nostalgic indie.

RED RIVER

Red River Street, at the eastern edge of the 6th Street district, represents the lifeblood of Austin's live music scene. Once the territory of crack dealers and vagabonds, this four-block stretch is now the vibrant core of the city's rock-and-roll culture. Anchoring the strip is **Stubb's Bar-B-Q** (801 Red River St., 512/480-8341, www.stubbsaustin.com), which hosts the city's best road shows in an outdoor amphitheater with room for 1,800 and accommodates smaller acts on an indoor stage. As the name implies, Stubb's also serves some fine smoked meats, but the bands bring the heat most nights. Artists ranging from Wilco and Willie Nelson to Big Thief and Vampire Weekend grace the main stage, while the more intimate inside stage has hosted local stalwarts such as The Gourds and The Derailers. Incidentally, Stubb's holds perhaps the most memorable New Year's Eve bash in town.

Nearby **Mohawk** (912 Red River St., 512/666-0877, www.mohawkaustin.com)

features indie rock bands from Austin and afar and draws one of the trendiest crowds in Capital City. The multiple-terraced outdoor patios offer cool views of downtown and quiet places to drink cheap beer.

For a true Austin experience, head to **Cheer Up Charlie's** (900 Red River St., 512/431-2133, www.cheerupcharlies.com), a welcoming spot with an amazing outdoor stage and patio for live indie rock, lounging, dancing, and smoking trendy cigarettes. The locally brewed *kombucha* and draft beer are also big hits.

Just down the street are a few down-and-dirty establishments offering local cow-punk and alternative bands along with cheap beer specials most nights of the week. The best of the bunch are **The Side Bar** (602 E. 7th St., 512/322-0697, www.sidebaraustin.com) and **Swan Dive** (615 Red River St., www.swandiveaustin.com). Note: Over the past few years, this area has become a bit dicey; although it isn't unsafe, be sure to keep an eye out for questionable characters after midnight.

WAREHOUSE DISTRICT

ACL Live at the Moody Theater (310 W. Willie Nelson Blvd., 512/225-7999, www.acl-live.com) has become the city's favorite place to see a show. The venue is impeccable, with its professionally designed acoustics and seating to accommodate the long-running namesake music show on PBS. With legendary blues acts, modern rock bands, stand-up comedy, and acoustic showcases, this is the best place in town to experience the "Live Music Capital of the World." An added bonus: The Willie Nelson statue outside the venue, officially dedicated at 4:20pm on April 20, 2012, is an ideal place to snap a selfie.

6TH STREET

There are still pockets remaining of old 6th Street—rock-and-roll venues and comfy dive bars—among the dance clubs, and they're worth checking out for the quality of live music being played most nights. One of the city's most notable venues is "Austin's Home

of the Blues," **Antone's** (305 E. 5th St., 512/814-0361, www.antonesnightclub.com). Although it has changed locations a few times, Antone's has been a fixture on the music scene for nearly three decades, staging legendary artists like B. B. King along with local blues and roots rock acts. Stevie Ray Vaughan got his start here, and people still line up to catch the latest homegrown and national acts on the big stage.

Consistently reliable is **The Parish** (214 E. 6th St., 512/473-8381, www.theparishaustin.com), featuring local and touring indie rock acts. Spoon spent a lot of time here on its rise up the indie-rock ladder, and occasional techno or hip-hop shows appear on the schedule. A couple of blocks east is longtime reggae club **Flamingo Cantina** (515 E. 6th St., 512/494-9336, www.flamingocantina.com). The Flamingo is a reliable source for local and national reggae and ska bands as well as cold Red Stripe beer and a lingering haze of green smoke.

SOUTH AUSTIN

Although this area covers a lot of ground geographically, the old-school soul of this part of town and the live music scene ties South Austin together. This is perhaps best represented at **The Continental Club** (1315 S. Congress Ave., 512/441-2444, www.continentalclub.com), the venerable South Congress venue that once hosted breezy artists like Glenn Miller in the 1950s. Now the tiny stage is a regular spot for local and national touring acts—most specializing in roots rock, bluegrass, rockabilly, and country. Celebrity sightings are fairly common, and the happy hours are a great way to experience authentic Austin.

Another local favorite is **The Saxon Pub** (1320 S. Lamar Blvd., 512/448-2552, www.thesaxonpub.com), featuring blues, singer-songwriters, and Americana. The venue itself isn't remarkable, with its limited seating and small stage, but the sound quality is excellent, and the artists are better than you'd expect to hear in a neighborhood bar.

Hollywood in Texas

Nearly 400 major features and made-for-TV movies have been filmed in Austin over the past couple of decades, and hundreds of commercials and independent projects have also used the state capital as a backdrop.

One of the city's first high-profile projects, aside from the classic *Texas Chainsaw Massacre*, was 1989's *Lonesome Dove*, which took full advantage of the Austin area's diverse scenery. Other big-name projects filmed in Austin include *Office Space, Dazed and Confused, Friday Night Lights, Tree of Life*, the *Spy Kids* series, and the seminal *Slacker*.

One of the main reasons filmmakers choose Austin is its diverse topography and moderate climate, suitable for year-round filming. The city has rolling hills to the west, flat prairies to the east, lakes, and pine forests all within a half hour of the production office. And because Austin is surrounded by small towns that haven't changed much in the past few decades, there are abundant locations to film period pieces that use historic county courthouses, Main Street storefronts, and vintage homes as scenery. Also, since the area has been a hot spot for filming since the early 1990s, there's a deep talent pool of qualified crew members.

Finally, as most Austinites will quickly and enthusiastically claim, the city is a fun place to be on location for a few months. Residents are welcoming without being starstruck, the restaurant and bar scene is a fun destination after a hard day's work, there are plenty of outdoor recreation opportunities, and the plethora of actors and directors make for a wealth of qualified available talent.

For a true Texas-style honky-tonk, check out the **Broken Spoke** (3201 S. Lamar Blvd., 512/442-6189, www.brokenspokeaustintx.net). Although this once-on-the-outskirts venue is now surrounded by a new condo, once you're inside, this is as real as it gets—the music, dancing, and atmosphere are purely Texas. On weekend nights, the dance floor is crowded with crisp-jeaned ranchers and tattooed hipsters, all two-stepping in a smoothly rotating counterclockwise pattern. Legends who've graced this low-ceilinged, no-frills establishment during its prominent past include Willie Nelson, Bob Wills, Ernest Tubb, and George Strait.

The Alamo Drafthouse

The classic "dinner and a movie" date received a major upgrade when the **Alamo Drafthouse** (www.drafthouse.com) opened in 1997. There are now six Austin locations and dozens across the country, from Los Angeles to New York City. The concept is genius in its simplicity: offer restaurant-quality food and alcohol to movie patrons. Narrow tables between seats allow waiters to take orders and deftly navigate the theater without disturbing viewers. Menu items include the "Royale with Cheese" burger and "Poultrygeist" pizza, and the cold draft beer, cocktails, and fine wines offer an ideal accompaniment. The food is often paired with the movie (spaghetti Westerns, or recreating meals from *Big Night* and *Like Water for Chocolate*), and there are clever promotions galore—screening 1980s B movies with appearances by the actors, a karaoke-style movie scene reenactment contest called "videoke," sing-alongs, open screen nights, and rolling road shows.

Entertainment Weekly named the Alamo the "best theater in America," and its tremendous popularity is an Austin success story. The Austin locations are Ritz/Downtown (320 E. 6th St.), South Lamar (1120 S. Lamar Blvd., 512/476-1320), Village (2700 W. Anderson Lane, 512/476-1320), Slaughter Lane (5701 W. Slaughter Lane, 512/861-7060), Mueller (1911 Aldrich St., Suite 120, 512/572-1425), and Lakeline (14028 N. U.S. 183, Bldg. F, 512/861-7070).

Events
SOUTH BY SOUTHWEST MUSIC FESTIVAL

What started as a small collection of bands and industry reps in a single downtown hotel has expanded to one of the largest multimedia music festivals in the country. Each March, thousands of musicians and their critics, businesspeople, and groupies flock to Austin for **South by Southwest** (512/467-7979, www.sxsw.com) for the ideal weather, beer, barbecue, Tex-Mex, and every kind of music under the sun. During 10 days, Austin becomes the epicenter of the music industry, complete with international media coverage, splashy promotional events, and plenty of black leather.

The original concept was to expose bands and sign contracts for up-and-coming artists (acts that got their first major buzz at the festival include the White Stripes, Katy Perry, Janelle Monae, Alabama Shakes, Odd Future, and Hanson). SXSW has evolved into an enormous showcase hosting big names and reunion gigs (Lady Gaga, Kanye West, Big Star) for the publicity factor. The festival has scaled back in recent years to focus on its original mission of showcasing new artists. You need to fork over nearly $1,000 for an unrestricted festival pass, but there are still hundreds of fun, worthwhile, and free music options during SXSW week for less expense, mostly daytime parties featuring bands who'll play anywhere possible—a back alley, a street corner, a front lawn—to maximize exposure. SXSW organizers work with the city to stage free shows at the downtown park Auditorium Shores, where past notables include Spoon, Public Enemy, and Cheap Trick.

AUSTIN CITY LIMITS MUSIC FESTIVAL

Literally one of the country's hottest festivals, scheduled annually in the inferno of Austin's September-October, **Austin City Limits Music Festival** (www.aclfest.com) features searing temperatures and equally scorching bands. The event takes place over two weekends, allowing the flexibility to find out which acts are a "can't-miss" after the first weekend. Presented by the organizers of the long-running PBS show of the same name, ACL Fest premiered in 2002 and has become a premier event among music fans. Artists range from rock legends like Paul McCartney and David Byrne to big names like Lizzo, Kanye West, and Wilco. Over the years, fest organizers have learned some valuable lessons about hosting a successful event by offering dozens of exclusively local food vendors, shade and misting tents, free water stations, and an Austin Kiddie Limits stage. Despite the sweltering conditions, 70,000 fans snap up tickets each year.

THE STAR OF TEXAS FAIR AND RODEO

Most years, the rodeo takes place at the same time as South by Southwest, in mid-March, in an apt representation of Austin, with progressive music and an old-fashioned livestock show. Even the rockers can enjoy The **Star of Texas Fair and Rodeo** (512/919-3000, www.rodeoaustin.com), with its roping and barrel-racing competitions, carnival rides, Texas food vendors, and live music. The rodeo attracts huge crowds from across the state, drawn by the excitement of the bull-riding competition—it's far more intense in person than on TV—and by the quality musicians. Past performers include diverse acts such as Nelly, Maroon 5, and Lady Antebellum.

SHOPPING

Once home to numerous slacker music stores and bookstores, Austin now has trendy clothing boutiques featured on national TV shows and fashion magazines. Several new upscale malls have also popped up recently, but they haven't displaced too many distinctive local shops—vinyl records, obscure books, and custom-made boots are still available in not-so-trendy places off the beaten path.

South Congress

South Congress Avenue just south of the Colorado River used to be desolate, with undercover cops stalking drug dealers and prostitutes. The area transformed during the 1990s, most notably when a dot-com start-up replaced an aging adult theater. Other new businesses followed suit, and the streetscape soon was revitalized with cafés, galleries, and trendy clothing stores. There were marketing efforts to brand the strip with the moniker "SoCo," but locals don't refer to it by that name.

Several of the strip's anchors are antiques and clothing shops. The best-known is longstanding **Lucy in Disguise** (1506 S. Congress Ave., 512/444-2002, www.lucyindisguise. com), the quintessential thrift store, featuring the city's coolest vintage threads and accessories along with bodacious costume rentals.

South Congress is also a haven for trendy boutiques. Among the most popular is **Stag** (1423 S. Congress Ave., 512/373-7824, www. stagprovisions.com). As its name implies, Stag offers rugged and hearty men's clothing for those who want to appear ready for a hunting adventure at a moment's notice. From stylish work boots to Americana shirts and heavyweight denim, Stag is a tougher breed than most of the other South Congress boutiques.

At the other end of the spectrum is **By George** (1400 S. Congress Ave., 512/441-8600, www.bygeorgeaustin.com), a vibrant shop known for its laid-back vibe, popular designers (Current-Elliot, Madison Marcus), playful accessories, and pricey clothes. Customers are inevitably won over, however, when the staff offers them a beer as they peruse the clothing and jewelry.

Nearby, **Maya Star** (1508 S. Congress Ave., 512/912-1475, www.mayastar.com) has developed a strong reputation for its selection of affordable designer clothing, jewelry, and impeccable customer service.

Farther down the road, **Creatures Boutique** (1206 S. Congress Ave., 512/707-2500) has a hip edge, particularly with its eclectic selection of purses and shoes.

Though certainly not as trendy, one of the best apparel shops on the entire South Congress strip is **Allens Boots** (1522 S. Congress Ave., 512/447-1413, www. allensboots.com), a refreshingly low-key establishment among the much-hyped boutiques. Knowledgeable employees help customers find a perfectly fitting boot and explain the differences among styles and brands. In addition to the extensive boot selection, Allens offers a broad range of shirts, hats, jeans, and belts.

The Domain

Austin's upscale mall, **The Domain** (11410 Century Oaks Terrace, 512/873-8099) is considered a godsend by those in search of big-city shopping options. The Domain includes more than 60 stores in a sprawling indoor-outdoor configuration in the rapidly growing northern reaches of the city. There's no denying this shopping center brings a slice of Dallas to Central Texas. Appropriately enough, The Domain is anchored by Dallas-born Neiman Marcus, known for its quality merchandise and name-brand products—especially women's shoes—with knowledgeable and helpful customer service. Other high-end retailers include Tiffany & Co. and Calypso. Since Austin is a computer-savvy town, one of The Domain's most popular establishments is the Apple Store.

6th and Lamar

It's hard to believe this vibrant busy intersection was once a collection of used-car lots. Now the vehicles bustling around these streets are hybrids, convertibles, and scooters en route to the city's coolest large-scale stores. This intersection is a microcosm of Austin's prototypical population—literate, organic, outdoorsy music fans.

The veteran of the group is **Waterloo Records** (600 N. Lamar Blvd., 512/474-2500, www.waterloorecords.com), regularly voted one of the country's top music stores. Waterloo is a music lover's paradise, with thousands of CDs and vinyl catering to every style, refreshingly categorized in alphabetical order as opposed to genre. Waterloo hosts in-store appearances by big-name artists on a small stage and is one of the few remaining places where music fans can hang out with like-minded souls to share their latest musical discoveries.

Across the street is **Book People** (603 N. Lamar Blvd., 512/472-5050, www.bookpeople. com), another nationally recognized independent retailer where customers often find themselves spending an entire afternoon. Billing itself the largest bookstore in Texas, Book People is a destination for literary types across the state, especially for readings and appearances by world-renowned authors and politicians.

North Austin Western Wear

You're more likely to see flip-flops and ironic T-shirts on Austinites than cowboy hats and big belt buckles, but the city still boasts several big ol' Western shops that remind visitors they're deep in the heart of Texas.

Two of the city's most popular Western wear stores are chains, but considering the products involved are cowboy-related, these spots don't carry the stigma of big-box retailers. **Boot Barn** (5451 N. IH-35, 512/582-2521, www.bootbarn.com) is an enormous store brimming with boots, hats, shirts, belts, jeans, and anything else you'd ever need to make your ride on a mechanical bull appear more authentic. This is perhaps the best place in town for aspiring cowgirls to stock their wardrobe, since many similar stores cater more to men's wear.

If you're hankering for a pair of affordable boots and jeans, look no farther than **Cavender's Boot City** (8809 Burnet Rd., 512/451-7474, www.cavenders.com), with quality low-priced boots and apparel for cowboys, cowgirls, and cowkids.

FOOD

Austinites eat out so often they've been accused of not having kitchens in their homes. Indeed, the city is well known for its diverse mix of quality and affordable restaurant options, and Austin is tops some national hotspot lists for foodies. Locals enjoy keeping

up with the latest trends and chefs without abandoning their traditional favorite comfort-food spots. No matter where you go, you'll hear somebody talking about Austin's restaurant scene. Fortunately, most of the talk is good.

Downtown
AMERICAN

Downtown on Congress Avenue, have a meal at **Swift's Attic** (315 Congress Ave., 512/482-8842, www.swiftsattic.com, Mon.-Thurs. 11am-10pm, Fri. 11am-11pm, Sat. 5pm-11pm, Sun. 10:30am-3pm, $13-42). Ascend a flight of stairs from the busy streetscape and escape into this small-plate cozy upstairs space for modern comfort food. Start with a signature ice-ball cocktail (a ball of ice surrounded by an enticing blend of liquors) and soak up the trendy laid-back scene. Menu highlights include pork belly, fish-and-chips, grilled salmon, and corn fritters.

Upscale rustic food can be gimmicky unless it's done right, like **Moonshine Patio Bar & Grill** (303 Red River St., 512/236-9599, www.moonshinegrill.com, Mon.-Thurs. 11am-10pm, Fri.-Sat. 11am-11pm, Sun. 9am-2pm and 5pm-10pm, $12-26) does. Across the street from the convention center, this is an escape into a historic limestone home. Down-home favorites like macaroni and cheese, baked chicken, and ribs get the high-end treatment with top-quality ingredients and attention to detail. One of the best items on the menu is an appetizer—beer-battered asparagus served with a tangy dipping sauce. Make sure to save room for dessert, particularly the chocolate peanut butter pie.

On the other side of downtown, **Ranch 616** (616 Nueces St., 512/479-7616, www. theranch616.com, Mon.-Fri. 11am-2pm and 5pm-10pm, Sat.-Sun. 5pm-10pm, $11-24) offers American fare with a Texas and Southwestern twist. The Gulf Coast is represented in the seafood options (shrimp quesadillas, fish tacos), and the kitchen does Texas and the South proud with its tasty biscuits, chicken-fried quail, and fried pies. Ranch

616 also draws a lively happy hour crowd, many who come for the dozens of premium tequilas.

You'll find some of Austin's most popular Cajun cuisine at the laid-back, local favorite **Shoal Creek Saloon** (909 N. Lamar Blvd., 512/474-0805, www.shoalcreeksaloon. com, daily 11am-11pm, $9-18). It's a bit divey, but you can get down-home Cajun fare like shrimp po'boys, duck gumbo, and crawfish étouffée. Don't be surprised by the giant New Orleans Saints helmet on the roof—it's a sign of Shoal Creek's Louisiana roots.

To experience the old-school Austin so many old-timers complain about losing, head to the stalwart **Texas Chili Parlor** (1409 Lavaca St., 512/472-2828, daily 11am-2am, $8-18). Step into 1980s Austin by ordering a big bowl of red (a Texas term for chili—order it XX if you like the heat), a cold Lone Star beer, and classic cosmic cowboy music. The chicken verde enchiladas are surprisingly amazing, and the burgers are almost as good as the legendary chili. You won't regret this time-travel trip.

BARBECUE

Cold beer, live music, and barbecue is the holy trinity for laid-back Southerners, and in Austin, believers flock to **Stubb's Bar-B-Q** (801 Red River St., 512/480-8341, www. stubbsaustin.com, Mon.-Thurs. 11am-10pm, Fri.-Sat. 11am-11pm, Sun. 11am-9pm, $16-38). The hickory-smoked barbecued brisket is legendary, and the sauce is the best in town: a perfect combination of vinegary tang and peppery bite. Save room for savory sides like jalapeño-creamed spinach and collard greens. Stubb's Sunday Gospel Brunch (held at the slacker hours of 11am and 1pm) is virtually required, more for the soulful music than the hearty breakfast. Reservations are recommended.

Benefiting from a prime spot next to the Austin Convention Center, **Iron Works Barbecue** (100 Red River St., 512/478-4855, www.ironworksbbq.com, Mon.-Sat. 11am-9pm, $12-33) has exposed more out-of-staters to Texas-style barbecue than anywhere else in town. Fortunately, it's a worthy ambassador, offering succulent beef brisket, tender pork ribs, and flavorful sausage to first-time barbecue lovers since 1978.

For a genuine taste of Texas barbecue in the urban core, drop by **Cooper's Old Time Pit Bar-B-Que** (217 Congress Ave., 512/474-4227, www.coopersbbqaustin.com, daily 11am-10pm, $11-29). Cooper's serves up Texas-style barbecue (beef brisket and ribs, sausage) based on time-honored traditions and recipes from the original outpost in Llano, 75 miles (120 km) west of town.

If you're downtown and looking for something slightly fancier, check out **Lambert's Downtown Barbeque** (401 W. 2nd St., 512/494-1500, www.lambertsaustin.com, Mon.-Sat. 11am-3pm, Sun.-Wed. 5pm-10pm, Thurs.-Sat. 5pm-10:30pm, $15-41). In a historic mercantile store, Lambert's offers a rare combo of urban and rural that works—cloth napkins, expensive cocktails, and big-city ambience blend seamlessly with the authentic smoked meats, quality sauce, and down-home service.

MEXICAN AND TEX-MEX

One of the most popular destinations in Austin's hopping 2nd Street "district" (block) is the higher-end **La Condesa** (400 W. 2nd St., 512/499-0300, www.lacondesa.com, Mon.-Fri. 11:30am-2:30pm and 5pm-10pm, Sat.-Sun. 11am-3pm and 5pm-10pm, $16-36). A step up from traditional Tex-Mex, La Condesa is a classy modern spot with quality twists on classic dishes, including scallop ceviche, pork belly and bleu cheese tacos, and *dulce de leche* sponge cake.

With a 30-year history, **Manuel's Downtown** (310 Congress Ave., 512/472-7555, www.manuels.com, Mon.-Thurs. 11am-10pm, Fri.-Sat. 11am-11pm, Sun. 10am-10pm, $10-19) is an Austin tradition with an emphasis on fresh seafood dishes (ceviche, shrimp tacos) and interior Mexican (mole enchiladas). Manuel's offers consistent quality, but it can get really loud on weekend nights.

The Barbecue Trail

Central Texas is the state's barbecue capital and therefore, in the eyes of Texans, the barbecue headquarters of the world. There's some truly tasty stuff, and the smorgasbord of top-notch restaurants can be mind-boggling. Fortunately, you can't go wrong at most locally owned family-run places, especially if you see the stacks of hardwood logs out back and smell the hearty smoke burning. The good news is, most small towns in Texas are brimming with restaurants like this. Look for the long lines forming out the door at lunchtime.

CUEING FOR 'CUE

Barbecue purists typically mention three must-taste towns on the barbecue trail—all accessible from I-35. Taylor, just north of Austin, is best known as the home of **Louie Mueller Barbecue** (206 W. 2nd St., Taylor, 512/352-6206, www.louiemuellerbarbecue.com, Mon.-Sat. 11am-6pm, $14-30). Open since the 1940s, Louie Mueller's has been featured on food programs around the globe and is famous for its succulent smoked brisket. The place oozes weathered, smoke-drenched, rustic charm and serves up tender beef with a slightly peppery sauce and accompanying sweet sides (potato salad, coleslaw).

Just down the road is the town of Elgin, known for its delicious "hot guts" (sausage). One of the city stalwarts since 1882 is **Southside Market & Bar-B-Q Inc.** (1212 Hwy. 290 E., Elgin, 512/281-4650, www.southsidemarket.com, Mon.-Thurs. 8am-8pm, Fri.-Sat. 8am-10pm, Sun. 9am-8pm, $10-24). Sausage is the main event here, and it's still made with fresh meats in the German tradition and served on butcher paper.

Long considered the holy grail of the barbecue trail is the community of Lockhart. This small town is big on legendary barbecue establishments, each offering a distinctive approach to preparing the meat. Purists swear by **Kreuz** (619 N. Colorado St., Lockhart, 512/398-2361, www.kreuzmarket.com, daily 10:30am-8pm, $15-44), which doesn't provide sauce because it would compromise the savory, smoky taste, but others remain loyal to **Black's** (215 N. Main St., Lockhart, 888/632-8225, www.blacksbbq.com, Sun.-Thurs. 10am-8pm, Fri.-Sat. 10am-8:30pm, $15-48) or **Smitty's** (208 S. Commerce St., Lockhart, 512/398-9344, www.smittysmarket.com, Mon.-Fri. 7am-6pm, Sat. 7am-6:30pm, Sun. 9am-6:30pm, $15-39) because the sauce and sides provide the perfect complementary flavor. People are usually willing to do the extensive research involved to find out what combination of smoke and meat results in the ultimate Texas barbecue experience.

In Austin, you can't go wrong with **Franklin Barbecue** (900 E. 11th St., Austin, 512/653-1187, www.franklinbarbbq.com, Tues.-Sun. 11am-3pm, $19-44). *Bon Appétit* declared it the best barbecue in America, and there's regularly a three-hour-plus line. The brisket is succulent, with smoky goodness infusing the exceptional beef to create a wonderful blend of hearty goodness. Although you only need to sample the brisket, make a point to order the savory pork ribs or spicy sausage

Just north of downtown is the excellent **Fresa's Chicken al Carbon** (915 N. Lamar Blvd., 512/428-5077, www.fresaschicken.com, Sun.-Wed. 11am-10pm, Thurs.-Sat. 11am-11pm, $8-16). Known for wood-grilled chicken, Fresa's offers a unique take on Mexican fare. You can order a taco or two, or make it an experience by grabbing a few friends and ordering a whole grilled chicken. It's carved into sections and bundled in waxed paper with a gaggle of tasty accompaniments, including grilled onions and peppers,

tortillas, and several salsas. Fresa's doesn't have a dining room, so grab an order to go and enjoy your feast at a nearby park.

South Austin
AMERICAN

One of the city's most popular culinary destinations is ★ **Odd Duck** (1201 S. Lamar Blvd., 512/433-6521, www.oddduckaustin. com, Mon.-Fri. 11:30am-10pm, Sat. 5pm-11pm, Sun. 10:30am-2:30pm and 5pm-10pm, $10-32). This is haute cuisine sourced from

Louie Mueller Barbecue

to complement the meaty meal. To skip the multiple-hour wait, a couple almost-as-good options with 30-minute waits beckon at **Stiles Switch** (6610 N. Lamar Blvd., Austin, 512/380-9199, www.stilesswitchbbq.com, Tues.-Thurs. 11am-9pm, Fri.-Sat. 11am-10pm, $12-41) and a local outpost of Lockhart's famous **Black's BBQ** (3110 Guadalupe St., Austin, 512/524-0801, www.blacksbbq.com, Sun.-Thurs. 11am-9pm, Fri.-Sat. 11am-10pm, $11-37).

BARBECUE'S BACKGROUND

So, how did Central Texas become such a meat mecca? Food historians believe African American Southern cooking customs and German meat markets primarily influenced the style of barbecue in this area. The concept of barbecued meats on a lunch plate likely came about when African American and Mexican American cotton pickers, familiar with their own traditional pit-style meat cooking, ordered sausage and ribs from the German butcher shops in small Central Texas towns. The workers weren't allowed into restaurants in the early 1900s, so after they got paid, they'd walk over to the market, order fresh-smoked meat on butcher paper, and eat it on-site. Before long, picnic tables and side items of vegetables (traditional German fare like potato salad and coleslaw) emerged, giving way to the restaurants that dot the landscape today.

local farmers. Odd Duck prides itself on using area resources, and diners are rewarded with incredibly fresh-tasting menu items. Local favorites include anything with pork belly (the slider is a good choice), accompanied by a tasty bit of arugula and garlic mayonnaise. Even more inventive is the chicken-fried fish head. Or try a fried quail sandwich, the beautifully presented and immensely flavorful redfish tacos, or grits mixed with mushrooms and parmesan topped with a delectable duck egg.

Burger and beer fans should hop to **Hopdoddy's** (1400 S. Congress Ave., 512/243-7505, www.hopdoddy.com, daily 11am-10pm, $9-18). You may have to wait in line, so grab a goblet of local craft beer and study the menu, since the inventive options on enormous Angus beef patties are tempting. Locals love the Llano Poblano's combo of smoked bacon, pepper jack cheese, seared poblano peppers, and chipotle mayo, or try a Terlingua—chili con carne, cheddar cheese, Fritos, and a spicy sauce.

According to the Food Network, some of the nation's best fried chicken is on the menu at **Lucy's** (2218 College Ave., 512/297-2423, www.lucysfriedchicken.com, Mon.-Sat. 11am-11pm, Sun. 10am-11pm, $9-29). Lucy's is deserving of high praise—the chicken is perfectly prepared, with a crispy exterior covering a high-quality meaty interior. Be sure to start things off with another chicken-based delicacy: deep-fried deviled eggs, which are just as tasty as they sound.

You can't go wrong with the consistently delicious **South Congress Cafe** (1600 S. Congress Ave., 512/447-3905, www.southcongresscafe.com, Mon.-Fri. 10am-10pm, Sat.-Sun. 9am-10pm, $13-30). In the heart of the trendy South Congress scene, this little restaurant is big on style and taste. Most dishes are Southwestern influenced, and all the portions are huge. The pork tenderloin, carrot cake, and blue-corn crepes are local favorites.

To get an authentic feel for the old-time Austin that locals pine for, drop by **Magnolia Café South** (1920 S. Congress Ave., 512/445-0000, www.themagnoliacafe.com, daily 24 hours, $9-18). This chilled-out, veggie-friendly, late-night spot offers Southern charm and hearty breakfasts all day—its famous gingerbread pancakes are especially appealing after a night on the town. Magnolia's Tex-Mex enchiladas are noteworthy, and the spicy Love Migas will test your heat index.

ITALIAN

Austin isn't known for its Italian cuisine scene, but locals will always suggest **Vespaio** (1610 S. Congress Ave., 512/441-6100, www.austinvespaio.com, Mon.-Sat. 11am-10pm, Sun. 5:30pm-10pm, $18-42). At this tiny 15-table trattoria, it's impossible to go wrong with any menu items or the extensive daily specials. Even basics like the bread, wine selection, and service are extraordinary. Appetizers include seared tuna and sliced bresaola with aged provolone. The mixed meat plate, seafood grill, spaghetti alla carbonara, and handkerchief pasta are just a few of the delectable options. Stick around for a post-meal port or brandy.

JAPANESE

Regularly perched atop Austin's "top restaurants" polls is ★ **Uchi** (801 S. Lamar Blvd., 512/916-4808, www.uchiaustin.com, daily 5pm-10pm, $18-55). This is a must for Japanese-food lovers or anyone looking to explore sushi beyond the basic crab and California rolls. Knowledgeable and friendly waitstaff politely explain and recommend items, and the atmosphere is comfortable yet romantic (although occasionally loud). All the menu items are spectacular, but some of the most popular include the Muscovy duck, striped bass sushi, rib eye *nigiri* with a quail egg, and baby bok choy. Not surprisingly, sushi is a specialty, and the sushi bar is a singles hot spot. Uchi remains one of the city's most popular restaurants, so reservations are strongly recommended.

MEXICAN AND TEX-MEX

Serving consistently quality Mexican food is South Congress stalwart **Guero's Taco Bar** (1412 S. Congress Ave., 512/447-7688, www.guerostacobar.com, Mon.-Wed. 11am-10pm, Thurs.-Fri. 11am-11pm, Sat.-Sun. 8am-10pm, $11-28). In a historic feed store with south-of-the-border charm, Guero's draws foodies and celebrities for its delectable Mexican food—perfectly seasoned chicken enchiladas in a tangy tomatillo sauce, savory beef and pork tacos, and a heavenly *queso flameado*. One of Guero's biggest fans is former president Bill Clinton, and the restaurant has a menu item named in honor of his favorite combo: chicken taco, beef taco, tamale, and guacamole salad.

One of the most popular Tex-Mex restaurants among longtime locals is the consistently reliable **Chuy's** (1728 Barton Springs Rd., 512/474-4452, www.chuys.com, daily 11am-10pm, $9-23), and for good reason. Now a major national chain, this Austin-born,

1: the legendary lines at Franklin Barbecue **2:** Dan's Hamburgers **3:** Black's BBQ **4:** Odd Duck in South Austin

funky, Elvis-obsessed establishment is a reliable source of classic Tex-Mex—enchiladas, tacos, and quesadillas—with a Southwestern flair (blue tortillas, green chilies). The margaritas are highly recommended, and the chips and salsa are so good you'll fill up on them before your entrée arrives. It's worth exercising some self-control for the whole (stacked) enchilada.

North and East of Downtown

Austin has distinctive neighborhoods, but its relatively small one-square-mile downtown means the areas historically referred to as North, South, West, and East Austin are only a few miles away from the city's core. For those visiting the University of Texas or staying near downtown for a festival, the following restaurants are within five minutes by car.

MEXICAN AND TEX-MEX

Until the 1980s, the highest-profile restaurant in Austin was **Fonda San Miguel** (2330 W. North Loop Blvd., 512/459-4121, www.fondasanmiguel.com, Mon.-Thurs. 5pm-9:30pm, Fri.-Sat. 5pm-10:30pm, Sun. 11am-2pm, $14-35). It's still a top-notch experience, but the trendy downtowners have overshadowed it lately. Fonda San Miguel remains the place to go if you're in search of authentic, flavorful interior Mexican food, and the hacienda-like atmosphere adds to the experience. Start off with a renowned margarita (mango is a popular choice) and continue with a pork, seafood, or enchilada dish (the mole sauce is especially succulent). Fonda San Miguel's Sunday brunches are legendary, so be sure to make reservations.

A classic trailer-to-mortar experience awaits at the tremendous **Torchy's Tacos** (2801 Guadalupe St., 512/494-8226, www. torchystacos.com, Mon.-Fri. 7am-10pm, Sat.-Sun. 8am-11pm, $5-11). Among the dozen menu options, exceptional are the fried avocado taco (hand-battered fresh avocados topped with lettuce, tomato, cheese, and an outstanding poblano sauce on a corn tortilla); the green chili pork (roasted pork *carnitas*

with green chilies topped with *queso fresco,* cilantro, and tomatillo sauce on a corn tortilla); and the Trailer Park (fried chicken, green chilies, *pico de gallo,* cheese, and poblano sauce on a flour tortilla)—be sure to get it "trashy," which substitutes the lettuce with a creamy smothering of queso.

Far less formal yet incredibly *delicioso* is **Vamonos** (4807 Airport Blvd., 512/474-2029, http://vamonos-texmex.com, Mon.-Wed. 11am-9pm, Thurs.-Sat. 11am-10pm, Sun. 11am-8pm, $11-30). Billed as "ranch-style Tex Mex," this tasty spot gets everything right, from the cocktails (the ranch water, with blue agave tequila, lime, and a bottle of Topo Chico), to the delectable near-perfect *queso,* to the authentically seasoned puffy tacos, to the sweet sopapillas for dessert.

If you're looking for something untrendy, old-school, and flavorful, head to **El Patio** (2938 Guadalupe St., 512/476-5955, Tues.-Sat. 11am-8:45pm, $9-16). It may not be cool, but it's comfort food to the max—cheesy enchiladas, crispy beef tacos, tasty chalupas, and some of the best chips and *queso* in the city. Sometimes it's nice to escape the contemporary bustle and experience old-school Austin (1954, to be exact). Although the waiters ditched their maroon jackets, they still offer diners a free dessert of their choice: sherbet or candy (a sweet buttery coconut-flavored praline).

AMERICAN

Consistently topping many of Austin's best-restaurants lists is the incomparable ★ **Barley Swine** (6555 Burnet Rd., 512/394-8150, www.barleyswine.com, daily 5pm-10pm, 10 courses prix fixe $95, reservations recommended). Described as "radically flavorful," this trailer-turned-restaurant specializes in a single menu, with each progressive course offering amazing flavor combinations prepared with high-quality ingredients. The menu, featuring nine savory and two sweet courses, changes often; notable past dishes include seasoned quail, inventive beet dishes, and eggs prepared in creative ways, from caramelized to frothy.

Just east of downtown is the fabulous **Launderette** (2115 Holly St., 512/382-1599, www.launderetteaustin.com, daily 11am-2:30pm and 5pm-10pm, $14-34). In a former laundromat in a rapidly changing part of town, Launderette offers a fresh take on quality classics, with plenty of unexpected and charming ingredients to make every menu item intriguing. A good starting place is the plate of fried olives, followed by tandoori prawns with bacon-based brussels sprouts. Save room for the cheddar apple pie.

North of the UT campus, locals and visitors experience Detroit's best culinary export at **Via 313** (3016 Guadalupe St., 512/358-6193, www.via313.com, daily 11am-10pm, $12-26). This Motown-style pizza is irresistible, with thick buttery crust, cheese, and fresh-tasting tomato sauce. Legend has it that the rectangular pans originated with a motor worker's creative use of a metal drip tray. Order a Detroiter (two kinds of pepperoni sausage) and pair it with a local pint or a Detroit-based Faygo pop.

A tantalizing brand of Southern cooking is on the menu at **Hoover's** (2002 Manor Rd., 512/479-5006, www.hooverscooking.com, daily 11am-10pm, $12-25), just east of I-35 downtown. Owner-cook Hoover Alexander brings a comprehensive collection of Southern influences to his dishes—his mama's home cooking, East Texas Cajun, pit-style barbecue, and Tex-Mex. The results are sublime: smothered pork chops, jerked chicken, spicy sausage. The gravy is the best in town, and the sides (mac and cheese, jalapeño creamed spinach) are legendary.

Good burger joints are a must in any college town, and Austin has several noteworthy locales. The king of the old-timers is **Dirty Martin's Kum-Bak Place** (2808 Guadalupe St., 512/477-3173, www.dirtymartins.com, daily 11am-11pm, $9-17). Much more appetizing than it sounds, Dirty's is a legendary burger stand that still offers carhop service. Inside, a thin layer of grease everywhere lets diners know they're in for the real deal—grilled patties oozing with cheese on a sweet bun accompanied by thin fries or, better yet,

tater tots. Washing it all down with a chocolate shake is mandatory.

A few miles north, **Dan's Hamburgers** (5602 N. Lamar Blvd., 512/459-3239, daily 6am-10pm, $5-12) is a classic 1950s-style burger joint. Utterly unpretentious, Dan's offers a perfect microcosm of Austin's population—rich, poor, old, and young fill this no-frills restaurant daily just to partake of reliable tasty burgers. Order a cheeseburger "all the way," Texan for lettuce, tomatoes, pickles, onions, and mustard. Incidentally, Dan's serves one of the best diner-style breakfasts in town. Biscuits and gravy, breakfast tacos, pancakes, and huevos rancheros provide an ideal way to start the day.

JAPANESE

Perhaps the best dining experience in Austin is ★ **Uchiko** (4200 N. Lamar Blvd., 512/916-4808, www.uchikoaustin.com, Sun.-Thurs. 5pm-10pm, Fri.-Sat. 5pm-11pm, $24-59). An offshoot of the now-legendary Uchi in South Austin, Uchiko delivers inventive, fresh, and high-quality food inspired by the founder's Filipino heritage and Texas culinary experience. Emerging as instant menu classics are bacon *onigiri* (fried pork belly, rice, *bánh mì* pickles), *hama chili* (yellowtail sashimi, sliced Thai chili, orange), and the *take nabe* (Japanese mushroom, *koshi hikari*, farm fresh egg, *bushi*). Each of the uniquely and unexpectedly crafted dishes are expertly explained by the waitstaff, who politely suggest menu items and recommend dishes based on the level of adventure and budget of each diner.

BARBECUE

Just east of downtown is the legendary ★ **Franklin Barbecue** (900 E. 11th St., 512/653-1187, www.franklinbarbecue.com, Tues.-Sun. 11am-3pm, $19-44). *Bon Appétit* declared Franklin's the best barbecue in America, and Food Network programs regularly feature the restaurant as the ultimate example of top-quality Texas barbecue. The first thing you'll hear about Franklin's is the line—a three-hour wait that's become its own

Brew for You

Jester King Brewery

Like most U.S. cities, Austin's craft brewing scene has exploded over the past decade, almost to the point of saturation. This is causing some beer hounds to worry that the scene's foam bubble may soon burst. In the meantime, there is an embarrassment of riches to sample; visit the comprehensive and helpful www.craftbeeraustin.com. Otherwise, the following breweries are consistently bustling and producing nationally recognized products.

Beer nerds travel from around the country for the opportunity to experience the exquisite ales at **Jester King Brewery** (13187 Fitzhugh Rd., 512/537-5100, www.jesterkingbrewery.com, Fri. 4pm-10pm, Sat. noon-10pm, Sun. noon-7pm), about 25 miles (40 km) west of Austin. Local culture and natural surroundings are part of the beer—check the website to learn about its spontaneous fermentation with a mixed culture of native yeast and bacteria, refermented with regional grapes. Most of the ales are tantalizingly sour and funky, but a few lighter options have local honey and fruit. The brewery's inviting grounds are a traditional Hill Country ranch with picnic tables beneath oak trees overlooking the fields. Make a point to devote some of your outdoor time to waiting in the inevitable lines for beer and Jester King's delectable food, including home-baked pretzels, inventive salads, and pizzas (the reuben-inspired Americana is a highlight).

On the east side of Austin is welcoming **Live Oak Brewing** (1615 Crozier Lane, 512/385-2299, www.liveoakbrewing.com, Sun.-Thurs. noon-8pm, Fri.-Sat. noon-10pm). The brew house offers beer lovers an escape from the city to enjoy crisp Pilz, tasty Hefeweizen, or hoppy Liberation IPA in the light-filled taproom or, better yet, on a picnic table under one of the many surrounding live oak trees.

For a road trip with your brewery-hopping, head 90 miles (145 km) east of Austin through the rolling Blackland Prairie to experience **Brazos Valley Brewing Company** (201 W. 1st St., Brenham, 979/987-1133, www.brazosvalleybrewery.com, taproom Fri.-Sun. afternoon). Big on charm and flavor, the beers favor the hoppy side of the spectrum. Be sure to try the Mama Tried IPA or Willin' Pale Ale, and sample a seasonal ale.

cultural phenomenon. There's a reason people are willing to wait this long for a plate of meat: It is absolute perfection. The brisket is succulent, with smoky goodness infusing free-range grass-fed beef. By the time you reach the front of the line, you'll be asked if you'd like the brisket "lean" or "fatty"; go with the fatty. Sample the brisket to make your Franklin experience complete, and make a point to order the savory pork ribs or spicy sausage to complement the meaty meal. Sides and sauces are also available but not necessary; go with the creamy coleslaw or potato salad and the espresso sauce. A meal at Franklin's is an unforgettable Austin experience.

Food Trailers

Austin's food trucks helped spark a statewide trend circa 2008. Although they aren't the hottest news anymore, they've had a big impact on the local culinary scene, especially with the number that transformed to brick-and-mortar locations, and they still offer inventive, accessible, inexpensive options. Most serve distinctive regional cuisine, with the only drawback the scenery—typically a parking lot or an urban streetscape. The heaviest concentration is near downtown. The following locales represent a sampling of the city's best options, from gourmet doughnuts to all-natural tacos. Due to their mobile nature and ever-changing city ordinances, food trucks have decreased in number over the past few years and often relocate based on property issues.

FOOD TRUCK SAMPLER

Start your mobile culinary journey at one of Austin's food truck parks near downtown, about 1 mile (1.6 km) outside the central business district. Locations change on a sometimes weekly basis, so confirm their current location ahead of time. The following are a sampling of the city's ever-evolving options.

If you only experience one food truck, make sure it's ★ **Veracruz All Natural** (2505 Webberville Rd., www.veracruzallnatural. com, hours vary, $5-11). Named one of the top five tacos in the nation by the Food Network,

the *migas* taco at Veracruz earns its distinction. The tortilla is an integral component—the perfectly prepared covering wraps around flavorful ingredients such as pork (the al pastor is sublime), steak, and chicken mole. Jimmy Fallon raved about these tacos during his *Tonight Show* visit.

Conscious Cravings (www. consciouscravingsaustin.com, hours vary, $5-12) is a popular destination for vegetarians and vegans. Eliciting the strongest cravings are the wraps encased in a hearty grilled tortilla. The options and flavors are dynamic, including black beans, mushrooms, and spicy chickpeas. Be sure to pair your wrap with superb rosemary french fries, and wash it all down with blueberry lemonade or a strawberry banana smoothie.

Fancy doughnut cravings will be satisfied in unexpected ways at **Gourdough's** (1503 S. 1st St., www.gourdoughs.com, hours vary, $3-8). Everything here is surprisingly delicious, but locals tend to gravitate toward the Porky's (Canadian bacon, cream cheese, and jalapeño jelly), the Son of a Peach (peach filling, cinnamon, sugar, and cake mix topping), the Dirty Berry (fudge icing with grilled strawberries), or the Mother Clucker (a fried chicken strip with honey butter). Wet your whistle with coffee or, for maximum sweet effect, a Dublin Dr Pepper, made with real cane sugar.

ACCOMMODATIONS

Austin has quite a few chain hotels, but its independently owned spots are big on charm and atmosphere. If you're planning well in advance, book a room at one of the funky South Congress locations—you won't experience anything like them elsewhere. Most downtown options are within walking distance from the entertainment districts.

South Congress
$100-150

You can't miss the distinctive sign in front of this retro establishment, a gateway to the hip South Congress scene: ★ **The Austin Motel** (1220 S. Congress Ave., 512/441-1157, www.

austinmotel.com, $140-260 d) is a SoCo stalwart for its kidney-shaped pool surrounded by funky old lounge furniture and enough vegetation to offer some privacy from the nearby street. The iconic South Congress landmark was renovated by famous local hotelier Liz Lambert (Hotel San Jose, Saint Cecilia). The motel features retro kitschy rooms with 1950s and 1980s styling, including curvy vinyl beds and enormous silkscreened music posters. Amenities include free Wi-Fi, complimentary coffee service in the lobby, 50-inch TVs, bathrobes, and free carport parking.

OVER $250

Considered by many to be the best lodging in Austin, the ★ **Hotel San Jose** (1316 S. Congress Ave., 512/444-7322, www. sanjosehotel.com, $280-435 d) is the definition of cool—simple, clean, bright, and relaxing. Vintage and modern furniture rests on smooth concrete floors, and garden areas offer songbirds, citrus trees, and peace. Enjoy San Jose's cozy pool, movie and music library, free Wi-Fi, in-room manicure-pedicure service, and charming room-service breakfasts in custom *bento* boxes.

Just off busy Congress Avenue in an adjacent tree-lined neighborhood is the unparalleled **Hotel Saint Cecilia** (112 Academy Dr., 512/852-2400 www.hotelsaintcecilia.com, from $385). Named for the patron saint of music and poetry, this cultural-minded boutique hotel is brimming with Austin charm. Consisting of several suites in the main house and small bungalows on the sprawling grounds, the Saint Cecilia is filled with luxurious curios and amenities, from vintage record players to tasteful furniture to top-notch cocktails and food.

Downtown
$100-150

Commendable for its prime location is **Extended Stay America** (507 S. 1st St., 512/476-1818, www.homesteadhotels.com, $126 d), within walking distance of downtown and Zilker Park and an ideal place to stay for the Austin City Limits festival. It's a bit rough around the edges but offers full kitchens with utensils, pet-friendly accommodations, and free Wi-Fi.

Location-wise, the **La Quinta Inn Austin Capitol** (300 E. 11th St., 512/476-1166, www. lq.com, $135 d) is superb, with easy access to good times, with major attractions and entertainment options in walkable distance. Other positive aspects include complimentary internet access and toiletries, a free continental breakfast, a fitness center, and occasionally impressive views.

$150-200

Perhaps the best skyline view in the city is from the riverside rooms at the ★ **Hyatt Regency** (208 Barton Springs Rd., 512/477-1234, www.hyatt.com, $179 d), one of the only hotels on the south side of Lady Bird Lake. Hyatt guests get an eyeful of the ever-expanding city skyline with bonus views of the Hill Country and the bats' celebrated evening emergence. The hotel also includes an outdoor pool, a whirlpool, a sundeck, and a health club.

$200-250

One of the finest downtown options is the slick, business-oriented **Hilton Austin** (500 E. 4th St., 512/482-8000, www.hilton.com, $209 d), alongside the Austin Convention Center. Amenities include an upscale health club and spa with an outdoor heated lap pool and a hot tub, as well as free Wi-Fi.

LINE Austin (111 E. Cesar Chavez St., 512/478-9611, www.thelinehotel.com, $226 d) overlooks scenic Lady Bird Lake and the Congress Avenue bat bridge. Get a backyard view of the city's famous summertime bat-watching festivities, or just enjoy the contemporary upgrade by Austin architect Michael Hsu, activity on the water, and shoreline hike-and-bike trail. Amenities include a large outdoor pool, a fitness center, and free Wi-Fi. Incidentally, the pool scene here is fun and crazy, so it's not a quiet respite.

The magnificent ★ **InterContinental**

Stephen F. Austin Hotel (701 Congress Ave., 512/457-8800, www.austin.intercontinental.com, $249 d) provides historical luxury on a large scale. Originally opened in 1924, the Stephen F. offers opulence in an ideal downtown location and features the best place in town to enjoy a beverage with a view. The hotel's terrace bar overlooks the busy epicenter of downtown, offering the only publicly accessible balcony with a view of the capitol building. Room amenities include minibars, elegant furnishings, and soft bathrobes.

The Residence Inn (300 E. 4th St., 512/236-8008, www.marriott.com, $249 d) is popular with the business crowd since it's across the street from the convention center. This is one of the city's cleanest hotels, and it's just blocks away from some of Austin's premier restaurants and bars. The hotel features an indoor pool, complimentary hot breakfast, and free Wi-Fi.

Dominating the Austin skyline from I-35 is the new and highly recommended Fairmont Austin (101 Red River St., 512/600-2000, www.fairmont.com, $229 d). With its stunning blue-glass exterior reflecting the sky's many moods, the Fairmont offers luxury in downtown Austin without five-star rates. Amenities include top-notch bedding, lavish baths, 50-inch TVs, and charging stations with USB outlets.

OVER $250

The spectacular ★ Driskill Hotel (604 Brazos St., 512/474-5911, www.driskillhotel.com, $259 d) exudes history, sophistication, and Texas. Built in 1886 as the showplace of a cattle baron, this historic downtown hotel offers guests a luxurious way to appreciate Austin's charms and attractions. The lobby alone is stunning, with its massive columns, marble floor, and stained-glass domed ceiling, and the rooms contain intricate woodwork, period furnishings, and sweeping views of downtown. Other highlights include the nationally recognized Driskill Grill and

a fitness studio with massage tables and a sauna.

Some of the coolest new digs in town are at Heywood Hotel (1609 E. Cesar Chavez St., 512/271-5522, www.heywoodhotel.com, from $269). Named one of the "world's best new hotels" by *Condé Nast Traveler,* the Heywood is an über-trendy boutique hotel in Austin's über-trendy East Side. Taking its inspiration from mid-century modern design, the has stylish furnishings, an internet jukebox, coffee service, free Wi-Fi, and bikes.

One of the newest and best hotels in Austin is the Hotel Van Zandt (605 Davis St., 512/542-5300, www.hotelvanzandt.com, $299 d). In the heart of the trendy fun-filled Rainey Street entertainment district, the Van Zandt is a true Austin original, named after local singer-songwriter Townes Van Zandt. Amenities include a free yoga mat in every room, pet-friendly accommodations, a full-service rooftop pool, a 24-hour fitness center, and free morning coffee service.

If you're participating in University of Texas activities, consider the expensive and more welcoming than it sounds AT&T Executive Education and Conference Center (1900 University Ave., 877/744-8822, www.meetattexas.com, $309 d). In a central location on the southern edge of the UT campus just north of downtown, this corporate lodging option is one of the few places to stay adjacent to campus. Aside from easy access to the university, the hotel features upscale bedding, wet bars, and free Wi-Fi.

A favorite of celebrities and jet-setters, Austin's Four Seasons (98 San Jacinto Blvd., 512/478-4500, www.fourseasons.com, $399 d) has luxury and exquisite views of Lady Bird Lake, the Congress Avenue Bridge, and the gently rolling Hill Country. Other exquisite amenities include a luxurious spa, a pool, and a fitness center overlooking the shoreline; private minibars; thick terry-cloth bathrobes; rental bikes; and a Texas authors lending library.

Arboretum Area

$100-150

Though it's far from the typical trendy Austin experience, the Arboretum area offers a pleasant environment adjacent to north-side shops and restaurants a 15-minute drive from downtown. Closer to the upscale Domain shopping destination is **Hampton Inn** (3908 W. Braker Lane, 512/349-9898, www.hamptoninn.com, $109 d). The Hampton's amenities include free high-speed Wi-Fi, a free hot breakfast or to-go bags with a bottle of water (Mon.-Fri.), a fitness center, and a pool.

Another good option in the Arboretum area is **Courtyard by Marriott** (9409 Stonelake Blvd., 512/502-8100, www.marriott. com, $119 d). Amenities include free Wi-Fi, a breakfast buffet (or add $10 to your nightly rate to include breakfast), and a fitness center with an indoor pool and a whirlpool.

$150-200

A clean and reliable option is **Staybridge Suites** (10201 Stonelake Blvd., 512/349-0888, www.ichotelsgroup.com, $150 d), with welcoming grounds of grassy hills and an outdoor recreation area, including a heated pool and sports courts. Inside is a fitness center, and rooms include Wi-Fi. Kids eat free with a standard room reservation; suite reservations include free breakfast for all guests.

For a step up in service, consider **Homewood Suites** (10925 Stonelake Blvd., 512/349-9966, www.homewoodsuites.hilton. com, $169 d). This all-suite hotel is in a tranquil parklike setting, and its one- and two-bedroom suites feature separate living and sleeping areas and kitchens with a fridge, a microwave, a stove, a dishwasher, and a coffeemaker. Homewood Suites are pet-friendly and offer complimentary hot breakfast daily as well as free Wi-Fi.

Camping

About 10 miles (16 km) southeast of downtown Austin, **McKinney Falls State Park** (5808 McKinney Falls Pkwy., 512/243-1643, www.tpwd.state.tx.us, $7 over age 12) offers a natural respite just down the road from Capital City. The 744-acre park is a great place for camping, hiking, biking, swimming in Onion Creek, picnicking, and fishing. Facilities include screened shelters with bunk beds (no mattresses) and dozens of campsites with water and electricity.

Another nearby camping area is **Pace Bend Park** (2501 N. Pace Bend Rd., 512/264-1482, www.co.travis.tx.us, primitive camping $15 per vehicle, improved camping $20 per vehicle). At 30 minutes away, it's worth the scenic Hill Country drive. This is a popular camping area, so show up early and carpool to take advantage of the beautiful lakeside park. Bring a radio or download the app to catch the rootsy, twangy sounds of Texas Rebel Radio (107.9 KFAN), the best campfire music you've ever heard.

INFORMATION AND SERVICES

Tourism Offices

The **Austin Visitor Center** (602 E. 4th St., 512/478-0098, www.austintexas.org, Mon.-Sat. 9am-5pm, Sun. 10am-5pm) is a good place to get started with the help of free maps and friendly staffers. The visitors center also contains headquarters for **Austin Duck Adventures** (www.austinducks.com), conducted in an amphibious vehicle, and **Austin Overtours** (www.aotoursaustin.com), held in the comfort of a van. Another good place to gather information, brochures, and maps about the city is the **Austin Convention and Visitors Bureau** (111Congress Ave., Suite 700, 512/474-5171, www.austintexas. org, Mon.-Fri. 8am-5pm).

Adjacent to the capitol, the **Capitol Visitors Center** (112 E. 11th St., 512/305-8400, daily 9am-5pm) provides helpful information about the capitol building and surrounding attractions and services.

Publications

The city's only metro daily paper is the **Austin American-Statesman** (www.statesman. com), known as much for its innovative design as its content. Friday's paper has up-to-date entertainment news in the Austin 360 supplement, or visit www.austin360.com. Offering a healthy alternative is the *Austin Chronicle* (www.austinchronicle.com), published every Thursday and packed with comprehensive articles devoted to local politics, culture, and entertainment.

GETTING THERE AND AROUND

Small yet easily navigable **Austin-Bergstrom International Airport** (AUS, 512/530-2242, www.austintexas.gov/airport) is 8 miles (12.9 km) southeast of downtown and features exclusively local restaurants and music by Texas artists. Check out the bands playing on stage at the Hill Country Bar.

If you're interested in local alternatives to Uber and Lyft, download the app for RideAustin. Otherwise, the city has three major cab companies: **American Yellow Checker Cab** (512/452-9999, www.yellowcabaustin.com), **Austin Express Cab** (512/666-4141), and **Lone Star Cab** (512/836-4900). Fares are around $30 from the airport to downtown. Another option is **Super Shuttle** (512/258-3826, www.supershuttle.com), with 24-hour shared-van service for $20-25 pp.

If you're feeling adventurous, the city's bus system, **Capital Metro** (512/474-1200, www.capmetro.org), provides service to downtown and the University of Texas campus. Buses run Monday-Saturday 5am-midnight, Sunday 6:30am-10:30pm. Check the website for fare information.

Vicinity of Austin

A weekend road trip to experience more Central Texas culture means barbecue, and some of the finest the Lone Star State has to offer is in the meat mecca of Lockhart. The region's other college towns offer a fresh take on university life outside a large metro area, and the Highland Lakes are renowned for placid water and abundant recreational opportunities.

THE HIGHLAND LAKES

A series of dams was built along the Colorado River in the late 1930s, resulting in the creation of seven lakes. The three most popular and usually navigable are Lakes Travis, LBJ, and Buchanan, 20-60 miles (32-97 km) northwest of Austin. These clear, clean bodies of water are a welcome respite from Texas's hot summers to swim, sail, fish, and water-ski.

Lake Travis

When it isn't depleted due to drought conditions, **Lake Travis** (www.laketravis.com) is an extremely popular destination for Austinites on weekend getaways. It's so popular that it's often difficult to navigate around all the party barges and ski boats that descend during the summer months, especially at Devil's Cove. Sailors, parasailers, windsurfers, fishers, scuba divers, Jet Skiers, and partiers occupy most of the space, and when things are hopping on the lake, it's quite a spectacle.

One of the busiest places is **Volente Beach** (16107 Wharf Cove, 512/258-5109, www.volentebeach.com, $20-25), offering sandy shores instead of the lake's typical limestone banks, along with waterslides, a swimming pool, volleyball courts, and a restaurant. Lake Travis boasts 18 parks, eight marinas, more than a dozen restaurants, several nature preserves, and a variety of fishing and sporting-goods businesses providing boat and equipment rental. For a comprehensive listing of lake services and events, visit the website. During the parched summer months, be sure to check ahead to make sure the shoreline hasn't receded too far from the marinas and swimming areas due to drought.

Lake LBJ

Named after President Lyndon B. Johnson, **Lake LBJ** (www.lake-lbj.net) is a 21-mile-long (34-km) constant-level body of water, making it ideal for sailing, boating, and other water sports. Along with Lake Travis, this is the most developed of the Highland Lakes, with hundreds of homes on the shoreline, most of them occupied by retirees and weekenders. To rent a condo or lakefront home in a quiet, relaxing environment for a few days, this is the place to be. Anglers flock to Lake LBJ for the abundant largemouth and Guadalupe bass, and the lake's white crappie population is considered the best of any of the Highland Lakes chain. Plenty of dining options are at the cafés and Tex-Mex restaurants in nearby communities of Horseshoe Bay, Kingsland, Granite Shoals, and Sunrise Beach.

Lake Buchanan

A big ol' lake in a sparsely populated area, **Lake Buchanan** (www.lake-buchanan.com) isn't a hot spot for partiers or retirees, and that's its appeal. Tree-lined shores and vast open stretches of water are dotted by boaters and anglers. Lake Buchanan is well known for its striper (striped bass) fishing, and the Texas Parks and Wildlife Department helps keep this reputation thriving by stocking the lake. Fishing guides are available to take visitors to the best spots. Like other nearby lakes, accommodations on Lake Buchanan range from campgrounds and RV parks to rental homes and even houseboats.

November-March, consider a unique opportunity to commune with nature. The **Vanishing Texas River Cruise** (800/474-8374, www.vtrc.com, $17-25) offers a rare chance to see one of the largest colonies of American bald eagles. The *Texas Eagle II*, a 70-foot (21-m), 120-passenger vessel, has two observation decks and covered viewing areas to glimpse the magnificent bird in its natural habitat.

Accommodations

The upper Highland Lakes region, northwest of Lake Travis, is surrounded by small communities, most with populations of about 5,000, so there's a wide range of accommodations, from cheap chains on the highways, upscale resorts on the lakeshore, and quaint bed-and-breakfasts in historic downtowns. The three largest towns in the region are Burnet (pronounced BUR-nit), Marble Falls, and Llano. A comprehensive list of accommodations in these communities and outlying areas is available at www.highlandlakes.com; the cabin listings are especially helpful. Most visitors to Lake Travis stay in Austin or at one of the nearby campgrounds.

Camping

Camping options in the upper Highland Lakes region are plentiful, but a few parks stand out among the rest. Lake Buchanan's immense size and absence of development make it a good place to enjoy remote, natural conditions (or a comfortable lodge, if you choose). One of the best places to pitch a tent is **Black Rock Park** (Hwy. 261, north of Hwy. 29, 512/793-3138, www.lcra.org, $5 entry fee, call for campsite and cabin fees). The 10-acre park offers 25 tent sites, 15 RV sites, and six cabins with heat and air conditioning. One of the park's biggest draws is its sandy beach, and the ample shoreline is also popular for bank fishing.

Less rustic is the nearby **Canyon of the Eagles** (16942 Ranch Rd. 2341, 800/977-0081, www.canyonoftheeagles.com, cottage or room about $169, campsite about $16), a 940-acre resort with campsites and 64 cottage and lodge rooms designed to blend in with the natural beauty of the surrounding Hill Country. Each cabin features wooden rocking chairs on the front porch, some with spectacular views of Lake Buchanan. Camping is in 25 spacious shaded sites that include a paved pad and a picnic table. Some of the sites have a limited view of the lake, and all have access to the property's amenities. Primitive camping is at Chimney Slough, in a peaceful cove on the lake with 23 tent sites and potable water, and Tanner Point, with 10 sites with no water.

Canyon of the Eagles also features a restaurant, a swimming pool, and a recreation room.

Another popular option is **Inks Lake State Park** (3630 Park Rd. 4 W., 512/793-2223, www.tpwd.state.tx.us, $7 over age 12). Camping, backpacking, hiking, swimming, and fishing are popular activities, along with the park's guided nature walks and canoe tours. Small cabins and primitive campsites are available, and the park includes a nine-hole golf course, a store with boats and bikes for rent, and Wi-Fi access.

Information and Services

The best way to get up-to-date lodging and event information is through the various chambers of commerce in the Highland Lakes region. They'll also provide plenty of handy maps and brochures with info about places to go and things to do.

For Lake Travis area information, visit www.laketravis.com or contact the **Lake Travis Chamber of Commerce** (1415 RR 620 S., Suite 202, 512/263-5833, www.laketravischamber.com). For the upper Highland Lakes, contact the **Burnet Chamber of Commerce** (229 S. Pierce, 512/756-4297, www.burnetchamber.org), the **Marble Falls/Lake LBJ Chamber of Commerce** (100 Ave. G, 830/693-4449, www.marblefalls.org), and the **Llano Chamber of Commerce** (100 Train Station Dr., 325/247-5354, www.llanochamber.org).

Getting There and Around

From Austin, take Highway 71 west to begin your Highland Lakes journey. The first lake (or last, from a downriver standpoint) is Lake Travis, accessible from Highway 71 or Highway 620, which runs north from Highway 71 in the town of Bee Cave. It's a 30-minute drive from Austin. Continuing westward on Highway 71, access Lakes LBJ and Buchanan by heading north on U.S. 281 toward breathtaking Marble Falls (Lake LBJ) and Burnet (Buchanan). It takes an hour to reach Lake LBJ from Austin, and closer to two hours for Lake Buchanan.

SAN MARCOS

Located 26 miles (42 km) south of Austin, San Marcos (population 63,509), home of Texas State University, is a college town that is well known for the laid-back recreational activity of tubing, where young adults lounge around half-dressed drinking beer while floating on an inner tube down a refreshingly cold river. Despite the appeal of this pursuit, it doesn't draw nearly as many visitors as the outlet malls on the outskirts of town.

Tubing the San Marcos River

Compared to New Braunfels, San Marcos's tubing scene is pretty tame. Despite the proximity of Texas State, tubing in San Marcos is marketed as a family activity, resulting in fewer booze cruises and less questionable activity than in New Braunfels. Regardless, the appeal remains the same—escaping from the Texas heat by floating in a refreshingly cold river (approximately 71°F/22°C) through picturesque countryside with a beverage in hand.

For the most part, the pace is slow and relaxing, but there are occasional swiftly flowing stretches, and a river chute on a dam creates a fun rapids effect. The entire trip takes about 1.5 hours. The best place to begin your trek, with equipment rental and transportation upriver, is **San Marcos Lions Club Tube Rental** (City Park, off Charles Austin Dr., 512/396-5466, www.tubesanmarcos.com, May Sat.-Sun., June-Sept. daily, tube rental $14, $20 tube deposit).

Meadows Center Glass-Bottom Boats

The San Marcos springs release millions of gallons of water daily and are the focal point of Texas State University's **Meadows Center for Water and the Environment** (921 Aquarena Springs Dr., 512/245-7570, www.meadowscenter.txstate.edu, daily 10:30am-3:30pm, $9.75 adults, $8 seniors, $6 ages 3-12). For much of the 1900s, the area was a resort and entertainment park known as Aquarena Springs, featuring amusement park-style rides, water shows with mermaids, and Ralph, a pig that performed amazing aquatic tricks. Although Ralph is no longer a featured attraction, glass-bottom boats remain as a fun option for visitors to explore the depths of the site's Spring Lake.

A knowledgeable and laid-back guide (usually a TSU student) pilots the small boat around the former pool while visitors peer into an opening with a large slab of glass—the crystal-clear view is pretty spectacular, especially when fish dart by or a percolating spring is visibly bubbling. TSU purchased the aging theme park in 1994 and transformed it into a nonprofit nature center dedicated to conserving natural resources and educating the public about the role water plays in daily life. After taking a boat ride, visitors are encouraged to explore the site's wetland boardwalk and discovery center with hands-on exhibits and archaeology displays featuring 12,000-year-old artifacts.

Wonder World

Take a break from shopping to visit **Wonder World** (1000 Prospect St., 512/392-3760, www.wonderworldpark.com, Memorial Day-Labor Day daily 8am-8pm, Sept.-May Mon.-Fri. 9am-5pm, Sat.-Sun. 9am-6pm, $26 adults, $19 seniors and ages 6-12). The main attraction is an enormous cave formed by a prehistoric earthquake along the Balcones fault line, resulting in distinctive geographic formations not found in typical erosion-based caves. At the end of the tour, visitors ascend the 146-foot-tall (46-m) Tejas Tower via elevator, offering a spectacular bird's-eye view of the region's geographic features. Other park attractions include a train ride through a wildlife park, a petting zoo, and a wacky antigravity house.

Shopping

San Marcos's outlet stores rank among the top destinations in Texas. Depending on your perspective, this is either fascinating or depressing. Regardless, shopping for bargains is a phenomenon that's unlikely to wane in popularity anytime soon, so people will continue to flock to San Marcos to spend hours or even days sifting through racks of clothes, shoes, accessories, and housewares in search of the ultimate deal at 250 stores in two main centers.

The biggest is **Premium Outlets** (3939 I-35 S., 512/396-2200, www.premiumoutlets. com, daily 10am-9pm). Unironically designed after a classic shopping plaza in Venice, Premium Outlets offers more than 130 luxury and brand-name shops such as Last Call by Neiman Marcus, Gucci, Lacoste, Salvatore Ferragamo, Saks Fifth Avenue Off 5th Outlet, and Polo Ralph Lauren. The other main attraction, just south of Premium Outlets, is **Tanger Outlet Center** (4015 I-35 S., 512/396-7446, www.tangeroutlet.com, Mon.-Sat. 9am-9pm, Sun. 10am-7pm), which contains more than 100 stores, including Calvin Klein, Charlotte Russe, Cavender's Boot City, Express Factory Outlet, and Wilsons Leather Outlet.

Food
TEX-MEX

One of San Marcos's most popular restaurants is the consistently satisfying ★ **Herbert's Grocery & Taco Hut** (419 Riverside Dr., 866/721-3530, Mon.-Thurs. 10am-9pm, Fri. 10am-10pm, Sat. 7am-9pm, $8-18). Originally a takeout taco stand, Herbert's has evolved over the decades into a first-rate Tex-Mex establishment and salsa enterprise, drawing students and locals with its flavorful tacos and extremely prompt service (food often arrives in mere minutes). One of the biggest draws is the restaurant's exquisite flour tortilla—these homemade gems are perfection, with just the right texture and buttery taste to practically make an entire meal. The most popular dish is Herbert's Special, a combo plate featuring a hearty beef taco, tangy cheese enchilada, and crunchy bean chalupa.

Another well-known Mexican food joint is **Mamacita's Restaurant** (1400 Aquarena

1: Meadows Center for Water and the Environment
2: Root Cellar Cafe in downtown San Marcos

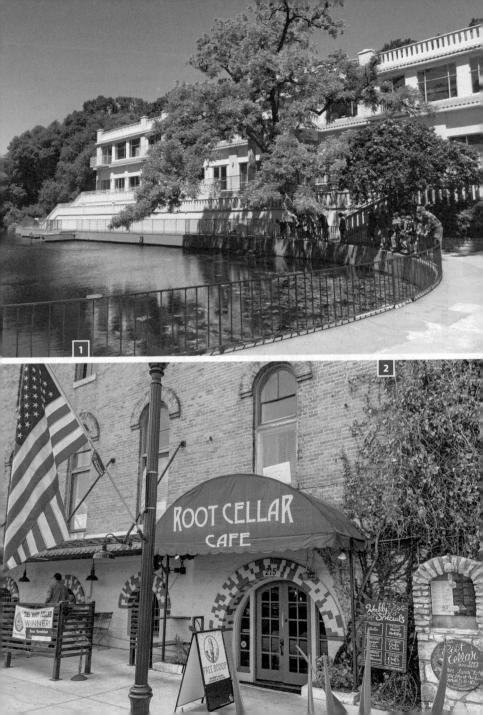

Springs Dr., 512/353-0070, www.mamacitas.com, Sun.-Thurs. 11am-9:30pm, Fri.-Sat. 11am-10pm, $9-18). This family-friendly spot is a favorite for quick lunches and group outings, and it's an ideal place to take newcomers, since the spices are relatively mild. Popular dishes include the sour cream chicken enchiladas and the beef fajitas.

AMERICAN

A favorite among locals and students is the remarkable **Root Cellar Cafe** (215 N. LBJ Dr., 512/392-5158, www.rootcellarcafe.com, Tues.-Sun. 7am-10pm, $10-21). There's something instantly warm and inviting about descending into a basement-level establishment with a warm and cozy vibe and ferns everywhere. Breakfast and lunch are the most popular meals—the bacon and waffles are consistently flavorful, the shrimp and grits are legendary, and the burgers and sandwiches (the tuna, in particular) are way above average. Lunch, dinner, and happy hour are enhanced by Root Cellar's house-made brewed beer selection, with the pale ale and vanilla cream ale among the favorites.

There's something to be said for a college-town restaurant that's endured for 45 years. **Grin's** (802 N. LBJ Dr., 512/392-4746, www.grinsrestaurant.com, daily 11am-10pm, $10-22) is a classic all-American family restaurant that's been putting smiles on people's faces for decades with its tasty burgers, steaks, and sandwiches. The chicken-fried chicken is another signature dish. Just up the hill from Texas State University, Grin's is popular with students and families, and the huge tree-shaded deck is an ideal place to enjoy a meal.

Accommodations

If you're looking for an affordable hotel to go with your bargain purchases at the outlet mall, one of the better deals in San Marcos is **University Inn** (1635 Aquarena Springs Dr., 512/353-8011, $69 d). It's rough around the edges, but within walking distance of Bobcat Stadium at Texas State University, and offers a free continental breakfast, Wi-Fi access, and an outdoor pool.

If proximity to the outlet malls is a top consideration, it doesn't get much closer than **Baymont Inn & Suites** (4210 I-35, 512/392-6800, www.wyndhamhotels.com, $89 d). The hotel features an indoor pool (heated Nov.-Mar.), a fitness center, free Wi-Fi, and a free continental breakfast.

A bit pricier yet slightly more upscale is **Hampton Inn & Suites** (106 I-35, 512/754-7707, www.stonebridgehotels.com, $142 d), offering free Wi-Fi, a free continental breakfast, an outdoor pool, and an exercise room.

Get away from the hustle and bustle at **Crystal River Inn** (326 W. Hopkins St., 888/396-3739, www.crystalriverinn.com, $120-175), a bed-and-breakfast and garden complex with 13 rooms in three buildings. The quaint structures surround a garden with roses, fountains, and stately pecan trees, and Crystal River's gourmet breakfasts offer a wonderful way to fuel up for a day of shopping without dropping.

Information and Services

San Marcos has two visitors centers offering helpful brochures and maps about attractions in the area. For general information, contact the **Tourist Information Center** (617 I-35 N., 512/393-5930, www.toursanmarcos.com, Mon.-Sat. 9am-5pm, Sun. 10am-4pm). Another reliable source is the **San Marcos Convention and Visitor Bureau** (202 N. C. M. Allen Pkwy., 512/393-5900, www.toursanmarcos.com, Mon.-Fri. 8:30am-5pm).

Getting There and Around

San Marcos is a quick drive south on I-35 from Austin. It takes about 40 minutes when traffic is moderate; take the exit for FM 12, or just look for the signs for Texas State University.

BRYAN-COLLEGE STATION

Best known as home to Texas A&M University, the Bryan-College Station area (population about 150,000) is truly representative of the

A (agriculture) in A&M. Ranches, farms, and rolling prairies surround the two cities, which serve as supply and market centers for the small surrounding communities. Despite rumors to the contrary from Austin, College Station is a cultural asset that draws educated instructors and students and regularly schedules impressive exhibits and speakers.

College Station's influence—particularly from Texas A&M University—has had a major impact on the region's development. Texas A&M opened in 1871 as Texas Agricultural and Mechanical College, a male-only military institution with Corps of Cadets participation required. During the early 1900s, Texas A&M kept a strong military association, but in 1963 the university's name changed to Texas A&M, women were officially admitted, and the Corps of Cadets became voluntary. An enrollment surge followed, from 8,000 students to 25,000 by 1976.

Texas A&M has created opportunities that otherwise wouldn't exist in this part of the state, including professional connections, diversity, and a lot of money, all of which have improved the lives of people in Bryan-College Station.

Texas A&M University

Home to 62,000 students, Texas A&M University is one of the country's premier schools for agriculture-related studies, especially in veterinary medicine, geosciences, and landscape architecture. Aggieland is truly a phenomenon—the immense school pride manifests itself in ubiquitous "Gig 'em Aggies" signs and stickers, the omnipresent maroon hue, and "yell practice," a pep rally event. Aggies' attempts to insult UT (referring to the school as "TU" and calling them "tea sippers") don't tend to rile the Longhorns, but the Aggies' nostalgic sense of being true to their school is endearing.

The school still has the largest uniformed cadet corps in the nation outside the military academies. More than 2,000 male and female students serve as military cadets each year, and their Fightin' Texas Aggies Band, which performs mesmerizing precision-filled routines at football halftime shows, is the world's largest military marching band.

To tour the campus, contact the **Appelt Aggieland Visitor Center** (1st Fl., Rudder Tower, 979/845-5851, www.tamu.edu/visitors, Mon.-Fri. 8am-5pm).

SAM HOUSTON SANDERS CORPS OF CADETS CENTER

On campus, visitors can experience the **Sam Houston Sanders Corps of Cadets Center** (979/862-2862, www.corps.tamu.edu, Mon.-Fri. 8am-5pm), showcasing the proud history of the university's iconic cadets. Dozens of displays feature artifacts and pictures documenting the cadets' rituals such as Fish (freshmen) Drill Team, yell practice, 12th Man, and the Aggie Band.

GEORGE BUSH PRESIDENTIAL LIBRARY AND MUSEUM

One of College Station's biggest claims to fame is former U.S. president George H. W. Bush. He didn't even attend Texas A&M, but Bush was so impressed with the school after accepting an invitation to deliver a commencement address that he agreed to have his presidential archives preserved and displayed here. It's worth making the trip to Aggieland for the **George Bush Presidential Library and Museum** (1000 George Bush Dr. W., 979/691-4000, www.bush41.org, Mon.-Sat. 9:30am-5pm, Sun. noon-5pm, $9 adults, $7 seniors, $3 ages 6-17). The museum has become especially important for visitors wishing to pay homage to the president, who died in 2018.

The museum's main exhibits demonstrate the life and times of Bush Senior via interactive touch-screen and video displays (check out the clip of Bush's first steps in 1925). Popular displays include a section of the Berlin Wall, a Gulf War exhibit, an Avenger similar to the plane Bush flew in World War II, and a replica of the White House situation room. One of the most memorable portions of the museum is the Oval Office exhibit that allows visitors to sit in the "seat of power" and have their photo taken behind the president's desk.

Another popular draw is the White House in Miniature, offering visitors a peek into the residence Bush once called home. In addition to these exhibits, the site also contains archives with 38 million pages of personal papers and official documents from his vice presidency and presidency, an extensive collection of audiovisual and photographic records, and approximately 60,000 historical objects, including personal items and gifts from individual Americans. Of particular interest is the exhibit dedicated to gifts given by international dignitaries and supporters, ranging from small painted rocks to a gilded replica fortress.

Brazos Valley Museum of Natural History

Regional heritage is on display at Bryan's small yet interesting **Brazos Valley Museum of Natural History** (3232 Briarcrest Dr., 979/776-2195, www.brazosvalleymuseum. org, Tues.-Sat. 10am-5pm, $5 adults, $4 seniors and ages 4-17). The museum has plugged steadily along since 1961, increasing public awareness of the region's cultural and natural heritage with permanent displays of artifacts, maps, and photos, highlighting the events and people that shaped the area's history along with regular traveling exhibits.

Food
AMERICAN

You can't go to College Station without stopping by the **Dixie Chicken** (307 University Dr., 979/846-2322, www.dixiechicken.com, daily 11am-2am, $8-17). Better known as a bar than a restaurant, "the Chicken" can squawk about its tasty food too. Pub grub (burgers, sandwiches, fried stuff) is served in a unique atmosphere, with mounted animal heads looming over deeply carved tables and walls, and the place reverberates with the sounds of college students—clinking beer bottles, whoops and laughs, and classic country music. Order a Shiner and soak up the scene. Sister

property **Chicken Oil Co.** (3600 S. College Ave., 979/846-3306, Sun.-Thurs. 11am-9pm, Fri.-Sat. 11am-10pm, $7-13) serves up the best burger in Aggieland. Despite the name (a reference to a former service station), this restaurant offers top-notch beef in a down-home atmosphere.

Slightly more refined is **Blue Baker** (201 Dominik Dr., 979/696-5055, www.bluebaker. com, daily 7am-9pm, $7-16), which prides itself on made-from-scratch breads, pastries, and pizza dough. Patrons can watch the bread-making and baking process while waiting for a signature brick-oven pizza, mouthwatering sandwich, or chocolate chip cookie.

Another classic College Station hangout is **Layne's** (106 Walton Dr., 979/696-7633, www.layneschickenfingers.com, Mon.-Tues. 10:30am-10pm, Wed.-Sun. 10:30am-11:30pm, $5-11), with a distinctive niche in the local culinary scene. Layne's serves one type of food only: chicken, specifically chicken fingers. It's known for its dipping sauce (a secret peppery recipe) and funky, some might say dumpy, atmosphere. Layne's only other menu items are a chicken finger sandwich and a grilled cheese.

For those who still have yet to sample the Southern delicacy known as chicken-fried steak, head straight to **Bryan's Longhorn Tavern Steak House** (1900 Hwy. 21 E., 979/778-3900, Mon. 11am-3pm, Tues.-Thurs. 11am-9pm, Fri.-Sat. 11am-9:30pm, $10-29). People come from miles around to satisfy their craving for the Longhorn's famous CFS, but there are other worthy items on the menu—sirloins, rib-eyes, T-bones, and New York strips.

TEX-MEX

Enormous burritos are the specialty at **Freebird's World Burrito** (319 University Dr., 979/846-9298, www.freebirds.com, daily 10:30am-10pm, $6-12) and its four other locations. Diners choose beef, chicken, rice, cheese, veggies, and salsa as they proceed down the counter. The natural ingredients come with a healthy side of good-natured attitude from the employees, and patrons are encouraged to create sculptures from the left-over tinfoil overwrap.

For a modern and tasty twist to the typical taco experience, head to **Mad Taco** (404 Jane St., 979/704-6266, www.madtaco.com, Sun.-Wed. 11am-9pm, Thurs.-Sat. 11am-10pm, $5-13). Start things off with a cerveza or Mad 'Rita (the beet option is a nice change of pace), then settle in for the main attraction: mad tacos. Although all the protein options (beef, pork, chicken, seafood, mushrooms) are commendable, try the jerk chicken—the aioli seasoning and chili oil offer an especially distinctive flavor combo.

Another popular Mexican restaurant is **Fuego Tortilla Grill** (108 Poplar St., 979/703-1804, www.fuegotortillagrill.com, Tues.-Sun. 24 hours, $7-14), serving inventive fare with comfortable ingredients, including a hearty steak taco (The King), a chicken and waffle combo, and an amazing salsa. An added bonus: Fuego is open 24 hours (except Mon.).

Down the road in Bryan is local legend **Pepe's Mexican Cafe** (3312 S. College Ave., 979/779-2457, www.pepesmexicancafe.com, Sun.-Thurs. 6:30am-10pm, Fri.-Sat. 6:30am-11pm, $8-17). Considered the original fast-food restaurant in Bryan, Pepe's still offers freshly made tacos, burritos, enchiladas, and other Tex-Mex specialties.

Accommodations

One of the more affordable A&M-area options is the **College Station Super 8** (301 Texas Ave., 979/846-8800, www.super8.com, $80 d). Three blocks from campus, the hotel offers free internet and a complimentary breakfast. The **Comfort Inn & Suites** (2313 Texas Ave. S., 979/680-8000, www.choicehotels.com, $99 d) features free internet access, a free hot breakfast, an exercise room, and a seasonal outdoor pool. Another noteworthy spot is **Courtyard College Station** (3939 Hwy. 6 S., 979/695-8111, www.marriott.com, $129 d), offering a free healthy breakfast and complimentary Wi-Fi.

Just down the road in downtown Bryan is the beautifully restored **LaSalle Hotel** (120 S. Main St., 979/822-2000, www.lasalle-hotel.com, $109-159 d), a 1928 boutique hotel that's listed on the National Register of Historic Places. The LaSalle exudes vintage charm with modern amenities, including free internet access in each room. Complimentary breakfast is served. Those willing to splurge on a suite ($139) receive the extra benefits of a fridge, a microwave, a jetted tub, a separate living room with a pullout sleeper sofa, and TVs in the bedroom, living area, and bath.

Information and Services

To learn more about Texas A&M or to take a campus tour, contact the **Appelt Aggieland Visitor Center** (1st Fl., Rudder Tower, 979/845-5851, www.tamu.edu/visitors, Mon.-Fri. 8am-5pm). For information about the Bryan-College Station area, including maps and brochures on attractions and lodging, stop by the **Bryan-College Station Convention & Visitors Bureau** (715 University Dr. E., 979/260-9898, www.visitaggieland.com, Mon.-Fri. 8am-5pm, Sat. 10am-2pm).

Getting There and Around

Bryan-College Station is about 1.5 hours east of Austin. Take U.S. 290 east to Highway 21 (about 25 minutes), then head east on Highway 21 until you reach the outskirts of Bryan-College Station. Signs point toward Bryan or to Highway 47 to reach College Station.

LOCKHART

Lockhart (population 13,924) is the true mecca for barbecue lovers, with four legendary restaurants offering enough lore and smoked meat to satisfy connoisseurs of this Texas food style. Barbecue is Lockhart's biggest draw, making it an ideal place for a quick 30-minute road trip from Austin. Visitors can walk off their brisket- and sausage-induced coma by strolling around the small historic downtown, punctuated by the majestic and magnificently restored Caldwell County Courthouse.

★ Black's Barbecue

Vying for the crown of best barbecue in Texas is **Black's Barbecue** (215 N. Main St., 888/632-8225, www.blacksbbq.com, Sun.-Thurs. 10am-8pm, Fri.-Sat. 10am-8:30pm, $15-48), the place to go for time-honored, perfectly smoked, mouthwatering barbecue. There are no pretensions here—the pork ribs, chops, and loins are all fantastic, with hardwood smoke perfectly accentuating the succulent flavor accented by the basic salt-and-pepper dry rub.

Equal in quality is the sausage, available in a flavorful beef-and-pork combo, garlic blend, and spicy jalapeño version. Most barbecue joints aren't known for their ambience, and Black's is no exception, but the black-and-white photos of bygone high school football teams and the longhorns and antlers looming above them lend a touch of rural charm. The sign outside Black's boasts "8 Days a Week," a reference to the seemingly endless amount of time restaurant staffers have prepared and doled out their delicious fare since 1932, and the fact it's open every day except Thanksgiving and Christmas.

Kreuz Market

For many barbecue aficionados, this is the traditional mainstay that represents the best old-school approach to smoking meats. **Kreuz Market** (619 N. Colorado St., 512/398-2361, www.kreuzmarket.com, daily 10:30am-8pm, $15-44) is legendary, but since the Austin barbecue explosion occurred over the past decade, it has slipped in comparative quality. Still, you won't find the typical barbecue combo plates offered at most Texas restaurants.

First, there's no sauce—why would you taint the perfectly smoked high-quality meat? Second, orders are placed at the meat counter in close proximity to the massive fire pits, where succulent sausage, thick pork chops, and hearty ribs and brisket are served by the pound on butcher paper. Third, there aren't any utensils, except for the plastic knife that's used for slicing off chunks of meat, cheese, avocado, tomato, and jalapeño. These side items, along with crackers, bread, pickles, and onions, stem from Kreuz's origins as a meat market and grocery store, where ranchers and farmhands would buy vegetables, bread, and meat and eat their purchases on-site, using a pocket knife. The food at Kreuz remains as expertly prepared as it has been since 1900, and it's worth a visit for the pork chops alone. Wash it all down with a Shiner Bock or Dr Pepper or Big Red.

The Caldwell County Courthouse in Lockhart

Smitty's Market

The business hasn't been around as long as the others (it opened in 1999), but the rustic building is legendary at **Smitty's Market** (208 S. Commerce St., 512/398-9344, www. smittysmarket.com, Mon.-Fri. 7am-6pm, Sat. 7am-6:30pm, Sun. 9am-6:30pm, $15-39). Smoked meat has been a specialty for more than a century, and visitors get an up close view of the decades-old fire-and-smoke-spewing brick pits adjacent to the line that snakes out the back door most weekends. By the time you sit down to eat, you won't even notice your smoke-drenched clothes. The brisket and sausage are specialties, and the tender and delicious pork ribs are available on weekends only. Smitty's also offers traditional sides such as potato salad, coleslaw, and pinto beans.

Chisholm Trail BBQ

In a town filled with world-famous barbecue restaurants, the locals' favorite is **Chisholm Trail BBQ** (1323 S. Colorado St., 512/398-6027, www.lockhartchisholmtrailbbq.com, Mon.-Wed. 7am-8pm, Thurs.-Sat. 7am-9pm, Sun. 8am-8pm, $11-29). A relative newcomer, Chisholm Trail holds its own, perhaps because it doesn't have the *New York Times* and Food Network hawking its food across the country. Chisholm Trail offers quality barbecue that would be a stand-alone knockout in most other Texas towns. The seasoned sausage is a specialty, and locals line up for the ribs, chicken, and turkey. Chisholm Trail has a large cafeteria-style bar with a plethora of sides, including fried okra, potato salad, coleslaw, pinto beans, green beans, squash, and various salads. What sets it apart from the other barbecue restaurants in town is its expanded menu, offering chicken-fried steak, catfish, and other Southern specialties.

Information and Services

Lockhart doesn't have an official visitors bureau, but you can direct general questions about area attractions and lodging to the city hall (512/398-3461, www.lockhart-tx.org). Another helpful resource is the **Lockhart Chamber of Commerce** (631 S. Colorado St., 512/398-2818, www.lockhartchamber. com).

Getting There and Around

From Austin, it takes 40 minutes to reach Lockhart via U.S. 183 southbound. There's an optional tollway along U.S. 183, but it only saves five minutes and costs about $4. Once you reach Lockhart, signs everywhere direct you to the "best" barbecue in Lockhart. They can each make a rightful claim.

Waco

In the late 19th century, cotton was king in Waco (population 138,183), weaving its way through the vivid heritage of this colorful town. The dark rich soil of the Blackland Prairie proved ideal for growing the crop, and like the oil that would be discovered later, it attracted a rush of immigrants.

Before the advent of river steamers and railroads, cotton buyers employed teamsters to make the overland trek to markets in the East. Eventually, trails and railroads converged in cotton boomtowns like Waco, which became known as "The Crossroads of Texas." Baylor University, the world's largest Baptist university, moved to Waco in the late 1800s, and by the early 20th century the city's manufacturing base increased from agricultural business to include standard service industries, two domino factories, and several soft drink companies: Dr Pepper became nationally famous, while the cream-soda-ish Big Red remained a sensation in the South.

Waco attained a "Wacko" reputation in 1993 when eccentric Branch Davidian sect

Be a Pepper

Dr Pepper Museum's historic building

The Dr Pepper Company bills itself as "the oldest major manufacturer of soft drink concentrates and syrups in the United States" and is proud of its status as a native Texas product. To experience this history, visit Waco's **Dr Pepper Museum** (300 S. 5th St., Waco, 254/757-1025, www.drpeppermuseum.com).

In the 1880s pharmacist Charles Alderton was intrigued with the various fruit syrup flavor smells wafting around the pharmacy and soda fountain in Waco, so he decided to create a drink that tasted like that smell. He kept a journal, and after many experiments created a mixture to his liking. Alderton offered his new drink to his customers, and word soon got out about the tasty beverage at Morrison's soda fountain. He knew he was onto something when crowds arrived and began ordering it by asking him to "shoot me a Waco." The origin of the name remains a mystery—one rumor is that Alderton named it after his horse, while another claims that combining its "peppiness" with the "Dr." prefix made it sound healthier.

Dr Pepper continued to gain in popularity throughout the 20th century and went on to have several memorable slogans, including "Drink a bite to eat at 10, 2, and 4," "The friendly Pepper-upper," "Be a Pepper," and the most recent campaign, focusing on the 23 flavors that give the drink its distinctive taste.

leader David Koresh defended his Mount Carmel compound against the U.S. government in a highly publicized attack that drew worldwide media coverage. Things turned more positive in the mid-2010s when HGTV's Magnolia franchise, a product of local heroes Chip and Joanna Gaines, became a national phenomenon.

SIGHTS
★ Magnolia Market
Magnolia Market (601 Webster Ave.,

254/235-0603, http://magnoliamarket.com, Mon.-Sat. 7:30am-6pm) is Waco's top travel destination by far. Local couple Chip and Joanna Gaines's *Fixer Upper* show on HGTV is a national phenomenon, based on the comfy styles they developed over the past decade at their Waco home decor shop. Their biggest rehab project ever—a 2015 expansion and upgrade at the iconic silos in downtown Waco—launched their TV show and location into the stratosphere, resulting in 25,000 visitors a week. Their headquarters, known as the

Magnolia Silos, include a crazy-popular retail store in a former grain barn, a garden area, an amazing bakery, a food truck court with local vendors, and a huge lawn for family activities and games.

Arrive early or on a weekday if you want to avoid the entry lines and the crowds that pack the retail store. Many people depart the site with bags full of goodies, although it's also common to see visitors strolling the grounds snapping photos of every charming item they see. Even if you aren't a fan of the enterprise, Magnolia Market is a comfy place to walk around with a food-cart coffee while watching frolicking families play Wiffle ball and snap selfies in front of the silos. The silos date to 1912, when the Brazos Valley Cotton Oil Co. extracted oil from cotton seeds. They aren't currently in use but serve as a beacon and photo op, with future plans to renovate them for use as an undisclosed Magnolia-related attraction.

Waco Mammoth National Monument

The **Waco Mammoth National Monument** (6220 Steinbeck Bend Rd., 254/750-7946, www.nps.gov/waco, daily 9am-5pm, $5 adults, $4 seniors and students) is a fascinating look at prehistory 70,000 years ago. It opened to the public in 2009, but its modern story began in 1978 when a bone protruding from a dry creek bank was reported to scientists at nearby Baylor University. Subsequent investigations and digs revealed dozens of mammoths.

It's worth waiting for the guided tour, which provides insight and context. For example, the guides explain the history of this type of mammoth (Columbian, not woolly), and point out the creature's gargantuan size by using the height of nearby light posts for comparison. In an effort to retain the integrity of the dig site, a special protective building was constructed around the bones. A walkway offers an amazing overhead view of the site, where visitors can snap photos while being surrounded by brightly painted images of the

mammoths in their heyday. The one-hour tour is worthwhile for adults and families, although parents with toddlers should consider the less-talky self-guided option.

Dr Pepper Museum

Discover what makes the world's oldest major soft drink pop at the **Dr Pepper Museum** (300 S. 5th St., 254/757-1025, www.drpeppermuseum.com, Mon.-Sat. 10am-5:30pm, Sun. noon-5:30pm, $10 adults, $8 seniors, $6 students). This fun museum takes visitors through the history of Waco-born Dr Pepper and Texas's soft drink industry. Dr Pepper originated in 1885 at a Waco drugstore, where a pharmacist concocted the recipe while mixing up different flavoring syrups for curious customers.

The main museum is housed in the Artesian Manufacturing and Bottling Company building, where the product was made in the early 1900s. The mixture of flavors in Dr Pepper remains a closely guarded secret, but visitors can learn about some of the theories and the history of the beverage from the museum's educational and interactive exhibits. The extensive collection of soft drink cans and bottles exhibiting design and logo styles through the ages is particularly fascinating. A new museum wing recently opened in an adjacent warehouse. The historic building is now home to a "cooking with Dr Pepper" laboratory, a mock bottling line, and a historical transportation display about soda distribution. Appropriately, the tour ends with an authentic soda fountain, serving Dr Pepper in its original incarnation, with pure cane sugar instead of corn syrup.

Mayborn Museum Complex

Baylor University's most noteworthy public entity is the impressive **Mayborn Museum Complex** (1300 S. University Parks Dr., 254/710-1110, www.maybornmuseum.com, Mon.-Wed. and Fri.-Sat. 10am-5pm, Thurs. 10am-8pm, Sun. 1pm-5pm, $9 adults, $8 seniors, $7 ages 2-12). In fact, this enormous 142,000-square-foot complex is arguably the finest natural history museum in Central Texas. Spend time investigating the strange and surreal objects in the museum's first room, dedicated to curiosities collected by the previous natural history museum's director—from bizarre stuffed rodents to a colossal skull from a 3,000-pound whale.

Waco's crossroads legacy is highlighted through the museum's collection of natural, cultural, and historical exhibits on the landscapes and people of Central Texas. Eye-catching features include a Native American grass house and a replica of the Waco Mammoth National Monument beneath a Plexiglas see-through floor. Incidentally, kids can spend hours in the museum's hands-on discovery center, where they'll experiment with water structures, musical instruments, and wind- and electrical-powered energy experiments. Be sure to set aside some time for the outdoor historic village behind the main building, where you can enter a mercantile store, ring a school bell, and play a church piano.

Cameron Park Zoo

Similar in approach to the highly respected Fort Worth Zoo is Waco's **Cameron Park Zoo** (1701 N. 4th St., 254/750-8400, www.cameronparkzoo.com, Mon.-Sat. 9am-5pm, Sun. 11am-5pm, $12 adults, $11 seniors, $9 ages 4-12). Dirt paths and wooden bridges connect habitats featuring animals from Africa, Asia, and the Americas in recreated environments simulating their homelands. The herpetarium is particularly impressive, with lush plants and waterfalls surrounding dozens of species of reptiles and amphibians. Drop by to visit the buffalo, jaguar, and aquarium fish, or check in on the lions, lemurs, and gibbon island. The zoo represents its Texas roots with the Brazos River Country exhibit, where visitors follow the footsteps of early Spanish explorers who searched for the seven cities of gold through the seven habitats of plant and animal life along the mighty river.

Waco Suspension Bridge

Once the largest suspension bridge in the country, the city's most famous landmark was built in 1870 as a 475-foot-long (145-m) toll bridge, spanning the Brazos River, along the Chisholm Trail. Traffic crossed under the bridge's lofty towers for a century, but it has been pedestrian-only since 1971. The steel cables and girders are a testament to bygone days, and the large bronze longhorn statues at the entrance to the bridge offer a reminder of its historical origins. The bridge is considered an icon of Waco history and serves as the backdrop and centerpiece for festivals and events throughout the year. Access the bridge via University Parks Drive between Franklin and Washington Avenues. Worth noting: The dozens of empty plastic bags tied to the west side of the bridge aren't trash—they're remnants of a Baylor University student tradition of attempting to toss tortillas onto a nearby bridge post.

Texas Ranger Hall of Fame and Museum

You're not going to encounter too many other museums like the **Texas Ranger Hall of Fame and Museum** (106 Texas Ranger Trail, 254/750-8631, www.texasranger.org, daily 9am-5pm, $8 adults, $7 seniors, $4 children). Stephen F. Austin introduced these legendary hired hands to the state's lexicon in 1823 when they were brought on board to help protect settlers against Native Americans along the westward-expanding frontier. They played significant roles in Texas's history—participating in the revolution against Mexico, bringing down Bonnie and Clyde—but by 1935, the state government roped them in under the jurisdiction of the Texas Department of Public Safety, where their primary role has been to focus on special investigations.

Although they currently number only about 100, the Rangers remain famous for their sharp skills and are considered some of the elite law enforcement officers of the modern era. The museum showcases their legacy through exhibits featuring documents, artifacts, and firearms. The Hall of Fame honors the most distinguished Rangers in history, and the research center contains archives, books, original clippings, genealogies, and photographs.

Texas Sports Hall of Fame

Another uniquely Lone Star State experience is the **Texas Sports Hall of Fame** (1108 S. University Parks Dr., 254/756-1633, www. tshof.org, Mon.-Sat. 9am-5pm, $8 adults, $7 seniors, $3 ages 5-18). Sports are an integral part of life in Texas, and the museum pays homage to the state's mythical stories and most accomplished athletes, including Nolan Ryan, Troy Aikman, George Foreman, Roger Clemens, David Robinson, Earl Campbell, and Tom Landry. The facility is divided into four separate wings—the Texas Sports Hall of Fame, the Texas Tennis Hall of Fame, the Texas High School Football Hall of Fame, and the Texas High School Basketball Hall of Fame. Video clips show highlights of Texas sports moments and athletes' achievements, and visitors can view sports artifacts and a display showcasing the evolution of tennis rackets.

FOOD

With Magnolia's takeover of Waco, the food scene has increased dramatically in quality. The food trucks at the silos site are consistently interesting, and the affiliated Magnolia Table has become a major foodie destination. Otherwise, one of Waco's old-school gastronomic specialties is chicken-fried steak, and several spots in town serve up some of the best Texas has to offer, along with regular steak and continental fare.

American

It's worth the effort to experience the magnificent breakfast and lunch dishes at ★ **Magnolia Table** (2132 S. Valley Mills Dr., 254/235-6111, www.magnolia.com/table, Mon.-Sat. 6am-3pm, $12-42). HGTV stars Chip and Joanna Gaines opened their highly

anticipated restaurant in 2018, immediately drawing curious customers from across the country. Wait times can be an hour or two, but the down-home fare is top-notch, featuring fresh ingredients in the flavorful breakfast tacos, Gaines Brothers burger, and "Gaines family favorite" Frito pie, a savory chili dish accompanied by some of the tastiest cornbread you'll ever eat.

Since most Waco visitors end up near the Magnolia Silos downtown, plan to be there around lunch or dinner to take advantage of the impressive local food trailer options. Although food trailer parks are naturally ever-evolving, one long-standing option at Magnolia is **Cheddar Box** (601 Webster Ave., 850/501-2076, www.cheddarboxwaco. com, daily 11am-6pm, $7-14). Who knew grilled cheese could be elevated to such an art form? Although you can't go wrong with any of the compelling options, the best include the Boss (bacon, gouda, and basil), Guac This Way (guacamole, salsa, and pulled pork), and Sweet Granny (granny smith apples, cream cheese, honey, and cinnamon). Other food-truck options include barbecue, pizza, sandwiches, and ice cream. Enhance the entire comfy experience by eating at a picnic table overlooking Magnolia's Great Lawn.

A popular upscale yet casual eatery is **1424 Bistro** (1424 Washington Ave., 254/752-7385, www.1424bistro.com, Tues.-Sat. 5pm-10pm, Sun. 5pm-9pm, $14-35), one of the few places in town where there can be a wait due to demand and the limited seating area. Specializing in seafood and Italian dishes, 1424 is an ideal place for a quality meal in a pleasant setting. Nightly seasonal specials are prepared using natural ingredients, and the head chef often makes the rounds to discuss dishes with the diners.

Lunch

Within walking distance of Magnolia is the local legend **Schmaltz's Sandwich Shoppe** (105 S. 5th St., 254/753-2332, wwwschmaltzs-sandwichshop.com, Mon.-Fri. 10am-8pm,

Sat. 10am-4pm, $6-13), an old-school lunch-counter spot offering a nice change of pace from the nearby trendy trailers and fast-food options. Schmaltz's signature item is its round homemade bun—a perfect accompaniment to the fresh veggies and tasty deli meats. You'll feel like a local in the small dining room, over-hearing conversations about Baylor sports and wacky weather.

One of the busiest hangouts for pub grub is **Cricket's Grill and Draft House** (211 Mary Ave., 254/754-4677, www.cricketsgrill.com, daily 11am-2am, $9-17). The emphasis is on the draft, but the pizza and fried-food items are worthy companions.

Burgers are also a must, and Waco's legendary locale is the not aptly named **Health Camp** (2601 Circle Rd., 254/752-2081, www.health-camp-waco.com, daily 11am-9pm, $6-14). A classic 1950s burger joint, Health Camp offers greasy yet immensely satisfying burgers made from high-quality beef and perfect onion rings. Not to be overlooked is **Dubl-R Old Fashioned Burgers** (1810 Herring Ave., 254/753-1603, www.dubl-r.com, Mon.-Fri. 10am-6:30pm, Sat. 10am-2pm, $7-15). Another 1950s-style joint, Dubl-R serves up delicious meaty handmade patties on soft sweet buns.

Coffee

Downtown in the shadow of the city's lone skyscraper, the 22-story Alico Building, is the stylish and welcoming **Dichotomy** (508 Austin Ave., 254/714-1710, www.dichotomycs.com, Sun.-Thurs. 6am-midnight, Fri.-Sat. 6am-2am, $4-9). With its attention to design and high-quality ingredients, Dichotomy feels like a big-city experience, yet the extremely friendly baristas in hip garb are a reminder you're still in Waco. And you'll be glad you are, because the perfectly prepared and decorated lattes, exceptional customer service, and fetching details will make you want to soak up the local scene and the excellent java for hours.

ACCOMMODATIONS
Motels and Hotels

Waco isn't teeming with trendy or historic places to spend the night; chain hotels are virtually the only option, and fortunately they're mostly clean and affordable. The best of the bunch are downtown near Baylor University, including **Super 8 Waco** (1320 S. Jack Kultgen Freeway, 254/754-1023, www.super8.com, $69 d), which features free hot breakfasts and free Wi-Fi. Another good option near Baylor is **La Quinta Inn** (1110

Magnolia Table in Waco

S. 9th St., 254/752-9741, www.lq.com, $149 d), offering free internet access, a complimentary continental breakfast, and an outdoor pool.

The newest option in Waco, coinciding with the influx of Magnolia visitors, is the trendy and upscale **Hotel Indigo** (211 Clay Ave., 254/754-7000, www.ihg.com, $181 d). On prime real estate downtown, it allows guests to walk along the Brazos River and to Magnolia Market. Amenities include an indoor-outdoor pool, a fantastic restaurant and bar, free Wi-Fi, and contemporary furnishings.

One of the most upscale options in town is the **Hilton Waco** (113 S. University Parks Dr., 254/754-8484, www.hilton.com, $209 d). The recently renovated high-rise, adjoining the Waco Convention Center, overlooks the mighty Brazos River and is across the street from the city's warehouse entertainment center. Rooms include free Wi-Fi, and the hotel contains a fitness center, an outdoor pool, a hot tub, and a tennis court.

Bed-and-Breakfasts

Consider staying at one of the city's bed-and-breakfasts as an alternative to the chain hotels. The best of the bunch is **Bed and Breakfast on White Rock Creek** (267 Ruby Dell Lane, 254/799-9783, www.whiterockcreek.com, from $125). Accommodations are in a historic home overlooking the scenic creek. The B&B features comfortable rustic furnishings,

gourmet breakfasts, and the peace and privacy of country living.

Camping

The most popular destinations for camping are the series of parks along the shores of Lake Waco operated by the U.S. Army Corps of Engineers. Sites include Speegleville Park, Midway Park, and Airport Park (254/756-5359), each providing basic drive-in pads and spaces with water and electricity.

INFORMATION AND SERVICES

The helpful and friendly folks at the **Waco Convention and Visitors Bureau** (254/750-5810 or 800/321-9226, www.wacoheartoftexas.com) operate a valuable **Tourist Information Center** (106 Texas Ranger Trail, 254/750-8696 or 800/922-6386, daily 8am-5pm). Pick up free maps, visitors guides, and brochures about Waco attractions or ask the staff for insight about their city.

GETTING THERE AND AROUND

Waco is 90 minutes from both Austin and Dallas-Fort Worth, so most travelers arrive via I-35, the main north-south thoroughfare. The **Waco Regional Airport** (ACT, 866/359-9226) is served by American Eagle. Cab service from the airport is available via **Waco Yellow Cab** (254/756-1861); the average fare to downtown Waco is around $25.

The Hill Country

The Hill Country of west Central Texas is a charming landscape of rolling vistas, cool breezes, and German heritage. City dwellers in Austin and San Antonio spend summer weekends at bed-and-breakfasts and ranches in the Hill Country, where the slow pace of life and the prospect of perfect peaches provide a welcome getaway. Despite the moniker, the hills aren't really dramatic—heights

of 1,400-1,700 feet (425-520 m) are the norm—but the increase in elevation and decrease in humidity are welcome respites for heat-drenched lowlanders. The views don't quite qualify as breathtaking, but the chill of the region's spring-fed rivers will prompt gasps. Cabins, lodges, resorts, and dude ranches dot the landscape, many offering access to the nearby Frio, Sabinal, Guadalupe, Medina, and

Pedernales Rivers, where visitors can swim, canoe, fish, or tube in the cool clear water.

★ FREDERICKSBURG

This small Hill Country town of 11,000 people is a favorite weekend destination for Texans, and the community's German heritage is a major draw, with dozens of restaurants and shops specializing in German food, drink, and crafts. Several annual events celebrate Fredericksburg's German pioneers, including the Wild Game Dinner (for men only) and the Damenfest (for women only). Some of the town's longtime residents still speak German as a first language.

Fredericksburg was one of several German settlements from the Texas Gulf Coast to the Hill Country. The first wagon train of 120 pioneers arrived from New Braunfels in 1846, and dubbed their community Fredericksburg after Prince Frederick of Prussia. The town was laid out like traditional German villages along the Rhine, with one wide main street paralleling Town Creek.

Today, this road is U.S. 290, which remains the main thoroughfare, and it's regularly filled with visitors from across the country who descend upon Fredericksburg—often via tour buses—to explore the art galleries, beer gardens, German bakeries, and antiques shops.

National Museum of the Pacific War

You can't miss the towering three-story steamboat-esque tower presiding over the entrance to the ★ **National Museum of the Pacific War** (340 E. Main St., 830/997-4379, www.pacificwarmuseum.org, daily 9am-5pm, $18 adults, $14 seniors, $8 students), and you shouldn't miss it. This enormous six-acre site, owned by the Texas Historical Commission, is the only institution in the continental United States dedicated exclusively to the Pacific battles of World War II. Why is it in Fredericksburg? The museum was originally known as the Admiral Nimitz Museum, named after Fredericksburg native Chester Nimitz, leader of the Pacific campaign. As

a boy in Fredericksburg, Nimitz lived in the family's famous steamboat-shaped hotel, and he went on to have a highly decorated military career, highlighted by his position as fleet admiral during World War II.

The George H. W. Bush Gallery, a state-of-the-art 33,000-square-foot exhibit, focuses on the inspiring story of the U.S. war in the Pacific during World War II. The gallery features 40 media installations, 900 artifacts, and hundreds of historic photographs.

The original portion of the museum offers a fascinating collection of equipment, artifacts, and models related to the Pacific campaign, including a B-25 bomber, a submarine, battleship artillery, and a comprehensive collection of uniforms, weapons, and scale-model destroyers and aircraft carriers. Elaborate walk-through dioramas bring the island combat scenes to life, and though the Nazi flags and uniforms cause an involuntary shudder, they put the war and the era in context. Even if you're not a history buff, you'll find the well-preserved and simply interpreted artifacts and memorabilia intriguing.

Outside the exhibit halls are a memorial courtyard honoring war veterans, a Plaza of Presidents dedicated to the 10 commanders-in-chief who served in World War II, and the remarkable Japanese Garden of Peace, an inviting natural sanctuary containing the three basic elements represented in a traditional Japanese garden: stone, plants, and water. The garden was a gift to the American people from the military leaders of Japan, who held Admiral Nimitz in high regard.

The museum's newest component, the Pacific Combat Zone, is located one block away and features informative exhibits about combat boats, life for soldiers on the Pacific, and "living-history shows," offering families an opportunity to see flamethrowers and re-enacted battle scenes.

Pioneer Museum Complex

Bookending Fredericksburg's bustling Main Street scene is the city's other major history-related attraction, the **Pioneer Museum**

The Hill Country's Dance Hall Heritage

Texas's dance halls have been hosting bands for a century.

On any given weekend night during summer, you're bound to hear music, whoops, and hollers emanating from rustic old buildings along the Hill Country's rural ranch roads. Dozens of historic dance halls still stand in the region, where German immigrants built sturdy structures for festivals and community gatherings more than a century ago.

To experience these authentically Texas destinations, check their websites to see who's playing and what time they take the stage—most shows are on weekends, starting around 7pm. You can buy tickets in advance for some shows, but for local acts you should bring $10-20 cash to pay at the door. Most people will be sporting Western wear, including cowboy hats, pressed jeans, and starched shirts.

Among the most famous is in tiny **Luckenbach,** population 3, just east of Fredericksburg (412 Luckenbach Town Loop, 830/997-3224, www.luckenbachtexas.com). The scenic rural roads leading to this musical hamlet in the Hill Country set the stage for the laid-back experience. Although the dance hall here was built circa 1849, it wasn't until the early 1970s when Texas troubadours put it on the map with their cosmic country singalongs under the oak trees.

To get an authentic old-fashioned dance hall experience, head to the tiny towns off the beaten path that draw mostly local crowds. Some of the best options that keep the tradition alive, around 90 minutes west and southwest of Austin, include **Kendalia Halle** (1135 FM 3351, Kendalia, 210/863-1100, www.kendaliahalle.com), **Anhalt Hall** (2390 Anhalt Rd., Spring Branch, 830/438-2873, www.anhalthallcom), **London Hall** (17430 U.S. 377, London, 325/475-2921) and **Twin Sisters Dance Hall** (6720 U.S. 281, Blanco, 830/833-5773).

The buildings were feats of engineering. Designed with Texas's hot climate in mind, most included walls of windows that were propped open with long sticks to catch the breeze. Thanks to their solid construction, many of the original structures remain standing in rural areas where German immigrants settled, including Fredericksburg, Luckenbach, and near Austin. Some are in dire need of a face-lift, but many still serve their original purpose as community gathering places for friends and family.

Up-and-coming artists can still make a name for themselves at these low-profile locales, and families continue to gather at these historic halls to hear country music and dance on the well-worn floors.

Complex (325 W. Main St., 830/990-8441, www.pioneermuseum.net, Mon.-Sat. 10am-5pm, $7.50 over age 17, $3 ages 6-17). This is the kind of museum found in many small towns, distinguished here by German settlers.

This collection of late-1800s and early-1900s buildings is based on the original house, smokehouse, and barn of Henry Kammlah, one of the city's early residents. The home is filled with furniture and equipment from pioneer life, but several aspects of Kammlah's home are unique to his heritage—the cool damp basement contains a large wooden beer keg, and visitors can almost smell the savory scent of sausage emanating from the old smokehouse in back.

The remainder of the complex contains a barn with old farm and kitchen equipment, a collection of horse buggies, and an old schoolhouse complete with desks and a chalkboard with lessons written in German. Serving as an entryway to the complex is the Dambach-Besier House, a 1969 limestone residence relocated to the site and now serving as the welcome center for the museum and as the Fredericksburg Convention and Visitors Bureau.

Vereins Kirche Museum

If you still can't get enough of the German Hill Country heritage, drop by the small **Vereins Kirche Museum** (100 block of W. Main St., at Marktplatz Center, 830/997-7832, Tues.-Sat. 10am-4:30pm, free). Like the Pioneer Museum Complex, the museum is operated by the Gillespie County Historical Society and features archives and exhibits of photos and artifacts dedicated to the Fredericksburg area's history, particularly the rugged life experiences of the German settlers and everyday life on the frontier. Housed in a 1936 replica of the 1847 Vereins Kirche (Society Church), the octagonal building honors one of the first structures erected in Fredericksburg.

Shopping

Hill Country heritage aside, Fredericksburg's big draw is the shopping. The town's sidewalks are lined with chalkboard signs, and sweet smells of flowery domestic products entice passersby. Most offer similar pricey country-kitchen-style furniture and knickknacks, but there are some worthy boutiques and galleries featuring uncommon objects and rustic home furnishings.

Among the more popular establishments is **Carol Hicks Bolton Antiques** (301 S. Lincoln St., 830/997-5551, www.carolhicksbolton.com), specializing in antique and modern furniture, from small sconces to enormous armoires. Another popular spot is the nearby **Phil Jackson's Granite & Iron Store** (206 E. Main St., 830/997-4716), specializing in Mr. Jackson's signature custom tables, most featuring rare granite slabs and intricate ironwork. The home decor items here are also noteworthy, including tasteful lamps, clocks, pottery, and mirrors.

Finally, a stroll down Main Street would be incomplete without stopping by **Fredericksburg Fudge** (218 E. Main St., 830/997-0533, www.fbgfudge.com). This traditional candy shop has been doling out thick chunks of rich, sweet, made-from-scratch fudge for decades and provides the perfect souvenir.

Food

How often do you get to eat authentic German food? Fredericksburg is the ideal place to explore sauerkraut and wiener schnitzel. A good starting point is the ★ **Fredericksburg Brewing Company** (245 E. Main St., 830/997-1646, www.yourbrewery.com, Mon.-Fri. 11:30am-9pm, Sat. 11am-10pm, Sun. 11am-7pm, $13-29). In the middle of the action, this brewpub provides a taste of German culture and cuisine, with finely crafted homebrews made on-site in the shiny copper tanks near the dining room and a *biergarten* out back. The beers are immensely satisfying compared to mass-produced products. Although the Peacepipe Pale Ale isn't as

---

1: National Museum of the Pacific War
2: Fredericksburg Brewing Company

hoppy as most bitter brews of this type, it has a sweet, full flavor; the Pioneer Porter, meanwhile, is everything a rich dark beer should be. Menu items include *jägerschnitzel*, sausage, and the incomparable *überbackene schweineschnitzel* (a tasty pork chop smothered with tangy cheese, colorful peppers, and a sweet apple cider cream sauce), along with local specialties such as chicken-fried steak and venison chili.

For a slightly more formal meal, go to **Der Lindenbaum** (312 E. Main St., 830/997-9126, www.derlindenbaum.com, Wed.-Mon. 11am-10pm, $15-33), in a historic limestone building. The standard German dishes (schnitzels, steaks, homemade breads) are worth sampling, but the restaurant's specialties are more traditional meals such as sauerbraten (Rhineland-style sweet-and-sour marinated roast beef) and *schweinekotelett* (pork chops in mustard sauce). Save room for the strudel.

A dozen bakers in town serve pastries and light lunches. One of the best is **Twisted Sisters Bake Shop** (111 S. Washington St., 830/990-7999, Tues.-Sat. 7:30am-5:30pm, Sun. 7:30am-noon, $7-16), tucked away in a pleasant courtyard behind busy Main Street. It's a wonderful place to enjoy a tasty breakfast of delectable pastry. The homemade bread is outstanding, but the desserts are the main draw. Try the sausage *kolach,* chorizo breakfast bowl, or blueberry scone.

Another noteworthy place to pick up sweets is the **Old German Bakery** (225 W. Main St., 830/997-9084, http://oldgermanbakeryandrestaurant.com, daily 7am-3pm, $7-16), which specializes in homemade goodies and hearty lunches. The cookies are well known, and people flock here to pick up potato pancakes and fresh bread.

For a fine meal away from Main Street, head to **Hill Top Cafe** (10661 N. U.S. 87, 830/997-8922, www.hilltopcafe.com, Tues.-Sat. 11am-2pm and 5pm-9pm, Sun. 11am-2pm and 5pm-8pm, $14-33). About 10 miles (16 km) west of town, this restaurant features an upscale Cajun take on comfort food. Menu highlights include the rubbed tenderloin with Greek seasoning, fried Port Arthur shrimp, frog legs, and catfish. Save room for the peach cobbler or raspberry pie.

Another nice option outside town is **Cotton Gin Restaurant & Lodging** (2805 S. Hwy. 16, 830/990-5734, www.cottonginrestaurant.com, Tues.-Sat. 5pm-10pm, $16-48). In a beautiful outdoor setting with a koi pond and mellow musicians often accompanying your meal, the Cotton Gin features delectable items such as the grand chicken-fried pork steak, jumbo lump crab gratin, and an amazing rib-eye steak.

Accommodations

Fredericksburg is the ultimate bed-and-breakfast town, with hundreds of options from rustic ranch cabins to luxurious châteaus to a historic railroad sleeper car. Many travelers begin their search with a B&B locator service such as **First Class Bed & Breakfast Reservation Service** (909 E. Main St., 888/991-6749, www.fredericksburg-lodging.com). You can also peruse the many options listed at the **Visit Fredericksburg** (www.visitfredericksburgtx.com) website.

Not everyone visiting Fredericksburg is required to stay at a B&B. For a quilt-free evening, book a room at **La Quinta Inn & Suites** (1465 E. Main St., 800/531-5900, www.lq.com, $149 d). The hotel features free internet access, a fitness center, an outdoor pool and jetted tub, and free continental breakfast. A nicer option near the heart of downtown is **Hampton Inn & Suites** (515 E. Main St., 830/997-9696, www.hamptoninn.com, $187 d), offering free internet access, complimentary breakfast and beverage service, an exercise room, and an outdoor pool.

Information and Services

A good starting point to get a handle on Fredericksburg's myriad shopping, eating, and lodging options is the **Visitor Information Center** (302 E. Austin St., 830/997-6523 or 888/997-3600, www.visitfredericksburgtx.com, Mon.-Fri. 8:30am-5pm, Sat. 9am-5pm, Sun. noon-3pm). The friendly staff will provide maps and brochures, and visitors can watch an informative nine-minute video about the town and its attractions.

Getting There and Around

From Austin, Fredericksburg is a 90-minute drive west on U.S. 290. It's a beautiful stretch of prime Hill Country scenery, so take your time and enjoy the ride.

BANDERA

Proudly billing itself as the "Cowboy Capital of the World," Bandera (population 898) is a quaint little Western town surrounded by working and guest ranches for city folk to experience life on a dude ranch. Bandera is also proud of its rodeo heritage, with more champions than any Texas town of its size. Visitors can witness this legacy at public rodeo events throughout summer, or get in touch with their inner cowboy or cowgirl through the myriad horseback riding opportunities around town.

Dude Ranches

Bandera's main draw is its dude ranches. Some are hokier than others, but all offer a natural escape. Families, mostly from San Antonio, spend weekends in the country surrounded by docile horses, wooded trails, swimming holes, outdoor barbecues, campfires, and hayrides. It allows bonding with other families at the ranch-style community meals and recreational events. Activities are optional, so guests can choose to spend as much time as they like inside rustic cabins and lodges or outdoors.

One of the best known is the **Dixie Dude Ranch** (833 Dixie Dude Ranch Rd., 830/796-7771, www.dixieduderanch.com, adults average $160 pp, children $80). Unlike many, the Dixie is a working stock ranch, operating since 1901. Guests can partake of planned activities such as horseback riding, swimming, fishing (gear provided), hiking, and hayrides, or venture out on their own to explore the ranch on hiking trails, hunt for fossils and arrowheads, or visit the 100-year-old barn and cemetery. Chow time means meals

in the family-style dining house, outdoor barbecues, fried chicken, or a cowboy breakfast. Accommodations are in duplex cabins, cottages, a two-story bunkhouse, and a main lodge. All have two or more beds with private baths, air-conditioning, and heat.

A resort ranch, as opposed to a working ranch, is the renowned **Mayan Ranch** (off Pecan St., 1.5 mi/2.4 km west of Bandera, 830/796-3312, www.mayanranch.com, adults average $170 pp, children $80, 3 meals and 2 horseback rides included). Guests at the Mayan can pony up for a full day of optional activities, including a cowboy breakfast cookout, trail rides, a poolside lunch, swimming, cowboy games, tubing on the adjacent Medina River, dancing, and even fireworks. Afterward, guests sleep soundly in individual cottages with up to three bedrooms or a large lodge room overlooking the Hill Country.

Another popular Bandera getaway is the **Silver Spur Guest Ranch** (9266 Bandera Creek Rd., 830/796-3037, www.silverspurranch.com, minimum 2-night stay, adults about $160 pp, children $75, 3 meals and 2 hours of horseback rides included). Alongside an enormous state park, the Silver Spur offers the activities of a well-heeled dude ranch, including trail rides, outdoor cookouts, and hayrides, with additional features such as a junior Olympic-sized swimming pool and an arena for barrel racing, pole bending, and other riding activities. The main lodge and cabins offer modern and comfortable amenities.

Bandera boasts nearly a dozen more dude ranches in the general vicinity, each offering a varied range of rustic charm and cowboy-related activities. For a comprehensive list of options and a sneak peek at what they have to offer, check in with the Bandera County Convention and Visitors Bureau (800/364-3833, www.banderacowboycapital.com).

Horseback Riding

Most of Bandera's dude ranches offer horseback riding as part of the package, but not everyone visiting the area up for the ranch experience. Several independent stables in the area will arrange horseback rides by the hour, day, or even overnight. Options include **Bandera Historical Rides** (www.banderahistoricalrides.com, 830/328-2203) and **Bar M Guest Ranch** (830/796-9096, www.bar-mranch.com).

Frontier Times Museum

Don't expect interactive, hands-on exhibits at **Frontier Times Museum** (510 13th St., 830/796-3864, www.frontiertimesmuseum.org, Mon.-Sat. 10am-4:30pm, $6 adults, $4 seniors, $3 ages 6-17), a decidedly old-school museum. Instead you'll find an amazing collection of random stuff deemed important by townspeople since 1933. Western relics abound, including old household items, photos, farming equipment, and rodeo memorabilia, as well as an eclectic mix of "exotic" items from Asia and Europe, such as rare bells, plates, and a gong from the Ming Dynasty. The museum also includes a gallery of Western art.

Hill Country State Natural Area

One of the crown jewels of the Texas parks system is the **Hill Country State Natural Area** (10600 Bandera Creek Rd., 830/796-4413, www.tpwd.state.tx.us, Feb.-Nov. daily, Dec.-Jan. weekends, day use $6 over age 12, overnight $3 over age 12). Secluded and undeveloped, this ruggedly beautiful 5,400-acre park offers opportunities for equestrians, hikers, and mountain bikers to traverse trails across valleys, streams, and limestone hills. Primitive backcountry camping areas are available to equestrian and non-equestrian campers.

Most of the parkland was donated by the Merrick Bar-O-Ranch, which stipulated that it "be kept far removed and untouched by modern civilization, where everything is preserved intact, yet put to a useful purpose." The terrain ranges from flat creek bottoms to rocky canyons reaching 2,000 feet (210 m) in elevation. Several spring-fed streams provide swimming holes and water for horses, but the humans among the herd are encouraged to bring their own drinking water.

Food and Entertainment

Despite being a town of nearly 1,000, Bandera has several noteworthy restaurants catering to city slickers who invade the community most weekends. To get a true taste of Bandera, drop by the **OST Restaurant** (305 Main St., 830/796-3836, Thurs.-Tues. 6am-8pm, Wed. 6am-2pm, $9-20). The acronym stands for Old Spanish Trail, which used to run through the area, and the Western theme permeates everything from the menu to the John Wayne-inspired decor. The OST's specialty is breakfast, including staples such as biscuits and gravy, hash browns, and huevos rancheros, served any time. The soups and chicken-fried steak are local favorites. For an authentic experience in the Cowboy Capital, you can literally saddle up to the bar at the OST.

Another busy downtown place to get good country vittles is **Busbee's Bar-B-Q** (319 Main St., 830/796-3153, Wed.-Mon. 10:30am-8pm, $9-19). Busbee's serves up traditional Texas barbecue—brisket, sausage, and ribs—along with standard side dishes like coleslaw, potato salad, and beans. For a good Tex-Mex fix, visitors can stick close to downtown for their fill of tacos, enchiladas, quesadillas, and breakfast burritos at the tiny **El Jacalito** (1207 Cedar St., 830/460-3853, Tues. 6:30am-2pm, Wed.-Fri. 6:30am-2pm and 4pm-9pm, Sat. 6:30am-noon, Sun. 7am-noon, $8-16).

For entertainment, the most famous establishment in Bandera is **Arkey Blue's Silver Dollar Saloon** (308 Main St., 830/796-8826, call for hours, live music Wed.-Sun.). Established in the 1930s, Arkey's is a classic honky-tonk with a sawdust-covered dance floor. The scene is more authentically Western than many of the nearby resort ranches, and the crowds (especially the veteran two-steppers) will give out-of-towners a true sense of country living. Over the years, the saloon has hosted many high-profile guest performers, including Willie Nelson, Ernest Tubb, and Bruce and Charlie Robison.

Far less famous yet certainly entertaining in its own right is the **Chikin Coop** (402 Main St., 830/796-4496, www.chikincoop.com, daily 11am-2am). Located among the restaurants and bustle of downtown, the saloon hosts live music on the deck overlooking Main Street every Thursday-Saturday. This is a good spot for dancing, drinking, and people-watching, and if you happen to arrive on horseback, you're in luck—tie up to the hitching post out front, and you might even receive an "I got a horse" discount the whole time you and your horse are there.

Accommodations
MOTELS AND HOTELS

As unbelievable as it may seem, not everyone visiting the Bandera area wants to stay at a dude ranch. Other worthwhile alternatives include the charming **River Front Motel** (1004 Maple St., 830/460-3690, www.theriverfrontmotel.com, cabins average $109). The simple, rustic motel has 11 cabins near the river, each offering a microwave, a fridge, coffee, cable TV, a private bath, and a covered front porch.

Other nearby options include the affordable but not-quite-as-charming **Bandera Lodge** (700 Hwy. 16 S., 830/796-3093, www.banderatxhotel.com, $99 d), containing 21 rooms with microwaves and fridges as well as free internet access and an outdoor pool.

BED-AND-BREAKFASTS

For some, a trip to the country necessitates a stay in a bed-and-breakfast, where gentle breezes land on soft downy pillows and days begin with gourmet coffee and egg dishes. The **Diamond H Ranch Bed and Breakfast** (5322 Hwy. 16 N., 830/796-4820, www.diamondhbanb.com, from $110), 4miles (6.4 km) northwest of Bandera, is a comfortable, laid-back locale along the Medina River. The main house has seven Western-style bedrooms with private baths, air-conditioning, heat, porches, and patios, and the main room includes a pool table, games, and a large fireplace.

Cool Water Acres (3301 FM 470, 830/796-4866, www.coolwateracres.com, $125) is on a five-acre spring-fed lake offering crisp, clear water for swimming, snorkeling, fishing, and relaxing. The cabin is part of an 1870 homestead that holds three adults comfortably. Property features include complimentary fruit and farm fresh eggs on arrival, a private floating dock, and a nearby barn with friendly horses, cats, and chickens.

Bandera is brimming with other B&Bs—a comprehensive list is available at the **Bandera County Convention and Visitors Bureau's** website (www.banderacowboycapital.com).

Information and Services

Bandera has plenty of visitor services overseen by the **Bandera County Convention and Visitors Bureau** (126 Hwy. 16 S., 830/796-3045 or 800/364-3833, www.banderacowboycapital.com). The website is particularly helpful for comparing amenities, and the office staff offers expert advice and provide brochures, maps, and directions to the hard-to-find destinations tucked among the hills.

Getting There and Around

Bandera is closer to San Antonio than Austin, but its Hill Country status makes it a Central Texas community. From Austin, take I-35 South to the Hwy. 1604 outer loop of San Antonio (about an hour away), then head westward, continuing on Highway 16, which becomes Main Street in Bandera.

JOHNSON CITY

Most people assume Johnson City (population 1,734) is named for its legendary native son, Lyndon Baines Johnson, the 36th president of the United States. It's actually named after his grandfather's nephew James Polk Johnson, even though he never achieved the same level of recognition as LBJ. The Johnson family, however, is an ideal representation of the determined, down-to-earth folks who settled in this rugged part of the state more than 150 years ago and whose descendants remain on the rocky terrain. A visit to this small town, especially the incredible LBJ Ranch, reveals the gritty and tenacious nature of the region, reflected in the no-nonsense approach of LBJ himself. This was truly far from Camelot.

★ Lyndon B. Johnson National Historical Park

TOP EXPERIENCE

Even if you're just passing through the Hill Country, be sure to set aside a few hours to tour the remarkable **Lyndon B. Johnson National Historical Park,** with two visitors centers (100 Lady Bird Lane, Johnson City; and LBJ Ranch, Hwy. 290, near Stonewall, 14 mi/22.5 km west of Johnson City, 830/868-7128, www.nps.gov/lyjo, daily 8am-5pm, Texas White House tour $3 adults).

As visitors soon find out, LBJ remains a larger-than-life figure who brought acclaim (and electricity) to the Hill Country. To get a full appreciation for this mythical man, start at Johnson City's LBJ State Park and Historic Site—his boyhood home and the Johnson Settlement (his grandparents' log cabin home)—which put his formative years in context.

Afterward, make the 14-mile (22.5-km) drive west to the LBJ Ranch near Stonewall. The family residence, a.k.a. the Texas White House, is open to the visitors, who can view the president's office, living room, and dining room, and the Johnsons' bedroom suites. The self-guided driving tour on the ranch property reveals the one-room schoolhouse LBJ would sneak into as a four-year-old, and the small graveyard with the modest granite blocks marking the graves of Lyndon and his beloved wife, Lady Bird.

The ranch's interpretive center includes informative exhibits about the history of LBJ and the Hill Country, including a post office display with audio versions of letters describing the harsh environs of the region to relatives on the East Coast and in Germany.

Hill Country Science Mill

One of Johnson City's newest attractions is in one of its oldest buildings. The **Hill Country Science Mill** (101 S. Lady Bird Lane, 830/263-6406, www.sciencemill.org, Wed.-Sun. 10am-4pm, $11 adults, $9.50 ages 3-18). In an 1880 feed mill punctuated by eye-catching rustic silos, the Science Mill offers an intriguingly different approach. Curiosity is key here, as students of all ages are drawn to experiment with dozens of fun and educational displays to test their brains. A highlight is Mindball, offering kids and parents a chance to test their telekinetic skills by strapping on an electrical headband and attempting to control a ball via brain waves. Other fun exhibits include a banana-powered musical program, a racetrack for custom-built toy cars, and a fascinating sandbox that allows visitors to create hills and valleys, which are immediately tracked with colored topographical lights.

Exotic Resort Zoo

There's plenty of land in the Hill Country, and apparently it's somewhat similar to the environment of the creatures that roam the spacious grounds of the **Exotic Resort Zoo** (235 Zoo Trail, 830/868-4357, www.zooexotics.com, daily 9am-6pm, $17 adults, $14 children), 4 miles (6.4 km) north of Johnson City. Visitors take a guided open-bus tour through the expansive property while guides describe the characteristics of the zoo's animals, including giraffes, lemurs, kangaroos, zebras, bears, ostriches, and bison. Some of the friendly beasts will even let visitors pet them (the treats handed out by the guides offer an incentive). The Exotic Resort Zoo operates several cabins, three with kitchenettes, for those who really want to experience life on the range.

Pedernales Falls State Park

One of the most pleasant and scenic spots in Central Texas is **Pedernales Falls State**

1: Lyndon B. Johnson National Historical Park
2: Hill Country Science Mill 3: Pecan Street Brewing
4: Enchanted Rock State Natural Area

Park (2585 Park Rd. 6026, 830/868-7304, www.tpwd.state.tx.us, $6 over age 12), 9 miles (14.5 km) east of Johnson City. Set on 5,200 acres of rolling hills and flowing water, the park's main attraction is namesake Pedernales Falls, visible from a scenic overlook at the north end of the park.

Park activities include camping, hiking, swimming, tubing, mountain biking, fishing, and, most popular of all, bird-watching. The park has a covered bird-viewing station with feeders (food is provided year-round) and a drip bath. Quails, doves, rufous-crowned sparrows, western scrub jays, and the endangered golden-cheeked warbler nest in the park and visit the feeders. Facilities include campsites with water and electricity, primitive campsites, restrooms with and without showers, 20 miles (32 km) of hiking and mountain biking trails, and 14 miles (22.5 km) of backpacking trails.

Food

For a town of nearly 2,000 people, Johnson City has several worthy restaurants, perfect for fueling up before a day at the LBJ Ranch or Pedernales Falls State Park. The best of the bunch is Pecan Street Brewing (106 E. Pecan Dr., 830/868-2500, www. pecanstreetbrewing.com, Tues.-Sun. 11am-9pm, $11-32). Located across from Johnson City's magnificent historic courthouse, Pecan Street Brewing does comfortable, down-home cuisine just right. Pizza and beer are the big draws—the 1897 Jailbreak IPA, Screwloose Blonde, and Chain Gang Oatmeal Stout are highlights, and the brick-oven pizzas are family-pleasing favorites.

Another popular eatery is East Main Grill (209 E. Main St., 830/868-7710, Wed.-Thurs. and Sun. 11am-2:30pm, Fri.-Sat. and Mon. 11am-2:30pm and 5pm-9pm, $14-31), in a historic lumberyard alongside several antique shops, offering upscale country fare in a pleasant environment. Choose from standards like chicken-fried steak, bronzed catfish, bratwurst, or tenderloin steak. Local

singer-songwriters such as John Arthur Martinez and Mike Blakely enhance the Hill Country experience with their mellow acoustic tunes.

The other reliable local restaurants in town serve standard Tex-Mex fare. You can't go wrong with either El Charro Restaurant (502 N. Hwy. 281, 830/868-7040, daily 6:30am-10pm, $8-15) or nearby El Agave (408 N. Hwy. 281, 830/868-0812, daily 6am-11pm, $8-13). Both feature classic cheesy and beefy Tex-Mex dishes such as enchiladas, tacos, quesadillas, and burritos.

Accommodations

Those looking for a reliable hotel experience have limited options, and the best among them is the Best Western Johnson City Inn (U.S. 281 at U.S. 290, 830/868-4044, www. bestwestern.com, $139 d). The hotel offers free Wi-Fi, a complimentary continental breakfast, and an outdoor swimming pool.

Information and Services

Information about accommodations, restaurants, and other visitor needs, including maps and brochures, is available at the Johnson City Chamber of Commerce (830/868-7684, www.lbjcountry.com).

Getting There and Around

From Austin, Johnson City is about an hour's drive west on U.S. 290. Be on the lookout for the several-mile stretch of U.S. 290 that joins U.S. 281 north before continuing westward.

HILL COUNTRY SIDE TRIPS

Visitors often turn a Hill Country excursion into an extra-long weekend, with day trips to one of the region's scenic parks for hiking and biking or an afternoon cruising down a canyon-walled river in a canoe, kayak, or inner tube. Fans of outlaw country music—particularly Willie, Waylon, and the boys—are virtually required to make a pilgrimage to the tiny yet fabled Luckenbach.

★ Enchanted Rock State Natural Area

Serving as a natural beacon for millennia is the enormous pink granite dome at the heart of **Enchanted Rock State Natural Area** (16710 Ranch Rd. 965, 830/685-3636, www.tpwd.state.tx.us, $6 over age 12), 18 miles (29 km) north of Fredericksburg. Visitors have only been coming to the state park since 1984, but people have been drawn by its surreal magnitude for more than 11,000 years. The rock is a massive granite exfoliation dome rising 1,825 feet (556 m) above sea level and is one of the largest batholiths (an underground rock formation uncovered by erosion) in the country.

The Tonkawa people believed the rock was mystical, and Spanish explorers in the mid-1700s were equally intrigued by the natural structure. Legend has it that Comanche people held human sacrifices at its base, but this has been disputed. Most anthropologists agree the Native Americans were fearful of the rock because they believed it to be haunted. These days, New Agers occasional seek spiritual power from the iridescent reflections emanating from the sparkling granite on full-moon nights. Even if it's not a full moon, it's worth ascending the rock at dusk for the 360-degree sunset views and incredible stargazing.

Hundreds of visitors come on weekends for hiking, rock climbing, backpacking, camping, and stargazing, and the parking often reaches capacity on weekends and closes early, sometimes by 10am. Call ahead to gauge accessibility. The park contains a 4-mile (6.4-km) hiking trail through the granite formations, and a short steep trail leading to the top of the rock. Those not in peak physical condition will likely have to take several breaks along the way. For adventurous non-claustrophobic types, there are several small caves along the back of the dome that are worth exploring for a short distance.

Park amenities include an interpretive center, hike-in primitive sites, restrooms with showers, tent pads, picnic sites for day-use with tables and grills, and a group picnic area with a pavilion and restrooms. Vehicle camping is not permitted. Contact the park for camping fees and restrictions, which vary depending on the number of people and type of use.

Frio and Sabinal Canyons

The geological structures along the Frio and Sabinal Rivers could be referred to as "mini canyons." Even though they're not dramatic in scale, these canyons are beautiful wonders of nature. Most Texas rivers traverse hills and plains, so these are spectacular in comparison—especially from the vantage point of a canoe or inner tube. True to its name, the Frio River (*frio* means "cold" in Spanish) is refreshingly brisk on a 100°F (38°C) summer day. Visitors to this area relish the rural scenery and the abundant opportunities to camp in primitive areas or stay in rustic hillside cabins and lodges.

GARNER STATE PARK

One of the most popular state parks in Texas is **Garner State Park** (234 Ranch Rd. 1050, 830/232-6132, www.tpwd.state.tx.us, day use $6 over age 12, overnight $4 over age 12), 8 miles (12.9 km) north of Concan. Boasting 1,420 acres of natural beauty along the Frio River, the park attracts hundreds of thousands of visitors annually to swim, boat, tube, and fish in the chilly water; hike the park's remarkable nature trails; dance at the nightly concession stand gatherings during summer; and even golf at the nearby miniature golf course, lighted for nighttime play.

Most visitors camp at primitive tent sites, although there are a limited number of high-demand cabins for rent. The park is open year-round, but it's busiest Memorial Day-Labor Day. Like Enchanted Rock, the popularity of the park occasionally results in parking capacity issues, forcing officials to close the gates by noon. Contact the park regarding camping fees and restrictions, which vary depending on the number of people and the type of use. The popular summertime dances can reach maximum parking capacity as well, so call ahead.

LOST MAPLES STATE NATURAL AREA

Northerners take note: Fall colors are virtually nonexistent in Texas, so don't be surprised to hear about frenzied and overcrowded conditions to catch a rare glimpse of the leaves at **Lost Maples State Natural Area** (37221 Ranch Rd. 187, 830/966-3413, www.tpwd.state.tx.us, Oct.-Nov. day use $6 over age 12, overnight $3 over age 12, Dec.-Sept. day use $5 over age 12, overnight $3 over age 12), 5 miles (8 km) north of Vanderpool. The maples add a welcome splash of color to the region's normally uninspired fall palette of browns and yellows. They're deemed "lost" since they grow hundreds of miles from their native habitats due to the cooler and wetter conditions provided by the surrounding canyon walls. The trees hit their colorful peak in late October-early November, resulting in huge crowds and parking-capacity issues (limited to 250 vehicles). Call ahead to determine accessibility, or better yet, arrive on a weekday when it's less crowded.

Even when the fall foliage isn't taking center stage, visitors are attracted year-round to the park's limestone canyons, cool spring-fed streams, and wooded trails. Since the beloved maples have a shallow root system, hikers are encouraged to stay on the trail to avoid damaging the trees. Park amenities include campsites with water and electricity, restrooms with showers, and primitive camping areas. Camping is in primitive campsites ($8) and sites with water and electric hookups ($18).

CANYON COMMUNITIES

This part of the state is dotted with small riverside towns filled with resorts, retirees, and the descendants of the German settlers who migrated here in the 1800s. Concan is a tiny community (population 200) surrounded by gorgeous scenery in the tree-topped hills and cliffs overlooking the crystal-clear Frio River. The meandering drive along U.S. 83 to the town is unlike any other in Texas, with the adjacent canyons beckoning drivers to pull over and explore scenic overlooks.

The best place to experience this view is 3 miles (4.8 km) southwest of Concan at one-of-a-kind **Neal's Lodges** (Hwy. 127, 830/232-6118, www.nealslodges.com, 3-night minimum stay in summer, cabins $90-375 for up to 8 people). Established in 1926, Neal's offers 74 cabins that range from funky to upscale. The most basic options are one-room wooden structures with evaporative coolers, and the nicest are upscale Hill Country lodges. In between are cinderblock structures overlooking the Frio and the "best swimming hole in Texas." All but four of the cabins have kitchenettes. Other on-site amenities include a grocery store, a restaurant, and laundry facilities. One of the biggest draws for Frio frolickers is the massive 83-foot-long (25-m) slide that allows guests to fly into the river. RV hookups and tent sites are also available, and Neal's rents inner tubes for floating the Frio, with a return stop on the property's riverbank.

Another reliable option is **Frio River Cabins** (6978 S. U.S. 83, Concan, 830/232-5996, www.cabinsfrioriver.com, $125-250), with more than a dozen rustic cabin options, ranging from modest wooden structures to charming stone cottages. The main draw is the cool river—visitors can while away an entire day with a beer in hand, basking in the refreshing water beneath the cypress trees.

Just up the road on U.S. 83 is Leakey (pronounced LAY-key), another small community (population 439) with riverside lodging and multigenerational Hill Country settlers. This is one of the closest towns to Garner State Park, so visitors often stay in a Leakey cabin to visit the park during the day. One of the best lodging options in town is the **Historic Leakey Inn** (527 S. Hwy. 83, 830/232-5246, www.leakeyinn.com,

$84-149). The three-acre property includes 4 rooms and 11 cabins with free Wi-Fi, a lounge, a pool, a covered pavilion, barbecue grills, and picnic tables.

Kerrville

This charming Hill Country town (population 22,931) isn't quite as quaint as it used to be, but it's still worth visiting—especially for the arts scene. Artists, musicians, and writers are continually drawn to its rolling hills, cool breezes, and laid-back lifestyle.

KERRVILLE FOLK FESTIVAL

Kerrville is best known for the annual **Kerrville Folk Festival** (830/257-3600, www.kerrville-music.com), held for 18 days in late May-early June, which draws more than 100 singer-songwriters specializing in folk, Americana, country, and roots rock for three weeks of scheduled concerts and improvisational jams on stages and around campfires in the hills. Several big-name artists played Kerrville early in their careers, including Willie Nelson, Lyle Lovett, Robert Earl Keen, Lucinda Williams, and Nancy Griffith. Other nationally known artists like Arlo Guthrie, Judy Collins, and Janis Ian make regular appearances. While many people attend the evening main-stage shows, the soul of the festival is in the campgrounds, where artists and amateurs spend hours singing and strumming in guitar circles under the oaks and the starry sky.

MUSEUM OF WESTERN ART

One of the city's most impressive attractions is the **Museum of Western Art** (1550 Bandera Hwy., 830/896-2553, www.museumofwesternart.com, Tues.-Sat. 10am-4pm, $7 adults, $5 students). The building exterior is framed in hardy timbers and rugged limestone, and life-size bronze statues occupy the grounds. Inside, the Wild West comes to life through artwork featuring cowboys, cowgirls, Native Americans, and frontier settlers. A 5,000-volume library of art and history draws students and scholars, and the museum features distinguished artists in permanent and rotating exhibits following the tradition of Remington and Russell in their celebration of the Old West.

ACCOMMODATIONS

Kerrville offers a wide range of accommodations in guest ranches, river cabins, bed-and-breakfasts, hotels, motels, RV parks, and campgrounds. The **Kerrville Convention and Visitors Bureau** (2108 Sidney Baker St., 800/221-7958, www.kerrvilletexascvb.com, Mon.-Fri. 8:30am-5pm, Sat. 9am-3pm, Sun. 10am-3pm) offers a comprehensive list of options. The friendly staff is happy to lend a hand via phone or in person.

Luckenbach

Luckenbach (population 3, really) is perhaps best known as the subject of a classic 1977 Waylon Jennings tune "Luckenbach, Texas (Back to the Basics of Love)." The song painted a mythical picture of a simple place to unwind "with Waylon and Willie and the boys." Decades later, people are still making a pilgrimage to this tiny Hill Country town on Ranch Road 1376, about 52 miles (84 km) northwest of San Antonio and 75 miles (121 km) west of Austin.

The thriving "downtown" contains three buildings—a blacksmith shop, a rustic tavern and general store, and a historic dance hall. During the summer months, you'll find Texas troubadours gathered beneath the enormous oak trees picking tunes on their banjos and guitars. Even during the off-season winter months, there's music to be enjoyed in the 1849-era general store. Step back in time as you walk across the well-worn wood floors (holes are patched with old license plates) back to the bar, where local musicians regale visitors with entertaining tunes and tales. Belly up to the bar and order a Shiner Bock as you sit back and soak up this distinctively Texas experience.

Bigger shows are held in the historic Luckenbach Dance Hall several times a month, with themes such as Wacky Waylon Wednesday and the Thursday Songwriters' Circle. Tickets for these shows run $15-30. For more information, visit www.luckenbachtexas.com or call 830/997-3224.

Finding the town can be a challenge, since people often steal the "Luckenbach" signs pointing the way. From Fredericksburg, head east on U.S. 290 for 6 miles (9.7 km) to FM 1376, then head south for another 4 miles (6.4 km) to Luckenbach. Take the second left, Luckenbach Road.

San Antonio and South Texas

Most of South Texas is defined by its Tejano

heritage. It contains a scattering of German and other European settler communities, but the majority of South Texas culture is tied to
Mexico, including the legendary Alamo, constructed along with four
other San Antonio missions in the early 1700s to help expand Spain's
influence in the New World.

Despite the well-known phrase, people typically don't remember
the Alamo in its actual historical context. The 1836 siege at the Alamo
site, by then an abandoned mission complex, resulted in a loss for the
Texans, who subsequently used the defeat as a motivational rallying
cry ("Remember the Alamo!") in their victorious battle at San Jacinto
a month later.

San Antonio and
   Vicinity 172
Del Rio 208
Laredo. 214
Rio Grande Valley 222

Highlights

Look for ★ to find recommended sights, activities, dining, and lodging.

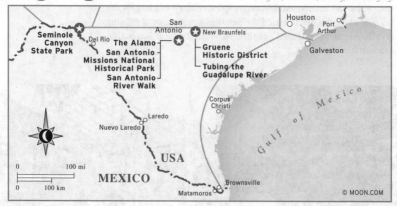

© MOON.COM

★ **Remember the Alamo.** This "Shrine of Texas Liberty" stands as a monument to the sacrifice of men who fought to their deaths for Texas (page 175).

★ **Bike through history,** riding between four magnificent colonial mission buildings. **San Antonio Missions National Historical Park** transports visitors to the mid-1700s and Spanish rule (page 176).

★ **Wander the San Antonio River Walk,** enjoying its impressive assortment of shops, restaurants, and nightclubs. You can even enjoy the river itself by boat (page 178).

★ **Hit the dance floor** at Texas's oldest operating dance hall. There's also a rustic restaurant and enough shopping to keep a family stocked with jewelry and T-shirts for years in the **Gruene Historic District** (page 203).

★ **Tube the Guadalupe River.** Kick back and let the lazy current carry you down a tree-lined waterway on a hot summer day (page 205).

★ **See ancient Native American rock art.** Some of the mesmerizing pictographs at **Seminole Canyon State Park** date back more than 4,000 years (page 208).

San Antonio and South Texas

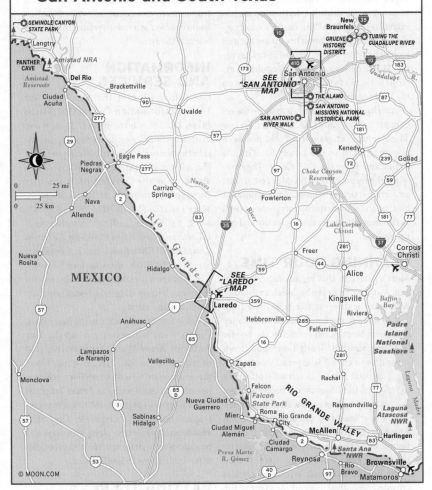

Settlers continued to descend on this sun-drenched tropical region throughout the 19th-20th centuries, many from Mexico, and others from ports on the Gulf Coast. The Mexican cowboys known as vaqueros had a cultural impact on the region that would ultimately affect the entire state's image. These professional ranch hands passed along their knowledge of roping, branding, and riding to the Anglos who arrived in droves in the mid-1800s and acquired vast amounts of South Texas ranch land. The evacuation of long-horn and other cattle from area ranches to San Antonio, Fort Worth, and markets to the north along the legendary Chisholm Trail was the largest migration of livestock in history.

Previous: San Antonio's River Walk; Seminole Canyon State Park; Mission San José

The urban but not quite cosmopolitan intrigue and abundant business opportunities in San Antonio made it a destination for immigrants in the 19th-20th centuries, but significant recent population booms are in cities along the Texas-Mexico border. Brownsville and McAllen have experienced population explosions thanks to the major factories built on the banks of the Rio Grande.

Also having an economic impact on the region are the snowbirds, a.k.a. winter Texans. These retirees migrate from cold northern climes to roost in the Lower Rio Grande Valley and along the Gulf Coast. They frequent the region's many Tex-Mex restaurants and are particularly fond of the abundant birding and ecotourism opportunities as well as the museums and historic sites throughout the region.

PLANNING YOUR TIME

Most visitors to this region either stay in San Antonio or near the Mexican border. Although the three- to five-hour drive from San Antonio to the Lower Rio Grande Valley may seem lengthy, experiencing the border culture is worth it. South Texas food (from sopapillas to citrus) is especially outstanding. Now that Mexico is virtually off-limits to travelers, the closest many people will get to a genuine Mexican meal is along the border.

Allow at least two or three days in San Antonio. The city's friendly atmosphere draws visitors into its laid-back vibe. The Alamo and the nearby River Walk are must-sees despite being heavily touristed. Weekdays are less crowded; save the weekend for visiting the missions, the Institute of Texan Cultures, and the San Fernando Cathedral, or take an extra day to enjoy the amusement at SeaWorld or Six Flags.

In the San Antonio area, the historic charm of New Braunfels offers a nice destination for a day trip, especially if there's a show at Gruene Hall. Otherwise, the pleasant yet small city of Del Rio is a more ambitious day trip, about 2.5 hours away.

For a taste of border culture, spend several days in the Valley, especially Brownsville and McAllen. Brownsville offers the history and traditions of two countries, while McAllen features newer attractions related to ecotourism and the arts.

INFORMATION AND SERVICES

Get information at the **San Antonio Visitor Information Center** (317 Alamo Plaza, 210/207-6700 or 800/447-3372, www.visitsanantonio.com, daily 9am-5pm), inside the historic Crockett building between the Alamo and the River Walk. You can also drop by the **Convention & Visitors Bureau's corporate offices** (203 S. St. Mary's St., 2nd Fl., 210/207-6700 or 800/447-3372, daily 8am-5:30pm). Another useful resource is the **Greater San Antonio Chamber of Commerce** (602 E. Commerce St., 210/229-2100, www.sachamber.org), which offers a comprehensive website with extensive listings of hotels, restaurants, attractions, and events.

For information specific to the River Walk and its many businesses, contact the **San Antonio River Walk Association** (110 Broadway, Suite 500, 210/227-4262, www.thesanantonioriverwalk.com). For a regional perspective, check with the **Texas Tropical Trail Region** (361/592-4603, www.texas-tropicaltrail.com) in Kingsville. They offer an informed perspective along with maps and brochures on heritage tourism and other cultural destinations in South Texas.

GETTING THERE AND AROUND

Travelers arrive in South Texas by plane at San Antonio airport, and there are smaller regional airports in Del Rio, Laredo, and Brownsville. San Antonio and the midsize cities have bus and taxi services; otherwise, travelers navigate by car. San Antonio's freeway system was well designed in anticipation of increased traffic, unlike other cities (ahem, Austin). As a result, rush hour traffic isn't a nightmare.

Two Days in San Antonio

DAY 1

Ideally, you've spent the night at a hotel near the Alamo and River Walk, so you can visit before the lines get too long. Despite its touristy reputation, **the Alamo** has a one-of-a-kind story. Afterward, stroll along the River Walk and have lunch at the **Esquire Tavern.** Work off your full belly by renting a **Bike Share** and hitting the **San Antonio Missions Trail** for an afternoon of exercise, history, and scenery. For dinner, head back to the River Walk for cocktails and a hearty plate of nachos at **Acenar,** then meander along the river to **Casa Rio,** where you can enjoy a traditional Tex-Mex combo plate dinner on the riverbank. Wrap up your evening at **Alamo Plaza** for an ice cream cone, which you can enjoy while sitting on a wall in front of the dramatically lit Alamo.

DAY 2

Head 1 mile (1.6 km) west of the River Walk to experience another historic aspect of San Antonio—the Main Plaza district. Start off at the **San Fernando Cathedral,** then head to the 1730 **Spanish Governor's Palace.** Sample some enchiladas at **Mi Tierra,** then take a **Go Rio** water taxi to the **Museum Reach** for an afternoon of culture at the **San Antonio Museum of Art** and **McNay Art Museum.** Enjoy a local beer and appetizers at **Southerleigh Fine Food and Brewery** in the Historic Pearl Brewery District, then head back downtown for a marvelously meaty meal at **Maverick's.** If you feel like dancing off dinner, head out to **Floore Country Store** for some traditional Texas-style two-stepping.

The **San Antonio International Airport** (SAT, 9800 Airport Blvd., 210/207-3411, www.sanantonio.gov) is a small but good-looking facility and is easy to navigate. About 12 miles (19.3 km) north of downtown, the airport has flights on 10 U.S. and 3 Mexican airlines.

Most travelers choose use a ride-share or rent a car to explore beyond downtown. The major rental companies at the airport include Alamo (of course), Budget, Enterprise, and Dollar. It's a straight shot down U.S. 281 to downtown, which takes 20-30 minutes, depending on the time of day.

For those not using a ride-share, taxis cost about $40 and take about 20-30 minutes between the airport and downtown. Taxi stations are outside the airport terminals, and unlike most cities, up to four people can share a cab for the same fare without paying additional per-person or luggage fees.

Also unique to San Antonio is the respectable public transportation system, considered efficient, inexpensive, and accessible. **VIA Metropolitan Transit** (210/362-2020, www. viainfo.net, from $1.20) runs 100 bus lines and a downtown streetcar service.

A unique way to get around town is via water taxi on the river with **Go Rio Cruises** (202 E. Nueva St., 210/227-4746, www.goriocruises.com, $13.50 adults, $10.50 seniors, $7.50 ages 1-5), which specializes in tours but can also arrange for transportation. Shuttle tickets ($19.50) allow passengers to get off and on the shuttle at their pace, throughout the downtown and museum reaches, for the entire day.

San Antonio is accessible by **Amtrak** (350 Hoefgen St., 800/872-7245) *Sunset Limited* and *Texas Eagle* trains at the depot on the east side of downtown, and on intercity buses run by **Greyhound** (500 N. St. Mary's St., 210/270-5868) at the downtown bus station.

Smaller airports in this region include the **Laredo International Airport** (LRD, 5210 Bob Bullock Loop, Laredo, 956/795-2000, www.ci.laredo.tx.us), with daily flights to Dallas-Fort Worth, Houston, Las Vegas, and other cities on three major airlines. **Del Rio International Airport** (DRT, 1104

W. 10th St., Del Rio, 830/774-8538, www.cityofdelrio.com) has American Airlines flights to Houston several times daily, and the **Valley International Airport** (HRL, 3002 Heritage Way, Harlingen, 956/430-8600, www.flythevalley.com) has Southwest, United, and American as the main airline carriers.

San Antonio and Vicinity

San Antonio is an internationally legendary city whose beginnings predate the founding of the United States by half a century. The Alamo is its cultural icon, and the city's missions represent a fascinating era of Spanish colonialism. Add the lure of the River Walk, amusement parks, and the city's welcoming lack of pretense, and it's no surprise that San Antonio regularly appears on top-10 lists of favorite travel destinations.

San Antonio (population 1,532,233) is the seventh-largest city in the country, but that's not evident to visitors savoring long lunches at downtown patio cafés alongside casually dressed office workers. Nor is it obvious when you're sitting atop the Tower of the Americas, surveying the modest skyline, devoid of egocentric glass monuments to power and prosperity. It's certainly not noticeable in the genuine greetings and friendliness you'll encounter around every corner.

Ideally suited for a getaway, San Antonio has no stressful hustle and bustle, just a steady flow of activity amid historic buildings and modern conveniences. Many visitors come on a pilgrimage to see the Alamo, even though its historical significance is not widely known. The nearby River Walk is one of the top destinations in the state, but its vibrant energy doesn't represent the soul of this city.

The city's origins are tied to the 1718 San Antonio de Bexar Presidio (fort) and the nearby village of San Fernando de Bexar, chartered in 1731 by a group of people from the Canary Islands. several of San Antonio's most significant structures were constructed around this time on two of the major plazas, Military and Main. The Spanish Governor's Palace was completed in 1749, and, 10 years later, the San Fernando de Bexar Church was built around the corner.

San Antonio became a hub of activity during the Texas Revolution and was the site of several notable clashes, including the 1835 Siege of Bexar and the memorable 1836 Battle of the Alamo. Once Texas entered the Union in 1845, migrants arrived in droves from the eastern United States and European nations, mainly via the port of Galveston. Many of the newcomers were in the cattle industry, and aspects of city life soon revolved around agriculture, since most early trail drives went through San Antonio. Ranching was facilitated on the city's main plazas at banks, saloons, mercantile stores, and fancy hotels like the Menger, St. Anthony, and Gunter. The more prosperous ranchers had homes in the tony King William District just south of downtown.

The cowboys who gathered at the plazas and stockyards were ambassadors of San Antonio's multicultural makeup, since their skills and equipment were based on the vaqueros who drove cattle and worked the ranches in Mexico before Anglos started arriving in Texas. From branding to roping to riding, the Mexican influence on ranching in Texas was profound, and in San Antonio, the impact reached beyond the barbed wire.

San Antonio flourished in the late 1800s-early 1900s thanks to the railroads and highway systems that kept the economy strong with agricultural trade and the military bases that proliferated in the area. By the middle of the 20th century, the city had gained a reputation as a major travel destination due to its moderate climate, dynamic history, and appealing mid-continent location for conventions.

San Antonio

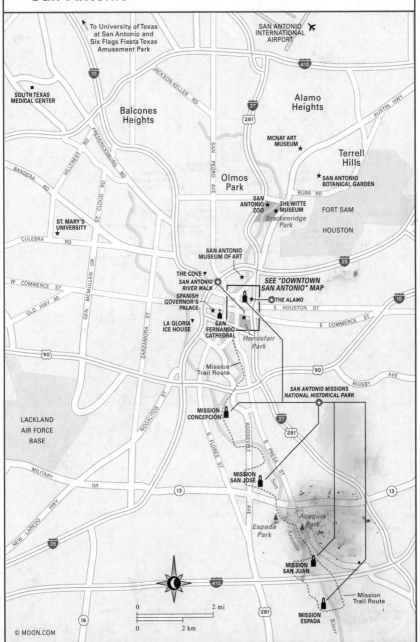

To University of Texas at San Antonio and Six Flags Fiesta Texas Amusement Park

SAN ANTONIO INTERNATIONAL AIRPORT

SOUTH TEXAS MEDICAL CENTER

JACKSON-KELLER RD

Balcones Heights

Alamo Heights

AUSTIN HWY

MCNAY ART MUSEUM

Terrell Hills

Olmos Park

SAN ANTONIO BOTANICAL GARDEN

BURR RD

FORT SAM

ST. MARY'S UNIVERSITY

SAN ANTONIO ZOO

THE WITTE MUSEUM

HOUSTON

Brackenridge Park

CULEBRA RD

SAN ANTONIO MUSEUM OF ART

SEE "DOWNTOWN SAN ANTONIO" MAP

THE COVE

W COMMERCE ST

SAN ANTONIO RIVER WALK

THE ALAMO

OLD HWY 90

SPANISH GOVERNOR'S PALACE

E HOUSTON ST

LA GLORIA ICE HOUSE

SAN FERNANDO CATHEDRAL

E COMMERCE ST

Hemisfair Park

Mission Trail Route

RIGSBY AVE

SAN ANTONIO MISSIONS NATIONAL HISTORICAL PARK

LACKLAND AIR FORCE BASE

MISSION CONCEPCIÓN

MILITARY DR

NEW LAREDO HWY

MISSION SAN JOSE

Espada Park

Acequia Park

MISSION SAN JUAN

Mission Trail Route

MISSION ESPADA

0   2 mi

0   2 km

© MOON.COM

Downtown San Antonio

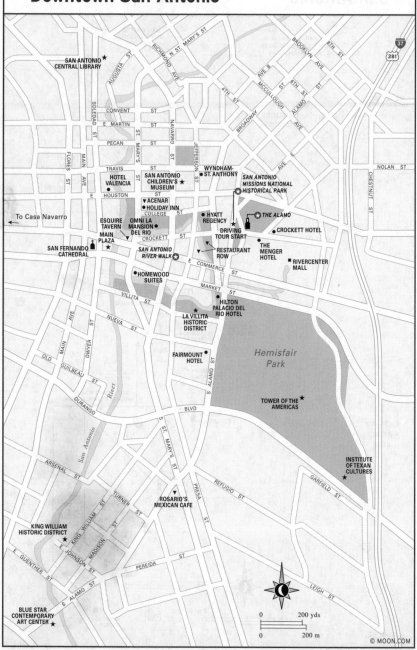

SAN ANTONIO
CENTRAL LIBRARY ★

RICHMOND AVE

N ST. MARY'S ST

AUGUSTA ST

4TH ST

BROOKLYN AVE

7TH ST

AVE. B

MCCULLOUGH AVE

6TH ST

ALAMO

37
281

SOLEDAD ST

CONVENT ST

E MARTIN ST

NAVARRO ST

BROADWAY

PECAN ST

ST. MARY'S ST

JEFFERSON ST

AVE

NOLAN ST

FLORES ST

MAIN AVE

TRAVIS ST

E HOUSTON ST

HOTEL
VALENCIA ●

WYNDHAM-
ST. ANTHONY ●

SAN ANTONIO
CHILDREN'S
MUSEUM ★

COLLEGE ST

SAN ANTONIO
MISSIONS NATIONAL
HISTORICAL PARK ★

CHESTNUT ST

To Casa Navarro ←

ESQUIRE
TAVERN ●

▼ ACENAR
● HOLIDAY INN

OMNI LA
MANSION
DEL RIO ●

CROCKETT ST

HYATT
REGENCY ●

DRIVING
TOUR START ★

★ THE ALAMO

CROCKETT HOTEL ●

MAIN
PLAZA ★

SAN FERNANDO
CATHEDRAL

SAN ANTONIO
RIVER WALK ✦

▼ RESTAURANT
ROW

E COMMERCE ST

THE
MENGER
HOTEL ●

RIVERCENTER
MALL ■

● HOMEWOOD
SUITES

VILLITA ST

MARKET ST

NUEVA ST

LA VILLITA
HISTORIC
DISTRICT ★

HILTON
PALACIO DEL
RIO HOTEL ●

MAIN AVE

DWYER ST

OLD GUILBEAU ST

River

FAIRMOUNT
HOTEL ●

S ALAMO ST

Hemisfair
Park

DURANGO BLVD

San Antonio River

ARSENAL ST

S ST. MARY'S ST

TOWER OF THE
AMERICAS ★

INSTITUTE
OF TEXAN
CULTURES ★

GARFIELD ST

TURNER ST

KING WILLIAM ST

ROSARIO'S
MEXICAN CAFE ▼

PRESA ST

REFUGIO ST

KING WILLIAM
HISTORIC DISTRICT ★

E GUENTHER ST

JOHNSON ST

MADISON ST

PEREIDA ST

LEIGH ST

S ALAMO ST

BLUE STAR
CONTEMPORARY
ART CENTER ★

0   200 yds

0   200 m

© MOON.COM

ORIENTATION

San Antonio is an ancient city by Texas standards, with Spanish mission structures dating to the early 1700s and a dense downtown boasting centuries-old homes, plazas, and commercial buildings. It's worth exploring beyond the Alamo and River Walk to discover the city's many cultural charms.

Alamo Plaza and River Walk Area

This is where the action is, and it's possible to spend a few days in this part of town without tiring of the history, culture, and people-watching. Consider booking a historic hotel like the Menger or the Crockett, adjacent to the Alamo, and walk to the shops and restaurants along the River Walk and nearby Market Square.

King William District and Southtown

Just south of downtown, this area is ideal for exploring on foot or by car. In the 25-block King William District, stately and ornate Victorian, Greek Revival, and Italianate homes stand on pleasant tree-lined streets. Take a walking tour to soak up the late-1800s architecture, or enjoy the scenery from an air-conditioned vehicle if it's a sweltering summer day. The surrounding Southtown boasts funky boutiques, art galleries, and restaurants.

Midtown

This centrally located part of San Antonio is close to all the action. Although it's primarily residential, Midtown offers a nice option to soak up the local culture of the historic homes and businesses. Hot spots in Midtown include the recently restored Pearl Brewery district and picturesque Trinity University.

Deco District

Northwest of downtown, this up-and-coming neighborhood is becoming a favorite destination for unique shopping and dining. With commercial and residential buildings reflecting the city's early-1900s art deco period, this area anchored by Fredericksburg Road boasts distinctive art galleries and trendy Tex-Mex restaurants.

Alamo Heights

Technically an independent municipality, Alamo Heights is the upscale part of San Antonio with high-end restaurants and fancy hotels. The enormous homes are visual attractions, and the top-notch clothing boutiques, fashionable dining options, and tony nightclubs offer a slice of glitz in Alamo City.

SIGHTS

TOP EXPERIENCE

★ The Alamo

The Alamo (300 Alamo Plaza, 210/225-1391, www.thealamo.org, fall-spring daily 9am-5:30pm, summer daily 9am-7pm, free, guided tours $20 in advance via the website) is referred to as the "Shrine of Texas Liberty": Visitors are asked to remove their hats and refrain from taking photos out of respect. If that word conjures up a sacred fortress drawing faithful devotees, the Alamo certainly qualifies. Once visitors get past the site's unexpected urban setting—unlike in textbook sketches, the Alamo isn't in its rustic frontier-era isolated state—they can appreciate its historical significance. A major "reimagining" of Alamo Plaza is getting underway in 2020, so keep an eye out for road closures and construction near the site.

The Alamo's historical significance is explained in a 20-minute presentation inside the main building. Without lecturing, Alamo experts discuss the complex series of events that led to the infamous battle. Established in 1718 as a mission to spread Catholicism and protect Spain's colonial interests, it had subsequent incarnations as a hospital and cavalry post. In March 1836 the Alamo siege saw thousands of Mexican troops descend on San Antonio, raising a red flag of "no quarter" (no mercy), and a few hundred Texans and

Tejanos fought to the death "in the cause of liberty and humanity."

The Alamo site was in bad shape in 1905 when the Texas legislature entrusted the care and maintenance of the grounds to the Daughters of the Republic of Texas. Later the Alamo's stewardship transferred to the State of Texas, resulting in some grand plans for the future. The site's website outlines the coming vision for the property, including the connection with pop music's Phil Collins and his collection of Alamo artifacts.

In addition to the famous mission building, the grounds include the **Long Barrack Museum** (closed due to construction in early 2020), a lush courtyard with a well dating to the mission era (1724-1793), an informative timeline displayed on large outdoor panels, and a jam-packed gift shop befitting a world tourism destination.

★ San Antonio Missions National Historical Park

The extraordinary San Antonio missions stand among urban scenery as the **San Antonio Missions National Historical Park** (various locations, 210/534-8875, www. nps.gov/saan, daily 9am-5pm, free). The five structures, including the Alamo, serve as testament to the role Texas played in history during the early 18th century. One of the best ways to explore the missions is by bike—the sites are loosely connected by a **San Antonio Missions Trail** (map at www.sanantonioriver. org), and rental bikes are available at **Bike Share** (www.sanantonio.bcycle.com) stations throughout downtown. By helping expand Spain's religious and secular influence in the New World, the missions became a focal point for European powers and their quest to claim to the land that would eventually become Texas.

The first to be developed was San Antonio de Valero (the Alamo), in 1718. It went on to infamy and is therefore designated as its own separate historic site. The remaining missions—Concepción, Espada, San José, and San Juan—were established 1720-1731 and offer a window to a past that predates Texas's typical Main Street buildings and Victorian homes.

In 1690 Spain established six missions in East Texas to establish its presence in the New World and convert Native Americans to Catholicism. Plans were made to construct new missions along a natural stopping point on a meandering Rio Grande, where the Spanish gathered to celebrate the feast of Saint Anthony (San Antonio).

The legendary Alamo

Missions Accomplished

San Antonio's five magnificent Spanish missions are unlike any other historic structure in Texas, representing a bygone era when Native Americans still occupied the land and European powers were staking claims in the New World. The missions:

SAN ANTONIO DE VALERO

Now known as **The Alamo,** this mission was founded in 1718 and was the first established on the San Antonio River. Like the other missions, it served to protect the interests of Spain and spread Catholicism; it is best known as the fort that was attacked during Texas's War for Independence from Mexico in 1836.

CONCEPCIÓN

The mission **Nuestra Señora de la Purísima Concepción** was relocated from East Texas in 1731, and the church appears as it did in the mid-1700s, when it served as the mission's center of religious activity. Once covered with colorful geometric patterns on its exterior and interior surfaces, they have long since faded.

Mission Espada

ESPADA

The oldest of the original East Texas missions was founded in 1690 as San Francisco de los Tejas. In 1731 the compound was moved to the San Antonio River and renamed **San Antonio de la Espada.** This mission's church appears almost as remote today as it did in the mid-1700s since it's the farthest south from the urban environs of San Antonio.

SAN JOSÉ

Known as the "Queen of the Missions," this compound's enviable size and organization gave it a reputation as being a model of mission life. San José was a major social center, featuring distinctive architecture and plentiful pastures.

SAN JUAN

Mission San Juan Capistrano was originally established in East Texas as San José de los Nazonis. In 1731 it was relocated to the San Antonio River and renamed San Juan. Decades later, it became a major regional supplier of agricultural produce thanks to its rich farmlands.

Meanwhile, the missions farther north were struggling with drought and disease, so several relocated to the San Antonio River valley in 1731. The missions thrived in the 1740s-1780s, and Native American "recruits" hunted, built structures, gardened, cooked, and made soap. Although they indoctrinated as Catholics and adopted many Spanish customs, the Native Americans continued practicing their own traditions, typically under the pretext of Catholic festivals.

By the late 1700s, mission life became more difficult, with Apache and Comanche people pushing back on Spanish territorial claims and political maneuvers in Europe threatening the missions' roles. To support his military ventures in Europe, Napoleon Bonaparte's signed a treaty that resulted in the Louisiana Purchase, signaling the end for the missions.

The missions were in decline for other reasons—European diseases had decimated much of the Native American population, and successful colonization made the missions' original objectives obsolete. In 1824 the missions were secularized, the land was redistributed, and the chapels in the complexes were transferred to the secular clergy.

★ San Antonio River Walk

It's easy for people to dismiss the **San Antonio River Walk** (210/227-4262, www. thesanantonioriverwalk.com) as a crowded tourist attraction, but there's a reason people flock to this location: It is a genuinely festive environment punctuated by laughter, yucca plants, and riverboats packed with people wearing silly hats and sunglasses. The immediate access to so many different types of authentic high-quality Texas food alone is worth the visit.

The city has made efforts to extend the River Walk beyond the core area to allow exploration of additional cultural resources. The Museum Reach encompasses a few extra miles north of the city to allow walkers, joggers, and cyclists to visit the San Antonio Museum of Art, Witte Museum, and the Pearl Brewery district. Discover the Mission Reach section just south of downtown, offering access to the historic King William District and four missions in the San Antonio Missions National Historical Park.

The main portion of the River Walk is a scenic horseshoe-shaped stretch of the San Antonio River, flanked by tropical foliage, cobblestone walkways, and a fascinating collection of shops, restaurants, and nightclubs. The whole blissfully detached scene exists a level below the busy streets and sidewalks used by businesspeople, allowing River Walkers to operate separately.

For those looking to stretch their legs beyond the main loop, the River Walk extends throughout downtown, linking many of the city's main attractions, including Alamo Plaza, La Villita, HemisFair Park, and Rivercenter. The River Walk also plays a major role in the city's annual Fiesta San Antonio, with a river parade featuring flower-bedecked "floats" that actually float on the water.

The modern-day version of the River Walk began in 1961, when one of the companies responsible for designing Disneyland drafted a plan recommending the buildings be developed with riverside access in an early Texas or Mexican colonial style. The city developed a River Walk District, and the parks department completed a major landscape project by adding 17,000 assorted trees, shrubs, vines, and ground cover. Next came the hotels, which brought pedestrian traffic that boosted the restaurants and retail establishments along the 3 miles (4.8 km) of scenic riverside walkways. Before long, word spread about this distinctive attraction, annually drawing hundreds of thousands of visitors, conventioneers and families, to its tree-lined banks.

One of the most popular ways to experience the River Walk is via boat. To get on board, contact **Go Rio** (202 E. Nueva St., 210/227-4746, www.goriocruises.com, $13.50 adults, $10.50 seniors, $7.50 ages 1-5). The boat rides are about 30 minutes and include a narrated description of sites along the San Antonio River. Visit the website for boat stations and ticket counters.

Institute of Texan Cultures

The gargantuan 50,000-square-foot structure just east of downtown is the magnificent **Institute of Texan Cultures** (801 E. Durango Blvd., 210/458-2300, www.texancultures.com, Mon.-Sat. 9am-5pm, Sun. noon-5pm, $12 adults, $9 seniors and ages 6-17). The building's main ground-floor exhibit reveals that Texans are a remarkably diverse bunch, with cultural and ethnic backgrounds from all corners of the globe. Although more than 250 groups exist in the Lone Star State, just 26 are showcased in the exhibits. A large sign

---

1: San Antonio Museum of Art **2:** SeaWorld of Texas **3:** San Antonio River Walk

announcing each group's name hangs from the ceiling, and the display cases below feature objects and artifacts representing the culture, with a focus on its Texas connection. An enormous globe at the entryway conveys the message that Texas is a melting pot.

The institute offers other resources in the halls above and beyond the massive main exhibit space. They include a research library and offices related to the annual Texas Folklife Festival, an immensely entertaining multicultural event held the second weekend in June, with international food, music, dance, arts, and crafts to celebrate Texas's unique heritage. The 22-acre institute is also home to a museum store and a living-history area known as the Back 40.

San Antonio Museum of Art

A world-class facility, **San Antonio Museum of Art** (200 W. Jones Ave., 210/978-8100, www.samuseum.org, Tues. 10am-9pm, Wed.-Sun. 10am-5pm, $20 adults, $17 seniors, $12 students and military, free Tues. 4pm-9pm and Sun. 10am-noon) is housed in the historic Lone Star Brewery building on the River Walk's Museum Reach and contains artwork from around the world.

Best known for its colossal holdings in Latin American art, in the Nelson A. Rockefeller Center for Latin American Art (the former vice president provided his extensive collection to the museum), the facility includes an overview of 3,000 years of art. The museum's pre-Columbian collection has stone, ceramic, and metal objects as well as more recent works from Maya, Aztec, Zapotec, and Inca cultures.

Another noteworthy section is the Egyptian gallery, where an enormous statue of the goddess Sekhmet from 1350 BC greets visitors. Ceramics and stone objects testify to the longevity of the artwork—these beautiful objects were crafted by human hands more than 3,000 years ago. The fascination continues with the museum's remarkable Greek and Roman art.

McNay Art Museum

A 5-mile (8 km) jaunt north of downtown is the remarkable **McNay Art Museum** (6000 N. New Braunfels Ave., 210/824-5368, www.mcnayart.org, Wed. and Fri. 10am-6pm, Thurs. 10am-9pm, Sat. 10am-5pm, Sun. noon-5pm, $20 adults, $15 seniors, students, and military, free under age 13). Ohio-born heiress Marion Koogler McNay moved to San Antonio in 1926 and lived in the 24-room Spanish Revival mansion that would become the core of the museum. She collected 19th-20th-century European and American paintings and Southwestern art, ultimately leaving her 700 works, house, and surrounding 23 acres to establish "the first museum of modern art in Texas."

The McNay opened in 1954 and has expanded to 20,000 works, including medieval and Renaissance art, and an impressive collection of 19th-21st-century European and American paintings, sculptures, and photographs. The 19th-20th-century paintings are notable; don't be surprised to encounter a Picasso, Cézanne, Matisse, Van Gogh, or Pissarro. Stroll the magnificent lush Spanish-influenced courtyard, and check ahead for temporary exhibits.

King William Historic District

To get a sense of San Antonio's high society at the turn of the 20th century, take a walking tour through the **King William Historic District,** just south of downtown on the east side of the San Antonio River. Stately and ornate Victorian, Greek Revival, and Italianate homes stand on pleasant tree-lined streets in a 25-square-block area, one of the first Texas neighborhoods to be listed on the National Register of Historic Places. On a hot day the enormous trees provide a shady canopy over most streets. Get a guide brochure at the **San Antonio Conservation Society** (107 King William St., 210/224-6163, www.saconservation.org, Mon.-Fri. 8:30am-4:30pm), at the northern edge of the neighborhood.

Although a majority of the district's houses are private homes or bed-and-breakfasts, two sites are open for tours. The 1859 **Guenther House** (205 E. Guenther St., 210/227-1061, www.guenther-house.com, Mon.-Sat. 8am-4pm, Sun. 8am-3pm, free) is the outstanding home of the family that founded Pioneer Flour Mills—you can't miss the gigantic factory behind it, with Pioneer on the tower. The house features a small informative museum of milling history and a popular restaurant. A block north is **Steves Homestead** (509 King William St., 210/225-5924, daily 10am-3:30pm, $10 over age 12, $8 seniors), a stunning three-story 1876 mansion. Guided tours showcase the home's ornate furnishings as well as the carriage house, servants quarters, and the city's first indoor swimming pool.

San Fernando Cathedral

The magnificent **San Fernando Cathedral** (115 Main Plaza, 210/227-1297, www.sfcathedral.org, Mon.-Fri. 9am-5pm, Sat. 8am-7pm, Sun. 8am-6:30pm) was set up in 1731 by a group of Canary Islands families and has been a centerpiece of San Antonio ever since. This stunning building went through several incarnations before the current Gothic Revival construction in 1873. The enormous cathedral has a distinctive European feel, with lofty arches, a gilded 24-foot-tall (7-m) altar, and gigantic stained-glass windows. People gather at the church throughout the day for tours, religious activities, or to sit in the serene surroundings. Not exclusively a Catholic church, it bills itself as "a center of unity and harmony," drawing than 5,000 parishioners to mass every week.

Spanish Governor's Palace

Just around the corner from the cathedral is the circa-1730 **Spanish Governor's Palace** (105 Military Plaza, 210/224-0601, www.spanishgovernorspalace.org, Tues.-Sat. 9am-5pm, Sun. 10am-5pm, $5 adults, $3 military, seniors, and ages 7-13), which served as the headquarters and residence of the presidio of San Antonio de Bexar's captain, the ranking representative of the king of Spain in the absence of the governor. The National Geographic Society called the palace "the most beautiful building in San Antonio," and its three-foot-thick (1-m) stuccoed stone walls are striking, as are its eclectic mix of historic furniture and artifacts. The palace's highlight by far is the magnificent courtyard, a natural patio with a canopy of live oaks stretching over lush tropical plants. Chirping birds, a soothing fountain, and gentle breezes transport visitors to an oasis far from the surrounding urban environment.

SeaWorld of Texas

When you need a break from Texas history, **SeaWorld** (10500 SeaWorld Dr., 800/700-7786, www.seaworld.com, hours vary by season, from $70) is a 250-acre perfect destination on a hot summer day, with water rides, water shows, and water games to keep the family entertained and refreshed. The main attraction has shifted from Shamu the performing whale to *Orca Encounter,* which focuses more on education.

One of the park's most popular summertime attractions is the Lost Lagoon area, a mini water park featuring a giant wave machine, a mellow tube ride, and several twisty waterslides. Kids ages 1-6 will love the Happy Harbor, a small area in the center of the park with several rides, a large ship festooned with climbing and crawling features, an infant play area, and a water zone with every kind of soaking device imaginable.

Adults can have fun too by experiencing SeaWorld's water rides, such as Journey to Atlantis, and roller coasters like the Texas Stingray, and Riptide Rescue. The Wave Breaker Rescue Coaster has the perfect level of excitement for people who like roller coasters but don't love them, and the Steel Eel and Great White are for hard-core coaster lovers. Be sure to smile sweetly and hold back your lunch at the bottom of the first big hill, since a camera captures everyone's expressions for souvenir keepsakes. The Rio Loco river ride gets you completely wet from cruising under the waterfall. If it's a cool day, there are

Talking 'Bout a Revolution

Presidio La Bahia in Goliad

The Texas Revolution of 1836 still looms large in the hearts and travel plans of many Texans. The triumphant war for independence from Mexico created the Republic of Texas, which lasted a decade (1836-1845) until statehood; its legacy still survives at historic sites east of San Antonio.

About 90 miles (145 km) southeast of the city in the town of Goliad is the stunning **Presidio La Bahia** (217 U.S. 183, 361/645-3752, www.presidiolabahia.org, daily 9am-4:45pm, $5 adults, $4.50 seniors, $2 children), which dates to 1721, when an original fort on a Gulf Coast bay *(la bahía)* was established. On March 27, 1836, Texas colonel James Fannin and 300 of his men were in the site's chapel after surrendering to the Mexican army. Under order of Mexican general Santa Anna, the men were executed. Known as the Goliad Massacre, the event roused the Texas troops, who used the rallying cry "Remember Goliad!" in their decisive victory at the Battle of San Jacinto.

These stories are told in exhibits throughout the fortress-like presidio building, with impressive stone walls complete with turrets and cannons, a traditional courtyard, and reportedly haunted guest chambers; if you can rouse the courage, contact the site about spending the night here.

A few hours northeast is the Texas Historical Commission's **San Felipe de Austin State Historic Site** (220 2nd St., San Felipe, 979/885-2181, www.visitsanfelipedeaustin.com, daily 9am-5pm, $10 adults, $8 seniors and veterans, $5 children). San Felipe was founded in 1824, and the following year it was second in population to San Antonio. San Felipe was the political, social, and economic center of Stephen F. Austin's colony. Today, visitors can get a sense of life in San Felipe at the site's impressive new museum, which features enormous state-of-the-art touch screen displays and fascinating exhibits with rare artifacts.

body-size dryers at the exit gate to un-drench you; it's worth the $5.

Of course, animals are a featured attraction at SeaWorld, particularly in exhibits and shows featuring sea lions and dolphins. A new feature called Animal Encounters allows guests to swim alongside a dolphin, beluga whale, or sea lion. The penguin habitat,

with its replicated Antarctic environment, is especially fascinating. Throughout the park families will find midway-style games, snack stands, and gift shops.

Casa Navarro State Historic Site

The smooth whitewashed stucco blanketing

Casa Navarro State Historic Site (228 S. Laredo St., 210/226-4801, www.visitcasanavarro.com, Tues.-Sat. 10am-5pm, Sun. noon-5pm, $4 adults, $3 students) doesn't quite mesh with the surrounding urban environment. Once inside, however, this cozy home of Tejano patriot José Antonio Navarro radiates a charm not found beyond the house's thick adobe walls. Named a National Historic Landmark, Navarro's home reflects his simple yet refined environment, including interpretive panels, Texas law books, and other period furnishings offering insight about his family and city during the mid-late 1800s.

Most of the home was constructed circa 1848, and its acquisition by the Texas Historical Commission has helped raise its profile. Navarro's service to Texas is legendary—he served in the legislature under Mexico, the Republic of Texas, and the state of Texas, and he signed the Texas Declaration of Independence in 1836, representing San Antonio. Most historians consider Navarro the first Tejano to write about Texas history. Enjoy interactive features such as tablet games and exhibits, streamlined interpretation, and even a multisensory feature that includes alluring smells of food cooking in a traditional kitchen.

The Witte Museum

The **Witte Museum** (3801 Broadway St., 210/357-1900, www.wittemuseum.org, Mon. and Wed.-Sat. 10am-5pm, Tues. 10am-8pm, Sun. noon-5pm, $14 adults, $13 seniors, $10 ages 4-11) focuses on South Texas history and science and features impressive permanent and rotating galleries and hands-on exhibits. This is an ideal place to bring the kids—they're omnipresent, especially during school hours—to learn about Texas culture. Dinosaurs take up a big portion of the ground floor, along with other animals and nature. The 2nd floor is devoted to permanent exhibits, including displays related to mummies and the 4,000-year-old rock art of Texas's Lower Pecos region. Outside are several historic buildings adjacent to the San Antonio River.

La Villita Historic District

The downtown **La Villita Historic District** (418 Villita St., 210/207-8614, www.lavillitasanantonio.com, most shops daily 10am-6pm) reflects the Spanish, European, and Anglo influences that helped shape San Antonio's history. Once the site of a Coahuiltecan village, La Villita subsequently thrived as a residential area containing Mexican houses of caliche block or stucco-covered brick and German (and later Swiss and French) structures before the neighborhood deteriorated into a run-down barrio in the early 1900s. In 1939, La Villita was restored by the city, and following another major renovation in the early 1980s, the neighborhood now houses scores of tourist-friendly boutiques, art galleries, and restaurants. One of the most popular attractions is the historic Little Church, a 19th-century stone chapel that frequently hosts weddings and festival activities.

San Antonio Central Library

The **San Antonio Central Library** (600 Soledad St., 210/207-2500, www.mysapl.org, Mon.-Thurs. 9am-9pm, Fri.-Sat. 9am-5pm, Sun. 11am-5pm), known around town as "Big Red," is the color of a red enchilada and enormous at 240,000 square feet. It has become an attraction and is considered one of the city's most important architectural accomplishments. On the site of an old Sears department store, the six-floor library was designed by renowned Mexican architect Ricardo Legorreta, who used natural light, color, water, and some unexpected angles and sight lines to create this urban cathedral of knowledge. The library also features an intriguing mural by San Antonio artist Jesse Treviño, depicting a slice of life in the city during World War II.

Six Flags Fiesta Texas Amusement Park

A big draw for family fun is **Six Flags Fiesta Texas** (I-10 W. and Loop 1604, 210/697-5050, www.sixflags.com, late May-late Aug.

¿Cómo Se Llama?

In Spanish classes across the United States, one of the first things most students learn is the question *"¿Cómo se llama?"* (What's your name?). The words translate literally as "What do you call yourself?"—a question many Mexican Americans are asking themselves these days thanks to the varying categorical terminology being used.

San Antonio's former Museo Alameda has been credited as a media source to help clear up some of the confusion. Although Alameda representatives claimed it's ultimately up to the individual to determine what they want to be called, they offered the following definitions, with the stipulation that ethnic identifiers vary by region:

- **Mexican American:** A U.S. citizen of Mexican descent whose roots trace to the racial mixture that resulted from the 16th-century conquest of Mexico.

- **Hispanic:** A term created by the U.S. Census Bureau to denote people of various Latin American and Spanish origins.

- **Latino:** A U.S. resident with cultural and historical ties to Latin America and the Caribbean.

- **Chicano:** A generational designation rooted in the idea of self-determination. The term arose from the civil rights movement in the 1960s.

- **Tejano:** A Texan of Mexican descent.

Mon.-Sat. 10am-9pm, Sun. 11am-9pm, weekend hours vary Sept.-May, $84, $70 under 48 inches tall). Most of the rides and attractions at this 200-acre facility are standard amusement park fare, but Six Flags' nine roller coasters are the main draw, with the new Batman coaster and the "floorless" Superman Krypton Coaster generating the most buzz, along with the Boomerang's trio of loops. The old wooden-coaster standby, the Rattler, still remains a crowd pleaser, even though park officials had to reduce the length of its first downward plunge after many complaints about it being "too intimidating and aggressive."

The park contains several Texas-themed areas with shows and rides related to the Lone Star State's history, and the entire complex is partially surrounded by 100-foot (30-m) cliffs from a former limestone quarry. Six Flags Fiesta Texas also operates a water park (included in the admission fee), with waterslides, family raft rides, and a lazy river tube ride. The park also stages a variety of shows and concerts.

San Antonio Zoo

Visitors often overlook the worthy 56-acre **San Antonio Zoo** (3903 N. St. Mary's St., 210/734-7184, www.sazoo.org, daily 9am-5pm, $19 adults, $15 ages 3-11), set among the cliffs of an old limestone quarry in Brackenridge Park and home to 3,500 animals representing 600 species. The big animals are in an area called the Savanna, where guests can view lions, tigers, and kangaroos. One of the zoo's highlights is the giraffe area, thanks to the viewing platform at the animals' head level. Employees are often on hand to talk about these fascinating creatures and even let guests feed them. Be sure to look down from the platform—you might see a zebra running below.

The extensive exhibits include an impressive bird collection (make a point to visit the penguins), an African antelope collection, and an exhibit of the endangered whooping crane. The children's area, called the Tiny Tot Nature Spot, is for kids under age five to get out of their strollers (and shoes and socks) to interact with the natural world by digging up worms and bugs and occasionally feeding them to nonthreatening animals like the guinea pig.

San Antonio Children's Museum: The DoSeum

A cool indoor alternative to the big amusement parks is the **San Antonio Children's Museum** (2800 Broadway Ave., 210/212-4453, www.thedoseum.org, Mon.-Thurs. 10am-5pm, Sat. 9am-6pm, Sun. noon-5pm, $14 age 1 and up). Dozens of exhibits entertain kids most of the day, outlasting parents' patience. The interactive activities are well maintained and even educational. Highlights include the Sound Zone, the Explore area with maps and models, the Innovation Station, which featuring tools and robots, and a large supermarket where kids can play customer and cashier.

Blue Star Contemporary Art Center

In an enormous former warehouse complex on the city's south side is the eye-catching and thought-provoking **Blue Star Contemporary Art Center** (116 Blue Star St., 210/227-6960, www.bluestarcontemporary.org, Thurs.-Fri. 10am-8pm, Sat.-Sun. 10am-6pm, $5 adults, $3 seniors). Anchored by the contemporary art center, Blue Star embodies the word *eclectic*—from performance art to trendy jewelry to avant-garde photography. The exterior is somewhat uninspiring, but visitors are greeted by colorful, bizarre, and beautiful artwork inside. Local and nationally known artists grace the walls, floors, and halls of the many distinctive galleries.

RECREATION

San Antonio's warm weather most of the year makes it ideal place for outdoor recreation. The city's biggest claim to sports fame, the five-time NBA champion San Antonio Spurs, play indoors at the raucous AT&T Center, but residents also attend sporting events outside, including the Missions minor league baseball team, golfing, hiking, biking, and strolling the city's colorful gardens.

Mexican Rodeo

Who needs major sports when you have Mexican rodeo? This exquisite custom captures everything essential about a sporting event—drama, heroics, compassion, and grace. The **San Antonio Charro Association** (6126 Padre Dr., 210/846-8757, www.sacharros.org) promotes monthly *charreadas* April-November. Don't miss seeing the daring and graceful *charros* in action on horses, bulls, and wild mares. One of the most jaw-droppingly suspenseful acts is *el paso de la muerte* ("the pass of death"), where a *charro* tries to leap from his own bareback horse to a wild bareback horse (all without reins) and ride it until it stops bucking. The death-defying element? All the while, three other mounted *charros* are chasing the wild mare around the arena. As if all this weren't enough, sometimes the *charros* perform this act backward just for show. This event, along with other macho roping and riding feats, are tempered with the beauty and grace of the *escaramuza* equestriennes. Check the website for show dates and locations.

Professional Sports

The beloved **San Antonio Spurs** (210/444-5000, www.nba.com/spurs), the city's only professional sports franchise, enjoyed an unusually long run of success in the early 2000s. In their nearly 40 years on the court, the Spurs have won 20 division titles (the most in the NBA during that time), yet they're often frustratingly overlooked as a basketball powerhouse on the national sports scene. The team plays at the AT&T Center just east of downtown.

The **San Antonio Missions** (210/675-7275, www.samissions.com) are a AA minor-league baseball team in a city that has a major affinity for baseball. The Missions play two levels below the big leagues and are affiliated with the Milwaukee Brewers. The team remains a popular draw, with fans filling 6,300-capacity Wolff Stadium (5757 U.S. 90 W.), just west of town. A handful of the spectators will admit to being there only to see

"Henry the Puffy Taco" race the kids around the bases during the seventh-inning stretch. The team plays April-September.

Golf

Golf is an obsession in semitropical areas like San Antonio, with year-round play on fairways lined with palm trees. The city boasts two dozen private, public, and municipal golf courses. For a comprehensive list of courses, including ratings, greens fees, and golfers' comments, visit www.sanantoniogolf.com.

A scenic and somewhat challenging round is just 10 minutes from downtown at **The Quarry** (444 E. Basse Rd., 210/824-4500, www.quarrygolf.com), rated one of America's Top State Golf Courses by *Golf Digest*. The front nine has long open holes with several water hazards, and the back nine winds through a former rock quarry with 100-foot (30-m) walls as a backdrop.

City Parks and Gardens

One of the city's most pleasant destinations is the inviting **San Antonio Botanical Garden** (555 Funston Place, 210/207-3250, www.sabot.org, daily 9am-5pm, $15 adults, $13 seniors, military, and students, $12 ages 3-13). Texas's diverse landscape is well represented with native wildflowers, grasses, bushes, and trees. Visitors experience individual environments, a large courtyard, and a pond. The 33-acre complex also includes a tearoom, a gift shop, and an impressive conservatory of 100,000 square feet, accessed through a tunnel 16 feet (4.8 m) below ground to several greenhouse areas dedicated to the tropics, the desert, palms, and ferns.

A popular expanse of public green space is **Brackenridge Park** (3910 N. St. Mary's St., 210/207-7275, www.brackenridgepark. org, daily 5am-11pm). This century-old, 344-acre park is busy on weekends, but the crowds are dispersed. Most congregate in three main areas—the San Antonio Zoo, Brackenridge Golf Course, and the Japanese Tea Gardens. The Tea Gardens are a natural oasis of lush foliage, stone bridges, a 60-foot (18-m) waterfall,

carp ponds, and shaded walkways. The name was changed to "Chinese Tea Gardens" during World War II, and it was also known as Sunken Gardens before reclaiming its original name.

Other Brackenridge Park highlights include a 3.5-mile (5.6-km) miniature train known as the Brackenridge Eagle; the Skyride, a cable car system providing aerial views of the city and zoo; and a 60-horse carousel. Standard features include hike and bike trails, sports courts and fields, playgrounds, and picnic facilities.

ENTERTAINMENT AND EVENTS

San Antonio's music scene may not get the same attention as Austin's, but it should, especially considering its eclectic mix of wide-ranging styles—conjunto, country, blues, punk, and even polkas. For an authentic taste of San Antonio's culture, visit during one of the annual festivals.

Performing Arts

San Antonio doesn't have a lot of professional performing arts groups, and many residents prefer their cultural experiences to be country and western or conjunto dancing. For a highbrow evening, it doesn't get much better than the **San Antonio Symphony** (www. sasymphony.org), with performances at the Tobin Center for the Performing Arts (100 Auditorium Circle, 210/233-8624) and the Majestic Theatre (224 E. Houston St., 210/226-3333). The season runs late September-June and features a mix of classical, pops, family, and community programs, often with high-profile guest artists.

Long considered the crown jewel of San Antonio's performing arts venues is the magnificent 1929 **Majestic Theatre** (224 E. Houston St., 210/226-3333, www.majesticmpire.com). Originally constructed as an "atmospheric" palace for vaudeville shows and motion pictures, it now serves as the home of the San Antonio Symphony and hosts an eclectic schedule of touring shows, from

The San Antonio Sound

Ask a Texas musician about the San Antonio sound, and many will mention heavy metal. Over the past few decades, the city has developed a reputation for rocking hard, serving as a regular tour stop for bands in black leather. Rewind 50 years and the city's best-known sound is much sweeter. Dubbed Chicano soul or the West Side sound, the music is tremendously enjoyable but overlooked.

Emerging from the late-1950s influences of rhythm and blues and doo-wop, the San Antonio sound captured an innovative blend of soulful Motown-style harmonies and melodies with Mexican-influenced accents from brass and reed instruments. The combination is instantly catchy, and it remains puzzling why it never caught on beyond San Antonio.

CHICANO SOUL

One song—Sunny and the Sunglows' "Talk to Me"—found a broader audience, and it peaked at number 11 on the *Billboard* charts in September 1963. Similar songs from bands with quaint names like Danny and the Dreamers, the Royal Jesters, and Little Jr. Jesse and the Teardrops were mostly unknown.

This Tejano take on R&B music never gained a national following, but the Mexican influence on pop music made a splash later in California, where acts like Richie Valens ("La Bamba"), the Champs ("Tequila"), and the Mysterians ("96 Tears") had hit singles. San Antonio's only contribution to the national music scene at the time was the garage-rocker "She's About a Mover" by the Sir Douglas Quintet.

Still, the city's Chicano soul movement was celebrated locally, and the style has experienced a resurgence and newfound appreciation thanks to music blogs and online radio programs. For those interested in lending an ear to these delightful sounds, several sweet-sounding compilations were released called *Chicano Soul: San Antonio's Westside Sound,* vols. 1-3.

Broadway productions to world-renowned concert artists. Recent events have included *Mozart Extravaganza* and comedian Jay Leno.

The Majestic interior is described as "a Mediterranean amphitheater in a Moorish-Baroque style." The main lobby includes ornately decorated plaster sculptures and a colossal ornamented chandelier, and the elaborate auditorium contains colorfully illuminated alcoves and grottoes topped off by a simulated night sky, complete with twinkling stars and floating clouds.

Country Music Venues
LIVE MUSIC
Though it's 15 miles (24 km) northwest of town, no other place is quite as authentic as **Floore Country Store** (14492 Old Bandera Rd., 210/695-8827, www.liveatfloores.com). A sign outside this historic honky-tonk reads "Willie Nelson Every Sat. Nite," and although

those days are long gone, the Red-Headed Stranger still makes a point of playing occasional gigs at this big ol' Texas dance hall. The walls are covered with photos of other country legends who have graced the stage (Ernest Tubb, Hank Williams), and the venue still hosts contemporary and classic country acts such as Lyle Lovett, Dwight Yoakam, Jack Ingram, and Bruce Robison.

Another legendary honky-tonk on the outskirts of town is the **Hanging Tree Saloon** (18424 2nd St., Bracken, 210/651-5812), which opened in 1915 as a two-lane bowling alley for nine-pin, a game popular in German pioneer communities. In 1989, mythically named Texan Big John Oaks converted the bowling alley into a roadhouse honky-tonk, using wood from the lanes to construct the bar. The stage stands where the pins were once placed. This classic venue hosts local country bands on the weekends and occasionally features well-known regional acts such as Johnny Bush, Gary P. Nunn, and Johnny Rodriguez. To get there, take FM 2252 north from Bracken, turn right at the first road past the railroad tracks, go four blocks, and then turn left.

DANCING

If you'd rather have your conversation drowned out by prerecorded sounds instead of a live band, head to **Cowboys Dance Hall** (3030 NE Loop 410, 210/646-9378, www.cowboysdancehall.com), which features a cavernous dance floor and bull riding. Saturday nights feature a rodeo with live bull riding, or try your eight seconds of luck on the mechanical bull any time. The music is the big draw, and on some nights live shows (including a bona fide house band) replace DJs.

Conjunto and Tejano Clubs

San Antonio's conjunto clubs, which specialize in accordion-based Tejano dance music, are typically in neighborhood bars that appear unassuming during the week but get mighty spicy on weekend nights. One of the city's most popular venues is a sports bar with a large dance floor and a disco ball: **Reptilez Sports Bar** (5418 Enrique M. Barrera Pkwy., 210/432-8840), where conjunto reigns on Sunday thanks to the bouncy beats of house band Fred Saldana y Los Camaroneros. One of the newer venues in town is the colorful **Squeezebox** (2806 N. St. Mary's St., 210/314-8805), or there's always an old-school classic-car hangout like **Sanchez Ice House** (819 S. San Saba St., 210/223-0588).

River Walk Bars

The River Walk is touristy by design, so it's not surprising that the bars lack scruffy neighborhood charm. For a slick place to enjoy a fancy drink, try the swanky **V-bar at Hotel Valencia** (150 E. Houston St., 210/227-9700), on the 2nd floor. Contemporary lighting and furnishings give the place an air of sophistication, and the sprawling scene—particularly the inviting terrace overlooking the River Walk—makes for a romantic experience.

Equally savory is ★ **Havana** (1015 Navarro St., 210/222-2008), at the Havana Riverwalk Inn. The swanky vibe is evident as you descend the stairs into the cavernous bar space, lit only by red wall lamps. Mellow out on a soft leather couch and have a heavy martini. The tapas, particularly the empanadas, are worth ordering, or if you're in the mood for dessert, consider the handmade chocolate sampler.

It's hard to escape the hotel scene on the River Walk, but some places are tucked away from the crowds. The best of the bunch is **Esquire Tavern** (55 E. Commerce St., 210/222-2521, www.esquiretavern-sa.com), recently nominated for a James Beard Award. Dating to 1933, the Esquire is the place to go for a classic cocktail or local craft beer—especially if you can find a spot at the incredible wooden bar, reportedly the longest in Texas. Make a point to arrive at happy hour, lunch, or dinner to sample some of the savory bites, from fried beets to flavorful empanadas. This place is always packed, so consider booking space ahead of time via the website.

Less swanky is **Howl at the Moon** (111 W. Crockett St., 210/212-4770, www.howlatthemoon.com), a raucous dueling piano bar where visitors regularly let loose with the abandon of being anonymous in an unknown city. Patrons "sing" along with their favorite tunes (think "Sweet Caroline," "Crocodile Rock," and, of course, "Piano Man") as they're pounded out on the ivories, along with good-natured banter. Complement the boisterous scene with a Jell-O shot or a fuzzy navel.

Downtown Lounges

San Antonio's Latino culture takes center stage at **Azuca Nuevo Latino** (713 S. Alamo St., 210/225-5550), a restaurant by day and bar by night. Arrive around 10pm and take advantage of both the classic Latin American fare and contemporary dance scene. Have a drink at the Nuevo Latino bar and shake a leg on the dance floor.

Nearby is the slightly upscale yet decidedly low-key **Bohanan's Bar** (221 E. Houston St., 210/271-7472), the lounge associated with an adjacent steak house. The patio is a perfect place to chill on a warm summer evening, or belly up to the long black granite bar for a hearty cocktail.

Just down the block is the comfortably upscale **SoHo Wine & Martini Bar** (214 W. Crockett St., 210/444-1000), a place to see and be seen, but since it lacks pretension, the atmosphere is refreshingly comfortable. Enjoy a live jazz band while sipping on a custom martini.

Events
SPRING

The winters aren't too harsh in San Antonio, but that doesn't stop people from celebrating the warmer spring weather with festivals and gatherings. One of the city's first major annual events, **Battle of the Alamo Commemoration** (210/273-1730, www.thealamo.org), is held the first weekend of March. A stirring sunrise ceremony honors the Texans who died at the Alamo siege, and much of the daytime activity involves living-history reenactments, music, demonstrations, and food.

Another distinctive event in March is the **St. Patrick's Day River Parade** (210/273-1730, www.thesanantonioriverwalk.com). City officials use 35 pounds of environmentally safe green dye to tint the San Antonio River the color of the Irish and rechristen it River Shannon. Residents and visitors celebrate Celtic culture throughout the weekend with a pub crawl, a river parade, and Irish music and dance.

The city's biggest and best annual celebration, **Fiesta San Antonio** (210/227-5191, www.fiestasanantonio.org) is a massive 10-day event in April and is the cultural highlight of the year for 3.5 million attendees. Festivities range from colorful parades to fashion shows to art exhibits, concerts, and a legendary oyster bake. The pageants and parties are important social events, and the carnivals and galas celebrate the city's Latino heritage.

SUMMER

Another major event drawing nearly a million people annually is the **Texas Folklife Festival** (801 S. Bowie, 210/458-2224, www.texancultures.com), held each June at the Institute of Texan Cultures to celebrate the Lone Star State's cultural diversity through art, crafts, music, and plenty of amazing food. Cultures not always associated with Texas proudly represent the state each year, including Scotland, China, Norway, India, Greece, and the Canary Islands.

September is still summertime in San Antonio, and the biggest cultural events of the month are related to **Fiestas Patrias,** particularly Mexican Independence Day, also referred to as Diez y Seis (Sept. 16). Celebrations that include dances, food booths, and carnivals take place at Market Square, La Villita, and Guadalupe Plaza.

FALL AND WINTER

Those in the San Antonio vicinity on November 2 shouldn't be afraid to take part in the events of **El Dia de Los Muertos** (Day of the Dead, 210/432-1896). This Mexican custom welcomes back departed family members and friends for one day through offerings (skulls made of sugar, marigolds), parades (many participants dress as skeletons), and grave decoration.

The Christmas season in San Antonio officially kicks off with the **Ford Holiday River Parade** (210/227-4262) on the Friday after Thanksgiving. More than 122,000 colorful lights are simultaneously lit, bathing the River Walk in bright festive hues, while decorated floats glide along the sparkling water.

This is Texas, after all, so San Antonio residents proudly head 'em up and move 'em out to the **Stock Show and Rodeo** (723 AT&T Center Pkwy., www.sarodeo.com) for two weeks in early February. All the traditional events are here—calf roping, barrel racing, bull riding—as well as popular children's events such as the calf scramble and mutton bustin' (sheep riding).

SHOPPING
River Walk

The River Walk is truly the beaten path, so

it's no surprise that the shopping options are run-of-the-mill tourist spots offering T-shirts, knickknacks, art, and decorative furnishings. For some reason, the most popular shopping experience along the River Walk is the **Rivercenter Mall** (849 E. Commerce St., 210/225-0000, www.shoprivercenter.com), a three-story structure that offers a cool respite on hot days. Rivercenter contains the shops and food options found at malls across the country, but there are a couple distinguishing features—the Rio San Antonio Cruises depart from a "lagoon" on the ground level, and the IMAX theater showcases an Alamo movie to complement the real deal just around the corner.

Market Square

For a more authentic San Antonio shopping experience than the River Walk, head six blocks west to **Market Square** (514 W. Commerce St., 210/207-8600, www.marketsquaresa.com), referred to as the largest Mexican marketplace outside of Mexico. This bustling pedestrian area often has a south-of-the-border appearance, with roaming mariachis and hordes of street vendors selling pottery, blankets, handmade crafts, and authentic Mexican food.

Speaking of food—a trip to Market Square, also referred to as El Mercado by locals, would be incomplete without stopping by **Mi Tierra Cafe & Bakery** (218 Produce Row, 210/225-1262, www.mitierracafe.com). Whether you're in the mood for a sweet snack of its famous *pan dulce* or a hearty meal—everything from huevos rancheros to charbroiled steak—this 24-hour establishment is a must. Next door is the welcoming craft shop **Little Mexico Imports** (202 Produce Row, 210/226-7765). This stylish building is packed with colorful clothing and folk art.

La Villita

Falling somewhere between the River Walk and Market Square (tourism-wise, not geographically) is **La Villita** (418 Villita St., 210/207-8610, most shops daily 10am-6pm).

Adjacent to the River Walk, La Villita is known as much for its interesting heritage as for shopping, which runs the gamut from trendy boutiques to upscale galleries to comfy cafés. The vernacular architecture adds a charming appeal to this "little village," as do the working artisans—glassblowers, pottery spinners, and the like—who create their wares for all to see.

One of the more popular shops is **Casa Manos Alegres** (418 Villita St., Suite 600, 210/313-7293), offering Mexican and Guatemalan imports such as enormous colorful papier-mâché animals, quaint woodcarvings, and pottery. Another intriguing shop is **Nueva Street Gallery** (507 E. Nueva St., 210/229-9810), specializing in watercolor paintings, photography, handmade stoneware, and porcelain pottery. One of the best places to eat lunch in La Villita is **La Villita Cafe** (418 Villita St., 900, 210/223-4700, www.lavillitacafe.com), which serves fresh sandwiches and frosty ice cream.

Mexican Goods

Market Square is home to several of San Antonio's best Mexican import shops, with everything from guayaberas (the short-sleeved, open-collared shirts worn in tropical Latin locales) to copper sinks and tin ornaments and Mexican wrestling masks. For the basics, head to **Perales Mexican Imports** (514 W. Commerce St., 210/223-4802) or **Naturaleza Celestial** (514 W. Commerce St., 210/227-9254). For something unique, drop by **Old Mexico Imports** (888/522-8434), which specializes in *talavera* goods. *Talavera* is a white-glazed ceramic plates, bowls, tiles, and furnishings with simple or colorfully decorated designs.

Western Wear

Highly respected bootmaker **Lucchese** (255 E. Basse Rd., 210/828-9419, www.lucchese.com) claims to have outfitted "all the great cowboys, including Gene Autry and John Wayne" with their handsome boots, custom-made since 1883 with top-notch leather, lemon-wood pegs, and quality finishing (ask for your initials to be stitched or inlayed). These boots take time but will last for years. Lucchese has a retail store in the Alamo Quarry Market with standard sizes of boots, shirts, cowboy hats, belts, and other Western accessories.

Another local legend is **Little's Boots** (110 Division Ave., 210/923-2221, www.littlesboots.com), a family operation that's been in business for a century, specializing in custom boot-making, specialty makeup, and made-to-measure boots. Customers can choose from a variety of leathers—kangaroo, ostrich, alligator, lizard, and eel—or simply have their worn-out boots repaired.

In the Menger Hotel on Alamo Plaza, take a gander at the impressive Western apparel at **Silver Spur** (212 Alamo Plaza, 210/472-2210, www.silverspurboutique.com). Much of the clothing is embedded with rhinestones and crystals for a night out on the town. Silver Spur also has a limited selection of clothing for men as well as an extensive jewelry collection, hats, belts, handbags, and other accessories.

Not quite as charming but appealing in its immense size and selection is the chain option **Boot Barn** (Military Dr., 210/338-8907, and 6201 NW Loop 410, 210/681-8230, www.bootbarn.com). These stores are practically warehouses of Western clothing, including decent moderately priced boots, cowboy hats, jeans, shirts, belts, and the obligatory big buckles.

FOOD

The food is fabulous in San Antonio, and not surprisingly, the focus is on Mexican-inspired restaurants. The sheer number of Tex-Mex, Cal-Mex, and Interior Mex eateries offers a wide variety. Several well-regarded establishments have locations on the River Walk, and other downtown areas offer some of the best-quality Mexican food in Texas.

River Walk
AMERICAN AND SOUTHWESTERN

The **Esquire Tavern** (55 E. Commerce St., 210/222-2521, www.esquiretavern-sa.com, Sun.-Wed. 11:30am-midnight, Thurs.-Sat. 11:30am-2am, $12-26) dates to 1933 and is known for its wooden bar, reportedly the longest in Texas. It also garners attention for its innovative cuisine: Start with the fried pickled beets or tacos *con papas* (potatoes), then proceed to a classic hearty burger (the organic bison is a special treat) or the immensely tasty Big Red Empanada, packed with short-rib meat and tomatillo salsa and topped with a zesty chimichurri sauce.

Upscale **Boudro's** (421 E. Commerce St., 210/224-8484, www.boudros.com, Sun.-Thurs. 11am-11pm, Fri.-Sat. 11am-midnight, $18-44) is one of the few places on the River Walk that can entice locals to wade through the crowds. Be sure to call ahead for a reservation. For local flavor, start with a prickly pear margarita accompanied by chips and fresh-made guacamole prepared at your table (note the fresh squeeze of orange as opposed to lemon or lime—the difference is subtle yet spectacular). Entrées run the gamut from seafood to steaks to upscale Southwestern dishes, and Boudro's desserts, including bread pudding, flan, and crème brûlée, are legendary.

An upscale eatery drawing locals is **Biga on the Banks** (203 S. St. Mary's St., 210/225-0722, www.biga.com, daily 5:30pm-10pm, $18-48). In the city's former central library, Biga's has a reputation for serving some of the finest cuisine in the state. Enjoy complimentary champagne upon arrival as you browse the impressive menu of savory items, including smoked pork chops, seared tuna, roasted lamb, grilled steaks, and wild game. Many dishes are accompanied by bold touches such as curry sauces and foie gras. Make reservations to ensure a seat at this exquisite establishment.

The River Walk would be an incomplete Texas tradition without a barbecue restaurant. Some of the best is at the **County Line** (111 W. Crockett St., 210/229-1941, daily 11am-10pm,

Cocina de México

What comes to mind when someone asks if you're in the mood for Mexican food (besides "Yes!")? Most people drool at the thought of tacos, burritos, and nachos, but in Texas, there's way more on the menu. Mexican food can mean many things—cuisine from the interior of Mexico with savory sauces and meats, or border-inspired Tex-Mex with thick cheese, seasoned beef, and tortillas.

TEX-MEX

Tex-Mex prevails in the Lone Star State. Although fancy tacos are becoming trendy, the familiarity of Tex-Mex makes it a genuine comfort food.

- **Enchiladas, tacos,** and **tamales:** The main ingredients are simple: ground beef, chicken, cheese, and tortillas, combined in different ways for a variety of tasty options, including a crispy or soft beef taco; a beef, cheese, or chicken enchilada; and a pork tamale. Rice, beans, guacamole, lettuce, and tomato are typically side accompaniments. Where to try it: River Walk's **Casa Rio** (430 E. Commerce St., San Antonio, 210/225-6718, www.casa-rio.com, daily. 11am-10pm, $12-27)

INTERIOR MEXICAN

Interior cuisine is distinguished by more complex ingredients, especially the chilies (ancho, poblano), cheeses (queso fresco, queso panela), sauces (moles with nuts, chilies, and chocolate), and meat (duck, seafood, venison).

- **Chile relleno:** A prime example of interior Mexican food, legend has it that Spanish friars in the 1500s used Mexico's native poblano pepper as the basis for the dish. They filled it with ingredients they'd brought from the Old World, like potatoes, raisins, and cinnamon. The world relleno is Spanish for "filled." Later incarnations of the chile relleno would add beef and light pan-frying in an egg-based flour batter. Where to try it: **Rosario's Mexican Cafe** (910 S. Alamo St., San Antonio, 210/223-1806, www.rosariossa.com, Mon.-Thurs. 11am-10pm, Fri.-Sat. 11am-11pm, Sun. 11am-9pm, $11-27)

DESSERTS

Save space for dessert, since Mexico is home to many sweet delicacies, known as dulces.

$14-29), with authentic Texas-style 'cue. Load up on tender brisket, meaty beef ribs, and flavorful sausage, accompanied by classic sides like potato salad and coleslaw. Wash it down with a cold Shiner Bock or Dr Pepper.

MEXICAN AND TEX-MEX

Among the best for consistent quality and service are ★ **Casa Rio** (430 E. Commerce St., 210/225-6718, www.casa-rio.com, daily 11am-10pm, $12-27), the first restaurant on the River Walk in 1946. Interior walls and patio umbrellas radiate festive colors, complementing the equally tantalizing food. You can't go wrong with the basics: crispy beef tacos, hearty chicken enchiladas, savory pork tamales, and cheesy quesadillas, accompanied by a margarita or cerveza. Snag a seat on the patio or riverbank for optimal people-watching and wandering mariachi bands. Be sure to arrive early, since the usual wait at noon and 6pm is 30-45 minutes.

Another classic Tex-Mex spot with an amazing deck overlooking the riverbank is **Rio Rio Cantina** (421 E. Commerce St., 210/226-8462, www.rioriocantina.com, daily

traditional Tex-Mex combo plate

- *Tres leches:* This is a cake soaked in three kinds of milk (the name translates to "three milks": evaporated, condensed, and whole. *Tres leches* is a light cake filled with air bubbles, so the "soaking" doesn't bog down the consistency, but rather complements the sweet creamy taste. Where to try it: **Acenar** (146 E. Houston St., San Antonio, 210/222-2362, www.acenar.com)

- **Sopapillas:** Fried pastries made from flat bread, these puffy treats are made by deep frying the pressed bread, causing it to expand with a large air pocket in the center, creating its distinctive pillowy shape. Sopapillas are typically served with honey or a mixture of powdered sugar and cinnamon sprinkled on top. Where to try it: **Casa Rio** (430 E. Commerce St., San Antonio, 210/225-6718, www.casa-rio.com)

Several other standard Mexican delicacies don't qualify as authentic native products, but you'll find them on the dessert menus of Mexican restaurants. **Flan** and **churros** have Spanish origins, and **pecan pralines** are tied to New Orleans via France.

9:30am-10pm, $11-27). Bring your appetite, since the portions are enormous. Bring patience too, since the food can take a while to arrive; order another margarita while you're waiting. Try chicken enchiladas with green salsa, the *camarónes Yucateco* (spicy shrimp), and even the standard fajita plate, containing enough beef and chicken to feed an entire river-barge crew. Kids will love the quesadillas, and their parents will appreciate the noisy chatter drowning out their incessant questions about the pervasive pigeons.

A step up from Tex-Mex is ★ **Acenar** (146 E. Houston St., 210/222-2362, www.acenar. com, Sun.-Thurs. 11am-10pm, Fri.-Sat. 11am-11pm, $15-33), one of the largest restaurants on the River Walk, its multiple levels and tables with stellar views consistently packed. Start with sturdy chips and smooth and tasty *queso* dip. Acenar's tacos are packed with unconventional fillings like crab and oyster, and any dish with the savory mole sauce is magnificent. Try duck crepes and *entomatadas* (a chicken- and sweet potato-filled tortilla covered in an roasted tomato sauce with *queso fresco*). Accompany your meal with one of

Acenar's signature "hand-shaken" margaritas, and save room for the exquisite *tres leches* cake or coconut flan.

PEARL BREWERY DEVELOPMENT

At the far northern edge of the River Walk's Museum Reach, the Pearl Brewery complex is a sight to behold. The surrounding new eateries are among the best in town. Note that several establishments are closed Monday.

Garnering much attention and rave reviews is ★ **La Gloria Ice House** (100 E. Grayson St., 210/267-9040, www.lagloriaicehouse.com, daily 11am-10pm, $10-29), with authentic Mexican street food. Designed like a Mexican *mercado* taco stand, La Gloria specializes in delicious tacos, gorditas, and *tortas* prepared in regionally diverse styles. Tacos come three per order, so resist the temptation to sample everything on the menu, and start with just one or two—they'll get cold if they arrive all at once, and you'll be encouraged to place additional orders. Notable dishes include the *al pastor* pork tacos, the crispy-battered fish tacos, the tacos *potosinos* (rolled tortillas in chili sauce with fried carrots and potatoes), and the avocado *tlayuda* (pizza). Another immensely popular and flavorful menu item is the *tamal del día*, featuring a seasoned meat combined with spices (cinnamon, cloves) and fruit (apricots, dates) wrapped in a banana leaf. *¡Que sabor!*

Among the most popular venues at the Pearl complex is **Southerleigh Fine Food and Brewery** (200 E. Grayson St., 210/455-5701, www.southerleigh.com, Mon.-Thurs. 11am-10pm, Fri.-Sat. 11am-11pm, Sun. 10am-9pm, $12-35), a welcoming restaurant and brewery with cross-cultural Gulf Coast and Southern cuisine. Start with a house-made Gold Export Lager or Darwinian IPA, coupled with an appetizer of goat cheese and roasted beets. Worthy menu options include the Galveston Bay shrimp boil, cracker-crusted gulf redfish, charcoal-broiled rib-eye, and plump dinner burger.

For cutting-edge dishes from future chefs, head to the Culinary Institute of America's

Savor (312 Pearl Pkwy., 210/554-6484, www.naorestaurant.com, $11-31), a place to sample the tasty creations from students, including a four-course meal featuring squash, mussels, pork collar, and *panna cotta.*

On the weekend, stop by the **Pearl Farmers Market** (next to La Gloria, Sat. 9am-1pm, Sun. 10am-2pm), open rain or shine. Vendors offer fresh local seasonal vegetables, fruit, meat, herbs, baked goods, pecans, goat cheese, eggs, jams, and salsas.

Downtown Area
AMERICAN

Mexican food isn't the only option, and in a touristy area like the River Walk, the best bet is often an American-style restaurant with a local twist.

Marvel at the meaty goodness of the Southside's magnificent ★ **Maverick** (710 S. St. Mary's St., 210/973-6050, http://mavericktexas.com, Mon.-Thurs. 4pm-10pm, Fri. 11:30am-11pm, Sat.-Sun. 10:30am-2pm and 5pm-11pm, $17-53), billed as a Texas brasserie. The handsome black-and-white styled restaurant focuses on quality meat and expert service. Start with a cocktail or red wine and savor the refined comfortable scenery. Steak, pork, or seafood can be prepared grilled, smoked, sautéed, or roasted. Go whole hog and order the mixed grill, including Texas quail, sausage, pork belly, and tenderloin. Sautéed trout and rotisserie duck are other worthy options.

San Antonio's **Liberty Bar** (1111 S. Alamo St., 210/227-1187, www.liberty-bar.com, Mon.-Fri. 11am-midnight, Sat.-Sun. 9am-midnight, $13-31) merits mention for its creative high-quality cuisine. The focus is on sauced and seasoned pot roast, lamb sausage, herbed chicken, and other meat. The bread, spreads, and iced tea make a big impression, and the vegetables are always perfectly prepared. The Liberty draws its largest crowds on Sunday morning

1: Blue Star Brewing Company **2:** Casa Rio on the River Walk **3:** the mighty Maverick restaurant **4:** Pearl Brewery Development

for its legendary brunch (10am-2pm), with sumptuous egg dishes and perfect french toast.

Stunning sweeping views are the main course at **Chart House** (739 E. Cesar Chavez Blvd., 210/223-3101, www.chart-house.com, $14-36), the revolving restaurant atop the Tower of the Americas. Normally eateries in the round aren't known for top-notch food, but this restaurant is owned by Landry's, a seafood establishment, and most of the menu options are surf and turf, including tasty shrimp. Incidentally, the tower is 750 feet (230 m) tall and was built for the HemisFair, the 1968 World's Fair. A "4-D" multisensory theater is on the ground level.

It may not be native-born, but people line up for perfect steaks at **Morton's** (300 E. Crockett St., 210/228-0700, www.mortons.com, daily 4:30pm-10pm, $19-47). It looks, smells, and tastes like an upscale steak house should—dark wood, tuxedoed waitstaff, clanging steak knives, and delectable cuts of prime beef. Highlights include the porterhouse, double-cut filet mignon, and the bone-in prime rib.

A traditional alternative spot is **Madhatters** (320 Beauregard St., 210/212-4832, www.madhatterstea.com, Mon.-Thurs. 7am-6pm, Fri.-Sat. 8am-9pm, Sun. 9am-3pm, $6-12), an Alice in Wonderland-inspired teahouse turned café. It's a little warped, in a metaphorical sense, and the incredible variety of teas is the focal point, but the healthy salads and tasty sandwiches are worthy. The Spinach Mad Scramble with a side of fresh-squeezed orange juice will leave you grinning like the Cheshire Cat.

For a traditional family getaway, take a trip to **The Cove** (606 W. Cypress St., 210/227-2683, www.thecove.us, Tues.-Thurs. 11am-10pm, Fri.-Sat. 11am-11pm, Sun. 11am-10pm, $9-25), just north of downtown. The Cove has an Austin vibe, with an emphasis on organic ingredients, kids meals, veggie options, quality beer selections, live music, a safe and visible playground, and the weirdness of having a laundromat and car wash on-site. Beyond the comfy and eclectic scene, the food is outstanding—opt for the fish taco or spinach salad combo, Texas burger (local beef with refried beans, corn chips, salsa, and avocado), accompanied by sweet potato fries with Sriracha mayo.

On the River Walk's Mission Reach, stop by the **Blue Star Brewing Company** (1414 S. Alamo St., 210/212-5506, www.bluestar-brewing.com, Tues.-Thurs. 11am-9pm, Fri. 11am-midnight, Sat. 10am-midnight, Sun. 11am-9pm, $9-21). Beers are the main draw—the best are Cinco Peso Pale Ale, Belgian-style King William Ale, and perfectly dry Southtown Sour. The food is standard, but highlights include the brisket tacos, porterhouse pork chop, and Frito pie.

MEXICAN AND TEX-MEX

The gigantic selection of Mexican restaurants in San Antonio is overwhelming, and there's a combo plate for everyone. A great place to start is the original location of ★ **Rosario's Mexican Cafe** (910 S. Alamo St., 210/223-1806, www.rosariossa.com, Mon.-Thurs. 11am-10pm, Fri.-Sat. 11am-11pm, Sun. 11am-9pm, $11-27), on the edge of the King William Historic District. The food is more Mexican contemporary than traditional Tex-Mex; instead of beef, there's fresh avocado. Many dishes contain pleasant surprises (diced cactus, exotic peppers, a touch of cinnamon) rather than standby rice and beans. The deliciously smoky roasted-pepper salsa that comes to the table with the tortilla chips is a good indication of the quality to come. The spectacular chile relleno contains ranchero sauce and sweet raisin undertones, and the chili itself is perfectly breaded. On weekend nights, Rosario's becomes a hot spot for the singles scene, with salsa, merengue, and jazz bands playing for enthusiastic dancing crowds.

More traditional is **Mi Tierra Cafe & Bakery** (218 Produce Row, 210/225-1262, www.mitierracafe.com, daily 24 hours, $10-23), the legendary 24-hour Market Square restaurant. The scene alone is worth a visit—the ceilings are decked with Christmas lights, and mariachis stroll the grounds crooning their *canciones.* A lot of people come for the tasty *dulces* (sweet breads) and impressive tequila selection. Pastry fans should order an *empanada de calabaza* (pumpkin turnover). The homemade tortillas are soft and flavorful, and the standard combo plates with enchiladas, tacos, and tamales are a classic Tex-Mex fix. Get a perfect pecan praline or a to-go pastry for a late-night snack.

In the King William Historic District, busy **Azuca Nuevo Latina** (713 S. Alamo St., 210/225-5550, www.azuca.net, Mon.-Thurs. 11am-9:30pm, Fri.-Sat. 11am-5:30pm, Sun. 5pm-9:30pm, $12-29) specializes in Latin American and Caribbean food and consistently ends up on best-of lists. Try the mixed meat grill (chicken, beef, pork, and sausage), pork loin, and anything with plantains and coconut shrimp. The Curry Latino offers a blend of spices and seafood, and even the steaks have a Caribbean marinated flavor. Stick around for salsa, mojitos, and merengue bands on weekend nights.

Another local Tex-Mex institution is **La Fonda on Main** (2415 N. Main Ave., 210/733-0621, www.lafondaonmain.com, Mon.-Thurs. 11am-9:30pm, Fri.-Sat. 11am-10:30pm, Sun. 10:30am-9:30pm, $12-29). Other unaffiliated La Fondas in town don't offer the same quality of food. This excellent restaurant is in a historic building on the near-north side of town. The menu features standard Tex-Mex with a slightly more upscale approach (fancier tortillas, sauces in zigzag patterns), and classic Interior Mexican fare (mole dishes, black beans). The margaritas are some of the best in town, and if the weather's nice, grab a spot on the patio.

Outside Downtown

Expensive yet consistently excellent **Silo Elevated Cuisine** (434 N. Loop 1604 E., 210/483-8989, www.siloelevatedcuisine.com, daily 11am-3pm and 5:30pm-11pm, $15-45) is a stylish restaurant in a lofty second-story perch accessible via elevator. The food ascends beyond the city's other upscale options. The wine selection is superb (the waitstaff will bring samples if you're feeling indecisive), as are the entrées, including premium steaks, shrimp and grits, seared yellowfin tuna, and Silo's famous chicken-fried oysters. Silo features live entertainment several nights a week. Reservations are strongly advised.

For some of the best craft beer in the region, head to **Freetail Brewing Co.** (4035 N. Loop 1604 W., 210/395-4974, www.freetailbrewing.com, Mon.-Sat. 11am-midnight, Sun. noon-midnight, $10-26), named after Texas's official flying mammal, the Mexican free-tailed bat. The brews are largely seasonal, so expect hearty homemade porters during the cooler winter months and crisp pilsners on the patio in summertime. Local favorites include the Rye Wit (a flavorful wheat beer), the smoky Rubio Fumando, and a purple-tinged prickly pear variety. The waitstaff is knowledgeable and friendly. Load up on quality pub grub like nachos, pepper fries, mac and cheese, and pizza; the barbecue brisket pie is especially cheesy and delicious.

A 15-minute drive north from downtown is **Los Barrios** (4223 Blanco Rd., 210/732-6017, Mon.-Thurs. 10am-10pm, Fri.-Sat. 10am-11pm, Sun. 9am-10pm, $10-19). Start with a smooth tangy margarita to accompany warm chips and Argentina-style garlicky pesto salsa. Puffy tacos are the specialty, and the enchiladas are highly recommended—opt for the rich and flavorful chicken mole or hearty Mexicana sauce. The fresh homemade tortillas and flautas are also excellent choices. Food Network fans will appreciate that Bobby Flay "threw down" with Los Barrios (and lost). Don't be surprised if the owners drop by to make sure everything is *perfecto.*

Named by *Texas Monthly* one of the top five Mexican restaurants in the state, **SoLuna** (7959 Broadway St., 210/930-8070, www.solunasa.com, Mon. 11:30am-9pm, Tues.-Fri. 11:30am-10pm, Sat.-Sun. 8am-9pm, $14-34) offers consistently tasty cuisine with an emphasis on interior influences. The *chile en nogoda* (a poblano pepper with beef or pork seasoned with spices and cooked fruits) is an especially memorable dish, and the *pescado* *veracruzana* is a simple yet exquisite snapper fillet with capers, olives, and tomatoes. SoLuna's takes enchiladas to a new level; the SoLuna special features three enchiladas with tantalizingly different cream-based sauces.

More Austin than San Antonio is the organic-minded **Twin Sisters Bakery & Cafe** (6322 N. New Braunfels Ave., 210/822-0761, Mon.-Fri. 7am-9pm, Sat. 7am-2pm, Sun. 9am-2pm, $6-18). Although it has a strong veggie focus, carnivores can still find meat at this comfy spot. Favorites include a tasty avocado sandwich and Greek salad, while meat eaters enjoy the enchiladas and stews. Omnivores love the fresh-baked muffins, breads, pies, and cookies. On weekends, Twin Sisters transforms into a mellow hangout with live acoustic music.

Step back in time with a visit to **Texas Pride Barbecue** (2980 Hwy. 1604 Loop, Adkins, 210/649-3730, www.texaspridebbq. net, Tues.-Wed. 11am-8pm, Thurs.-Sat. 11am-9pm, Sun. 11am-6pm, $14-37), an old-school 'cue joint complete with vintage equipment and traditional flavors in a rural venue. Order meats by the pound (a half pound of the mesquite-smoked brisket and pork ribs is a good way to go) and walk your tray to a picnic table outside. On the weekend, stick around for authentic live country music and two-stepping with the locals.

ACCOMMODATIONS

San Antonio has lots of downtown lodging within walking distance of major attractions. The River Walk hosts a wide range, and although the city's historic downtown hotels are more expensive, they are a memorable experience in a vibrant urban environment. To save a few bucks, myriad affordable chain options are 20 minutes outside downtown on Loop 410, especially on the north side of the city near the airport.

The River Walk-Alamo Vicinity
$50-100

It's difficult to find a worthy bargain hotel in downtown San Antonio, but a few options

offer basic amenities. These spots tend to be pretty noisy due to freeway, train, and foot traffic. The best of the bunch is **Red Roof Inn** (1011 E. Houston St., 210/229-9973, www. redroof.com, $99 d), a 10-minute walk under the freeway from Alamo Plaza. The hotel offers complimentary Wi-Fi in all rooms, free continental breakfast, and an outdoor pool.

Within 1 mile (1.6 km) of the River Walk is another budget option that features a prime location instead of top-notch amenities: **Days Inn Downtown** (1500 S. I-35, exit 154B, 210/271-3334, www.dayssanantonio.com, $99 d), including a free breakfast, an outdoor pool, and free Wi-Fi.

$100-150

Several moderately priced options offer reliable service and clean compact rooms downtown on the River Walk. A family favorite is **Holiday Inn** (217 N. St. Mary's St., 210/224-2500, www.holidayinn.com, $149 d), in the middle of the action. It has a small but comfortable heated outdoor pool and whirlpool, free internet access, an exercise facility, and on-site parking.

Consider the fully equipped kitchen suites at **Residence Inn** (425 Bonham St., 210/212-5555, www.marriott.com, $149 d). Near the Alamo, the hotel also offers complimentary internet access and a free breakfast buffet, and it's pet-friendly.

$150-200

Most of the River Walk hotels fall in this price range, although it's worth checking the discount travel websites, since many of the following recommended locations are often available for $30-40 less.

A nice option in the middle of all the action is the **Drury Plaza Hotel** (105 S. St. Mary's St., 210/270-7799, www.druryhotels.com, $180 d). Housed in the stately 24-story Alamo Bank Building, the hotel covers a city block and retains much of its 1929 elegance and style in the lofty ceilings, travertine flooring, chandeliers, and stained-glass windows, along with its legendary rooftop weather spire. The Drury offers free Wi-Fi in all rooms, complimentary hot breakfast, and an outdoor rooftop whirlpool and swimming pool, billed as the highest swimming pool in San Antonio.

A reliable option is the towering **Wyndham Riverwalk** (111 Pecan St. E., 210/354-2800, www.wyndham.com, $189 d), offering internet access in all rooms, a heated rooftop pool, a sauna, and a whirlpool, and a full fitness center.

A clean commendable choice is **Hyatt Place Riverwalk** (601 S. St. Mary's St., 210/227-6854, www.hyatt.com, $189 d), downtown on the San Antonio River, not in the thick of the River Walk activity. The rooms are fairly large and feature microwaves, fridges, a separate workspace, and free Wi-Fi. The hotel also offers a 24-hour on-site restaurant (breakfast is free for Hyatt members), and an outdoor heated swimming pool.

A nice hotel in a great location is **Homewood Suites** (432 W. Market St., 210/222-1515, www.homewoodsuitesriverwalk.com, $191 d). This prime location is ideal for traveling with kids as it includes fully equipped kitchens for snack storage and leftovers, separate living and sleeping rooms, plus complimentary internet access in all rooms and an included hot breakfast.

$200-250

If you're willing to shell out some extra cash, the upscale lodging options along the River Walk will ensure a memorable stay in San Antonio.

A distinctive classy location is the stylish ★ **Hotel Valencia** (150 E. Houston St., 210/227-9700, www.hotelvalencia.com, $209 d). This 213-room contemporary luxury hotel bills itself as "classic meets hip." Corridors and rooms are too shadowy at times, with dramatic lighting and trendy detailing. Guests won't want to leave their room thanks to the exceptional city views, a minibar, free internet access, and luxurious linens; the baths are welcoming with classic bathtubs and waffle-weave robes. The Valencia is at the end of the River Walk, so crowds aren't usually an issue.

This is a good spot for couples rather than families.

At the gateway to the River Walk, a popular mainstream option is the **Hyatt Regency** (123 Losoya St., 210/222-1234, www.sanantonioregency.hyatt.com, $229 d), just a block from the Alamo. The Hyatt is a modest-size hotel with a 16-story atrium and rooftop terrace offering an outdoor swimming pool, a spa, and an adjoining 2,800-square-foot health club. Rooms are decked out in Southwestern decor and include a fridge, a microwave, and 65-inch TVs. There is usually a fee for Wi-Fi.

A consistently reliable and oft-recommended option is the welcoming **Westin** (420 W. Market St., 210/224-6500, www.marriott.com, $239 d), distinguished from other chain options on the River Walk by its private-balcony rooms overlooking the river. Rooms are inviting, with historic Texas decor, big comfy beds, marble baths, and views of the river and the city. The Westin also features an outdoor heated pool, a fitness center, and a sauna.

OVER $250

A truly memorable experience awaits at ★ **Hotel Havana** (1015 Navarro St., 210/222-2008, www.havanasanantonio.com, $249-399). Nestled inside a building constructed in 1914 are 27 rooms featuring pine floors and decorated with antique furniture and vintage Cuban artwork. Each room also contains a stocked minibar with local and international snacks and drinks, and complimentary Wi-Fi, flat-screen TVs, and boutique accessories (radios, lamps, fridges) with a charming rustic quality.

Historic Downtown Hotels
$100-150

For those who appreciate a little history with proximity to the action, Best Western's 1914 **Historic Travelers Hotel** (220 Broadway St., 210/455-3473, www.bestwestern.com, $149 d) was once considered an upscale extended-stay establishment for businesspeople. It fell into disrepair by the early 2000s and was renovated and reopened as a spruced-up lodging option. Just a block from the Alamo and two blocks from the Riverwalk, Travelers Hotel is steps from attractions and restaurants. Amenities include free Wi-Fi, complimentary breakfast, and a tiny open-air pool.

In the fancy 1883 Dullnig Building is the 17-room **Riverwalk Vista** (262 Losoya St., 210/223-3200, from $149), a luxury boutique hotel less than a block from the River Walk. The more-affordable rooms are pretty small, but the hotel's historic decor and thoughtful amenities make it a worthwhile experience. Rooms include bottled water as well as feather blankets, cordless phones, ottomans, and fancy baths containing bathrobes, slate showers, lighted makeup mirrors, and plush cotton towels. The Vista's food is a big draw—fresh-baked cookies are served every afternoon along with glasses of wine, and the mega breakfasts include empanadas, quiche, muffins, cereal, and fruit.

Directly behind the Alamo is the remarkable **Crockett Hotel** (320 Bonham St., 210/225-6500, www.crocketthotel.com, $149 d). This magnificent historic establishment is just 18 paces from the Alamo, according to hotel reps, and a five-minute stroll from the River Walk. The lobby is modest yet welcoming, and the rooms are tastefully decorated, with soothing colors and boutique-style features such as interior shutters and regional artwork. The Crockett's amenities include free internet access and a complimentary breakfast offering a tasty egg casserole, pastries, fresh fruit, and cereal. In 2020, extensive upgrades were planned for Alamo Plaza, so check for updates about hotel access and parking.

$150-200

The second-most-famous building on Alamo Plaza is the outstanding ★ **Menger Hotel** (204 Alamo Plaza, 210/223-4361, www.mengerhotel.com, $169 d), a highly recommended 1859 hotel across the street from the Alamo that has been a destination for travelers, ranchers, and dignitaries throughout its 160 years. The busy Victorian-era lobby conjures San Antonio's bygone bustling heyday, when famous guests such as Babe Ruth, Mae West, and Theodore Roosevelt walked the halls (some claim their ghosts now do the roaming). Roosevelt's time at the hotel is well documented in photos and news clips, especially in the Menger Bar, where he recruited Rough Riders and shot bullets into the wall (the holes are still there). The hotel boasts downtown's largest heated swimming pool, a wonderful place to take a dip at night under the stars (don't forget to pack a swimsuit!). The charming historic rooms have extremely high ceilings, antique furnishings, quality bedding, and fantastic views of either the Alamo, the courtyard, or the pool. Additional amenities include a full-service spa, a fitness room, a whirlpool, and free Wi-Fi. In 2020, extensive upgrades were planned for Alamo Plaza, so check for updates about hotel access and parking.

Billing itself the "Jewel of San Antonio" is the magnificent 1906 Victorian-style **Fairmount Hotel** (401 S. Alamo St., 210/224-8800, www.thefairmounthotel-sanantonio.com, $199 d), a block from La Villita, the historic neighborhood turned shopping area and just down the street from the River Walk and the Alamo. The Fairmount features 37 individually decorated rooms and suites in a stately brick building with wrought-iron verandas. The lobby overlooks a jeweled granite and marble courtyard with a fountain and palmetto trees with romantic garden seating. Most of the Fairmount's rooms are intimate suites featuring period furnishings, silk fabrics, fancy tiling, canopy beds, and internet access.

OVER $250

Especially impressive and historic is the **St. Anthony** (300 E. Travis St., 210/227-4392, www.marriott.com, $269 d), an ornate refined Victorian property three blocks from

1: Hotel Havana 2: Historic Travelers Hotel
3: Menger Hotel on Alamo Plaza

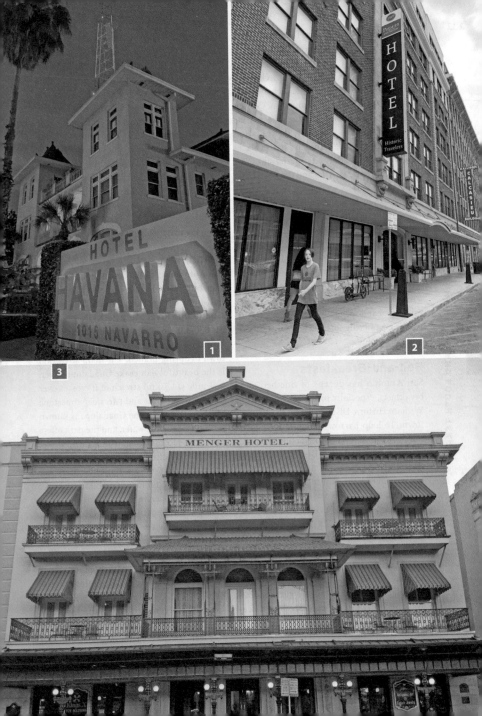

the Alamo and one block from the River Walk. Built in 1909, the hotel is designated a National Historic Landmark and is legendary for its "Peacock Alley" lobby, decked out with 8-foot-wide (2.4-m) crystal chandeliers and original artwork by Remington, Cartier, and DeYoung. The rooms feature Queen Anne decor with custom-tailored bedspreads and antique replicas. The baths have stylish black-and-white-tiled baths and pedestal sinks. All rooms feature free Wi-Fi, and the hotel has a pool and spa tub.

One of San Antonio's fanciest lodging options is the luxurious **Omni La Mansion Del Rio Hotel** (112 College St., 210/518-1000, www.omnihotels.com, $299 d), a Spanish colonial hacienda-style place on the River Walk. Nonguests are drawn to La Mansion for its excellent margaritas. Hotel amenities include a magnificent courtyard with a heated swimming pool and spa along with historical stylish rooms offering internet access, minibars, and plush robes.

Bed-and-Breakfasts

San Antonio has dozens of fine bed-and-breakfasts, especially in the charming King William Historic District just south of downtown. To help narrow the options by location, price, and level of interaction required, visit the **San Antonio Bed & Breakfast Association** (www.sanantoniobb.org).

Considered the finest B&B in town is the **Brackenridge House B & B Inn** (230 Madison St., 210/271-3442, www.brackenridgehouse.com, $139-184), in the King William District. Cozy without being too cute, there are antique furnishings in each room, accompanied by a microwave, a fridge, and free Wi-Fi. Added amenities are drinks, chocolates, and sherry in the guest rooms, and the breakfast is legendary—a three-course feast in the formal dining room. Also distinctive to this B&B is the backyard pool and hot tub.

Rivaling the Brackenridge is the remarkable **Oge Inn** (209 Washington St., 210/223-2353, www.ogeinn.com, from $149). This elegant 1857 mansion is on the banks of the river, and its architectural significance has placed it on the National Register of Historic Places and as a Texas Historical Landmark. Once the home of pioneer Texas Ranger, cattle rancher, and businessperson Louis Ogé, the home now contains 10 guest rooms luxuriously decorated with period antiques, private baths, fireplaces, and fridges, all with free internet access. Non-morning people will appreciate the Oge Inn's private tables, where a full breakfast is served in view of the fireplace or on the majestic front veranda.

Camping

San Antonio isn't a big destination for camping, but several state parks are within a half-hour drive of downtown. The best is **Guadalupe River State Park** (3350 Park Rd. 31, 830/438-2656, www.tpwd.state.tx.us, $7 over age 12), 29 miles (47 km) north of downtown in Spring Branch. The main attraction is the beautiful namesake Guadalupe River. A 9-mile (14.5-km) stretch of it crosses over four natural rapids and two steep limestone bluffs in the park. The Guadalupe is known for its crystal-clear water, and the park offers easy access to canoeing, fishing, swimming, tubing, picnicking, hiking, and camping. The park has a 5-mile (8-km) equestrian trail that's also open for mountain biking.

To stay closer to town in an RV park, the **KOA Campground** (602 Gembler Rd., 210/224-9296, www.koakampgrounds.com) is just a few miles east of town. KOA offers free Wi-Fi and is adjacent to a recreational lake and a golf course. Another option 3 miles (4.8 km) south of the city is **Travelers World RV Park** (2617 Roosevelt Ave., 210/532-8310, www.carefreervresorts.com), offering a city bus line at the main gate, a nearby hike and bike trail, a heated swimming pool, and Wi-Fi. Fees for both campgrounds vary based on site type; visit the websites for details.

INFORMATION AND SERVICES

Tourism Offices

The **San Antonio Visitor Information Center** (317 Alamo Plaza, 210/207-6700 or 800/447-3372, www.visitsanantonio.com, daily 9am-5pm) is in the historic Crockett building between the Alamo and the River Walk. Maps, guides, brochures, souvenirs, and expert advice from professional staff are available. Drop by the **San Antonio Convention & Visitors Bureau** (203 S. St. Mary's St., 210/207-6700 or 800/447-3372, www.visitsanantonio.com, daily 8am-5:30pm) to get the scoop on where things are and how to get there. Another handy service organization is the **Greater San Antonio Chamber of Commerce** (602 E. Commerce St., 210/229-2100, www.sachamber.org), with comprehensive listings of hotels, restaurants, attractions, and events on its website.

For specific information about River Walk businesses, including hours and locations, contact the **San Antonio River Walk Association** (110 Broadway, Suite 500, 210/227-4262, www.thesanantonioriverwalk.com).

Publications

San Antonio's daily newspaper, the *San Antonio Express-News,* is a good source about South Texas politics and culture. The *San Antonio Current* is the city's alternative newsweekly, featuring local writers and critics covering politics, arts, music, and food. It's distributed every Wednesday at hundreds of locations citywide, including most downtown coffee shops and bars.

GETTING THERE AND AROUND

The **San Antonio International Airport** (SAT, 9800 Airport Blvd., 210/207-3411, www.sanantonio.gov) is 12 miles (19.3 km) north of downtown and hosts flights on 10 U.S. and Mexican airlines. For those not using a ride-share, taxis cost about $40 and take about 20-30 minutes between the airport and downtown. Taxi stations are outside the airport terminals, and unlike most cities, up to four people can share a cab for the same fare without paying additional per-person or luggage fees.

San Antonio has a reliable public transportation system, **VIA Metropolitan Transit** (210/362-2020, www.viainfo.net, from $1.20), that runs 100 bus lines and a downtown streetcar service.

A unique way to get around town is via river taxi with **Go Rio Cruises** (202 E. Nueva St., 210/227-4746, www.goriocruises.com, $13.50 adults, $10.50 seniors, $7.50 ages 1-5), which specializes in tours but can also arrange for transportation. Shuttle tickets ($19.50) allow passengers to get off and on the shuttle at their pace, throughout downtown and the museum reaches, for the entire day.

NEW BRAUNFELS

New Braunfels is synonymous with German heritage and tubing (floating in an inner tube on the river). This town of 84,612, just northeast of San Antonio, started when German immigrants used the dependable strong-flowing Comal Springs and Guadalupe River as a source for power and navigation. By the mid-1800s, New Braunfels was a growing agricultural area and manufacturing center supplying wagons, farm equipment, clothing, and furniture for Central Texas pioneers. The subsequent population boom resulted in New Braunfels being the fourth-largest town in Texas in 1850. People continued to arrive after the Civil War, and agriculture grew with the population. By the mid-1900s, the area had become a recreational hot spot catering to San Antonio residents with second homes on nearby Canyon Lake or the scenic Guadalupe River. Motels, resorts, and tubing companies soon followed, cementing New Braunfels's reputation as a unique spot to relax on the water or spend time at the numerous antiques shops and German restaurants.

★ Gruene Historic District

Quaint can mean frilly quilts, tea sets, and

doilies, but when combined with the authentically rustic, it can be downright charming. The modest **Gruene Historic District** (Gruene is pronounced "green"), a few miles northwest of New Braunfels, is a heritage tourism destination. The several-block area retains its authentic character from the late 1800s, when German immigrant Henry D. Gruene built a mercantile store and later a cotton gin and dance hall to serve the sharecroppers who settled in the area. The small community was bustling until the 1920s, when Depression and a nasty plague of boll weevils wiped out the cotton business and, consequently, the town. In the 1970s, several San Antonio and New Braunfels entrepreneurs saw potential in the abandoned buildings, and people seeking recreation on the nearby Guadalupe River added shopping and dancing to their weekend itineraries.

The district's most remarkable structure is the magnificent 1878 **Gruene Hall** (1281 Gruene Rd., 830/606-1281, www.gruenehall. com), the oldest continually running dance hall in Texas. This Hill Country treasure's sturdy German-constructed wooden floors and long tables have witnessed more than a century of country and roots rock music. Overlooking the scene are reproduced beer and soft-drink ads. Americana artists play Gruene Hall several nights a week and include well-known regional acts like Robert Earl Keen, Kelly Willis and Bruce Robison, and Delbert McClinton, and some heavy-hitting national stars like George Strait and Lyle Lovett. Check the website for upcoming performances.

Shopping in Gruene isn't too overwhelming—there are only a couple of main streets, and the historic buildings are spaced apart. One of the highlights is the 1875 **Gruene General Store** (1610 Hunter Rd., 830/629-6021, www.gruenegeneralstore.com, daily 9am-sunset), containing everything you'd expect to find in an old-time mercantile business, from Texas-made candy, coffee, jams, and trinkets to home decor and clothing.

The adjacent **Grapevine** (1612 Hunter Rd., 830/606-0093, www.grapevineingruene.com, Mon.-Fri. 10am-8pm, Sat.-Sun. 10am-9pm) is a wine-tasting store featuring quality Texas wines, specialty beers, and gourmet gifts and food. The **Gruene Antique Company** (1607 Hunter Rd., 830/629-7781, www.grueneantiqueco.com, daily 10am-9pm) is an enormous space containing antiques and collectibles in H. D. Gruene's 1903 mercantile building. The **Tipsy Gypsy** (1710 Hunter

the legendary Gruene Hall in New Braunfels

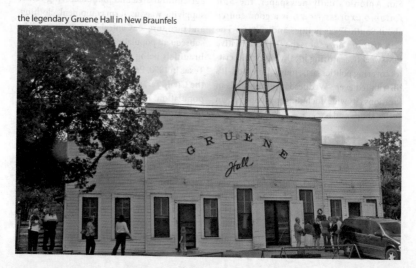

Rd., 830/625-4431, Mon.-Fri. 10am-5pm, Sat.-Sun. 10am-6pm) is a funky boutique with colorful and flashy new and consignment items.

McKenna Children's Museum
McKenna Children's Museum (386 W. San Antonio St., 830/606-9525, www.mckennakids.org, Mon.-Sat. 10am-5pm, $7.50 over age 1) rivals big-city facilities in San Antonio and Austin and will keep kids occupied and educated for hours. On hot days, head to the outdoor area, where a raised water canal offers fountains, hoses, bridges, movable dams, and so many boats and rubber ducks you won't hear the parental command of "share." Inside, an imagination world awaits with miniature environments offering kids the chance to play in a town square, grocery store, hospital, tool shed, ranch house, and campground. There's also a Tot Spot for barely walking babies, an outer space area, and a large hall for traveling kid-oriented art and educational exhibits.

★ Tubing the Guadalupe River
Grab an inner tube (a cooler full of beverages is standard or optional, depending on who you ask), plop it in the Guadalupe River, and let the lazy current carry you down a refreshing tree-lined waterway. It's a pleasant way to spend a hot summer day, even though city officials have adopted ordinances that prohibit tubers from carrying coolers with capacities of more than 16 quarts to reign in the college-age drinkers. The party-on-the-water atmosphere left empty beer cans and bottles littering the scenic river. Now the shenanigans can continue, but the scene is cleaner and more family-friendly.

Dozens of reliable companies provide tube rental service. Check out the River Outfitters link at the website of the **New Braunfels Chamber of Commerce** (www.playinnewbraunfels.com). The following are recommended by veteran tubers.

River Sports Tubes (12034 FM 306, 830/964-2450, www.riversportstubes.com, Sun.-Fri. 9am-7pm, Sat. 8am-7pm), 12 miles (19.3 km) west of town, has a prime spot on the Guadalupe in the busy Horseshoe Loop. Tubers have the option of taking short, medium, or long floats, and when they're done, the shuttle returns them to home base. Tube rental is $20, a cooler costs $10, and the shuttle is $5.

In Gruene, the local hot spot is **Rockin' R River Rides** (1405 Gruene Rd., 800/553-5628, www.rockinr.com), the only river outfitter in New Braunfels with locations on both the Guadalupe and Comal Rivers. Tube rental is $23.

Another popular rental spot is **Roy's Rentals & Campground** (6530 River Rd., 830/964-3721, www.roysrentals.com). Campsites are available, and in addition to rental tubes ($20), Roy's provides inflatable canoes, regular canoes, and rafts.

Schlitterbahn Waterpark
For three months a year, the German word *Schlitterbahn* (slippery road) is on every South Texas kid's lips, the ubiquitous summertime slogan of **Schlitterbahn Waterpark** (381 E. Austin St., 830/625-2351, www.schlitterbahn.com, June-Aug. daily, Apr.-May and Sept. Sat.-Sun., $51 adults, $39 children). "Water park" doesn't begin to describe this summer wonderland, featuring more than 3 miles (4.8 km) of tubing "trails," 17 waterslides, seven water playgrounds, a surfing machine, and three unique "uphill water coasters." Attractions include dueling speed slides, tube chutes, and soft slides for toddlers. Teens can get their adrenaline rush on the speedy downhill racing slides while parents spend time leisurely inner tubing on the slow-moving Kristal River ride, and the little ones can splash in the kiddie pools. Admission covers tubes, life jackets, and a souvenir cup with free refills.

Natural Bridge Caverns
About 12 miles (19.3 km) west of town, the otherworldly **Natural Bridge Caverns** (26495 Natural Bridge Caverns Rd., 210/651-6101, www.naturalbridgecaverns.com, Oct.-Feb. daily 9am-4pm, Mar.-Sept. hours vary, $21-25 adults, $14-15 ages 3-11, tours every

10-40 minutes) are an escape from the heat: The caverns' temperature is a steady 70°F (21°C), although the 99 percent humidity makes it feel like Houston. Visitors descend 200 feet (60 m) below ground via cement walkways to a surreal world of natural formations with names like soda straws, chandeliers, flowstones, and cave ribbon. Strollers are difficult to operate here, and toddlers might not have the patience or interest.

Several tours are available: The standard North Cavern Tour is a 75-minute half-mile trek past stalagmites, stalactites, flowstones, and formations such as the King's Throne and Sherwood Forest. The Flashlight Tour, takes place in a 120-foot-deep (37-m) chamber filled with delicate formations like the brittle soda straws. Each person gets a flashlight to check out the nooks and crannies at their leisure. The Adventure Tour ($100) is a physically demanding three-plus-hour excursion allowing visitors to climb, rappel, and explore the cavern; gear is provided.

Sophienburg Museum

New Braunfels's cultural history is on display at the **Sophienburg Museum** (401 W. Coll St., 830/629-1572, www.sophienburg.org, Tues.-Sat. 10am-4pm, $8 adults, $4 students, $2 ages 6-12). The town's German heritage takes center stage, with hundreds of artifacts telling the story of settlers in the mid-1800s. Docents describe how the original village was founded by Prince Carl of Solms Braunfels, and historic photos and documents chronicle these events. A replica town containing a castle, a general store, a pharmacy, a doctor's office, and a saloon transport visitors to this bygone era.

Food

★ **The Gristmill** (1287 Gruene Rd., 830/625-0684, www.gristmillrestaurant.com, Sun.-Thurs. 11am-9pm, Fri.-Sat. 11am-10pm, $12-31) is a must in Gruene. In a historic cotton gin building beneath the iconic Gruene water tower, it embodies tastefully done rustic comfort. This multilevel establishment overlooks the scenic Guadalupe River. Start with an order of perfectly breaded sweet onion rings and proceed to anything on the Southern-tinged menu. The beef tenderloin sandwich with avocado and horseradish sauce is especially tasty, as are the burgers, fried catfish, and tomatillo chicken. Good luck saving room for the delectable fudge pie.

For a German experience in this German town, try **Friesenhaus** (148 S. Castell St., 830/237-8862, www.friesenhausnb.com, Mon.-Sat. 11am-10pm, Sun. 11am-9pm, $10-27), named for the family's home in northern Germany. Breaded pork schnitzel is the specialty, but the steaks, sausage, and seafood are equally tempting. Sample some of the flavorful breads and rolls made daily in the bakery, and stick with the German tradition by accompanying everything with local beer.

Better known as a national meat delivery company, the **New Braunfels Smokehouse** (140 S. Hwy. 46, 830/625-2416, www.nb-smokehouse.com, Mon.-Fri. 10:30am-6pm, Fri.-Sat. 7:30am-8pm, Sun. 7:30am-6pm, $13-33) has a restaurant just off the freeway that serves savory hickory-smoked meats on a plate rather than in a box. Sausages are the most popular items, but locals return for the brisket, ham, ribs, and chicken and dumplings. At breakfast, don't miss the eggs and smoked sausage or pork chop combos. Lunches feature smoked ham, turkey, pastrami, and Canadian bacon sandwiches on homemade bread.

A break from the German and Hill Country scene is the popular downtown **Huisache Grill & Wine Bar** (303 W. San Antonio St., 830/620-9001, www.huisache.com, daily 11am-10pm, $13-33). Housed in a modest late 19th-century building with beautiful woodwork and abundant natural light, Huisache features freshly prepared eclectic cuisine in a comfy setting. You can't go wrong with the mixed grill of beef tenderloin kebabs, wild boar sausage, and seared duck, or baked salmon.

Accommodations

BED-AND-BREAKFASTS

New Braunfels is a B&B town, especially in the Gruene Historic District. San Antonio and Austin residents make weekend getaways to Gruene B&Bs to tube and shop. A popular destination is **Gruene Mansion Inn** (1275 Gruene Rd., 830/629-2641, www.gruenemansioninn.com, weekends usually 2-night minimum, $195). This Victorian home of the town's namesake, Henry D. Gruene, is now listed on the National Register of Historic Places. Gruene's mansion was converted into 30 guest rooms, each with its own entrance, private bath, and porch, and the rooms are decorated with a heavily furnished "Victorian rustic elegance." Free Wi-Fi is available, and breakfast is a buffet with hot items, pastries, breads, and fruit.

Highly regarded **Gruene Homestead Inn** (832 Gruene Rd., 830/606-0216 or 800/238-5534, www.gruenehomesteadinn.com, from $165) is a collection of historic farmhouses on eight acres. Amenities include private baths and porches, free Wi-Fi, and full breakfast. Guests have access to the swimming pool and hot tub, and family accommodations on this former German homestead are in cottages and guest houses that sleep up to five. Catch a local blues or Americana band on the inn's grounds at Tavern in the Gruene, a live music venue featuring a full bar, a shuffleboard table, and a horseshoe pit.

HOTELS

New Braunfels has several decent nonchain accommodations, including the fancy 1929 **Faust Hotel** (240 S. Seguin Ave., 830/625-7791, www.fausthotel.com, from $149 d), with an on-site microbrewery. The Faust Brewing Company beer garden serves tasty housemade brews, including a crisp *hefeweizen*. The rooms have period furnishings and free Wi-Fi. The hotel also provides free breakfast.

Not as upscale is the tuber-friendly collection of cottages on the river at **The Other Place** (385 Other Place Dr., 830/625-5114, www.theotherplaceresort.com, cabins $180-300). This natural spot was founded as Camp Giesecke in 1910, and its four wooded acres are bordered by 1,400 feet (430 m) of river frontage in the horseshoe bend of the Comal River. Each unit has central air and heat, a full kitchen with dishes and utensils, a dining area, Wi-Fi access, and a private porch overlooking the river. There are no phones or TVs in the rooms.

Information and Services

The sheer number of tubing options and German tourism activities can be mind-boggling. Drop by the **New Braunfels Chamber of Commerce** (390 S. Seguin Ave., 830/625-2385 or 800/572-2626, www.playin-newbraunfels.com), where friendly staffers will provide brochures and directions.

Getting There and Around

From San Antonio, New Braunfels is a quick 30-minute drive north on I-35. Take exit 185 and head north on Spur Street. To reach Gruene, continue through the city for about 1 mile (1.6 km) on the same road, which becomes Common Street.

Del Rio

Del Rio (population 35,954) is a worthy destination for the Native American pictographs and archaeological sites in Amistad National Recreation Area and Seminole Canyon State Park. Although it seems isolated, Del Rio is under two hours' drive west of San Antonio. Make a day trip or an overnight for the ancient Native American rock art.

Del Rio's history is tied to the San Felipe Springs, which gush 100 million gallons of clear cool water each day. Native Americans and later Spanish settlers used the springs to forge irrigation systems, eventually developing a canal system that diverted water to 1,500 acres of surrounding land.

Soon after the canal system was formalized in 1871, two major railroads linked up just west of the city, and the resulting economic boom established Del Rio as a burgeoning border town and division headquarters for the railroad. By the 20th century, a large portion of Del Rio's economy was government: the border patrol, Laughlin Air Force Base, customs offices, and a federal courthouse.

Del Rio's cultural legacy has an intriguing tale in the border blaster radio saga. In the late 1950s "Dr." John R. Brinkley made international waves when he advertised his controversial hormone-enhancing medical procedures (involving goat gland transplants) from his radio station in Ciudad Acuña, across the border from Del Rio. U.S. radio stations were federally regulated as how powerful their signals could be, but Brinkley's Mexican station, XER, at broadcast 250,000 watts, five times the U.S. limit. In the early 1960s, he hired a gravelly voiced deejay named Wolfman Jack, who became a vital figure in early rock-and-roll history thanks to the high voltage beaming his voice throughout the continent.

SIGHTS
★ Seminole Canyon State Park

The steep narrow canyons of the Rio Grande and Pecos River have provided shelter for thousands of years and preserved ancient materials. Some of the most impressive examples are ancient Native American artwork, the focal point of **Seminole Canyon State Park** (U.S. 90, 432/292-4464, www.tpwd.state.tx.us, daily, $4 over age 12), 38 miles (61 km) west of Del Rio. The park's main attraction is Fate Bell Shelter, containing an mesmerizing array of ancient pictographs, including shamanic figures, animal images, and soul-stirring handprints.

The intention of the paintings is lost with the people who made them, but that makes them intriguing. What were they communicating with these drawings? What do the mystic shamanic figures represent? What were conditions like in this region so many millennia ago? What is known is that the various Native American groups, collectively referred to as the people of the Lower Pecos River, lived in small bands and subsisted off small animals and wild plants. The pictographs, made with rust-colored paint derived from animal oils and plant materials, depict many of these animals, along with shamanic figures. Some historians suggest the shamans are symbols of medicine men or spiritual beings connecting them to different levels of consciousness via hallucinogenic herbs and plants.

The park's **Fate Bell Shelter Tour** (June-Aug. Wed.-Sun. 10am, Sept.-May Wed.-Sun. 10am and 3pm, $8 adults, $5 ages 5-12) involves a fairly rugged hike to the bottom of the canyon and then up to the art-filled rock shelter. Volunteers with the nonprofit **Rock Art Foundation** (888/762-5278, www.rock-art.org) conduct the tours, and the group also offers weekend trips to the region's other noteworthy rock art sites, including the Galloway

Lower Pecos Rock Art

Panthers, shamans, deer, and abstract figures adorn the walls of hundreds of rock shelters in the Lower Pecos region, just west of Del Rio, where the Pecos and Devils Rivers join the Rio Grande. Known as rock art or pictographs, these ancient images, believed to be 3,000-4,000 years old, represent possibly the largest collection in North America.

Evidence of human habitation in the Lower Pecos region dates back at least 10,000 years, and archaeologists estimate the rock art was created 3000 BC-AD 1880. Several distinct types of pictographs include the Archaic-age Pecos River style, with scenes depicting stylized figures and humans; the Late Archaic period's tiny dark-red rock art; the Late Prehistoric period's multicolored (red, orange, and yellow) solid human and animal figures; and the Historic style, including drawings showing European influence.

Controversially, some archaeologists think hallucinogenic peyote, mountain laurel beans, and jimson weed may have influenced the artists' work. Many depict shamans, who served an important role in Native American communities as healers, diviners, and guardians who journeyed to the spirit world through altered states of consciousness.

White Shaman Preserve, the Casper Site, and the Curly Tail Panther Site.

Although Seminole Canyon is primarily devoted to ancient pictographs, there are other things to do between visits to rock shelters. The park includes an insightful and well-researched interpretive center, campsites with water and electricity, 8 miles (12.9 km) of multiuse trails for hiking and mountain biking, and nature and interpretive trails.

Panther Cave

Panther Cave has been referred to as the Sistine Chapel of American rock art. This mesmerizing rock shelter, featuring 4,000-year-old Native American pictographs, is only accessible by boat (call 830/775-7491 to make arrangements), and even at a choppy 45 mph (72 km/h) it takes an hour to get there. After traversing Lake Amistad, an artificial reservoir on the Rio Grande just west of Del Rio, visitors ascend a steep steel staircase along the canyon wall to see this spectacular rock art.

Stretched across a 100-foot-wide (30-m) canvas of limestone are more than 100 rust-colored images depicting animals and magnificent shamanic figures created by Native Americans long before the ancient Egyptians built the Great Pyramid. The centerpiece is

the cave's namesake 10-foot-long (3-m) panther, a reddish-brown profile of a massive cat on its hind legs with spiky hair on its back and an unusually long tail. Visitors will be transfixed. A chain-link fence limits up-close interaction with the paintings, and there are nearby informative panels.

The National Park Service manages Panther Cave with Seminole Canyon State Park. Droughts can result in lower lake levels and occasional loss of access to the cave.

Amistad National Recreation Area

Lake Amistad (Spanish for "friendship") was created in 1969 by Amistad Dam, an enormous structure containing two bronze eagles at the center, symbolizing the spirit of cooperation between the United States and Mexico. The National Park Service manages the **Amistad National Recreation Area** (830/775-7491, www.nps.gov/amis) and its impressive 67,000 surface acres of water along 540 miles (870 km) of U.S. shoreline. The lake is a popular destination for year-round boating, fishing, swimming, scuba diving, water-skiing, and bird-watching. Most of the water activity originates at one of the lake's marinas, where visitors can arrange slip rentals and purchase fuel, bait, ice, snacks, and beverages.

Border Radio

Way before MTV and blogs, people relied on the radio for exposure to new music. Most cities had AM stations with news and religious broadcasts, but a different animal took to the airwaves in the 1960s: Wolfman Jack became a legendary growly voiced DJ spinning records from a small radio studio just across the Rio Grande from Del Rio. A modest exhibit about this distinctive saga in media history is at Del Rio's **Whitehead Memorial Museum** (1308 S. Main St., 830/774-7568, www.whiteheadmuseum.org, Tues.-Sat. 10am-6pm, Sun. 1pm-5pm, $8 adults, $6 seniors, $3 ages 13-18, $2 ages 6-12).

Whitehead Memorial Museum

Known as border radio or border blasters, these stations became powerful ambassadors of early rock-and-roll because their high wattage—often operating at five times the power allowed by U.S. regulators—transmitted the broadcasts across the entire hemisphere. In the 1930s, Americans as far away as New York and Seattle were exposed to Western swing and Mexican folk music; by the 1950s-1960s the sounds of Southern blues and early rhythm and blues bands spread via transistor radios.

The most famous of the border radio stations was XER, later called XERA, home of Wolfman Jack and controversial "goat-gland doctor" John Brinkley. Brinkley made a fortune from his bizarre medical procedure—a gland transplant operation from goat to man to supposedly increase libido. He used his wealth to open the radio station in neighboring Ciudad Acuña and a hospital in Del Rio. The 300-foot-tall (90-m) border blaster transmitters in Mexico advertised the procedure across the continent and brought occasionally unwanted attention to Del Rio. Regardless, the country and rock music had a lasting cultural impact on the United States and inspired many would-be musicians to pick up a guitar and imitate the sounds they heard on "good ol' XER."

FISHING

Professional anglers are hooked on Amistad Reservoir's high-quality year-round fishing, especially for largemouth, smallmouth, and striped bass. By boat or on shore, fishers also cast lines for channel and blue catfish, crappie, various species of sunfish, and alligator gar. Catch-and-release is encouraged. What's required, however, is a valid Texas fishing license for the U.S. side of Amistad Reservoir. Mexico also requires a fishing license for boaters in its waters. Numbered buoys running along the main channel of the Rio Grande indicate the border with Mexico. The permits are available at **Fisherman's Headquarters** (in the Chevron, U.S. 90 W. and U.S. 277 N., 830/774-5670).

BOATING

At any given time of year you'll see boats on Amistad Reservoir. Personal watercraft, ski boats, sailboats, and houseboats are commonly seen on the clear lake thanks to the mild weather. A lake use permit is required for the U.S. side, and Mexico also requires a boat permit for use of its waters. Boating permits can be purchased at **Amistad Visitor Information Center** (U.S. 90 W., 830/775-7491, daily 8am-5pm), 5 miles (8 km) west of the park headquarters. Permits are available at ATM-type machines at Diablo East, Rough Canyon, Box Canyon, and the Pecos. The National Park Service also charges a lake use fee for all watercraft requiring state registration. The fees are $4 daily or $10 for a three-day pass.

CAMPING

Don't expect fancy camping accommodations or RV hookups at Amistad. The lake's four campgrounds are for hard-core campers, with the only amenities being site pads, covered picnic tables, and grills. The only campground offering potable water is **Governors Landing** (4121 Veterans Blvd., 830/775-7491, www.nps.gov/amis), with sites ($4) for tents or RVs under 28 feet (8.5 m).

Historic Buildings

Like other border towns, Del Rio has retained an impressive number of historic structures, due to economic forces rather than a strong preservation ethic. Ultimately the economic struggle means that border communities like Del Rio have magnificent structures from the early 1900s that were bulldozed in other places in the 1950s. For a guide detailing the location and background of 30 historic buildings in town, drop by the **Del Rio Chamber of Commerce downtown office** (1915 Ave. F).

One of the city's gems is in the heart of downtown, the 1887 **Val Verde County Courthouse** (400 Pecan St.). Noted for its distinctive tan-colored limestone, it features handsome stonework forged by Native American masons. Del Rio celebrated the restoration of this magnificent Classical Revival structure through the Texas Historical Commission's Texas Historic Courthouse Preservation Program. Nearby **Sacred Heart Church** (320 Mill St.) is another spectacular example of regional architecture. Construction of this native limestone church began in 1891, and the Gothic Revival building was enlarged and remodeled in 1929.

Just up the street is the fetching **Firehouse Gallery** (120 E. Garfield St., 830/775-0888, www.delrioarts.com), now housing the Del Rio Council for the Arts. This charming two-story structure, which hosts arts-related programs and exhibits, once served as city hall, a jail, and a fire station. Just a few blocks away is Del Rio's historic downtown district, featuring a fascinating combo of late-1800s buildings and mid-century modern slipcovers and storefronts.

Historic for different reasons is the **Brinkley Mansion** (512 Qualia Dr.). Built in the early 1930s, this Spanish Eclectic-style residence was home to the infamous "goat-gland doctor" John R. Brinkley of border radio fame. The house serves as a monument to one of the country's biggest medical frauds, a procedure known as the "Brinkley operation," where a gland transplant from a goat supposedly restored virility in men. Patients and money rolled in, and Brinkley used his profits to establish the 250,000-watt XER radio station across the border, where Wolfman Jack and early rock-and-roll were introduced to the continent. He also enhanced his home with flashing colored lights, elaborate water features, and speakers connected to a pipe organ inside. Locals would gather outside this local landmark to dance to the music and enjoy the light show.

Whitehead Memorial Museum

Local history is the main draw at the **Whitehead Memorial Museum** (1308 S. Main St., 830/774-7568, www.whiteheadmuseum.org, Tues.-Sat. 10am-6pm, Sun. 1pm-5pm, $8 adults, $6 seniors, $3 ages 13-18, $2 ages 6-12). Named for a local ranching family who preserved the historic 1871 Perry Store, the open-air museum contains a two-acre frontier village featuring the store and 20 other exhibit sites, including a replica of local legend Judge Roy Bean's famous combined saloon-courtroom building as well as Bean's actual gravesite. Also featured are a portion of the San Felipe irrigation canal, an exhibit on the Black Seminole Indian tribe, and a building dedicated to border radio.

San Felipe Springs

Del Rio's **San Felipe Springs** were a vital watering stop for indigenous people and later settlers on the historic Chihuahua Road. Nearly 100 million gallons of clear, clean water flow from the springs daily. It no longer fills the historic irrigation canals that

1

2

Chunto's Mexican Restaurant

run throughout town, but it still sustains of Del Rio and nearby Laughlin Air Force Base. Locals use the springs to cool off on hot afternoons. Moore City Park has stone banks offering a safe and shallow place for kids to play, and the swimming hole at Horseshoe Park is popular for a dip. To reach the source of San Felipe Creek, take U.S. 90 west into town; look for San Felipe Country Club on your right. The road through the golf course, San Felipe Springs Road, leads to the source.

Brackettville

Take a few hours to visit **Brackettville** (population 1,784), on U.S. 90 about 30 miles (48 km) east of Del Rio. A main attraction is **Fort Clark Springs** (830/563-2495, www.fortclark.com, call ahead for reservations and accessibility), a spectacular hotel, pool, museum, and golf course that combines military history and modern-day recreation at the site of a former U.S. Army fort. Stay in the recently restored barracks, which offer modest comfortable rooms. Stroll the old fort grounds, where former officers' quarters are now residences, including the home of famed General George S. Patton. The highlight is a massive spring-fed pool that has offered a cool respite for centuries.

The fort's historical significance lies in its role as the base for the Army's Black Seminole Scouts, enslaved people displaced from Florida who gained respect as soldiers along the Mexican border after the Civil War. The **Seminole Indian Scout Cemetery,** just west of Brackettville on FM 693, honors their legacy.

FOOD

American

In a faux log cabin, **Cripple Creek Steakhouse** (U.S. 90 W., 830/775-0153, Mon.-Sat. 5pm-10pm, $9-27) is one of the best places in town for standard steak and seafood dishes. The mesquite-grilled steaks are

popular, as is the seafood, including lobster, swordfish, shrimp, and crab. A small outdoor petting zoo keeps the kids entertained before, during, and after the meal. A bonus for locavores: Cripple Creek serves wine from Del Rio's very own Val Verde Winery.

Another favorite local hangout is **Blue Oasis Bar & Grill** (3806 Veterans Blvd., 830/313-7088, Sun.-Thurs. 11am-10pm, Fri.-Sat. 11am-11pm, $8-18), a no-frills establishment that focuses more on hearty food than quaint atmosphere. The Corona Chicken is a signature menu item, and other popular dishes include the barbecue sandwich and meaty burgers and steaks.

Mexican and Tex-Mex

Since it's no longer considered safe to cross to nearby Ciudad Acuña in Mexico, opt to sample Del Rio's restaurants.

At the top of the list is **Memo's** (804 E. Losoya St., 830/774-1583, www.memosrestaurant.com, Mon.-Sat. 11am-2pm and 5:30pm-9:30pm, $7-18), known for its history more than its respectable Tex-Mex fare and steaks. Since 1936 the restaurant has been operated by the Calderon family, including "Blondie" Calderon, who achieved fame as the lead piano player and conductor for Ray Price's Cherokee Cowboys Band. The restaurant hosts Latin-themed jam sessions on Thursday nights. Food favorites include the Tampiqueña dinner (tenderized steak in a spicy sauce with a cheese enchilada on the side) and Blondie's *guizado* (*carne guisada* and an enchilada).

Known for tremendous tacos and a fabulous collection of Mexican wrestling masks, **Chinto's Super Taco** (400 E. 6th St., 830/774-1592, daily 6am-2:30pm, $6-14) is a hot spot for Tex-Mex breakfast and lunch, with line-ups for breakfast tacos and lunch specials. The al pastor pork tacos are a specialty, and the tortillas are handmade. Sit at a table near the wall of *luchador* masks—the wrestling costumes come in a fascinating array of colors and styles, a perfect accompaniment to your meal.

One of the newest options is **Manuel's Steakhouse** (1312 Veterans Blvd.,

1: downtown Del Rio's county courthouse
2: Chinto's Super Taco

830/488-6044, www.manuelssteakhouse. com, Tues.-Sun. 11am-10pm, $8-19), straddling Tex and Mex in a rare opportunity to experience a Mexican restaurant (the original location is in Ciudad Acuña) without crossing into Mexico. Steaks are the specialty, but the Mexican menu is extensive and delicious, with northern Mexico favorites such as *pericos* (fancy nachos), quail legs, and *mollejas* (sweetbreads). The fresh guacamole is some of the best the border has to offer.

ACCOMMODATIONS
Hotels

Among the reliably consistent chains are **La Quinta Inn Del Rio** (2005 Veterans Blvd., 830/775-7591, www.lq.com, $64 d), featuring free internet access in all rooms, a free deluxe continental breakfast, and an outdoor pool. Another worthy option is **Best Western Inn of Del Rio** (810 Veterans Blvd., 830/775-7511, www.bestwesterntexas.com, $74 d), offering "the largest rooms in the area," complete with microwaves and fridges, along with free Wi-Fi, a free breakfast, and an outdoor pool and hot tub.

A modest step up in price and quality is **Hampton Inn & Suites** (2219 N. Bedell Ave., 830/775-9700, www.hamptoninn.com, $109 d). Amenities include a free hot breakfast, free internet access and lap desks, an outdoor swimming pool, and a fitness center.

Camping

Del Rio's camping options are no-frills campsites for fishers and hunters, and full-service parks for RVs. For tent camping, the best place is close to the action at Amistad National Recreation Area. For the RV crowd, there's **Holiday Trav-L Park** (11490 W. Hwy. 90, 830/775-7275, www.holidaytrav-l-park.com, $33-36), with free Wi-Fi access (with tech support), bathhouses, a swimming pool, free coffee and breakfast, and car rentals. Another option is Lonesome **Dove RV Ranch** (4832 W. Hwy. 90, 830/774-1823, $28), offering full hookups, showers, a swimming pool, and a laundry room.

INFORMATION AND SERVICES

The **Del Rio Chamber of Commerce** (1915 Veterans Blvd., 830/775-3551, www.drchamber.com) distributes maps and brochures, and provides visitor information about the area. Check with them for details about walking and driving tours of Del Rio, and information about the latest news in Ciudad Acuña.

GETTING THERE AND AROUND

It's an easy two-hour drive from San Antonio to Del Rio on U.S. 90 west. You'll see signs for downtown Del Rio (Ave. J).

Laredo

Although Laredo's (population 261,639) reputation as a fun destination was tarnished by drug cartel violence in neighboring Nuevo Laredo, the city is safe to visit, with authentic Mexican culture, historic buildings, and abundant birding opportunities.

Laredo is the only place within the state's current borders to have fallen under seven flags, including the short-lived Republic of the Rio Grande, created in 1840 by a constitutional convention after several prominent

Laredoans joined a revolt to protest the Mexican government. Violent clashes erupted, including a brutal battle that ended with the execution of the republic's chief army lieutenant, Antonio Zapata. His severed head was displayed as a warning. Representatives ultimately surrendered later that year, ending the Republic of the Rio Grande after 283 days.

Unlike many border towns in the Lower Rio Grande Valley, Laredo has retained its Hispanic culture without yielding to the religious and architectural influences European settlers imposed on other Texas cities. Anglo settlers here married into Mexican families and assimilated, rather than enforcing their culture on the older residents. Local historians refer to it as a comfortable "Hispanicization," with newcomers easily picking up the language and customs.

This resulted in the Rio Grande being considered more a psychological dividing line than a physical border, at least until the recent gang-related violence in Nuevo Laredo made Mexico a dangerous destination. Laredo's ties to northern Mexico are long-standing; the city was split when the international boundary was established as the Rio Grande in 1755. Until recently, families freely traversed the border, living and working on both sides of the river. This binationalism is reflected in the city's architecture, referred to as border vernacular, with downtown buildings combining traditional Mexican adobe or mission elements with U.S. neoclassical style.

SIGHTS
San Agustin Plaza

A center of activity is **San Agustin Plaza,** formerly a thriving town square near the Rio Grande with traditional Mexican elements such as a cathedral, a hotel, mercantile stores, and a central park. The most striking feature is **San Agustin Cathedral** (214 San Bernardo Ave.), a focal point on the east side of the plaza. The parish was established in 1778, and the current building dates to 1872. The masonry Gothic Revival structure boasts a spectacular five-story tower and spire, making it the second-tallest building in Laredo. The cathedral is the seat of the Catholic Diocese of Laredo.

On the south side of the plaza is the compelling **La Posada Hotel** (1000 Zaragoza St.), in remarkable Spanish colonial-style architecture. The site dates to 1767, when it served as city hall. It later became Laredo's first convent before transforming into Laredo High School and subsequently a hotel in 1966.

On the La Posada grounds is the **Washington's Birthday Celebration Museum** (956/722-1701, Tues.-Sat. 11am-4pm, free), featuring costumes, photos, and exhibits related to Laredo's 115-year-old fiesta honoring George Washington. The city holds Washington in high regard for his role in making the United States welcoming for the many cultures that influenced Laredo's heritage. The celebration itself is held in February, drawing 400,000 people for parades, a carnival, concerts, fireworks, and traditional exchange of *abrazos* (hugs) representing the "friendly" relationship between the United States and Mexico.

Next door to La Posada is the **Republic of the Rio Grande Museum** (1005 Zaragoza St., 956/727-3480, Tues.-Sat. 9am-4pm, $4) in a circa-1830 Mexican vernacular home that served as the capitol building for the short-lived republic. The museum features artifacts related to the republic, which existed for a scant 283 days in 1840, along with other documents and photos showcasing Laredo's history.

Local history is also on display at the nearby **Villa Antigua Border Heritage Museum** (810 Zaragoza St., 956/727-3480, www.webbheritage.org, Tues.-Sat. 9am-4pm, $6). In a historic Italianate-style home, the museum offers photos and artifacts relating to regional history along with traveling exhibits.

Laredo Center for the Arts

Laredo isn't a hotbed of artistic activity, but the **Laredo Center for the Arts** (500 San Agustin Ave., 956/725-1715, www.laredoartcenter.org, Tues.-Sat. 11am-4pm, free) "promotes the artistic creativity of all people" by hosting artistic and cultural events such as international art exhibits, dance performances, lectures, musical performances, and art education classes. The center is also home to the Webb County Heritage Foundation and hosts a gallery for the Laredo Art League. Three galleries showcase the work of local student artists.

Fort McIntosh

Fort McIntosh (west end of Washington St., www.laredo.edu), on the campus of Laredo

Laredo

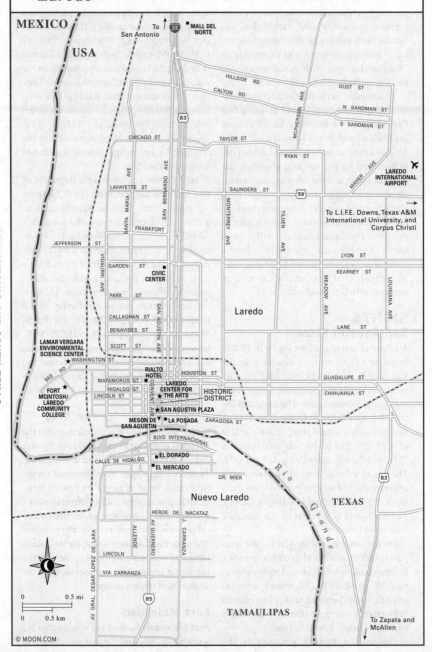

MEXICO

USA

To San Antonio

MALL DEL NORTE

HILLSIDE RD

CALTON RD

GUST ST

N SANDMAN ST

S SANDMAN ST

MCPHERSON AVE

CHICAGO ST

TAYLOR ST

RYAN ST

MAHER AVE

LAREDO INTERNATIONAL AIRPORT

LAFAYETTE ST

SAUNDERS ST

To L.I.F.E. Downs, Texas A&M
International University, and
Corpus Christi

SANTA MARIA AVE

SAN BERNARDO AVE

MONTERREY AVE

TILDEN AVE

FRANKFORT

JEFFERSON ST

LYON ST

GARDEN ST

CIVIC CENTER

PARK ST

KEARNEY ST

MEADOW AVE

LOUISIANA AVE

Laredo

CALLAGHAN ST

BENAVIDES ST

SCOTT ST

SAN AGUSTIN AVE

LANE ST

LAMAR VERGARA
ENVIRONMENTAL
SCIENCE CENTER

WASHINGTON ST

BEE RD

FORT
MCINTOSH/
LAREDO
COMMUNITY
COLLEGE

VIDAURRI AVE

RIALTO HOTEL

MATAMOROS ST

HIDALGO ST

LINCOLN ST

HOUSTON ST

LAREDO
CENTER FOR
THE ARTS

CONVENT AVE

SAN AGUSTIN PLAZA

HISTORIC
DISTRICT

GUADALUPE ST

CHIHUAHUA ST

MESON DE
SAN AGUSTIN

LA POSADA

ZARAGOSA ST

BLVD INTERNACIONAL

CALLE DE HIDALGO

EL DORADO

EL MERCADO

DR. MIER

Rio Grande

83

Nuevo Laredo

TEXAS

HEROE DE NACATAZ

AV GRAL CESAR LOPEZ DE LARA

ALLENDE

AV GUERRERO

J. CARRANZA

LINCOLN

VIA CARRANZA

85

TAMAULIPAS

To Zapata and
McAllen

0   0.5 mi

0   0.5 km

© MOON.COM

Community College, was established by the U.S. Army in 1848 following the Mexican War and was among a series of border forts guarding against attacks. It outlasted other border forts that protected settlers in the mid-late 1800s. Because of its position on an international border, Fort McIntosh was in continuous use for nearly a century.

The fort is now part of Laredo Community College, which has incorporated several of the historic buildings—barracks, chapel, infirmary, guardhouse, commander's house, and commissary—as administrative facilities and housing for faculty and students. Fort McIntosh is marked by four distinct architectural eras: early Fort McIntosh (1848-1861), Civil War to Spanish-American War (1861-1898), modern Fort McIntosh (1900-1945), and Laredo Community College period (since 1946). The street names honor fort commanders, officers, and soldiers.

Lamar Vergara Environmental Science Center

Also on the Laredo Community College campus is the **Lamar Vergara Environmental Science Center** (west end of Washington St., 956/764-5701, www.laredo.edu, Mon.-Fri.

8am-6pm, free), dedicated to plant and animal life in the Rio Grande watershed. The property features four ponds containing alligators, turtles, and fish, and a garden area with 50 types of native vegetation, including cacti, wildflowers, and regional brush species. Indoor exhibits showcase amphibians, reptiles, rodents, and fish. The Paso del Indio Nature Trail (you can't miss the giant entryway sign) overlooks the Rio Grande and is peppered with informational panels about the history and culture of the area.

Birding

Like many border towns along the Rio Grande, Laredo has abundant birding opportunities. Birders flock here during migratory periods for the geographical diversity. The mix of species includes the rare green parakeet and white-tipped dove, the green jay, and the white-collared seedeater. Hot spots for bird-watching include River Road on the **Laredo Community College** campus, the **Paso del Indio Nature Trail** (accessible behind the Lamar Vergara Science Center), and areas near the **Laredo Independent School District**'s central office (1702 Houston St.).

Laredo's San Agustin Cathedral

Border Crossings

the international bridge at Brownsville/Matamoros

Years ago, people were able to cross the Rio Grande sans passport, free to roam the pleasantly slow-paced Mexican border towns in search of cheap treasures and tasty tacos. These days, the once-simple jaunt across the bridge is considered too dangerous.

People in border communities are wary of the violence across the river associated with warring drug cartels, which don't always limit the violence to people they know. Fortunately, law enforcement has a strong presence on the U.S. side, where cities tend to be some of the safest in the state, while the opposite is true across the river in Mexico.

However, if you must cross the border, one safe option is Boquillas, Mexico, across the Rio Grande from Big Bend National Park, where you can arrange to make the brief voyage (if you have your passport). Boquillas is a tiny village, but its cantinas and folk art stands are representative of many border towns.

The violence in Mexico has subsided for the time being, but it has only been a few years since there were official warnings against visits the neighboring country. It is still advisable for travelers in Texas not to cross to Mexico. Many of the restaurants on the Mexican side have addressed the drop in cross-border business by opening new locations on the Texas side of the Rio Grande. They may not offer the same international flavor, but equally palatable is your safety.

SHOPPING

Rather than trendy boutiques, Laredo has several interesting spots for elusive treasures. A good starting place is San Bernardo Avenue between Hidalgo and Matamoros Streets near downtown, with several quality import stores. Most carry similar ceramics, glassware, furniture, papier-mâché artwork, small musical instruments, leather goods, home furnishings, and metalwork, although some are higher quality than others.

Among them are **Martinez Imports** (3302 San Bernardo Ave., 956/727-9828), the low-key **Diana's Imports** (3104 San Bernardo Ave., 956/337-9419), and the upscale **Vega's Interiores Mejicanos** (4002 San Bernardo Ave., 956/724-8251).

For furniture, drop by the city's noteworthy antiques shops. Prices are still reasonable at **Timeless Treasures** (2619 Salinas Ave., 956/727-2300, http://timelesstreasureslaredo.com). Far less spectacular is the most popular shopping destination in Laredo, **Mall Del Norte** (5300 San Dario Ave., 956/728-1536, www.malldelnorte.com), featuring Macy's, Dillard's, and 150 other stores along with a kids play area, a food court, and a movie theater.

FOOD

Laredo has some of the best Tex-Mex, with its own variety of standard fare, such as *panchos* (nachos) and mariachis (breakfast tacos), as well as *cabrito* (goat). There are other types of restaurants in town, but most are chains. The following locales offer a good sampling of the Mexican food in this bountiful border town.

Skip the hotel breakfast and start your day at **Marla** (5904 McPherson Ave., 956/729-9878, daily 7am-3pm, $7-17), a Texas version of a Mexican institution that does breakfast *migas* (eggs with crispy tortilla chips and savory peppers) and biscuits topped with beans.

Once a hidden restaurant frequented only by those in the know, ★ **El Meson De San Agustin** (908 Grant St., Mon.-Sat. 11am-4:30pm, Fri.-Sat. 7pm-11pm, $6-15) is more visible these days—a small sign now hangs above the door—but its reputation as an enigmatic lunch destination endures. The modest back-street facade fades as you enter the small yet homey dining room, packed with customers and colorful decorations. Traditional cuisine is the main draw, especially hearty *caldo* (flavorful beef soup with rice, vegetables, and chunks of corn). The best of the menu includes *enmoladas de pollo* (tortilla-wrapped chicken) and the *carne de puerco* (pork with peppers). Speaking Spanish is a plus here.

★ **La India Packing Co. and Tasting Cafe** (1520 Marcella Ave., 956/723-3772, www.laindiaherbsandspices.com, Mon.-Fri. 11am-4pm, $8-16) has been providing seasonings and herbal remedies since 1924. The family-run business began as a small grocery store and evolved to a large-scale distribution company, still on-site behind the modest retail shop and restaurant. Sample the seasonings in dishes expertly prepared in a small back-room kitchen. The most memorable meal is the chicken mole, a sublime blend of tastes from hints of chocolate and cinnamon to a rich nutty flavor, served on authentic family decorative plates.

Locals love **Tacolare** (6102 McPherson Ave., 956/753-0116, daily 11am-11pm, $6-13), which elevates the ordinary taco to a lofty delicacy. Some have crafty ingredients like ham and sausage while others are uniquely constructed, like the *sincronizada,* a sandwich-like stacked tortilla concoction.

Semi-swanky **Tono's Bar & Grill** (1202 E. Del Mar Blvd., 956/717-4999, Mon.-Sat. 11:30am-10pm, $9-31) has authentic interior Mexican-style meals, with entrées like *huevos montados* (sunny-side-up eggs over tortillas, beans, cheese, and sausage), beef *milanesa* (a Mexican-fried steak with chipotle sauce in place of gravy), and upscale meat and seafood dishes like tenderloin medallions and sea bass. Look for live music in the bar most weekends.

One of Laredo's favorite establishments is **Fonda Don Martin** (9652 McPherson Rd., 956/723-7778, www.fondadonmartin.com, daily 7am-3pm, $8-25), an amazing restaurant in an uninspiring strip mall. Upon entering and seeing the tortilla-making stand, you know you're in for a treat. Order the *enchiladas callejeras* (cheese-filled goodness topped with a spicy sauce) or the *heftier cortadillo del res* (seasoned beef).

ACCOMMODATIONS

Stay in a downtown historic hotel to get a true sense of the city's culture. Compared to other Texas cities, rates are affordable. Hotels are downright cheap in other parts of the city, particularly the reliable chains on I-35, a few miles north of downtown.

Downtown

The best way to experience Laredo is at ★ **La Posada Hotel** (1000 Zaragoza St., 956/722-1701, www.laposada.com, $119 d). With its remarkable Spanish colonial-style architecture,

the hotel is a focal point on the San Agustin Plaza. The site dates to 1767, when it served as a city hall, and its hacienda appearance makes it a welcoming regional building. Recently renovated, La Posada features a fully equipped fitness center, lush courtyards, and free Wi-Fi in all rooms.

Another worthy downtown option is the historic **Rialto Hotel** (1219 Matamoros St., 956/725-1800, www.rialtohotel.net, $119 d), offering classic features with modern amenities. This 47-room boutique hotel includes a fitness center and free internet access in all rooms, along with a microwave and fridge.

North of Downtown
One of the best budget options in town is the independently owned **Family Garden Inn & Suites** (5830 San Bernardo Ave., 956/723-5300 or 800/292-4053, www.familygardeninn.com, $68 d). Amenities include a free continental breakfast and evening social gathering, an outdoor pool, a fitness center, a playground, and rooms with fridges and microwaves.

Nearby is the **Courtyard Laredo** (2410 Santa Ursula Ave., 956/725-5555, www.marriott.com, $97 d), catering to business travelers and featuring free internet access, a swimming pool, breakfast, a whirlpool, and an exercise room.

For the comforts of home, including a fully stocked kitchen and several large rooms, **Residence Inn Laredo del Mar** (310 Lost Oaks Blvd., 956/753-9700, www.marriott.com, $99 d) offers a complimentary breakfast and free internet access in all rooms.

Camping
The best place to camp near Laredo is just east of town at **Lake Casa Blanca International State Park** (6101 Bob Bullock Loop, off U.S. 59, 956/725-3826, www.tpwd.state.tx.us, $4 over age 12). The park offers restrooms with showers, campsites with water and electricity, and playgrounds, sports courts, an amphitheater, a boat ramp, and 2 miles (3.2 km) of mountain bike trails.

INFORMATION AND SERVICES
The **Laredo Convention and Visitors Bureau** (501 San Agustin Ave., 956/795-2200 or 800/361-3360, www.visitlaredo.com, Mon.-Fri. 9am-5:30pm, Sat. 9am-1pm) is a good place to pick up maps and brochures, and staffers can handle inquiries about border crossing. The CVB also has a booth at the airport.

GETTING THERE AND AROUND
Most Laredo visitors arrive via I-35, but the small **Laredo International Airport** (LRD, 5210 Bob Bullock Loop, 956/795-2000, www.cityoflaredo.com/airport) offers daily flights to Dallas-Fort Worth, Houston, Las Vegas, and several other cities on three airlines.

1: La India Packing Co. and Tasting Cafe
2: La Posada Hotel in downtown Laredo

Rio Grande Valley

Known simply as "the Valley," this four-county area in South Texas extends from the mouth of the Rio Grande for 100 miles (160 km) upriver. For most of its history it was semiarid coastal plains, but things changed dramatically when irrigation and railroads were introduced in the early 20th century. Property near present-day McAllen sold for 25 cents an acre in 1903, and three years later for $50. The subsequent migration of farmers from the Midwest and from Mexico led to enormous population growth.

Irrigation on the fertile river delta soil created ideal conditions for citrus farming. Texas grapefruit, including the famous ruby red, and several varieties of oranges became big-time cash crops. Counties in the region remain tops in the state in acres of fruit and vegetables harvested.

The Valley's mild year-round climate draws travelers and seasonal residents to its beaches and resorts. McAllen, Brownsville, and other Valley communities have become winter homes for 125,000 northerners. The local population remains the leading cultural force, with 85 percent of Valley residents being Hispanic.

BROWNSVILLE

Brownsville (population 183,392) offers the history and traditions of two countries, and its towering palm trees and warm Gulf Coast breezes complement its bird-watching and beachcombing opportunities. The city is one of the few in the Valley with history dating to the mid-1700s; most border communities are tied to the development of the railroad in the early 1900s.

Brownsville was the site of two important battles—Palo Alto and Palmito Ranch—in the U.S.-Mexican War (1846-1848), significant because its outcome extended the United States from sea to sea. The city also played a role in the Civil War thanks to its access to the Gulf

of Mexico, allowing Confederate trade to continue with Europe without Union retaliation.

Agricultural trade, particularly cotton, was essential to the Brownsville region. Cotton merchants and riverboat entrepreneurs such as Charles Stillman, Mifflin Kenedy, and Richard King made fortunes in their business dealings, resulting in massive land purchases leading to the birth of Texas's ranching industry. Citrus farming later became a major industry, and the construction of a bridge over the Rio Grande led to increased trade with Mexico. In the 1930s, a ship channel was constructed, connecting Brownsville to the Gulf Coast. By the 1960s, the Border Industrialization Program was another economic boost that brought 100 manufacturing companies to Brownsville.

Museums

The city's multicultural past is on display at the **Historic Brownsville Museum** (641 E. Madison St., 956/548-1313, www.brownsville-history.org, Tues.-Sat. 10am-4pm, $6 adults, $4 seniors, $2 students), in the remarkable 1928 Southern Pacific Railroad Depot, the city's best example of Spanish Revival architecture. Abundant informative exhibits feature the history of namesake Fort Brown, historic artifacts, regional artwork, and a Baldwin railroad engine.

Local history is also the draw at the **Stillman House Museum** (1325 E. Washington St., 956/542-3929, Tues.-Sat. 10am-noon and 2pm-4pm, $6), in the 1850 downtown home of town elder Charles Stillman. Historic images and items depict the city's ranching, education, and religious heritage along with mid-19th-century Stillman family furnishings. The facility offers tours and a research library. Adjacent Brownsville Heritage Museum displays impressive large-scale photos and significant artifacts related to the area's multicultural history. Check out

Brownsville

BROWNSVILLE TOURIST
INFORMATION CENTER

To Staybridge
Suites and Hampton
Inn & Suites

802

VALLEY REGIONAL
MEDICAL CENTER

Resaca de la Palma

77
83

BEST WESTERN ROSE
GARDEN INN & SUITES

CENTRAL BLVD

TACO PALENQUE

THE VERMILLION

BOCA CHICA BLVD

To
Trevino's
Restaurant

4

To South Padre Island
and Boca Chica

To
Airport

Brownsville

PALM BLVD

GLADYS
PORTER
ZOO

BROWNSVILLE
MUSEUM OF
FINE ART

E. 6TH ST

E. 7TH ST

E. 13TH ST

INTERNATIONAL BLVD

SOUTHMOST RD

1419

E. ADAMS

E. WASHINGTON

HISTORIC
BROWNSVILLE
MUSEUM

E. 12TH ST

E. 14TH ST

E. ELIZABETH

E. LEVEE

STILLMAN HOUSE
MUSEUM

MEXICO ST

COLONIAL
HOTEL

CIVIC
CENTER

UNIVERSITY OF TEXAS AT BROWNSVILLE

USA

TEXAS

Fort
Brown
Resca

AV ALVARO OBREGON

AV TAMAULIPAS

CALLE UNO

Rio Grande

MI PUEBLITO

HIDALGO
HERRERA
BUSTAMENTE
BRAVO

MARKET

PLAZA
HILDALGO

AV CD DE MEXICO

GONZALES

MORELOS

SANTOS DEGOLLADO

TAMAULIPAS

SENDERO
NACIONAL

AV CUAHUTEMOC

CALLE 7

CALLE 6

CALLE 4

AV LAURO VILLAR

AV CANALES

Matamoros

0   0.5 mi
0   0.5 km

MEXICO

© MOON.COM

SAN ANTONIO AND SOUTH TEXAS
RIO GRANDE VALLEY

Vaqueros

The mythical American cowboy would be all hat and no cattle if it weren't for the Spanish and Mexican vaqueros who preceded them. These colonial herders and 19th-century ranch hands set the stage for the modern cowboys by passing along the tricks of the trade to Anglo settlers on the South Texas plains.

Spanish vaqueros in colonial times were rough and rowdy and acknowledged for their cattle-driving skills and horsemanship. As ranching progressed northward through Mexico to Texas, they were on the front line of Hispanic colonization and became associated with a *patrón* (a rancher with a land grant from the king) and stayed with the ranch and family for generations.

When Anglos arrived in the early 1800s, the vaqueros were the experts in the field, and they passed along their ranching techniques. Items associated with the cowboys of the Wild West—saddles, lassos, spurs, sombreros, bandanas, and chaps—came from the vaquero traditions. These elements of the ranching and cattle-driving culture eventually became attached to Texas cowboys, reaching fabled heights in books and movies celebrating the rugged people of the plains.

the huge 1909 German limousine in the back of the museum, reportedly custom-made for former Mexican president Porfirio Díaz.

A preeminent art museum is the **Brownsville Museum of Fine Art** (600 Ringgold St., 956/542-8909, www.brownsvillemfa.org, Wed. 10am-8pm, Thurs.-Sat. 10am-4pm, $5 adults, $2.50 seniors and ages 6-12), next to the Gladys Porter Zoo. The museum prides itself on regional and international art as well as daily art classes. Exhibits range from local school competitions to renowned paintings and works of sculpture. Classes in different media are held in the historic 1850 Neale House, and the museum is home to the original Fort Brown Bandstand.

Birding

Ecotourism is a big draw to the Brownsville area, and bird-watching is the most popular activity. Virtually all migratory species from the eastern United States and the Midwest pass through in spring and fall, and an increasing number of nature preserves and sanctuaries host exotic and rare birds. One of the best places for birding is the **Sabal Palm Sanctuary** (8400 Southmost Rd., 956/541-8034, www.sabalpalmsanctuary.org, daily 7am-5pm, $5 adults, $3 students), 557 acres of preserved land with many endangered birds and plants, including the marvelous sabal palm. Take a self-guided tour of the

sanctuary's 3 miles (4.8 km) of nature trails for face-to-beak contact with long-billed thrashers, buff-bellied hummingbirds, and chacalacas. Drop by the recently restored 1892 Rabb Plantation House to learn about local history.

Los Ebanos Preserve (27715 Hwy. 100, 956/399-9097, www.losebanospreserve.com, call for hours and appointments, prices vary), north of Brownsville in San Benito, is an 82-acre park for bird and butterfly species. Tropical landscaping and gardens entice the winged wonders while visitors track their activity through binoculars. Several trails include self-guided tours and the opportunity to see the elusive and tiny Brownsville common yellowthroat, previously thought to be extinct.

Just west of town is the **Resaca de la Palma State Park** (3301 S. International Blvd./FM 1015, 956/585-9156, www.worldbirdingcenter.org, tours by appointment only), 4 miles (6.4 km) west of Brownsville, offering the World Birding Center network's largest tract of native habitat. Its 1,200 acres of semitropical property offer a diverse birding environment. Colorful species abound—if you're lucky, you may spy an American redstart or a yellow-breasted chat.

Immaculate Conception Cathedral

On the edge of downtown is the **Immaculate**

Conception Cathedral (1218 E. Jefferson St., 956/546-3178, www.immaculateconceptioncathedral.org) a stunning 1859 Gothic Revival building on the National Register of Historic Places. Although not set up as a tourism destination, you can go inside to see the cathedral's remarkable sky-blue ceiling of stretched canvas, colorful stained-glass windows, and the angelic sound of recorded choral music.

Palo Alto Battlefield National Historic Site

The National Park Service's desolate **Palo Alto Battlefield** (FM 1847 and FM 511, 956/541-2785, www.nps.gov/paal, daily 8am-5pm, free) is 5 miles (9.7 km) north of downtown Brownsville. On May 8, 1846, this unassuming site, marked by prickly pear cactus, spiky yucca plants, and miles of sandy soil, was the scene of a violent clash in the U.S.-Mexican War (1846-1848), a conflict that shaped U.S. history. The visitors center's small theater puts it in context with the insightful and interesting 15-minute video *War on the Rio Grande*. Stroll along the boardwalk, where informative displays point out significant military activities in the now-pristine field.

Gladys Porter Zoo

One of the city's most popular attractions is the small yet satisfying **Gladys Porter Zoo** (500 Ringgold St., 956/546-2177, www.gpz. org, daily 9am-5pm, summer longer hours, $13 adults, $10.50 seniors, $8 ages 2-13), with 1,600 animals representing 400 species from Africa, Asia, Indo-Australia, and tropical America. Built on an old channel of the Rio Grande, the zoo allows animals to live in open exhibits surrounded by natural waterways. Drawing the largest crowds are the gorillas, bears, sea lions, and the tropical birds that live in the zoo's foliage. There are also warthogs, and kids love Small World, a nursery and petting zoo where they can touch and interact with domesticated animals.

Food

Brownsville's best eating establishments are Mexican restaurants. For the ultimate Mexican street taco experience, head to ★ **El Ultimo Taco** 938 N. Expressway, 956/554-7663, daily 11am-3am, $3-9). Flavorful tacos draw aficionados from across the state and they only cost $1.09. Don't let the suburban strip mall ambiance fool you; this is the real deal. Start with the *bistec* (beef) and *al pastor* (pork). The immensely flavorful meat is

Sabal Palm Sanctuary near Brownsville

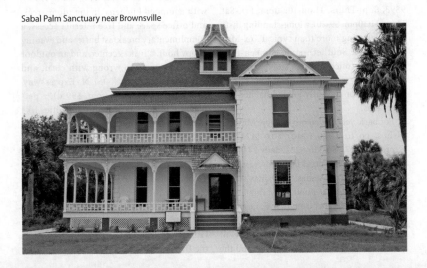

enhanced by the perfect corn tortilla and topping of avocado with *queso blanco*. Squeeze a dash of the *rojo* (red) sauce on top to enhance the goodness. The other two options are for the adventurous types—the *moella* (gizzard) and *barbacoa* (stewed cheek) are almost as tasty, but might have a gamey flavor.

At the unique **Trevino's Restaurant** (54 Boca Chica Blvd., 956/544-7866, Mon.-Sat. 7am-3am, Sun. 7am-midnight, $5-14), visitors know they're getting fresh-made fare since the restaurant doubles as a tortilla factory, bakery, and grocery store.

Another popular spot near downtown is **Mejia's Easy to Go** (2974 East Ave., 956/544-7266, Mon.-Sat. 11am-10pm, Sun. noon-9pm, $8-17), specializing in consistently tasty standards such as tacos, enchiladas, tostadas, fajitas, and flautas.

Another local favorite is **Taqueria y Antojito's Rico's** (714 Military Rd., Suite 281, 956/546-0014, Mon.-Thurs. 4pm-midnight, Fri.-Sat. 4pm-2am, Sun. noon-midnight, $6-13). You can't go wrong with any of the beef-based items (*bistec* tacos, fajita tacos, and beef flautas are recommended), and the fresh avocados on the plates and in the guacamole are worth the trip.

Just north of downtown is **The Vermillion** (115 Paredes Line Rd., 956/542-9893, Sun.-Thurs. 11am-10:30pm, Fri.-Sat. 11am-11:30pm, $9-20), a long-standing institution offering more than typical Tex-Mex. Down-home Southern-style chicken-fried steak, charbroiled chicken, and fried catfish make this a true Tex-Mex option. Diners flock here for the fully loaded nachos and beef tacos.

For basic yet consistently reliable Mexican dishes, go to **Taco Palenque** (4227 N. Expressway 77, 956/350-8232, daily 24 hours, $7-17) to line up for breakfast tacos, tasty tortillas, enchiladas, tostadas, and fajitas.

For 1950s-style seafood, head downtown to the historic **Oyster Bar** (1057 E. Levee St., 956/542-9786, Mon.-Sat. 11:30am-4:30pm, $8-19). The seafood is fresh because the Gulf Coast is only 20 miles (32 km) away, and the atmosphere is homey, with wood-paneled walls and local knickknacks. The food is the main draw, with perfectly fried shrimp, locally famous oysters, and enough baked potatoes and iceberg lettuce to remind you that you can't go wrong with the classics.

Accommodations

Like other border towns, Brownsville's accommodations are relatively affordable, although the lower-tier options tend to be rough. To be safe, go with one of the more expensive chains along U.S. 77/83.

On the northern edge of downtown is the reasonably priced **Best Western Casa Villa Suites** (4317 S. Expressway 83, 956/412-1500, www.bestwesterntexas.com, $89 d), offering a free breakfast buffet, an outdoor pool with a hot tub, and internet access. A bit closer to town is **Hampton Inn & Suites** (3000 N. Hwy. 77/83, 956/548-0005, www.hamptoninn.com, $89 d), with a free hot breakfast buffet, a swimming pool, a whirlpool, a fitness center, and Wi-Fi.

Farther north of downtown on U.S. 83 are several higher-end options, which tend to be newer and oriented toward business clients. For fully furnished rooms, consider **Staybridge Suites** (2900 Pablo Kisel Blvd., 800/970-4654, www.staybridge.com, $99 d), with equipped kitchens, living room areas, and office space and free internet access, a complimentary breakfast buffet and evening happy hour, a fitness center, and an outdoor pool. You can't go wrong with clean and reliable **La Quinta** (5051 N. Expressway, 956/350-2118, www.lq.com, $99 d), a pet-friendly place that provides amenities like free Wi-Fi, free breakfast, and an outdoor pool.

Information and Services

The best place to stock up on maps and brochures is the **Brownsville Convention & Visitors Bureau** (2305 N. Hwy. 77/83, 956/546-3721, www.brownsville.org). Offering info about businesses in the area is the **Brownsville Chamber of Commerce**

(1600 University Blvd., 956/542-4341, www.brownsvillechamber.com).

MCALLEN

McAllen's (population 143,433) initial development was so slow that the town ceased to exist about a century ago. The railroad and citrus industries kept the village afloat, and it went on to become an important agricultural center with one of the busiest access points between Mexico and Texas.

Like other Valley cities, McAllen's mild temperatures and subtropical climate make it a destination for winter Texans and birders. It doesn't have the dense historical fabric of other border towns, but McAllen's newest residents have had a distinct cultural impact on the community. Wildlife refuges, a renowned art museum, and the city's status as the "Square Dance Capital of the World" reflect local values.

International Museum of Art and Science

The finest cultural experience in the region is McAllen's **International Museum of Art and Science** (1900 Nolana Ave., 956/682-1564, www.theimasonline.org, Tues.-Wed. and Fri.-Sat. 9am-3pm, Thurs. 9am-8pm, Sun. 1pm-5pm, $7 adults, $5 over age 54, $4 ages 4-12). Spanning several centuries of art, with European masters, Mexican folk art, and enormous sculptures, the museum is a destination for those intrigued by intellectual endeavors. The fine art and pre-Columbian objects join items in the Earth Science Gallery, including fossils, geological samples, and dinosaur prints. The museum's primary focus is its impressive collection of objects from the Americas, represented by folk art such as masks and ceramics.

La Lomita Chapel

A Valley treasure is **La Lomita Chapel** (FM 1016, Mission, no phone, generally open sunrise to sunset, free). This profoundly serene site dates to 1899 and provides a respite from modern distractions, with its historic adobe architecture, gleaming white walls, and heavenly breezes.

Los Ebanos Ferry

Though border-hopping is discouraged these days, you can still watch the operation of **Los Ebanos Ferry** (off U.S. 83 at FM 886, $1.25 each way), west of McAllen. This "ancient" (1954) mode of transport is the last hand-pulled ferry on the Rio Grande. Crew members use ropes and pulleys to carry a maximum of three cars and a small number of pedestrians across the river on a modest metal barge. Border inspection stations are set up on both banks of the river, and the journey takes a scant five minutes. Passports are required just to pass the entry gate, and the ferry doesn't run on a consistent schedule, so it's occasionally unavailable.

Birding

McAllen is home to several acclaimed birding sites catering to thousands of annual visitors. The city helps operate the World Birding Center's **Quinta Mazatlan** (600 Sunset Ave., 956/688-3370, www.worldbirdingcenter.org, Tues.-Sat. 8am-5pm, $3 adults, $2 seniors and children), near downtown, the site is an oasis (*quinta* is Spanish for "country estate") offering 15 acres of tropical gardens, native woodlands, and a beautiful 10,000-square-foot historic Spanish Revival adobe hacienda. Naturalists enjoy the walking trails, butterfly garden, nature exhibits, birding feeding stations, and bird meadow, with elusive local bird species such as the black-bellied whistling duck, buff-bellied hummingbird, and olive sparrow.

At Mission's ★ **National Butterfly Center** (3333 Butterfly Park, Mission, 956/583-5400, www.nationalbutterflycenter.org, daily 8am-5pm, adults $10, $5 ages 5-12), ecotourists explore trails and perch on the banks of the Rio Grande to catch a rare photo or glimpse of elusive bird and butterfly species. Migratory traffic is especially dense because birds and butterflies take routes that hug the South Texas coastline to avoid flying over the Gulf of Mexico, just 60 miles (97 km) away.

A few miles east of town near the community of Alamo is the highly regarded **Santa Ana National Wildlife Refuge** (FM 907, off U.S. 281, 956/784-7500, www.fws.gov, trails daily dawn-dusk, driving tour summer Sat.-Sun. 8am-4pm, $3 per vehicle). Nearly 400 bird species live in this 2,000-acre refuge, established in 1943 to protect the thousands of birds that funnel through the region as they migrate to and from Central and South America. This small patch of semitropical thorn forest that once dominated the area also hosts nearly half of all butterfly species found in the United States. The refuge contains a visitors center offering field guides, insect repellent, bird lists, and binoculars, and many visitors opt to experience the property via a 90-minute interpretive tram tour (three daily trips Thanksgiving-Apr., $3 adults, $1 children).

The **Bentsen-Rio Grande Valley State Park** (2800 S. Bentsen Palm Dr., Mission, 956/585-1107, www.tpwd.texas.gov, daily 7am-10pm, $5 over age 11, $3 seniors) bills itself as the "crown jewel of Rio Grande Valley parks." Just west of McAllen in the town of Mission, its claim is supported by the World Birding Center, headquartered at this one-of-a-kind 760-acre park. Birders flock here for species found exclusively in this region. Park officials strive to retain the natural state by maintaining the woodlands and recreating the flooding that previously nourished the land. These conditions and the park's feeding stations draw species popular with the birding crowd, such as the chacalaca, green jay, broad-winged hawk, and the northern beardless tyrannulet. Visitors can ride the tram, bike, or walk through the park, which offers observation decks, bird blinds, bike rentals, nature programs, and a visitors center surrounded by butterfly gardens and hummingbird feeders.

Food

There's no shortage of quality food in McAllen. The city's Mexican food is commendable, and there are other worthy eateries offering fresh takes on American classics.

TEX-MEX

★ **Rex Cafe** (321 S. 17th St., 956/686-9074, www.rexcafebakery.com, daily 6am-8pm, $6-16) is a multiple-generation family establishment serving traditional Tex-Mex classics since the 1950s. The bakery is famous for Mexican pastries—the cinnamon rolls are exquisite, and the fruit-filled empanadas are perfect to eat on-site or later from a to-go bag. Breakfast is equally delicious, especially the huevos rancheros. Order them over-medium with some extra flour tortillas.

Reliable local hangout **La Justica Restaurante** (5421 N. 23rd St., 956/928-1905, Mon.-Sat. 6:30am-9pm, Sun. 7:30am-3pm, $6-15) offers a dose of rustic charm. Start with the *caldo de pollo,* a savory chicken soup loaded with meat and potatoes and fresh jalapeño, onion, and cilantro on the side. Then feast on a sumptuous entrée, such as the chicken mole with smooth spicy sauce.

More upscale is the fantastic **Costa Messa** (1621 N. 11th, 956/618-5449, daily 7am-9pm, $9-26), where authentic Tex-Mex meals are accompanied most weekend nights by a trio of guitarists or even a mariachi band. The *botana* platter sampler is a tantalizing mix of fajitas, quesadillas, flautas, and fried zucchini. Order the fresh guacamole, served with crispy fried tortilla halves.

For a reliably tasty lunch, **La Casa del Taco** (1100 W. Houston Ave., 956/631-8193, daily 7am-10pm, $6-14) is a Valley stalwart featuring better-than-average standards such as tacos, burritos, and enchiladas. The margaritas are particularly popular and potent.

One of the finest Mexican spots in town is the slightly more expensive **Palenque Grill** (606 E. Hwy. 83, 956/618-5959, www.palenquegrill.com, Sun.-Thurs. 11am-11pm,

---

1: Palo Alto Battlefield National Historical Site **2:** Immaculate Conception Cathedral **3:** Brownsville's El Ultimo Taco **4:** National Butterfly Center near McAllen

Fri.-Sat. 11am-midnight, $9-30). Fancy fajitas are a specialty, and not just because they spare you the spectacle of bringing them out on a sizzling skillet. The quality of the beef, shrimp, and chicken is top-notch, and the fresh flour tortillas provide a tasty wrapping. Other fine options include pork *al pastor* and the *sarandeado* fish.

Not nearly as fancy is local mainstay **Delia's** (4800 S. 23rd St., 956/630-3502, Mon.-Sat. 6am-8pm, Sun. 7am-6pm, $4-10), known for its tamales. Tucked in a shopping center corner, Delia's offers tasty tamales of all types—chicken, pork, and sweet and spicy varieties.

AMERICAN

If you live on a ranch, you'll feel right at home at the **Republic of the Rio Grande** (1411 S. 10th St., 956/994-8385, www.therepublicoftheriogrande.com, Mon.-Thurs. 11am-10pm, Fri.-Sat. 11am-11pm, $13-29). This knickknack-stocked establishment specializes in down-home cuisine, including steaks, seafood, chicken, and the enormous Lone Star Burger, doused in tangy homemade barbecue sauce. Snag a seat on the patio by the fountain if possible, and save room for the almond taco dessert, a sweet shell filled with fruit and cream.

Accommodations

Because it's relatively new, McAllen doesn't have many funky historic lodging options. There's a wide range of affordable chains with standard amenities. One of the few independently owned options is **La Copa Hotel** (2000 S. 10th St., 956/686-1741, www.lacopainn.com, $67 d), featuring a free hot Belgian waffle breakfast and free Wi-Fi in all rooms, as well as a heated pool, a fitness room, and a jetted tub.

A step up in price and quality is the remarkable ★ **Renaissance Casa de Palmas** (101 N. Main St., 956/631-1101, www.marriott.com, $109 d), a stunning Spanish Revival structure dating to 1918 in the heart of downtown. Lush tropical landscaping on the surrounding grounds and an inviting interior courtyard set this hotel apart, along with its state-of-the-art fitness center, minibars, Spanish Room restaurant, and free Wi-Fi.

One of the nicest and most expensive places in town is **Embassy Suites** (1800 S. 2nd St., 956/686-3000, www.embassysuites.com, $187 d), with its welcoming tropical courtyard and fountain, fitness room, pool, free cooked-to-order breakfast, and nightly manager's reception, and rooms featuring fridges, microwaves, and free Wi-Fi.

Information and Services

The **McAllen Convention & Visitors Bureau** (1200 Ash Ave., 956/682-2871, www.mcallenchamber.com, Mon.-Fri. 8am-5pm) is a great source of information and personal service along with maps, brochures, and guides.

HARLINGEN

Harlingen (population 65,436) is more a Valley city than a border town, with small-town American sensibility. The traditional grid-patterned Main Street-style downtown is based on the railroad, differing from the Mexican plaza-inspired border communities.

Border-town residents go to Harlingen specifically for its folksy Americana. Jackson Street, the main drag of the city's historic commercial district, hosts traditional downtown shops and restaurants. What sets it apart are the towering palm trees and occasional Tejano music drifting from a lunch counter or passing vehicle.

Geographically, the Lower Rio Grande is a rich river delta, and the fertile soil was the main draw for the citrus farmers who came here in the late 1800s and early 1900s. Harlingen grew even more when the railroad arrived in 1904, connecting it to larger coastal cities Brownsville and Corpus Christi.

The railroad spurred development as Harlingen's plentiful produce was packed in the city's icehouses and shipped north on the rails. Harlingen didn't see a notable population increase until the 1920s, when local legend claims the railroad companies advertised the Harlingen area's fertile and affordable land before loading northerners on trains to see this "land of opportunity." When the trains got to the dry, dusty, and desolate King Ranch area, developers would lower the window shades and open bottles of booze so potential property buyers would be in good spirits by the time they arrived in Harlingen's tropical environs. Many enthusiastically purchased plots of land on sight, and the region's population went from around 1,700 people to nearly 12,000 in 10 years.

Harlingen Arts and Heritage Museum

At the former Harlingen Army Air Field site, the **Harlingen Arts and Heritage Museum** (2425 Boxwood St., 956/216-4901, Tues.-Sat. 10am-4pm, Sun. 1pm-4pm, $2 adults, $1 children) complex contains several facilities representing Harlingen's colorful past. A main attraction is the relocated 1904 Lon C. Hill Home, where Harlingen's founding father lived with his eight children. The home features a compelling collection of historic photos and period antiques chronicling family and frontier life in the early 1900s. Other notable attractions include the relocated 1850s

Harlingen Arts and Heritage Museum

Stagecoach Inn and 1923 Harlingen Hospital, with its strange antique medical equipment. The Harlingen Arts and Heritage Museum also contains a modern main building with rotating cultural exhibits and touring art shows.

Iwo Jima Memorial and Museum

Harlingen's most recognizable attraction is its **Iwo Jima Memorial and Museum** (320 Iwo Jima Blvd., 956/421-9234, www.mma-tx.org). This massive outdoor structure is the original working model used by sculptor Dr. Felix de Weldon while casting the official bronze version in Washington DC. Not surprisingly, the monument is just as powerful as the final rendering, with six inspirational figures stirring patriotic emotions among the veterans and visitors who make regular pilgrimages here. The structure was donated to the nearby Marine Military Academy to inspire young cadets and to acknowledge the regional connection to one of the soldiers depicted in the monument.

The nearby **museum and gift shop** (Mon.-Sat., 10am-4pm), associated with the Marine Military Academy, feature exhibits and displays primarily related to the U.S.

SAN ANTONIO AND SOUTH TEXAS RIO GRANDE VALLEY

Marine Corps. Other attractions include an educational film about the Battle for Iwo Jima and the Iwo Jima Veterans Hall of Fame.

Rio Pride Orchards

A visit to the Valley would be incomplete without paying homage to the citrus industry that paved the way for the region's development. The famous ruby red grapefruit comes from this area, and one of the most-visited sites in the Valley is the Harlingen-based **Granny Clare's Citrus at Rio Pride Orchards** (14748 Hoss Lane, 956/423-1191, www.grannyclarescitrusatrioprideorchards.com, Mon.-Fri. 8am-5pm, Sat. 9am-1pm). The orchard is at its peak November-March, when grapefruit and oranges ripen. Drop by the orchard for some flavorful fresh fruit and a history lesson about the agricultural industry that put the Rio Grande Valley on the map.

Hugh Ramsey Nature Park

A top natural attraction is the spectacular 55-acre **Hugh Ramsey Nature Park** (1001 S. Loop 499, 956/216-5951, www.theworldbirdingcenter.com, daily 6am-9pm), a paradise for nature lovers, who flock to this pristine swath of Valley vegetation and its dozens of species of rare birds, subtropical plants, and colorful butterflies. Although the park is most popular during winter months, its peaceful gardens and pleasant walking paths are pleasant year-round. Bring bug repellent, since the mosquitoes are relentless in this naturally lush area.

Food

Since border-hopping is no longer a safe option, Harlingen has several worthy Mexican food options, including **Pepe's Mexican Restaurant** (117 S. 77 Sunshine Strip, 956/423-3663, Mon.-Sat. 11am-9pm, $8-18). Don't skip the chips and salsa, one of the highlights, using crispy tortillas and slightly spicy salsa. The entrées are some of the best in the region, including chicken mole that captures the rich flavor you'd expect in a traditional mole sauce, and the enchiladas verdes, the

perfect balance of tangy tomatillo sauce and heartily seasoned chicken.

Another option with more Mex, less Tex is **La Playa Mexican Café** (502 S. 77 Sunshine Strip, 956/421-2000, Sun.-Mon. 11am-9pm, Tues.-Thurs. 11am-10pm, Fri.-Sat. 11am-11pm, $9-19). The first thing you may notice is that the mariachi band is quite loud (in a good way), allowing you to focus on the margaritas instead of conversation. You'll also appreciate that the *queso* isn't Velveeta yellow; instead, it's a white cheese served with fried flour tortilla chips. Main dishes are inventive and flavorful, ranging from shrimp *amarrados* (cheese and jalapeño-stuffed shrimp wrapped in bacon), chipotle chicken enchiladas, and shrimp and scallop-stuffed eggplant.

For traditional Tex-Mex in a casual atmosphere, try **Los Asados** (210 N. 77 Sunshine Strip, 956/421-3074, www.losasados.com, Sun.-Thurs. 11am-9:30pm, Fri.-Sat. 11am-10pm, $8-17). In a group, be sure to order the *botana,* a platter crammed with beef and chicken fajita, beans, cheese, guacamole, and jalapeños. Other specialties include verde enchiladas, crispy beef tacos, and chicken burritos.

Accommodations

A good bargain is **Best Western Casa Villa Suites** (4317 S. Expressway 83, 956/412-1500, www.bestwestern.com, $81 d), with a complimentary hot breakfast Monday-Friday and continental breakfast on weekends, a free newspaper, an outdoor pool and hot tub, an exercise room, and free Wi-Fi service.

One of the best lodging deals in Harlingen is **Country Inn & Suites** (3825 S. Expressway 83, 956/428-0043, www.countryinns.com, $84 d). Amenities include an outdoor pool and whirlpool, an on-site fitness center, free Wi-Fi, complimentary hot breakfast daily, and free 24-hour coffee and cookies in the lobby.

Holiday Inn Express (501 S. P St., 956/428-9292, www.hiexpress.com, $89 d) features an outdoor heated pool with an adjacent whirlpool, a fitness center, and a free breakfast bar. For a slight increase in price and quality, consider **Hampton Inn & Suites** (1202 Ed Carey Dr., 956/428-9800, $99 d). The Hampton offers Wi-Fi, a free breakfast, an exercise room, and an outdoor pool.

Information and Services

The **Harlingen Convention and Visitors Bureau** (311 E. Tyler St., 956/423-5440 or 800/531-7346, www.visitharlingentexas.com) can assist with brochures, maps, and advice. Another helpful resource is knowledgeable **Downtown Harlingen** (956/216-4910, www.myharlingen.us), which can help discover local businesses and hard-to-find resources.

Getting There and Around

Some travelers fly to the region for spring break or to avoid the long stretch of uninspiring ranchland driving. **The Valley International Airport** (HRL, 3002 Heritage Way, Harlingen, 956/430-8600, www.flythevalley.com) has flights on Southwest United, and American.

By car, the long drive is through vast stretches of King Ranch on U.S. 77. From San Antonio, take I-37 south to U.S. 77. The drive takes about 3.5 hours. Be sure you have enough gas before the desolate 45-minute stretch between Sarita and Raymondville.

Houston and East Texas

Houston 239
Vicinity of Houston 275
Piney Woods 279

Like the mountains to the west, the pine forests

of East Texas are a natural wonder not typically associated with the Lone Star State. Not surprisingly, the cultural gap between the two regions is as wide as their distance apart.

East Texas has a distinct Southern influence, reflected in the region's food, heritage, and even the dialect. Locals are much more likely to regale visitors with long stories in their laid-back, drawn-out speaking style than their twangy, tight-lipped West Texan counterparts. Standing apart from this rural Southern character is the megalopolis of Houston, the fourth-largest city in the country and home to NASA, oil-related industries, a world-class medical district, and some of the preeminent museums in the country.

Highlights

Look for ★ to find recommended sights, activities, dining, and lodging.

★ **Walk with butterflies** at the most popular exhibit at the **Houston Museum of Natural Science.** Covering everything from dinosaurs to ancient Egypt and Latin American cultures, it offers adventures for the family (page 243).

★ **Appreciate the European masters** at Texas's largest art museum. Spanning several city blocks, **Museum of Fine Arts, Houston** boasts 64,000 works, ranging from antiquity to the present (page 244).

★ **Explore the ever-changing exhibits** at one of the country's most compelling modern art facilities, the **Contemporary Arts Museum of Houston,** which is housed in a stunning stainless-steel building (page 244).

★ **Re-live the Apollo missions** in the meticulously restored Mission Control room at the otherworldly **NASA Space Center** (page 252).

★ **Celebrate Texas independence.** The legendary battle where General Sam Houston's troops defeated the Mexican Army in 1836 is commemorated at the 1,200-acre **San Jacinto Battleground Historic Site** (page 254).

★ **Reconnect with nature.** A gaggle of species from the Gulf Coast, Central Plains, and Southeastern forests coexist alongside creatures from the deserts, bayous, woods, and swamps in the **Big Thicket National Preserve** (page 279).

★ **Ride the rails.** A rickety locomotive from the historic **Texas State Railroad** chugs, clanks, and charms its way through the East Texas Piney Woods (page 291).

★ **Swim in Caddo Lake.** Texas's only natural lake offers hiking, fishing, and boating with a backdrop of wispy Spanish moss and outstretched cypress trees (page 301).

© MOON.COM

East Texas has long been the gateway to the Lone Star State: Native Americans, European explorers, Anglo settlers, and African Americans arrived primarily from the East. One of the first things they encountered was the dense acreage now known as the Piney Woods, which includes several national forests and the Big Thicket Preserve.

The first to inhabit the area were the Caddo People, an advanced society with sophisticated trade networks throughout the region. The Caddo are credited with inspiring the name Texas, as they welcomed the Spanish explorers by referring to them as *tejas,* meaning "friends" or "allies." By the 1700s, Spain attempted to fortify its presence in the area by establishing a series of missions to protect their political interests, especially against France, and to convert the indigenous population to Catholicism. Neither of these ventures was very successful, and the land remained relatively unoccupied until Anglo homesteaders began arriving in large numbers in the early 1800s. In the southern portion of this region, just west of modern-day Houston, a group of settlers known as the Old Three Hundred established Stephen F. Austin's initial colony. After the fall of the Alamo in March 1836, droves of frightened frontier families fled to East Texas in an event known as the Runaway Scrape.

By the late 1800s, the region became associated with industry. Railroad expansion and European immigration brought an increased population and entrepreneurs, and the new railroad lines provided access to the Piney Woods's interiors, allowing the lumber industry to flourish. A few decades later, Texas's identity was forever changed when the 100-foot-high (30-m) oil spout known as the Lucas Gusher blew in (the industry term for "erupt") near Beaumont. As soon as word spread about the gusher's subterranean Spindletop oil field, tens of thousands of people flocked to the area. The colorfully named roughnecks and wildcatters worked the fields, while the entrepreneurial-minded investors made the money.

In 1901, the first year of the boom, three major oil companies—Gulf, Humble (later Exxon), and Texas (later Texaco)—formed in Beaumont, and by the following year there were 500 corporations in town. The impact of Spindletop and other oil fields discovered near Tyler is immeasurable, as it brought billions of dollars to Texas through oil companies and related industry endeavors. Houston benefited the most, since the oil business ultimately shifted headquarters and shipping operations to the city, which grew at phenomenal rates throughout the mid-1900s.

As a result, East Texas has a remarkable number of heritage destinations to explore, including Caddo burial mounds, historic logging towns, Southern plantation homes, oil boomtowns, and five national forests.

PLANNING YOUR TIME

Houston has become a major destination for culinary-minded travelers and remains a popular convention location. Those who visit Houston will discover several days' worth of intriguing activities.

To maximize your time, first head to the Museum District, where nearly a dozen attractions, from the enormous Museum of Natural Science to the Buffalo Soldiers Museum, appeal to a wide spectrum. Visitors typically make it to about three destinations in a day before losing steam, so pick specific museums to make the most of them.

Nowhere else can claim Houston's distinctive connection to the space program. NASA is about a half hour from downtown, so you'll need at least half a day. Other uniquely Houston sites such as the impressive San Jacinto Monument and Battleship *Texas* also involve a 30-minute drive.

The remaining vast expanse of East Texas is worth three or four days of exploring.

Previous: Houston's skyline; a Space Shuttle exhibit at NASA's Space Center; Texas State Railroad

Houston and East Texas

Paris
TEXAS
Red River
ARKANSAS
Texarkana

Cooper Lake
Mount Pleasant
Lake o' the Pines
Jefferson
LOUISIANA

Plano
Lake Fork Reservoir
Longview
Marshall
CADDO LAKE
Shreveport

DALLAS
Lake Tawakoni
Kilgore
Tyler
Mansfield

To Austin
Trinity River
Henderson
Lake Palestine

Jacksonville
Mount Enterprise
Caddo Mounds State Historic Site
Sabine N.F.
Toledo

Fairfield
TEXAS STATE RAILROAD
Rusk
Alto
Nacogdoches
St. Augustine
Bend
To Lafayette

Palestine
Weches
Ratcliff
Milam
Angelina
Reservoir

Marlin
Kennard
Lufkin
N.F.
Lake Sam Rayburn Res.

Davy Crockett N.F.
Zavalla
Neches River
Jasper

Lake Livingston
Woodville
Steinhagen Lake
Bon Wier

Bryan
Huntsville
Livingston
BIG THICKET NATIONAL PRESERVE

College Station
Coldspring
Sam Houston N.F.
Silsbee
To Lake Charles and New Orleans

Conroe
Kountze
Lumberton

To Austin
Brenham
GEORGE BUSH INTERCONTINENTAL AIRPORT
Beaumont
Orange
Waterway

CONTEMPORARY ARTS MUSEUM OF HOUSTON
MUSEUM OF FINE ARTS, HOUSTON
HOUSTON
SAN JACINTO BATTLEGROUND HISTORIC SITE
Port Arthur
Sabine Lake

HOUSTON MUSEUM OF NATURAL SCIENCE
Trinity Bay
Gulf Intracoastal

Rosenberg
WILLIAM P. HOBBY AIRPORT
NASA SPACE CENTER
Galveston Bay

Hallettsville
El Campo
Galveston
Gulf of Mexico

Freeport

0   30 mi
0   30 km

© MOON.COM

Two Days in Houston

DAY 1

Kick the day off in the Museum District to get a feel for the city's cultural story. Prioritize the Houston Museum of Natural Science, the Contemporary Arts Museum of Houston, and the Museum of Fine Arts, Houston. For a nearby lunch, go with new-school Vietnamese cuisine at Lua Viet Kitchen or old-school comfort food at Benjy's. Continue discovering Houston's cultural legacy at the Menil Collection (the Rothko Chapel will provide welcoming serenity), then venture a few miles southeast of town to experience unique folk art at The Orange Show. Afterward, enjoy an incredible Southern dinner at Lucille's, then head down to Main Street for cocktails at Dean's Credit Clothing.

DAY 2

Skip the hotel breakfast and beat the lines at Breakfast Klub, where the delectable chicken and waffles are still drawing crowds. Then hit the road for an out-of-this-world experience at NASA, where you can see the recently restored Mission Control Center and learn about the Apollo and Space Shuttle programs. Then head north for an afternoon of history at the San Jacinto Battleground. Drive back to Houston for some strolling along Buffalo Bayou then have a hearty dinner—for Mexican food, head to Hugo's; for a traditional Houston steakhouse, go to Pappas Brothers Steakhouse. Top off the evening with craft beers at Hay Merchant or live music at the Continental Club.

Beaumont is a fun day trip from Houston, less than two hours away, especially to learn about Texas's oil legacy. Naturalists should set aside a day or two to explore the Big Thicket National Preserve and other nearby national forests, and visitors interested in old-fashioned Southern culture can spend a few days in the northern portion of the Piney Woods, where the cities of Tyler, Lufkin, and Jefferson exude Texas heritage.

INFORMATION AND SERVICES

Knowledgeable staff members at the Greater Houston Convention and Visitors Bureau (701 Av. de las Americas, 713/437-5200, www.visithoustontexas.com, daily 7am-10pm) can handle almost any request. Similar services are southwest of town at Visit Bay Area Houston (604 Bradford Ave., Kemah, 281/474-9700, www.visitbayareahouston.com).

Tours of Houston and the surrounding area are available with Houston City Tours (832/388-8434, www.texascitytours.us) by activity types or location. Another company,

Houston Tours Inc. (8915 Bellaire Blvd., 832/630-9188, www.houstontours.com) features traditional bus tours of downtown, outlying neighborhoods, and treks to Galveston.

To venture beyond Bayou City, the Texas Forest Trail Region (headquarters 202 E. Pilar St., Suite 214, Nacogdoches, 936/560-3699, www.texasforesttrail.com) is an ideal place to prepare for a Piney Woods adventure. Check out the website or drop by the main office to get help with an East Texas itinerary.

Entering East Texas by vehicle from Louisiana, look for the Texas Department of Transportation's Travel Information Center at two spots on the state border. The largest is in Orange (1708 E. I-10, 409/883-9416) on I-10 en route from New Orleans. The other is in Waskom (1255 N. I-20 E., 903/687-2547), on I-20 from Shreveport. Visit www.txdot.gov for road-related travel information.

GETTING THERE AND AROUND

Several East Texas cities have small regional airports, and Houston is so big it has two. Houston's major airport is George Bush

Intercontinental Airport (IAH, 2800 N. Terminal Rd., 281/230-3100, www.airport-houston.com), just north of Houston and one of the major hubs for United Airlines. The city's old airport, William P. Hobby Airport (HOU, 7800 Airport Blvd., 713/640-3000, www.fly2houston.com), is now the center of activity for Southwest Airlines.

Super Shuttle (281/230-7275, www.supershuttle.com) offers shuttle service to and from area hotels and both Houston airports. If you're not using a ride-share, local cab companies include Houston VIP Taxi (281/616-5838), Liberty Cab Company (713/444-4444), and Yellow Cab (713/236-1111).

All the major rental car companies are accessible from the shared Rental Car Center (281/230-3000, www.fly2houston.com) at Bush Intercontinental Airport, about five minutes by bus from the terminals; the rental companies share a shuttle system that runs about every five minutes.

Buses and trains are a viable option in Houston. Buses arrive and depart at Houston Greyhound (2121 Main St., 713/759-6565 or 800/231-2222, www.greyhound.com). Amtrak's *Sunset Limited* trains arrive and depart three times a week at the Houston Amtrak station (902 Washington Ave., 713/224-1577 or 800/872-7245, www.amtrak.com).

Houston's public transportation system, the Metro, a.k.a. the Metropolitan Transit Authority of Harris County (713/635-4000, www.ridemetro.org), offers local and commuter light rail and bus service. Tickets are available from vending machines at each station. The Metro's red line serves 16 stations near downtown's busiest commercial and recreational sites.

Houston

Houston's humongous growth (population 2,325,502) has it closing in on Chicago as the third-largest city in the country, and it was recently named the nation's most diverse metropolis. The city is named after larger-than-life Sam Houston, president of the Republic of Texas, who led the fight for independence from Mexico as a general of the Texas Army.

The Bayou City is notorious for its lack of zoning ordinances and its high humidity, resulting in unmitigated sprawl and unbearably hot summers. But it's not without its charm—Houston has world-class cultural and medical facilities, and its international population contributes to a truly cosmopolitan setting with world-renowned services and restaurants.

The city started with grand ambitions: In the late 1830s, New York City brothers and entrepreneurs Augustus and John Allen claimed the town would become the "great interior commercial emporium of Texas," with ships from New York and New Orleans sailing up Buffalo Bayou. For most of the late 1800s, Houston was a typical Texas town, fueled by cotton farming and railroad expansion. The oil industry boom that started in 1901 changed Houston forever, with major corporations relocating to the city and using its deep ship channel for oil distribution.

Houston had another identity shift and financial surge in the mid-1900s, when it became headquarters for the aerospace industry. NASA established its Manned Spacecraft Center in 1961, which eventually became the epicenter of the U.S. space program's Gemini and Apollo missions.

With the proliferation of air-conditioning around that time, Houston's brutal humidity was no longer a year-round deterrent, resulting in corporations relocating from colder climes. The population boomed in the 1970s, when the OPEC oil embargo caused Houston's petroleum industry to become a vital asset.

Houston

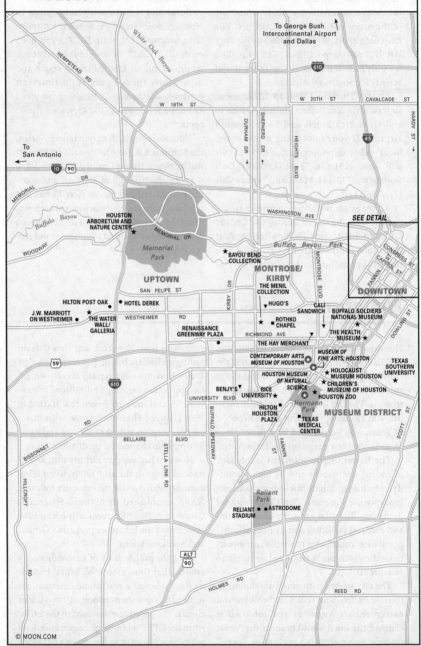

To George Bush
Intercontinental Airport
and Dallas

HEMPSTEAD RD

White Oak Bayou

W 18TH ST

W 20TH ST

CAVALCADE ST

HARDY ST

DURHAM DR

SHEPHERD DR

HEIGHTS BLVD

To San Antonio

MEMORIAL DR

Buffalo Bayou

WOODWAY

WASHINGTON AVE

Buffalo Bayou Park

SEE DETAIL

HOUSTON ARBORETUM AND NATURE CENTER ★

MEMORIAL DR

Memorial Park

CONGRESS ST

CAPITOL ST

FANNIN

★ BAYOU BEND COLLECTION

MONTROSE/ KIRBY

MONTROSE BLVD

DOWNTOWN

UPTOWN

SAN FELIPE ST

KIRBY DR

THE MENIL COLLECTION

HILTON POST OAK ● HOTEL DEREK

▼ HUGO'S

CALI SANDWICH

BUFFALO SOLDIERS NATIONAL MUSEUM

DOWLING ST

J.W. MARRIOTT ON WESTHEIMER ● ● THE WATER WALL/ GALLERIA

WESTHEIMER RD

★ ● ROTHKO CHAPEL

THE HEALTH MUSEUM ★

RENAISSANCE GREENWAY PLAZA ●

RICHMOND AVE

MUSEUM OF FINE ARTS, HOUSTON

TEXAS SOUTHERN UNIVERSITY

THE HAY MERCHANT ●

CONTEMPORARY ARTS MUSEUM OF HOUSTON ✪

HOLOCAUST MUSEUM HOUSTON

HOUSTON MUSEUM OF NATURAL SCIENCE

CHILDREN'S MUSEUM OF HOUSTON ★

BENJY'S ▼

RICE UNIVERSITY ★

HOUSTON ZOO

SCOTT ST

UNIVERSITY BLVD

BUFFALO SPEEDWAY

HILTON HOUSTON PLAZA ●

Hermann Park

MUSEUM DISTRICT

BELLAIRE BLVD

STELLA LINK RD

FANNIN ST

■ TEXAS MEDICAL CENTER

BISSONNET

HILLCROFT

Reliant Park

RELIANT ■ ■ ASTRODOME STADIUM

HOLMES RD

REED RD

© MOON.COM

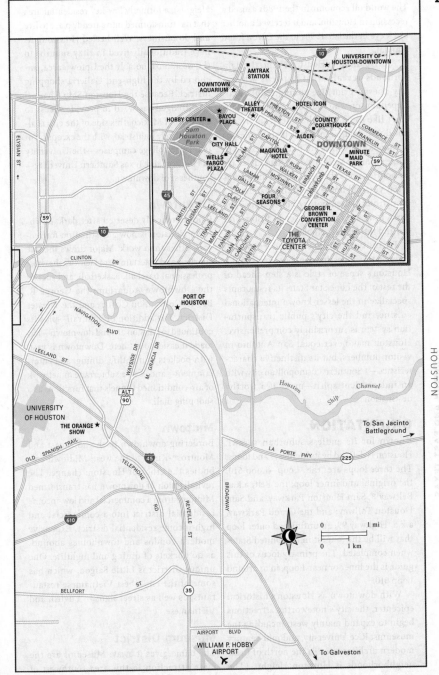

The world oil economy in the 1980s caused a recession in Houston, and it received another black eye in the late 1990s in the Enron fraud scandal.

A drive through Houston's central neighborhoods reveals what happens when a city doesn't prioritize zoning regulations. Depending on who you ask, it's good (Texans don't like to be told what they can or cannot do) or bad (significant historic neighborhoods and homes are routinely leveled to make room for McMansions). Regardless, it's part of Houston's character, even if that means a 150-year-old home sits in the shadow of a monstrous contemporary house across the street from a gargantuan pseudo-historic retail and residential complex.

Texans typically don't consider Houston a viable travel destination, but they should. Houston's sense of style is a step ahead of the rest of the Lone Star State, its restaurants specialize in the lesser-known international cuisine, and the city's public transportation system is surprisingly comprehensive. Houston may never equal San Antonio in visitor numbers, but its distinctive characteristics—a Southern cosmopolitan city with an independent spirit—make it a worthy destination.

ORIENTATION

Known for its endless suburban sprawl, Houston is defined by its highways and loops. The three loops are "the" Loop—Loop 610, the original and inner loop; the Belt, a.k.a. Beltway 8, Sam Houston Parkway, and Sam Houston Tollway; and the Grand Parkway, a.k.a. Highway 99, an unfinished outer loop that will be the longest in the United States when completed. The primary focus of this guide is the inner or near-Loop, in or around Loop 610.

With downtown as Houston's historical epicenter, the city's noteworthy attractions begin to expand mainly west, including the museums, Rice University, and mid-century modern architecture. To the north of these neighborhoods is Houston Heights (The

Heights), a formerly low-key residential area that has transformed into a trendy place to live and do business. Well-heeled Houstonians have traditionally lived in ritzy suburbs to the west, most notably the Uptown area, anchored by the high-end Galleria shopping district. Because the Houston Ship Channel was dredged eastward to provide access to the Gulf of Mexico, this side of the city is almost entirely industrial, with the exception of two large college campuses—the University of Houston and Texas Southern University—southeast of downtown.

Downtown

Once practically deserted after dark, downtown Houston is now a destination for reasons other than work. Major draws include sporting and entertainment facilities that host professional baseball, basketball, and soccer; the Downtown Aquarium; the George R. Brown Convention Center; and the Theater District. The addition of light rail—plus its continued expansion around downtown—has made it easier to get here. Downtown is vast, with pockets of nightlife, dining, and entertainment—and even a subterranean network of air-conditioned tunnels that functions as a shopping mall.

Midtown

Bordering downtown to the northeast and Montrose-Kirby to the west, Midtown embodies the ethos of Houston: change. The revitalization of downtown has transformed Midtown from a commercial and low-income residential district into a commercial and high-income residential district. Expensive modern condos and townhomes abound, as do pockets of dining and nightlife. One unique district is Little Saigon, which has some of the city's best Vietnamese restaurants, as well as street signs in English and Vietnamese.

Museum District

The name gives it away: Museums are the main attraction in this area southwest of

Midtown, and many major medical facilities are also here. With more than a dozen museums to explore within a manageable area, this is Houston's most-visited neighborhood, with welcoming greenery in manicured parks and lush tree canopies.

Montrose-Kirby

Long the antithesis of Houston's sterile suburbs, the Montrose-Kirby area has been the bastion of the LGBT community, artists, hippies, punks, and bohemian types for decades. The scene has lost some of its edge of late: The forces of gentrification have been at work for decades, and Montrose-Kirby today is less seedy and has higher rents and upscale dining. That said, it remains an avant-garde and artsy hub, with world-class museums and galleries, eclectic nightlife, and renowned restaurants.

West University

Officially known as West University Place or West U for its proximity to Rice University, this enclave is predominantly residential, with a mix of cottages and bungalows attracting professorial types and wealthy families. The adjacent Rice Village is a 16-block zone packed with shops, restaurants, and bars.

The Heights

If the Heights' Victorians and tree-lined roads could speak, they might report on the massive social changes in the district. The journey from streetcar suburb to city center has taken a predictable path: from desirable residential neighborhoods to postwar decline to revitalization and gentrification. The constant throughout has been the residential vibe. While it has a laid-back and somewhat bohemian feel like Montrose-Kirby, it is known more for its antiques shops and thrift stores than its of-the-moment clubs and boutiques.

Uptown

Anchoring Uptown is the Galleria, one of the largest shopping centers in the United States and a major Houston attraction. Just west of Loop 610, the Galleria's lavish sensibility infuses the district surrounding it, which features more upscale shops, hotels, and offices. Uptown is the second major business district in Houston after downtown. Beyond the business district, the vast and hard-to-define Uptown has many exclusive residential neighborhoods.

Greater Houston

Not surprisingly, this category represents the outlying parts of town, typically beyond Loop 610. Attractions include cultural sites like NASA, the Kemah Boardwalk, and the San Jacinto Battleground to the southeast and east. To the west are shopping and dining destinations Chinatown and the Kirby Outlet Malls. Otherwise, Greater Houston is mainly sprawling suburbs.

SIGHTS

A city of Houston's size offers countless cultural attractions. The Museum District is a loose collection (not logically planned, like most of Houston) just southwest of downtown. The urban core features occasional historic buildings and theaters among the modern skyscrapers, and offbeat spots outside town include the folk-art wonder of The Orange Show and the historically significant state park featuring the San Jacinto Battleground site.

Museum District

More inspiring than its name implies, the city's Museum District just south of Midtown spans several miles, with parks and medical facilities and 19 museum attractions. Realistically, visitors can make it to about three destinations each day before losing steam.

★ HOUSTON MUSEUM OF NATURAL SCIENCE

One of the best places in Houston for a family adventure is the **Houston Museum of Natural Science** (1 Hermann Circle Dr., 713/639-4629, www.hmns.org, daily

9am-5pm, $25 adults, $16 seniors and students, extra fees for some exhibits, free Thurs. 2pm-5pm). An overwhelming array of exhibits and artifacts covers everything from dinosaurs to gems and minerals to ancient Egypt. Its permanent collection is especially impressive in the Hall of the Americas, with exhibits on how people arrived, including Mayan, Aztec, and other Native American cultures, and their lifeways.

The museum's wing devoted to paleontology features dramatically lit dinosaur fossils and exhibits on evolution and early humans, with action-packed scenes of predators and prey.

Children won't want to leave the museum's Discovery Place on the lower level, featuring interactive exhibits dedicated to light and sound waves; machines with levers, pulleys, and gears; and a simulated weather studio. The Energy Hall is an extensive area showcasing the oil and gas industry. Interactive hands-on and touch-screen displays cover oil density, drilling, and delivery. Kids will be interested in the museum's large gemstone exhibit, featuring colorful and sharply cut gems in fascinating backlit displays.

The museum's butterfly exhibit ($10-12) is worthwhile to see the thousands of colorful winged creatures in the towering domed Mayan rainforest habitat. A lengthy waterfall flows gently in the background, and butterflies occasionally drop by for a personal visit.

★ MUSEUM OF FINE ARTS, HOUSTON

Billing itself "the largest art museum in America south of Chicago, west of Washington, D.C., and east of Los Angeles," the **Museum of Fine Arts, Houston** (1001 Bissonnet St., 713/639-7300, www.mfah.org, Tues.-Wed. 10am-5pm, Thurs. 10am-9pm, Fri.-Sat. 10am-7pm, Sun. 12:15pm-7pm, $19 adults, $16 seniors and ages 6-18, free Thurs.) contains several buildings with 300,000 square feet of display space and 18 acres of public gardens drawing two million people

annually. Look for the main entrance on Bissonnet Street, since the museum complex stretches over several blocks.

The museum's collection of 64,000 pieces of world art dates from antiquity to the present. It's challenging to soak up the significance of each collection in a half-day visit, so consider visiting the museum's website ahead of time. European masters include Italian Renaissance paintings and the French impressionist works. The Arts of North America wing offers nascent American landscape paintings, black-and-white photographs, vintage jewelry, and renowned works of sculpture. The ancient Asian holdings are especially notable, including sculpture from Japan's pre-Buddhist days and a Chinese boat dating to circa 2400 BC. Other significant collections include masterworks by famed Western artist Frederic Remington, and the Glasswell Collection of African Gold, considered the best of its kind in the world.

★ CONTEMPORARY ARTS MUSEUM OF HOUSTON

As big-city museums go, this is one of the best, with intriguing objets d'art down every hall. In the heart of the Houston Museum District, the **Contemporary Arts Museum of Houston** (5216 Montrose Blvd., 713/284-8250, www.camh.org, Tues.-Wed. and Fri. 10am-7pm, Thurs. 10am-9pm, Sat. 10am-6pm, Sun. noon-6pm, free) is unmistakable, in a distinctive stainless-steel building designed by architect Gunnar Birkerts.

As a non-collecting museum, the focus is on current and new directions in art, with changing exhibits. The museum grew steadily in the 1970s-1980s and features contemporary still-life painting, thematic installations, performance pieces, and other media. The museum's store is a step above similar shops, featuring whimsical toys, large posters, and decorative items.

1: Museum of Fine Arts, Houston **2:** Children's Museum of Houston **3:** Houston Museum of Natural Science

Houston's Mid-Century Mod

Now that modern architecture is becoming historic, the term "mid-century" is emerging as a distinctive style from the 1950s-1960s. Since Houston experienced one of its population booms during this era, the city known in architectural circles for its mid-century buildings that have so far survived the wrecking ball.

Houston Mod (www.houstonmod.org), an organization dedicated to 1960s architecture, is making impressive efforts to document and preserve dozens of the city's significant mid-century structures. Perhaps most iconic is the Astrodome, which opened in 1965 and served as home field for the Astros baseball and Oilers football during the teams' glory years. Finding a new use for the building, once hailed as the Eighth Wonder of the World, has been a challenge.

Another historically significant structure is the 1963 Humble Oil Building. The 600-foot-tall (180-m) 44-story edifice is one of downtown Houston's most recognizable mid-century buildings. For a short time, it even boasted the title of "tallest building west of the Mississippi."

Also instilling pride in Houston's mid-century fans is the Alley Theatre building, which opened in 1968. Known for its flowing and curvilinear use of raw concrete, the Alley is also associated with an architectural style known as Brutalism, coined in 1953 and referencing the French term *béton brut* (raw concrete).

THE HEALTH MUSEUM

Since Houston is a leading medical center, it makes sense there's a corresponding Health Museum (1515 Hermann Dr., 713/521-1515, www.mhms.org, Mon.-Sat. 9am-5pm, Sun. noon-5pm, $10 adults, $8 seniors and ages 3-12, fees for some exhibits). In the Museum District, this modest-size facility educates mostly children about the importance of health. In the Amazing Body Pavilion, experience a human body by walking through it, entering through the mouth and exploring the various systems and organs via innovative interactive displays. Vocal cords, lung capacity, stomach acids, and blood content are portrayed through games, hands-on activities, and informative models. The museum also features traveling exhibits related to children's health and a gift shop with fun toys, games, and knickknacks.

HOUSTON ZOO

Consistently rated a top attraction, the lush and welcoming Houston Zoo (6100 Hermann Park Dr., 713/533-6500, www.houstonzoo.org, daily 9am-5pm, $23 ages 12-64, $18 seniors and ages 2-11) has 5,000 animals on 55 acres of worldwide ecosystems. Drop by the World of Primates, the Asian elephant habitat, the lion and tiger exhibit, and the grizzly bear habitat.

Kids will love the Children's Zoo, featuring a petting area with farm animals, and the "Meet the Keeper" program, offering behind-the-cage insight. Families with children will want to set aside time for an excursion on the train, which takes a short journey through the park along the zoo's border. If you have children in tow, consider bringing extra clothes, since most kids love the water play area and will undoubtedly get soaked.

CHILDREN'S MUSEUM OF HOUSTON

A must-see in the Museum District is the Children's Museum of Houston (1500 Binz St., 713/522-1138, www.cmhouston.org, Tues.-Wed. and Fri.-Sat. 10am-6pm, Thurs. 10am-8pm, Sun. noon-6pm, $12, $11 seniors). The building itself is a sight to behold—a playful take on classical architecture with giant colorful details. Inside, nine galleries engage children's minds in science, geography, performing arts, and history. One of the most popular and informative attractions is the multilevel exhibit *How Does It Work?* Parents may pick up a few pointers on how mobile phones function and how turning a key gets an engine running. Younger kids relish the opportunity to sit in a model car with the freedom to push and pull every button and lever in sight. Other fun activities include an interactive Mexican village, art stations, live shows, and a café with healthy snacks. An added bonus: The Teacher and Family Resource Center has loads of books and items related to child development and parenting.

BUFFALO SOLDIERS NATIONAL MUSEUM

The specialized **Buffalo Soldiers National Museum** (3816 Caroline St., 713/942-8920, www.buffalosoldiermuseum.com, Mon.-Fri. 10am-5pm, Sat. 10am-4pm, $10 adults, $5 students, free Thurs. 1pm-4pm) recently moved from a modest-size facility to a larger building. The name is derived from the term associated with the African American troops who served in the U.S. Army and protected the Texas frontier in the late 1800s. Native Americans reportedly called them as Buffalo Soldiers due to their bravery and valor. Fittingly, the museum honors the legacy of African Americans' contributions to military service for the past 150 years. This is a unique collection of materials dedicated to a compelling aspect of U.S. heritage. Two stories of exhibits feature artifacts, photos, and maps. It's a true learning experience, and inspiring to see students making connections with the past as interpretive guides offer insight about the uniforms, flags, and equipment.

HOLOCAUST MUSEUM HOUSTON

A somber subject is handled admirably at the **Holocaust Museum Houston** (5401 Caroline St., 713/942-8000, www.hmh.org, Mon.-Fri. 9am-5pm, Sat.-Sun. noon-5pm, $15 adults, $10 seniors, not recommended under age 10). The museum's mission is to educate people about the dangers of prejudice and hatred, and it makes an impact on everyone who walks through its doors. Visitors learn about the historical and personal stories associated with the Holocaust in the museum's permanent exhibit, called *Bearing Witness:*

A Community Remembers, which focuses on the stories of Holocaust survivors living in the Houston area. Displays chronicle the Nazi rise to power and the concentration camps. Artifacts, photos, films, informative panels, and a research library serve as testament to the suffering, with the hope that this educational experience will help prevent similar future atrocities.

HOUSTON CENTER FOR PHOTOGRAPHY

One of the best small museums in the region is the **Houston Center for Photography** (1441 W. Alabama St., 713/529-4755, www. hcponline.org, Wed.-Sun. 11am-7pm, free), in a funky building at the edge of the Museum District. The HCP's mission is to encourage and educate people about art and photography. Exhibits showcase local and national photographers, and programs stimulate dialogue about the art form through digital workstations and presentations about methods and critique.

ASIA SOCIETY TEXAS CENTER

Even if you're not an architectural aficionado, you'll be impressed by the contemporary building that houses the **Asia Society Texas Center** (1370 Southmore Blvd., 713/496-9901, www.asiasociety.org/texas, Tues.-Sun. 11am-6pm, free, exhibits $5). In a residential neighborhood a block from the Museum District, the graceful structure blends in with its surroundings, offering panoramic views of downtown Houston from enormous second-story windows. Designed by Harvard-educated Yoshio Taniguchi, the 40,000-square-foot building is impeccable, with clean sight lines and exquisite materials. Research and community outreach are the center's primary focus, but there are public displays and an outdoor sculpture garden.

Downtown

There are plenty of shiny skyscrapers, hotel and convention facilities, and sports arenas downtown, but not many cultural sights for travelers. Regardless, the downtown area reveals Texas's version of cosmopolitan life—and a bizarre subterranean tunnel system.

HOUSTON'S DOWNTOWN AQUARIUM

Mingle with marine life at the modest-size **Downtown Aquarium** (410 Bagby St., 713/223-3474, www.aquariumrestaurants. com, Sun.-Thurs. 10am-9pm, Fri.-Sat. 10am-10:30pm, $15 adults, $13 seniors, $12 children, additional fees for rides and parking). Not as extensive or awe-inspiring as some big aquariums, Houston's version is focused on fun. Families will marvel at the enormous tanks, touch pools, and midway rides outside.

It's awe-inspiring to stand face-to-face with a grouper, piranha, or shark. One of the aquarium's highlights is the Shark Voyage, where a train takes visitors into a clear tunnel surrounded by blacktips, whitetips, and zebra sharks. Other notable exhibits are the Gulf of Mexico tank, with barracuda and snappers, and the Discovery Rig, where kids can get a handle on horseshoe crabs and stingrays. The aquarium also includes an interesting exhibit with several majestic white tigers.

The on-site restaurant is better than expected, so plan your visit around a meal to enjoy a decent seafood plate while gazing at still-living sea creatures in the surrounding 150,000-gallon aquarium. Stick with the basics here: the flaky and flavorful whitefish or succulently seasoned shrimp.

Step outside and pony up for a few of the midway rides: A medium-size Ferris wheel offers spectacular views of downtown Houston, and the merry-go-round (with sea creatures in place of horses) will bring genuine smiles of delight to your family's faces.

HERITAGE SOCIETY AT SAM HOUSTON PARK

Offering a welcome historical respite downtown is the **Heritage Society at Sam Houston Park** (1100 Bagby St., 713/655-1912, www.heritagesociety.org, Tues.-Sat.

10am 4pm, Sun. 1pm-4pm, museum gallery free, guided tours $15 adults, $12 seniors, $6 ages 6-18). Ten historic structures represent Houston 1823-1905. Although the buildings were relocated to the park from other parts of town, their collective stories illustrate life in the burgeoning boomtown. For a quick overview, the Kellum-Noble House gallery showcases the Heritage Society's early preservation efforts in a city that often didn't place value on protecting its past.

SAINT ARNOLD BREWING COMPANY

Just north of downtown in a semi-industrial neighborhood is the highly recommended **Saint Arnold Brewing Company** (2000 Lyons Ave., 713/686-9494, www.saintarnold. com, beer hall Sun.-Thurs. 11am-10pm, Fri.-Sat. 11am-11pm, free tours 1pm, 3pm, 5pm, and 7pm). Billing itself as Texas's oldest craft brewery, Saint Arnold's dates to 1994 and makes 10 different year-round beers, six seasonal varieties, and a handful of special series. The best place to sample them is in the beer hall—a welcoming room with long tables and German-inspired design. Bartenders are happy to offer suggestions based on personal tastes. Always reliable options include the Elissa IPA, Weedwacker hefeweizen, and 5 O'Clock Pils. Make a point to visit at lunch or dinner, since the beer hall's café serves German food; the bratwurst on a pretzel roll is superb.

DOWNTOWN TUNNELS

Houston's bizarre **Downtown Tunnels** (713/650-3022, tour info 713/392-0867, www. houstonhistoricaltours.com) are more a local shopping destination than a tourist attraction. The 6-mile (9.7-km) subterranean system connects dozens of downtown buildings, offering an air-conditioned respite from triple-digit surface temperatures. The tunnels started by connecting three downtown theaters in the 1930s; now, tunnel-goers can find scores of banks, restaurants, clinics, and boutiques, all 20 feet (6 m) below the surface.

Little Saigon, the Sequel

Traditional Vietnamese cuisine is available in many Houston neighborhoods.

In the 1960s, hundreds of Vietnamese residents fled their country and settled in and around Houston, where they found jobs in fishing, shrimping, manufacturing, and retail in a humid coastal environment reminiscent of their homeland. Today, Houston's Vietnamese community of more than 80,000 is the nation's largest outside California.

During the past few decades, tens of thousands of Vietnamese residents relocated from California and from Vietnam to purchase homes and open businesses, mostly along a 4-mile (6.4-km) stretch of Bellaire Boulevard in southwestern Houston. Comparatively cheap housing drew the Californians, many of whom lived in the Los Angeles area's famed Little Saigon district.

Word spread that Vietnamese families were selling their pricey California abodes and purchasing homes in Houston for a third the cost. The profits were often invested in new Vietnamese-centered businesses, including restaurants, real estate firms, medical facilities, and supermarkets.

The result is a vibrant community, and neighboring Chinese, Latino, and Pakistani enclaves add to Houston's cosmopolitan and diverse atmosphere. The Vietnamese restaurant scene is top-notch, with options ranging from inexpensive to upscale.

HOUSTON AND EAST TEXAS
HOUSTON

The tunnel system is accessed by elevators, stairways, and escalators inside commercial buildings and parking garages. The only buildings offering direct access to the tunnels from the street are **Wells Fargo Plaza** (1000 Louisiana St.) and the **McKinney Place Garage** (930 Main St.). It's an appealing getaway on a sweltering summer day in Houston.

Once below ground, there are maps and wayfinding signs to help you get oriented. You'll need them to keep track of your location. Things move quickly in the tunnels, and you'll see that most people are mostly running

errands and grabbing food. If you want to plan ahead, consult the maps on the website.

Montrose-Kirby
THE MENIL COLLECTION

What do you do when you have too much fine art? Renowned art collectors John and Dominique de Menil opened their own museum. **The Menil Collection** (1515 Sul Ross St., parking at 1515 W. Alabama St., 713/525-9400, www.menil.org, Wed.-Sun. 11am-7pm, free) is set among comfortable homes at the edge of the trendy Heights neighborhood, and it's an ideal place to spend a few hours soaking up some magnificent art spanning many ages. The grounds are expansive and inviting, with an abundance of trees, installation artwork, and even a wooden swing. The Menils left a legacy of 17,000 paintings, sculptures, prints, drawings, photographs, and rare books, most modern with an emphasis on surrealism, but there are also African pieces and works from the Byzantine period.

The compound includes several noteworthy structures near the main museum. Two blocks south of the main building is a fascinating Dan Flavin light installation, inside a former grocery store. The vertical-oriented fluorescent tubes on the side walls are a sensory delight, toying with color in your peripheral vision. Set aside at least 15 minutes to experience the **Rothko Chapel,** a block east of the main building. From the outside, the chapel is disarmingly stark, with bland rectangular brick walls. Inside, it's similarly subdued, but the silence screams reverence. Even if you're not religious, the experience of being completely quiet in a public space is absolutely sacred.

BAYOU BEND COLLECTION

The affluent home of the unfortunately named Ima Hogg, a respected Texas philanthropist, now houses the **Bayou Bend Collection** (6003 Memorial Dr., 713/639-7750, www.mfah.org, guided tours Tues.-Thurs. 10am-11:45am and 1pm-2:45pm, Fri.-Sat. 10am-11:15am, regular hours Tues.-Sat. 10am-5pm, Sun. 1-pm, guided tours $12.50 adults, $11 seniors, $6.25 ages 10-18). This spectacular 1928 home is one of Houston's cultural treasures, filled with nearly 5,000 antique objects showcasing American decorative arts 1620-1870. "Miss Hogg," as she was known, also had a hand in the design of the opulent home and grounds, featuring lush gardens and distinctive decorations spanning colonial to antebellum times. Call in advance to make tour reservations, and note that children under age 10 are not permitted in the home.

RIENZI

Another art museum in an impressive homestead is **Rienzi** (1406 Kirby Dr., 713/639-7800, www.mfah.org, tour only Wed.-Sat. 10am, 11am, 1:30pm, 2:30pm, 3:30pm, Sun. 1pm-4pm every 30 minutes, $12.50 adults, $10 seniors and students, free under age 13). Dedicated to European decorative arts, Rienzi features paintings, furnishings, and miniatures in the former home of local philanthropists Carroll Sterling Masterson and Harris Masterson III. The home was designed by Houston architect John Staub in 1952, and the museum is named after Harris Masterson's grandfather Rienzi Johnston, a Houston newspaperman and politician.

The collection is best known for fine English ceramics and furniture, European jewelry, and sculpture, including the main attraction, an early-1800s white marble Venus. The surrounding four-acre grounds are impressive, with welcoming shade trees and lush gardens. Drop-in visits are welcome, but reservations are advised.

RICE UNIVERSITY

One of the best universities in the South, Rice University is an oasis of intellectualism and vegetation in this sprawling metropolis. With an exclusive undergraduate enrollment of 6,700 students, the university has a reputation for high-quality instruction in medical, science, and engineering fields. Consider dropping by the **Rice Student Center** (6100 Main St., 713/348-4096) to pick up a T-shirt or ball cap, grab a coffee, visit the gardens, and even have a beer at Willy's Pub.

Garnering the most attention these days is the spectacular Skyspace building, adjacent to the university's Shepherd School of Music. The open-air structure was designed for music, but the visual effect of the two-story construction appears as a large grass-covered mound topped by a futuristic light show that

1: The Menil Collection's Rothko Chapel **2:** San Jacinto Battleground Historic Site **3:** The Orange Show

projects LED-based colors onto the enormous 72-foot-wide (22-m) square roof, which opens to the sky.

Uptown
HOUSTON ARBORETUM & NATURE CENTER

Experience Houston's often forgotten natural side at the **Houston Arboretum & Nature Center** (4501 Woodway Dr., 713/681-8433, www.houstonarboretum.org, grounds daily 7am-7pm, Discovery Room Tues.-Sun. 10am-4pm, free). On the west side of near-downtown Memorial Park, the 155-acre nature sanctuary is a green oasis in a city known for sprawling concrete. Native plants and animals are the focal point, with interactive exhibits and activities. The park area is beautifully landscaped, and kids will love the Discovery Room's pondering pond and learning tree. Stroll the 5 miles (8 km) of trails, hear the birds, and get a glimpse of Houston's version of the natural world.

THE WATER WALL

Houstonians take immense pride in their beloved **Water Wall** (2800 Post Oak Blvd., 713/621-2011, daily 8am-9pm). In a strangely unoccupied area among office buildings and Galleria parking garages, this six-story structure is a giant wall of cascading water that needs to be experienced to be appreciated. The structure is semicircular, and the hypnotic sound of falling water is mesmerizing. The gentle mist provides respite from a hot summer day, and the experience is even cooler at night thanks to the dramatic lighting and evening temperatures.

Considered the most romantic spot in town, the Water Wall is typically bustling with couples on dates, getting married, or taking selfies. The nearby 64-story Williams Tower offers an urban complement to the scene. Parking can be a hassle—instead of driving around in search of a street spot, head to the nearby West Drive parking garage, which is free on weekends.

Greater Houston

★ NASA SPACE CENTER

Light-years from ordinary cultural attractions is the **NASA Space Center** (1601 NASA Pkwy., 281/244-2100, www.spacecenter.org, Mon.-Fri. 10am-5pm, Sat.-Sun. 10am-6pm, summer longer hours, $30 adults, $28 seniors, $25 ages 4-11). NASA is about as big as it gets for Houston attractions, and it's one of the few cities in the United States to host such a distinct icon.

Start at the far end of the main building with the open-air tram tour, which transports visitors to the space center's significant buildings, including the remarkably restored Mission Control Center. Here, visitors learn about the fascinating saga of the Apollo piloted spacecraft missions.

A knowledgeable and entertaining guide takes you on a descriptive tour spacecraft experience as you peer through a glass partition at the iconic aquamarine-paneled equipment and flat monitor screens. The entire room was meticulously restored and reopened in 2019 for the 50th anniversary of the first human moon landing.

Goosebumps may rise on your neck as you realize you're in the room where the words "The *Eagle* has landed" and "Houston, we have a problem" were first heard. Nearby, you'll get to see real astronauts in action at the Space Vehicle Mockup Facility, containing space shuttle orbital trainers, an International Space Station trainer, a precision air-bearing floor, and a partial-gravity simulator. One of the highlights of the tour is a visit to the enormous structure housing the immense Saturn V rocket, an awe-inspiring sight that must be seen to be believed.

Most of the NASA facility features educational and entertainment-related elements, including Starship Gallery, containing impressive space-related artifacts such as the Apollo 17 command module, the Gemini 5 capsule, lunar rovers, and even a moon

Houston, We Have a Legacy

Space exploration used to be major international news; now, we hardly know when a mission is taking place. Throughout the past four tumultuous decades, the **NASA Space Center** (1601 NASA Pkwy., 281/244-2100, www.spacecenter.org, Mon.-Fri. 10am-5pm, Sat.-Sun. 10am-6pm, summer longer hours, $30 adults, $28 seniors, $25 ages 4-11) in Houston has been the hub of American spaceflight. The facility was established in 1961 as the Manned Spacecraft Center and renamed the Lyndon B. Johnson Space Center in 1973. The center will forever be associated with its early Gemini and Apollo missions.

the iconic Mission Control building at NASA

The Mission Control Center is the nerve center of the U.S. piloted space program, and the facility's remarkable guided tours shed light on what took place here. In 2019, NASA reopened the meticulously **restored Mission Control room** for visitors. See restored details like the aquamarine-colored metal consoles, stark monitor screens, and even authentic ashtrays, bringing the Apollo missions to life as visitors absorb the significance of being in the same room where the words "The *Eagle* has landed" and "Houston, we have a problem" were first heard.

OUTER REACHES

Mission Control previously handled the activity related to the space shuttle and International Space Station programs. Training for these missions took place at an adjacent building, where astronauts and engineers prepared for their time in orbit using the Space Vehicle Mockup Facility. This enormous edifice still houses an International Space Station trainer, a precision air-bearing floor, and a partial-gravity simulator.

Although the future of the space program remains unclear (Mars missions are being discussed), NASA expects to play a role in space exploration. For over 50 years, the space center has helped humans transcend the physical boundaries of Earth to enhance our knowledge about the universe.

rock. Additional attractions include interactive flight simulators and Independence Plaza, with a model of the space shuttle *Independence,* which visitors can walk through to see what astronauts experienced, including the robotic arms they operated and even the toilets they used.

THE ORANGE SHOW

You know that occasional burst of inspiration that enters your brain? Jeff McKissack, a Houston postal worker turned artist, acted on it and built an enormous folk art monument dedicated to oranges. McKissack glorified

his favorite fruit with 3,000 square feet of space filled with orange-related folk art now known as **The Orange Show** (2402 Munger St., 713/926-6368, www.orangeshow.org, usually Sat.-Sun. noon-5pm, $5). Standing among modest suburban homes just east of downtown, this bizarrely compelling artwork is primarily brick and concrete, accompanied by metal sculptures, mosaic tilework, and various objects that include birdhouses, windmills, and statues.

McKissack once delivered oranges throughout the South and became obsessed enough to fashion this whimsical collection of objects found along his mail route. The absurdity factor is fascinating, and the devotion to his subject is admirable. McKissack apparently believed his life work (it took him 25 years to assemble his collection into a publicly accessible venue) would become a major tourism destination. It never quite caught on, but it remains an intriguing folk art environment unlike any other you'll encounter. You'll know you're in the right spot when you see the colossal 70-foot-tall (21-m) blue saxophone, an enormous sculpture comprising oil-field pipes, an entire VW Beetle, and even a surfboard.

KEMAH BOARDWALK

About 25 miles (40 km) southeast of downtown on Galveston Bay, the popular **Kemah Boardwalk** (215 Kipp Ave., 281/535-8100, www.kemahboardwalk.com, open daily, amusement rides Mon.-Thurs. noon-7pm, Fri. noon-9pm, Sat. 10:30am-10pm, Sun. 10:30am-9pm, all-day ride pass $25 adults, $19 children) features restaurants, shops, fountains, and an impressive collection of amusement park rides at the water's edge. Touristy by nature, it draws suburbanites by the thousands for a summertime diversion of nostalgic family fun. The restaurants are more notable for their bayside views than the food, but there's plenty of excitement in rides, including a roller coaster, a Ferris wheel, and a double-decker carousel. Other attractions include a 50,000-gallon aquarium with 100 species of tropical fish, a marvelous meandering train, and an interactive stingray reef.

TOP EXPERIENCE

★ SAN JACINTO BATTLEGROUND HISTORIC SITE

A significant historical attraction lies near the Houston Ship Channel, just 20 miles (32 km) east of the city. After driving through miles of stark petroleum plants, visitors to **San Jacinto Battleground State Historic Site** (3523 Hwy. 134, 281/479-2431, www.thc.texas.gov, daily 9am-6pm, free) encounter the welcoming beacon of Texas independence, where the stories of valiant warriors defending Texas's independence come alive.

The battleground site, with its remarkable 570-foot-tall (174-m) monument, 15 feet (4.6 m) taller than the Washington Monument, commemorates Texas's victory in its fight for independence. The 1,200-acre site, now owned by the Texas Historical Commission, preserves and interprets the legendary battleground where Texas Army troops under General Sam Houston defeated the Mexican Army in an 18-minute battle on April 21, 1836. The magnificent monument—topped by a 34-foot (10-m) star symbolizing the Lone Star Republic—is dedicated to the "Heroes of the Battle of San Jacinto and all others who contributed to the independence of Texas."

The ground level houses the **San Jacinto Museum of History,** containing 400,000 objects, documents, and books spanning 400 years of Texas history. The display case dedicated to Sam Houston is a highlight, containing personal artifacts and inspiring writings. Be sure to watch the fascinating 30-minute movie *Texas Forever!* The site's highlight is the observation deck, a 490-foot-tall (150-m) vantage point offering stunning sweeping views of the battlefield, ship channel, reflecting pool, and surrounding scenery. Don't be discouraged by the historic 1930s-era elevator—it's a quick ride to the top, where you'll be rewarded with an amazing panoramic view and enviable photo opportunities.

GEORGE RANCH HISTORICAL PARK

A step back in time and away from the urban pace is **George Ranch Historical Park** (10215 FM 762, Richmond, 281/343-0218, www.georgeranch.org, Tues.-Fri. tours only, Sat. 9am-5pm, $15 adults, $12 seniors, $10 ages 5-15). About 30 miles (48 km) southwest of downtown near the community of Richmond, the 484-acre living-history site showcases four generations of the George family, settlers who began ranching operations here in the 1820s.

Visitors discover what life was like for Texans on a working cattle ranch through exhibits and displays at the pioneer farmstead, an 1890s Victorian mansion, and a 1930s ranch house. Nearby barns and working pens focus on 1930s-1940s ranching operations. Plan a few hours to explore this truly Texan locale, with daily demonstrations on tending to horses, pigs, and chickens, hands-on activities such as corn-grinding and weaving, and a chance to help harvest seasonal crops. You can even watch cowhands roping cattle. When it gets too hot outside, escape to the air-conditioned ranch house for exhibits, photographs, and artifacts about pioneer and farming life on the George Ranch.

RECREATION

Houston is home to several professional sports franchises, most notably the Texans football team, as well as myriad opportunities for outdoor activities such as golf, hiking, and cycling.

Parks

Houston's showcase central park is Hermann Park, just outside downtown in the Museum District. Memorial Park is a haven for local hikers and bikers, a contrast to Hermann Park's strollers. The city operates dozens of neighborhood-oriented parks (visit www.houstontx.gov/parks). An outdoor experience near NASA is the Armand Bayou Nature Center.

HERMANN PARK

The huge green swath in the middle of the city map is **Hermann Park** (6001 Fannin St., 713/524-5876, www.houstontx.gov). In the heart of the Museum District just southwest of downtown, Hermann Park is a 400-acre magnet for joggers, dog walkers, bikers, and families, a rare green space in a city known for rampant development. Trails and trees are abundant, as are amenities and services, including a theater, a golf course, and a garden center. The park is filled with statues: Look for monuments to Sam Houston, Mahatma

Gandhi, and the park's namesake George Hermann.

MEMORIAL PARK

Hugging the northwest corner of the city's inner loop is **Memorial Park** (6501 Memorial Dr., 713/845-1000, www.houstontx.gov), distinguished by its recreational facilities, primarily the hike and bike trails. Set on 1,400 acres that was once the World War I-era Camp Logan, Memorial Park is now a magnet for hiking and biking, and includes a full-service tennis center, a swimming pool, a golf course, a fitness center, baseball diamonds, a croquet field, and sand volleyball courts.

ARMAND BAYOU NATURE CENTER

Farther outside town but worth the 30-minute drive is **Armand Bayou Nature Center** (8500 Bay Area Blvd., Pasadena, 281/474-2551, www.abnc.org, Tues.-Sat. 9am-5pm, Sun. noon-5pm, $6 adults, $4 seniors and ages 4-12). Located near NASA on the west side of Galveston Bay, the nature center offers residents and visitors a chance to learn about native plant and animal species, hike on the discovery trails, or see the live animal displays featuring bison, hawks, and spiders. The main area of the park contains a boardwalk traversing the marshes and forests, providing a glimpse of the beautiful bayou region of East Texas. The best way to experience this natural wonder is by boat—consider taking a tour on the pontoon boat or signing up for a guided canoe tour.

Hiking

Despite reports claiming Houston and the South in general are the least-fit places in the nation, many residents are interested in exercise and health, although the city does not offer an abundance of hiking trails and coordinated recreational facilities.

The city's most popular outdoor destination for exercise is Buffalo Bayou, known as a biking destination. A slightly less-crowded area is nearby **Seymour Lieberman Exercise Trail** in Memorial Park. The 3-mile

(4.8-km) trail is popular for daily workouts and has exercise stations and restrooms along the route. Dedicated runners use the nearby asphalt timing track to work on speed and develop skills, while the **Memorial Park Picnic Loop** offers a smooth surface for in-line skaters, traditional roller skate enthusiasts, and hikers. Dogs are welcome at the park—canine drinking fountains are at ground level along the jogging trails. Keep your pooch on a leash and bring waste bags.

A few miles outside town is the scenic tree-filled **Houston Arboretum & Nature Center** (4501 Woodway Dr. 713/681-8433, www.houstonarboretum.org, daily 7am-dusk). The arboretum's outer loop is a 2-mile (3.2-km) trail for hikers to combine exercise with bird and wildlife viewing. Its lush natural setting allows an escape from the concrete cityscape. For a topographically diverse alternative, consider a trek on the R. A. Vines Trail, offering up-close views of shallow wetlands, fish, and a boardwalk.

Biking

Cyclists enjoy the challenging terrain along the city's **Buffalo Bayou** (1800 Allen Pkwy., 713/845-1000, www.buffalobayou.org), an urban greenbelt with the namesake waterway as its centerpiece. With the towering Houston skyline as a backdrop, the park draws bikers, joggers, art lovers, and walkers to its riverside trails and bustling activity. In addition to the smooth wide trails, the 124-acre park contains exercise stations, a recreation center, a disc golf course, a children's playground, and a popular dog recreation area. Public art abounds along the jogging trail, from stainless-steel objects representing tree roots on an overpass to the large stone block sculptures that remain from the city's demolished civic auditorium. Visit the park's website to download PDFs of trail maps. The southwest section of adjacent Memorial Park contains color-coded trails with maps at the trailheads, and Infantry Woods provides an advanced trail for those with superior skills.

Golf

Houston's **Parks and Recreation Department** (www.houstontx.gov) operates seven respectable municipal golf courses. Three of the most popular are within the loop, drawing golfers and hackers to well-maintained grounds and offering affordable greens fees.

The gem of the downtown-area municipal courses is **Memorial Park Golf Course** (1001 E. Memorial Loop Dr., 713/862-4033), a 600-acre oasis of rolling fairways and challenging greens. Originally a nine-hole sand green course for soldiers at Camp Logan (now Memorial Park), the links feature lush landscapes, putting and chipping greens, a golf museum, a contemporary clubhouse, and an always-packed driving range offering shade and lighting.

Adjacent to the city's Museum District, **Hermann Park Golf Course** (2155 Cambridge St., 713/526-0077) is another natural escape from the surrounding urban scenery. Lengthy fairways, snug out-of-bounds, and occasional water hazards make Hermann a favorite among serious golfers, who appreciate the shade of the ancient oaks and steady surface of the Bermuda grass greens. While at the turn, be sure to order a hot dog or two from the clubhouse kitchen.

Farther south of town is **Gus Wortham Park Golf Course** (7000 Capitol St., 713/928-4260), a former private course now operated by the city. The sportiest of the three downtown-area courses, Wortham Park features hilly terrain, tight turns, and several short par-fours. The course also offers a practice green and bunker, a chipping green, and a full driving range.

Spectator Sports

Houston is a football town. Once home to the storied Houston Oilers, the city has hosted the NFL's **Houston Texans** (832/667-2000, www.houstontexans.com) since 2002. The Texans have become a formidable franchise that continues to draw substantial crowds to see defensive end J. J. Watt at NRG Stadium (1 NRG Pkwy.).

Sports fans are also drawn to the venerable **Houston Astros** (713/259-8000, www.houston.astros.mlb.com). In 1965, the Astros became the primary occupants of the then-futuristic Astrodome, billed as the "Eighth Wonder of the World." It was a welcome respite from Houston's horrendous humidity, and the Astros assembled some worthy teams in the 1980s, most notably with hometown hero Nolan Ryan, and two decades later, local legend Roger Clemens, and a powerhouse offense in the "Killer B's"—Craig Biggio, Jeff Bagwell, and Lance Berkman. The Astros fled to their current home in downtown's Minute Maid Park (501 Crawford St.), a classic urban ball field with a modern retractable roof. The Astros gained national prominence in 2017 when they won the World Series, before their bright star was tarnished in 2019 by a cheating scandal.

Basketball isn't as big a draw in Texas as football, but the **Houston Rockets** (713/627-3865, www.nba.com/rockets) have always had a considerable following. Their successful 1990s teams, featuring top-notch talent such as Clyde "The Glide" Drexler and Hakeem "The Dream" Olajuwon, were the talk of the NBA during their glory years, when they won the NBA title in 1993 and 1994. The Rockets hold court at the downtown Toyota Center (1510 Polk St.).

ENTERTAINMENT AND EVENTS

The Urban Cowboy legend was born in Houston in the early 1980s, and in some parts of town, visitors can still get a feel for true honky-tonk nightlife. Houston has a healthy blues scene, and the downtown bars and dance clubs are reminders of the city's cosmopolitan culture. The performing arts in Houston truly befit the nation's fourth-largest city, particularly its internationally renowned opera and ballet companies and spectacular symphony.

Nightlife

With the fluid nature of clubs, instead of attempting to capture the moment's trendy venue, the following listings focus on established sites that have proven their venerability as the trends come and go.

DOWNTOWN

Surprisingly, pockets of downtown Houston are completely quiet at night, and the urban core doesn't tend to be a scene. Still, visitors can find notable clubs that boast a distinctive vibe.

An interesting spot to grab a cocktail is **Dean's Credit Clothing** (316 Main St., 713/227-3326, www.deansdowntown.com, Tues.-Sun. 5pm-2am). That's not a misprint: Inside a downtown 1930s clothing store, Dean's strives to maintain as much of its early charm as possible. Grab a spot at the low-lit bar, or sink into one of the comfy vintage couches. Original features from the 1893 building include the ornate flooring and exposed bricks. The craft cocktails are strong and well-made, with clever names referencing old-time department stores like Woolworth's and Penney's. On Sunday nights, Dean's hosts an acoustic lounge act or small jazz combo.

The energy picks up a few doors down at the hipper **Nightingale Room** (308 Main St., 832/968-3370, www.nightingaleroom.com, Tues.-Sat. 4pm-2am). Cocktails are a major draw, and the bourbon-based Godfather is a big hit. So is the booming sound system, evident when the 2nd-floor DJ helms the turntables and spins hip-hop from the impressive collection of vinyl behind the bar.

A few blocks away is the low-key and comfy **Warren's Inn** (307 Travis St., 713/247-9207, Mon.-Fri. 11am-2am, Sat. noon-2am, Sun. 2pm-2am). A longtime downtown lounge, Warren's is a dark and mellow place where the regulars look like they've occupied their spots at the bar for decades. Fortunately, the happy hour prices are similarly retro, with cans of brew offered for $2-3. Be sure to check out the jukebox with appropriate soundtrack music from the 1940s-1960s.

If you're not interested in the latest trends or worried about specifically appropriate footwear, head to **La Carafe** (813 Congress St., 713/229-9399, daily 1pm-2am). Known for its laid-back vibe and legendary jukebox, La Carafe is in a historic brick building that exudes character. Order wine, punch in Otis Redding on the jukebox, and settle in for a cozy evening.

THE HEIGHTS

Transcending its former trendy reputation is **Max's Wine Dive** (4720 Washington Ave., 713/880-8737, www.maxswinedive.com, Mon.-Thurs. 11am-midnight, Fri.-Sat. 10am-2am, Sun. 10am-midnight), just south of The Heights. "Dive" is a misnomer, since the dimly lit and comfortable locale caters to an upscale clientele, but the pairings of drink and food are down and dirty. You never realized a glass of red wine would complement a burger so well, or a flute of champagne with fried chicken. More than 150 wines are available by the glass or bottle, and many are available to go. An added bonus: Most of the beverages and food are Texas organic products.

If you'd rather dress down than up, The Heights is especially accommodating. Soak up a true Lone Star State experience at **Alice's Tall Texan** (4904 N. Main St., 713/862-0141, Sun.-Fri. 10am-midnight, Sat. 11am-1am), with no-frills cafeteria-style seating in a modest brick building and friendly folks chatting above the din of classic jukebox country music and cheap beer. For just $2.50 you can order a giant goblet of Lone Star or Shiner draft beer accompanied by a $1 bag of popcorn.

Another dive-ish option is **Big Star Bar** (1005 W. 19th St., 281/501-9560, www. bigstarbar.com, daily 4pm-2am). Dimly lit with a classic checkerboard floor, Big Star is a comfy place to kick back with a cheap bottle of beer and shoot a few rounds of pool while listening to Johnny Cash. An outdoor patio with a chain-link fence offers a friendly place to chat and hangout, and the vintage furniture and picnic tables were designed with chilling in mind.

Just north of The Heights in Garden Oaks-Oak Forest is the welcoming **Petrol Station**

(985 Wakefield Dr., 713/957-2875, Mon. 5pm-midnight, Tues.-Fri. 2pm-midnight, Sat. noon-1am, Sun. noon-10pm). Petrol Station is known for an impressive selection of local beers and its burgers—some of the heartiest and tastiest in town. Choose from lamb, beef, or veggie, and top it with flavorful mushrooms and grilled onions.

UPTOWN

For a reliable cocktail and above-average bar food, check out the **West End** (5320 Westheimer Rd., 713/590-0616, www. westend-houston.com, Mon.-Fri. 3pm-2am, Sat.-Sun. 11am-2am). The West End is an ideal place to take things up a notch from typical bar fare. The margaritas are a bit stronger, with higher-quality ingredients, and the burgers and wings are extra flavorful.

For those in search of a classic British-style pub, head to **Richmond Arms** (5920 Richmond Ave., 713/784-7722, www. richmondarmspub-houston.com, daily 11am-2am). It's an ideal place to watch a soccer game on TV, and you can easily identify fellow fans at the outdoor picnic tables painted with team and national flags. Not surprisingly, there are plenty of fine British ales on tap, and the food is surprisingly good.

MONTROSE

One of the most colorful places to spend a late night is **Poison Girl** (1641 Westheimer Rd., 713/527-9929, daily 4pm-2am). The first thing you'll notice are the bright pink walls; next are the incredible selection of bourbons and pinball machines. Even if you're not a bourbon fan, chat with the bartender to help pick your, um, poison. Spend some time on the back patio, where you'll be in the presence of a fun-loving crowd and the largest statue of the Kool-Aid Man you'll ever see (or attempt to climb).

For the craft-beer crowd, it doesn't get much better than ★ **Hay Merchant** (1100

1: Minute Maid Park, home of the Houston Astros **2:** Dean's Credit Clothing bar **3:** Warren's Inn in downtown Houston **4:** The Continental Club

Westheimer Rd., 713/528-9805, www.
haymerchant.com, Mon.-Fri. 3pm-2am,
Sat.-Sun. 11am-2am). Locals love the affordable sandwiches and rotating variety of
beer. Bartenders will suggest brews based on
specific preferences, and the food is always
a step above normal bar fare. The Korean
fried-chicken sandwich is a perfect example
of a comfort food taken to the next level with
a slightly spicy gochujang sauce and crispy
exterior.

Far more refined is the cocktail-minded
Anvil Bar & Refuge (1424 Westheimer Rd.,
713/523-1622, www.anvilhouston.com, daily
4pm-2am), a place where steady crowds take
their booze seriously. The bartenders shun
the term "mixologists," but they're deft at
concocting perfect cocktails. One of the bar's
most popular is the Nitro Cuba Libre, the fanciest rum and Coke you'll ever experience,
dispensed via a nitrogen tap. Also consider a
First Growth, made with gin, pineapple juice,
elderflower, and sage.

WEST UNIVERSITY

Many Houstonians associate pub crawls
with West University's Rice Village area,
where a collection of English-style brew-
pubs has kept nearby students out of the libraries for decades. Two locales for a freshly
poured pint, the jukebox of your dreams,
and the freewheeling college scene are **The
Ginger Man** (5607 Morningside Dr., 713/526-
2770, www.gingermanpub.com, Mon.-Fri.
2pm-2am, Sat.-Sun. 1pm-2am) and nearby
Little Woodrow's (5611 Morningside Dr.,
713/522-4438, Mon.-Fri. 3pm-2am, Sat.-Sun.
noon-2am).

Gay Bars

Houston has perhaps the largest gay scene in
the South, centered on the city's Montrose
district, west of downtown, where most of the
gay bars are, both understated and overblown.
One of the most popular clubs is **JR's** (808
Pacific St., 713/521-2519, www.jrsbarandgrill.
com), drawing a semi-professional crowd for
drink specials, karaoke, and male dancers.

Parking is hard to find, so use the valet service across the street.

Next door is the popular **South Beach**
(810 Pacific St., 713/521-0107, www.
southbeachthenightclub.com, Thurs. 9pm-
2am), a hot spot for dancing. South Beach attracts a primarily gay clientele, but everyone is
welcome on the dance floor, where suspended
jets spray liquid ice on the crowd to keep
things cool. Nearby is **Ripcord** (715 Fairview
St., 713/521-2792, daily 1pm-2am), reportedly
the second-oldest gay bar in Texas. Pool is a
popular draw, as are the cheap drinks.

Live Music
BLUES
Mention blues towns and most people think
of Memphis or Chicago, but Houston belongs
in the mix, with a long-standing tradition
of swampy bayou blues. Some of the gritti-
est and most soulful players have emerged
from the city's downtown African American
neighborhoods.

The **Continental Club** (3700 Main St.,
713/529-9899, www.continentalclub.com,
Thurs. 6pm-2am, Fri. 7pm-2am, Sat. 8pm-
2am) doesn't stage blues exclusively—roots
and alternative rock acts are often on the
bill—but the local and touring blues bands
that play here are typically the best around.
An offshoot of the legendary Austin venue,
Houston's version of the Continental is appropriately more sprawling but still dedicated to
soulful music.

Consistently topping Houston's annual
"best blues club" lists is West University's
**The Big Easy Social and Pleasure
Club** (5731 Kirby Dr., 713/523-9999, www.
thebigeasyblues.com, daily 7pm-2am). The
quality musicianship is the epitome of integrity. Weekends are set aside for top-notch
touring acts and Houston's premier local blues
bands, while weeknights offer themes like
open jams and dance parties. Sunday-night
zydeco is another highlight.

Another local favorite is **The
Shakespeare Pub** (14129 Memorial Dr.,
281/497-4625, www.shakespearepub.net,

daily 5pm-2am). Locals rule the stage here, including luminaries such as John McVey, Eugene Moody, and Texas Johnny Brown. If you get a chance, drop by at dinnertime on Sunday for Spare Time Murray's weekly Early Blues Jam.

COUNTRY AND WESTERN

Houston is the home of the Urban Cowboy, so grab those boots if you're fixin' to head out for some two-stepping at one of these fine dance halls, including the city's big-box country music venues. Near the Galleria among the trendy upscale dance clubs is the refreshingly unhip **Firehouse Saloon** (5930 Southwest Freeway, 713/977-1962, www. firehousesaloon.com, Sun.-Wed. 7pm-11pm, Fri.-Sat. 5pm-2am). There's some flashiness here—big ol' shiny belt buckles, fancy light machines, Vegas-style video games—but the crowd is genuinely friendly. Cover bands take the stage most nights, but you'll find the occasional worthy local band.

For an overwhelming dose of Lone Star State culture, drop by the **Big Texas Dance Hall and Saloon** (803 E. NASA Blvd., 281/461-4400, www.bigtexassaloon.com, Wed.-Sat. 7pm-2am). It's a bit hokey, with pseudo-rustic decor of cacti and Western "artifacts," but the scene is vibrant, especially for singles. Live music is the big draw on Thursday, when regional acts get boots scootin', but DJs fill the dance floor most weekends.

For drinking and country music without dancing, drop by **Goode's Armadillo Palace** (5015 Kirby Ave., 713/526-9700, www. thearmadillopalace.com, Tues.-Thurs. 11am-11pm, Fri. 11am-2am, Sat. 4pm-2am), among the cluster of Goode Company barbecue and Texas restaurants. The Armadillo has a huge bar in the middle and tiny stage in the corner, and fortunately the pure honky-tonk sounds from the bands are huge enough to fill the venue and get a few people two-stepping in the limited space near the stage.

JAZZ

One of the many benefits of being a music fan in a big city is access to quality jazz clubs. Houston is a major player on the jazz circuit and a hotbed for the genre's rising stars. The stalwart on the scene is **Sambuca** (909 Texas Ave., 713/224-5299, www.sambucarestaurant. com, Mon.-Wed. 11am-11pm, Thurs. 11am-midnight, Fri. 11am-1am, Sat. 4pm-1am, Sun. 4pm-11pm). In the stunning historic Rice Hotel, Sambuca is a jazz fan's dream—a classy downtown venue offering nightly performances from local and national performers. Get a juicy steak from the acclaimed restaurant, and visit the cigar room after your meal or during the set break.

Intimate **Cezanne** (4100 Montrose Blvd., 713/522-9621, www.cezannejazz.com, Fri.-Sat. 9pm-midnight), a 40-seat venue in the trendy Montrose district, is considered Houston's premier jazz club, where aficionados get to sit feet from national acts. Every seat is a good one, and you'll feel every note being played.

CONCERT VENUES

Since Houston is such a business and convention-oriented city, visitors often have expense accounts to afford the pricey tickets for familiar rock acts. Virtually every touring act makes a stop in Houston. Browse the online calendar for the downtown entertainment complex **Bayou Place** (500 Texas St., 713/227-0957, www.bayouplace.com).

Away from the hassle of downtown, head to folky **Anderson Fair** (2007 Grant St., 832/767-2785, www.andersonfair.net), tucked away in the Montrose area and hosting up-and-coming folk and roots rock acts for decades. It continues to stage some of Texas's most popular Americana acts. Note: Anderson Fair is only open on weekends.

Performing Arts
THE HOUSTON GRAND OPERA
A big city deserves a big-time opera company, and Houston has the **Houston Grand Opera** (713/228-6737, www.houstongrandopera. org). Performances are held at the downtown

Wortham Theater Center (501 Texas Ave., 832/487-7000, www.houstonfirsttheaters. com). It's the only opera company on the planet to win a Tony, two Emmys, and two Grammy awards, and it has a reputation for commissioning and performing new works, with dozens of world premieres over 50 years. The company tours extensively, bringing productions to Europe, Japan, and Egypt, and has been lauded for accessibility: Tickets for some shows start at $15, and the casual dress series is popular among young people.

THE HOUSTON BALLET

World-class Houston Ballet (601 Preston St., 713/523-6300, www.houstonballet.org) also utilizes the beautiful Wortham Theater Center and has developed a national reputation for making stars of principal dancers as well as staging contemporary edgy ballets. In recent years, the company has taken its show to China, London, Canada, and Washington DC's Kennedy Center.

THE HOUSTON SYMPHONY

Highly respected Houston Symphony (713/224-4240, www.houstonsymphony.org) has been impressing audiences at the magnificent downtown Jones Hall (615 Louisiana St.) since 1966. Shows include a classical season, a pops series, *Messiah* performances at Christmas, and family concerts. In the summer, the symphony performs outdoor shows and stages children's performances throughout the region.

THEATER

Houston boasts several high-quality theater companies, but two consistently emerge at the top. The Alley Theatre (615 Texas Ave., 713/220-5700, www.alleytheatre.org) stages productions in a Brutalist fortress in the heart of downtown that's separated into two stages. Classic and contemporary performances consistently draw diverse audiences.

Also drawing rave reviews is the Ensemble Theatre (3535 Main St., 713/520-0055, www. ensemblehouston.org). Billed as the largest African American professional theater company in the country with its own productions and facility, the Ensemble regularly stages acclaimed dramas, comedies, and musicals for enthusiastic crowds. The company also runs an educational touring program and a popular summer training program for youth.

Events
WINTER

Each year in mid-January, the Antioch Missionary Baptist Church of Christ is a gathering site for the Gardere Martin Luther King Jr. Oratory Competition (500 Clay St., 713/867-3286, www.gardere.com). Sponsored by the Gardere law firm for nearly two decades, the event is a highly anticipated contest for elementary school students, who research, write, and deliver inspiring speeches dedicated to Dr. King's legacy. The competition also includes a spirited performance by the Salvation Army Choir.

In mid-February, the Texas Home and Garden Show (8400 Kirby Dr., 800/654-1480, www.texashomeandgarden.com) offers interactive displays and more than 1,500 exhibitors at the Reliant Center to help with spring gardening plans.

SPRING

Every March, the University of Texas Health Science Center presents the popular Brain Night for Kids (7000 Fannin St., 713/521-1515, www.thehealthmuseum.org), featuring presentations about how the brain works, a dissection of a sheep's brain, an informative video, and other brainy activities.

In April, don't miss the Bayou City Cajun Fest (7979 N. Eldridge Pkwy., 281/890-5500, www.tradersvillage.com) at Traders Village. Patrons enjoy crawfish, po'boys, zydeco bands, and all kinds of Cajun culture. Another popular annual springtime event is the AsiaFest (11903 Bellaire Blvd., 713/784-1112, www.asiasociety.org), featuring an impressive parade, food booths, and cultural activities at the Alief Community Park in southwest Houston each May.

SUMMER

It gets sweltering in Houston during the summer months, but that doesn't deter locals from celebrating. One of the best-known annual events is **Juneteenth** (7800 Airport Blvd., 713/558-2600, www.houstonculture.org), commemorating the day in June that enslaved Texans learned about their freedom via the Emancipation Proclamation. Juneteenth activities include national gospel, blues, and jazz acts taking the stage at Hermann Park, along with plenty of good eats and revelry.

September is still the height of the summer in Houston, and residents celebrate by enjoying hot jazz at the **Houston International Jazz Festival** (520 Texas Ave., 713/839-7000, www.jazzeducation.org), with local and nationally known jazz artists at the Bayou Music Center.

FALL

Get your ghoul on with the city's annual **Ghost Tour** (www.houstonghosttour.com) throughout October. Hauntees gather in the scary suburb of Spring, where they can get freaked out by various urban legends and recreated historical death scenes.

People descend en masse on downtown neighborhoods on November 2 for the **Dia de Los Muertos Festival** (4912 Main St., 713/343-0218, www.hispanichouston.com). This Latin American cultural event includes parades and festivals honoring deceased family and friends.

SHOPPING

Mention "shopping" and "Houston" and most people immediately think of the Galleria, a sprawling community unto itself on the western edge of the city's outer loop. It's a glassy, bustling, commercial destination that inspires some and intimidates others. Plenty of shopping options run from exclusive high-end (Galleria) to funky bargain-basement (The Heights). Despite being associated with the Urban Cowboy mystique, Houston does not have an overabundance of specialty shops with Western gear, although you're likely to find flashy rhinestone-esque clothing.

Downtown

One of the most popular downtown shopping destinations is the pleasantly modest **Shops at Houston Center** (1200 McKinney St., 713/759-1442, www.shopsathc.com, hours vary), 50 specialty stores and boutiques beneath a canopy-style atrium. Look for jewelry, home decor, and quick bites in the two-block complex. The shops are connected to Houston's **Downtown Tunnels** (713/650-3022, tour info at 713/392-0867, www.houstonhistoricaltours.com), a 6-mile (9.7-km) system of air-conditioned subterranean walkways that links dozens of downtown buildings.

The Heights

Shopping destinations in The Heights reflect the neighborhood's funky and trendy vibe. A good example is **Casa Ramirez** (241 W. 19th St., 713/880-2420), featuring Latin American folk art, clothing items, and traditional Latin American wares, from furniture to handbags and paintings. Look for Mr. or Mrs. Ramirez, who can provide suggestions and explain the shop's many interesting items.

See the culture of rural America at **Wabash Antiques and Feedstore** (4537 N. Shepherd Dr., 713/863-8322, www.wabashfeed.com), with high-end pet food and the sounds and sights of farms, including antique equipment, lawn art, and plenty of hens, turkeys, kittens, and rabbits.

Texas-style fashion boutique **Hello Lucky** (1025 Studewood St., 713/864-3556, www.hellolucky.com) is in a small historic home and filled with Texas-themed clothing and knickknacks. Featured items include jewelry, T-shirts, tote bags, and accessories like gold armadillo cufflinks.

Uptown

One of the city's most popular shopping destinations is the colossal **Galleria** (5085 Westheimer Rd., 713/622-0663, www.

galleriahouston.com). This city within a city—the fourth-largest mall in the country—draws 30 million visitors annually. Noted for its remarkable glass atriums and suspended balconies, the Galleria contains a popular ice-skating rink, two high-rise hotels, and 400 shops, including high-end Nordstrom, Saks Fifth Avenue, Neiman Marcus, Cartier, Gucci, and Tiffany & Co. The best time to experience the Galleria is Saturday afternoon: It's an absolute madhouse, and you won't get much shopping done, but the people-watching is the best the city has to offer. Grab a latte and keep an eye out for the girls in flashy gowns celebrating their *quinceañera,* a Latin American rite of passage dedicated to a girl's 15th birthday.

West University

Another of Houston's most popular shopping destinations is **Rice Village** (Rice Blvd. and Kirby Dr., 713/302-8918, www.ricevillagedistrict.com), just west of Rice University. This 16-block complex has been a favorite place for bargain hunting, browsing, and people-watching since the 1930s. The Village features scores of independent shops and eclectic boutiques along with local restaurants and services, some in historic homes, others in modest 1950s strip centers.

Independent **Brazos Bookstore** (2421 Bissonnet St., 713/523-0701, www.brazosbookstore.com) is fiercely loved by local book people—it was rescued from closure by a group of concerned citizens. Spend an afternoon out of the heat browsing, reading, and chatting with the knowledgeable and friendly staff.

Greater Houston

An eclectic mix of Asian shops and restaurants awaits on **Harwin Drive,** roughly between Gessner and Fondren Streets. The area offers an epic mash-up of the strip malls and gaudy signs of American suburban sprawl with the cultural diversity of Thai, Pakistani, Indian, and Chinese vendors and eateries. Spend an afternoon browsing for unexpected

gems and bargain clothes, accessories, furniture, and knickknacks. Just a few miles west on Harwin is **Chinatown,** a concentrated collection of Chinese establishments, including a mall with bookstores, music, gifts, and cooking items.

FOOD

Houston has 11,000 restaurants, and recently the city's culinary scene has drawn the attention of national food critics and restaurateurs, regularly earning high marks. People here love eating out, so the array of options ranges from fast food to haute cuisine. The city's enormous international population means there is regional cuisine rarely seen elsewhere. Home-grown varieties include barbecue, Tex-Mex, and Southern cooking. The following suggestions don't represent the trends in Houston's always-evolving culinary scene but are examples of the impressive variety, with an emphasis on long-standing eateries.

Downtown
STEAK

A steak house doesn't have to be stodgy, and the scene is downright comfortable at **III Forks** (1201 Fannin St., 713/658-9457, www.3forks.com, Mon.-Thurs. 11am-10pm, Fri. 11am-11pm, Sat. 4pm-11pm, $16-49). Sumptuous steaks take center stage, with featured double-cut strip, filet mignon, and porterhouse. Sides cost extra but are ideal accompaniments, including the popular spinach and six-cheese potatoes. Save room for the Texas pecan cake.

Well-heeled nontraditional downtown steak house **Vic & Anthony's** (1510 Texas St., 713/228-1111, www.vicandanthonys.com, Mon.-Fri. 11am-10pm, Sat.-Sun. 5pm-10pm, $18-51) is chic, minimalist, and tightly packed. Vic & Anthony's sticks with the basics—a simple menu of high-quality cuts of meat and a few seafood and chicken options. Outstanding salads and appetizers include the pear salad and oysters, and the wine selection is impressive if pricey. Steaks are enormous, and the bone-in rib-eye is considered the best in town.

CAJUN

With direct access to seafood, sauces, spices, and swamps, Houston is one of the few places in the country with authentic Cajun cuisine. It doesn't get much better than the legendary New Orleans establishment ★ **Brennan's** (3300 Smith St., 713/522-9711, www. brennanshouston.com, Sun.-Fri. 11am-2pm and 5pm-10pm, Sat. 5:45pm-10pm, $13-41). In a historic brick mansion, Brennan's offers classic Louisiana flavors such as étouffée, lump crab cakes, and pecan-crusted amberjack. Breakfasts are legendary, and the eggs and delectable sauces taste even better paired with live jazz music during the weekend New Orleans Jazz Brunch.

Less formal is the popular downtown lunch chain **Treebeard's** (315 Travis St., 713/228-2622, www.treebeards.com, Mon.-Sat. 11am-2:30pm, $8-16). All the Creole classics are here—shrimp étouffée, jambalaya, gumbo, and a hearty dose of red beans and rice. Be sure to order a side of jalapeño cornbread, and save room for the bread pudding with whiskey sauce. Treebeard's isn't open for dinner.

TEX-MEX

For true Tex-Mex, **Irma's Original** (22 N. Chenevert St., 713/222-0767, www. irmasoriginal.com, Mon.-Wed. 8am-3pm, Thurs.-Fri. 8am-10pm, Sat. 4pm-10pm, $13-28) was named for founder Irma Gonzalez Galvan, a Rio Grande Valley native who moved to Houston with her family in the 1940s and became one of the city's most famous chefs. Her authentic recipes are the ultimate Texas comfort food, including *caldo* (corn-based chicken soup), fajitas, and especially the enchiladas—try the mole sauce and green tomatillo options. The service may not be spectacular, but the food is supreme.

BREAKFAST

The Breakfast Klub (3711 Travis St., 713/528-8561, www.thebreakfastklub.com, Mon.-Fri. 7am-2pm, Sat.-Sun. 8am-2pm, $9-24) is known for its long line and its famous chicken and waffles, worth waiting up to an hour to experience. The line moves fairly quickly and is shorter if you arrive before 9am. The diversity of your fellow line-mates offers a refreshing perspective on this international city and its love for good food. The chicken and waffles are perfectly prepared, with tender and flavorful centers. The "biskuits" and gravy are flaky and flavorful.

The Heights
BARBECUE
Possibly Houston's best barbecue, ★ **Gatlin's Barbecue** (3510 Ella Blvd., 713/869-4227, www.gatlinsbbq.com, Mon.-Thurs. 11am-8-pm, Fri.-Sat. 11am-9pm, $12-36) is in an uninspiring strip mall with perfectly smoked meat. Order a Gatlin sandwich just to taste the amazing bun, a buttery toasted delight. The meat is the main draw, with tender succulent brisket and savory smoked sausage.

Uptown
STEAK
Although Uptown lacks the historical charm of downtown, it has a few of the city's most esteemed steak houses. A favorite is **Pappas Brothers Steakhouse** (5839 Westheimer Rd., 713/780-7352, www.pappasbros.com, Mon.-Thurs. 5pm-10pm, Fri.-Sat. 5pm-11pm, $17-53), where steak lovers gather for perfectly marbled cuts of top-notch beef. The filets are Pappas Brothers' specialty, and the somewhat lofty prices (upper $40s) feel like a wise investment once you're savoring each tender bite. The sides are also top-notch; suggested options include potatoes au gratin and asparagus.

Just down the street is **Chama Gaucha** (5865 Westheimer Rd., 713/244-9500, www. chamagaucha.com, Mon.-Fri. 11:30am-2:30pm and 5pm-10pm, Sat. 4:30pm-10pm, Sun. 3pm-9pm, $13-44), a Brazilian-style steak house where the staff serves a plethora of meat options with sharp and shiny knives. The filet mignon and sirloin are excellent, but other styles to consider are the bacon-wrapped variety and a cut of lamb. The introductory salad bar may tempt you with its leafy goodness, colorful vegetables, and bread medallions, but don't overdo it at the expense of the magnificent meat.

LEBANESE

Uptown contains several noteworthy informal lunch venues, the best among them serving savory Lebanese food. **Mary'z Lebanese Cuisine** (5825 Richmond Ave., 832/251-1955, www.maryzcuisine.com, daily 11am-midnight, $8-19) is tiny, but the tastes are huge, especially in freshly made kebabs, falafel, shawarma, and baba ghanoush. Complement your meal with a Lebanese beer like Almazo. At night, Mary'z becomes a hot spot for young adults who toke on hookahs.

AMERICAN

One of the finest meals in town is at ★ **Lucille's** (5512 La Branch St., 713/568-2505, www.lucilleshouston.com, Tues.-Thurs. 11am-9pm, Fri. 11am-10pm, Sat. 10am-3pm and 4pm-10pm, Sun. 10am-3pm, $13-39), in a cozy historic home run by chefs Chris Williams and Khang Hoang. Chris's great-grandmother Lucille was a local African American culinary pioneer, and Lucille's replicates some of her most famous recipes. This is Southern cooking at its best, with an emphasis on traditional dishes featuring exquisite sauces and sides. Order shrimp and grits, catfish and grits, or cheesy grits, or step it up and get the bone-in pork chop or smothered steak. One of the best items on the menu is the braised oxtail—the savory sauce makes this hearty dish a delectable meal.

Locals can't get enough of classy **Cafe Annie** (1800 Post Oak Blvd., 713/840-1111, www.cafeanniehouston.com, Mon.-Fri. 11:30am-10pm, Sat. 5pm-10:30pm, $12-43). Elegance exudes from the decor and the tantalizing appetizers of goat cheese crepes and entrées like the cinnamon-roasted pheasant and cocoa-roasted chicken. Haute Texas cuisine is represented in the cilantro-enhanced

mussel soup and barbecued sweet potatoes. Reservations are strongly advised.

The enormous sandwich spot **Kenny & Ziggy's** (2327 Post Oak Blvd., 713/871-8883, www.kennyandziggys.com, Mon.-Fri. 7am-9pm, Sat.-Sun. 8am-9pm, $13-35) is a deli, a rarity in Texas. The corned beef and pastrami are favorites, especially piled high on a reuben. Portions are enormous, so consider splitting a plate. Save space for the potato salad and pickles.

MEXICAN

Molina's Cantina (7901 Westheimer Rd., 713/782-0861, www.molinascantina.com, Tues.-Sat. 11am-9:30pm, Sun.-Mon. 11am-9pm, $9-20) is a traditional Mexican restaurant on the western edge of Uptown. A Houston institution since 1941, Molina's is the ultimate destination for old-school Tex-Mex, and the signature Mexico City Dinner captures it all: chili con queso, tamale, tostada, taco, and enchilada with rice and beans.

Montrose-Kirby

JAPANESE

Houston's version of **Uchi** (904 Westheimer Rd., 713/522-4808, www.uchirestaurants.com, Sun.-Thurs. 5pm-10pm, Fri.-Sat. 5pm-11pm, reservations strongly advised, $17-49) is as good as the original, with exquisite flavor combinations. Order a bottle of wine and the fried brussels sprouts to start—the smoky caramelized flavors are perfect with the leafy green vegetables. The sushi rolls are a delight, with disparate yet instantly perfect intertwined tastes. Examples include the salmon and Asian pear or yellowfin tuna and oranges. The *hamachi nabe* is tuna topped by a soy-based broth and an egg. Each of the uniquely crafted dishes are expertly explained by the waitstaff, who politely suggest menu items and recommend dishes based on your level of adventure and budget.

1: Treebeard's in downtown Houston **2:** Houston's famous Irma's Original **3:** Lucille's **4:** Lua Viet Kitchen

AMERICAN

Close to the Rice University campus is contemporary, classy, and casual **Local Foods** (2424 Dunstan Rd., 713/521-7800, www. houstonlocalfoods.com, daily 10am-8:30pm, $13-35), an ideal spot for lunch in a welcoming environment. The restaurant is best known for its scrumptious Crunchy Chicken sandwich; the pretzel bun is worth ordering on its own. Pair it with the clean-tasting lemongrass soup and the flavorful kale.

Houstonians go berserk over **Backstreet Café** (1103 S. Shepherd Dr., 713/521-2239, www.backstreetcafe.net, Mon.-Fri. 11am-10pm, Sat. 10am-11pm, Sun. 10am-9pm, $12-30), a wildly popular two-story New American venue revered for its crafty chef, Hugo Ortega of Hugo's, who specializes in quality comfort food. Backstreet is known for its "crusted" dishes, including mustard-crusted salmon and sesame-crusted shrimp. The most popular entrée is the meat loaf tower, an aptly named stack of seasoned meat, garlic mashed potatoes, sautéed spinach, and mushroom gravy. Backstreet breakfasts are legendary, as is the Sunday jazz brunch (11am-3pm).

Popular with locals is ★ **Benjy's** (2424 Dunstan Rd., 713/522-7602, www.benjys.com, Tues.-Thurs. 4pm-10pm, Fri.-Sat. 4pm-11pm, Sun.-Mon. 4pm-9pm, $13-33), a contemporary venue with outstanding food and service. Things change often, from the artwork to the menu, keeping things fresh. Seafood is the specialty (smoked salmon, seasoned shrimp), but Benjy's also serves comfort food with modern flair, including sandwiches and entrées such as the pecan- and pistachio-crusted chicken with mixed potato gratin. Locals flock to Benjy's for brunch, and the Bloody Marys are some of the best in the city, with wasabi instead of horseradish.

MEXICAN

A visit to this part of town is incomplete without a meal at the tremendous ★ **Hugo's** (1600 Westheimer Rd., 713/524-7744, www. hugosrestaurant.net, Mon.-Thurs. 11am-10pm, Fri.-Sat. 11am-11pm, Sun. 10am-9pm, $15-39), a chic open-air hacienda serving trendy Mexican dishes. Start with Hugo's signature velvety margarita, paired with a tantalizing appetizer such as the squash-blossom quesadillas or one of four ceviches. Entrées range from savory pork *carnitas* to tender snapper Veracruzana. Desserts are legendary, especially the flan and Mexican hot chocolate, containing freshly roasted and ground cocoa beans.

ITALIAN

Montrose residents can't get enough risotto, and several worthy Italian options satisfy their craving, chief among them fresh, authentic, and homemade **Divino Italian Restaurant** (1830 W. Alabama St., 713/807-1123, www. divinoitalian.com, Tues.-Thurs. 5:30pm-10pm, Fri.-Sat. 5:30pm-10:30pm, $14-49). Locals love the Parma-style risotto, though the boar sausage-style is also commendable. In-house pasta specialties include Merlin's papardelle for mushroom lovers. The seasonal seafood dishes are consistently excellent.

Another notable destination is quaint and upscale **DaMarco Cucina E Vino** (1520 Westheimer Rd., 713/807-8857, www. damarcohouston.com, Tues.-Thurs. 11:30am-2pm and 5:30pm-10pm, Fri. 11:30am-2pm and 5:30pm-10pm, Sat. 5:30pm-10pm, $16-51), known for top-notch ingredients and the inventive flavor combos of renowned chef Marco Wiles. Diners choose Tuscany- and Texas-inspired dishes, including savory chianti-braised pork ribs, sea bass with grilled grapefruit, and roasted Texas quail. Other suggested menu items include the flavorful lamb chops with a tasty cumin-based yogurt sauce, truffle pasta, served table-side, and the sweet corn lobster ravioli.

VIETNAMESE

Houston has an abundance of Vietnamese restaurants, some long-standing and consistently serving quality food.

For a modern fresh take, head to ★ **Lua Viet Kitchen** (1540 W. Alabama St., 346/227-7047, www.luavietkicten.com, Sun.-Thurs.

11am-9pm, Fri.-Sat. 11am-10pm, $9-26), in contemporary space with suspended vertical lighting. Locally sourced ingredients (a list of contributing Houston-area farmers is on the menu) include the salt-and-pepper shrimp and shaking beef. Amazing rice-based dishes include the five-spiced hen. Lua's also has an extensive vegetarian menu.

Known for its late hours as much as its food, **Mai's** (3401 Milam St., 713/520-5300, www.maishouston.com, Mon.-Thurs. 11am-3am, Fri.-Sat. 11am-4am, $8-27) draws enthusiastic revelers and foodies for dishes like *tom xao thap cam* (shrimp with mixed vegetables in a sumptuous sauce), *bun bo hue* (a flavorful soup with just the right amount of spice), and *mi xao don* (savory meats atop crispy noodles).

If you're craving tasty Vietnamese food and only have a few bucks to spare, head to **Cali Sandwich and Pho** (3030 Travis St., 713/520-0710, Mon.-Sat. 10am-9pm, $5-10). The *bánh mì* sandwiches are delicious and cost only $4. Fresh veggies and hearty pork, tofu, or chicken are packed in a perfect French roll. For a big bowl of flavorful soup, order a *bun bo hue*, which is on the spicy side. Lunchtime is especially busy; try to arrive before noon or after 1pm.

LUNCH

Most restaurants in this traditionally trendy part of town have impressive lunch menus, but a few are noteworthy for their vibrant scenes, including **Goode Co. Barbeque** (5109 Kirby Dr., 713/522-2530, www.goodecompany.com, daily 11am-10pm, $11-29), a funky spot always packed with students, young professionals, and working-class carnivores. Goode's specializes in classic 'cue—sausage, ribs, chicken, and the signature tender and juicy brisket, all topped with succulent smoky sauce. The side items are better than average, including sweet coleslaw and jalapeño cornbread.

On the opposite end of the spectrum is the sleek **Ra Sushi** (3908 Westheimer Rd., 713/621-5800, www.rasushi.com, daily 11am-midnight, $7-22). Drawing a young crowd, Ra is known for its stylish social scene as much

as its hip sushi rolls. Popular items include the spicy lobster roll, scallop dynamite, and Viva Las Vegas roll with light tempura, crab, tuna, and lotus root. Order a seaweed salad or a more substantial item from the Pacific Rim-themed full menu. Stick around for the happy hour scene at Ra's Flying Fish Lounge.

ACCOMMODATIONS

For all its cosmopolitan charm, Houston remains a business destination, reflected in its hotels. A few upscale independent options include the ZaZa and Derek, but most lodging is on the interstates, with easy access to business centers. Rooms are easy to book year-round and are mostly generic in their amenities.

Visitors can take advantage of the business orientation by booking upscale downtown rooms at affordable weekend rates (around $130). With the absence of work-related traffic on weekends, it's easy to drive to Museum District sites from a high-end historic downtown hotel like the Magnolia.

Downtown
$100-150

A worthwhile option just outside the inner loop is the clean and spacious **Best Western Plus Downtown Inn and Suites** (915 W. Dallas St., 713/571-7733, www.bestwestern. com, $119 d). Rooms and suites include microwaves, fridges, and free Wi-Fi, and the hotel offers a free full breakfast every morning, a fitness center, a spa, and an outdoor pool.

One of the best ways to experience Houston at an affordable rate is at the fabulous ★ **Magnolia Hotel** (1100 Texas Ave., 713/221-0011, www.magnoliahotelhouston. com, $139 d), a historic downtown gem that hosts business guests and events in a cosmopolitan 1926 building within walking distance of attractions and restaurants. Rooms are on the small side, and the Magnolia's complimentary services include Wi-Fi, downtown car transportation, and free milk and cookies at bedtime. The minibar is stocked with beverages and snacks, and the library and billiards room is stocked with an eclectic collection of books. There is a rooftop fitness center with a lap pool and a hot tub.

A deluxe downtown lodging experience is the **Sam Houston** (117 Prairie St., 832/200-8800, www.hilton.com, $149 d). "The Sam" offers near-luxury accommodations. Pamper yourself in this contemporary setting with amenities such as upscale baths (granite walls and glass-walled showers with plush robes and towels), quality bedding (down comforters and pillows, pillow-top mattresses), gourmet snacks, a minibar, and free Wi-Fi.

$150-200

Hotel Icon (220 Main St., 713/224-4266, www.hotelicon.com, $152 d) offers dynamic contemporary lodging in the heart of downtown. This 12-story hotel in a former bank is filled with bold colors and lavish details, including marble countertops, antique claw-foot tubs, luxury robes, and plush linens. Other amenities include free Wi-Fi, a stocked mini-bar, and fresh-cut flowers.

In the middle of the action is **Hilton Americas** (1600 Lamar St., 713/739-8000, www.hilton.com, $169 d), an enormous visually striking hotel with 1,200 rooms towering over downtown. A big-time business destination attached to the convention center, weekends are a cheaper time to stay, since the hotel's many amenities are more accessible. Highlights include three restaurants, several bars and lounges, and an impressive spa and health club with downtown views. Rooms feature free Wi-Fi, upscale linens, and an in-room refreshment center.

The comforts of home in a historical urban setting are at the **Residence Inn Houston Downtown** (904 Dallas St., 832/366-1000, www.marriott.com, $169 d), in the spectacular 1921 Humble Oil Building. Well-restored Classical Revival details include brass elevator doors, tall ceilings, and stately rose marble. Hotel amenities include free Wi-Fi, a large pool, a fitness center, and spacious suites with fully equipped kitchens and separate sleeping and living areas. An unexpected complimentary service: Leave a grocery list at the front desk and return in the evening to a stocked kitchen.

In a historic setting, the elegant yet comfortable ★ **Hotel Lancaster** (701 Texas St., 713/228-9500, www.thelancaster.com, $199 d), one of Houston's original small luxury hotels, is in the heart of the Theater District. The lobby is decorated with large oil paintings and dramatic lighting, and there's a sense of European opulence in the hotel's decor. Guest rooms capture this charm with dark-wood two-poster beds, feather pillows with the softest sheets imaginable, and brass furnishings. The breakfast buffet is cosmopolitan—muesli, salmon, and olives accompany sausage, eggs, and waffles. Guests notice the attention to detail and customer service. The Lancaster offers Wi-Fi, a bountiful breakfast, and car service to nearby attractions for a $15 service fee.

$200-250

Some of the most upscale lodging in town is at the **Westin Houston Downtown** (1520 Texas Ave., 713/228-1520, www.innattheballpark.com, $209 d), within earshot of Houston Astros games. The location is one of the prime amenities, since the other services are not overly inspiring. The Westin offers free transportation services around town and a fitness center, but there are fees for in-room internet access and breakfast.

The luxurious five-star **Four Seasons** (1300 Lamar St., 713/650-1300, www.fourseasons.com, $299 d) has skyline views and outstanding services, including the exquisite spa and salon, a spacious pool and fitness center, complimentary downtown car service, a tasty antipasti bar, and rooms featuring plush bathrobes, minibars, and Wi-Fi.

Uptown
$50-100

Some of the best bargains in the city are in the busy Uptown area west of downtown near the

1: Hotel Lancaster **2:** Magnolia Hotel **3:** Houston's Main Street at night

Galleria. Among them are **La Quinta Inn & Suites** (1625 W. Loop S., 713/355-3440, www.lq.com, $89 d), with a heated pool and spa, a fitness center, a free continental breakfast buffet, and rooms with free internet access.

Similarly priced and amenity packed is the adjacent **Drury Inn and Suites** (1615 W. Loop S., 713/963-0700, www.druryhotels.com, $99 d), offering a free hot breakfast, a fitness center, an indoor-outdoor pool, and a whirlpool. Guest rooms feature free Wi-Fi, microwaves, and fridges.

$100-150

Worth considering is **Hotel Indigo at the Galleria** (5160 Hidalgo St., 800/465-4329, www.ichotelsgroup.com, $116 d), featuring bold design and inspiring colors throughout, room options with separate sitting and work areas, free internet access and printing capacity, a fitness center, and an outdoor pool.

Unique and memorable ★ **Hotel Derek** (2525 W. Loop S., 866/292-4100, www.hotelderek.com, $119 d) is an independent option with consistently reliable service. Hotel Derek's highlights include an outstanding pool with a gushing waterfall, day-spa treatments, and a chauffeured car providing free transportation to the Galleria's nearby shopping locales. Rooms feature free Wi-Fi, minibars, bathrobes, and beds with goose-down duvets. The hotel's restaurant, Revolve Kitchen + Bar, is a destination itself.

Another worthy consideration is the impressive **Hilton Post Oak** (2001 Post Oak Blvd., 713/961-9300, www.hilton.com, $119 d). Each room includes a balcony offering impressive skyline views as well as Wi-Fi, minibars, and fridges. The hotel also offers complimentary shuttle service to destinations within a 3-mile (4.8-km) radius.

The reliable **Doubletree Guest Suites** (5353 Westheimer Rd., 713/961-9000, www.doubletree.com, $141 d) has an ideal location and spacious one- and two-bedroom suites with free Wi-Fi, an upscale fitness center, and a large outdoor pool area with a sundeck and a whirlpool.

$150-200

Galleria visitors enjoy **Embassy Suites** (2911 Sage Rd., 713/626-5444, www.embassysuites.com, $162 d). Hotel amenities include an impressive atrium, an indoor pool and whirlpool, a large fitness center, and an included cooked-to-order breakfast. Rooms offer a private bedroom and separate living area with a sofa bed, a minibar, a fridge, a microwave, and free Wi-Fi.

Another option favored by many Galleria shoppers is the **JW Marriott Houston** (5150 Westheimer Rd., 713/961-1500, www.marriott.com, $169 d), a stately 23-floor hotel featuring Wi-Fi, a fitness center, indoor and outdoor pools, and a whirlpool.

Connected to the country's fourth-largest mall, the **Westin Galleria Houston** (5060 W. Alabama St., 713/960-8100, www.marriott.com, $194 d) is in a prime location, allowing guests to walk straight from the hotel to the massive shopping center. After shopping, unwind in a spacious room with internet access (for a fee) and attractive furnishings.

West University

Downtown is quiet most nights, but the West University area is usually hopping. Visitors stay here for the abundant nearby nightlife and cultural attractions. One of the best deals is the **Doubletree Greenway Plaza** (6 Greenway Plaza E., 713/629-1200, www.marriott.com, $104 d), featuring spacious rooms with walk-in closets, luxury bedding, internet access, a fitness center, and an outdoor pool.

A similar bargain is **Courtyard Houston West University** (2929 Westpark Dr., 713/661-5669, www.marriott.com, $98 d), offering an outdoor pool and whirlpool, an exercise room, a book-filled library, and free Wi-Fi. Another worthy option is the enormous **Hilton Houston Plaza** (6633 Travis St., 713/313-4000, www.hilton.com, $149 d). The Hilton includes large suites, minibars, internet access, a fitness facility, a heated swimming pool, and free transportation within a 3-mile (4.8-km) radius of the hotel.

The lodging jewel of the city is ★ **Hotel ZaZa** (5701 Main St., 713/526-1991, www. hotelzaza.com, from $219), just east of the university neighborhood on the edge of the Museum District. Billed as an "urban resort with a mix of glamour and warmth, high style, and creature comforts," the ZaZa is in a league of its own. Amenities include a poolside retreat and outdoor bar with private cabanas, the luxurious ZaSpa and fitness center, nightly turndown service, cordless phones, free Wi-Fi, ZaZa guest robes, upscale linens, fridges, and an in-room "grab and go gourmet refreshment bar."

Greater Houston

A 30-minute jaunt up I-45 is the luxurious and relaxing ★ **Woodlands Resort** (2301 N. Millbend Dr., The Woodlands, 281/367-1100, www.woodlandsresort.com, from $229), contemporary accommodations with several pools, a tubing river, whirlpool tubs, a pampering spa, and tasty cuisine. Sheets and couches are incredibly soft and the bath is opulent in the modern rooms. The Forest Oasis Waterscape pool area has multiple swimming areas, waterslides, and the über-enjoyable lazy river tube ride. If you have kids in tow in summer, take advantage of the "dive-in" movies and poolside s'mores. Schedule a massage, facial, or manicure at the Woodlands Resort Spa. Two lush golf courses and an extensive tennis center with clay, hard, and indoor courts accompany the trail system, allowing guests to ride bikes (rentals are available) or hike and jog among in the pine and hardwood forest.

A resort getaway would be incomplete without a memorable meal at **Robard's Steakhouse** (281/364-6400, www. robardssteakhouse.com, Mon.-Thurs. 4pm-10pm, Fri.-Sat. 4pm-11pm, $16-53). Robard's mission is to offer "the perfect cut" of beef, and it's hard to argue with the results. Each steak is selected from the in-house butchery and prepared to order. The steaks are exquisite when paired with one of the hundreds of wine or craft beer options, flavorful sides, and delectable desserts.

Tech-minded **Element Houston Vintage Park** (14555 Vintage Preserve Pkwy., 281/379-7300, www.elementhoustonvintagepark.com, $119 d) is an environmentally sustainable lodging option. Part of a "lifestyle center" in the bustling northwestern part of town, Element touts its environmentally friendly design and construction, as well as its provision of widespread Wi-Fi for computers, phones, and portable online devices. Other amenities include a hot breakfast, and open-flow guest rooms with fully equipped kitchens.

Camping

Houston's best camping is about 30 miles (48 km) southwest of the city at **Brazos Bend State Park** (21901 FM 762, 979/553-5102, www.tpwd.state.tx.us, $7 over age 12). Covering 5,000 acres, this popular park offers hiking, biking, equestrian trails, and fishing on six easily accessible lakes. Visitors are cautioned about alligators, which are numerous in some areas of the park. Facilities include restrooms with showers, campsites with water and electricity, screened shelters, primitive equestrian campsites, and a dining hall. Many visitors make Brazos Bend a weekend destination due to its abundant activities, including free interpretive programs and hikes. A nature center with informative displays contains a hands-on alligator discovery area, a model of the park, a freshwater aquarium, live native snake species, and the George Observatory.

INFORMATION AND SERVICES

Tourism Offices

The **Greater Houston Convention and Visitors Bureau** (701 Avenida De Las Americas, 713/437-5200, www. visithoustontexas.com, daily 7am-10pm) office is of literature and knowledgeable staff members. Similar services are available southwest of town at **Visit Bay Area Houston** (604 Bradford Ave. in Kemah, 281/474-9700).

If you're entering East Texas by vehicle from Louisiana, look for the **Texas Department of Transportation's** Travel

Information Center at two spots on the state border. The largest facility is in Orange (1708 E. I-10, 409/883-9416) on I-10 en route from New Orleans. The other is in Waskom (1255 N. I-20 E., 903/687-2547) on I-20 from Shreveport. Visit www.txdot.gov for road-related travel information.

Publications

The best source for news and information in Houston and southeast Texas is the *Houston Chronicle* (www.chron.com), with thorough coverage of city and state happenings as well as detailed listings of restaurants and entertainment venues. For specific information about local politics, touring shows, and movie listings, pick up a free copy of the *Houston Press* (www.houstonpress.com) at bars and coffee shops across town.

GETTING THERE
Air

The major air hub in this part of the country is **George Bush Intercontinental Airport** (IAH, 2800 N. Terminal Rd., 281/230-3100, www.airport-houston.com), just north of the city. This is one of United's major hubs, with flights to 170 cities around the world, and it's typically bustling at all hours. The city's older airfield, **William P. Hobby Airport** (HOU, 7800 Airport Blvd., 713/640-3000, www.fly2houston.com) is now the center of activity for Southwest Airlines and several other carriers. Located 10 miles (16 km) southeast of downtown, Hobby is more accessible than Bush and costs $20 less by taxi from downtown, but it's showing its age.

Super Shuttle (281/230-7275, www.supershuttle.com) offers shuttle service to and from area hotels and both airports. Look for the company's ticket counters in the lower-level baggage claim areas. Many downtown-area hotels offer free shuttle service to and from Bush Intercontinental Airport, but check first to make sure they're running.

Train

Amtrak's *Sunset Limited* passenger train runs cross-country between Orlando and Los Angeles. Look for three weekly arrivals and departures at the **Houston Amtrak station** (902 Washington Ave., 713/224-1577 or 800/872-7245, www.amtrak.com).

Bus

Intercity buses are run by **Houston Greyhound** (2121 Main St., 713/759-6565 or 800/231-2222, www.greyhound.com).

GETTING AROUND
Car

Rent a car at Bush Intercontinental Airport's **Rental Car Center** (281/230-3000, www.fly2houston.com). All the major rental companies are at this shared location about five minutes from the terminals. Shuttle buses, located outside the terminal, are marked "Rental Car Shuttle."

Public Transportation

Houston has a decent public transportation system, but it can be confusing. A little homework can help to strategize plans to use the Metro, a.k.a. the **Metropolitan Transit Authority of Harris County** (713/635-4000, www.ridemetro.org, $1.25), with light rail and bus lines. Tickets for trains are available in vending machines at each station. Metro's red line serves 17 stations near downtown's busiest commercial and recreational sites.

Taxi

Ground transportation employees outside each terminal of Bush Intercontinental Airport and near the lower-level baggage claim area (curb zone 1) of Hobby Airport will half-heartedly hail travelers a taxi. All destinations within Houston's city limits to or from Bush Airport are charged a flat zone rate or the meter rate, whichever is less. For more information on rates, see the Ground Transportation section at www.fly2houston.com. Arrange for cab pickup service within the city with **Houston VIP Taxi** (281/616-5838), **Liberty Cab Company** (713/236-1111), and **Taxis Fiesta** (713/225-2666).

Vicinity of Houston

BEAUMONT

Beaumont (population 118,428) isn't an average midsize Texas city. It's more connected to the eastern United States than the South, it has a working-class union element, and it has a denser historic downtown than sprawling West Texas cities. Its proximity to New Orleans and the Gulf Coast have earned it, along with nearby Port Arthur and Orange, the nickname "the Cajun Triangle."

The city's fate was forever changed on January 10, 1901, when the Lucas Gusher erupted from the Spindletop oil field. Tens of thousands of people flocked to Beaumont to capitalize on the oil boom and built an impressive collection of churches, civic buildings, and residences. Beaumont became an American melting pot, with Italian and Jewish influences combined with Cajun and African American inspirations. The city's architectural treasures give downtown its distinctive historical charm.

The corporate oil scene would eventually move to Houston, 80 miles (129 km) southwest, but Beaumont's petroleum legacy remains its true identity. In 1901, the first year of the boom, three major companies formed—the Gulf Oil Corporation, Humble (later Exxon), and the Texas Company (later Texaco). One year later, more than 500 corporations were doing business in Beaumont.

The boom soon went bust, as Spindletop fell victim to an overabundance of wells. Two decades later, new advancements in the oil industry allowed riggers to dig wells deeper, resulting in another Spindletop boom. In 1927, the oil field yielded its all-time annual high of 21 million barrels. Beaumont never experienced another major surge, but the city prospered during World War II as a shipbuilding center, and the petrochemical industry continued to sustain the economy for decades to come.

The nearby coastal communities of Port Arthur and Orange benefited from the oil money, opening art museums, forging a soulful music identity, and capitalizing on its Cajun culture by developing fabulous dining.

Sights

SPINDLETOP-GLADYS CITY BOOMTOWN MUSEUM

To get a sense of the craziness that befell Beaumont on the discovery of the Spindletop oil field, visit the **Spindletop-Gladys City Boomtown Museum** (5550 Jimmy Simmons Blvd., 409/880-1750, www.lamar.edu, Tues.-Sat. 10am-5pm, Sun. 1pm-5pm, $5 adults, $3 seniors, $2 ages 6-12). Near the site of the famous Lucas Gusher, the museum offers a self-guided tour of 15 clapboard building replicas from the oil-boom era, including a general store, a saloon, a post office, a stable, and a blacksmith shop. The buildings and associated photos and interpretive panels tell the story of the massive and unprecedented boomtown saga, where Beaumont transformed from a village of several hundred to a city of 30,000 in a matter of weeks. The museum also features wooden oil derricks of the era, including a weekly water-spewing gusher that keeps families entertained and refreshed during the hot summer months.

MCFADDIN-WARD HOUSE

One of the city's top destinations is the remarkable 1906 **McFaddin-Ward House** (1906 Calder Ave., 409/832-2134, www.mcfaddin-ward.org, Tues.-Sat. 10am-3pm, Sun. 1pm-3pm, closed at lunch, over age 7 only, $5 guided tours). This impressive beaux arts mansion features decorative exterior detailing and opulent interior furnishings reflecting the lifestyle of William McFaddin, a Texas Army veteran who created a cattle and oil empire from the land he received for his military service. The guided tours of his home and adjacent carriage house provide anecdotal and architectural background information along with up-close views of furniture, artwork, and mementos.

TEXAS ENERGY MUSEUM

Among Beaumont's best museums is the downtown Texas Energy Museum (600 Main St., 409/833-5100, www. texasenergymuseum.org, Tues.-Sat. 9am-5pm, Sun. 1pm-5pm, $3 adults, $2 seniors and ages 6-12), a spacious two-story facility that features a fascinating collection of exhibits dedicated to oil-based energy sources. Interactive displays highlight the history of oil and provide information about the global significance of this local commodity. The name is somewhat misleading—there aren't any power plants or lightbulbs here—but the museum educates visitors about the remarkable history and relevance of the petrochemical industry.

FIRE MUSEUM OF TEXAS

The nearby Fire Museum of Texas (400 Walnut St., 409/880-3927, www. firemuseumoftexas.org, Mon.-Fri. 8am-4:30pm, free) is a small unexpected gem. In the 1927 Beaumont Fire Department Headquarters Station, it is dwarfed by the massive black-and-white-spotted "world's largest fire hydrant" out front. Now considered the third-largest in the world, this 24-foot-tall (7-m) hydrant was donated to the museum by Disney Studios on the release of the movie 101 Dalmatians. Inside, the facility showcases the importance of firefighters in Texas and across the country through vintage fire engines and equipment, educational exhibits, and the Texas Firefighter Memorial.

BABE DIDRIKSON ZAHARIAS MUSEUM

Babe who? You'll be telling everyone about her after experiencing the captivating Babe Didrikson Zaharias Museum (1750 I-10 E., 409/833-4622, www.babedidriksonzaharias. org, Mon.-Sat. 9am-5pm, free). Port Arthur native Zaharias was a pioneer in women's sports voted the world's greatest woman athlete in a poll by the Associated Press. Nicknamed "Babe" after swatting five home runs in one baseball game, Zaharias was an accomplished Olympic athlete, tennis player, basketball player, diver, bowler, and, most notably, golfer. She won every major professional golf championship at least once and is credited with single-handedly popularizing women's golf. The museum features trophies, golf clubs, photos, newspaper clippings, Olympic medals, and films representing her athletic career.

Food
AMERICAN

For lively dinner-and-drinks atmosphere, go to Madison's (4020 Dowlen Rd., 409/924-9777, daily 11am-2am, $9-26). Classic American fare is the best option here, with reliable huge burgers, chicken, and fried food. Try the bacon-wrapped shrimp with jalapeño. Things pick up at Madison's after dark, when bands often take the stage and the bar gets busy.

More inspiring than its name implies is The Grill (6680 Calder Ave., 409/866-0039, www.theaspgrill.com, Tues.-Sat. 3pm-10pm, $11-34), with fine dining in Beaumont style: quality food with attentive service in a refined atmosphere. Recommended items include parmesan-crusted Chilean sea bass, grilled rack of lamb, and au poivre tournedos (beef tenderloin with a tasty cognac mushroom sauce). Save room for the amazing tres leches cake, topped with a velvety goat's milk caramel.

CAJUN AND SEAFOOD

Beaumont is one of the best places in Texas to get authentic Cajun food, and the city's proximity to the Gulf of Mexico means the seafood is always fresh. A local favorite is no-frills Kajun Seafood and Wings (597 S. 11th St., 409/832-9988, Tues.-Sat. 10am-8:30pm, Sun. 10am-7pm, $10-25). Beaumonters love the succulent and slightly spicy shrimp and wings, an ideal representation of Beaumont's distinctive cuisine. Other popular items include the broiled seafood platter and fried, grilled, or blackened catfish.

Locals line up at consistently delectable **Vautrot's Cajun Cuisine** (13350 Hwy. 105, 409/753-2015, Tues.-Fri. 11am-2pm and 5pm-9pm, Sat. 11am-9pm, $9-12). Start with the tasty crawfish étouffée or jam-packed gumbo, or proceed directly to the ridiculously large and flavorful Uncle Emrick's Seafood Sampler, containing the gumbo and étouffée along with fried crawfish, fried catfish, fried shrimp, fried oysters, onion rings or french fries, and a salad.

Floyd's Cajun Seafood (2290 I-10 S., 409/842-0686, www.floydsbeaumont.com, Sun.-Thurs. 11am-10pm, Fri.-Sat. 11am-11pm, $10-22) is a small regional chain that's huge on authentic flavor. Reliable standards include crawfish, shrimp, oysters, and catfish. Floyd's specializes in southern Louisiana home-style cooking, with regional favorites like po'boys (go for the shrimp or crawfish), gumbo, and étouffée.

Accommodations

Beaumont lacks downtown hotels within walking distance of its many museums and cultural attractions. A popular and reliable option is **Econo Lodge Inn & Suites** (2030 N. 11th St., 409/892-6700, www.choicehotels. com, $69 d), featuring free Wi-Fi, a free deluxe continental breakfast, a fitness center, and an outdoor pool.

The best bang for the buck is ★ **Holiday Inn Beaumont-Plaza** (3950 I-10 S., 409/842-5995 or 800/465-4329, www.holidayinn.com, $99 d). An enormous three-story cascading waterfall greets guests in the spacious garden atrium, and the renovated rooms provide clean and comfortable accommodations. The Plaza location (not to be confused with Holiday Inn Midtown) features free Wi-Fi, an indoor pool and whirlpool, a full fitness center, and free meals for kids under age 13.

Regional chain **MCM Elegante** (2355 I-10 S., 409/842-3600, www. mcmelegantebeaumont.com, $115 d) features a tropical outdoor pool, an upscale fitness center, free Wi-Fi, fridges, and microwaves.

Another consistently solid choice is **Homewood Suites by Hilton** (3745 I-10 S., 409/842-9990, www.homewoodsuites3. hilton.com, $149 d), 4 miles (6.4 km) from downtown. The suites feature separate living and sleeping areas, fully equipped kitchens with full-size fridges, and free Wi-Fi. Accommodations include a full breakfast each morning and a complimentary grocery shopping service. Homewood Suites is a dog-friendly hotel.

Information and Services

To get a handle on the layout of the city, contact the friendly folks at the **Beaumont Convention & Visitors Bureau** (505 Willow St., 409/880-3749 or 800/392-4401, www. beaumontcvb.com, Mon.-Fri. 8am-5pm).

Getting There and Around

The 75-minute drive on I-10 to Houston is considered by some a suburban commute. The cities have completely different identities, and the proximity makes Beaumont an easy day trip.

The closest airports are in Houston: **George Bush Intercontinental Airport** (IAH, 2800 N. Terminal Rd., 281/230-3100, www.airport-houston.com), just north of Houston, is one of the major hubs for United Airlines. Houston's old airport, **William P. Hobby Airport** (HOU, 7800 Airport Blvd., 713/640-3000, www.fly2houston.com), is the center of activity for Southwest Airlines.

In Beaumont, it's easy to get anywhere in about 15 minutes. If you don't have a car, cab companies include **Royal Taxi** (409/289-9950) and **King Cab** (409/242-8136). If you're feeling adventurous, you may even consider tackling the **Beaumont Municipal Transit System** (409/835-7895, www.beaumonttransit.com) buses.

PORT ARTHUR

It's worth the 20-mile (32-km) drive from Beaumont to Port Arthur (population 55,018) to spend an afternoon at a museum or sample some seafood. With several major oil refineries, Port Arthur's economy remains petroleum-centered. Named for Arthur Stillwell, a Kansas City businessperson who brought the railroad to town, this low-key community has been tied to the shipping industry since a navigable canal was dredged in the early 1900s.

Aside from oil and shipping, Port Arthur is known for churning out music stars (Janis Joplin, the Big Bopper, Johnny Winter, and Tex Ritter) as well as Cajun food, fishing, and a legendary Mardi Gras celebration, drawing tens of thousands of people each February.

Sights

Get a grasp on the region's illustrious history at the **Museum of the Gulf Coast** (700 Proctor St., 409/982-7000, www.museumofthegulfcoast.org, Mon.-Sat. 9am-5pm, $8 adults, $6 seniors, $4 ages 4-18). In a large downtown building that was once a bank, the two-story museum covers prehistory to the Texas Revolution artifacts to the modern era, and a comprehensive representation of cultural events in the region.

Check out the replica of Janis Joplin's painted psychedelic Porsche in the museum's music exhibit, where visitors can play songs on a jukebox for free and browse displays dedicated to the surprising number of musicians from the area, including Joplin, George Jones, the Big Bopper, Tex Ritter, and members of ZZ Top. Nearby, a large number of sports legends and celebrities feature in the pop-culture exhibit, including Jimmy Johnson, Bum and Wade Phillips, and, head-scratchingly, two stars of the *Police Academy* film, G. W. Bailey and Charles "Bubba" Smith.

The **Sabine Pass Battleground State Historic Site** (6100 Dick Dowling Rd., 512/463-7948, www.visitsabinepassbattleground.com, free), 12 miles (19.3 km) south of town, is worth visiting even if you aren't a history buff. Owned and operated by the Texas Historical Commission, this 58-acre site tells the story of a fierce Civil War battle where severely outnumbered Confederate troops prevailed over a formidable Union fleet. Interpretive panels in a large concrete kiosk, historical markers, and a bronze statue help portray the conflict. Visitors have access to walking trails and camping facilities overlooking the Sabine Ship Channel.

The **Buu Mon Buddhist Temple** (2701 Procter St., 409/982-9319, www.buumon.org) was the first Buddhist center in Beaumont (inspiration for its name) and moved to Port Arthur into a former Baptist and Vietnamese Catholic church. A stupa replaced the steeple, and a 7-foot-tall (2-m) gilt bronze Buddha rests on the altar. The temple's annual spring garden tour attracts hundreds to the lotus garden. Monks are always on hand to guide visitors through the temple and the garden and even offer a cup of freshly brewed green tea.

Food

Port Arthur is known for seafood and Cajun restaurants. One of the best spots in town is the bland-looking yet consistently tasty **Bruce's Seafood Deli** (6801 9th Ave., 409/727-3184, Mon.-Sat. 10am-9pm, $9-21). You can't go wrong with the basics—shrimp, crawfish, and catfish. Just about everything is deep-fried and incredibly flavorful and fresh. The uninspiring decor (it was once a fast-food chain restaurant) allows you to focus on the fine seafood.

Another favorite Bayou-style eatery is **Larry's French Market and Cajun Cafeteria** (3701 Atlantic Hwy., Groves, 409/962-3381, www.larrysfrenchmarket.com, Mon.-Wed. 11am-2pm, Thurs. 11am-9pm, Fri. 11am-2pm and 5pm-10pm, Sat. 5pm-11pm, $9-24), offering an all-inclusive combo in the Captain's Platter, featuring fresh and flavorful shrimp, catfish, oysters, barbecue crabs, fried crawfish, seafood gumbo, and Cajun fries. Alternate menu options include the "boiled water critters" (crawfish and crab) served with corn, potatoes, and a dipping sauce, as well as fried critters (alligator, frog legs). Larry's often hosts live music, so check the website for showtimes.

Locals tend to loiter at the traditionally minded and classically decorated (a.k.a. dated) **The Schooner** (1507 S. Hwy. 69, 409/722-2323, www.theschoonerrestaurant.com, Mon.-Sat. 11am-10pm, $9-27). Seafood is the main catch, from fresh fillets to fried platters. Popular menu items include broiled fillet of snapper, stuffed crab, and oysters.

Piney Woods

The Piney Woods are the natural heart of East Texas, comprising several national forests and not much else. Most of this vast area remains as it was centuries ago, when Native Americans and pioneers hunted wild game in the dense woods by day and slept under the pine canopy by night.

The name Piney Woods is a Texas colloquialism describing this forested region, not typically associated with the wide-open landscape of the Lone Star State. These aren't dense lush groves of evergreens but rather shortleaf and loblolly pines, sprinkled with hardwoods such as oak, elm, ash, and maple. The combination is appealing in autumn, when bursts of changing color offer a pleasant outdoor escape.

Nearly 750,000 acres of East Texas pine forests remain standing due to federal protection. The trees were mostly clear-cut during the zealous timber harvesting of the early 1900s, but the U.S. Forest Service eventually became administrator of the vast woodlands, allowing them to be responsibly harvested and replenished. Several of the forests, Angelina in particular, feature logging-related trails and historical exhibits. A highlight is the abandoned and ghostly Aldridge Sawmill in Angelina National Forest.

The four national forests of East Texas make a natural weekend getaway for camping, hiking, and mountain biking, and there are rivers and lakes for canoeing and fishing, drawing tens of thousands. Texans frequent the forests year-round, but out-of-staters will most enjoy the temperate months of spring and late fall.

These wooded areas provided shelter and sustenance for the region's earliest inhabitants, the Native Americans displaced by westward frontier expansion. The legacy of the Caddo people is evident in Piney Woods communities like Nacogdoches, and the Alabama-Coushatta Tribe is a vital cultural presence on its land in the Big Thicket National Preserve.

★ BIG THICKET NATIONAL PRESERVE

The Big Thicket National Preserve's name is misleading: There are dense, seemingly impenetrable forests, but this National Park Service preserve is mostly woodsy, with pines, oaks, and swamplands dominating the landscape. The tremendous variety of habitats and the thicket's geographic location result in a unique destination for nature lovers and wildlife enthusiasts.

Species from the Gulf Coast, Central Plains, and Southeastern forests coexist with critters from the deserts, bayous, woods, and swamps. Birds from all regions of the country share airspace as they pass through on migration. There are 85 tree species, 186 kinds of birds, and 50 reptile species, including a small and rarely seen population of alligators.

Sights

A good place to start is the **Big Thicket visitors center** (6102 FM 420, 409/951-6725, daily 9am-5pm), 7 miles (11.3 km) north of Kountze at the intersection of U.S. 69 and FM 420, with brochures, maps, and a discovery room with interactive educational exhibits. The Big Thicket consists of nine separate land

Logging Time with the Company

the historic Aldridge Sawmill ruins

From the 1880s until the 1920s, East Texas's Piney Woods saw a "lumber bonanza" with 18 million acres of timber being cut. Lumber production started with small owner-operated sawmills and eventually evolved into large operations that dominated the East Texas economy. These corporations built their own railroads into the forests and connected their isolated sawmills with major cities and shipping points.

FACTORY TOWN

The men who worked in the sawmills and on cutting crews were encouraged to remain with a company long-term, with the incentive that their wives and children could live in the lumber company towns. The companies would choose a location on a rail line and construct a makeshift town, complete with homes, schools, churches, stores, and hospitals. Workers were often paid with credits they could use for food, merchandise, and services in the company town facilities. Learn about this phenomenon at Diboll's **History Center** (102 N. Temple St., Diboll, 936/829-3543, www.thehistorycenteronline.com, Mon.-Fri. 8am-5pm, Sat. 9am-1pm, free).

Sometimes the towns would pick up and move with the ever-changing frontier of virgin forest. Homes in railcars allowed for easy mobility, leaving behind a ghost town of clapboard buildings and dirt roads. By the 1920s, the depletion of the East Texas timber resources and the subsequent Great Depression caused the decline of the lumber bonanza. Some of the companies went bankrupt, while the larger timber corporations moved to the Pacific Northwest.

units over an expanse of East Texas. View the visitors center's 30-minute orientation film and talk to an NPS nature guide about taking a short excursion to several of the ecosystems found in the preserve.

LAKE TOMBIGBEE

Lake Tombigbee is in one of only three Native American reservations in Texas, the **Alabama-Coushatta reservation** (936/563-1100, www.alabama-coushatta.com). The tribe no longer runs its museum or tourism activities, but visitors can use the reservation's **Lake Tombigbee Campground** (936/563-1221 or 800/926-9038), with cabins, tent sites, primitive camping sites, full-capacity RV stations, restrooms with bathhouses, swimming areas, and hiking and nature trails. Fishing is popular on the lake; bring your own equipment as rental operations are scarce.

Recreation

HIKING

Eight trails offer 45 miles (72 km) of mild hiking terrain through the muggy forest. The ideal time to hike in Big Thicket is late fall-early winter or spring, since the summer is brutally hot. The trails include wheelchair-accessible half-mile loops to an 18-mile (29-km) cross-forest trek. The best slices of Big Thicket life:

- **Beaver Slide Trail:** In the southeast corner of the preserve's Big Sandy Creek Unit, this 1.5-mile (2.4-km) trail encircles several ponds formed by old beaver dams. The towering shaggy-barked cypress trees are a main attraction.

- **Kirby Nature Trail System:** This group of trails offers a lot of flexibility with distance and environments. A printed guide at the trailhead is handy to have in your back pocket, providing basic maps and information about the ecosystems and trails, ranging from a half-mile loop through a cypress slough to a 2.4-mile (3.9-km) hike traversing the southern edge of the Turkey Creek Unit.

- **Pitcher Plant Trail:** For a distinctive trek through diverse ecosystems, take this 1-mile (1.6-km) trail through a mixed pine forest to a wetland savanna to a mixed hardwood-pine forest. Watch for the sundews and pitcher plants along the wooden boardwalk.

- **Turkey Creek Trail:** Environmental highlights of the preserve's Turkey Creek Unit and its namesake creek along this lengthy 15-mile (24-km) trail include baygalls, floodplains, sandhill pine uplands, and mixed forests.

BIKING

Big Thicket is remote, and cyclists should bring their own bikes, as you won't find bike rentals.

Bikes are only allowed on the **Big Sandy Creek Horse/Bike Trail** in the southern portion of the Big Sandy Creek Unit. It is the Big Thicket's longest trail, offering 18 miles (29 km) of beautiful natural scenery. Highlights include a diverse hardwood forest of sweetgum, basket oak, and hornbeam; dense and fragrant upland pine forests; and a mixed area with loblolly pines and beech-magnolia trees. Be sure to check ahead about trail access, as it's occasionally closed during hunting season, and keep an eye out for horses.

BIRD-WATCHING

Several popular trails, including the **Big Thicket Loop** and **Sundew Trail,** offer opportunities for birders, with 185 species in the park either year-round or on two migratory flyways. Bird migration peaks March-May, and the most sought-after species include the red cockaded woodpecker and the Bachman's sparrow. In the spring, bird and wildflower enthusiasts flock to the Sundew Trail in the park's Hickory Creek Savannah Unit to see the rare brown-headed nuthatch or an eye-catching pitcher plant.

PADDLING

The Big Thicket is gaining a reputation for its paddling opportunities. Canoeists and kayakers are fond of the Village Creek area, where they can explore the lush waterway and find camping opportunities. Another popular area is the Lower Neches River Corridor, a larger body of water with East Texas-style bayous and swamps leading south to the Gulf of Mexico. Equipment rentals and shuttles are available—check with the visitors center for a list of companies.

BACKCOUNTRY CAMPING

The Big Thicket is a hard-core camping destination. There are no developed sites with water and electricity; campers are required to procure a Backcountry Use Permit for a primitive site. The permit is available for free at the visitors center or headquarters office (409/951-6725, visit www.nps.gov/bith).

Naturalist activities are available with reservations or on selected weekends. Call to find out more about making reservations.

Food and Accommodations

Since the Big Thicket is spread across a large geographic area, there is no specific town for food or lodging. The preserve's sections range 80 miles (129 km) west-to-east from Livingston to Kirbyville, with dozens of small communities between, and 70 miles (113 km) north-to-south from Jasper to Beaumont. Nearby communities with services include Woodville and Kountze. Beaumont is less than an hour from most of the Big Thicket's nine areas, so consider budgeting time to drive to this comparatively big city for food and lodging.

Information and Services

Get trail maps, boating conditions, and information on nearby restaurants at the Big Thicket **visitors center** (409/951-6725, www. nps.gov/bith, daily 9am-5pm). It's 7 miles (11.3 km) north of Kountze at the intersection of U.S. 69 and FM 420.

For fishing or camping on the **Alabama-Coushatta reservation** (936/563-1100, www.alabama-coushatta.com), call 936/563-1221 or 800/926-9038.

SAM HOUSTON NATIONAL FOREST

Approximately 40 miles (64 km) north of Texas's largest city, Sam Houston National Forest comprises 162,984 acres of shortleaf and longleaf pine, hardwood forests, and abundant recreational opportunities. Camping is the main draw, complemented by daytime activities on Double Lake and Lake Conroe and the 140-mile-long (225-km) Lone Star Hiking Trail.

Recreation

The **Lone Star Hiking Trail** is 140 miles (225 km) of walkways open to foot travel only. The trail traverses the Sam Houston

National Forest through woodlands, swamps, and meadows via five loops to accommodate various starting points and parking for day hikers or overnight backpackers. Trail maps and brochures are available at the park headquarters in New Waverly.

Cyclists will enjoy the 8-mile (12.9-km) trail on the east side of the forest custom-built by mountain bikers. Most East Texas forests are devoid of significant slopes, but this hilly trek offers terrain-filled passages winding through the pine forests.

The 22,000-acre **Lake Conroe** is a big draw in Sam Houston Forest for swimming, boating, fishing, and sailing. The lake is stocked with bass and bluegill, and boats are available for rent at several marinas along the lakeshore.

Food

When in East Texas, stick with what the locals know best: Southern food.

When it comes to burgers, one of the most popular spots is in the small town of Coldspring: **The Hop** (14801 Hwy. 150 W., Coldspring, 936/653-4889, Mon.-Sat. 10:30am-9pm, $9-17). This down-home, charmingly cluttered local establishment is a classic 1950s-style burger joint, so you can't go wrong with a big ol' burger, fries, and chocolate milk shake. Pop a few dollars in the corner jukebox to complete your classic Americana experience.

Just up the road from Coldspring in the slightly larger town of Livingston is **Courthouse Whistlestop Cafe** (318 N. Washington Ave., Livingston, 936/327-3222, www.courthousewhistlestop.com, daily 6am-2pm, $8-16). Across from the stately Polk County Courthouse in the historic downtown district, the Whistlestop is an ideal place to grab a hearty breakfast before a hike or a paddle. Start with a mug of strong coffee and a meaty omelet or stack of buttermilk pancakes. For lunch, opt for a big deli sandwich (the reuben is a local favorite) or a bowl of chili. Order a side of fried okra.

Down-Home Southern Cooking

a traditional plate of chicken-fried steak

Texas is in a geographically undefined region—it isn't really the South, and it doesn't quite qualify as the Southwest. Although Southern cooking is on the menu in most Texas cities, it's especially prevalent in East Texas, with geographical proximity to the South. Like everything else, Texas puts its own spin on down-home country cuisine.

- **Chicken-Fried Steak:** One of the best examples of Southern cooking in Texas is chicken-fried steak, a thin cut of cube steak that's tenderized, breaded in a seasoned flour mixture or egg batter, pan fried in lard or vegetable oil, and served smothered in peppered cream gravy. The term "chicken-fried" refers to the similar process used in frying chicken. Where to try it: **Dolli's Diner** (116 S. Pecan St., Nacogdoches, 936/305-5007, Mon.-Wed. and Thurs.-Sat. 7am-5pm, Sun.9am-4pm, $7-19)

- **Catfish:** Another East Texas fried favorite is catfish. Near the Gulf Coast, some chefs take a Cajun-style approach by dipping the fillet in hot sauce and milk before dredging it in a traditional blend of cornmeal, salt, pepper, paprika, and cayenne and frying it in a cast-iron skillet until golden brown. Where to try it: **Vautrot's Cajun Cuisine** (13350 Hwy. 105, Beaumont, 409/753-2015, Tues.-Fri. 11am-2pm and 5pm-9pm, Sat. 11am-9pm, $9-12)

- **Fried Okra:** A cornmeal-based covering is common for fried okra. A basic batter starts with whisked egg and buttermilk with a covering of cornmeal, flour, brown sugar, salt, peppers, and seasoning before frying in a skillet. Where to try it: **Courthouse Whistlestop Cafe** (318 N. Washington Ave., Livingston, 936/327-3222, www.courthousewhistlestop.com, daily 6am-2pm, $8-16)

Another Southern cooking tendency is to include **meat in veggie dishes.** Texans spruce up their beans, greens, and black-eyed peas with ham hock or bacon. Lard or bacon grease can add an extra dimension of flavor to just about any vegetable or bread recipe.

One more Southern-tinged trait: If you order tea in a Texas restaurant, you'll get **iced tea** (usually unsweetened, but East Texans often prefer the sweetened variety). Finally, never skip an opportunity to order a **fruit cobbler** or **pecan pie** for dessert.

Camping

Sam Houston National Forest contains three developed campgrounds. **Cagle Recreation Area** (936/344-6205, $20-30) is a campground with 48 sites with electricity, water, and sewer; hot showers; lakeshore hiking, biking, and equestrian trails; fishing; and swimming. **Double Lake Recreation Area** (936/653-3448, $20-30), constructed in 1937 by the Civilian Conservation Corps, surrounds a 24-acre lake with campsites that have a tent pad, parking, and a picnic table; some have water, sewer, and electrical hookups. There is a swimming area and a beach, a concession stand, and a bathhouse. **Stubblefield Recreation Area** (936/344-6205, $8-15) has 28 campsites, hot showers, and access to fishing and hiking.

Double Lake is by reservation, while Cagle and Stubblefield are first-come, first-served only. Call ahead for availability and fee information.

Information and Services

For more information about recreational opportunities at the forest, including maps, contact the **Sam Houston National Forest headquarters** (394 FM 1375, 936/344-6205 or 888/361-6908, www.fs.usda.gov/texas, Mon.-Fri. 8am-4:30pm), 2 miles (3.2 km) west of I-45 and New Waverly. For campground reservations, call 877/444-6777 or go to www.recreation.gov.

Getting There

Since the national forests are in rural areas of East Texas, the only way to access them is by car. From Houston, take I-45 north for 40 miles (64 km) to the small town of New Waverly. The forest's visitors center is a few miles west of the I-45 at New Waverly. Drivers can also take U.S. 59 northeast from Houston. When you reach Cleveland or Shepherd, look for signs directing you to county roads heading west into the forest.

DAVY CROCKETT NATIONAL FOREST

For hikers, the Davy Crockett National Forest is a wild frontier, with 160,000 acres of scenic woodlands just west of Lufkin and some of the region's best opportunities for hiking and horseback riding.

Recreation

The most popular hiking trail in the forest is the **Four C National Recreation Trail,** named after the Central Coal and Coke Company, which logged the forest's trees 1902-1920. The 20-mile (32-km) trail traverses moderate terrain amid lofty pines, swampy bogs, and hardwood forests. Horses and hikers share the woodsy, mossy, and boggy 50-mile (80-km) **Piney Creek Horse Trail.**

The **Ratcliff Lake Recreation Area** was built in 1936 by the Civilian Conservation Corps around a 45-acre lake that was once a log pond and source of water for the Central Coal and Coke Company Sawmill. The area offers camping, a swimming beach and a bathhouse, an interpretive trail, showers, boating, and fishing.

The forest's abundant wildlife includes deer, turkeys, doves, quail, and various waterfowl. The endangered red-cockaded woodpecker also lives in a managed habitat within the forest.

Food

Since Lufkin is just 10 miles (16 km) east of the forest's boundaries, it's worth heading to there for the better restaurant options than in the small towns around the forest's perimeter.

Camping

Some of the forest's most scenic camping sites are along the Four C Trail at the **Walnut Creek campsite** (5 tent pads, a shelter, and a pit toilet) and at another small campsite, farther north, with two tent pads. Another option is the **Ratcliff Lake Recreation Area.** For primitive sites, head to the nearby **Neches Bluff Overlook** at the north end of the trail, with a panoramic view of pine-hardwood forest in the Neches River bottomlands. Call the forest headquarters (936/655-2299) for availability and fee information.

Information and Services

To obtain a trail map of the forest or to learn more about camping and boat accessibility, contact the **Davy Crockett National Forest headquarters** near Kennard (Route 1, Box 55 FS, 936/655-2299, www.fs.usda.gov). The ranger district office is near Ratcliff on Highway 7, about a quarter mile west of FM 227.

Getting There

By car from Houston, take I-45 north to Highway 19 in the town of Crockett. Turn right onto Highway 7, and in a few miles you'll find the main visitors center in Ratcliff. You can also take U.S. 59 northeast from Houston. When you reach Lufkin, take a left onto Highway 103, which turns into Highway 7 and leads to the visitors center.

ANGELINA NATIONAL FOREST

Just east of Lufkin, the 153,179-acre Angelina National Forest is popular for fishing and boating. Angelina encapsulates most of massive 114,500-acre Lake Sam Rayburn, formed on the Angelina River by Sam Rayburn Dam in the early 1960s.

The forest is gently rolling landscapes covered with shortleaf and loblolly pine, hardwoods, and a swath of longleaf pine in the southern portion. When the federal government took on its management in 1935, Angelina was in bad shape—most of the land had been clear-cut. The Texas Forest Service's fire prevention efforts resulted in much of the land naturally seeding in, a practice that continues to this day.

Aldridge Sawmill

Angelina is about water-based activities, but the most memorable experience in the forest is a surreal and spooky abandoned sawmill.

All that's left of the Aldridge Sawmill are huge concrete structures. A century ago, thousands of people thrived in a busy logging community called Aldridge, bustling with several saloons, hotels, and churches, before abandoning the site practically overnight. Aldridge workers logged East Texas's largest longleaf pines, some more than 30 inches in diameter. When the trees were depleted by 1920, the residents and their families moved on to the next woodland, leaving behind several large-scale mill facilities.

The enormous stark concrete walls of these buildings offer an eerie juxtaposition to the surrounding natural beauty of the second-growth forest. Similarly intriguing are the remnants from local teenagers—graffiti, beer bottles, and flip-flops—who frequent the ghost town. A U.S. Forest Service guide noted, "A lot of innocence has been lost here."

Forest officials discourage publicizing Aldridge's location to deter even more teenagers from discovering and destroying it, but legitimate visitors can get a map and directions (look for the Sawmill Hiking Trail) from the visitors center.

Recreation

Lake Sam Rayburn is a popular destination for anglers seeking the lake's abundant largemouth bass, crappie, and catfish. Recreational boating is a major activity, with water-skiers, sailboats, and personal watercraft dotting the surface. Even if you don't have a boat, drive across Lake Sam Rayburn on the long Highway 147 bridge. On the east side of the bridge, an access road leads to **Jackson Hill Park,** where you can explore the lakeside and catch a picturesque sunset.

Wildlife in the Angelina Forest includes deer, wild turkey, woodcock, quail, and a year-round resident population of wood ducks. In winter, bald eagles live near the reservoir, and the forest is also home to the endangered red-cockaded woodpecker, a small black-and-white bird that is difficult to locate.

Food

Nearby food options are minimal, so make the 15-mile (24-km) drive to Lufkin for quality regional cuisine. In the Zavalla area, basic **Carlene's Place** (594 E. Main St., 936/897-2900, daily 6am-8:30pm, $8-14) features a buffet of fried food and a salad bar along with standard American fare like burgers, chicken-fried steaks, and sandwiches.

Camping and Lodging

The park's two main recreation areas, **Caney Creek** and **Sandy Creek,** offer camping, boating, and fishing on the shores of Lake Sam Rayburn. Also popular are **Bouton Lake Recreation Area** and **Boykin Springs Recreation Area,** including historic structures built by the Civilian Conservation Corps, and offering camping, swimming, fishing, and canoeing. Call the park office (936/897-1068) for campsite availability and fee information.

Information and Services

To learn more about the campsite availability and fees, lake access points, and trail maps, contact the **Angelina National Forest park office** (111 Walnut Ridge Rd., Zavalla, 936/897-1068, www.fs.usda.gov, Mon.-Fri. 8am-4:30pm).

Getting There

Take U.S. 59 northeast from Houston. At Lufkin, turn right onto Highway 103. To reach the visitors center, head southeast from Lufkin on U.S. 69 to Zavalla.

SABINE NATIONAL FOREST

The 160,656-acre Sabine National Forest is the easternmost of Texas's four national forests, dominated by the massive Toledo Bend Reservoir along the Louisiana border. The second-largest lake in Texas and the fifth-largest reservoir in the United States, Toledo Bend offers extensive recreation, from boating and fishing to swimming and lakeshore camping.

Recreation

Outdoor recreation includes fishing, hunting, camping, hiking, horseback riding, and mountain biking. A popular destination is the 12,369-acre **Indian Mounds Wilderness Area,** designated by Congress as a site "to allow the Earth's natural processes to shape and influence the area." Unfortunately it was misnamed, since the mounds are actually just natural hills that host beautiful flora, including American beech, southern magnolia,

National Forest Service sign in East Texas

yellow lady's slipper orchids, and broad beech ferns.

Hike the 28-mile (45-km) **Trail Between the Lakes,** extending from the Toledo Bend Reservoir's Lakeview Recreation Area to U.S. 96 near Lake Sam Rayburn. Contact park headquarters for a map showing the many miles of roads throughout the forest that are open to mountain bikers and horseback riders.

Fishing draws people to the **Lake Sam Rayburn** reservoir, ideal for catching striped bass. The forest's rivers and creeks teem with crappie, bass, and bluegill.

Birders flock to the area during spring and fall to glimpse of migratory waterfowl and other neotropical migratory songbirds, hawks, and shorebirds. As in the other East Texas forests, the red-cockaded woodpecker, an endangered species, receives special habitat management.

Food

One of the best food options is 15 miles (24 km) east of the state line in Leesville, Louisiana, at a homey spot called **Mustard Seed** (1152 Entrance Rd., Leesville, 337/537-1933, Mon.-Fri. 11am-8pm, Sat. 11am-3pm, $9-21). Go for the local specialty, crispy and tender fried catfish and savory chicken or sausage gumbo. Side dishes include Louisiana-style collard greens and brown gravy.

One of the only recommended barbecue options is **Hemphill BBQ** (3285 S. Bayou Rd., Hemphill, 409/787-1814, Mon.-Sat. 11am-8pm, $9-21) in the small town of Hemphill. In East Texas the specialties tend to shift away from beef toward pork, so order the baby back ribs or a pulled pork sandwich. The sides tend to be sweeter in this part of the state, which works well for Hemphill's coleslaw and potato salad. Locals come for the homemade desserts, so save room for a pie or pastry.

Camping

Get a primitive camping spot at **Indian Mounds Wilderness Area.** Less primitive is the **Ragtown Recreation Area,** offering opportunities for hiking, fishing, and bird-watching atop a bluff that faces the lake. Camping with electrical hookups is available at **Red Hills Lake** and **Boles Field.** Call the forest headquarters (409/787-3870) for availability and fee information.

Information and Services

For a comprehensive list of Toledo Bend Reservoir services—fishing guides, private resorts, and boat launch sites—visit www.toledo-bend.com. To learn more about Sabine Forest's campsites and fees, lake access points, and trail maps, contact the **Sabine National Forest headquarters** (201 S. Palm St., Hemphill, 409/787-3870). To learn more about the park's recreational opportunities and seasonal news, visit www.fs.usda.gov.

Getting There

Take U.S. 59 northeast from Houston. At Lufkin, turn right onto Highway 103. To reach the park's visitors center, head south on Highway 87 in Milam for 3 miles (4.8 km).

LUFKIN

Lufkin (population 35,510) played a unique role as a major logging town. Founded in 1882 as a stop on the Houston, East & West Texas Railway, the town was named for Abraham P. Lufkin, a Galveston cotton merchant and close friend of the railroad company president.

The construction of railroad lines in the early 1880s allowed access to the forests' interiors, and the lumber industry and regional economy began to boom. Between 1890 and 1900 the forest industry contributed more to Texas's economy than any other industry, including cattle and cotton. As a result, lumber company towns sprang up in the Lufkin area. The corporations provided jobs for men and prioritized family life by building schools, churches, and medical facilities. Workers were often paid in credits redeemable for merchandise and services in company town facilities. Although some sawmill workers were later drawn to the oil fields for higher wages, many chose to stay with their families in the lumber company towns for the community environment.

The lumber industry continues to play a significant role in Lufkin's economy. Each year, the region produces more than a million board feet of saw timber as well as a significant manufacturing of pulpwood from the nearby pine and hardwood forests.

Antiques shoppers and history buffs are drawn to downtown Lufkin's quaint mix of restaurants and retail shops. A walking tour showcases several remarkable historic buildings, including the 1925 Pines Theater and the location of the first Brookshire Brothers grocery store. Along the way, look for the five colorful murals by artist Lance Hunter that depict historic area businesses and stories.

Sights
TEXAS FORESTRY MUSEUM
An essential stop in Lufkin is the **Texas Forestry Museum** (1905 Atkinson Dr., 936/632-9535, www.treetexas.com, Mon.-Sat. 10am-5pm, free), offering a look at the region's lumber industry in a forest history wing and the resource and management wing.

Highlights include a compelling exhibit about life in a lumber company town, complete with model buildings and a collection of artifacts from early logging camps. Historic equipment, a fire lookout tower cab, a paper mill room, and an educational exhibit detail the natural succession of a forest. The scenic Urban Wildscape Trail runs behind the main building.

MUSEUM OF EAST TEXAS
The **Museum of East Texas** (503 N. 2nd St., 936/639-4434, www.metlufkin.org, Tues.-Fri. 10am-5pm, Sat.-Sun. 1pm-5pm, free) isn't as grand as it sounds. Built in 1976, it showcases regional artists as well as occasional traveling shows and science or children's exhibits. The museum hosts occasional lectures, performances, classes, kids art camps, and publications on the character and heritage of East Texas.

ELLEN TROUT ZOO
Expectations are exceeded at the large and impressive **Ellen Trout Zoo** (402 Zoo Circle, 936/633-0399, www.cityoflufkin.com/zoo, daily 9am-5pm, $7 adults, $3.50 ages 4-11), home to 700 animals from all over the planet. The zoo contains a surprising variety of rainforest beasts, tropical birds, and swamp creatures in a well-organized and spacious setting. Spend 3-4 hours to fully appreciate animals typically seen only in big-city zoos, including monkeys, a giraffe, rhinos, and hippos. Keep an eye out for alligators, seals, and birds around every corner.

A highlight for families is the miniature train that circles the zoo and then makes an unexpected detour across Ellen Trout Lake (look for the elusive gators), followed by a loop through the nearby forest.

THE HISTORY CENTER
Just 11 miles (17.7 km) outside Lufkin in the small town of Diboll is a fascinating attraction known simply as **The History Center** (102 N. Temple St., Diboll, 936/829-3543, www. thehistorycenteronline.com, Mon.-Fri. 8am-5pm, Sat. 9am-1pm, free). Diboll is one of the oldest continually operated forest company sites in Texas, and the 12,000-square-foot History Center is technically a public archives dedicated to East Texas history. That makes it sound boring, which it's not.

The vaguely named History Center did not get a more specific moniker because organizers did not want it to be classified as just a museum or a library. Although it contains many reference materials, it's more than a research center. It features artifacts but it's not really a museum. It's best described as a public history and archive center that collects, preserves, and explores the heritage of East Texas.

Visitors are drawn to the exquisite woodwork, consisting of cypress walls preserved from the 1950s along with floors of locally harvested yellow pine. Exhibit panels feature century-old photos showcasing Diboll's

---

1: The History Center in Diboll **2:** downtown Lufkin

dynamic past as a lumber company town along with an impressive collection of archives, including 70,000 photos, decades of community newspapers, and lumber company log books.

For children, the History Center's highlight is parked behind the building: an authentic 1920 Baldwin 10-wheel, 68-ton steam locomotive, which visitors can explore by climbing in, on, and around it. Pull on a rope to hear the engine's steam whistle blast across the courtyard.

Recreation

With its proximity to four national forests, Lufkin is surrounded by boating, hiking, camping, and biking. In town, the city manages 16 municipal parks through **Lufkin Parks and Recreation** (936/633-0250, www. lufkinparks.com) to jog or walk your dog. Check the website for hours and accessibility to swimming pools, jogging trails, playgrounds, and picnic areas.

Food
BARBECUE
Lufkin Bar B Q (203 S. Chestnut St., 936/634-4744, www.lufkinbbq.com, Mon.-Sat. 10am-9pm, $10-21) is in an unassuming 1950s-era strip mall. The lightly fried rolls served before the meal are so tasty you'll be tempted to make a meal of them. Save space for the main event: succulent brisket and spicy sausage barbecue, or try a chipped beef sandwich for a smaller quantity.

AMERICAN
Lufkin has many generic chains and a few admirable local eateries. Mingle with the locals at **Mar Teres Tea Room** (3157 Ted Trout Dr., 936/875-6200, Tues.-Fri. 11am-2pm, reservations suggested, $10-23), a classic luncheon spot filled with antiques and pink decor. This tightly packed home is the ultimate destination for quality cuisine in Lufkin. The almond tea is the talk of the town, and entrées like chicken spaghetti, chicken salad, and French onion soup are

outstanding. Desserts are top-notch, especially the lemon cake, coconut pie, and old-fashioned chocolate cake.

More down-home and low-key is **Mom's Diner** (900 W. Frank Ave., 936/637-6410, Mon.-Fri. 11am-7pm, $7-16) with the best chicken-fried steaks in the area as well as juicy burgers, fried chicken, and outstanding peppered cream gravy.

For old-time greasy and tasty burgers, locals love the classic 1950s feel and fare of **Ray's Drive In Cafe** (420 N. Timberland Dr., 936/634-3262, Mon.-Sat. 10am-10pm, $7-12), including the mouthwatering bacon cheeseburger with onion rings, mushroom burger, chili dog, and chocolate milk shake. Classic oldies music completes the nostalgic scene.

TEX-MEX
Lufkin is known more for barbecue than Tex-Mex, but a couple places in town draw sizable lunch crowds. Consistently reliable **Cafe Del Rio** (1901 S. 1st St., 936/639-4471, daily 11am-10pm, $9-19) has crispy chips, spicy salsa, loaded nachos, and sizzling fajitas. Also recommended is **Casa Ole** (2109 S. 1st St., 936/632-2653, daily 11am-10pm, $8-17), offering tasty tacos and hearty enchiladas.

Accommodations
Lufkin's lodging options are limited, but several chains offer reliable rooms and amenities. An affordable commendable hotel is **La Quinta** (2119 S. 1st St., 936/634-3351, www. lq.com, $53 d). Features include an outdoor pool, free continental breakfast, and free Wi-Fi. Also worthwhile is **Hampton Inn & Suites** (4400 S. 1st St., 936/699-2500, www. hamptoninn.com, $92 d), featuring a free hot breakfast, to-go breakfast bags on weekdays, and free Wi-Fi. A step up is **Best Western Crown Colony Inn & Suites** (3211 S. 1st St., 936/634-3481, www.bestwesterntexas. com, $119 d), offering spacious rooms with microwaves and fridges, free Wi-Fi, deluxe continental breakfast, an outdoor pool, and a fitness room.

Information and Services

To get the scoop on lodging and dining options or to pick up a map or brochure, stop by the **Lufkin Convention & Visitors Bureau** (1615 S. Chestnut St., 936/633-0349 or 800/409-5659, www.visitlufkin.com, Mon.-Fri. 8:30am-5pm).

NACOGDOCHES AND VICINITY

Nacogdoches (population 33,542) claims to be Texas's oldest town, and there's no denying the wealth and breadth of its heritage and culture. Named for the Nacogdoche Caddo people that live in the area, Nacogdoches was an active Native American settlement until 1716, when Spain established a mission at the site. In 1779 Nacogdoches received official designation from Spain as a pueblo, prompting locals to deem it Texas's first official "town."

Nacogdoches became a center of trading activity, much of it illicit, primarily among the French and Americans, centered around the Old Stone Fort. With the town's strategic location on major trade routes, Nacogdoches was prominent in early military and political activities.

By the mid-1800s Nacogdoches lost its distinction in these areas due to its lack of modern steamboat and railroad transportation. Growth remained stagnant until the 1920s, when the Stephen F. Austin State Teachers College (now Stephen F. Austin State University) opened, bringing jobs and cultural activities. With a current enrollment of 13,000, the university remains the lifeblood of Nacogdoches.

Sights

OLD STONE FORT MUSEUM

The **Old Stone Fort Museum** (1936 North St., 936/468-2408, www.sfasu.edu/stonefort, Tues.-Sat. 9am-5pm, Sun. 1pm-5pm, free) on the Stephen F. Austin State University campus is a 1936 replica of the home of Don Antonio Gil Y'Barbo, the founder of present-day Nacogdoches. The original building, dating to the 1700s, was the oldest stone structure

in Texas before it was torn down amid much protest in 1902. Now historic itself, this replica is a Nacogdoches landmark, featuring a permanent exhibit on the history of the building that served as a trading post, church, jail, private home, and saloon, but never an official fort. The Old Stone Fort Museum contains artifacts related to the early history of East Texas, with a special focus on the Spanish and Mexican periods (1690-1836).

STERNE-HOYA HOUSE

One of the oldest homes in East Texas is the 1830 **Sterne-Hoya House** (211 S. Lanana St., 936/560-5426, www.ci.nacogdoches.tx.us, Tues.-Sat. 10am-4pm, free admission and tours). Built by Adolphus Sterne, a leader of the Texas Revolution, the home stands on its original site, which is rare for the era, as most were moved or demolished. Prominent figures of the time, including Davy Crockett, Sam Houston, and Cherokee chief Bowles, visited the Sterne home in the mid-1800s. Tour guides explain the significance of the period antiques and the prominent families who occupied the home, now listed on the National Register of Historic Places.

★ TEXAS STATE RAILROAD

All aboard the **Texas State Railroad** (Hwy. 84 W., Rusk, 877/726-7245, www.texasstaterr.com, $40-75 adults, $25-45 ages 2-12). The depot is in Rusk, 30 miles (48 km) northwest of Nacogdoches, where passengers board for a historic journey through the East Texas Piney Woods. Trains have plied these 25 miles (40 km) from Rusk to Palestine since 1881, when the state prison system began constructing the railway to transport iron ore and timber.

The 90-minute trek is an enjoyable and relaxing journey into the past, with gently rolling train cars clickety-clacking over bridges and through the dense green forest. Sit back while the steam locomotive's whistle bellows and the genial conductor checks your ticket. Before you know it, you'll be at the Victorian-style depot at the end of the line, where you'll

Caddo Communities

Most of East Texas was originally occupied by the **Caddo people,** a large nation comprising dozens of distinct groups or "families" in modern-day Texas, Oklahoma, Arkansas, and Louisiana. To learn all about their heritage and culture, go to **Caddo Mounds State Historic Site** (1649 Hwy. 21 W., 936/858-3218, www.visitcaddomounds.com).

When Europeans arrived in the 1500s and 1600s, they encountered Caddo communities along streams and rivers. The Caddo were farmers who grew corn, beans, squash, sunflowers, and other crops that flourished in the humid and rainy East Texas environment.

Although the Caddo people lived in remote river and stream valleys, their leaders usually lived in larger villages, where tall temples built of poles and thatched grass often stood atop earthen mounds. These centers were where community members gathered for festivities or during times of crisis.

The vast lands of the Caddo provided them much protection, but they also had a reputation as fierce and skilled warriors. When threatened, groups would band together. The Caddo were known for their pottery skills. Caddo women made everything from 3-foot-tall (1-m) storage jars to tiny bowls as well as smoking pipes and earspools. The Caddo traded bison hides and horses for French guns and merchandise.

Today, descendants of this great nation make up the Caddo Nation of Oklahoma, with nearly 4,000 members. The nation's headquarters is 45 miles (72 km) west of Oklahoma City in the town of Binger.

find historical exhibits, gift shops, and food service.

Round-trip excursions depart Saturday-Sunday at 11am year-round from both the Rusk and Palestine depots, and return to their point of origin by 3:30pm. Yes, the tickets are pricey, but the experience is one-of-a-kind. A 90-minute layover is scheduled at the opposite train depot, where a variety of lunch options are available. Snacks, beverages, and restrooms are available on the train.

CADDO MOUNDS STATE HISTORIC SITE

Just south of Rusk near the small town of Alto is the **Caddo Mounds State Historic Site** (1649 Hwy. 21 W., 936/858-3218, www. visitcaddomounds.com, Tues.-Sun. 8:30am-4:30pm, $2 adults, $1 students). Caddo-speaking farmers built these ceremonial burial mounds more than 1,200 years ago, and historians now say they are the southwesternmost structures of the legendary Mound Builders of the eastern North American woodlands. Three of these earthen mounds, used for burials, temples, and religious ceremonies,

still rise from the East Texas forests. Visitors can walk among the gently sloping structures and explore the interpretive center's exhibits and displays. Note that a devastating tornado struck the site in 2019, so a temporary visitors center is in operation while the permanent museum is built.

THE FREDONIA BREWERY

Not historic but drawing a large number of heritage travelers is the **Fredonia Brewery** (138 N. Mound St., 936/305-5125, www. fredoniabrewry.com, Thurs. 5pm-9pm, Fri. 4pm-9pm, Sat. 2pm-10pm), just a block north of downtown. The founders, both Nacogdoches natives, opened the 15-barrel brew house in 2017. Their shared love of beer and local history is evident in the pine taproom and the beers, including the tasty Nine Flags Amber Ale and Pine Cove Porter. Even the brewery's name and logo reference local history: the Fredonia Republic (1826-1827), "Brewed with the independent spirit that created Texas."

1: Sterne-Hoya House **2:** The Fredonia Brewery

Recreation

HIKING

For a quiet retreat to the surrounding woodlands, hoof it to the **Stephen F. Austin Experimental Forest** (6598 FM 2782, 936/564-8924, www.srs.fs.usda.gov), 8 miles (12.9 km) southwest of Nacogdoches. Not as compelling at its name implies, the forest is dubbed "experimental" for its crazy variety of tree species planted in the 1940s. A century ago, the area was logged and abandoned for use as cotton fields, but the U.S. government's purchase of more than 600,000 acres of East Texas land—eventually becoming the region's national forests—allowed for the reforestation of hardwoods and pines that would eventually populate the area. The Experimental Forest contains 3 miles (4.8 km) of trails with interpretive signs. Walk the wooded trails to glimpse 150 species of birds and 80 kinds of butterflies at this peaceful site.

BIKING

A scenic and pleasant hour's ride is the campus of **Stephen F. Austin State University** (1936 North St., 936/468-3200, www.sfasu.edu). Enjoy the tree-lined streets and classic collegiate structures while keeping an eye out for the thousands of meandering-while-texting students.

For a lengthy ride with cyclists knowledgeable about the area, consider meeting up with the **Nacogdoches Bicycle Club** (www.bikenacogdoches.org). The group meets several times a month for a 30-mile (48-km) ride on the rolling rural roadways outside town. Membership is not required, and visitors are welcome to drop in. The group meets Saturday morning near the SFASU campus at **Java Jack's** (1122 North St., 936/560-3975, www.javajacks.com).

Food

AMERICAN

If you're downtown at lunch, drop by the wonderful **Dolli's Diner** (116 S. Pecan St., 936/305-5007, Mon.-Wed. and Thurs.-Sat. 7am-5pm, Sun. 9am-4pm, $7-19), a classic lunch spot on the square with everything you'd expect from a small-town diner, including the best chicken-fried steak in the region, hearty sandwiches, healthy salads, big burgers, and friendly waitstaff.

Another popular lunch spot is the campus-area **NacBurger** (3205 N. University Dr., 936/564-3588, Mon.-Sat. 11am-7pm, $5-10). Students and professors line up at this shopping-center deli for tasty burgers and chicken sandwiches accompanied by bacon cheddar fries and a large iced tea.

Locals also love the regional chain **Clear Springs Cafe** (211 Old Tyler Rd., 936/569-0489, www.clearspringsrestaurant.com, Mon.-Thurs. 11am-9pm, Fri.-Sat. 11am-10pm, $7-21). Seafood is the main draw, including popular dishes such as the pan-seared tilapia, salmon or crawfish salad, and catfish étouffée.

BARBECUE

CC's Smokehouse (2709 Westward Dr., 936-462-8880, Mon.-Sat. 11am-8:30pm, $10-21) is classic East Texas-style barbecue done right: delicious brisket, savory sausage, and meaty pork ribs. Not quite as reliable is **The Barbeque House** (704 N. Stallings Dr., 936/569-9004, daily 11am-8:30pm, $9-22). The brisket and chicken are popular, and the sausage is a bit spicy but worth ordering.

MEXICAN

Nacogdoches isn't known for quality Mexican restaurants, but a couple options include **Tacos Dona Pancha** (112 W. Seale St., 936/559-9995, daily 6am-7pm, $8-18), with authentic tacos in tasty tortillas—opt for the beef with cilantro and onions. Don't be concerned by the surrounding iron gates and possibility that you'll have to order by pointing at menu items.

Another option is **Restaurant El Ranchero** (123 King St., 936/569-2256, daily 10:30am-9pm, $8-18), featuring some of the hottest and heartiest salsa in town, along with traditional favorites such as quesadillas, fajitas, and flautas. Call in advance to see if El

Ranchero is offering its semi-regular "two free margaritas" special.

Accommodations

Nacogdoches's lodging options are primarily chains, with most located near the Stephen F. Austin campus. The best budget choice is **Best Western Inn of Nacogdoches** (3428 South St., 936/560-4900, www.bestwestern. com, $74 d), offering rooms with free internet access along with microwaves and fridges, a free continental breakfast, and an outdoor pool.

One of Nacogdoches's few locally run establishments is the wonderful downtown six-story ★ **Fredonia Hotel** (200 N. Fredonia St., 936/564-1234, www.thefredonia.com, $99 d). Deemed "as modern as an atomic submarine" when it opened in 1955, the Fredonia's contemporary architectural style has French-inspired details in its decorative ironwork. This mid-century modern masterpiece is within walking distance of restaurants, coffee shops, and bars. The Fredonia features free Wi-Fi, a large and stylish outdoor pool, a good on-site restaurant, and a fitness center.

Moving into the slightly-more-expensive range is the clean and comfortable **Hampton Inn & Suites** (3625 South St., 936/560-9901, www.hamptoninn.com, $116 d), offering free internet access, a complimentary hot breakfast buffet, an outdoor pool, and a fitness center.

A popular option with business travelers is the nearby **Holiday Inn Express Hotel & Suites** (3807 South St., 936/564-0100, www. hiexpress.com, $126 d), with amenities such as free Wi-Fi, an upscale fitness center, and an outdoor pool.

Information and Services

While strolling historic downtown Nacogdoches, drop by the town's two main tourism offices. The **Nacogdoches Convention & Visitors Bureau** (200 E. Main St., 888/653-3788, www.visitnacogdoches. org, Mon.-Fri. 9am-5pm, Sat. 10am-4pm, Sun. 1pm-4pm) has information about the city's history and local sites of interest. Just around the corner is the headquarters of the **Texas Forest Trail Region** (202 E. Pilar St., 936/560-3699, www.texasforesttrail.com, Mon.-Fri. 8:30am-5pm). Operated by the Texas Historical Commission, the Forest Trail Region oversees heritage travel destinations and cultural activities in Nacogdoches and the East Texas Piney Woods region. Drop by to pick up brochures and maps, and to talk to the friendly and knowledgeable staff.

Information and Services

While strolling historic downtown Nacogdoches, drop by the town's two main tourism offices. The **Nacogdoches Convention & Visitors Bureau** (200 E. Main St., 888/653-3788, www. visitnacogdoches.org, Mon.-Fri. 9am-5pm, Sat. 10am-4pm, Sun. 1pm-4pm) has information about the city's history and local sites of interest.

Just around the corner is the office headquarters of the **Texas Forest Trail Region** (202 E. Pilar St., 936/560-3699, www. texasforesttrail.com, Mon.-Fri. 8:30am-5pm). Operated by the Texas Historical Commission, the Forest Trail Region oversees heritage travel destinations and cultural activities in Nacogdoches and the entire East Texas Piney Woods region. Drop by to pick up brochures and maps, and to talk to the friendly and knowledgeable staff.

TYLER

Slow-moving Tyler will never be confused with fast-paced Austin, but this large town or small city (population 105,729) certainly has a distinctive feel: Southern. From stately plantations to hospitable residents to deep-fried cooking, Tyler has a strong cultural connection to the Deep South.

One of the city's big draws is its roses. Tyler now provides nearly 20 percent of the roses in the United States. The Tyler Municipal Rose Garden contains tens of thousands of rose bushes representing hundreds of varieties. The gardens attract bees, butterflies, and

Boom! Goes the Town

In the early 1900s, East Texas was a land of opportunity, with prospectors speculating about the location of the next big oil field. More often than not, their efforts were unsuccessful, but when they guessed correctly and tapped into a fertile patch of petroleum, the fortunes of everyone associated with the discovery exploded like the gusher of oil.

These stories, along with photos and artifacts, are on display at local history museums in East Texas. For a full look at the region's oil boomtown years, visit Kilgore's comprehensive **East Texas Oil Museum** (1301 S. Henderson Blvd., Kilgore, 903/983-8295, www.easttexasoilmuseum.com), at the intersection of U.S. 259 and Ross Street.

After Beaumont, another East Texas boomtown was Kilgore, 30 miles (48 km) east of Tyler. Kilgore's glory years began in 1930, when the first oil gusher arrived; within weeks, the town's population surged from 500 to more than 10,000. Before well-spacing regulations were adopted, Kilgore boasted a small section of downtown that became known as the "World's Richest Acre," where 24 oil wells once stood.

At the height of Kilgore's boom, residents woke up to find their yards filled with strangers covered with boxes, sacks, and newspapers. People installed iron doors on their homes for protection from the influx of newcomers, and they stopped hanging their clothes out to dry since they'd be stolen off the line.

Not surprisingly, the oil boom brought con artists, criminals, and prostitutes to these small East Texas towns. The Texas Rangers were assigned to clean up the area, and they often had to resort to unorthodox means—like the time they "remodeled" an old church into a makeshift prison, with padlocked prisoners lining the interior walls—to address the newfound population of ne'er-do-wells.

thousands of people annually from around the world. Many visitors come for the Texas Rose Festival, held each October since 1933, featuring the queen's coronation, the rose parade, the queen's tea, and the rose show.

Tyler changed dramatically in 1930, when the discovery of the nearby East Texas oil field turned this small agricultural and railroad city into a major destination for workers and corporations. The town received an added boost in the 1940s when Camp Fannin was established nearby, including a troop capacity of 19,000 at the height of World War II.

In the following decades, Tyler's economic base shifted from agriculture to industry. Most were petroleum related, but other manufacturing plants soon followed, including metal and fabricating companies, railroad and machine shops, furniture and woodwork manufacturers, aluminum foundries, and air-conditioning and refrigeration plants.

In the 1970s-1980s, Tyler was best known as the hometown of football legend Earl Campbell, who earned the Heisman Trophy at the University of Texas and went on to become a Hall of Fame running back in the National Football League. Campbell's nickname, "The Tyler Rose," forever linked him with his hometown.

Sights
TYLER MUNICIPAL ROSE GARDEN AND MUSEUM

The region's most popular attraction is the **Tyler Municipal Rose Garden and Museum** (420 Rose Park Dr., 903/597-3130, www.parksandrec.cityoftyler.org, Mon.-Fri. 8am-5pm, Sat. 9am-5pm, Sun. 1pm-5pm, free), with numerous displays showcasing the elaborately jeweled, hand-sewn gowns worn by rose queens dating back to 1935. Check out the scrapbook pages from each rose queen, including memorabilia, personal recollections, and photos, including one with a queen and her freshly killed deer. Visitors can also view videos about the history of Tyler's rose industry and rose festival, and experience an interactive "attic" exhibit with an eclectic collection of antiques from Tyler's past.

The municipal garden is the primary draw, however, with its sea of colorful roses—35,000 bushes representing 500 varieties. The blooming period is May-November, and early May is the peak of the flowers' natural growing cycle. This is when the garden's 14 acres burst with the bright sight and sweet scent of fresh roses.

PLANTATION MUSEUMS

Tyler's heritage is on full display at Tyler's three plantation museums, where the Old South comes to life through historic furniture, artifacts, and photos. This lifestyle, typically associated with the Deep South, wasn't prevalent in most of Texas, and these sites provide a feel for the ornate homes and luxurious grounds. If you're lucky, the docents and tour guides may be dressed in period costume.

The **Goodman-LeGrand House Museum** (624 N. Broadway Ave., 903/531-1286, www.cityoftyler.org, Tues.-Sat. 10am-4pm, free) was the home of Dr. W. J. Goodman, a local doctor and Civil War surgeon. His son, also named Dr. William Jeffries Goodman, was a Civil War Major and chief surgeon, who bought the house from his father. The family lived in the home for 73 years and four generations. Originally built in 1859, the house is Tyler's first property to be listed on the National Register of Historic Places. The museum features original furnishings, including hand-carved tables and chairs, a grandfather clock from the colonial era, surgical tools and medical cases, and fine silver and china. It's open for walk-in tours.

Just as impressive is the 1854 **Dewberry Plantation** (14007 FM 346 W., 903/825-9000, www.dewberryplantation.com, by appointment, tours $8 adults and seniors, $5 ages 6-18). The plantation site served as a campground for the officers of the Army of the Republic of Texas prior to their final battle with the Cherokee people. The home, billed as the only original two-story pre-Civil War house still standing in Smith County, was built for War of 1812 hero Colonel John Dewberry, who moved to Tyler in 1835.

Also noteworthy is the grand 1878 **McClendon House** (806 W. Houston St., 903/592-3533, www.mcclendonhouse.net, Fri.-Sat. 10am-4pm, tours $7). Once a hub for Tyler's elegant Victorian society, the home was eventually purchased by the McClendon family, whose youngest daughter, Sarah, became a noted Washington DC journalist with a presidential-coverage career spanning Franklin D. Roosevelt to George W. Bush. The home is now primarily used as a wedding and events site but is open for tours.

CALDWELL ZOO

One of the best-run and most highly acclaimed zoos in the state is **Tyler's Caldwell Zoo** (2203 W. Martin Luther King Jr. Blvd., 903/593-0121, www.caldwellzoo.org, Mar.-Labor Day daily 9am-5pm, Labor Day-Feb. daily 9am-4pm, $11.60 ages 13-54, $10 seniors, $8.40 ages 3-12). What started in 1938 as a backyard menagerie of squirrels and parrots for schoolchildren has evolved into an 85-acre zoo containing 2,000 animals from East Africa and North and South America. Animals on display in naturalistic habitats include monkeys, rhinos, elephants, giraffes, cheetahs, and mountain lions.

TYLER MUSEUM OF ART

For a dose of traditional culture, visit the respectable **Tyler Museum of Art** (1300 S. Mahon Ave., 903/595-1001, www.tylermuseum.org, Tues.-Sat. 10am-5pm, Sun. 1pm-5pm, $5 adults, $3 students), on the east side of the Tyler Junior College campus. The museum showcases local and regional artists with an emphasis on contemporary works; occasional traveling exhibits feature centuries-old European paintings, Japanese artwork, and Native American pottery and ceramics. It contains three galleries on the main level, a smaller gallery for special exhibits upstairs, and a children's gallery.

DISCOVERY SCIENCE PLACE

With the family in tow, this is the place to go: **Discovery Science Place** (308 N. Broadway, 903/533-8011, www.discoveryscienceplace. org, Mon.-Sat. 10am-5pm, Sun. 1pm-5pm, $8 adults, $6 children and seniors) offers three large exhibit halls with fun interactive features like the earthquake shake, a cavern crawl, a dinosaur exhibit, and a bat cave.

Entertainment and Events

For a city of 100,000, Tyler has a surprising number of entertainment options, perhaps due to the increasing number of Dallas-area retirees moving to Tyler for its slower-paced lifestyle. The quality of the local arts scene has grown over the past decade, resulting in top-notch ballet, symphony, and cultural offerings.

BALLET TYLER

An organization drawing plenty of local attention is **Ballet Tyler** (4703 D. C. Dr., Suite 105, 903/596-0224, www.artandseek.org). A convergence of two programs, the School of Ballet Tyler and the Tyler Junior College dance program, has helped raise the group's profile. Dancers range in age 11-20, and the company stages several performances throughout the year. Visit the website for schedules and tickets.

EAST TEXAS SYMPHONY ORCHESTRA

One of Tyler's enduring cultural entities is the **East Texas Symphony Orchestra** (522 S. Broadway Ave., Suite 101, 903/526-3876, www. etso.org). Newly named to encompass the larger region, the orchestra has also bumped up its mission to bring classical music to a larger segment of the community. The organization offers a wide range of concerts, from contemporary to Renaissance.

COWAN CENTER

For big-name touring acts, Tyler residents and visitors head to the University of Texas-Tyler's **Cowan Center** (3900 University Blvd.,

903/566-7424, www.cowancenter.org), the stage for international and touring stars in comedy, jazz, and Broadway shows. Past performers and performances include Bill Cosby, David Copperfield, Lyle Lovett, *Cats*, *Stomp*, and Larry Hagman.

Shopping
EAST TEXAS FRESH FARMER'S MARKET

Tyler isn't a major shopping destination, but locals spend time and money at the **East Texas Fresh Farmer's Market** (2112 W. Front St., May-Aug. Tues. and Sat. 7am-1pm). The market features regional vendors offering fresh produce, flowers, and wares. Soak up the local scene and support the local farming community.

Food

Tyler's quality restaurant options are better than you'd expect in a smallish city in a rural part of the state.

AMERICAN

A stalwart on the scene is ★ **Rick's on the Square** (104 W. Erwin St., 903/531-2415, www.rix.com, Mon.-Fri. 11am-10pm, Sat. 4pm-1am, $13-39), a swanky lunch and dinner joint and rowdy blues bar by night. In the heart of downtown in an old saloon and theater, Rick's has tempting shrimp and oyster appetizers, gigantic juicy burgers with chunks of fried potatoes on the side, and exquisite entrées ranging from chicken dumplings to the recommended crawfish-stuffed filet mignon.

The popular **Potpourri House** (3200 Troup Hwy., 903/592-4171, www. potpourrihouse.com, Mon.-Sat. 10am-3pm, $11-32) is a welcoming spot combined with a retail establishment offering candles, antiques, jewelry, more candles, and potpourri. The restaurant's offerings range from club sandwiches to baked fish, chicken, and prime rib.

A local legend and a must-experience for barbecue fans is ★ **Stanley's Famous Pit Bar-B-Q** (525 S. Beckham Ave., 903/593-0311, www.stanleysfamous.com, Mon.-Fri. 7am-7pm, Sat. 11am-8pm, $7-19). The smoked ribs are atop "best of" barbecue lists across Texas—their tender, succulent taste will have you thinking about them for days. Try the smoked turkey and sausage, or sample a sliced brisket sandwich. Better yet, tackle the Brother-in-Law sandwich, teeming with sausage, chopped beef, and cheese.

TEX-MEX

Tyler is far from the border but has a few worthy Mexican restaurants, including popular homegrown regional chains.

If you're downtown, drop by **Posado's** (2500 E. 5th St., 903/597-2573, daily 11am-9:30pm, $9-19). Mission-style decor adds to the authentic Mexican-inspired taste, including interior-style dishes such as marinated quail fajitas and shrimp or fish platters. The classics include chicken enchiladas and spicy beef tacos.

Locals also love **Taqueria El Lugar** (1726 E. Gentry Pkwy., 903/597-4717, Mon.-Thurs. 9am-9pm, Fri.-Sat. 9am-10pm, $10-20). As the name implies, tacos are the specialty, listed on the menu by number. Order anything with the amazing guacamole and tasty beef (the cabbage isn't quite as recommendable), and be sure to ask for it on a corn tortilla.

Accommodations

Chain hotels are the only choice in Tyler. The available options are safe, reliable, and relatively affordable. On the lower end of the price spectrum is **La Quinta** (1601 W. Southwest Loop 323, 903/561-2223, www.lq.com, $69 d), featuring free Wi-Fi, a free continental breakfast, and an outdoor pool.

Perhaps the best deal in town is the **Comfort Suites at South Broadway Mall** (303 E. Rieck Rd., 903/534-0999, www.choicehotels.com, $99 d), offering rooms with free Wi-Fi, microwaves, and fridges, and hotel amenities such as an exercise room, free continental breakfast, and an indoor heated pool and whirlpool. The only drawback is its location, far from the downtown activity.

On Broadway, about 10 minutes from downtown, is the recommendable **Country Inn & Suites** (6702 S. Broadway Ave., 903/561-0863, www.countryinns.com, $105 d). There's plenty of space to spread out, with a mini kitchen (fridge, microwave) and rooms offering free Wi-Fi. The free breakfast includes meat, eggs, bagels, and cereals.

Nearby is the city's largest hotel—the comfortable **Holiday Inn Select** (5701 S. Broadway Ave., 903/561-5800 or 800/465-4329, www.holidayinn.com, $109 d), which features free Wi-Fi service, an outdoor pool, a full-feature fitness center, and free meals for kids under age 13.

Information and Services

The **Tyler Convention & Visitors Bureau** (315 N. Broadway Ave., 903/592-1661 or 800/235-5712, www.visittyler.com) is just a few blocks north of the downtown square on the 1st floor of the historic Blackstone building. The friendly staffers provide brochures, maps, and general information to help you get around the Rose Capital.

Getting There

American Airlines flies regional jets to **Tyler Pounds Regional Airport** (TYR, 700 Skyway Blvd., 903/531-9825, www.cityoftyler.org) several times a day from Dallas-Fort Worth. Most visitors opt to drive, which takes 3.5 hours from Houston.

JEFFERSON

Set aside a few hours to explore Jefferson (population 1,967). This quaint Deep South community is nestled in the forest, offering a pleasant escape to the Piney Woods's past. In its glory days of the mid-19th century, Jefferson was a burgeoning boomtown containing a kaleidoscope of cultures, including entrepreneurial East Coast shop merchants, newly freed enslaved people, and westward-moving pioneers. For more than a decade, Jefferson welcomed a steady flow of steamboats bringing worldly influences and people.

In 1870, Jefferson had a population of 4,180

and was the sixth-largest city in Texas, and 1867-1870, steamboats became important in the town's commercial trade, which grew from $3 million to $8 million. By 1870, only the port of Galveston exceeded Jefferson in volume. In 1873, things changed dramatically for Jefferson. The destruction of the Red River raft, a natural dam on the river, lowered the water level of the surrounding lakes and streams, making navigation to Jefferson via steamboat impossible. Also that year, the Texas and Pacific Railway, which bypassed Jefferson, was completed. Without steamboat or railroad access, Jefferson shrank.

In the mid-1900s, locals began looking at Jefferson's distinctive past as a way to preserve and promote the town's heritage, particularly its remarkable 100-plus recognized historic structures. Known as the "Bed and Breakfast Capital of Texas," tourism is now Jefferson's economic base.

Sights
HISTORIC BUILDINGS
With so much Southern heritage in such a small town, it's necessary to visit some of the sites that make Jefferson historically significant. One of its crown jewels is the **House of the Seasons** (409 S. Alley St., 903/665-8000, www.houseoftheseasons.com, tours Mon.-Sat. 11am, $10). Built in 1872 by Colonel Benjamin Epperson, a prominent businessperson and friend of Sam Houston, this magnificent home contains Greek Revival, Italianate, and Victorian architectural elements. The name is from the glass encasement on top of the house, with colored glass representing each of the seasons.

A visit to Jefferson is incomplete without a stop at the **Jefferson General Store** (113 E. Austin St., 903/665-8481, www. jeffersongeneralstore.com, Sun.-Thurs. 9am-6pm, Fri.-Sat. 9am-10pm). Walking through the creaky screen doors offers a step back in time, with vintage trinkets and current-day souvenirs mingling in a historic 1870s mercantile setting. Touches of bygone days are everywhere, in the signature five-cent cup

of coffee, the homemade pecan pralines, and the soda fountain. Jams, salsas, T-shirts, and candy round out the experience.

Also worth a visit is **The Grove** (405 Moseley St., 903/665-8018, www.thegrove-jefferson.com, call for tour information, $6). Referred to as "the most haunted house in Jefferson," The Grove is a private residence built in 1861 and listed on the National Register of Historic Places. An hour-long tour offers a fascinating glimpse into the home, along with stories about the supernatural experiences of the owners, including a woman in a white dress who always takes the same path through the house. Its paranormal activity is so legendary, *This Old House* placed it on its list of Top 12 Haunted Homes, and it graces the cover of the book *A Texas Guide to Haunted Restaurants, Taverns, and Inns.*

THE ATALANTA RAILROAD CAR
The Atalanta (210 W. Austin St., 903/665-2513, daily 10am-3pm) was a private railcar used by railroad tycoon Jay Gould. It's rather odd that this elaborately designed and elegantly furnished car ended up in Jefferson, since the city rejected Gould's plans to bring a railroad through the town. Upon being spurned, he left, predicting Jefferson's demise; he was partly right, since the town never regained its steamboat-era splendor of the 1860s. *The Atalanta* features a dozen rooms containing opulent mahogany, crystal light fixtures, and silver bath accessories. Across from the Excelsior House downtown, it remains a major attraction of Jefferson's heritage tourism. Tours are $5, and guides are available at the adjacent Excelsior House Hotel.

SCARLETT O'HARDY'S GONE WITH THE WIND MUSEUM
The campy and somewhat strange **Scarlett O'Hardy's Gone with the Wind Museum** (408 Taylor St., 903/665-1939, www. scarlettohardy.com, Thurs.-Sat. 10am-4pm, $3 adults, $1 under age 13) is jam-packed with everything imaginable related to the classic

film *Gone with the Wind,* including posters, photos, costume reproductions, dolls, and seats from the Atlanta theater where the movie premiered in 1939. Perhaps most interesting is the collection of autographs from the movie's stars, most notably Clark Gable, Vivien Leigh, Leslie Howard, Hattie McDaniel, and Butterfly McQueen.

LAKE O' THE PINES

Nearby **Lake o' the Pines** (903/755-2597, www.lakeothepines.com) is as charming as its name implies. The popular destination is known for bass, catfish, and crappie fishing as well as boating for waterskiing, sailing, pontoon boats, party boats, and "floating cabins," all available at several lakeside marinas. Campers flock to Lake o' the Pines, pitching tents and parking RVs at four U.S. Army Corps of Engineers parks and privately owned campgrounds. Other options include guesthouses, cabins, and motels.

★ CADDO LAKE

For the area's premier recreational destination, head just downriver from Jefferson to **Caddo Lake,** the only natural lake in Texas (all the others were created by dams). Stringy Spanish moss and outstretched cypress trees surround this mysteriously beautiful and sometimes marshy lake. The Caddo people say a massive flood formed the lake, but scientists believe logjams blocked the Red River, causing it to back up into the Cypress Bayou watershed, which formed the lake. Popular lake activities include camping, hiking, swimming, fishing, and boating. Among the many attractions at Caddo Lake is the Texas Parks and Wildlife-operated **Caddo Lake State Park** (FM 2198, via Hwy. 43, 903/679-3351, www.tpwd.state.tx.us). The park offers access to diverse fishing, canoe rentals, and quaint cabins built by the Civilian Conservation Corps in the 1930s.

Food

Because of its modest size, most restaurants in Jefferson are within walking distance of the historic downtown shopping and lodging attractions. One of the stalwarts is the tremendous **Joseph's Riverport Barbecue** (201 N. Polk St., 903/665-2341, Tues.-Sun. 11am-6pm, $10-22). This is traditional East Texas-style 'cue, with sweet spicy sauce covering savory smoked meats, including pork ribs, brisket, and chicken. The turkey and chopped beef sandwiches are amazing, and the potato salad, coleslaw, and beans as sides are way better than average. Drop by Friday night for a catfish feast.

For a fancier dining experience, make reservations at the top-notch **Stillwater Inn** (203 E. Broadway St., 903/665-8415, www.stillwaterinn.com, Tues.-Sat. 5:30pm-9pm, $12-35). In an 1890s Victorian house, this busy upscale restaurant is famous for its grilled seafood and steak, veal specials, and roasted rack of lamb.

Accommodations

BED-AND-BREAKFASTS

Jefferson claims to be the "Bed and Breakfast Capital of Texas." The dozens of B&Bs far outnumber the few hotel options, and the town is a Victorian-era playground.

Among the popular choices is the **Claiborne House Bed & Breakfast** (312 S. Alley, 903/665-8800, www.claibornehousebnb.com, $109-199), a stately Greek Revival home built in 1872 and offering six rooms—four in the main house and two in the carriage house, each named after romantic poets (Yeats, Wilde, Dickinson). All rooms have a framed poem, a book of the poet's work, free Wi-Fi, private baths, and TVs. A full Southern gourmet breakfast is served at 9am, and a day spa is available for massages, body wraps, hot rock treatments, and salt scrubs.

The **Old Mulberry Inn and Cottages** (209 Jefferson St., 903/665-1945, www.oldmulberryinn.com, $89-189) is recommended by *Southern Living* magazine and even the *New York Times.* The antebellum home contains five guest rooms and two cottages with private baths that feature claw-foot tubs, family heirlooms, cable TV, and free Wi-Fi. The three-course gourmet breakfasts include delectable items such as artichoke quiche, baked pears with cranberries, Rocky Mountain grits, and mulberry almond coffee cake.

HOTELS

For those who insist on staying in a normal plush-free hotel in the B&B Capital of Texas, there's really only one option: the **Executive Inn & Suites** (200S. Walcott St., 903/665-3700, www.executiveinnjefferson.com, $85 d). There's nothing fancy here, but it's new and pleasant, with a free hot breakfast, suites with jetted tubs, and free Wi-Fi. A word of caution: The whistles from the trains across the highway can be loud in the night.

The historic **Excelsior House** (211 W. Austin St., 903/665-2513, www.theexcelsiorhouse.com, $129 d) is technically a hotel but feels like a B&B. It's rich in history and ghosts and has hosted guests since the 1850s. Fans of paranormal activity claim this is one of the most haunted locations in town. During Jefferson's prosperous days, guests

included Ulysses S. Grant, Rutherford B. Hayes, and Oscar Wilde, and its 150-plus years of operation make it one of the oldest establishments of its kind still in business in Texas.

Information and Services

To find out more about the dozens of available B&Bs or other area attractions, pick up a map or brochure from the kind folks at the **Marion County Chamber of Commerce** (101 N. Polk St., 903/665-2672, www.jefferson-texas.com).

Getting There

Like the other destinations in the Piney Woods region, Jefferson is accessed via U.S. 59, which runs north-south to Houston, passing through Lufkin, Nacogdoches, and Marshall. The drive can take four hours if you're doing things right—making time to soak up the forest views, stopping for a bite to eat, and waiting patiently to pass the logging trucks. From Dallas, the drive is two hours eastbound on I-20 before heading north on U.S. 59 for Marshall and Jefferson or south for Nacogdoches and Lufkin.

The Gulf Coast

Stretching more than 350 miles (560 km) along the Gulf of Mexico, this region of sun, sea, and sand offers the ultimate escape. Moderate beaches and waves don't attract crowds the way Florida's mighty surf does, but draws casual beachcombers, anglers, and families.

Occasionally referred to as the country's "Third Coast," the gulf region offers quiet natural seashores, crazy spring break parties, and world-class museums. The constant breeze off the ocean keeps sailors and windsurfers cruising, and temperatures are a few degrees cooler than inland, although the humidity is always hair-curling. The ocean is warm and inviting, sometimes uncomfortably warm in summer, and is technically responsible for stirring up the horrific hurricanes far

Galveston 308
Brazosport Area 326
Corpus Christi 330
Mustang Island 343
Kingsville 348
South Padre Island 352

Highlights

Look for ★ to find recommended sights, activities, dining, and lodging.

★ **Window shop on The Strand.** Galveston's thriving historic district hosts hotels, restaurants, art galleries, and boutiques amid 19th-century splendor (page 308).

★ **Get a feel for seafaring life.** Walk the sturdy wooden decks of **The *Elissa*,** one of the oldest operational sailing vessels in the world (page 310).

★ **Experience the depths of the Texas Gulf.** Start with birds and gators at sea level before descending to oil-rig depths with menacing sharks and hundreds of other slippery species at the **Texas State Aquarium** (page 330).

★ **Tour a 33,000-ton floating museum.** The decommissioned aircraft carrier **USS *Lexington* Museum** transports you back to World War II with vintage aircraft and an impressive collection of historic memorabilia (page 332).

★ **Watch sea turtles hatch.** You can also witness the migrations of thousands of birds along **Padre Island National Seashore,** the longest undeveloped barrier island in the world (page 343).

★ **Experience cowboy culture.** At 825,000-acre **King Ranch,** genuine cowboys herd longhorn cattle in wide-open spaces, evoking the Texas mystique (page 349).

© MOON.COM

★ **Take in views from Port Isabel Lighthouse.** It's well worth climbing the 74-step spiral staircase for the sight of the gorgeous Laguna Madre stretching to Port Isabel (page 354).

out at sea. Hurricanes Ike (2008) and Harvey (2017) wreaked havoc on the Gulf Coast, and the Deepwater Horizon oil spill (2010) caused visitors to avoid the beaches.

All along the Gulf Coast are anglers of different stripes, from solo artists casting lines off a pier or at surf's edge to groups on charter deep-sea boats with professional guides. The promise of fresh flounder, trout, bull reds, snapper, and even shark and tuna is one of the region's main draws.

Naturalists come for the abundant birding opportunities. The Great Texas Coastal Birding Trail links 300-plus miles (480 km) of shoreline, from hummingbird sighting near Galveston to whooping cranes and tropical species on Padre Island. Two major migratory flyways intersect along the Gulf Coast, allowing birders to photograph elusive species.

In addition to the recreational opportunities along the shore, the cool air-conditioning at numerous Gulf Coast museums offers a welcome respite. Galveston's Moody Gardens and several Corpus Christi attractions are world-class facilities for learning about regional history, wildlife, and art. Top your day off with a fresh catch from a seaside restaurant.

Aside from Galveston's festive springtime Mardi Gras and South Padre's spring break, most of the Gulf Coast is a slow-moving year-round vacationland, where the biggest challenge is determining the day's activities—swimming, fishing, shell collecting, sunbathing, surfing, boating, or building sand castles. Visitors responding to the call of the sea find the region to be as low-key as the gulf's lightly lapping waves.

ORIENTATION

With 350 miles (560 km) of shoreline, Texas's Gulf Coast is challenging to characterize but uniquely Texan—from oil refineries to spring break beach parties, the coastline stretches from urban playgrounds to a national seashore.

The northern part of Texas's coast is dominated by Galveston Island, just 45 minutes from Houston. It can be crowded with urban escapees on weekends, but Galveston has small-town charm with a fascinating past and impressive historic buildings. Just an hour down the coast is the Brazosport Area (that's its actual name), a collection of communities known for oil refineries and chemical plants balanced by welcoming beaches and fishing.

Three hours farther south, Corpus Christi offers a less urban vibe. Visitors flock here for birding, fishing, seafood, and recreation. The final stretch of coastline is three hours' drive from Corpus to South Padre along an uninspiring inland highway through the enormous King Ranch. The drive culminates at gorgeous South Padre Island, with pristine beaches and tasty waves.

PLANNING YOUR TIME

Coast-bound travelers tend to stay for a weekend in one area—Galveston, Brazosport, Corpus Christi, or South Padre—at a beach condo or fishing village, as opposed to roaming the entire region. If you have time and money to spare, you can cruise along the coast in a rented boat.

The two main types of Gulf Coast travelers are busy families on a getaway from the burbs, and anglers on a getaway from the family. The South Padre Island beaches are the nicest, so if quality sand and surf are priorities, that's the place to start. Spend at least two or three days in the sun, soft white sand, and gentle surf.

Farther up the coast, the beaches tend to be less scenic—the sand is darker and civilization is more apparent in the oil rigs, tankers, and commercial buildings. The lure of the sea is just as strong, but there is more traffic and crowds. Spend a long weekend in Corpus

---

Previous: Corpus Christi beach scene; The *Elissa*; The Pleasure Pier's ferris wheel

The Gulf Coast

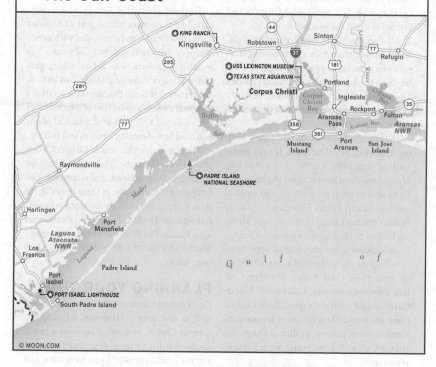

KING RANCH
Kingsville

Robstown

Sinton

44

37

77

Refugio

285

USS LEXINGTON MUSEUM
TEXAS STATE AQUARIUM

181

Portland

281

Corpus Christi

Corpus
Christi
Bay

Ingleside

Rockport

35

Fulton

77

Baffin

Bay

358

361

Aransas
Pass

Aransas Bay

San Jose
Island

Aransas
NWR

Raymondville

Mustang
Island

Port
Aransas

PADRE ISLAND
NATIONAL SEASHORE

Madre

Harlingen

Port
Mansfield

Laguna
Atacosta
NWR

Los
Fresnos

Padre Island

Laguna

G   u   l   f   o   f

Port
Isabel

PORT ISABEL LIGHTHOUSE
South Padre Island

© MOON.COM

Christi on pleasant Mustang Island or nearby Padre Island National Seashore. Corpus's USS *Lexington,* Texas State Aquarium, and Museum of Science and History are a family-friendly, air-conditioned change of pace.

The Brazosport Area offers fewer cultural amenities, and anglers spend quiet weekends here sans water parks and booming car stereos. Things are more laid-back and less commercial here, where retirees, anglers, and professional beachcombers peacefully coexist.

Galveston is where Houston folk go to spend money to get their beach and seafood fix. It's the least pristine of all the Gulf Coast beaches, but the waves are welcoming, and the shopping and restaurant scene in the historic Strand district are deserving of two travel days.

INFORMATION AND SERVICES

Most communities along the Gulf Coast have visitors bureaus to inquire about directions, equipment rental, and other travel-related assistance. Contact the following entities before your trip with questions about logistics or scheduling. Their physical addresses and hours of operation are included at the end of each destination section in this chapter.

Brazosport Area Chamber of Commerce (979/285-2501, www.brazosport.org), **Corpus Christi Area Convention & Visitors Bureau** (361/881-1800 or 800/766-2322, www.visitcorpuschristitx.org), **Galveston Island Convention & Visitors Bureau** (409/763-4311 or 888/425-4753, www.galveston.com), **and South Padre Island Convention & Visitors Bureau**

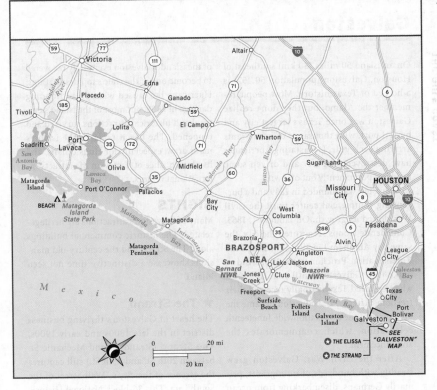

(956/761-6433 or 800/767-2373, www.sopadre.com).

GETTING THERE AND AROUND

Most travelers arrive on the Gulf Coast by car. Commercial flights are available to Corpus Christi International Airport and at Brownsville South Padre Island International Airport.

Since most of the coastline is undeveloped, no major freeways link the coastal cities. Highway 35 is primarily a rural road between Houston and Corpus Christi, passing through dozens of small towns along the way. The lengthy Padre Island National Seashore is only accessible via the park road near Corpus Christi. Otherwise, the trek to South Padre beaches is 20 miles (32 km) inland via

U.S. 77 through Kingsville, Harlingen, and Brownsville.

Corpus Christi International Airport (CRP, 1000 International Blvd., 361/289-0171, www.corpuschristiairport.com) has flights on American Eagle, United, and Southwest. South Padre is accessible via the **Brownsville South Padre Island International Airport** (BRO, 700 Amelia Earhart Dr., 956/542-4373, www.flybrownsville.com), served by United and American Eagle. Galveston is an hour's drive from Houston's **George Bush Intercontinental Airport** (IAH, 2800 N. Terminal Rd., 281/230-3100, www.airport-houston.com) or **William P. Hobby Airport** (HOU, 7800 Airport Blvd., 713/640-3000, www.fly2houston.com). Rental cars are available at each airport.

Galveston

On an island 50 miles (80 km) southeast of Houston, Galveston (population 50,457) is a hotbed of Texas history. Most people remember the Alamo, but they don't realize Galveston was once Texas's largest city and busiest port, with thousands of immigrants arriving each year. Devastating hurricanes have destroyed property and driven some residents permanently out of town.

Galveston was founded in 1839 and a burgeoning commercial center until the Civil War slowed its growth. On January 1, 1863, Confederate troops recaptured the city, the same day Abraham Lincoln signed the final Emancipation Proclamation. Word didn't make it to Galveston until June 19, 1865, when enslaved Texans finally received their freedom. Afterward, Galveston became the birthplace of the now nationwide Juneteenth celebration, which commemorates the announcement.

After the Civil War, Galveston grew steadily with hundreds of immigrants, primarily Germans, disembarking from ocean liners each day. Trade was prosperous, especially cotton exports, and for a while Galveston was known as the "Wall Street of the South" due to its robust economy and cosmopolitan amenities, such as electric light, telephones, and modern streetcars. The stately mansions and downtown commercial buildings of this era still stand as the heart of Galveston's historic district. Most of these ornate homes are now museums that draw visitors from around the globe.

Galveston was forever altered in 1900 when a massive hurricane destroyed a third of the island's buildings. The torrential 120-mph (190-km/h) windstorm caused an estimated 6,000 deaths. As a result of the devastation, Galveston's industries and residential population shifted to Houston.

Thanks in part to the construction of a massive seawall to protect the northern part of the island, Galveston eventually recovered to become one of the state's top destinations. Hurricane Ike caused widespread flooding damage in 2008, but most of the island's cultural and historical attractions survived and reopened. The beach remains the island's main draw, especially for Houstonians, and its pleasant slice of Victorian life attracts international visitors.

SIGHTS

Many of Galveston's attractions are heritage-related. The historic commercial buildings along The Strand and the century-old mansions showcase a distinctive time not seen inland.

★ The Strand

The heart of Galveston's thriving business district in the late 1800s and early 1900s, **The Strand** (Strand St. and Mechanic St. between 20th St. and 25th St.) still captures the essence of the city's "Wall Street of the South" era. This 36-block National Historic Landmark District features New Orleans-style hotels, restaurants, art galleries, and boutiques, most of which escaped the devastation of the 1900 hurricane. Today, visitors are drawn to antiques and clothing shops, art studios, and seasonal festivals, including the popular Dickens on the Strand and Mardi Gras celebrations.

Pleasure Pier

The smile-inducing amusement park **Pleasure Pier** (2501 Seawall Blvd., 855/789-7437, www.pleasurepier.com, hours vary, $20-27 day pass, $4 individual rides) harks back to a 1940s facility with the same name, although the gangsters of yore have been replaced with families and couples. The current Pleasure Pier is the third iteration—two earlier sites were knocked out by hurricanes.

Spend a few hours exploring 16 rides,

Galveston

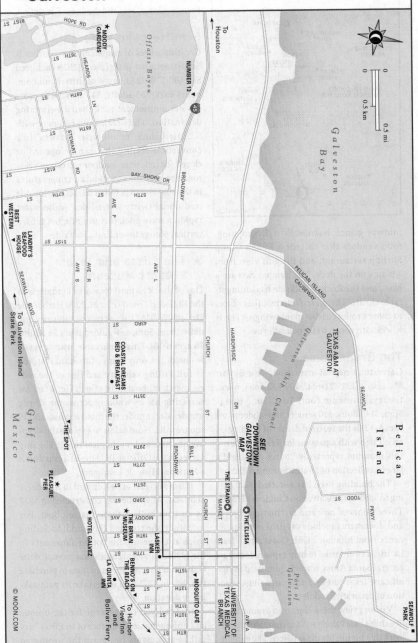

To Houston

HOPE RD

★ MOODY GARDENS

Offatts Bayou

81ST ST
81ST ST
HEARDS LN
79TH ST
69TH ST
61ST ST
STEWART RD
59TH ST
61ST ST

NUMBER 13

45

BAY SHORE DR

BROADWAY

57TH ST
57TH ST

AVE P

● BEST WESTERN

▼ LANDRY'S SEAFOOD HOUSE

SEAWALL BLVD

To Galveston State Park

51ST ST

AVE S
AVE R

AVE L

PELICAN ISLAND CAUSEWAY

Galveston Ship Channel

TEXAS A&M AT GALVESTON

Galveston Bay

Pelican Island

SEAWOLF

Port of Galveston

TODD ST

SEAWOLF PKWY

SEAWOLF PARK ■

N

0   0.5 km
0   0.5 mi

Gulf of Mexico

43RD ST
35TH ST

CHURCH ST
HARBORSIDE DR

AVE P

COASTAL DREAMS BED & BREAKFAST

▼ THE SPOT

29TH ST
27TH ST
25TH ST
23RD ST

BALL ST
BROADWAY

SEE "DOWNTOWN GALVESTON" MAP

THE STRAND ★

MARKET ST
CHURCH ST

● THE ELISSA

★ PLEASURE PIER

● HOTEL GALVEZ

MOODY AVE
19TH ST

★ THE BRYAN MUSEUM

LASKER INN

17TH ST
15TH ST

▼ BENNO'S ON THE BEACH

LA QUINTA INN

To Harbor View Inn and Bolivar Ferry

13TH ST
11TH ST
10TH ST
8TH ST

AVE A

▼ MOSQUITO CAFE

UNIVERSITY OF TEXAS MEDICAL BRANCH

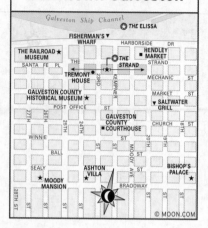

Downtown Galveston

Galveston Ship Channel

THE ELISSA

FISHERMAN'S WHARF

THE RAILROAD MUSEUM

HENDLEY MARKET

HARBORSIDE DR

SANTA FE PL

THE STRAND

STRAND

THE STRAND

TREMONT HOUSE

MECHANIC ST

GALVESTON HISTORICAL MUSEUM

MARKET ST

SALTWATER GRILL

POST OFFICE

GALVESTON COUNTY COURTHOUSE

CHURCH ST

WINNIE

BALL

SEALY

ASHTON VILLA

BISHOP'S PALACE

MOODY MANSION

BROADWAY

© MOON.COM

midway games, boardwalk-style shopping, food vendors that include a Bubba Gump Shrimp restaurant, and the gulf view from a bench on the deck. The bumper cars are a blast, and the Rock-n-Roll ride has unforgettable thrills. There aren't many other places to enjoy a roller coaster, giant swing, or Ferris wheel with ocean water beneath you.

The Bryan Museum

Galveston's newest attraction, **The Bryan Museum** (1315 21st St., 409/632-7685, www.thebryanmuseum.com, Tues.-Sun. 10am-5pm, $14 adults, $10 seniors and students, $4 ages 6-12) is the realized dream of J. P. Bryan, an oilman with a passion for Texas history—this museum reportedly houses the world's largest collection of Southwestern artifacts.

The building itself has a storied past, dating to 1895 as the Galveston Children's Home. Three floors of rare and fascinating objects and documents include original correspondence from infamous Gulf Coast pirate Jean Lafitte, a sword used to help capture Mexican general Santa Anna, historic guns used in significant Texas battles, and an amazing collection of decorative saddles.

Visitors view these objects in dramatically lit exhibit cases along with accompanying artwork that highlights the artifacts. The exhibits

begin with Native American history and progress chronologically to the Spanish and French colonial eras and the Texas Revolution.

Schlitterbahn Waterpark

Creating waves of excitement for families is **Schlitterbahn Waterpark** (2026 Lockheed St., 409/770-9283, www.schlitterbahn.com, hours vary, $53 adults, $41 ages 3-11), more a water amusement park than a swimming destination. The ocean can't compete with Schlitterbahn's "uphill water coasters" in a convertible facility that can be opened or closed for indoor or outdoor recreation year-round to keep the water and air temperatures in the 80s (27-31°C). Other attractions include traditional twisty waterslides, white-water rapids, a wave pool, playgrounds, hot tubs, a vertical plunge tower, and a surf ride.

★ The *Elissa* and Texas Seaport Museum

One of the city's most treasured landmarks is the 1877 ship *Elissa* (Pier 21, 2200 Harborside Dr., 409/763-1877, www.galvestonhistory.org, daily 10am-5pm, self-guided tours $8 adults, $6 ages 6-18). This remarkable historic vessel is one of the only ships of its kind restored to full sailing capacity and one of the oldest merchant boats still afloat. Get a feel for seafaring life by walking across the sturdy wooden decks under the massive masts and 19 square sails. Head below to explore the sleeping quarters and mechanical room. The ship serves as the Official Tall Ship of Texas and is a National Historic Landmark.

Elissa's origins are a shipyard in Aberdeen, Scotland, where she was constructed in 1877 as an iron-hulled, three-masted boat. For a century she traveled the world, including stops at Galveston for cotton shipments in the 1880s. This local connection prompted the Galveston Historical Foundation to purchase the ship in 1975 and undertake its painstaking restoration.

In April you can arrange for the unique and unforgettable experience of an *Elissa* "day sail." Participants can grasp the weathered

Hurricanes: Deadly Tropical Cyclones

Hurricane season is tumultuous for Gulf Coast residents. These devastating tropical cyclones can come ashore anytime June-November, though most strike in the hot summer months of **August-September.**

Hurricanes originate when ocean waters reach their highest temperatures, leading to thunderstorms with winds of up to 40 mph (64 km/h), officially a tropical storm. At this point, the National Hurricane Center names the storm, working from a predetermined alphabetical list of names. Tropical storms get their energy from warm humid air over the ocean, and they release this energy as powerful winds.

Traditionally the probability of a hurricane hitting Texas hasn't been high, but the past decade or so has been a different story. In September 2005, Hurricane Rita, a category 5 storm with intense 120 mph (190 km/h) winds, made landfall near Sabine Pass on the Texas-Louisiana border and caused $11 billion in damage and seven deaths. Even more devastating was Hurricane Ike, which slammed into Galveston Island in September 2008, leaving an enormous swath of destruction. Ike leveled several communities, and its 110 mph (175 km/h) winds ripped apart hotels, office buildings, and countless homes in Galveston, Houston, and the surrounding area. Devastation struck again in 2017, when Hurricane Harvey walloped Rockport, near Corpus Christi, with 130mph (210 km/h) winds. The associated storms resulted in unprecedented flooding in Houston.

WALLOPING WINDS

The statistical possibility of Texas being hit by a hurricane is once every six years along any 50-mile (80-km) stretch of the coast. The recent incidents, plus the memory of 2005's devastating Hurricane Katrina in New Orleans, have residents tuning in to the weather whenever the words *"tropical depression"* surface. Annual probabilities of a hurricane striking a 50-mile (80-km) segment of the coast range from 30 percent near Port Arthur to 40 percent at Matagorda Bay, northeast of Corpus Christi.

Some of the strongest hurricanes to hit the U.S. coast have come ashore in Texas historically typically in uninhabited areas. In 1970, meteorologists recorded wind gusts of 180 mph (290 km/h) near Aransas Pass, and in 1961, Hurricane Carla brought 175 mph (280 km/h) winds to Port Lavaca. By comparison, Katrina's wind speeds were 140 mph (225 km/h) at landfall, but Katrina's extremely low barometric pressure made it unusually intense.

In the wake of the devastating losses with Hurricanes Ike and Harvey, officials have organized emergency plans and evacuation routes for coastal cities. Public awareness campaigns focus on the importance of being informed and prepared. The unpredictable nature of these storms makes evacuation planning a challenge, but an increasing number of Gulf Coast residents pack up and move inland when an intensifying tropical storm is on the horizon.

---

lines and assist with raising the massive sails while enjoying a day at sea. A hardworking crew of volunteers serves guests a hearty lunch. Visit the Galveston Historical Foundation's website for dates and prices.

To learn more about the *Elissa*'s history and restoration, visit the adjacent **Texas Seaport Museum** (daily 10am-5pm) The portside facility features informative exhibits about maritime culture and a movie about Galveston's port-based heritage as the "Ellis Island of the West." The museum's database contains the names of more than 133,000 immigrants who entered the United States through Galveston. Admission to the museum is included in tickets for the *Elissa*.

The Bishop's Palace

Grand. Stately. Ginormous. However you choose to describe it, the spectacular 1886 **Bishop's Palace** (1402 Broadway St., 409/762-2475, www.galvestonhistory.org, daily 11am-6pm, guided tours hourly, $14 adults, $9 students) is the centerpiece of Galveston's historic Broadway Street. The American Institute of Architects designated

Bishop's Palace as one of 100 outstanding buildings in the country. This Victorian castle exudes elegance, with ornate fireplaces (one is lined with pure silver), grand stairway, stained-glass windows, and intricately carved furnishings and details. Galveston's most visited historical attraction, it transports visitors to another era. For a behind-the-scenes tour of the inner workings and rare views of the marvelous mansion, ask about the monthly Basement-to-Attic tour.

The Moody Mansion

Galveston entrepreneur W. L. Moody Jr. purchased the four-story, 32-room, 28,000-square-foot limestone and brick **Moody Mansion** (2618 Broadway St., 409/762-7668, www.moodymansion.org, daily 10am-5pm, $15 adults, $7 students) a week after the 1900 hurricane. The impressive and opulent home features rare hand-carved wood, coffered ceilings, stained glass, and heirlooms from the Moody family, whose financial empire was built on banking, ranching, and insurance. Marvel at the manicured grounds, exquisite furnishings, expansive ballroom, and the dining room's gold-leaf ceiling. Behind-the-scenes tours (Fri.-Sun. 4pm, $35 pp) are available.

Moody Gardens

Natural wonders await beneath three enormous glass pyramids at **Moody Gardens** (1 Hope Blvd., 409/744-4673, www.moodygardens.com, daily 10am-6pm, $65 day pass, $26-33 individual pyramid tickets), an elaborate collection of plants, animals, and educational exhibits inside the 100-foot-tall (30-m) structures. If you only have time to explore one area, go with the Rainforest Pyramid. The Aquarium Pyramid has more animals and features, but in the rainforest environment you'll find yourself face-to-face with African animals, tropical birds, and colorful reptiles, along with massive plants, cascading waterfalls, and the constant chatter of birds and insects. Check out the bat cave, with

various species of bats hanging upside-down and nibbling on fresh fruit.

The Aquarium Pyramid displays the world's oceans, viewed at the surface and underwater. Marvel at penguins as they waddle and dive, and catch an up-close view of sea lions as they glide and play. Sharks, sea turtles, rays, and tropical fish await below the surface, viewable in a traditional aquarium tank setting or from the underwater tunnel, surrounded by a million gallons of water.

The Discovery Pyramid features science and nature exhibits, and there are a ropes course, a zip line with a bird's-eye view of the pyramids, three IMAX theaters, kids' activities aboard a paddle-wheel boat, seasonal recreation at Palm Beach (swimming lagoons, whirlpools, volleyball, and paddleboats), formal gardens, a golf course, nature trails, and the Moody Gardens conference center, hotel, and spa.

One of the newest attractions is "animal experiences," offering guests the chance to interact one-on-one with river otters, seals, and adorable penguins in a secluded environment. Check the website for prices and timing.

Galveston Tree Sculptures Tour

Check out the East End Historical District's offbeat **Galveston Tree Sculptures Tour** (information and maps 409/797-5144, www.galveston.com). Hurricane Ike devastated Galveston in 2008 with a tidal surge that led to the demise of thousands of oak trees. Local artists honored the former foliage by creating carvings from the remains. Highlights include a large live oak containing a dozen carved birds called *Birds of Galveston,* and a carving named *Tin Man and Toto* at the birth home of *Wizard of Oz* director King Vidor.

Ashton Villa

Also of historical interest is the 1859 **Ashton Villa** (2328 Broadway St., 409/762-3933, www.galvestonhistory.org, call ahead for guided

---

1: the historic Bryan Museum **2:** Pleasure Pier

tours), built as the residence of wealthy businessman James Moreau Brown. It set the standard for the exquisite Galveston homes that followed. Experience the Victorian lifestyle through the home's grand entryway, life-size paintings, and beautifully landscaped grounds. The house contains artworks, furniture, and mementos the family acquired during travels to Asia. Ashton Villa's carriage house now houses a Galveston Island Visitors Center, open daily, but tours of the mansion are by appointment only.

The Railroad Museum

Anchoring Galveston's historic downtown Strand district is the former Santa Fe Union Station, home to **The Railroad Museum** (2602 Santa Fe Place, 409/765-5700, www. galvestonrrmuseum.org, daily 10am-5pm, $10 adults, $8 seniors, $5 students). More than 20,000 railroad items and several dozen vintage passenger, dining, and kitchen cars provide views of railroad life in the late 19th-early 20th centuries. The main terminal, at the heart of this impressive art deco building, contains interactive exhibits and a collection of unique plaster sculptures depicting "ghosts of travelers past." Kids will love the miniature model trains and the historic railcars behind the depot.

Ocean Star Offshore Drilling Rig and Museum

The **Ocean Star Offshore Drilling Rig and Museum** (1900 Harborside Dr., 409/766-7827, www.oceanstaroec.com, summer daily 10am-5pm, winter daily 10am-4pm, $10 adults, $8 students and seniors), just a block from the Strand historic district, is a distinctive small museum that educates visitors about the offshore oil and gas industry via a refurbished drilling rig. Visitors can take a self-guided tour through three levels of the retired rig to learn about oil exploration, drilling, and production through informative exhibits and videos.

The Galveston Naval Museum

The Galveston Naval Museum (100 Seawolf Park Blvd., 409/797-5114, www. galvestonnavalmuseum.com, daily 9am-6pm, $10 adults, $5 students) features historic World War II vessels on a guided or self-guided tour, allowing visitors to experience what it was like to patrol underwater in the Pacific or assist Allied forces in the Atlantic. Hop aboard the USS *Cavalla*, a submarine that sank a Japanese aircraft carrier involved in the Pearl Harbor attacks, or the USS *Stewart*, the only battleship of its kind preserved in the United States.

BEACHES

There are a few different kinds of beaches in Galveston—the touristy stretches near hotels and attractions, quiet areas frequented by locals, and the party spots. The Galveston Park Board recently helped organize an expansion project that widened existing beaches and added a significant amount of new beach, the largest restoration project of its kind in Texas history.

One of the most family-friendly spots is **Stewart Beach** (6th St. and Seawall Blvd., 409/765-5023, Mar.-mid-Oct., $12-15 per car), where you'll find parents and kids building sand castles, playing volleyball, and body-surfing. Nearby amenities include a children's playground with waterslides, umbrella and chair rentals, a concession area, a souvenir shop, restrooms, and a bathhouse.

Things get a bit crazier at **East Beach** (1923 Boddeker Dr., 409/762-3278, $12-15 per car), where Houston's young crowd comes to party and one of the few places where drinking is legal on the beach. As a result, there are more concerts, promotions, and festivals than at other beaches. Up to 7,000 cars pack the beach for drinking and sunbathing, and the bar area is a magnet for partiers. East Beach has restrooms with showers, volleyball courts, chair and umbrella rentals, and a souvenir shop.

1: The Bishop's Palace 2: a penguin at Moody Gardens 3: The *Elissa* 4: Grand 1894 Opera House

RECREATION

Recreational opportunities abound in Galveston. Outdoor-based activities have expanded in recent years as visitors increasingly search for physical challenges and workout opportunities on the coast.

Galveston Island State Park

A popular place to enjoy the outdoors is **Galveston Island State Park** (14901 FM 3005, 409/737-1222, www.tpwd.state.tx.us, $7 over age 12), with camping, hiking, biking, fishing, swimming, and birding, followed by a dip in the ocean or the simple pleasure of beachcombing. There are 4 miles (6.4 km) of trails through bayside salt marshes and prairie grassland. There are no lifeguards on the beach, but there are restrooms and rinse showers.

Biking

Bike rentals have become a popular way to experience Galveston, with no freeways or traffic jams. To rent a bike and learn about Galveston's best cycling areas, head to **Island Bicycle Company** (1808 Seawall Blvd., 409/762-2453, www.islandbicyclecompany. com). The shop claims to have the largest selection of rental bikes in the city and offers hotel pickup service. For $60, you can take a bike for a full-day self-guided tour that includes a ferry ride. The package includes a lock and a map.

Paddling

A slightly more adventurous way to explore Galveston Island is to rent a kayak, paddleboard, or canoe. Start at **Galveston Island State Park,** with convenient established put-ins and take-outs. Paddlers have three different water "trails": the 2.6-mile (4.2-km) Dana Cove Trail, beginning at Lake Como and meandering through shallow seagrass; the Oak Bayou Trail, a 4.8-mile (7.7-km) course beginning near the boardwalk and following the inlets and breakwaters of Galveston Bay; and the Jenikins Bayou Trail, a 2.8-mile (4.5-km) trail traversing a freshwater pond and a small inlet.

A worthy outfit for kayak rental and excursion info is **Gulf Coast Kayak Adventures** (979/215-6319, www. gulfcoastkayakadventures.com), offering shuttle service to specified locations, full-day rentals ($65 single kayak, $80 tandem). Guided kayak tours ($150 plus $60 pp) range from beginner trips exploring birding opportunities to advanced tours offering potential porpoise sightings.

Bird-Watching

The Gulf Coast is a birder's paradise, with ample opportunity to catch glimpses of flying species during migrations in spring and fall. Galveston Island offers a few incentives to stay for a while: The natural barrier island habitat provides protection and food-rich bayous and marshes.

Galveston Island State Park is an ideal perch for bird-watching opportunities. Keep an eye out for great blue herons, white ibis, great egrets, and white spoonbills as well as hawks, gulls, and terns.

Surfing

"Galveston" and "surfing" don't usually go together, but there are places where surfing exceeds expectations. Steady coastal winds allow for windsurfing, and there are often decent surfing conditions along the Seawall (between 21st St. and 51st St.). Waves are most consistent in spring, and their gentle nature offers an opportunity for beginners to hone their skills. Watch for the beach patrol's red-flag warnings on gusty days. The **Galveston Beach Patrol** (409/763-4769, www.galvestonislandbeachpatrol.com) provides current weather conditions. For information about surf equipment rental, contact one of the city's surf shops, like **Ohana Surf & Skate** (2814 Ave. R, 409/763-2700, www. ohanasurfandskate.com).

Fishing

Fishing opportunities abound, and a fishing license ($40 nonresidents, $20 residents) is required. Obtain one at the **Super Wal-Mart**

(6702 Seawall Blvd.), or the **Texas Parks and Wildlife Office** (800/895-4248) to purchase by credit card.

Spotted sea trout, black drum, and flounder can be caught along the shore at **Galveston Island State Park,** and a fish-cleaning station is at the end of the park road near the camping area. For information about conditions, contact the park's administrative office (409/737-1222).

One of the most popular fishing spots on the island is the **Galveston Fishing Pier** (90th St. and Seawall Blvd., 409/974-4383, www.galvestonfishingpier.com, $12 adults, $8 under age 12). The 300-foot-long (90-m) T-head is an ideal spot to view the shoreline while casting a line for redfish, jackfish, and sea trout. The pier offers equipment rental, bait, chairs, and mobile carts.

ENTERTAINMENT AND EVENTS
Nightlife

Like most beach towns, Galveston's nightlife scene is a mix of surfside venues (often the most fun and memorable options) and standard beer joints or restaurant-bar combos. Unlike other travel destinations, the bar scene tends to shut down early—10pm at many locations—so be sure to call ahead if you're planning a pub crawl.

During hot summer months, touristy and genuinely fun **Float** (2828 Seawall Blvd., 409/765-7946) has an outdoor pool where customers are encouraged to enjoy a cold beverage while floating. The atmosphere is like a supersize backyard pool party, with a full bar and views of the Gulf of Mexico. If you didn't bring a bathing suit or are visiting when temperatures are below 80°F (27°C), there's indoor seating and standard pub grub.

For those who take their drinking slightly more seriously, head directly to **Brews Brothers Brew Pub** (2404 Strand St., 417/230-6644). You won't find any commercial light beers here, and that's undeniably refreshing. The brewpub specializes in craft beers, and the staff is extremely knowledgeable and will gladly make recommendations.

To grab a meal followed by some drinks, people-watching, and a steady ocean breeze, drop by **Yaga's Café and Bar** (2314 Strand St., 409/762-6676, www.yagaspresents.com), in the heart of the Strand district adjacent to Saengerfest Park. Yaga's is known for its large outdoor patio and dance parties to live music on weekends.

Performing Arts

Nighttime entertainment tends to be bars rather than theaters, but Galveston has a few notable venues. Foremost is the **Grand 1894 Opera House** (2020 Post Office St., 409/765-1894, www.thegrand.com), which survived the devastating storms of 1900 and 1915 as well as more recent Hurricanes Carla, Alicia, and Ike. Listed on the National Register of Historic Places, the Grand was proclaimed "The Official Opera House of Texas" by the state legislature in 1993.

The building's rich history is apparent, with a grand staircase, wooden walls, and turn-of-the-20th-century furnishings. Friendly ushers offer stories to crowds who regularly pack the house for Texas legends (Lyle Lovett, Robert Earl Keen) and classic artists (Oak Ridge Boys, Kingston Trio).

Island Etc. (2317 Mechanic St., 409/771-0165, www.islandetc.org) is billed as Galveston County's only professional repertory theater company, staging up to six productions a year, mostly traditional shows such as *Cat on a Hot Tin Roof, Avenue Q,* and *Harvey.* The venue also screens classic movies, including *The Wizard of Oz, Rocky Horror Picture Show,* and *Back to the Future.*

Events

The biggest annual event in Galveston, and one of the biggest in Texas, is **Mardi Gras** (888/425-4753, www.mardigrasgalveston.com), held in February or early March. This all-out party draws a quarter million people (that's not a misprint). Held on the island for more than a century, the crazy days-long party features extravagant parades, exhibits, live entertainment, and galas. One of the biggest attractions is the three million beads thrown from floats and balconies.

Many beachside communities host sand castle competitions, but most aren't like Galveston's. The builders at Galveston's **annual sand castle competition** on East Beach in August are actual architects. Hosted by the Houston chapter of the American Institute of Architects since 1986, Galveston's event is a sight to behold. The imaginative and professionally designed sand structures have to be seen to be believed.

Aside from Mardi Gras, Galveston's most venerable event is **Dickens on the Strand** (502 20th St., 409/765-7834, www. galvestonhistory.org), held the first weekend of December to transports participants to the past for a weekend of 19th-century high society, Galveston style. Costumed revelers, carolers, entertainers, and attendees recreate the festive atmosphere of 1800s Galveston, then Texas's largest and richest city.

The city's other major holiday-related event is the **Moody Gardens Ice Land** (1 Hope Blvd., 800/582-4673, www.moodygardens. com), with a winter wonderland throughout the site's signature pyramid structures. The festival features a rarity in Texas: an outdoor ice-skating rink and Ice Slide ride.

SHOPPING

Shopping is among Galveston's main draws, with abundant fashion boutiques and knickknack shops throughout in the historic downtown area. Keep in mind that this is where wealthy Houstonians come to play, so prices reflect this clientele.

The Strand

The gaslit street lamps, ornate architectural detailing, and lofty display windows along the 36-block Strand district attract even non-shoppers with their Victorian-era charm. Start at the eclectic **Hendley Market** (2010 Strand St., 409/762-2610, www. hendleymarket.com), a fascinating emporium with Mexican imports, vintage jewelry, kitschy knickknacks, and antique medical instruments. Kids will love the baskets filled with handcrafted toys and plastic novelty trinkets. Not quite as charming yet equally beguiling in its array of objects is **Big House Antiques** (2212 Mechanic St., 409/762-0559). Shoppers will find many estate-sale pieces, including furniture, jewelry, decorative items, and books.

For something shiny and tasteful, head to **The Jewel Garden** (2326 Strand St., 409/766-7837), a fancy-yet-casual shop with a range of quality gifts, including silver jewelry, home decor objects, wind chimes, and hand-carved woodwork.

If you forgot your flip-flops or lost your sunglasses on the beach, drop by **Jammin Sportswear** (2314 Strand St., 409/763-4005). Every beach town needs T-shirt shops, and Jammin is one of the most popular on the island. Pick up towels, caps, sunscreen, or one of those bitey alligator toys. A step up is **Surf Styles** (2119 Strand St., 409/763-0147), where you can get a T-shirt for the beach and some stylish cruise wear for a night on the town. Brands include Stüssy, Miss Me Denim, Converse, and Lucky Brand.

A mandatory stop on The Strand is the venerable **Old Strand Emporium** (2016 Strand St., 409/515-0715). The longest-running spot in the district, it offers fresh fudge, ice cream, deli sandwiches, and cold drinks, including beers and wine. Texas foods are the specialty, including salsa, pecan pralines, and tangy barbecue sauce.

FOOD

There's no excuse not to eat seafood in Galveston, and the city is brimming with quality restaurants. After you've had your fill of shrimp, oysters, and snapper, try the Southern-style comfort food at one of the island's tremendous neighborhood joints.

Jellyfish Jam

"Jellies" on Texas's Gulf Coast refers to jellyfish, and despite their iridescent wiggly appearance, they cause much more pain than pleasure. One of the most common to wash up on the shore isn't technically a jellyfish, despite its translucent air bubble and blue tentacles. The Portuguese man-of-war (a.k.a. the blue bubble, blue bottom, or man-of-war) is actually a colony of organisms, each with its own distinct function. Its name comes from the air bubble's resemblance to the sails of a historical Portuguese war vessel. The man-of-war floats on ocean currents and is deposited on beaches during spring-late summer. These crafty carnivores feed on small fish and other small animals that get caught in their venom-filled tentacles.

The other washed-up organisms visitors may encounter are traditional jellyfish—gelatinous invertebrates with varying-size tentacles hanging from the main "body" of the organism (technically referred to as the mollusk). You won't find an abundance of these animals on a typical beach stroll, but watch for them, as their stings pack a wallop. They're much harder to see in the water, but a good indication of their presence is the appearance of washed-up organisms on the beach. The man-of-war is especially difficult to see since it's translucent and often blends in with sea foam.

Aside from avoiding areas of the ocean where you see beached jellies, make sure you don't step anywhere near the washed-up variety, since their stinging cells remain toxic even when the body has died. The tentacles are often nearly invisible, though you'll definitely feel the sharp shot of pain up your leg. If you step on one, scrape the tentacles off with a credit card. If a jellyfish stings you, place the affected area under hot water and apply hydrocortisone cream to relieve the itching. For a man-of-war sting, splash the area with saltwater, then apply vinegar or a diluted bleach solution (1 part bleach to 10 parts water) to the sting site without pressing too hard on the skin. The pain should go away within an hour.

Seawall and Vicinity
SEAFOOD

If you're staying in a hotel on Seawall Boulevard, your inaugural meal should be at ★ **Gaido's Seafood Restaurant** (3800 Seawall Blvd., 409/762-9625, www.gaidos. com, Sun.-Thurs. 11am-9pm, Fri.-Sat. 11am-10pm, $12-39), a venerable institution serving memorable meals since 1911. Its legendary reputation is evident in the time-honored trimmings, traditional menu, and attentive service. The shrimp bisque is amazing, the garlic snapper is succulent, and the crab cakes are outstanding. If it's on the menu, order the full snapper—head and bones and all, exquisitely prepared with complementary seasoning. A wide variety of local specialties are on the combination platter, including charcoal-grilled gulf shrimp, deep sea scallops, and catfish or snapper. Save room for a fun after-dinner cocktail by sharing a unique treat known as the Old Shoe (vanilla ice cream, coconut, and chocolate liqueurs).

Exceptional dining awaits at **Galvez Bar & Grill** (2024 Seawall Blvd., 409/765-7721, www.hotelgalvez.com, daily 6:30am-11am, 11:30am-2pm, and 5pm-10pm, $13-49), inside the historic Hotel Galvez and offering some of the highest-quality cuisine on the island. Menu highlights include fresh-caught seafood from nearby Pier 19, a sublime shrimp and polenta dish, and a grilled seafood platter with oysters, crawfish, and shrimp.

For an awesome lunch with an outstanding view, hit **The Spot** (3204 Seawall Blvd., 409/621-5237, www.thespotgalveston.com, Sun.-Thurs. 11am-10pm, Fri.-Sat. 11am-11pm, $9-23). After beachcombing, this is the place for a shrimp po'boy, fish-and-chips, or even a big ol' burger. The crunchy breading and homemade rolls are what set this spot apart, with crispy fresh-flavored seafood and sandwiches. The 2nd-floor deck offers panoramic views of the gulf.

A welcoming contemporary option on the island's East End is **Porch Café** (1625 E.

Beach Dr., 409/762-0808, www.porchcafe. com, Thurs. 5pm-10pm, Fri. 11:30am-3pm and 5pm-10pm, Sat. 9am-2pm and 5pm-10pm, Sun. 9am-2pm and 5pm-8pm, $12-33). Open and bright, Porch Café is an ideal place to linger for weekend brunch or an early dinner. Start with a light local lager paired with gulf white ceviche (shrimp and scallops) or seafood au gratin. Follow it with a crab cake-topped salad or a sumptuous plate of seafood linguini. A post-meal stroll on the adjacent beach is a necessity.

Although it's a regional chain, **Landry's Seafood House** (5310 Seawall Blvd., 409/744-1010, www.landrysseafoodhouse. com, Sun.-Thurs. 11am-10pm, Fri.-Sat. 11am-11pm, $9-31) is a respected eatery, even in a Gulf Coast town known for its local legends. Opt for the fresh catch Lafitte, gulf flounder, or broiled flounder. Landry's also does shrimp well, including a fried option stuffed with seafood.

Specializing in Cajun seafood is **Benno's on the Beach** (1200 Seawall Blvd., 409/762-4621, www.bennosofgalveston.com, Sun.-Thurs. 11am-10pm, Fri.-Sat. 11am-11pm, $9-20). This is an unassuming place until the food arrives, and it's apparent where Benno's focuses its resources. The shrimp dishes are perfectly seasoned with Cajun spices, and you can't go wrong with Benno's crawfish étouffée, jambalaya, spicy crab, or oysters.

For an ocean-side dining experience, have a meal at **Jimmy's on the Pier** (9001 Seawall Blvd., 409/974-4726, www. galvestonfishingpier.com, Mon.-Thurs. 11am-9pm, Fri.-Sat. 11am-11pm, Sun. 11am-9pm, $9-30). At the base of the popular T-head fishing pier, Jimmy's is a step above other pier restaurants, offering a variety of menu items, not just beach grub. Grab a table near the edge of the deck for optimal viewing of surfside activity and sunset. Jimmy's food ranges includes standard burgers, pizza, blackened fish, and broiled oysters. Everything on the menu is above average, especially paired with a St. Arnold's lager on tap.

Fresh and contemporary ★ **BLVD Seafood** (2804 Ave. R½, 409/762-2583, www.blvdseafood.com, Sun.-Thurs. 11am-9pm, Fri.-Sat. 11am-10pm, $9-36) serves a perfect lunch order: fish tacos topped with a red bell-pepper sauce and avocado, paired with a Galveston Island Brewery pale ale. You can't go wrong with a diversified seafood sampler for dinner, including the catch of the day, shrimp, scallops, and garlic butter sauce.

fish tacos at BLVD Seafood

AMERICAN

A few minutes from the shore is popular **Mosquito Café** (628 14th St., 409/763-1010, www.mosquitocafe.com, Tues.-Sat. 8am-9pm, Sun. 8am-3pm, $9-27). Have breakfast here at least once—the flavor-packed creative healthy food makes an impression. Grab a coffee and try to decide among the delectable options, such as Mosquito Benedict (a fresh-baked scone covered with portabella mushrooms, sautéed shrimp, sun-dried tomatoes, artichoke hearts, asparagus, and poached eggs topped with serrano hollandaise sauce), cinnamon-tinged french toast, fluffy pancakes, or bagels and lox. Lunch items include bowls of pasta with homemade pesto, olives, and feta cheese, or tasty sandwiches on delicious fresh-baked bread with hickory-smoked bacon, avocado salsa, and goat cheese.

For simple low-key fare, neighborhood stalwart **Sunflower Bakery and Cafe** (512 14th St., 409/763-5500, www.thesunflowerbakeryandcafe.com, daily 7am-5pm, $6-17) has fresh-made breads, pastries, and desserts as well as flavor-packed sandwiches (the turkey, bacon, and avocado on honey wheat bread is especially tasty), along with healthy salads and eclectic daily specials. The tomato basil soup is a local favorite. Family-owned Sunflower has a full menu complete with crab cakes, burgers, and po'boys, and this is the perfect place to order a to-go lunch for the beach—don't forget to include brownies and the legendary strawberry lemonade.

Strand Area
SEAFOOD

What else are you going to eat in Galveston? Fresh seafood is everywhere, and several of the best places are on the bay just a few blocks from The Strand.

Satisfy this urge for a plate of shrimp, oysters, snapper while overlooking the water downtown at **Willie G's** (2100 Harborside, 409/762-3030, www.williegs.com, daily 11am-9pm, $10-33). Opt for bayside seating and order some peel-and-eat shrimp to start—squeeze fresh lemon on top and dip them in tangy cocktail sauce—and proceed to the fresh catch of the day, from blackened snapper to grilled flounder to fried trout.

Next door is the larger and consistently dependable **Fisherman's Wharf** (Pier 22 and Harborside Dr., 409/765-5708, daily 11am-9pm, $9-33). Red snapper is the specialty, but shrimp kisses, oysters on the half shell, calamari, and even the steak and pasta are tasty. Ask for a table with a view of the bay, where you can sit on the deck and watch the shrimp boats glide by.

About a half mile inland is one of the finest restaurants in town. The fabulous ★ **Saltwater Grill** (2017 Post Office St., 409/762-3474, Mon.-Fri. 11am-2pm and 5pm-10pm, Sat. 4pm-10pm, Sun. 5pm-9pm, $14-42) feels urban and spare like Houston but tastes fresh and flavorful like a Gulf Coast restaurant should. Fresh is a genuine approach to food preparation: The restaurant utilizes a bizarre steam-kettle device that's linked to a large heater, pipes, and steel buckets that cause water to boil in three minutes. The result is rapidly cooked fresh seafood as opposed to reheated or perpetually boiled fare. Enjoy a plate of mussels, clams, or shrimp, and order the grand gumbo. Another must-taste is the appetizer with fried asparagus topped with crabmeat, and entrées such as the grilled yellowfin tuna, flounder, and seafood linguini. Reservations are recommended.

Enjoy a unique twist on island fare at **Rudy and Paco** (2028 Postoffice St., 409/762-3696, www.rudyandpaco.com, Mon.-Thurs. 11am-2pm and 5pm-9pm, Fri.-Sat. 11am-2pm and 5pm-10pm, $11-39). The seafood and meat dishes have a Central and South American flair, with distinctive seasonings and ingredients like *yuca* and roasted pork (the tacos de puerco are *fabuloso*). For dinner, order house specialty red snapper, crusted in plantains and topped with savory crab meat sauce. Rudy and Paco's has a low-key dress code for dinner; shorts are not allowed.

For old-school, affordable, flavorful seafood, head to **Shrimp n' Stuff** (3901 Ave. O,

409/763-2805, www.shrimpnstuff.com, daily 10:30am-8:30pm, $7-14). Skip the "stuff" and head for the shrimp—fried, boiled, or grilled. At this classic local joint, you order at the counter, get your food in a Styrofoam box, and sit in lively packed quarters.

AMERICAN

Step back in time at the charming and moderately priced **Star Drug Store** (510 23rd St., 409/766-7719, www.galvestonstardrug.com, daily 8:30am-3pm, $7-13). The historic neon and porcelain Coca-Cola sign out front sets the tone, featuring an a century-old horseshoe-shaped lunch counter with a soda fountain. Menu options are typical old-time lunch fare: burgers, reubens, pimiento cheese sandwiches, chicken salad, dilled pasta salad, and ice-cream floats. The drugstore's signature item is a tasty tomato-basil soup.

Despite its location on the Gulf Coast, Galveston doesn't have a strong Cajun flavor. That's not the case at **Little Daddy's Gumbo Bar** (2105 Post Office St., 409/744-8626, daily 11am-10pm, $9-21). The tasty seafood gumbo, packed with oysters, shrimp, and crab, is worth the trip. For something heartier, feast on the meaty Mumbo Gumbo, a concoction of sausage, prime rib, and chicken. *Bon temps!*

ITALIAN

For one of the finest meals on Galveston Island, head to ★ **Riondo's Ristorante** (2328 Strand St., 409/621-9595, www.riondos.com, Sun.-Thurs. 11am-9pm, Fri.-Sat. 11am-10pm, $14-52), with a delicious combination of Italian and seafood. Some of the best items include the gulf shrimp spaghetti carbonara, seafood ravioli pillows, and the cioppino, including clams, mussels, sea scallops, gulf coast shrimp, and homemade fettuccine.

Outside Downtown

It's worth making the 5-mile (8-km) drive west of downtown for the food and views at **Number 13 Prime Steak and Seafood** (7809 Broadway Ave., 409/572-2650, www.number13steak.com, Tues.-Thurs. 4pm-9pm,

Fri. 4pm-10pm, Sat. 11am-10pm, Sun. 11am-9pm, $13-51). Number 13 elevates the traditional surf-and-turf concept to haute cuisine. Steaks are available in wet-aged and dry-aged variety (the bone-in rib-eye rivals Houston's best steak houses), and the seafood ranges from iron-seared salmon to oak-grilled snapper. The wine list is top-notch, and the baked Alaska dessert is simply sublime.

For a step up from the standard touristy seafood joints, head to **Waterman's Restaurant** (14302 Stewart Rd., 409/632-0233, Tues.-Thurs. 4pm-9pm, Fri.-Sat. 11am-10pm, Sun. 11am-9pm, $12-35). There isn't anything too out of the ordinary, but the quality is noteworthy. Waterman's specializes in snapper; go with the Texas option, pecan and crabmeat. If you're not in the mood for fish, the flame-kissed Waterman Burger is ideal.

ACCOMMODATIONS

Galveston's popularity as a tourism destination means there's no shortage of lodging options, from cheap beachside motels to luxurious historic resorts.

Seawall Boulevard

For most visitors, the best way to experience an island vacation is on the shore. The following hotels aren't technically on the beach—you'll have to cross busy Seawall Boulevard to get your toes in the sand—but are close enough to smell the salty air and see the sailboats and barges.

At the affordable end of the scale is no-frills dependable **Gaido's Seaside Inn** (3700 Seawall Blvd., 409/762-9625, www.gaidosseaside.com, $69 d). Gaido's is perhaps best known for its incredible adjacent seafood restaurant, but the hotel has some tasty amenities, including free continental breakfast, an outdoor pool with a splash shower, and free coffee and juice in the lobby.

Well-regarded is **Commodore on the Beach** (3618 Seawall Blvd., 409/763-2375,

---

1: Waterman's Restaurant **2:** a full snapper dish at Gaido's **3:** Hotel Galvez **4:** Lasker Inn

www.commodoreonthebeach.com, $104 d). The Commodore features rooms with balconies facing the beach, a large pool with a welcoming cascading fountain, and several complimentary services, including Wi-Fi access, continental breakfast, coffee, and juice.

Corporate chain hotels are nearly outnumbered by independent establishments on Seawall, but some chains have competitive rates and reliable service, including **La Quinta East Beach** (1402 Seawall Blvd., 409/763-1224, www.lq.com, $149 d), featuring an outdoor pool, free continental breakfast, and internet access. The accommodations aren't luxurious, but there's something appealing about the comfy beach-town vibe and the ocean view outside your door. Farther down the island is **Red Roof Inn Beachfront Palms Hotel** (5914 Seawall Blvd., 409/740-1261, www.redroof.com, $177 d), offering a free continental breakfast, free Wi-Fi, and free cappuccino and hot chocolate.

Drop a little more cash at the remarkable ★ **Hotel Galvez** (2024 Seawall Blvd., 409/765-7721, www.hotelgalvez.com, $199 d). Known as the "Queen of the Gulf" when it opened in 1911, the Galvez is stunning in its Victorian elegance. Luxurious amenities include a pool with a swim-up bar, a heated saline outdoor pool, courtesy bikes and helmets, marble baths, free Wi-Fi, and an impressive spa and workout facility. Be sure to enjoy an incredible seafood meal at the on-site restaurant and have a cocktail at the classy lobby bar. Head downstairs for a history lesson—the walls are lined with stunning historic photos and informative exhibits about the Galvez's (and Galveston's) impressive cultural heritage.

Not nearly as historic yet conveniently located adjacent to the fun-filled Moody Gardens is the fancy **Moody Gardens Hotel** (7 Hope Blvd., 888/388-8484, www.moodygardenshotel.com, $249 d). After a day of exploring cultural attractions in the adjacent pyramids, unwind at the recently upgraded hotel with free Wi-Fi, plush bathrobes, and quality linens. Other amenities include an outdoor heated swimming pool with a jetted tub and a swim-up bar, an indoor lap pool, a full-service spa and salon, a 24-hour fitness center, an outdoor jogging track and sand volleyball courts, and a free weekend shuttle service to the Strand district.

Stylish **Hilton Galveston Island Resort** (5400 Seawall Blvd., 409/744-5000, www.galvestonhilton.com, $249 d), features large rooms with plush robes, free Wi-Fi, gulf-view rooms with private balconies, a tropically landscaped pool with a swim-up bar, and a fitness center.

Strand Area

If you'd rather be within walking distance of shopping than seashells, the exquisite Italianate-style ★ **Tremont House** (2300 Ship's Mechanic Row, 409/763-0300, www.wyndham.com, $269 d) is in the heart of the Strand historic district. The Tremont transports guests to Galveston's heyday as the "Wall Street of the South." Notice the lofty 14-foot (4.3-m) ceilings and incredibly tall windows. Wrought-iron beds, marble baths, antique furnishings, and a stylish black-and-white color scheme add to the elegant environment. Modern touches include free Wi-Fi and streaming TV.

Just down the street is the **Harbor House** (28 Pier 21, 409/763-3321, www.harborhousepier21.com, $269 d), fancy in a different way. It's not historic but offers an amazing vantage point of the busy harbor and bustling marina. One of the better seafood restaurants in town, Willie G's, is across the street, and the hotel provides free passes to a nearby fitness center. Amenities include free Wi-Fi and a free continental breakfast.

Bed-and-Breakfasts

With so many impressive historic structures, Galveston is an ideal place to stay in a B&B.

A popular and affordable option is **Avenue O Bed and Breakfast** (2323 Ave. O, 409/457-4255, www.avenueo.com, from $129), just a few blocks from the beach. This 1923 Mediterranean-style home is on a sizable property surrounded by tropical foliage. Breakfasts are hearty, and snacks are available throughout the day. Avenue O provides bikes for island excursions.

Ranked as Galveston's most popular bed and breakfast is the magnificent ★ **Lasker Inn** (1019 16th St., 409/497-4318, www.laskerinn.com, from $239). In one of Galveston's celebrated historic residential districts, the 1870 home originally served as a refuge for homeless children after the 1900 storm. Hospitality endures at the Lasker, where guests enjoy top-notch service and accommodations, including luxury bedding, elegant furnishings, and exquisite breakfasts featuring inventive egg dishes, fresh fruit, and high-quality coffee.

One of the island's newest B&B options is the classy **Carr Mansion** (1103 33rd St., 409/497-4740, www.carrmansion.com, from $289), a beautifully restored 19th-century Greek Revival home 10 blocks from the Seawall beaches. The property is rich with history, and the mansion hosts a complimentary happy hour every day, including two drinks and an appetizer.

Camping

In an RV or tent, **Galveston Island State Park** (14901 FM 3005, 409/737-1222, www. tpwd.state.tx.us, $7 over age 12, camping $15-25) is on the west end of Galveston Island, 10 miles (16 km) from town, with 140 campsites with electricity and water hookups and 10 screened camping shelters. Park facilities include 4 miles (6.4 km) of hike and bike trails, an interpretive center and nature trail, a concrete boat ramp, a fish-cleaning shelter, restrooms with showers, picnic sites, and Wi-Fi access.

The park is a great place for swimming, hiking, bird-watching, and mountain biking, with 2,000 acres of natural beauty along the Gulf Coast. Educational tours of the coastline's native plants and animals are available by appointment. You'll encounter trout, redfish, croaker, and flounder as well as tropical birds, ducks, marsh rabbits, and armadillos.

Less scenic yet more centrally located is the **Bayou Shores RV Resort** (6310 Heards Lane, 409/744-2837). Just off the causeway, the RV park offers standard hookups as well as a fishing pier and exercise facility.

INFORMATION AND SERVICES

The **Galveston Island Convention and Visitors Bureau** (2328 Broadway Ave., 409/797-5144, daily 9am-5pm, www. galveston.com) is a tremendous resource offering brochures and maps with friendly and remarkably helpful staff to answer questions. The website is information-packed and user-friendly. Contact the **Galveston Historical Foundation** (2228 Broadway, 409/765-7834, www.galvestonhistory.org) for information about the island's impressive historic attractions.

GETTING THERE AND AROUND

The only way to get to Galveston is via I-45. From Houston it takes about an hour, depending on the traffic. Once you reach the island, the only option is to turn onto Highway 87, which becomes Broadway Avenue.

Brazosport Area

Brazosport isn't a town name but a collection of eight Brazoria County communities southwest of Galveston, an unassuming mix of lightly developed beachfront and petrochemical plants. It's not as bad as it sounds—the beaches are pleasantly uncrowded most days, and the factories are beyond view from the shore. For the record, the Brazosport communities are Clute, Freeport, Jones Creek, Lake Jackson, Oyster Creek, Quintana Beach, Richwood, and Surfside Beach.

The state's earliest European explorers landed on nearby beaches 500 years ago, and Stephen F. Austin's first colony settled along the rich bottomlands of the Brazos, Colorado, and San Bernard Rivers in the early 19th century. The venerable Texas term "Old Three Hundred" refers to the 300 settlers who received land grants for Austin's first colony, where each family received up to 4,000 acres of fertile farm and ranch property in the area.

The massive Gulf Intracoastal Waterway carves a path along the coastal lowlands. This commercial boating canal, constructed in the 1940s, is the most valuable waterway in the country, transporting as much tonnage annually as the Panama Canal. The protected waterway stretches 1,000 miles (1,600 km) from Brownsville to Florida.

Visitors to the Brazosport region enjoy the small-town specialty and antiques shops, beach home rentals, and casual ocean-based recreation. Drive, walk, or swim along the 21-mile (34-km) stretch of beach or watch the seagulls and ocean barges lazily glide by. Other popular recreational activities include fresh- and saltwater fishing, boating, crabbing, and surfing.

SIGHTS

For a destination comprising several communities, the Brazosport Area offers an intriguing mix of cultural attractions. Fortunately, the communities are within a 20-minute drive of each other, so getting from one place to another takes the same amount of time as it does in a big city, just without the traffic or stoplights.

The Texas Historical Commission's Varner-Hogg Plantation

Lake Jackson Area Museums

A must-see attraction in the Brazosport Area is the spectacular **Sea Center Texas** (300 Medical Dr., Lake Jackson, 979/292-0100, www.tpwd.state.tx.us, Tues.-Sat. 9am-4pm, Sun. 1pm-4pm, free), combining several aquariums, an education center, and a fish hatchery along with an outdoor wetland exhibit and a kids fishing pond. The education center's main exhibit is a 50,000-gallon aquarium containing Gulf of Mexico marine animals such as nurse sharks, Atlantic spadefish, red drum, gray snapper, and an enormous moray eel. Other large aquariums house tropical species found in area salt marshes, coastal bays, jetties, and artificial and coral reefs. Kids will love the "touch pool," where they can handle several varieties of crabs, snails, and anemones.

Outside, the wetland exhibit is accessible by a long boardwalk over marsh areas. Families can bring a nature checklist and activity book to identify species, including green tree frogs, turtles, and a variety of birds. The adjacent hatchery has the capacity to produce 20 million spotted sea trout and red drum fingerlings each year for release into Texas coastal waters. Tours are available by advance reservation only.

Culture converges at **The Center for the Arts & Sciences** (400 College Blvd., Clute, 979/265-7661, www.bcfas.org, Tues.-Sat. 10am-4pm, Sun. 2pm-5pm, free), an all-inclusive facility home to the Brazosport Art League, the Brazosport Museum of Natural Science, the Center Stages Theater, and the Brazosport Planetarium. With so many cultural activities sharing space under one roof, you'll find an array of attractions, including a colossal collection of seashells, an art gallery and studio, and a theater staging regional productions. Most impressive is the natural science museum, containing wildlife, fossils, and an aquarium. Check out the exhibit featuring the lightning whelk (Texas's state shell) and the planetarium, which offers public viewings and previously served as a training facility for astronauts from NASA's nearby Johnson Space Center.

Varner-Hogg Plantation

Strolling beneath outstretched oaks provides a sense of the bygone world of Southern heritage at **Varner-Hogg Plantation** (1702 N. 13th St., West Columbia, 979/345-4656, www.visitvarnerhoggplantation.com, Tues.-Sun. 9am-5pm, $7 adults, $6 students). There's an undeniable charm to the lush grounds and distinguished historic buildings, occupied for most of the 1900s by the larger-than-life Hogg family, including the unfortunately named Miss Ima Hogg.

Owned by the Texas Historical Commission, the site showcases the Hogg family's remarkable 19th-century furnishings acquired from profits associated with the tremendous oil reserves discovered in the 1920s, which at one point brought in nearly $40,000 daily. Recent efforts have turned toward the era of Columbus Patton, the plantation's second owner after namesake Martin Varner. During insightful tours of the historic plantation home, knowledgeable guides educate visitors about the legacies of the three families connected to the property: Varner, Patton, and Hogg.

Brazoria National Wildlife Refuge

The protected habitats of the sizable **Brazoria National Wildlife Refuge** (24907 FM 2004, Angleton, 979/964-4011, www.fws.gov, Mon.-Fri. 9am-5pm) host 200 species of birds, one of the highest counts in the nation. In winter more than 100,000 snow geese, Canadian geese, teal, ducks, and sandhill cranes fill the numerous ponds and sloughs. In summer you'll find herons, egrets, white ibis, spoonbills, seaside sparrows, and scissor-tailed flycatchers. Alligators occupy the refuge year-round on Big Slough and in ponds. Look for their trails through the mud and "gator holes" in drier months.

San Bernard National Wildlife Refuge

The other major refuge in the Brazosport Area is **San Bernard National Wildlife Refuge** (6801 County Rd. 306, Brazoria, 979/849-6062, www.fws.gov, Mon.-Fri. 9am-5pm), a 24,000-acre protected area for snow geese, warblers, herons, egrets, ibis, gulls, and terns. Most of the refuge is closed to the public, but the accessible 3-mile (4.8-km) car tour and several miles of hiking trails offer access to high-quality wildlife viewing.

BEACHES

The words "Brazosport Area beaches" don't always prompt excitement or envy. These low-profile beaches can get crowded on summer weekends, but they're not major destinations. At Surfside and Bryan, the beachcombers' bodies aren't designed for a *Sports Illustrated* cover, and the vibe is easy and breezy.

Surfside Beach

If you don't mind a petrochemical plant just 1 mile (1.6 km) away (fortunately not dominating the view), **Surfside Beach** (979/233-1531, www.surfsidetx.org) is a delightful getaway for low-key recreation. Most people here are Houston residents looking for a respite from the Galveston crowds. Popular activities include fishing, swimming, sailing, camping, and shell collecting. For information about the village of Surfside Beach, including restaurants, shops, and lodgings, call or visit the website.

Bryan Beach

Near the community of Freeport is **Bryan Beach,** another casual and scenic stretch of sand. Grab a bucket for sand dollar collecting, a pole for shallow surf fishing, or a towel and sunscreen for sunbathing. Primitive campsites are available nearby. To reach the beach from Freeport, travel 2 miles (3.2 km) southwest of town on FM 1495, then 3 miles (4.8 km) south on Gulf Beach Road.

RECREATION

Popular activities in the Brazosport Area are swimming and birding. Fishing is one of the top draws, and kayaking and canoeing are emerging as viable options.

Fishing

Brazosport offers a multitude of facilities for fishing inshore or at sea. There are plenty of jetties, piers, and beaches where you can cast a line for speckled trout, flounder, redfish, sheepshead, and gafftopsail. Nearby marinas and beachside shacks sell tackle and bait. For deep-sea fishing, hire a charter boats to take you out farther for big-time catches, including snapper, marlin, king mackerel, and sailfish. A reputable outfit is **Johnston's Sportfishing** (979/233-8513).

A popular place for fishing, camping, and lounging is **Quintana Beach County Park** (979/233-1461, www.brazoriacountytx.gov), on a picturesque barrier island near Freeport. The park's multilevel fishing pier is a favorite among anglers, and the day-use facilities include shaded pavilions, restrooms, showers, and the historic Coveney House, containing a museum and natural history display. Camping sites ($15-27) include full hookups, showers, and laundry facilities. From Freeport, take FM 1495 south 2 miles (3.2 km) to County Road 723, then east 3 miles (4.8 km) to the park entrance.

Paddling

For low-impact coastal kayaking or canoeing, the **Christmas Bay Paddling Trail** (515 Amigo Lane, Freeport, 979/233-5159, www.tpwd.state.tx.us) is 19 miles (31 km) long, with a 4-mile (6.4-km) option. Known for fishing and birding opportunities, the trail also has extensive oyster reefs and a salt marsh.

Explore the **Brazos River Trail Gulf Prairie Run** via kayak. Part of a 125-mile (200-km) system stretching upriver to Houston, the water trail winds through the dense bottomlands, towering trees, and palmetto thickets. Paddlers can experience a wide variety of wildlife species and migrating birds. Launch points in the Brazosport Area are Brazos River County Park in Angleton and Wilderness Park in Lake Jackson.

FOOD

Surfside Beach has several good vacation-style eateries, and the best is **Red Snapper Inn** (402 Bluewater Hwy., 979/239-3226, www.redsnapperinn.com, Mon.-Fri. 11am-2pm and 5pm-9pm, Sat.-Sun. 11am-9pm, $10-28), a quality surf-and-turf restaurant best known for grilled boneless flounder stuffed with crabmeat dressing, the fried soft-shell crabs with rémoulade sauce, bacon-wrapped oysters, and sautéed garlic shrimp. Turf-wise, most diners opt for the spaghetti and char-broiled Greek-style meatballs or the classic chicken-fried steak.

For a good meal with a great view, head to **Seahorse Bar & Grill** (310 Ocean Ave., 979/239-2233, daily 8am-9pm, $7-15). The Seahorse has the best deck on the beach, featuring dozens of tables overlooking the surf and sand. Enjoy a cold beer and hearty burger on the porch.

Just around the corner, you can't miss **Kitty's Purple Cow** (323 Ocean Ave., 979/233-9161, Mon.-Fri. 10am-8:30pm, Sat.-Sun. 7:30am-8:30pm, $6-12). The food isn't quite as attention-grabbing as the restaurant's facade, a distractingly purple building just a block off the beach. Kitty's specializes in tasty meaty burgers and boiled shrimp on the "app-moo-tizers" menu. Breakfast options include hearty portions of biscuits and gravy and standard egg dishes.

Any beach town worth its weight in sand dollars has a place where locals loiter. Here it's the low-key **Jetty Shack** (412 Parkview St., 979/233-5300, daily 11am-11:30pm, $7-16), a beachside dive offering a tasty Angus burger, plenty of fried food, grilled cheese, and cold beer.

ACCOMMODATIONS

The Brazosport Area is overrun with local lodging options, with just a few chain hotel signs in sight. Independently owned hotels are the norm, and many travelers rent a beach house or cabin for the weekend.

Hotels

Clean, comfy, and within walking distance of the beach is the **Ocean Village Hotel** (310 Ocean Village Dr., Surfside Beach, 979/239-1213, www.oceanvillagehotel.com, from $119). This nice newish spot offers several amenities not found at other accommodations in the area: direct beach access and an attached restaurant and bar, the Sea Horse Grill. The hotel offers ocean-view rooms with large private decks, free Wi-Fi, pet-friendly rooms, and extended-stay suites with kitchens.

More casual and representative of the many sun-bleached and slightly shabby beach hotels is **Surfside Motel** (330 Coral Court, Surfside Beach, 979/233-4948, www.surfsidemotel.biz, $69-129). The motel offers kitchenette units with two queen beds, one twin, and a full kitchen, or two-room suites with one queen, a pullout bed, a small fridge, and a microwave. Check with the front desk if you need beach towels, board games, or horseshoes.

If slightly shabby isn't your thing, you'll have to venture 4 miles (6.4 km) off the coast to Clute for the chain hotels. One of the better options is **La Quinta** (1126 Hwy. 332 W., Clute, 979/265-7461, www.lq.com, $59 d), featuring free Wi-Fi, free continental breakfast, and an outdoor pool. A nicer choice is **Holiday Inn Express** (1117 Hwy. 332 W., Clute, 979/266-8746, www.hiexpress.com, $129 d), offering free Wi-Fi, a workout facility, and free continental breakfast.

Beach Home Rentals

Hundreds of rooms are available in cabins and beach homes along the gulf in the Brazosport Area. The best way to find a place that fits your specific needs regarding pets, kids, and beach access is to contact a rental locating service. Two of the more commendable outlets are **Beach Resort Services** (800/382-9283, www.beachresortservices.com) and **Brannan Resort Rentals, Inc.** (979/233-1812, www.brri.com). For a comprehensive list of companies, visit www.visitbrazosport. com and www.surfsidetx.org.

Camping

Families and RVers return to **Quintana Beach County Park** (979/233-1461, www. brazoriacountytx.gov, $15-27), featuring 56 paved and level camping sites, full hookups, primitive tent sites, and a bathhouse with restrooms, showers, and laundry facilities. Cabins ($135-160, depending on the season), complete with TVs, microwaves, kitchenettes, and charming wooden detailing, are also for rent.

A popular option for anglers is **Surfside Beach RV Park** (102 Fort Velesco Dr., 979/233-6919, www.surfsidebeachrv.com, $25-30), offering full-hookup RV sites, free parking for fishing boats, on-site laundry, and free Wi-Fi access.

INFORMATION AND SERVICES

The **Brazosport Convention and Visitors Council** (main office 300 Abner Jackson Pkwy., Lake Jackson, 979/285-2501 or 888/477-2505, www.brazosport.org, Mon.-Fri. 9am-5pm) provides details on area attractions, accommodations, and restaurants as well as brochures and maps.

GETTING THERE

From Houston, take Highway 288 south for about 45 minutes to Lake Jackson. From there, take Highway 332 east for 15 minutes to reach the beach.

Corpus Christi

Corpus Christi (population 326,554) is the largest city on Texas's Gulf Coast and one of the most popular destinations in the state for seaside fishing, sailing, swimming, and windsurfing.

The city's precipitous history saw drought and various wars preventing settlement from taking hold until the mid-1800s, when a trading post was established and a small village developed that eventually became known as Corpus Christi, "the Body of Christ." Just when the town started growing, a yellow fever epidemic decimated the population, and for decades it lacked a deepwater port.

In 1916 and 1919, torrential storms destroyed portions of the city, erasing grand hotels and palatial homes. As a result, the "Sparkling City by the Bay" can appear historically lackluster, with few significant structures reflecting its heritage. Historic homes and churches that escaped the hurricanes and wrecking ball exist in downtown neighborhoods. By the middle of the 20th century, Corpus, as it's known, became a petroleum shipping center. Also contributing to the economy were military bases and six petroleum refineries making use of the 1,500 oil wells in the area.

Despite its population, Corpus retains the feel of a small city, albeit with remarkable museums and top-notch seafood restaurants. Mild year-round temperatures and the inviting tropical climate draw visitors from across the country.

SIGHTS
★ Texas State Aquarium

The magnificent **Texas State Aquarium** (2710 N. Shoreline Blvd., 361/881-1200, www. texasstateaquarium.org, Mon.-Sat. 9am-5pm, Sun. 10am-5pm, $37 adults, $35 seniors, $27 ages 3-12) offers a quick break from the beach with the region's fascinating natural resources. The layout is clever, leading visitors into Texas's marine world at sea level with exhibits containing birds, alligators, and stingrays, and proceeding to explore the Gulf of Mexico at sequentially deeper levels.

Primary exhibits showcase menacing sharks, a 350-pound grouper, and hundreds

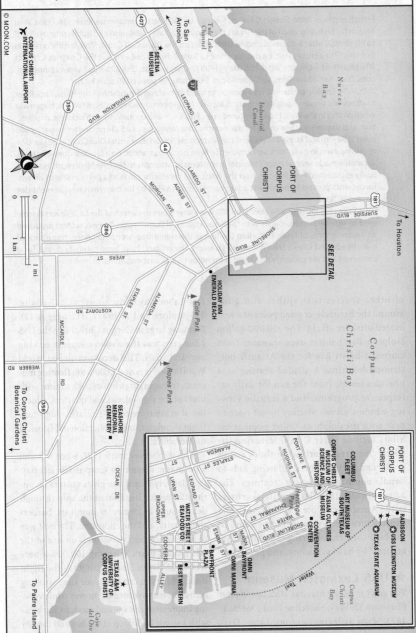

Corpus Christi

© MOON.COM

To San Antonio

Tule Lake Channel

Nueces Bay

CORPUS CHRISTI INTERNATIONAL AIRPORT

★ SELENA MUSEUM

LEOPARD ST

NAVIGATION BLVD

Industrial Canal

PORT OF CORPUS CHRISTI

To Houston

LAREDO ST

AGNES ST

MORGAN AVE

SURFSIDE BLVD

SHORELINE BLVD

SEE DETAIL

AYERS ST

HOLIDAY INN EMERALD BEACH

Cole Park

Corpus Christi Bay

KOSTORYZ RD

STAPLES ST

ALAMEDA ST

MCARDLE RD

WEBBER RD

Ropes Park

SEASHORE MEMORIAL CEMETERY

To Corpus Christi Botanical Gardens

OCEAN DR

TEXAS A&M UNIVERSITY OF CORPUS CHRISTI ★★

To Padre Island

Cayo del Oso

0   1 mi
0   1 km

Detail

ALAMEDA
STAPLES ST
HUGHES ST
PORT AVE E

CORPUS CHRISTI MUSEUM OF SCIENCE AND HISTORY ★

COLUMBUS FLEET

ART MUSEUM OF SOUTH TEXAS ★

PORT OF CORPUS CHRISTI

RADISSON
USS LEXINGTON MUSEUM
TEXAS STATE AQUARIUM ★

Heritage Park

CHAPARRAL ST

ASIAN CULTURES MUSEUM ★

CONVENTION CENTER

Corpus Christi Bay

LEOPARD ST

WATER ST

SHORELINE BLVD

UPPER BROADWAY

WATER STREET SEAFOOD CO. ■

STARR ST

MANN ST

BAYFRONT PLAZA ■

OMNI BAYFRONT
OMNI MARINA ●

LIPAN ST

BEST WESTERN ●

COOPERS ST

COOPERS ALLEY

Water Taxi

La Salle's Legacy

French explorer René-Robert Cavelier, Sieur de La Salle, left an enormous legacy in Texas. Well known for his exploration of the Great Lakes region, La Salle's ambition and hubris ultimately led to his demise after a doomed colonization effort on the Texas Gulf Coast. Many artifacts remain from his 17th-century visit, on display in the La Salle Odyssey collection at the **Corpus Christi Museum of Science and History** (1900 N. Chaparral St., 361/826-4667, www.ccmuseum.com, Tues.-Sat. 10am-5pm, Sun. noon-5pm, $12 adults, $9 seniors, $9 ages 3-12).

In 1684, La Salle embarked on a mission to build forts along the mouth of the Mississippi River to attack and occupy Spanish territory in Mexico. His expedition was a series of failures, beginning when pirates in the West Indies captured one of his ships and continuing with sickness, misdirection, and shipwrecks. Searching for the mouth of the Mississippi, La Salle missed his target by 500 miles (800 km) and landed at present-day Matagorda Bay on the central Gulf Coast of Texas. One of his ships was lost offshore, and another, La Belle, became stranded on a sandbar during a storm.

La Salle made several more ultimately unsuccessful attempts to find the Mississippi. He eventually established Fort St. Louis near the coast, and his attempt to lead a party in search of reinforcements proved to be his last adventure—he was killed by his own men near present-day Navasota, Texas.

La Salle's legacy would be rekindled 300 years later when the wreck of the La Belle was discovered by marine archaeologists with the Texas Historical Commission. The excavation produced an amazing array of finds, including the hull of the ship, three bronze cannons, thousands of glass beads, and even a crew member's skeleton. The artifacts have been carefully cleaned and preserved and are currently displayed at numerous Gulf Coast museums.

of other species that slither and glide around the barnacle-crusted poles of a replicated offshore oil rig. The 350,000-gallon Dolphin Bay habitat uses seawater from Corpus Christi Bay for the Atlantic bottlenose dolphins. A shaded seating area provides respite from the sun for daily interpretive programs, and a lengthy viewing window allows visitors to get nose to nose with the dolphins. Other popular exhibits include Otter Creek, featuring the frisky creatures cavorting on slides and in pools, and Living Shores, allowing kids to handle nonthreatening sea creatures. The aquarium also includes terrestrial critters in the Amazon rainforest exhibit, with boa constrictors and poison dart frogs, and in the bird theater, featuring "flight performances" by hawks, falcons, and parrots.

★ USS Lexington Museum

You can't miss the massive **USS Lexington Museum** (2914 N. Shoreline Blvd., 361/888-4873, www.usslexington.com, Labor Day-Memorial Day daily 9am-5pm, Memorial Day-Labor Day daily 9am-6pm, $17 adults, $15 seniors and military, $12 ages 4-12). Looming large in Corpus Christi Bay, the USS Lexington was the nation's longest-serving aircraft carrier. This decommissioned World War II vessel is now a 33,000-ton floating museum, transporting visitors back in time with tours of the ship's decks and quarters, educational exhibits, restored aircraft, a high-tech flight simulator, and a collection of historical memorabilia.

The ship served until 1991, when it found a permanent home in Corpus Christi Bay. Its relatively recent use gives visitors an authentic feel for life aboard the ship through details such as computer monitors, barbershop chairs, and the chow line. The best way to experience the Lexington is on one of the self-guided tours, covering 100,000 square feet on 11 decks. The highlight is the flight deck, where you can take your time strolling across the massive former runway while viewing impressive vintage and modern warbirds with a scenic backdrop of the bay and the city skyline.

Corpus Christi Museum of Science and History

To get a better sense of the area's colorful past, drop by the **Corpus Christi Museum of Science and History** (1900 N. Chaparral St., 361/826-4667, www.ccmuseum.com, Tues.-Sat. 10am-5pm, Sun. noon-5pm, $12 adults, $9 seniors, $9 ages 3-12), with myriad educational exhibits emphasizing the Gulf Coast's nature and culture. Noteworthy exhibits are maritime-related, including an interactive shipwreck display containing artifacts from three Spanish treasure ships that ran aground on Padre Island in 1554, an exhibit featuring artifacts related to French explorer René-Robert Cavelier, Sieur de La Salle's ill-fated *La Belle* shipwreck, and the Children's Wharf, a bustling learning area for youngsters. The remainder of the museum is a collection of 28,000 shells, Native American crafts, and bird and reptile eggs representing the history and culture of South Texas.

Heritage Park

Just down the street from the science museum is the city's **Heritage Park** (1581 N. Chaparral St., 361/826-3414, www.cctexas.com). These 12 restored Victorian-era historic homes were moved to the city's cultural area to protect them from demolition and to showcase the city's past. The centerpiece is the Cultural Center's Galván House, open for free tours by appointment. Otherwise, visitors can stroll among the homes to admire the different eras of coastal architecture.

Asian Cultures Museum

Also in the city's cultural district is the **Texas State Museum of Asian Cultures** (1809 N. Chaparral St., 361/882-2641, www.texasasianculturesmuseum.org, Tues.-Sat. noon-5pm, $6 adults, $5 students, $3 under age 13), offering an interesting array of objects and artwork from across the Pacific. What started as a local resident's personal collection of cultural objects has evolved into a full museum containing thousands of items representing a dozen Asian countries. Billie Trimble Chandler spent decades as a teacher and art collector in Asia, and she brought items back to share with Corpus residents and to educate them about faraway lands. Since then, the museum has grown to include clothing, furniture, paintings, dolls, statues, and other art objects from Japan, Korea, China, the Philippines, and Taiwan. The museum features international traveling exhibits and offers educational classes.

USS *Lexington*

Selena Museum

Latin-music fans often make a pilgrimage to the Selena Museum (5410 Leopard St., 361/289-9013, Mon.-Fri. 10am-4pm, $4). It's not easy to find—the museum is downtown off I-37 in a warehouse-type building with no sign (look for the painted mural of Selena on the outside). It was created by Corpus resident Abraham Quintanilla to honor the memory of his daughter, the famous Tejana singer who was killed by the president of her fan club in 1995. The museum showcases many of Selena's personal memorabilia, including the outfits and dresses she designed and wore at concerts, her red Porsche, pencil sketches, her prized egg collection, and letters of sympathy from fans across the world.

Art Museum of South Texas

Culture converges at the Art Museum of South Texas (1902 N. Shoreline Blvd., 361/825-3500, www.stia.org, Tues.-Sat. 10am-5pm, Sun. 1pm-5pm, $8 adults, $6 seniors and military, $4 over age 11). The three-story building is unmistakable, with bright white concrete walls and 13 rooftop pyramids overlooking the bay. Inside are galleries showcasing the museum's 1,300 artworks, primarily paintings and sculpture representing the Americas with a focus on Texas, Mexico, and the Southwest. The museum also contains an interactive kids playroom, classrooms, studios, a gift shop, and an auditorium.

Corpus Christi Botanical Gardens and Nature Center

To appreciate the area's natural beauty beyond the beach, the Corpus Christi Botanical Gardens and Nature Center (8545 S. Staples St., 361/852-2100, www.stxbot.org, daily 9am-6pm, $9 adults, $7 seniors and military, $4 ages 5-12) has exotic gardens and perfectly landscaped lawns, taking full advantage of the tropical climate to produce vibrant colors and lush landscapes. One of the center's showpieces is the Rose Garden, featuring 300 roses, a large pavilion, and a beautiful fountain. Other noteworthy areas

are the hummingbird garden, the orchid garden with 2,500 flowering plants, and the hibiscus garden.

BEACHES
City Beaches on the Bay

If you're staying downtown and need a quick beach fix, go to Corpus Christi Beach (just north of the USS Lexington, 361/880-3480). It's not quite picturesque, and the sand is coarse, but it's great for a leisurely stroll or swim with a pleasant view of Corpus Christi Bay. Local families are playing in the sand and flying kites, and there are several spots offering rinse-off showers, restrooms, and small cabana huts with picnic tables. Much smaller in size yet within walking distance of downtown hotels is Magee Beach (Shoreline Blvd. at Park St., 361/880-3461). This 250-yard (230-m) stretch of sand on the bay isn't designed for shell collecting, but it's a good place to get your feet wet without worrying about the undertow found on larger ocean beaches. Showers and restrooms are on the north end of the beach.

RECREATION
Paddling

Kayakers are increasingly flocking to Corpus Christi for saltwater kayaking and bay paddling. Both offer beginners and experienced paddlers a fun way to spend a few hours on the water. Saltwater kayaking, a.k.a. sea kayaking, is typically more difficult, since it can involve choppy and unpredictable conditions. It's often more fun, and the waves don't tend to reach intimidating heights. Sea routes can also be longer and less restricted.

Bay paddling is ideal for beginning kayakers, offering calmer conditions and shorter trail options. A good starting point is the Mustang Island State Park Paddling Trail (www.tpwd.state.tx.us), with several routes, including the 5-mile (8-km) Shamrock Loop to the 8.5-mile (13.7-km) North Trail, that meander through coves and marshes. The park's 7-mile (11.3-km) Ashum Trail traces the Corpus Christi Bay shoreline, offering quality birding and fishing.

Rental and tour options are available at **Coastal Bend Kayak** (1125 S. Commercial St., Aransas Pass, 361/557-7003, www.coastalbendkayaking.com).

Fishing

Corpus is a major destination for anglers, and there are plenty of locations and services to accommodate them. You'll see poles anchored in the sand at city beaches, including Corpus Christi Beach, where fishers gather at the **Nueces Bay Pier** at the end of Hull Street. Lines are also cast from the massive concrete downtown piers (known locally as T-heads), several spots along the seawall, and at lighted breakwater jetties. Another popular spot is **Bob Hall Pier** (15820 Park Rd. 22, 361/949-0499) at Padre Balli Park on North Padre Island. Its prime location and abundance of species (tarpon, mackerel, redfish, and even shark) have drawn anglers to this venerable productive spot since the 1950s.

To get out on the sea for big-game fishing, a charter or rental company can set you up with all the gear, guides, and advice. Deep-sea boats are available to troll for Gulf species such as marlin, sailfish, tuna, and kingfish. Reputable companies include **C&T Bay Charters** (1031 Whispering Sands, Port Aransas, 888/227-9172, www.ctbaycharters.com) and **Deep Sea Headquarters** (416 W. Cotter Ave., Port Aransas, 361/749-5597, www.deepseaheadquarters.com), providing private excursions to anglers of all ages and skill levels.

Windsurfing

Thanks to its constant easy breeze, averaging 15-20 mph (24-32 km/h), Corpus is a mecca for windsurfers. Some try their sails on the bay at city locales like **Cole Park** (near the 2000 block of Ocean Dr., restrooms available), but most windsurfers head to North Padre Island, particularly **Bird Island Basin** at the Padre Island National Seashore. This half-mile stretch of beach is internationally recognized as one of the top windsurfing sites on the U.S. mainland. If you've never grabbed hold of a sail, this is the best place to learn, since there's always a breeze. To set yourself up with all the gear, contact **Worldwinds Windsurfing** (11493 S. Padre Island Dr., 361/949-7472, www.worldwinds.net) or **Wind & Wave Water Sports** (10721 S. Padre Island Dr., 361/937-9283, www.windandwave.net).

Corpus Christi, a popular destination for windsurfers

Hiking and Biking

Recreational opportunities in Corpus are almost exclusively water-based. With so many options available in the bay and the gulf, the development of organized land-based trails for hiking and biking has not been a priority for governments or private organizations.

The primary hiking and biking option is the Bay Trail (www.ccparkandrec.com), an 8-mile (12.9-km) route hugging the bay. It's extremely scenic, offering views of downtown buildings and bird habitats. Another option is the hike and bike trail on the campus of Texas A&M Corpus Christi (www.tamucc.edu). Although students and faculty are the primary users of the 3-mile (4.8-km) route, it's open to the public and offers a well-lit paved path for safety.

Horseback Riding

Have you ever wanted to ride a horse on the beach, with the waves crashing at your steed's feet as the ocean breeze whips through your hair? Horses on the Beach (16562 S. Padre Island Dr., 361/949-4944, several rides daily, reservations required), just north of Padre Island National Seashore, has horses for first-timers, children, and experienced riders, and the stable owners also handle lessons. You're welcome to walk, trot, or ride your horse into the surf.

ENTERTAINMENT AND EVENTS

Bars and Clubs

Many visitors choose to sip their cocktails on the beach or in the hotel bar, but other options exist for live music and to mingle with the locals. The best place to soak up the scene without feeling like an outsider is the downtown Executive Surf Club (309 N. Water St., 361/884-7873, www.executivesurfclub.com). Adjacent to the Water Street Seafood Co., the Surf Club's decor reflects its name, with vintage surfboards on the walls and refurbished as tables. The scene is lively yet casual, with live music most nights (mainly Texas rock and blues acts, often with a cover charge), more than 30 beers on tap, and a kitchen serving up tasty grub.

Another friendly spot is the more up-scale Republic of Texas Bar & Grill (900 N. Shoreline Blvd., 361/886-3515, www.omnihotels.com). On the 20th floor of the Omni Bayfront hotel, the Republic of Texas is dimly lit and heavily wooded in a welcoming way. The views of the bay and city are outstanding, the drinks are expertly made, and the pianist provides a perfect soundtrack. Grab a scotch, margarita, or draft beer and soak up the scenery.

With a younger and more boisterous local crowd, Rockit's Whiskey Bar & Saloon (709 N. Chaparral St., 361/884-7634, www.rockitscc.com) is on a formerly vibrant stretch of Chaparral Street in the heart of downtown. Rockit's is still thriving, and it's still all about the blues: Live bands from Corpus and across the state play nightly, and the place can get rocking when the bands get rolling. Check the website for a music schedule and cover charges.

Performing Arts

The grande dame of Corpus Christi's performing arts scene is Corpus Christi Ballet (1621 N. Mesquite St., 361/882-4588, www.corpuschristiballet.com), staging several ballets annually, including classics like *The Nutcracker* and children's fare such as *Cinderella*. Corpus Christi Ballet is a first-rate classical company.

One of the most popular classical venues in town is the Performing Arts Center at Texas A&M Corpus Christi (6300 Ocean Dr., 361/825-5700, www.pac.tamucc.edu). The $18 million facility is known for its excellent acoustics and amenities. Performers are mainly classical, with featured names from past years including pianist Van Cliburn, mezzo soprano Frederica von Stade, and violinists Itzhak Perlman and Joshua Bell.

Perhaps the most venerable performing arts organization in Corpus Christi is the Harbor Playhouse (1 Bayfront Park,

Save the Sea Turtles

Padre Island National Seashore is undertaking extensive efforts to protect an endearing creature that nests along its shoreline and glides in the gentle waves. The Kemp's ridley is the most endangered species of sea turtle, and it was nearly lost forever in the 1960s due to massive exploitation of its eggs and meat at its primary nesting beach in Mexico. The 16-mile (26-km) stretch of sand at nearby Playa de Rancho Nuevo in Tamaulipas, Mexico, was home to 40,000 Kemp's ridleys in 1947. Fewer than 5,000 currently nest each year.

Park officials incubate turtle eggs and release the little guys into the gulf each summer. The public is invited to view this fascinating natural event—for release dates and directions to the site, call the Hatchling Hotline (361/949-7163).

Named for Richard M. Kemp, an angler who submitted the first documented specimen in 1906, the Kemp's ridley has been making a slow resurgence thanks to the devoted scientists of the National Park Service, which operates the Padre Island National Seashore between Corpus Christi and South Padre.

KEEPING KEMP'S

To help save the turtle, the U.S. and Mexican governments have been working together to re-establish a nesting beach at Padre Island National Seashore, utilizing the theory that turtles will return to the beach where they were born to lay their own eggs. In 1978-1988 scientists collected more than 22,000 eggs at Rancho Nuevo and transported them in Padre Island sand to a lab at the national seashore for incubation. The hatchlings were released on the beach, where they then crawled to the surf with the hope they'd naturally imprinted with the location in their memories for future reference.

Biologists have attempted to gauge the turtles' successful rate of return by marking their shells and fins with identification tags and even GPS devices. Their efforts appear to be productive, since each year more turtles revisit their birthplace. In fact, nearly 60 percent of the species' eggs are now found on Padre Island, making it the most important Kemp's ridley nesting beach in the United States.

Visitors who see a live or dead turtle on the beach should immediately contact a park ranger or the seashore's turtle biologist (361/949-8173). Messing with these endangered turtles in any way is a felony, with fines up to $20,000. Many Kemp's ridleys have been identified and protected as a result of visitors' efforts, so perhaps your next stroll on the beach will yield a finding far more valuable than an intact sand dollar.

361/882-5500, www.harborplayhouse.com), a nonprofit community theater that traces its history to 1925. Corpus residents have spent a century enjoying the group's staging of classic musicals and plays such as *Annie*, *The Sound of Music*, and *A Christmas Carol*.

SHOPPING

Corpus has several standard malls, and vacationers looking for trinkets and T-shirts opt for the souvenir shops in Port Aransas. There are several places that offer quality clothing, jewelry, and beach gear, including Pilar Gallery (3814 S. Alameda St., 361/853-7171), a colorful shop with quality women's clothing,

tapestries, rugs, and imported jewelry and folk art from Mexico and around the globe.

Every beach town needs a good surf shop, and Corpus has several rad options. Hodads to heroes will find boards, surf wear, kayaks, skateboards, and surf and skate accessories at Wind & Wave Water Sports (10721 S. Padre Island Dr., 361/937-9283, www.windandwave. net) or Worldwinds Windsurfing (11493 S. Padre Island Dr., 361/949-7472, www. worldwinds.net).

FOOD

Seafood is the favored item for most Corpus Christi diners, and the variety of restaurants in the downtown area offers plenty of options. The city has a large Hispanic population, so you'll also find high-quality Tex-Mex restaurants.

Seafood

You'll catch the city's best seafood at ★ **Water Street Seafood Co.** (309 N. Water St., 361/882-8683, www.waterstmarketcc.com, daily 11am-11pm, $10-26). If you're in Corpus for more than a day, it's practically eat a meal at this legendary downtown locale or at its adjacent sister location, Water Street Oyster Bar. Water Street combines fresh seafood, Mexican influences, Cajun flavors, and Southern cooking. For first-timers, start with fresh catches and daily specials like blackened snapper and broiled flounder. The regular menu features in-demand items such as crab cakes served with spicy rémoulade and mango salsa; seafood jambalaya packed with shrimp, chicken, sausage, and crawfish tails in a creamy tomato sauce; and Southern-fried catfish stuffed with shrimp. For those in search of a simple seafood delight, order a double-size peel-and-eat shrimp plate accompanied by a hoppy pale ale draft.

Slightly more upscale and not quite as family-oriented is the next-door **Water Street Oyster Bar** (309 N. Water St., 361/881-9448, www.waterstmarketcc.com, Sun.-Thurs. 11am-11pm, Fri.-Sat. 11am-midnight, $13-29), a great spot to have a few cocktails and order some freshly shucked gulf oysters on the half shell. The menu is the same as the Seafood Co.'s, so the aforementioned recommendations apply, and you'll enjoy them in a more refined atmosphere. Two additional recommendations: Order your salad with the walnut-based tangy dressing, and save room for the hot chocolate brownie with ice cream. The freshest addition to Water Street's empire is the Sushi Room, featuring traditional rolls without as strong an emphasis on local sourcing.

One of the fanciest places in town for seafood and ocean views is the **Yardarm Restaurant** (4310 Ocean Dr., 361/855-8157, www.yardarmrestaurantcorpuschristi.com, Tues.-Sat. 5:30pm-9pm, $13-37). Modestly sized and cozy, it offers tantalizingly fresh seafood, including oysters, shrimp, a snappy snapper papillote, and thick juicy steaks. Due to its limited size and popularity, reservations are recommended.

On the opposite end of the sophistication scale is the consistently tasty yet way casual ★ **Snoopy's Pier** (13313 S. Padre Island Dr., 361/949-8815, www.snoopyspier.com, summer daily 11am-10pm, winter daily 11am-9pm, $9-25). If you want to eat like a local and soak up the laid-back beach life, this is the place to be. On the water just below the causeway, Snoopy's is ideal to grab a cold beer and a plate of fried or boiled shrimp. Watch the sun set as you enjoy the flaky goodness of fresh catches such as flounder or drum.

If you're staying on Corpus Christi Beach, you'll find two quality laid-back seafood restaurants within walking distance. **Pier 99** (2822 N. Shoreline Blvd., 361/887-0764, www.pier99restaurant.com, Sun.-Thurs. 11am-9pm, Fri.-Sat. 11am-10pm, $10-27) is a Corpus Christi stalwart on the beach across from the massive USS *Lexington*. The portions are nearly as big, particularly the combo plates overflowing with shrimp, crab legs, oysters, crawfish, and catfish. Order a bowl of fresh seafood gumbo. Mellow live music keeps the atmosphere spirited most nights, providing a perfect Margaritaville moment.

Not quite as aesthetically pleasing yet reliable in its good food is the misleadingly named **Blackbeard's on the Beach** (3117 E. Surfside Blvd., 361/884-1030, www.blackbeards.restaurant.com, Sun.-Thurs. 11am-10pm, Fri.-Sat. 11am-11pm, $9-24), across the street from the Radisson and a couple of blocks from the shore. This is a casual family-friendly place where you'll find a bar full of bric-a-brac and hearty helpings of fresh seafood and Tex-Mex specialties.

1: Snoopy's Pier seafood restaurant **2:** Dragonfly restaurant near Corpus Christi

American

Beach towns are populated with casual eateries, but a special occasion restaurant is **Republic of Texas Bar & Grill** (900 N. Shoreline Blvd., 361/886-3515, Mon.-Sat. 5:30pm-10:30pm, Sun. 5:30pm-9pm, $14-50). On the 20th floor of the Omni Bayfront, this restaurant serves upscale Texas fare in a refined environment with stunning views. Meat is the main event, in a range of options and methods of preparation. Can't-miss items include château steak with sautéed asparagus and broccoli, pork rib chops in an apple-ginger glaze, Texas crab cake with lobster and cognac sauce, and perfectly prepared venison, buffalo, and redfish.

Katz 21 Steak & Spirits (317 N. Mesquite St., 361/884-1221, www.katz21.com, Mon.-Thurs. 5pm-10pm, Fri.-Sat. 5pm-11pm, $14-44) is a popular traditional steak house specializing in prime grade-A quality cuts of beef as well as fresh seafood, veal, and lamb. Unlike many traditional steak houses, Katz's offers a lighter lunch menu with soups, salads, sandwiches, and pastas. Popular items include the prime rib served au jus with horseradish sauce, bone-in rib-eye, rack of lamb, and veal *piccata*. Reservations are encouraged.

Steak lovers should also consider **Niko's Steakhouse** (5409 Saratoga St., 361/992-2333, www.nikossteakhouse.com, Mon.-Sat. 11am-11:30pm, $19-44). Prime rib is a favorite, but the rib-eye and sirloin steaks are worthy considerations. Sides play second fiddle to the meat, but several notable options include the asparagus and Yukon potatoes.

Slightly more trendy is **Dragonfly** (14701 S. Padre Island Dr., 361/949-2224, www. dragonflycuracaoblues.com, Tues.-Fri. 4pm-9pm, Sat. 5pm-10pm, $10-29), offering a fresh take on seafood and other standard fare, along with an extensive and interesting tapas menu. Dragonfly's salmon features a wonderful curry seasoning and is accompanied by a tasty side of baby bok choy and carrots, while the cheesy lasagna manages to be hearty without being overly filling. Other menu highlights include the slightly spicy shrimp skewer and

tasty grilled tuna. Dragonfly doesn't have a kids menu, but they'll whip up a bowl of creamy mac and cheese on request.

Tourist-friendly **Executive Surf Club** (309 N. Water St., 361/884-7873, www. executivesurfclub.com, Mon.-Thurs. 11am-11pm, Fri.-Sat. 11am-midnight, $9-22) specializes in comfort food in a casual atmosphere. Grab a juicy cheeseburger and a Shiner Bock while you contemplate your next beach activity. Standard bar fare is the main draw here, and the Surf Club delivers fish-and-chips, fried shrimp, tortilla wraps, and chicken-fried steak, all served on tables fashioned from old surfboards. Stick around after dinner for some local hot blues and rock bands.

For a hearty breakfast or lunch with colorful local residents, head to **Hester's Café and Coffee Bar** (1714 S. Alameda St., 361/885-0558, www.hesterscafe.com, Mon.-Sat. 7am-3pm, $9-24), a reliable spot for semi-fancy comfort food. Hester's offers classics like eggs and hash browns with delectable additions like fresh avocado and thick-cut bacon. Popular lunch options include the stacked Laguna Club sandwich with melted cheese on top, hearty Victoria Pasta, and fresh salads.

Asian

Corpus has a long connection with Asia, reaching back a century to the days when shrimpers and rice farmers arrived in the developing coastal town. More recent are Thai, Chinese, and Japanese restaurants, and among the most popular is **Yalee's Asian Bistro** (5649 Saratoga Blvd., 361/993-9333, Mon.-Fri. 11am-9:30pm, Sat.-Sun. 11am-11pm, $9-22). The counter-service approach may lower expectations, but the food is top-notch, including spicy *ma po* tofu and flavorful standards like *kung pao* shrimp and General Tso chicken.

Sushi fans should head to **Aka Sushi** (5301 Everhart Rd., 361/851-9191, Mon.-Thurs. 11am-2pm and 5pm-10pm, Fri. 11:30am-2pm and 5pm-10:30pm, Sat. 5pm-10:30pm, $11-27), with classic tuna and shrimp rolls to more elaborate options such as a dragon roll and its off-menu variation known as an ecstasy roll. The seaweed salad is popular, and the sake selection is impressive.

Only a handful of restaurants represent Thai options. **Thai Spice** (523 N. Water St., 361/883-8884, www.thaispicecc.com, daily 11am-11pm, $10-24) has popular coconut curry options, served in actual coconuts. The flavorful curry is tempered by the sweetness of the coconut and accompanying fresh pineapple. Another notable option is the lemongrass soup, though it can be a bit spicy for some.

Not quite as authentic, a similarly high-quality option is **Vietnam Restaurant** (701 N. Water St., 361/853-2682, www.vietnamrestaurant.com, Mon.-Thurs. 11am-2pm and 5pm-9pm, Fri. 11am-2pm and 5pm-10pm, Sat. 5pm-10pm, $11-25), the place to go for amazing soups, including *pho* and surprisingly tasty catfish soup. Seafood and veggie dishes are also worth ordering.

Tex-Mex

Unlike its seafood restaurants, most of Corpus Christi's Mexican spots are not on the waterfront. **La Playa** (5017 Saratoga Blvd.; 7118 S. Padre Island Dr., 361/986-0089, www.laplaya. cc, Sun.-Mon. 11am-9pm, Tues.-Sat. 11am-10pm, $9-24) is the place to go for top-notch traditional Tex-Mex. Feast on chicken enchiladas in a tangy tomatillo sauce or savor the sizzling beef fajitas. You won't regret ordering the stuffed fried avocados. This being a seaside town, you can also order Tex-Mex-style dishes featuring fresh fish and gulf shrimp.

Offering some coastal flair to the Tex-Mex offerings is **La Costenita** (4217 Leopard St., 361/882-5340, Mon.-Sat. 5:30am-6pm, $9-19), a downtown eatery that's small in size yet huge on taste, particularly the shrimp dishes and traditional enchilada and taco plates. The chips are amazing and the homemade salsa is perfectly spicy. Make sure you arrive before 5:30pm.

Locals flock to **Kiko's** (5514 Everhart Rd., 361/991-1211, Mon.-Thurs. 6:30am-9pm,

Fri.-Sat. 6:30am-9pm, $9-24) for the specialty enchiladas with zesty ranchero sauce. You can't go wrong with most menu items, including the green chili burrito, guacamole salad, and tortilla soup. Sample all the restaurant has to offer with the Kiko's platter, offering a signature cheese enchilada, beef fajita tacos, and a crispy chalupa.

Classic taqueria **Solis Mexican Restaurant** (3122 Baldwin Blvd.; 5409 Leopard St., 361/882-5557, Mon.-Sat. 6am-9pm, Sun. 7am-3pm, $9-20) draws crowds for its tasty tacos and enchiladas, all prepared with fresh homemade tortillas. Try the stuffed breakfast tacos, served all day, and *licuados* (fruity Mexican drinks).

ACCOMMODATIONS

There's no shortage of lodging in Corpus, and most have decent views, easy access to the bay, and reasonable rates. Budget options are in the airport and greyhound racetrack area, but most leisure travelers stay by the sea. For a nice spot away from the city, consider a condo with nightly rates on alluring Mustang Island or North Padre Island, 10-15 miles (16-24 km) from downtown on the Gulf Coast.

$50-100

Room rates at the beach are more affordable farther down the shore. One of the better deals in town is the bare-bones **Budget Inn & Suites** (801 S. Shoreline Blvd., 888/493-2950, www.budgetinnandsuitescc.com, $79 d), within walking distance of Cole Park, a premier windsurfing spot. Amenities include free continental breakfast, free Wi-Fi, and an outdoor pool and sundeck. Closer to the action is **Knights Inn** (3615 Timon Blvd., 361/883-4411, www.knightsinn.com, $99 d), a couple of blocks off the bay and offering private balconies, several ocean-view rooms, free Wi-Fi, fridges, microwaves, and an outdoor pool.

The best deal in this range is the family-friendly **Quality Inn & Suites** (3202 Surfside Blvd., 361/883-7456, www.qualityinn.com, $99 d), thanks to its prime location on Corpus Christi Beach in the shadow of the USS

Lexington and Texas State Aquarium. The hotel features an outdoor beachside pool and hot tub, free continental breakfast, and rooms with microwaves and fridges.

$100-150

Farther up the road in location and price is **Days Inn** (4302 Surfside Blvd., 361/882-3297, www.daysinn.com, $109 d), a block off Corpus Christi Beach. Amenities include rooms with microwaves, fridges, and free Wi-Fi, along with a complimentary continental breakfast and an outdoor pool. Closer to downtown is the **Plaza Inn** (2021 N. Padre Island Dr., 361/289-8200, www.plazainnhotels.com, $109 d), offering free hot breakfast in the morning. The Plaza Inn also has an outdoor pool, free Wi-Fi, and is pet-friendly. Just off busy South Padre Island Drive is the **Hampton Inn** (5209 Blanche Moore Dr., 361/985-8395, www.hamptoninn.com, $109 d), with free internet access, complimentary breakfast, to-go breakfast bags on weekdays, an outdoor pool, and a fitness center.

Another good option in this price range is the **Holiday Inn Express** (5213 Oakhurst Dr., 361/857-7772, www.hiexpress.com, $139 d), with free Wi-Fi, a complimentary hot breakfast bar, and a fitness center with an indoor pool and whirlpool. A bit farther east is **Hilton Garden Inn** (6717 S. Padre Island Dr., 361/991-8200, www.hiltongardeninn.hilton. com, $139 d), providing a heated outdoor pool with a whirlpool, complimentary internet, a microwave and mini-fridge in each room, and flat-screen TVs.

Also downtown is the **Best Western Corpus Christi** (300 N. Shoreline Blvd., 361/883-5111, www.bestwestern.com, $145 d), offering rooms with private balconies and marina views, free Wi-Fi, microwaves, fridges, a free continental breakfast, and an outdoor pool and exercise facility. Farther from the bay is **Staybridge Suites** (5201 Oakhurst Dr., 361/857-7766, www.staybridgecc.com, $144 d). Features include free hot breakfast, a fitness center, a whirlpool, an outdoor pool, and free Wi-Fi.

The best choice directly on the beach is the ★ **Radisson** (3200 Surfside Blvd., 361/883-9700, www.radisson.com, $149 d). Step out the back doors and onto the sand of Corpus Christi Beach, a pleasant stretch of shoreline on the bay that hosts a large number of frolicking families, flotsam and jetsam, and the USS *Lexington*. The rooms are bright and cheery, with private balconies, microwaves, fridges, and free Wi-Fi. The hotel features a splendid outdoor pool with swim-up bar service, a full-fledged fitness center, and a decent restaurant.

$150-200

Along the bayside is fantastic **Emerald Beach Hotel** (1102 S. Shoreline Blvd., 800/465-4329, www.hotelemeraldbeach.com, $199 d). This recently renovated hotel offers an independently owned option containing an indoor pool and fitness center along with an indoor recreation area for the kids, with a heated pool, table tennis, billiard tables, and vending machines. Emerald Beach features complimentary Wi-Fi and free meals for children.

Looming large along the Corpus Christi Bay are the **Omni Marina and Bayfront** (707 and 900 N. Shoreline Blvd., 361/887-1600, www.omnihotels.com, $199 d). Within a block of each other, the towers are connected by a walkway to form a deluxe complex. They're similar in price and amenities, although the Bayfront Tower offers additional upscale room options. Both provide rooms with Wi-Fi access, free meals for kids, an upscale health club, an indoor-outdoor heated swimming pool, an in-house massage therapist, bike rentals, and free covered parking.

Camping

For RVers, **Puerto Del Sol RV Park** (5100 Timon Blvd., 361/882-5373, www. puertodelsolrvpark.com, $29-39) is at the northern edge of Corpus Christi Beach. Amenities include full hookups, a rec room, laundry facilities, restrooms with hot showers, internet access, and a book exchange. Farther out of town at the entrance to Padre

Island is Colonia Del Rey (1717 Waldron Rd., 361/937-2435 or 800/580-2435, $29-39), offering a heated pool, a hot tub, a recreation facility, a laundry room, a convenience store, and Wi-Fi. Nearby is the minimal yet affordable Padre Balli Park (15820 Park Rd. 22, 361/949-8121, $15-25), containing 54 paved campsites with water and electric hookups, 12 hardtop campsites for pitching a tent with water and electric hookups, and primitive camping on the beach. A bathhouse and laundry facility are also available.

INFORMATION AND SERVICES

The Corpus Christi Area Convention & Visitors Bureau (101 N. Shoreline Blvd., 361/881-1800 or 800/766-2322, www.visitcorpuschristitx.org, Mon.-Fri. 8:30am-5pm) displays scores of brochures, maps, and helpful information on local attractions and recreation. Similar information is available at the bureau's downtown Corpus Christi Tourist Information Center (1521 N. Chaparral St., 361/561-2000, daily 9am-5pm).

Mustang Island

When people say they're going to Corpus Christi to hit the beach, they're often referring to adjacent Mustang Island. Within 15 minutes, you can move from the city to the sea.

TOP EXPERIENCE

★ PADRE ISLAND NATIONAL SEASHORE

Just south of Mustang Island is Padre Island National Seashore (3829 Park Rd. 22, 361/949-8068, www.nps.gov/pais, $5 pedestrians and bikers, $10 vehicles), a low-key, nature-oriented, protected shoreline not to be confused with the commercial-minded party atmosphere of South Padre Island, a three-hour drive south. Padre Island National Seashore is the longest remaining

GETTING THERE AND AROUND

For those driving from Central Texas (Austin, San Antonio) to Corpus, take I-35 south, then I-37 south from San Antonio. It takes 3.5 hours from Austin and 2 hours from San Antonio. Most Houstonians get their beach fix at nearby Galveston, but some travel down the coast via I-69 and U.S. 59 south to Victoria (a 2-hour drive) before heading south on U.S. 77 and U.S. 181 to Corpus (about 1 hour).

Five miles (8 km) west of downtown, the Corpus Christi International Airport (CRP, 1000 International Blvd., 361/289-0171, www.corpuschristiairport.com) offers flights on Southwest, United, and American Eagle, including to Monterrey, Mexico. The city's bus system, Regional Transportation Authority (1806 S. Alameda St., 361/883-2287, www.ccrta.org), provides citywide service. Check the website for fare and route information.

undeveloped stretch of barrier island in the world and appeals to naturalists who delight in its primitive shoreline and birding and fishing opportunities. Bird-watchers arrive in droves in the fall and spring migration seasons, when thousands of birds drop by the island, including sandhill cranes, hawks, and songbirds.

The park is also considered the most important nesting beach for the most endangered sea turtle, the Kemp's ridley. Park officials incubate sea turtle eggs found along the coast and release the hatchlings into the gulf during summer. You can watch this fascinating event—for release dates and directions to the site, call the Hatchling Hotline (361/949-7163).

Other popular activities at the park include

swimming, fishing, windsurfing, and beach-combing. Visit the website for detailed information about camping locations and fees. To reach the park from Corpus, take South Padre Island Drive (Hwy. 358) to Padre Island, then head south on Park Road 22 for 13 miles (21 km) to the Malaquite Visitor Center.

MUSTANG ISLAND STATE PARK

Don't miss the beautiful shoreline along **Mustang Island State Park** (17047 State Hwy. 361, 361/749-5246, www.tpwd.state.tx.us, $5 over age 12). Named for the wild horses that escaped from Spanish explorers and roamed free across this 18-mile-long (29-km) island, Mustang Island State Park comprises 5 miles (8 km) of pristine beach for swimming, fishing, sunbathing, hiking, biking, and even low-intensity surfing. Birding is popular on this 4,000-acre island, notable for its distinctive ecosystem of 20-foot-high (6-m) sand dunes that protect the bay and the mainland and can reduce powerful hurricane-driven waves. To get there from Corpus, take South Padre Island Drive (Hwy. 358) to Padre Island, then head north on Highway 361 for 5 miles (8 km) to the park headquarters.

SAN JOSE ISLAND

If you're seriously into beachcombing—we're talking shell collections, mounted driftwood, maybe even a metal detector—San Jose Island is your paradise. This privately owned property across the bay from Port Aransas is almost as untouched as it was when the Karankawa people lived here a thousand years ago. In the 1830s, locals found the remains of a pirate camp on the island, and legend has it that pirate Jean Lafitte's Spanish dagger with a silver spike is still somewhere guarding his booty of silver and gold.

These days, visitors can access "Saint Joe" via a short boat ride to go swimming, fishing, sunbathing, and treasure hunting on this beautiful unspoiled property. To arrange transport, drop by Port A's **Fisherman's**

Wharf (900 N. Tarpon St., 361/749-5448, www.wharfcat.com, call for rates).

PORT ARANSAS

At the northern tip of Mustang Island is Port Aransas, or Port A, as it's known locally, a charming little beach town. Port A took a major hit from Hurricane Harvey in 2017, but it is slowly returning to its status as a laid-back, charming destination.

The origins of Port Aransas (population 4,143) trace to an English farmer who used the area as a sheep and cattle grazing station in the mid-1800s. Decades later, New Jersey entrepreneur Elihu Ropes attempted to organize a massive project to dredge a 30-foot (9-m) shipping channel across Mustang Island to allow access to the deep waters of the gulf. He was ultimately unsuccessful, but his efforts resulted in the town briefly being named Ropesville in his honor.

By the mid-20th century, Port Aransas had become synonymous with recreation, drawing tens of thousands of anglers, swimmers, boaters, and beachcombers to its open sands and seaside village atmosphere. The town's population swelled from 824 residents in 1960 to several thousand by the end of the century. As many as 20,000 vacationers descend on Port Aransas during peak periods, packing the island's motels, beach houses, and restaurants.

To get here from the mainland, travel across the South Padre Island Drive causeway from Corpus on the southern edge of the island, or take the ferry from nearby Aransas Pass (daily 24 hours). Look for dolphins behind the ferry as they tumble over each other in the bay snatching up fish in the boat's wake.

Sights

Port A doesn't have cultural attractions, and the only real destination besides the beach is beach-related. The **Marine Science Institute** (630 E. Cotter Ave., 361/749-6729, www.utmsi.utexas.edu, Mon.-Fri. 8am-5pm, Sat.-Sun. 11am-3pm, free) is the oldest marine

1: Marine Science Institute 2: Trout Street Bar & Grill

research station on the Texas Gulf Coast, dedicated to the ecology, biochemistry, and physiology of the plants and animals of the sea. The visitors center offers educational movies (Mon.-Thurs. 3pm) and self-guided tours of marine-related research project exhibits, stunning photographs, entertaining interactive displays for children, and several aquariums containing local sea life, including a funky flounder with two eyes on one side of its body.

Recreation

When it comes to activities in Port Aransas, the key word is "outside," and there are noteworthy places to explore year-round.

FISHING

Port Aransas is a fishing mecca. Some claim the area is overfished, and it's clear to see why it's popular—easy access to the bay and deep-sea gulf fishing provide fishing year-round. Fish for free from beaches, jetties, or Charlie's Harbor Pier, Ancel Brundrett Pier, and J. P. Luby Pier, all lighted and extending into the Corpus Christi Ship Channel.

It's worth the $2 for the popular well-lit **Horace Caldwell Pier** (230 North on the Beach, 361/749-5333, www. keepersportaransasfishingpier.com), 1,200 feet (365 m) long and open daily 24 hours, with bait, tackle, rental equipment, and munchies at the concession stand. This is a one-stop-shop for people who don't have much experience fishing. Friendly locals are happy to assist with your bait, offer advice, and, if you're lucky, help remove your catch from your hook.

Many anglers prefer the challenge of the larger deep-sea species, including kingfish, mackerel, flounder, tuna, and shark. Group boats offer bay and deep-sea fishing, and popular fishing tournaments take place throughout summer. The Deep Sea Roundup, held each July, is the oldest fishing tournament on the Gulf Coast. As a testament to the overwhelming allure of fishing in Port A, the town has several hundred fishing guides. Inquire about group fishing at **Fisherman's Wharf** (900 N. Tarpon St., 361/749-5448, www. wharfcat.com). To arrange a private rental, contact **Woody's Sports Center** (136 W. Cotter Ave., 361/749-5252, www.woodys-pa. com).

SWIMMING

The best swimming is at Mustang Island State Park, but you can access portions of the wide welcoming beach among the condos and private land just off the island's main road (Hwy. 361). Visitors can also swim and camp at the northern tip of the island just outside Port A at 167-acre **Magee Beach Park** (321 North on the Beach, 361/749-6117, www.nuecesbeachparks.com, $12-20 nightly for camping). Not as breathtaking as other portions of Mustang Island or San Jose Island, it's a good spot to swim. A park office offers limited visitor information, and the beach bathhouse contains publicly accessible showers.

Food
SEAFOOD

One of the best seafood restaurants on the Gulf Coast is the unassuming ★ **Shells Pasta & Seafood** (522 E. Ave. G, 361/749-7621, www.eatatshells.com, Wed.-Mon. 11:30am-2:30pm and 5pm-9pm, $12-36). Inside a modest building, Shells is a tiny place—nine tables with plastic chairs—with an enormous reputation for quality fresh seafood and pasta. Order from the blackboard or the regular menu, featuring classic seafood such as the signature pan-seared amberjack, grilled shrimp, blue crab cakes, or sumptuous shrimp linguine in a creamy Alfredo sauce. This is elegant food in a casual shorts-wearing environment, and Shells will be a highlight of your trip to Port A.

Locals love **Lisabella's** (224 E. Cotter Ave., 361/749-4222, Tues.-Sat. 5:30pm-9pm, $10-31) mermaid soup, a tasty concoction of lobster, shrimp, coconut milk, curry, and avocado. The crab cakes and sautéed grouper are similarly enticing.

A casual spot where you can wear T-shirts and flip-flops among old fishing nets, mounted marlin, and a marina is **Trout Street Bar & Grill** (104 W. Cotter Ave., 361/749-7800, www.tsbag.com, Sun.-Thurs. 11am-8pm, Fri.-Sat. 11am-9pm, $11-30). Sit outside on the covered veranda to watch the ship channel activity while feasting on peel-and-eat shrimp, fish tacos, drum po'boys, grilled amberjack, snapper, tuna, or steak. Complement the fantastic flavors with a local *hefeweizen*. A bonus: Trout Street will cook your fresh-caught fish as long as it's cleaned and ready for the kitchen.

Another venerable seafood spot is **Fins** (420 W. Cotter Ave., 361/749-8646, www. finsgrillandicehouse.com, Mon.-Fri. 11am-9pm, Sat.-Sun. 11am-10pm, $9-29). The views and menu are amazing, and shrimp is the specialty. Order the Bayou Combo (sautéed whitefish and gulf shrimp topped with a zesty sauce) and savor the flavor. Fins is family-friendly, so bring the whole crew and order some burgers and chicken nuggets.

A popular new destination in town is **Tortuga's Saltwater Grill** (429 N. Alister St., 361/749-2739, www.tortugassaltwatergrill. com, Mon.-Fri. 11am-9pm, Sat.-Sun. 11am-10pm, $10-20). There's something immensely satisfying about sipping well-crafted specialty beer while waiting for your fresh seafood to arrive. Pair it with the shrimp tacos, fried gulf fish, or islander brick-oven pizza.

ITALIAN

Port A has both beach grub and upscale Italian. For a quick slice of pizza in an ultra-laid-back environment, check out the immensely popular **Port A Pizzeria** (407 E. Ave. G., 361/749-5226, www.portapizzeria. com, daily 11am-10pm, $9-20). The biggest draw is the buffet, allowing diners to devour hot slices. Some diners choose to wait a few minutes for the tasty calzone. The big crowds ensure a quick turnaround.

The fancy Italian option is the consistently top-notch **Venetian Hot Plate** (232 Beach Ave., 361/749-7617, www.venetianhotplate.

com, Tues.-Sat. 5pm-10pm, $13-35). Named for the sizzling iron plates some of the meals arrive on, this upscale spot specializes in tender succulent filet mignon medallions, veal, and lamb. The wine selection is excellent, and desserts are spectacular. Reservations are recommended.

Accommodations
INNS

A memorable experience in this quaint seaside village is the charming ★ **Tarpon Inn** (200 E. Cotter Ave., 361/749-5555, www. thetarponinn.com, $99-199). An "inn" in every sense of the term, this historic establishment offers a slice of life in the late 1800s. You won't find a TV or phone in your room, but Wi-Fi is available. Old-fashioned activities include reading, relaxing in a rocking chair, playing croquet and horseshoes, and talking. Rooms are small, with vintage beds and furniture, but are refreshingly uncluttered. Check out the old tarpon fish scales on the wall in the lobby, including those autographed by famous actors and politicians. The trolley stops out front every day to take guests to the beach or nearby shops.

Not quite as charming but appealing in its localness is **Alister Square Inn** (122 S. Alister St., 361/749-3003, www.portaransastexas.com, $99-199). A bit rough around the edges, this welcoming accommodation appeals to families and anglers alike with two-bedroom apartments, kitchenette suites, and standard hotel rooms, each featuring microwaves, fridges, and Wi-Fi access. Alister Square is within walking distance of the beach, shopping, and restaurants.

HOTELS

In Port Aransas, familiar chain hotels cost more than local inns. Just a couple of blocks from the beach is the **Holiday Inn Express** (727 S. 11th St., 361/749-5222, www. ichotelsgroup.com, $159 d), offering a fitness center, a pool and spa area, free continental breakfast, and rooms with microwaves, fridges, and free Wi-Fi. Among the more expensive options is **Best Western Ocean Villa** (400 E. Ave. G, 361/749-3010, www.bestwestern.com, $219 d), within walking distance of beaches, fishing piers, and local shops. Amenities include rooms with microwaves, fridges, and free internet access, along with free continental breakfast and an outdoor swimming pool.

CONDOS
Condos proliferate on Mustang Island's shoreline like barnacles on a shrimp boat. Condos make perfect sense in a beach environment—visitors can traipse back and forth to the surf, sand gathers on all surfaces, and beers and pizza fill the fridge. Hurricane Harvey damaged many of the condos, but in 2020 individual units were increasingly available via AirBNB.

Among the most popular still taking building-wide reservations is **Beachgate CondoSuites & Motel** (2000 On the Beach Dr., 361/749-5900, www.beachgate.com, $225-325). Adjacent to Mustang Island—meaning walking the boardwalks or long trails through the dunes isn't necessary—Beachgate offers everything from efficiency-size motel rooms to full-size three-bedroom condos, accommodating everyone from the solo angler to the sizable family reunion. Larger options contain fully equipped kitchens, and all units

have small fridges, microwaves, and coffee-makers. Additional amenities include a fish-cleaning facility, boat parking, washers, and horseshoe sets for fun on the beach.

Information and Services
Pick up a handy brochure with island info and a map of the trolley route at the **Port Aransas Chamber of Commerce and Tourist Bureau** (403 W. Cotter St., 361/749-5919, www.portaransas.org). **The Flexi-B** (361/749-4111, $0.25), a.k.a. "the B" and "the 94 shuttle," will take you anywhere in Port A, including the beach, the wharf, shops, and your hotel. It's particularly handy when you're drinking and dinner is calling.

Getting There
The **Port Aransas Ferry System** (361/749-2850) provides free transportation year-round daily 24 hours. It's a unique and charming way to cross the water—you can even get out of your car during the "ride" and look for the dolphins that swim behind the boat. The 15-minute ride connects Port Aransas with the mainland at Aransas Pass, north of Corpus Christi. Six ferries, each carry up to 20 vehicles. During the busy season, particularly holidays and some summer weekends, you may have to wait up to 45 minutes, but typically the wait is no longer than 5-10 minutes.

Kingsville

About 40 miles (64 km) southwest of Corpus Christi, Kingsville (population 25,487) is the birthplace of the American ranching industry. It's the main commercial center of the legendary King Ranch, which sprawls across 825,000 acres and boasts 60,000 head of cattle.

The community is named for the famous riverboat baron and rancher Richard King, who used his business profits to purchase the vast piece of property that would become the eponymous ranch. Kingsville's roots as a city are traced to the St. Louis, Brownsville and

Mexico Railway, which put the town on the map when its tracks were laid in the early 1900s. Most of Kingsville's early business was related to the King family, who started a weekly newspaper and built a hotel, an ice plant, and a cotton gin. Kingsville went on to become a busy trade center for ranching families across South Texas.

Kingsville's population grew significantly when Exxon relocated a district office here in the 1960s. A surge in enrollment at the Texas College of Arts and Industries, now Texas

King's People

At the heart of the King Ranch are the Kineños (King's people), a group of several hundred ranch employees whose families have operated the property for generations, training horses, clearing fields, and promoting the King Ranch's original cattle breed. The Kineños provide a link with the ranch's past and maintain its legacy. To learn more about this remarkable chapter of Texas history, plan a trip to **King Ranch** (2205 Hwy. 141 W., 361/592-8055, www.king-ranch.com, tours Mon.-Sat. 10am, noon, and 1pm, Sun. 12:30pm and 2pm, $20 adults, $15 seniors, $6 ages 5-12).

If you visit the ranch or take one of the tours, you'll get a chance to visit with one of these Kineños. Several now serve as guides, even though they occasionally take on some of their traditional ranching duties. Many of the Kineños are men in their 80s.

Some Kineños spent their early days breaking thoroughbred horses. In the 1940s-1950s, King Ranch trained racing horses and developed well-known successful thoroughbreds. The Kineños also worked extensively with the ranch's quarter horses, using the handling techniques passed down through generations of vaqueros. Others worked closely with the Santa Gertrudis cattle breed, specifically developed and marketed by the ranch, by attending livestock shows around the world. They even slept in the barns with the animals and woke early to clean, feed, water, and brush the cattle in preparation for the shows. Kineños also administered vaccinations, helped in the pastures, and maintained records.

Some of these stories have been captured in print. Pick up a copy of Alberto "Beto" Maldonado's book *The Master Showmen of King Ranch*.

A&M Kingsville, brought even more folks to town, with a population of 30,000 by the late 1970s. Exxon closed its regional office in 1985, and the population has slowly declined since then.

Kingsville remains a draw for birders and naturalists, who delight in the area's million acres of habitat. The historic downtown area has boutiques and antiques stores that reflect the heritage of King Ranch.

SIGHTS

TOP EXPERIENCE

★ King Ranch

King Ranch is the embodiment of the Lone Star State's legacy. Longhorn cattle, vast ranchlands, and genuine cowboys evoke a sense of mystique and grandeur. America's ranching legacy was revolutionized by a man who arrived on Texas's Gulf Coast as a preteen stowaway. Richard King, who left New York City in 1835 aboard a cargo ship, went on to become a steamboat baron along the

Rio Grande before overseeing his ranching empire.

The origins of King Ranch, now a National Historic Landmark, date to 1853 when Richard King purchased 68,500 acres of property that had been Spanish and Mexican land grants. Between 1869 and 1884 King sent more than 100,000 head of livestock from his ranch to northern markets on now-legendary routes like the Chisholm Trail. Many were marked with the iconic symbol for the King Ranch, the running-W brand, which first appeared in the 1860s. Though the origins of this distinctive shape aren't known, local legends claim it represents the sweeping horns of a longhorn bull, or a slithering diamondback rattlesnake.

One of King Ranch's claims to fame is the development of the western hemisphere's first strain of beef cattle, Santa Gertrudis. Based on the name from the property's original land grant, the breed was developed in the 1920s to produce cows that could withstand the oppressive South Texas conditions—heat, humidity, and biting insects. To accomplish this, breeding experts, including Richard

King's grandson, crossed Indian Brahman cattle with British shorthorns.

King was also one of the first ranchers to move Texas longhorns from Mexico to markets in the Midwest, and the innovations developed at his ranch, from breeding and disease control to improving the bloodlines of the quarter horse to well drilling, earned it the title "birthplace of American ranching."

Today, King Ranch sprawls across 825,000 acres, larger than the state of Rhode Island. The **King Ranch Visitor Center** (2205 Hwy. 141 W., 361/592-8055, www.king-ranch.com, tours Mon.-Sat. 10am, noon, and 1pm, Sun. 12:30pm and 2pm, $20 adults, $15 seniors, $6 ages 5-12) offers daily guided tours along an old stagecoach road past majestic longhorns with the iconic running-W brand on their hindquarters, and a 100-year-old carriage house with a mission-style roofline and distinctive arches. Other highlights include the Victorian-era cabin homes of King's working families, known as Kineños, and a horse cemetery with graves of famous racing thoroughbreds from the 1950s. It gets hot on the ranch, but you'll be in air-conditioned comfort in a plush utility vehicle with water breaks and a friendly guide to answer questions and point out fascinating information. Special tours

devoted to birding, wildlife, and agriculture are available in advance by reservation.

A couple of miles down the road is the **King Ranch Museum** (405 N. 6th St., Kingsville, 361/595-1881, www.king-ranch.com, Mon.-Sat. 10am-4pm, Sun. 1pm-5pm, $10 adults, $8 seniors and students, $4 ages 5-12). Housed in a historic downtown ice plant, the museum contains stunning 1940s photos of the ranch by award-winning photographer Toni Frissell, fancy saddles and firearms, antique coaches and carriages, and other historic ranch items. One of the most intriguing objects is "El Kineño," a custom-designed 1949 Buick Eight hunting vehicle—complete with rifle holders and a shiny running-W hood ornament—made by General Motors especially for Congressman R. M. Kleberg Sr.

Another must-see is the restored 1909 Ragland Mercantile Building that now houses the leather-filled **King Ranch Saddle Shop** (201 E. Kleberg Ave., 877/282-5777, www.krsaddleshop.com, Mon.-Sat. 10am-6pm). Originally used to supply gear exclusively to the King Ranch Kineños, the store now offers leather goods and clothing to the world, and its website does brisk business. The charming downtown shop also contains exhibits and photos on ranch history and information

a historic barn at King Ranch

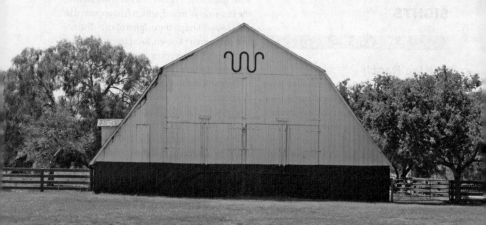

about the governors, presidents, and foreign dignitaries it has outfitted.

1904 Train Depot and Museum

A block from the saddle shop is the restored **1904 Train Depot and Museum** (102 E. Kleberg Ave., 361/592-8515, www.kingsvilletexas.com, Mon.-Fri. 8am-5pm, free), offering a glimpse into Kingsville's bustling past. Photos and artifacts, including an operational telegraph, highlight the historical significance of this hub of regional activity.

Kenedy Ranch Museum of South Texas

Richard King isn't the only famous rancher in these parts. His longtime pal Mifflin Kenedy also accumulated great wealth and property in commercial and ranching endeavors. His legacy is on display at the **Kenedy Ranch Museum of South Texas** (200 E. La Parra Ave., Sarita, 361/294-5751, Tues.-Sat. 10am-4pm, Sun. noon-4pm, $4 adults, $3 seniors and ages 13-18). Located 20 miles (32 km) south of Kingsville in the little town of Sarita, the museum showcases Kenedy's illustrious past through exhibits dedicated to family, particularly his wife, Petra Vela de Vidal, of prominent Mexican heritage. Kenedy accumulated 400,000 acres of Gulf Coast property and was among the first ranchers to hold cattle inside wire fences. Housed in the 1927 Kenedy Ranch headquarters, the museum also details the family's philanthropic programs.

John E. Conner Museum

Regional history and the natural world are the main areas of interest at the **John E. Conner Museum** (905 W. Santa Gertrudis Ave., 361/593-2810, www.tamuk.edu, Mon.-Fri. 8am-5pm, Sat. 10am-4pm, free). On the campus of Texas A&M-Kingsville, this modest museum offers exhibits devoted to the groups that have occupied the area, from Native Americans to Spanish, Mexican, and American settlers. Native plant and animal species are also on display, as well as artwork from students and Texas artists.

FOOD
American

Kingsville isn't a destination for fine dining, but one of the best places to eat in the region is 20 miles (32 km) south of Kingsville in the tiny town of Riviera. ★ **King's Inn** (1116 S. County Rd. 2270, Riviera, 361/297-5265, www.mybighouseonline.com, Tues.-Sat. 11am-10pm, $13-29) doesn't look like much from the outside, and the outdated ambience isn't charming, but that won't matter when the food arrives. Order the lightly breaded fried shrimp, accompanied by the famous spicy tartar sauce (the waiter claimed to be sworn to secrecy, though he eventually let it slip that the tartar sauce contained bread crumbs, "lots of eggs," and serrano peppers). This stunning sauce enhances everything from the interesting choice of fish (drum) to the homemade bread to the avocado salad with accompanying slices of tomato. It's worth the 20-minute detour to eat like a king.

For lunch, just south of downtown Kingsville is the occasionally rowdy **Big House Burgers** (2209 S. Brahma Blvd., 361/592-0222, daily 11am-10pm, $8-15). The sports bar atmosphere can be overwhelming on weekends, reminding you there's a college in this town, but the noise and blaring TVs are worth it for the immense and flavorful burgers. Try the quadruple burger if you dare. Split some of the crunchy fries or crispy onion rings with a pal.

Tex-Mex

Grab an authentic Tex-Mex meal at **El Tapatio Mexican Restaurant** (630 W. Santa Gertrudis St., 361/516-1655, Mon.-Sat. 6am-10pm, Sun. 6am-2pm, $9-18), on the edge of the Kingsville A&M campus. The food is standard Tex-Mex fare, with a few items that set it apart. The *carne guisada* has hearty gravy that brings out the rich flavor of the beef. Like the salsa, it has an extra kick and after-bite that leaves your mouth feeling satisfied.

Lydia's Homestyle Cooking (817 W. King Ave., 361/592-9405, Mon.-Sat. 6am-1:30pm, $9-19) is known for its tremendous breakfast taquitos (try the potato, eggs, and sausage) and the *machacado* plate, featuring shredded dry beef scrambled with eggs and grilled onions, tomato, and serrano peppers. Lydia's lunches are legendary, including the *barbacoa* plate, tamales, and chicken flautas. You can also order gringo burgers and sandwiches.

Reputable **El Dorado** (704 N. 14th St., 361/516-1459, Mon.-Sat. 6am-10pm, Sun. 6am-2pm, $8-15) has traditional Tex-Mex fare that's consistently decent, including the beef tacos, chicken enchiladas, and burritos.

ACCOMMODATIONS

Only a few lodging options are available in Kingsville. On the affordable side is **Best Western Kingsville Inn** (2402 E. King Ave., 361/595-5656, www.bestwestern.com, $69 d). Amenities include a complimentary hot breakfast, free Wi-Fi, standard rooms with microwaves and fridges, and a "soothing outdoor swimming pool and hot tub."

For a little more money, consider **Holiday Inn Express** (2400 S. Hwy. 77, 361/592-8333, www.hiexpress.com, $109 d), offering a free hot breakfast bar, complimentary Wi-Fi, and a heated outdoor pool.

INFORMATION AND SERVICES

For information about area attractions, accommodations, and restaurants, visit the **Kingsville Convention and Visitors Bureau** (1501 Hwy. 77, 361/592-8516, www. kingsvilletexas.com, Mon.-Fri. 9am-5pm, Sat. 10am-2pm).

GETTING THERE

The main route to Kingsville is U.S. 77. From Corpus, get on Highway 44 west for 15 minutes before linking up with U.S. 77, a drive of about 45 minutes total.

South Padre Island

The massive 130-mile-long (210-km) Padre Island is home to the longest sand beach in the United States. Never more than 3 miles (4.8 km) wide, the island was formed by sea erosion and deposition. The northern portion, adjacent to Corpus Christi, has a modest collection of hotels and residences and is mostly recreation-oriented; the central portion is the protected Padre Island National Seashore; and the southern tip is a major resort area lined with hotels and restaurants.

South Padre Island isn't technically an island, but rather the resort community (population 2,830) at the southern portion of the big island. The town is flanked by the Gulf of Mexico to the east, a narrow ship channel to the north, and Laguna Madre, the narrow bay leading to the Texas mainland.

Spanish explorers visited the area in the 1500s, but the seashore remained barren and pristine until the 1950s, when a causeway

connected Port Isabel to South Padre Island. It provided access to the nicest beaches on the Texas coast, and the community remained a low-key resort destination until the late 1970s, when insurance companies were required to provide hurricane coverage and the population increased dramatically from 314 to 1,012 residents thanks to the growing emphasis on tourism. For the past two decades, it has become a major spring break destination for college students, who descend on the small town by the thousands for revelry and recreation each March.

SIGHTS

Island time is good for the soul. Everything slows down, priorities shift to beach activities and seafood options, and even tightly wound drivers lay off their car horns. It may take a day or two to assimilate to South Padre mode, but you won't want to leave.

South Padre's soft smooth sand is more inviting and picturesque than the grainier, darker sand farther north. The resort community offers beachcombing, fishing, windsurfing, dolphin-viewing, biking, snorkeling, and scuba diving. Lodging options range from opulent resort condos to pitching a tent on the beach, and restaurants offer gulf-harvested oysters, shrimp, and fish. Make a point of taking a dolphin tour and visiting the sea turtle research center to get an appreciation of the sealife that doesn't end up on your dinner plate.

In winter you'll be surrounded by Midwestern license plates and polite retirees taking advantage of restaurant early-bird specials. In summer, Texas families flock to the island to play in the gentle waves and devour fried shrimp. The beach is pleasant year-round and the vibe is mellow, except during spring break.

It takes some effort to get to South Padre, but maneuvering around the small town is a breeze. After crossing the Queen Isabella Causeway, take a left onto Padre Boulevard to reach the main drag, with hotels, shops, and restaurants. Take a right off the causeway to reach the public beaches and seaside attractions.

Sea Turtle, Inc.

A heartwarming experience awaits at **Sea Turtle, Inc.** (6617 Padre Blvd., 956/761-4511, www.seaturtleinc.com, Tues.-Sun. 10am-4pm, donation), an unassuming little spot at the end of South Padre's main strip. Inside, tanks are full of various sea turtles, several native to the nearby Gulf Coast. Each turtle is identified in a separate tank, often with a tear-jerking tale about the unfortunate experience (boat propeller, fishing line, animal attack) that brought it to the rehab site. Arrive at 10am for the informative presentation that offers context about the friendly and fascinating creatures. Kids can feed the turtles, and everyone has a chance for a photo op. Marvel at these prehistoric animals—some can reach 450 pounds—and toss a few extra dollars in the box for this organization that works tirelessly to protect and promote these endangered creatures.

Dolphin Research and Sea Life Nature Center

Kids aren't the only ones who'll learn something at the nearby **Dolphin Research and Sea Life Nature Center** (110 N. Garcia St., Port Isabel, 956/299-1957, www.spinaturecenter.com, daily 10am-4pm, $3

a turtle at Sea Turtle, Inc.

Spring Break at South Padre

This low-key, unassuming beach community turns into a raucous party town for several weeks each March. Nearly 100,000 students from across the country descend on South Padre Island approximately March 10-20, prompting locals to leave their quiet seaside homes.

Rivaling Florida's Daytona Beach as the nation's ultimate spring break destination, South Padre has become party central for college students from Texas and the Midwest. The town doesn't have the infrastructure to handle the hordes—eight-hour waits on the causeway are common on peak arrival days—but it ultimately benefits from the millions spent on lodging, food, and DWI tickets (take the Wave shuttle if you've had a few drinks).

One of South Padre's biggest spring break assets is its beach consumption policy—unlike most U.S. seashores, it's legal to drink on the beach if you're 21 or older. The undercover Texas Alcoholic Beverage Commission agents are out in full force looking for minors in possession (MIPs). Rent a hotel with a kitchenette or a condo for easy access to a fridge, ice, and countertops.

Spring breakers often take advantage of package deals offered by travel agencies. Most involve flights and lodging, but several feature mini excursions around the area for a respite after days of drinking and sunbathing. One of the most popular activities is a professionally operated surfing lesson, complete with a board, a wetsuit, and individual instruction. For a change of scenery while downing drinks, sign up for a party yacht cruise, originating at Coconuts Bar and Grill.

donation). This low-key locale, just across the causeway from South Padre, contains 20 aquariums filled with sea creatures from the gulf waters. Shrimp, starfish, rays, and eels await, and a children's program (11am and 2pm, call ahead to make sure it's available) allows youngsters to handle and feed some of the nonthreatening species in the touch tanks. Knowledgeable staffers educate visitors about environmentally responsible ways to enjoy their time on the island.

★ Port Isabel Lighthouse

It's worth the 74-step climb up the tight spiral staircase of the historic **Port Isabel Lighthouse State Historic Site** (421 E. Queen Isabella Blvd., Port Isabel, 800/527-6102, www.thc.texas.gov, daily 9am-5pm), now owned by the Texas Historical Commission. The view stretches from Laguna Madre to the historic downtown Port Isabel. Constructed in 1852 at the request of sea captains frustrated by visibility along the low-lying Texas coast, the lighthouse was prominent until the early 1900s, when newer and more powerful towers were constructed. Sixteen similar lighthouses once graced the Texas coast, but the Port

Isabel Lighthouse is the only one still open to the public.

Pan American Coastal Studies Laboratory

Not as family-oriented as other area attractions, the **Pan American Coastal Studies Laboratory** (100 Marine Lab Dr., 956/761-2644, www.utrgv.edu/csl, Mon.-Fri. 1:30pm-4:30pm, free) is designed with researchers in mind. You'll learn things about the plant and animal life in the Laguna Madre and Gulf of Mexico through interactive displays (shark jaws, turtle shells) and a few aquariums.

BEACHES

The beach is everywhere at South Padre, so you won't have any trouble finding a place to park and tote your gear to the soft white sand (bring plenty of sunscreen and bottled water). Look for public beach access points every few blocks along Gulf Boulevard.

For more amenities—pavilions, picnic tables, and playgrounds in addition to the restrooms and showers—go to one of the county beach parks on the southern or northern ends of the island. The most popular is the southern option—**Isla Blanca Park** (33174

State Park Rd. 100, 956/761-5494, www.cameroncountyparks.com, daily 7am-11pm, $12 per vehicle). Referred to as the "crown jewel of the system," it features 1 mile-plus (1.6 km) of pristine white sand and bright blue water for swimming, surfing, and fishing. Parking is easily available, and beachcombers can step from the lot onto the beach, where they'll encounter pickup volleyball games, surfers, Frisbee dogs, and friendly folks strolling the low-key surf. There are also nearly 600 RV slots available.

At the northern end is **Andy Bowie Park** (7300 Padre Blvd., 956/761-3704, www.cameroncountyparks.com, daily 7am-11pm, $5 per vehicle). More rural in nature, Andy Bowie offers access to a beachfront road that eventually opens up to 20 miles (32 km) of scenic driving that qualifies as off-the-beaten-path. Horseback riding is popular, as is wade fishing and windsurfing on the bay side.

RECREATION
Water Sports

Your one-stop shop for all things recreational in South Padre is **South Padre Island Water Sports/Air Padre** (SPIWS, 5709 Padre Blvd., 956/299-9463, www.spiws.com). The company's credo says it all: "Beautiful South Padre island is best seen from the water." The following are compelling options:

Kayaks ($30-95) provide a steady vantage point of island scenery. SPIWS offers many kayaks for rent, including single, tandem, fishing, surfing, and even glass-bottom varieties.

Kiteboarding is another fun way to get a workout at South Padre, though you may spend more time looking at the sky than the sights. The island's steady winds and shallow water are optimal for this activity. SPIWS suggests scheduling an initial lesson (from $99) before venturing out on their rental equipment.

Windsurfing represents a step down in intensity from kiteboarding, though it's still an active pursuit requiring plenty of stamina. Fortunately, the island's steady 18 mph (29

km/h) winds make it easier to move consistently. Combined with Laguna Madre's calm water and shallow sandy floor, windsurfing offers a fun and easy way to zip around.

Traditional **surfing** remains an appealing option for many island visitors, and you'll see boards on most stretches of beach. The waves aren't major, but they're ideal for honing skills. One of the best ways to get your feet wet is through a SPIWS group lesson, offered daily. You'll find all the equipment you'll need for rent or purchase, including soft-stop surfboards, traditional longboards, and leashes.

Stand-up paddleboarding is low-key and the easiest water sport to experience South Padre. The wide boards help with stability and balance, and the canoe-style paddles provide plenty of propulsion power. SPIWS offers lessons for newbies and rental equipment.

Snorkeling and Scuba Diving

With clear water and fine sand, South Padre Island is a haven for scuba divers and snorkelers. The fish aren't varied or colorful like in tropical locales, but the marinelife among the reefs and rigs is intriguing.

Snorkeling and shallow shore dives are at the Mansfield Jetties, the beach at Dolphin Cove (look for sand dollars), and the adjacent Barracuda Bay. Scuba divers will enjoy the artificial reef (a wreck dive known as The Tug) 7 miles (11.3 km) southeast of the Brazos Santiago Pass Jetties. Farther out and most compelling for experienced divers are the oil rigs, where fish of all sizes are plentiful.

South Padre has several full-service dive shops offering equipment for rent and sale, organized excursions to prime spots, and instruction. One of the most reputable is **Southern Wave** (201 W. Pike St., 956/772-7245, www.sailspi.com). Another noteworthy option is **American Diving** (1 Padre Blvd., 956/761-2030, www.divesouthpadre.com).

Fishing

Fishing is a huge draw in South Padre. Everywhere you look are anglers with fishing poles—on the beach, jetty, pier, and chartered boats. Shoreline fishers tend to snag redfish, speckled trout, and flounder, while deep-sea adventurers seek tarpon, marlin, kingfish, mackerel, flounder, and wahoo.

Many anglers use the services of the venerable **Jim's Pier** (209 W. Whiting St., 956/761-2865, www.jimspier.com), which bills itself as the original South Padre Island fishing-guide company. Jim's provides boat slips, fueling docks, a launching ramp, and fish-cleaning facilities. The company also offers two bay fishing trips daily on its renowned 40-person party boat. To find out more about fishing locations and services, consult the **Port Isabel/ South Padre Island Guides Association** (www.fishspi.com), offering a list of endorsed professional fishing guides.

Dolphin-Viewing

Laguna Madre is home to myriad bottlenose dolphins, and there's nothing like the thrill of seeing them up close in their natural environment. The best way to get an intimate experience is through an independent tour company like **Fins to Feathers** (tours from Port Isabel's Sea Life Center, 956/299-0629, www.fin2feather.com, daily 7am-sunset, $25 pp). Enjoy a personalized experience from a small boat, allowing up-close views and interaction with the knowledgeable guide, a colorful character accompanied by a dolphin-finding dog. Anticipate the surge of excitement you'll feel when that first dorsal fin ascends from the water and the sun glistens off the smooth gray surface of these magnificent elegant creatures.

Hiking

South Padre is not a hiking destination, but there's plenty of shoreline to explore by foot. Head to **Andy Bowie Park** (7300 Padre Blvd., 956/761-3704, www.cameroncountyparks. com, daily 7am-11pm, $5 per vehicle), with access to a beachfront road (watch out for rogue vehicles) that eventually opens up to isolated areas.

Biking

Cyclists will enjoy the novel challenge of pedaling a Fat Sand Bike on the beach, a surprisingly quick and easy way to navigate the soft sand. Rentals are available at **South Padre Island Water Sports/Air Padre** (5709 Padre Blvd., 956/299-9463, www.spiws.com), from half days to a week ($40-250).

ENTERTAINMENT AND EVENTS
Bars and Clubs

After a day of in the ocean, relax and enjoy cold quality suds at **Padre Island Brewing Company** (3400 Padre Blvd., 956/761-9585, www.pibrewingcompany.com, Sun.-Thurs. 11:30am-10pm, Fri.-Sat. 11:30am-11pm, $9-21). Beer is the main theme, with home-brew supplies such as kettles, burlap sacks, and vintage bottles serving as scenery. It's a refreshing change from the ubiquitous corporate light-beer in most beach establishments. Fortunately, the handcrafted beer is commendable, particularly the Padre Pale Ale and Spotted Trout Stout. Food includes seafood and traditional bar fare like burgers, nachos, ribs, and sandwiches. Look for a seat on the second-floor outdoor deck.

For the ultimate island leisure activity, **Louie's Backyard** (2305 Laguna Dr., 956/761-6406, www.lbyspi.com, daily 11:30am-2am, $10-31) is party central during spring break, with multiple decks of dance floors and swirling light shows. The bartenders work quickly, and the drinks are potent. Before hitting the bar, consider the sumptuous buffet. Choose from boiled shrimp, crab legs, fish, and scallops along with ribs, pasta, and salad. The full menu has better options, including buttery, flaky flounder fillet and crispy fried shrimp. Top off your experience with a stunning view of the sunset over the bay while sipping Louie's signature cocktail, the multi-liquor and aptly named Whammy.

1: Port Isabel Lighthouse State Historic Site 2: view of South Padre from the lighthouse 3: Pier 19 on South Padre Island

A South Padre favorite bar has returned in a new location. **Parrot Eyes** (5801 Padre Blvd., 956/761-9457, Mon.-Fri. 11am-7pm, Sat.-Sun. 11am-9pm, www.parroteyesspi.com) is Buffett-esque, with a laid-back vibe and beach-loving patrons. Grab a drink and try to snag a spot on the small deck overlooking the bay. If you're feeling adventurous, order the Parrot-Head Paralizer, a crazy concoction of multiple liquors and fruit juices.

For the spring break vibe, head to **Coconut Jack's** (2301 Laguna Dr., 956/761-4218, daily 11am-11pm), with good food but known mainly for water sports rentals and recreation during the day, and in the evening an occasionally raucous bar scene with friendly and generously waitstaff.

Events

The community of South Padre knows a good time, as evidenced by several annual outdoor events. One of the first to draw big crowds each year is early February's **SPI Kitefest** (956/761-1248, www.sopadre.com). Held at the Sand Flats north of the SPI Convention Centre, Kitefest features hundreds of colorful kites punctuating the crisp blue sky. The steady ocean breeze helps keep even beginners' kites aloft, but there are also experts on hand to demonstrate new equipment and kite-flying skills and distribute prizes.

Of course, the community's biggest beach event is **spring break,** when tens of thousands of college students and other partiers descend on South Padre en masse. Revelers arrive throughout March, with the heaviest craziness during Texas Week, the second or third week of March.

Much mellower is the island's annual **Texas State Surfing Championship** (www.surftgsa.org), held in late April-early May, based on surf swell. This invitational competition for all ages is held in Isla Blanca Park on the southern tip of the island, considered the area's crowning jewel.

FOOD
Seafood

Even before you check in to your hotel room, drop by a low-key local eatery like **Palm Street Pier Bar & Grill** (204 W. Palm St., 956/772-7256, www.palmstreetpier.com, daily 11am-midnight, $9-20), known for tantalizing seafood and sunsets. Overlooking Laguna Madre, Palm Street Pier specializes in tasty fried and coconut shrimp. Don't miss the cheap margaritas and summertime Friday-night fireworks over the bay. Diners can bring their own fresh catch and have it expertly blackened, grilled, or fried with two side dishes. Palm Street operates on island time, so don't expect your food to arrive quickly.

Venerable and well-regarded **Blackbeard's** (103 E. Saturn Lane, 956/761-2962, www.blackbeardsspi.com, Sun.-Thurs. 11:30am-9pm, Fri.-Sat. 11:30am-10pm, $9-24) is a swashbuckling-themed spot with surprisingly refined food. Fresh gulf catches are the main draw, including flounder and tilapia, and equally commendable are charbroiled steaks and grilled chicken. The burgers here are some of the best on the island.

A local favorite in a new location is **Daddy's Cajun Kitchen & Seafood Market** (1801 Padre Blvd., 956/761-1975, http://daddysrestaurant.com, Sun.-Thurs. 11am-9pm, Fri.-Sat. 11am-10pm, $10-25). In a two-story building, Daddy's offers Creole and Cajun specialties such as jambalaya, gumbo, and crawfish étouffée, or one of the in-house lunch specials such as a crispy panko-breaded shrimp or almond-crusted fish fillet topped with crab and cheese sauce.

South Padre has upscale seafood, but in a casual town like this, you can still wear shorts and sandals. You can't go wrong with anything on the menu at ★ **Sea Ranch Restaurant** (1 Padre Blvd., 956/761-1314, www.searanchrestaurant.com, Sun.-Thurs. 4:30pm-9pm, Fri.-Sat. 4:30pm-10pm, $11-46), Options change regularly, focused on wild-caught seafood from the gulf. Signature dishes include grilled flounder, boiled king crab legs, gulf shrimp and bay oysters, and ahi tuna served rare with soy sauce and wasabi. Topping it off is an exceptional view of the sea. Reservations are advised.

Another popular seafood spot is **Pier 19** (1 Padre Blvd., 956/761-7437, www.pier19.us, $9-39), at the end of the road past the KOA Kampground. Located on the water, highlights at this restaurant include peel-and-eat, sautéed, and fried shrimp, blackened rockfish, and local flounder, pompano, and amberjack. The Baja tacos (with grilled shrimp) are especially tasty, bursting with the complementary flavors of savory shrimp, spicy jalapeño, and sweet mango. An added bonus: On some weekends, the staff "treats" diners to a pirate-themed show. Also watch for dolphins, known to make occasional appearances in the water below.

Beach Grub

If you've exhausted your craving for seafood, your next best bet is beach burgers, pizzas, and fried stuff, and, in South Padre, Tex-Mex. To combine all of these with cold suds is **Padre Island Brewing Company** (3400 Padre Blvd., 956/761-9585, www.pibrewingcompany.com, daily 11:30am-10pm, $9-21). The handcrafted beer is commendable, particularly the Padre Island Pale Ale and Spotted Trout Stout, to go with nachos, ribs, and sandwiches. Order a pale ale with a gulf-stuffed flounder, a flavorful fillet packed with crab and topped with creamy shrimp sauce. To enhance the experience, ask for a seat on the second-floor outdoor deck.

For a tasty burger and cold beer, head to **Tom & Jerry's Beach Bar & Grill** (3212 Padre Blvd., 956/761-8999, daily 11am-10pm, $8-22). The seafood dishes are commendable, but beach grub is the main draw, including burgers, chicken plates, chicken-fried steak, and a club sandwich. After your meal, head to the raised bar, where friendly staffers will pour draft beer or mix frozen concoctions.

ACCOMMODATIONS
Hotels

Lodging rates are high in the busy season and affordable the rest of the year. The following South Padre accommodations include prices for a weekend stay in midsummer, the busy getaway season in Texas, despite the high heat and humidity.

Among the affordable options is **South Beach Inn** (120 E. Jupiter Lane, 956/761-2471, www.southbeachtexas.com, $43-129), an independently owned 12-unit establishment among the palms just a block from the beach. One of the oldest hotels on the island, dating to 1961, South Beach offers kitchenettes with full-size stoves, fridges, microwaves, and toasters. Pets are welcome, and Wi-Fi is available.

Close to the Queen Isabella Causeway is the casual and consistent **Super 8** (4205 Padre Blvd., 956/761-6300, www.super8padre.com, $129 d), offering a heated outdoor pool, free continental breakfast, free Wi-Fi access, and mini microwaves and fridges. A step up that's closer to the action is the **Ramada Limited** (4109 Padre Blvd., 956/761-4097, www.ramadasouthpadreisland.com, $159 d), offering a free hot breakfast, an outdoor pool and hot tub, and rooms with microwaves, fridges, and free Wi-Fi. Pets are welcome at the Ramada.

Best Western Beachside Inn (4500 Padre Blvd., 956/761-4919, www.bestwestern.com, $164 d), features clean, simple rooms within walking distance of the beach, an outdoor pool with a hot tub, and kitchenettes with microwaves and fridges. A clean and reliable chain hotel is **Holiday Inn Express** (6502 Padre Blvd., 956/761-8844, www.hiexpress.com, $179 d). The massive aquarium in the lobby has dozens of colorful fish. Otherwise, the amenities are standard, including an outdoor pool, a fitness center, beach access, free Wi-Fi, and rooms with microwaves and fridges.

Resorts

A popular and affordable resort option is **La Copa Inn Beach Resort** (350 Padre Blvd., 956/761-6000, www.lacoparesort.com, $209 d). On the beach, La Copa is a pet-friendly spot with a breakfast buffet that includes a made-to-order omelet station, hot waffles, and free Wi-Fi.

Among the best-known resorts on the island is the **Isla Grand** (500 Padre Blvd., 800/292-7704, www.islagrand.com, $220 d), with perhaps the best beachfront location in town and excellent services. Rooms include free internet access, microwaves, and fridges. Condo suites have spacious rooms, a living area with a couch and a second TV, a fully equipped kitchen, and separate baths. The hotel's grounds have direct beach access, two outdoor swimming pools with a cascading waterfall, three whirlpools, four lighted tennis courts, shuffleboard courts, and plenty of lounge chairs.

For a step up, a hotel-to-resort renovation is the **Pearl South Padre** (310 Padre Blvd., 956/761-6551, www.pearlsouthpadre.com, $289 d). Occupying 15 tropical beachside acres, this former Sheraton is a comfortable fancy spot with ample amenities and several room types: standard guest rooms, kitchenettes, suites, and fully equipped two- and three-bedroom condominiums, all with private balconies. Other amenities include an enormous 6,000-square-foot swimming pool complete with a waterfall and a swim-up bar, a separate oversize whirlpool, volleyball nets, an exercise and weight room, and seasonal parasailing.

Just down the street is the upscale and pricey **Peninsula Island Resort & Spa** (340 Padre Blvd., 956/761-2514, www.peninsulaislandresort.com, $289 d), featuring one- to three-bedroom units with kitchenettes, a swim-up pool bar, a large pool and hot tub, rooms with fancy Brazilian furniture, a gym, and an on-site convenience store. Seasonal spa services are available.

Camping

Beachfront property is too valuable for camping in the commercial part of South Padre. Only a couple of options exist for RV campers.

The **South Padre Island KOA** (1 Padre Blvd., 800/562-9724, www.southpadrekoa.com, $30-60) is geared to RVs but has a few cabins and lodges available. Site amenities include an outdoor pool, a fitness center, a recreation room, and free Wi-Fi. The adjacent Pier 19 restaurant is one of the best places on the island to enjoy a quality seafood meal.

Another busy option for RVers is **Isla Blanca Park** (33174 State Park Rd. 100, 956/761-5494, www.cameroncountyparks.com, $25-40), referred to as the "crown jewel of the system," with 600 RV slots. Features include 1 mile (1.6 km) of pristine white sand and bright blue gulf water for swimming, surfing, and fishing.

You can pitch a tent or park an RV on the vast stretch of sand north of the major recreational activity. Officials caution that you should drive on the wet sand to avoid getting stuck in the soft tractionless powder farther from the surf. Bring your garbage back with you, as there are no trash cans in these remote areas, and take the "No trespassing" signs seriously.

INFORMATION AND SERVICES

The incredibly friendly and helpful people at the **South Padre Island Convention & Visitors Bureau** (600 Padre Blvd., 956/761-6433 or 800/767-2373, www.sopadre.com, Mon.-Fri. 8am-5pm, Sat.-Sun. 9am-5pm) will provide you with brochures, maps, and information about area attractions. Check with them about fishing, boating, and other ocean-based recreation.

GETTING THERE AND AROUND

The **Brownsville South Padre Island International Airport** (BRO, 700 S. Minnesota Ave., 956/542-4373, www.flybrownsville.com) is 27 miles (43 km) from South Padre and offers several American Eagle and United Airlines flights daily from Houston. Rental cars are available at the airport. The drive to South Padre from Dallas is nine hours, and from Houston or Austin approximately five hours.

Once on the island, you can ditch the car in favor of the city's reliable **Island Metro** (866/761-1025, www.spadre.com/thewave) transportation system; see the website for stops and schedules. The small buses typically operate 7am-9pm daily among local businesses and services, and late at night during spring break to shuttle impaired revelers. The belligerent scene on the ride back from the bar at 3am is one of the most insane experiences imaginable.

El Paso and West Texas

El Paso...............367

Guadalupe Mountains
    National Park........384

Midland and Odessa...388

Mention the word *Texas* to most people, and this region of the state is likely what they envision. West Texas is hot, dry, largely flat, and, yes, occasionally dotted with cactus and cow skulls.

The Chihuahuan Desert extends north into West Texas, accounting for its arid environment and temperature extremes. Portions of the region receive as little as eight inches of rain annually (compared to an average of 50 inches in East Texas), and temperatures typically range from the 40s overnight to daytime highs in the 80s. There's something to be said for the dry heat—most Texans find it a welcome respite from the oppressive humidity along the Gulf Coast and into the central prairies.

Highlights

Look for ★ to find recommended sights, activities, dining, and lodging.

★ **Follow the Mission Trail.** Three mesmerizing missions in El Paso will transport you back to the Spanish colonial era (page 368).

★ **Ride a gondola** in the country's largest urban park, **Franklin Mountains State Park,** for views of a geographically astonishing desert playground (page 375).

★ **Witness prehistoric wonders.** See rock art, colorful animal figures, and painted masks at **Hueco Tanks State Historic Site** for insight into the lives of Texas's first inhabitants (page 375).

★ **Hike to the highest point in Texas.** Enjoy stunning views of canyon walls and rugged outcroppings from the **Guadalupe Peak Trail** (page 387).

★ **Learn about a world-changing industry.** An enormous structure in Midland, **The Petroleum Museum** showcases every possible aspect of the product and industry that forever altered the fate of West Texas (page 389).

★ **Sand-surf** through the West Texas desert scrub. Otherworldly **Monahans Sandhills State Park** has miles of blinding-white dunes (page 393).

This region has been home to Native American tribes for more than 10,000 years, and several settlements date to the 17th century (considered ancient by Texas standards). The Ysleta and Socorro Missions east of El Paso were established after the Pueblo Revolt of 1680 sent Native Americans and Spaniards from present-day New Mexico south along the Rio Grande.

Centuries later, westward expansion would forever affect the region as thousands of people from the eastern United States braved the frontier in search of opportunity. Military personnel erected frontier forts along existing trade routes, ranchers explored the area in search of open land, and post offices popped up to serve the burgeoning communities. Travelers in West Texas can still see the natural splendor the region's settlers initially encountered—majestic mountains, dramatic river canyons, and the outstretched sky—as they zoom along at the posted speed limit of 80 mph on I-10 or U.S. Highway 90.

The residents of this far-reaching region tend to be fiery and independent-minded. Many live on large ranches and value their solitude without intrusion from neighbors, or particularly the "gub-mint." With such a low population density, West Texans are often ignored and disassociated with the rest of the state, and it's not surprising that people in El Paso have more in common with New Mexico and Old Mexico than Texas. The western portion of the region is even in a completely different time zone (Mountain) than the rest of the state.

The Wild West spirit thrives in this sun-baked region, where visitors can still find traces of the Old West in its charming, wind-swept communities. Oil derricks remain a common sight in the Midland/Odessa area, and breathtaking views of sheer cliffs, rock towers, and mountain passes prevail in Guadalupe Mountains National Park. This mythical part of the state draws visitors from around the world seeking the fabled image of Texas's rugged and independent spirit.

ORIENTATION

This region of West Texas isn't unified by many things, other than the desert-ish climate and I-10. Fortunately, the views along the interstate are impressive, ranging from mountains in the El Paso area to mesas and basins farther east. Keep in mind that there's a time zone border (Mountain and Central) in this region, located about an hour's drive east of El Paso.

El Paso Area

El Paso is Texas's sixth-largest city, but it's largely forgotten by the rest of the state (El Pasoans don't necessarily mind that). The city is unfortunately defined by I-10, which slices right through the middle of town and generally leaves an unfavorable impression on the many drivers who pass through en route to or from California. Travelers should make an effort to pull off the freeway for a while to soak up El Paso's unique borderland culture, featuring adobe neighborhoods, Wild West heritage, and some of the tastiest Mexican food in the state.

Midland-Odessa Area

About four hours to the east (just down the road in West Texas standards) is the only other slightly significant "metropolis" in this region. Midland-Odessa, known for its big ol' oil fields and football players, is on I-20 a few hours north of the break-off point with I-10. This is flat, dry, dusty territory, but visitors who make the effort are rewarded with distinctive cultural experiences associated with everything from petroleum to presidents.

PLANNING YOUR TIME

There's nothing compact about West Texas. In fact, locals consider the nearly four-hour drive between El Paso and Odessa a jaunt

---

Previous: Mission San Elizario; a Midland oil derrick; Guadalupe Mountains National Park

El Paso and West Texas

© MOON.COM

MEXICO

Chihuahua

45

16

MEXICO

CHIHUAHUA
TEXAS
USA

0   25 mi
0   25 km

Ojinaga

Presidio

Big Bend Ranch
State Park

67

Study
Butte

118

Big Bend
National
Park

USA
TEXAS
COAHUILA
MEXICO

90

385

Sanderson

Marathon

385

Sheffield

349

Seminole Canyon
State Park

90

Langtry

163

Amistad
Reservoir

Amistad N.R.A.

Ciudad
Acuña

Piedras
Negras

29

2   277

Eagle
Pass

Del Rio

90

Brackettville

Carta
Valley

Devils River

277

Sonora

163

277

Ozona

Barnhart

San
Angelo

Sterling City

163

Big
Lake

137

158

87

Big Spring

349

Odessa

THE PETROLEUM
MUSEUM

Midland

385

Mid Concho River

67

Fort
Stockton

18

Grandfalls

Monahans

MONAHANS
SANDHILLS
STATE PARK

20

Kermit

18

285

302

Pecos

285

20

Toyah

Pecos River

17

Kent

10

54

Van Horn

Sierra Blanca

180 62

Dell City

Guadalupe
Mountains
National Park

GUADALUPE
PEAK TRAIL

Pine Springs

62

HUECO TANKS
STATE HISTORIC SITE

EL PASO
MISSION TRAIL

Socorro

El Paso

FRANKLIN
MOUNTAINS
STATE PARK

Ciudad
Juárez

"SEE
'EL PASO'
MAP"

Rio Grande

10

45

NEW MEXICO

Alpine

Fort Davis

17

Marfa

90

Valentine

67

USA
TEXAS
CHIHUAHUA
MEXICO

down the road. Visitors may find the trek extensive, however, especially considering that one of the most enticing carrots on Odessa's cultural stick is a statue of the world's largest jackrabbit.

El Paso doesn't draw too many visitors as they zoom along busy I-10 on their way across the country, but it's worth spending a couple days in the Sun City to experience its intriguing mix of cultural influences. The centuries-old missions, the Tigua Indian tribe, and the distinctive variety of Mexican food deserve exploration.

Set aside another couple of days to soak up the natural beauty of Guadalupe Mountains National Park, an underappreciated Texas treasure. Visitors are drawn to the park's dramatic peaks and deep canyons for day hikes and overnight camping excursions.

For an all-inclusive West Texas experience, make the four-hour journey across the desert and into the Permian Basin for a day or two in Midland and Odessa. Known primarily for their petroleum and presidents, these cities put the *Friday Night Lights* and Bush family phenomena into perspective.

INFORMATION AND SERVICES

Visitors will find several information centers in West Texas where they can inquire about maps, brochures, directions, equipment rental, and other travel-related assistance. The biggest of the bunch is the **El Paso Convention Center and Visitors Bureau** (1 Civic Center Plaza, 915/534-0600, www.visitelpaso.com, Mon.-Fri. 8am-5pm). The Texas Department of Transportation operates a **Tourist Information Center** (8799 S. Desert Blvd., 915/886-3468, daily 8am-5pm) five miles west of town on I-10 with an extensive selection of Texas-related maps and publications.

If you're heading to Guadalupe Mountains National Park, contact the visitors center at Pine Springs on U.S. Highway 62/180 (915/828-3251, www.nps.gov/gumo, daily 8am-4:30pm Mountain Time).

For those planning a trip to Midland, contact the **Midland Convention & Visitors Bureau** (109 N. Main St., 432/683-3381 or 800/624-6435, www.visitmidlandtexas.com). In Odessa, get in touch with the **Odessa Convention and Visitors Bureau** (700 N. Grant, Ste. 200, 800/780-4678, www.discoverodessa.org).

For general information about cities and attractions in the region, the **Texas Mountain Trail** (432/284-0002, www.texasmountaintrail.com) is a helpful organization under the direction of the Texas Historical Commission covering the six westernmost counties of far West Texas. Its regional office is based in Alpine, and its website is packed with useful tidbits about the region. Another handy resource for exploring regional destinations is the **Texas Travel Information Center** (8799 S. Desert Blvd., Anthony, 915/886-3468), on the New Mexico border, where you'll find travel professionals ready to assist you concerning road conditions, trip planning, routings, points of interest, and events.

GETTING THERE AND AROUND

If you have a few extra days, consider making the drive to West Texas from points east (as opposed to flying). Marvel at the topographic transformation as the Hill Country slowly blends into basin and desert terrain complete with mini mesas and a surprising amount of color thanks to the wildflowers and stratified rock terrain. If you're pressed for time, hop aboard a cheap Southwest Airlines flight to **El Paso International Airport** (6701 Convair Rd., 915/780-4749, www.elpasointernationalairport.com), about five miles east of downtown. The airport operates international flights from most major airlines, including American, Delta, Southwest, and United.

If you're not taking a ride share, the airport has several taxi stands and staff members representing the major car rental companies. Since it's so close to I-10, cab fare to downtown

El Paso can run as little as $20. Renting a car is typically the best option, however, since most travelers will want to traverse the sprawling metropolis and the Wild West environs beyond its city limits.

The city's public transportation service, **Sun Metro** (915/533-1220, www.sunmetro.net), provides bus routes from the airport to downtown. Call or check the website for information about rates and routes to your destination.

Once in town, Sun Metro is a cheap way to get around as long as you're familiar with the stops and neighborhoods. A day pass costs $4. Dozens of bus lines run to all parts of the city, typically every 20-45 minutes. Sun Metro also operates an old-fashioned street car in a loop around downtown—it's worth taking for a spin if it's too hot outside. There is no public transportation across the border to Ciudad Juarez, and even though it's not as dangerous as it was a few years ago, casual visitation remains discouraged.

For those heading straight to Guadalupe

Mountains National Park, the closest airport is nearly 60 miles north in Carlsbad, New Mexico. Though service is provided only by Mesa Airlines from Albuquerque, it's an hour closer than El Paso. For Carlsbad flight information, contact **Cavern City Air Terminal** (575/887-3060). The El Paso airport is approximately 110 miles west of the park on U.S. Highway 62/180.

Midland is a good four-hour drive from El Paso, and Southwest Airlines flights are pretty cheap to this oil-based community occasionally referred to as the "tall city of the plains." **Midland International Airport** (9506 Laforce Blvd., 432/560-2200, www.flymaf.com) lies approximately 10 miles west of Midland and 10 miles east of Odessa, and offers flights from American, Southwest, and Continental Airlines. Located at a former army airfield in the heart of the petroleum-rich Permian Basin, the Midland airport typically has more private jets than commercial airliners on its dusty runway.

El Paso

In some ways, El Paso (population 682,669) doesn't really belong in Texas, and there are residents of this remote border town who would wholeheartedly agree. Culturally and geographically, El Paso has more in common with New Mexico and even Old Mexico, but the fiery Wild West spirit that permeates the town makes it a perfect fit for independent-minded West Texas.

The city's history is marked by renowned outlaws like Pancho Villa and Billy the Kid. One of the more colorful local legends claims Billy the Kid once broke *into* a jail just east of town, pointed a six-shooter at the jailer's face, and demanded he set his friend free. Afterward, he locked the jailer in the cell, threw away the keys, and rode off on horseback across the Rio Grande into Mexico.

The most significant aspect of El Paso's history, however, lies along the magnificent

Mission Trail east of the city. These significant structures have a rich heritage dating to the 1600s, and several are still active parishes. The seemingly ancient past they represent—Spanish colonial efforts to convert the native population to Catholicism—is nearly as fascinating as their compelling whitewashed adobe walls and rustic timber-laden interiors

Despite their magnitude, the missions only represent a slice of El Paso's vibrant history. For centuries the city's fate has been tied to Mexico, particularly the cross-border town of Ciudad Juarez. Commercial activity has existed for hundreds of years along the traditional north-south trading routes for Spaniards and Indians. The city's name, originally El Paso del Rio del Norte ("the pass of the river to the north"), is a geographical reference to the accessible location used by traders and travelers.

Throughout the 1900s, El Paso and Juarez significantly impacted each other's development, especially with industry and manufacturing endeavors such as mining, natural gas, and clothing production providing labor and administrative jobs on both sides of the border. The population of both cities shifted rather dramatically in the 20th century—El Paso had a population of approximately 100,000 in 1930 while Juarez had about 45,000 residents. Juarez currently has nearly 1.7 million people while El Paso has a population approaching 700,000. Locals note that 50 years ago, El Paso was considered an Anglo town with a strong Hispanic flavor; now it's thought of as a Hispanic town with an Anglo flavor.

Though residents used to freely cross the bridges over the Rio Grande to visit family and conduct business, this slowed considerably during the past decade of drug cartels and escalated violence. In fact, tens of thousands of people have moved from Mexico to El Paso in the past decade to flee the gunfire and kidnappings associated with the cartels and smaller groups exploiting the fear factor in Mexico. The influx has had a significant impact on El Paso—most have welcomed the restaurants and businesses that previously were only accessible by making a treacherous border run. A new downtown AAA minor league baseball stadium spurred development and changed the face of the landscape.

SIGHTS

In the past, visitors were drawn to El Paso for its proximity to Ciudad Juarez—the largest city along the Texas-U.S. border, where they could spend the day shopping for bargains and eat a cheap and tasty authentic meal. For several years, the drug cartels scared everyone off, and many potential visitors were also wary of El Paso due to its proximity to Juarez. Never fear—El Paso is regularly named one of America's safest cities. Although a border run remains a slightly dicey proposition, tourists are still encouraged to visit El Paso to experience the area's distinctive history—from Native Americans to Spanish conquistadors to

Mexicans and Wild West outlaws, the people of El Paso's past left a cultural legacy and related tourist attractions unique to Texas and the United States.

★ The Mission Trail

Even if you're only in El Paso one day, make a point of traversing the **Mission Trail,** an eight-mile route southeast of the city (accessible via marked exits on I-10, 915/534-0677, www.visitelpasomissiontrail.com, open mid-morning to mid-afternoon, free) containing three fascinating historic structures. The centuries-old and still active missions of **Ysleta** (131 S. Zaragosa Rd., 915/859-9848, www.ysletamission.org) and **Socorro** (328 S. Nevarez Rd., 915/859-7718) and the presidio chapel of **San Elizario** (1521 San Elizario Rd., 915/851-1682) were constructed in the 1800s, but their original settlements date to the 17th and 18th centuries.

Serving as lasting testaments to the Spanish colonial influence on the American Southwest, the missions originated as chapels designed to convert the native population to Catholicism. The success of the missions' mission may not be enduring, but these magnificent adobe buildings are truly a sight to behold.

The Ysleta and Socorro Missions have a particularly rich heritage. Native American tribe members and Spaniards fled present-day New Mexico to the El Paso area after the Pueblo Revolt of 1680. Subsequently, they established the communities that would become Ysleta (the foundation of the Ysleta del Sur Indian Pueblo) and Socorro two miles east. The first Catholic Mass in Texas was celebrated near present-day Ysleta on October 12, 1680, to commemorate the perilous trek across the desert.

Throughout the following century, flooding affected the mission's adobe structures, some ultimately destroyed and relocated by the ravaging waters. The fragile adobe material—comprised of sunbaked mud bricks and straw—was particularly susceptible to water damage. Painstaking efforts have been made to repair the structures—at Socorro, in particular, where experts and volunteers hand made more than 20,000 adobe bricks and conducted extensive structural repairs.

Fort Bliss

Fort Bliss is an integral part of El Paso's past and present. What started in 1849 as an isolated frontier military post has become a 1.1-million acre home of the U.S. Army's air defense headquarters.

In 1916, Fort Bliss served as the command center for the country's extensive efforts to capture Mexican revolutionary leader Pancho Villa, and during World War II, the fort transformed from the country's largest horse-cavalry post to its largest antiaircraft artillery training center. Fort Bliss has several interesting museums worth visiting, especially for military and history buffs. A forewarning: To access the museums and buildings, you'll need to have a government-issued ID. It's a good idea to call in advance to ensure you have the proper paperwork and permissions in place before making specific plans to spend time on the base.

The most intriguing attraction is the **Air Defense Artillery and Fort Bliss Museum** (Building 1735, Pleasanton Rd., 915/568-5412, www.bliss.army.mil, Tues.-Sat. 8:30am-4:30pm, free). Airplanes, Army history, and antiaircraft guns are the main attraction here, with an impressive collection of equipment from World War II through the present. Exhibits showcase the advances in military technology in the United States and enemy countries. For serious military enthusiasts, the reference library here contains volumes of material about the army's significant role along the Mexican border.

Also showcasing the history of the base is the **Old Fort Bliss Museum** (Pershing and Pleasanton Rds., 915/568-4518, www.bliss.army.mil, Mon.-Sat. 9am-4pm, free). Experience life at the fort as it was in the mid-1800s through replicas of original adobe fort buildings, outdoor displays, and military artifacts.

Worth noting: Scheduling a visit to a military base has become increasingly challenging, yet still doable. Be sure to call ahead to let the base know that you're planning to visit the museums to make sure you don't have to bring any additional identification.

Tigua Indian Cultural Center

Don't be fooled by the unassuming appearance of the **Tigua Indian Cultural**

Mission Socorro

El Paso

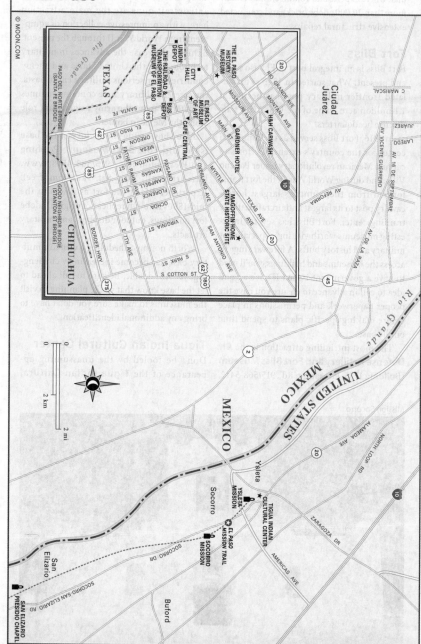

© MOON.COM

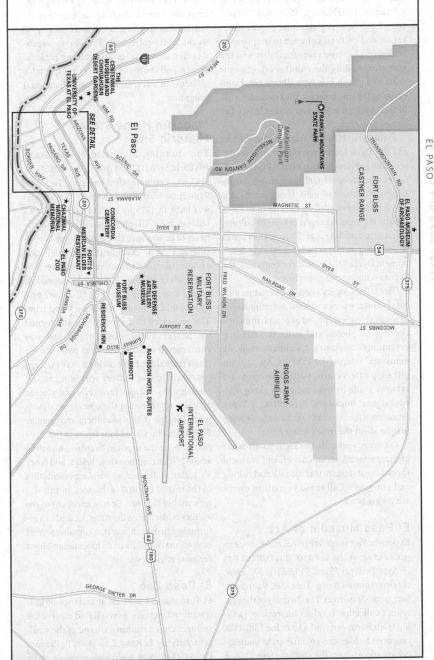

Center (305 Yaya Ln., 915/859-7700, www.ysletadelsurpueblo.org, Wed.-Sun. 10am-4pm, free). At first glance, the Tigua's reservation and cultural complex may appear to be empty. The streets are often quiet, and the area surrounding the cultural center's museum and gift shop is typically vacant. Upon entering the site, however, the resounding life of this steadfast tribe's fascinating legacy becomes apparent.

Founded in 1682, the Ysleta del Sur Pueblo, aka the Tigua Indian reservation, houses descendants of New Mexico's Isleta Pueblo's refugees who accompanied the Spanish during the Pueblo Revolt of 1680. The reservation is physically surrounded by the city of El Paso, but the tribe has managed to keep its culture, traditions, and language. Despite the threats of declining numbers and encroaching development during the past three centuries, the Tiguas remain strong survivors.

The tribe's legacy is on display at its cultural center, where a modest museum showcases past leaders, proud accomplishments, documents, photos, and artifacts, including ceremonial costumes, handmade cooking items, and interpretive exhibits. An adjacent gift shop offers crafts, pottery, jewelry, and artwork made by tribe members along with educational books and brochures. A Tigua representative is usually on hand to provide insight about the tribe's history.

On many weekends, the Tigua youth dance group performs social dances, and seasonal special events feature traditional bread baking and powwows. Call ahead to confirm events are taking place.

El Paso Museum of Art

Experience acclaimed regional and European works of art at the **El Paso Museum of Art** (1 Arts Festival Plaza, 915/532-1707, www.elpasoartmuseum.org, Tues.-Sat. 9am-5pm, Sun. noon-5pm, free). The diversity of the museum's collection is rather impressive, ranging from European works from the 13th-18th centuries to Mexican colonial art to contemporary pieces from the southwestern United States. Take your time strolling through the museum's five permanent galleries, offering a remarkable sampling of the more than 5,000 works in its collection. Temporary exhibits often showcase up-and-coming regional artists, and the museum offers a respectable schedule of lectures, films, and educational programs.

Magoffin Home State Historic Site

The stunning **Magoffin Home State Historic Site** (1120 Magoffin Ave., 915/533-5147, www.visitmagoffinhome.com, Tues.-Sat. 9am-5pm, $7 adults, $6 seniors, $ students) was built in 1875 by El Paso politician and businessman Joseph Magoffin. Now in the heart of downtown, this adobe home is considered a prime example of Territorial-style architecture, a distinctively Southwestern approach combining local adobe (sunbaked bricks comprised of mud and straw) and then-fashionable mid-Victorian wood trim. The one-story U-shaped compound owned by the Texas Historical Commission was constructed around a central patio with a plastered exterior to provide a masonry appearance. Inside, visitors will find historic photographs, antique furniture, and vintage artifacts representing the upscale yet down-home lifestyle of this prominent and popular El Pasoan who served four terms as the city's mayor. Note the exposed fireplace, revealing adobe bricks, traditional red bricks, and fancy Victorian wallpaper, an ideal representation of the mix of cultural influences on this significant heritage site. Be sure to check out the visitors center across the street, located in a refurbished historic home that contains several educational exhibits and information about regional attractions.

El Paso Zoo

El Paso doesn't have an abundance of kid-friendly attractions, so you'll find most of the younger crowd running around at the small yet satisfying **El Paso Zoo** (4001 E. Paisano Dr., 915/544-1928, www.elpasozoo.org, daily

Native Texans

El Paso's Tigua Indians live southeast of downtown on a small reservation known as the Ysleta del Sur Pueblo ("island of the south"). These tribe members are descendants of the Isleta Pueblo's refugees, who fled from their home in present-day New Mexico with Spanish colonists during the Pueblo Revolt of 1680. Now, as the Tiguas' Texas home is being encompassed by a larger city, the Tiguas' reservation remains an island attempting to maintain its proud heritage. Visitors can learn more about the tribe at the **Tigua Indian Cultural Center** (305 Yaya Ln., 915/859-7700, www.ysletadelsurpueblo.org).

Fortunately, the tribe has managed to keep its culture, traditions, and language intact for more than 325 years. Its pueblo and associated Spanish mission originated in 1682, allowing the Ysleta del Sur community to stake a claim as Texas's oldest town. The Tiguas are one of only three Native American tribes (aside from the Alabama-Coushatta and Kickapoo) living on reservations in Texas.

A LIVING LEGACY

The Tiguas are working diligently to preserve their legacy by retaining vital customs of their past. They are keeping their vanishing Tiwa language alive through classes for the reservation's children and teaching them traditional skills like pottery, painting, ceremonial dancing, and bread baking.

The Tiguas have long relied on the natural world to sustain them, and the tribe flourished when irrigation ditches from the Rio Grande allowed them to grow corn, pumpkins, and beans. To celebrate their agricultural heritage, the Tiguas hold the ceremonial Feast of Saint Anthony every June with a corn dance, traditional food preparation, and other cultural activities.

Although most of the tribe's customary rituals were eventually incorporated with Catholic holidays, its members still share a belief system with their forefathers—a way of living in unity and harmony with the forces of nature. They pay attention to the natural world around them and recognize their significant role in the universe beyond the borders of the Ysleta del Sur Pueblo.

9:30am-5pm, $12 adults, $9 seniors, $7.50 children ages 3-12). This 18-acre site just east of downtown is home to nearly 1,000 animals representing 240 species from across the world. The Animals of Asia area is the most impressive, with tigers, orangutans, tapirs, and an endangered leopard. Highlights of the Americas area include the must-see sea lion exhibit and a cage full of spindly spider monkeys. For a city of half a million people, the zoo seems rather limited in scope, but the effective use of desert foliage and squeals of delight from children make this a worthwhile experience.

The Centennial Museum and Chihuahuan Desert Gardens

The University of Texas at El Paso's **Centennial Museum** (500 W. University Ave., 915/747-5565, www.utep.edu/centennialmuseum, Tues.-Sat. 10am-4:30pm, free) is one of those old-school facilities with exhibits dedicated to history and culture that harkens back to the days of being a kid on a field trip. Judging by most of the dated dioramas and stuffed animals on display, nothing's changed much here since, but a few new exhibits (with video screens and fancy graphics) are a sign that things are slowly but surely progressing. Still, what's on display is pretty intriguing, dedicated primarily to the heritage of native groups and the cultural history of the southwestern United States and northern Mexico. The most compelling exhibits are on the top floor, particularly the artifacts from the Pueblo, Apache, and Navajo tribes.

The museum's outdoor **Chihuahuan Desert Gardens** 600-plus species in multiple areas are fascinating, especially for those unfamiliar with the diversity of desert plantlife. The educational component here is the importance of water conservation while landscaping in this arid region.

The Royal Road

Most of the western United States' traditional transportation corridors were established along wagon routes and trails associated with westward expansion. However, El Paso boasts the distinction of hosting a rare north-south route, the historically significant El Camino Real de Tierra Adentro ("the Royal Road of the Interior Lands").

The road, now roughly represented by I-25, played a significant role in the Southwest and Mexico as a trade route supporting cultural exchange and interaction among Spaniards, Native Americans, Mexicans, and Americans. Considered the earliest Euro-American trade route in the United States, El Camino Real de Tierra Adentro stretches more than 1,600 miles from Mexico City through El Paso to northern New Mexico. Based on ancient footpaths tying Spain's colonial capital at Mexico City to ancient Native American settlements in distant New Mexico, the route hosted historic parajes (camping grounds) created by the Spanish colonists that formed the basis for several modern cities along the Rio Grande and into New Mexico.

In 1598, Don Juan de Onate established the general route of El Camino Real de Tierra Adentro when he crossed the Rio Grande at El Paso del Rio del Norte ("the pass of the river to the north"), which eventually became the town of El Paso. He then followed indigenous routes along the river, eventually leading vast herds of livestock, traders, and settlers into New Mexico. The activity along the trail greatly affected the cultural development of the greater Southwest for nearly three centuries.

Although the route itself has been internationally designated, it doesn't yet contain a comprehensive interpretive element. Efforts are under way to incorporate signage and an organized educational component. To access a Geographic Information System interactive map or to find out more about tourism efforts, visit www.nps.gov/elca or call 505/988-6888.

Worth noting: Since the museum is located on a busy college campus, parking is problematic. There are several places to park behind the building, but you'll have to deal with the slight hassle of heading upstairs to find someone to give you a parking pass, since the campus police are aggressive about ticketing permit-less people.

El Paso History Museum

If the aforementioned Centennial Museum is old school in its approach to exhibiting the past, then the new school is represented by the **El Paso History Museum** (510 N. Santa Fe St., 915/351-3588, www.elpasotexas.gov/history, Tues.-Sat. 9am-5pm, Sun. noon-5pm, free). The two-story history museum is packed with informative displays and fun features. Visitors experience maps, artifacts, and photos related to all aspects of El Paso's past—from regional Native American tribes to the Wild West days to the city's role in the Mexican Revolution. The museum offers numerous eye-catching displays and interactive

exhibits, including computer touch screens with video clips, an amusing pop culture trivia game, audio stations with recordings about significant entrepreneurs, and hands-on architectural activities for the kids.

El Paso Museum of Archaeology

Though it is fairly far away from downtown, it's worth setting aside some time on your way to/from the Franklin Mountains State Park to visit the **El Paso Museum of Archaeology** (4301 Transmountain Rd., 915/755-4332, www.elpasotexas.gov/arch_museum, Tues.-Sat. 9am-5pm, free). Since this part of Texas is so rich with Native American heritage, this museum is stocked with intriguing history of regional tribes (especially from the southwestern United States and northern Mexico) in dioramas, artifacts, and pottery. Make a point of strolling through the 15-acre garden that surrounds the building, with more than 200 species of cacti and other flora representing the biodiversity of the Chihuahuan Desert.

★ Franklin Mountains State Park

A trip to El Paso is incomplete without experiencing the country's largest urban park. At 24,247 acres and covering nearly 37 square miles, the **Franklin Mountains State Park** (1331 McKelligon Canyon Rd., 915/566-6441, www.tpwd.state.tx.us, daily 8am-5pm, $5 ages 13 and older) provides a stunning natural backdrop to El Paso's city landscape. The Franklins are considered Texas's largest sustained mountain range, with a top elevation of 7,192 feet at the summit of North Franklin Peak. A pronounced gap in the range offering "the pass" through this rugged terrain provided the inspiration for the city's name. For more than 12,000 years, Native American groups, Spanish conquistadors, international traders, and adventurers have traversed the pass, and evidence of these ancient travelers remains in the form of rock art pictographs in several natural shelters throughout the park. Rangers offer tours on the first and third weekends of the month. Reservations are suggested. In addition, the park contains two pleasant hiking trails (accessible from Loop 375/Transmountain Road) and established rock climbing areas in McKelligon Canyon. A limited number of primitive tent-camping and RV sites are also available.

★ Hueco Tanks State Historic Site

It's well worth the 45-minute drive to witness the prehistoric wonders of **Hueco Tanks State Historic Site** (32 miles northeast of El Paso on U.S. Hwy. 62/180, then north on RR 2775, 915/857-1135, www.tpwd.state.tx.us, $4 ages 13 and older). The 860-acre park is named for the massive granite basins or "huecos" that provided priceless collected rainwater to Native Americans and travelers for thousands of years in this parched region of the country. These days, the invaluable attraction is the park's fascinating collection of pictographs created by area tribe members during the past several thousand years. Marvel at the mythological drawings and white- and rust-colored animal figures, each representing the lifeways of the region's bygone eras. Though the human and animal figures can be somewhat cryptic, the hundreds of masks—some clown-like, others menacing—painted by the ancient Jornada Mogollon culture are captivating and compelling. Park guides offer highly recommended pictograph tours, allowing visitors access to areas with rock art representing

Franklin Mountains State Park

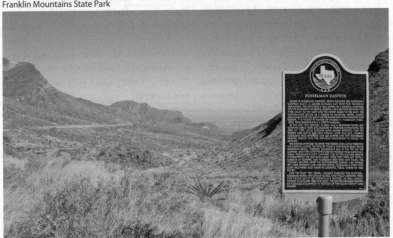

three distinct cultures. Tours are conducted primarily by reservation, so call a few days beforehand to let them know you're coming. Guides are available Wednesday-Sunday at 9am and 11am (May 1-Sept. 30) and 10:30am and 2pm (Oct. 1-Apr. 30).

Other park attractions include an interpretive center housed in a historic ranch house, ruins of a 19th-century stagecoach station, and abandoned ranch buildings. Visitors can also picnic, hike, camp, and rock climb. To reduce the threat of damage to the prehistoric pictographs, park officials limit the number of visitors to Hueco Tanks; therefore, advance reservations are required. For camping or tour reservations, call 915/849-6684. For other day-use reservations, call 512/389-8900.

ENTERTAINMENT AND EVENTS

Visitors to El Paso may not find the legendary saloons they've envisioned from the Wild West of yesteryear, but they'll discover surprisingly top-notch performing arts organizations and memorable border-spanning live music and international annual events.

Performing Arts

The cream of the city's cultural crop is the renowned **El Paso Symphony Orchestra** (1 Civic Center Plaza, 915/532-3776, www.epso. org). Established in the 1930s, the symphony bills itself as the oldest performing arts organization in town and the longest continuously running symphony orchestra in the state. The organization is respected among its peers for its ability to recruit highly qualified talent and international soloists. The symphony performs 12 classical concerts annually and hosts a variety of special events and educational programs drawing attendees from West Texas, southern New Mexico, and northern Mexico.

Equally grand in artistic ambition is the **El Paso Opera** (310 N. Mesa St., 915/581-2252, www.epopera.org), featuring national and international talent. The respected company stages several productions annually, with past performances including well-known

masterpieces such as Mozart's *Così fan Tutte* and Puccini's *Tosca*.

Newer to the scene is **El Paso Pro Musica** (915/833-9400, www.elpasopromusica.org), a chamber orchestra and choir group holding a series of concerts October-April at the El Paso Museum of Art (1 Arts Festival Plaza) and the University of Texas at El Paso's Fox Fine Arts Recital Hall (500 W. University Ave.). Pro Musica features instrumental and vocal ensembles, and hosts a popular annual Chamber Music Festival showcasing acclaimed artists from across the country.

If you're planning in advance, check to see if there's a show at the venerable **1930 Plaza Theatre** (125 Pioneer Plaza, www.elpasolive. com, 915/534-0600). This remarkably restored venue was once advertised as the largest theater of its kind between Dallas and Los Angeles. It was particularly well known for its fancy interior design and pioneering high-tech features (the Mighty Wurlitzer Organ rose from below the stage and provided sound effects for silent movies). Thanks to a spirited fundraising campaign, the theater was spared the wrecking ball in the 1980s and continues to host events, including the symphony, pop acts, and themed movie nights.

Bars and Clubs

El Paso's bar scene is fairly widespread, but the major centers of activity are downtown and near the UTEP campus. Don't expect too much from the university bars, a small collection of nondescript venues congregated near an intersection (misleadingly referred to as "the strip") and packed with indifferent college students.

If you're into local experiences, head directly to ★ **The Tap** (408 E. San Antonio Ave., 915/532-1848). This is the ultimate dive bar, with faded black and red velvet surroundings, recessed lighting, and so-bad-it's-good music on the jukebox. It's dark and dank in here with the occasional questionable character (members of the industrial rock band Ministry reportedly hang out at the bar), but that's exactly what a good dive bar should

From Robin Hood to Revolutionary

Born with the nonthreatening name Doroteo Arango, Pancho Villa was a notorious Mexican revolutionary who endeared himself to the country's poor and scared the hell out of countless Americans along the Texas border near El Paso.

As a teenaged cattle rustler in the late 1800s, Doroteo took the name Pancho Villa (reportedly after a lesser-known bandit named Pancho Villa died). His ability to evade the local law enforcement and his occasional tendency to pull off Robin Hood-style escapades made him a hero to poor folks across northern Mexico.

Villa officially became a revolutionary when he joined with Francisco Madero's forces opposing Mexico's Porfirio Diaz-led government in 1910. A year later, Villa made his first trip to Texas to meet with revolution sympathizers. After escaping from a Mexico City jail in 1913, he returned to El Paso to recruit followers and plot against Mexican general Victoriano Huerta. Villa's presence was welcome in El Paso, where he purchased an abundance of supplies and even temporarily relocated his family.

That changed in 1916, when the U.S. government recognized and supported Venustiano Carranza's regime in Mexico. Villa retaliated by raiding towns along the U.S.-Mexico border. He was no longer revered in El Paso; rather, he was exceedingly feared for his vindictive and violent tendencies.

In fact, U.S. president Woodrow Wilson even dispatched two punitive expeditions to capture Villa. Both were unsuccessful, ultimately endearing him to some Mexicans who viewed him as a triumphant menace to the meddling U.S. government.

In 1920, the Mexican government accepted Villa's surrender and bought his retirement by giving him an estate and a general's salary in his home state of Durango. Three years later, he was assassinated in Parral, Chihuahua.

be. The Tap solidifies this reputation with its cheap drinks and way-better-than-expected Mexican food. The nachos are legendary here, and they taste even better paired with a $2 can of Tecate.

"The strip" is comprised primarily of generic dance clubs where college kids gather to not dance. However, there are a couple places where you can order a quality beer or even just hang out and have a conversation without yelling. **Crave** (300 Cincinnati Ave., 915/351-3677) prides itself on its microbrews and imports, which are fairly limited by big-city standards but a welcome change of pace for this Bud Light-infused area. Next door is the comfy **Crawdaddy's Bar & Grill** (212 Cincinnati Ave., 915/533-9332, www.crawdaddys-ep.com), where you can order a cheap draft beer with a side of gumbo in a refreshingly laid-back environment.

Live Music

Geared toward the younger alternative crowd is **LQ New York** (4506 Montana Ave. 915/881-4080) a dance club featuring contemporary and salsa merigngue music. For what it's worth, don't be surprised if you get a security pat-down before entering.

A couple of traditional venues are within a few blocks of each other on a strip of highway northwest of town. For country and western dancing, drop by **Little Bit of Texas** (5500 Doniphan Dr., 915/585-2275). For blues, rock, and occasional Tejano bands, go to **Aceitunas** (5200 Doniphan Dr., 915/581-3260).

Gay and Lesbian

El Paso's only prominent gay bar is the **Briar Patch** (508 N. Stanton St., 915/577-9555). This dance club is known for its great music and open-mindedness.

Events

FIESTA DE LAS FLORES

One of El Paso's most beloved annual events is **Fiesta de las Flores** (at El Paso Coliseum,

4100 E. Paisano Dr., 915/755-2000, www. fiestadelasflores.org), held on Labor Day weekend each year. This popular event features a beauty pageant, live music, plenty of food, and the World Championship Huacha Tournament (a washer-pitching contest).

PILGRIMAGE TO MOUNT CRISTO

In 1934, a 12-foot wooden cross was placed on the summit of Mount Cristo, where Texas, New Mexico, and the state of Chihuahua, Mexico, meet. Later that decade, a shrine and an enormous limestone statue of "Christ the King" were erected. At more than 42 feet high, the monument is considered the largest of its kind in North America. Since the first pilgrimage in 1934, faithful worshippers have gathered each October at the base of the mountain (at the end of McNutt Road) to ascend the 5,650-foot, two-hour-long trek. Some carry wooden crosses, others walk barefoot over the rough path, and a few even climb on their knees. The anniversary Mass each October is observed at noon on the mount's summit and is performed in both English and Spanish.

THE SOUTHWESTERN INTERNATIONAL LIVESTOCK SHOW AND RODEO

The rodeo has been a customary event in El Paso since 1940. Referred to as the oldest sporting event in the city and the 17th-oldest rodeo in the nation, the venerable **Southwestern International Livestock Show and Rodeo** (915/755-2000) is held each September at Cohen Stadium (9700 Gateway N.) with the Franklin Mountains serving as a picturesque and appropriately rugged backdrop. The event features traditional rodeo activities such as bull riding, barrel racing, and roping.

SUN BOWL PARADE

More than a hundred floats and marching bands take to the streets (Montana St., specifically) for this annual Thanksgiving Day event. Held since the 1930s, the Sun Bowl Parade draws more than 200,000 revelers basking in El Paso's sunny winter weather.

SHOPPING

Portions of El Paso's downtown feel like marketplaces in Mexico, with discount clothing retailers and cheap trinkets lining the storefronts. They're interesting to browse, and they're pretty much the only way to do some authentic thrift shopping since a border run is no longer a safe option. Since this is the Wild West, you'll also find several reputable stores in El Paso offering quality Western wear and imports.

Boots and Western Wear

El Paso is one of the best places in Texas to find authentic Western wear. Boots and hats are required apparel as opposed to fashionable accessories in this sunbaked, windswept region. Besides, genuine cowboys live on surrounding ranches, so they need a place to get their work gear.

It's not the oldest place in town, but **Starr Western Wear** (two locations—112 E. Overland Ave., 915/533-0113, and 11751 Gateway Blvd., 915/594-0113, www. starrwesternwear.com) is the real deal. Ranching families and their workers have been outfitting themselves at this small store in the historic downtown shopping district for nearly 50 years. Starr's also carries ladies' and kids' Western wear and its durable line of Starr brand jeans and shirts. Look for traditional jeans (as opposed to fashionable) on the racks along with Wranglers, Levis, and Carhartts.

For boots, there's no excuse not to drop by one of the **Tony Lama Factory Stores** (particularly 7156 Gateway E., 915/772-4327, www.tonylamabootshop.com). A legendary boot maker for more than 80 years, Tony Lama is one of the most recognized names on the Western wear scene. Specializing in high-end handcrafted boots, Tony Lamas are made in El Paso and have been worn by famous customers such as Travis Tritt, the Texas Tornadoes, and ZZ Top. The factory outlets feature men's and ladies' boots and work boots, along with cowboy hats, belts, and Western-themed gifts.

Another established and beloved local institution is **Caboots** (2100 Wyoming Ave., 915/309-4791, www.caboots.com). This fourth-generation boot-making family primarily operates as an Internet company these days (call for an appointment), but their legacy continues with hundreds of different styles of boots, for cowboys, bikers, and kids to custom-made varieties fashioned from alligator, ostrich, python, stingray, and lizard. Fun fact: Champion's once outfitted many of the 1980s hair metal bands, including Bon Jovi and Mötley Crüe.

Yet another venerable Texas boot maker has been operating a factory store in El Paso for decades. San Antonio-based **Lucchese Boots Outlet** (6601 Montana Ave., 915/778-8060, or 40 Walter Jones Blvd., 915/778-3066) features high-quality footwear at significantly marked-down prices. For sheer volume, drop by **Cowtown Boots** (11401 Gateway Blvd., 915/593-2929), a 40,000-square-foot outlet store with an enormous selection of cowboy boots, leather goods, brand-name clothing, and accessories with affordable price tags.

Imports

For warehouse-style imports, be sure to set aside at least an hour to browse the massive **El Paso Saddleblanket** (6926 Gateway E., 915/544-1000, www.elpasosaddleblanket. com). This one-acre megastore features stacks, rows, and cases of items from Mexico and the Southwest. Colorfully patterned blankets and rugs are the main draw here, but you'll find just about anything else under the hot sun—furniture, pottery, jewelry, clothing, housewares, and artwork, to name a few.

SPORTS AND RECREATION

With more than half a million residents, El Paso is one of the largest cities in the country with no major professional sports teams.

However, much like Austin, fans are content to get their quality gamesmanship fix via Division 1-level college athletics (University of Texas at El Paso sporting events) and minor league teams.

Minor League Sports

The most popular sporting event in town, aside from the UTEP teams, is the **El Paso Chihuahuas** (1 Ballpark Plaza, www. epchihuahuas.com). El Paso residents love their AAA minor league baseball team, an affiliate of the San Diego Padres that regularly draws up to 10,000 fans to the new ballpark, located in the middle of downtown's urban landscape. The Chihuahuas play rival Pacific Coast League teams May-August.

University of Texas at El Paso

Most of the sports talk in town centers on the **UTEP Miners** (www.utepathletics.com), a nickname passed down from the school's origins as the State School of Mines and Metallurgy. As in the rest of Texas, football reigns supreme here, and fans experience the bonus of attending games at Sun Bowl Stadium, nestled among the sheer cliffs of the Franklin Mountains. The 52,000-seat stadium also hosts the venerable Sun Bowl game in late December each year.

The other major crowd-drawing UTEP athletic events are men's and women's basketball games. Both teams are perennial contenders on the brink of achieving national acclaim. The basketball teams play in the Foster Stevens Basketball Center.

FOOD

Not surprisingly, Mexican-inspired food is the most popular type of cuisine in El Paso. For a city of its size, El Paso is somewhat lacking in upscale restaurants, but its commendable mid-range Mexican, Tex-Mex, and down-home cookin' spots are plentiful.

Mexican and Tex-Mex

One of the most memorable places you'll ever have a Mexican meal is ★ **H&H Car Wash** (701

E. Yandell Dr., 915/533-1144, Mon.-Fri. 9am-4pm, Sat. 9am-3pm, $8-16). That's not a misprint—it's a real car wash. Let the professionals outside make your rig sparkle while their indoor counterparts whip up a spectacular feast. The decor is interesting if somewhat uninspiring—a 1960s-style coffee shop with minimal furnishings situated in the concrete desert just east of downtown. Regardless, most folks are here for the food, a tantalizing selection of fresh-made El Paso-style specialties such as chile relleno, burritos, red enchiladas (made with stacked or rolled tortillas filled with cheese and smothered in a spicy chile sauce), and carne picada—minced steak with diced jalapeños, onions, and tomatoes. One of the best menu items in town are the West Texas/New Mexico-style chiles rellenos, and H&H does 'em right, with a distinctive flavor bonus. Since the breaded chiles are heated on the same grill as the tasty (and greasy) burgers and sausage, the chiles' thin outer crust soaks up the goodness and adds an extra-flavorful kick.

For old-school Mexican food, head to downtown mainstay **Gonzalos G&R Restaurant** (401 E. Nevada Ave., 915/546-9343, Mon.-Sat. 8am-8pm, $8-17), a traditional spot that's blissfully operating in the past—you won't find any low-cal options or California influence here. G&R is an ideal place to order stacked red enchiladas, a regional specialty with layered tortillas, meat, and cheese that becomes even more of a local custom when you add a fried egg on top (it tastes way better than it sounds). G&R is also known for its creamy and spicy chile con queso and exquisite chiles rellenos.

Another classic Mexican joint just north of downtown is **Amigos Restaurant** (2000 Montana Ave., 915/533-0155, Tues.-Sun. 7am-8pm, Mon. 7am-3pm, $8-19). The food here is spicy New Mexico style (hot chiles), a welcome jolt for some but an unwanted kick for others. To be fair, not everything is four-alarm level here, but consider yourself warned about the enchiladas or anything else with chiles in the description. The crispy beef tacos, with the regional custom of potatoes mixed with the seasoned meat, are mild, and the chicken tampiquena, though spicy, offers a delightful blend of fresh flavors.

Locals are more likely to frequent the venerable Mexican restaurants outside of downtown, such as **L&J Cafe** (3622 E. Missouri Ave., 915/566-8418, daily 9am-9pm $8-17). Occasionally referred to as the "place by the graveyard" due to its location adjacent to Concordia Cemetery, the L&J is an El Paso institution dating to 1927 renowned for its cold beer and traditional Chihuahuan Desert-style dishes—caldillo (a flavorful beef, potato, and chile stew) and the green and red enchiladas with chicken, cheese, and multifaceted sauces.

If you only try one item at a Mexican restaurant in El Paso, make it the chiles rellenos at **Kiki's** (2719 N. Piedras St., 915/565-6713, www.kikisrestaurant.com, daily 10:30am-9pm, $9-18). These tasty delicacies are distinct to El Paso—an Anaheim chile (the long, green, and mild pepper) lightly fried in egg batter and filled with a velvety white cheese. Kiki's has perfected these supreme items, so do yourself a favor and load up on them while you're here.

To truly eat like a local, head to the eastern edge of downtown for the authentic taste of ★ **Forti's Mexican Elder Restaurant** (321 Chelsea St., 915/772-0066, www.fortisrestaurant.com, Mon.-Thurs. 9am-10pm, Fri.-Sat. 9am-11pm, Sun. 9am-8pm, $11-27). In a slightly run-down part of town in a somewhat dated hacienda-style building (like the best undiscovered local gems), Forti's is all about flavor—especially heat. Bordering on too spicy, some of the dishes (the red enchiladas, in particular) will test your heat index, but most are packed with local-style goodness. The chiles rellenos offer a perfectly smooth blend of velvety cheese and tangy pepper, and the gorditas are meaty and savory. Other menu highlights include the mole chicken enchiladas and pork al pastor tacos. If you're lucky, your meal may even be accompanied by a small band of musicians in the corner to perfectly complement your borderland experience.

Another popular spot is **Avila's Mexican Food** (6232 N. Mesa St., 915/584-3621, Mon.-Thurs. 11am-2pm and 4:30pm-8:30pm, Fri. 11am-8:30pm, Sat. 9am-8pm, Sun. 9am-3pm, $9-17), known for its semi-spicy chile dishes. To get an authentic sampling of local cuisine, order the tricolored enchilada plate, containing red, green, and sour cream enchiladas (the colors of Mexico's flag). Savor the flavors of these hearty desert chiles, coupled with the better-than-they-should-be beans and rice.

If you're simply looking for a quick bite to eat, drop by one of the several locations of **Chico's Tacos** (5305 Montana Ave., 915/772-7777, daily 9am-12:30am, $4-8), a local chain with a rabid following. The main draw here is the rolled taco—order two singles (three tacos per order) and gorge on the cheesy goodness. Strangely enough, Chico's is also known for its hot dogs, served on a hamburger bun with chili beans, pickles, and mustard.

If you're looking for that rare combo of high-quality food with a ridiculously low price tag (who isn't?), head straight to **Los Colorines** (201 E. Main Dr., Ste. 114, 915/544-5565, daily 7:30am-2:30pm, $6-12). As strange as it sounds, this is an easy yet difficult place to find. The physical landmark—the high-rise Chase bank building downtown—is pretty obvious, but the restaurant inside . . . not so much. You have to enter the building lobby and head past the escalators and around a corner to find the restaurant. It's definitely worth it. Since it's in an office building, Los Colorines is all about lunch—most tables are two-tops occupied by one businessperson—and therefore lunch specials (typically about $5-6). The tortilla soup is top-notch, with crunchy strips of fried tortilla accompanying a hearty chicken stock with fresh avocados, shredded chicken, and tasty cheese. Beef items are especially good here—the flautas are highly recommended—as are the guacamole and salsa. Top your meal off with a Mexican Coke and a smile.

American

El Paso's finest restaurant, ★ **Cafe Central** (109 N. Oregon St., 915/545-2233, www.cafecentral.com, Mon.-Sat. 11am-2am, $13-43) serves haute cuisine in a remarkable art deco building in the heart of downtown. Known for its impressive wine selection and sophisticated menu, Cafe Central is an ideal place for a fancy night on the town in a contemporary environment. Locals love the cream of green chile soup, the subtle yet savory sea bass, and the hearty grilled Angus tenderloin. Other popular menu items include the grilled pork chop with roasted brandied apples and the seared saku tuna crusted in sesame seeds.

For a thick steak with heaping sides of family activities, make the worthwhile trek to **Cattleman's Steakhouse** (30 miles northeast of El Paso in Fabens, 915/544-3200, www.cattlemanssteakhouse.com, Mon.-Fri. 5pm-10pm, Sat.-Sun. 12:30pm-9pm, $13-46). Out here in the Wild West, a 30-minute drive is just down the street, so locals drop by often to celebrate special occasions with the whole gang. Start your gastric juices flowing with the fluffy, buttery rolls, proceed to the ranch-style beans, and delve into the main attraction—the meaty, juicy prime beef. Attempt to choose from tantalizing options such as the T-bone, rib eye, New York strip, and filet mignon. Meanwhile, the kids will enjoy the outdoor petting zoo, snake pit, maze, playground, and livestock.

Breakfast

It's well worth making the five-minute drive from downtown to experience El Paso's **Bowie Bakery** (901 Park St., 915/544-6025, www.bowiebakery.com, daily 6am-9pm, $4-8). This small spot (note: there are no tables, so plan to take your items to go) is in the city's segundo barrio, a resurgent neighborhood near downtown filled with historic adobe homes and charming corner stores. The baked goods are the big draw here, particularly the traditional Mexican pastries. Bowie Bakery is a favorite among locals who line up

every morning for hot coffee and perfectly prepared *empanadas de pina* (delectable pineapple turnovers), *esponjas,* and a cream-filled swan pastry that tastes as sweet as it looks.

ACCOMMODATIONS

The majority of El Paso's lodging options are chains adjacent to the airport and Fort Bliss just northeast of downtown. Fortunately, most of the choices there and in the urban core are quite affordable (in the $100 range). El Paso's downtown used to have several historic hotels, but they've either closed their doors or declined to the point of not being recommendable.

Downtown

Budget travelers may want to consider the **Gardner Hotel** (311 E. Franklin Ave., 915/532-3661, www.gardnerhotel.com, $69 d), reportedly the oldest continually operating hotel in the city. Unfortunately, historic doesn't always mean quaint, as evidenced by the old furniture and bedding. Regardless, it's inexpensive and in a prime location. Amenities include Internet access and a fancy (in a dated way) lobby with memorabilia dating to the 1930s. There's also a hostel available for groups and backpackers on a budget.

For just a few dollars more per night, you'll find newer and cleaner accommodations a few miles away at the **Holiday Inn Express** (409 E. Missouri Ave., 915/544-3333, www.ichotelsgroup.com, $72 d), featuring a free continental breakfast, free Wi-Fi, a small fitness center, and an outdoor pool.

Located on the edge of the University of Texas at El Paso campus is the commendable **Hilton Garden Inn El Paso** (111 W. University Ave., 915/351-2121, www.hiltongardeninn.com, $99 d). The Hilton offers free wireless Internet access and refrigerators and microwaves in the rooms, as well as a fitness center and an outdoor pool.

Airport Area

The best bang for your buck in the airport vicinity is **Hyatt Place** (6140 Gateway Blvd. E., 915/771-0022, www.hyatt.com, $81 d), offering a slew of amenities, including rooms with 42-inch high-definition TVs, oversize sofa sleepers in a separate area, and free Wi-Fi along with a free continental breakfast and a fitness center. A bonus for cyclists (or those who just support cycling): Hyatt Place is a proud member of the Texas Mountain Trail Cycle Friendly Accommodations Program. Older yet still reliable is the nearby **Quality Inn & Suites** (949 Sunland Park Dr., 915/ 587-5300, www.qualityinn.com, $84 d), featuring a free full hot breakfast, an outdoor pool, free Wi-Fi, and refrigerators and microwaves in each room.

Another worthy option is **Radisson Hotel Suites** (1770 Airway Blvd., 915/772-3333, www.radisson.com, $108 d), offering rooms with Wi-Fi, refrigerators, and microwaves, as well as indoor and outdoor swimming pools, an exercise facility, and a nightly reception with complimentary cocktails. Not quite as fun yet similarly priced is the **Marriott** (1600 Airway Blvd., 915/779-3300, www.marriott.com, $109 d), with an indoor/outdoor pool, sauna, whirlpool, and exercise facility, and Internet access.

Popular with the business crowd and longer-range visitors is **Residence Inn** (6355 Gateway Blvd. W., 915/771-0504, www.marriott.com, $134 d), offering a free hot breakfast buffet daily, an evening social hour Monday-Thursday, a mini "market" with 24-hour access to snacks and drinks, large rooms with separate living areas, fully equipped kitchens with full-size appliances, and free Wi-Fi A bonus: Leave your grocery list at the front desk in the morning and come back to a fully stocked kitchen at night.

Camping

One of the nicer RV parks in West Texas is located 10 miles outside of town just over the New Mexico border. **El Paso West RV Park** (1415 Anthony Dr., Anthony, New Mexico,

---

1: the iconic H&H Car Wash **2:** downtown El Paso

575/882-7172, $20) offers free wireless, laundry facilities, and clean grounds with trees (a rarity in the desert). Another reputable option is **Mission RV Park** (1420 R.V. Dr. via exit 34 on I-10, 915/859-1133, www.missionrvparklp.com, $20) featuring free Wi-Fi, an enclosed heated pool, and on-site laundry facilities.

INFORMATION AND SERVICES

To gather maps, brochures, directions, and other travel-related assistance, visit the **El Paso Convention Center and Visitors Bureau** (1 Civic Center Plaza, 915/534-0600, www.visitelpaso.com, Mon.-Fri. 8am-5pm). Five miles west of town on I-10 is a handy **Tourist Information Center** (8799 S. Desert Blvd., 915/886-3468, daily 8am-5pm) operated by the Texas Department of Transportation. It's not quite as heavy on the El Paso info, but the selection of Texas maps and publications is extensive.

GETTING THERE AND AROUND

The quickest way to get to El Paso is via the **El Paso International Airport** (6701 Convair Rd., 915/772-4271, www.elpasointernationalairport.com), about five miles east of downtown. The airport services international flights of most major airlines, including American, Continental, Delta, Southwest, and United.

The airport offers taxi and car rental services (cab fare to downtown runs as little as $20), and El Paso's public transportation service, **Sun Metro** (915/533-1220, www.elpasotexas.gov), provides bus routes from the airport to downtown.

Once in town, Sun Metro is a cheap way to get around ($4 for a day pass), with dozens of bus lines running to all parts of the city.

Guadalupe Mountains National Park

Beckoning high in the distance to a surprisingly low number of travelers, the Guadalupe Mountains are an underappreciated natural wonder straddling the Texas-New Mexico border. Located 110 miles east of El Paso and 56 miles south of Carlsbad, New Mexico, Guadalupe Mountains National Park contains more than 86,000 acres with elevations ranging 3,650-8,749 feet—the summit of Guadalupe Peak, the highest point in Texas. Travelers who make the effort to visit this remarkably rugged and remote park are rewarded with deep canyons, the world's finest example of a fossilized reef, a rare mixture of plant and animal life, and West Texas's only legally designated wilderness.

Historically, this was the land of the Mescalero Apaches before western-bound settlers arrived in the mid-1800s. Though a proposed transcontinental railroad line through Guadalupe Pass never transpired, the Butterfield Overland Mail route traversed the area—look for the stainless-steel monument documenting the route's significance near the summit of Guadalupe Peak. By the late 1800s, ranchers and the military had established a presence in the mountains, driving away the Mescalero Apaches for good.

In the early 1920s, geologist Wallace Pratt with the then-tiny Humble Oil and Refining Company (now enormous Exxon) became captivated with the area while scouting for oil in the nearby Permian Basin. In subsequent decades, he bought a significant amount of property in the McKittrick Canyon and eventually donated nearly 6,000 acres that became the nucleus for Guadalupe Mountains National Park. The federal government purchased an additional 80,000 acres of adjacent property, and by 1972, the park was dedicated and formally opened to the public.

The park remains a compelling destination

Take a Peak

One of the few categories where Texans can't brag about having the biggest or best is mountains. Regardless, the mere fact the state boasts actual peaks—snow can even accumulate at its mile-and-a-half-high altitudes—is pretty impressive for a place typically associated with a flat, dry desert environment.

Geologically, the state claims 18 mountain ranges, all part of the rugged outcroppings of far West Texas. The most significant peaks are west of the Permian Basin between the New Mexico state line and the Rio Grande. Much of this uplifted area, particularly the Guadalupe Mountains on the New Mexico border, containing Texas's highest elevation (8,749 feet), is considered the far eastern edge of the Rocky Mountain system.

- **Guadalupe Peak:** This is the tip of Texas's top, and it's easier to access than most people realize. A well-maintained trail provides a somewhat-gradual ascent to the summit, where visitors are rewarded with breathtaking views of the majestic El Capitan peak, the colorful surrounding canyons, and diverse vegetation. One of the more bizarre items you'll find near the peak is a large steel pyramid erected in 1958 by American Airlines as part of a centennial celebration for the nearby Butterfield Overland Mail stagecoach route.

- **El Capitan:** This is perhaps the most recognized peak in Texas. With its distinctive blocky crown and sheer rock face, the mountain, at 8,085 feet tall, is the eighth-highest peak in the state. Unlike Guadalupe Peak, however, there isn't a trail to the top, so any attempts to ascend its summit should be cleared with the park's visitors center (a backcountry hiking permit is required). Expect plenty of loose rock, cactus, difficult terrain, and incredible views.

- **Mount Livermore:** Located in Davis Mountains State Park, this 8,206-foot-tall peak is a worthy contender. Although the most dramatic and picturesque mountains are in the Guadalupe and Big Bend National Parks, more Texans are familiar with the Davis and Chinati Mountains in the visitor-friendly Marfa and Fort Davis area just north of Big Bend. Historic hotels and lodges, fancy bed-and-breakfasts, and civilized campgrounds (with potable water, electricity) draw visitors from across the state who enjoy less-strenuous hikes

- **North Franklin Peak:** Don't forget about the Franklin Mountains, where this tip-top peak boasts a top elevation of 7,192 feet tall. Referred to as Texas's largest sustained mountain range, the Franklins provide an attractive natural backdrop to El Paso's urban landscape.

for hikers, backpackers, and campers who appreciate its solitude and challenging terrain. From jagged peaks to smooth sand dunes, deep canyons to sparkling springs, Guadalupe Mountains National Park is a distinctive destination offering inspiration in its remote and rugged beauty.

LAND AND CLIMATE

Rising upward of 8,000 feet above the Chihuahuan Desert, the Guadalupe Mountains occupy a traditionally arid landscape. Summertime temperatures regularly reach the mid-90s, while winter lows can dip into the teens.

Several hundred million years ago, this area was a vast sea, and the impressive rock formations currently on display—particularly El Capitan peak—are a result of a large leftover reef formed by sponges, algae, and the skeletal material of numerous aquatic organisms. In fact, the park's Capitan Reef, as it's known in the geological world, is recognized as one of the premier fossil reefs of the world. Incidentally, the millions of years of heat and pressure associated with the decomposition of this organic matter, most notably in the adjacent Permian Basin, transformed it to oil and gas.

Otherwise, the park's terrain is fascinatingly varied, shifting from dry creekbeds to tree-lined ridgetops to dramatic canyons and rippling springs. The resulting plant and animal life associated with each area is distinct to this region of the state, offering visitors the intriguing experience of viewing various exotic species.

The desert environment is a land of extremes, so visitors should plan accordingly—bring sunscreen and water in the summer and hats and gloves in the winter. Rain is fairly uncommon, but random showers can occur at any time, so sleeping under a tent or tarp is advisable. August and September are the rainiest times of the year (averaging about four inches monthly), and the mild temperatures of October and April draw the largest crowds. October is especially busy since Texans relish the rare opportunity to see vibrant fall colors on display.

PLANTS AND ANIMALS

Because of the uncommon intersection of desert, canyons, and highlands, the park is home to a variety of ecosystems serving as habitat for 60 species of mammals, 289 types of birds, and 55 species of reptiles as well as 1,000-plus varieties of plants.

Many of the park's animals are nocturnal, so you probably won't witness an abundance of scurrying critters during daytime hikes. At night, however, the desert comes to life when cooler temperatures prompt foxes, bobcats, badgers, bats, and even some howling coyotes to emerge from their dwellings in search of food. Early-morning and late-evening creatures include mule deer, javelina, and black-tailed jackrabbits.

Reptiles thrive in the Guadalupe Mountains' harsh daytime conditions, so be on the lookout for lizards (varieties include collared, prairie, and crevice spiny) and snakes (western diamondback rattlesnake, bullsnake, and coachwhip). Snakes tend to congregate in rocky areas like dry streambeds, so keep an eye and ear out for their presence. The park's rocky canyons are home to ring-tailed cats (a raccoon relative), rock squirrels, and a variety of reptiles including rock and black-tailed rattlesnakes and tree lizards. Also, don't be surprised if you come across one of the few dozen Rocky Mountain

elk descended from a herd brought to the area in the 1920s.

Plant-wise, the desert/mountain climate provides a diverse environment for a wide range of flora, from desert-floor cactus species (prickly pear, yucca, and sotol) to pine forests (ponderosa, Douglas fir) that thrive in the cooler elevations. The significant geographical variations in this rugged landscape result in various trees, grasses, and scrub brushes spanning thousands of acres with more than 6,000 feet of elevation difference.

You'll find some deciduous trees near water sources in the park's higher elevations that mimic the environment in northern climes, but much of the landscape is hardscrabble and arid. These areas produce hearty plants that can withstand severe temperature extremes, powerful winds, and a minimal water supply. Cacti have thick stems that store moisture and spines that help reflect the sun's radiant heat. The park's annual wildflowers grow during the rainy summer season—August and September—with a compacted life cycle to maximize the region's minimal moisture.

CAMPGROUNDS

Two of the park's most popular campgrounds, Pine Springs and Dog Canyon, are accessible by car, but the remaining nine wilderness sites are only reachable by foot. Those interested in roughing it to these remote areas are required to obtain a free backcountry use permit at the Pine Springs Visitor Center or Dog Canyon Campground, where detailed maps are also available. Due to the isolated nature of these sites, it's essential to bring at least a gallon of water per person per day, ample food (open fires are prohibited so a camp stove may also be necessary), and emergency gear such as a first-aid kit, compass, and extra batteries.

For those who enjoy a little potable water with their wilderness camping experience (and who doesn't?), spend the night at either the Pine Springs or Dog Canyon Campgrounds. Upon arrival, select a tent or RV site (no hookups or dump stations are available) and pay at the self-registration board near the restrooms. The fee is $8 per night per site.

Pine Springs

Near the park's headquarters and visitors center, Pine Springs is the largest of the two main campgrounds, featuring 20 tent and 19 RV sites in a simple desert camping area at the base of the mountain. Small trees shade most of the graveled tent sites, but the RV area is basically a big ol' paved parking lot. The campground features safe drinking water, accessible flush-toilet restrooms (no shower facilities), a utility sink, pay telephones, and a drink machine.

Dog Canyon

Sitting more than 6,200 feet above the desert, Dog Canyon Campground is in a secluded, tree-filled canyon on the north side of the park. Its higher elevation and sheltered location beneath steep cliff walls result in cooler temperatures than Pine Springs. However, the canyon also protects the area from strong winds that blast through this part of the park in winter and spring. Dog Canyon Campground has nine tent sites and four RV sites along with restrooms containing sinks and flush toilets but no showers. Cooking grills are available for charcoal fires since the area isn't quite as dry and windy as other parts of the park.

HIKING

If you're not up for an overnight stay, the best way to appreciate Guadalupe Mountains National Park is by putting boot to rocky terrain on one of the breathtaking hiking trails. More than a dozen options are available (check with the park's visitors center about length and difficulty), but visitors can experience several of the most popular treks— or at least the most scenic portions—in a day. In addition, smaller self-guided nature trails are available at the park's headquarters, McKittrick Canyon, and at Dog Canyon.

McKittrick Canyon Trail

To fully experience the majesty of McKittrick Canyon, considered by some to be one of Texas's most captivating natural wonders, allow most of the day to reach the high ridges. Start at the McKittrick Canyon Visitor Center (daily 8am-6pm), where you'll descend two miles into the canyon before reaching the first significant milestone— Pratt Cabin, a 1929 structure constructed for geologist and land donator Wallace Pratt. Continue another mile to the gorgeous Grotto Picnic Area, one of the most scenic areas in the entire canyon. If you have the extra time and stamina, continue four more miles to McKittrick Ridge for magnificent views of the colorful canyon walls and rugged surrounding outcroppings.

★ Guadalupe Peak Trail

Accessible from Pine Springs Campground, Guadalupe Peak Trail is highly recommended for the stunning views atop the highest point in Texas. Fortunately, the trail is in good shape, and despite the seemingly daunting task of ascending to an elevation of more than 8,000 feet, the trek isn't overly strenuous. At four miles long (one-way), the trail is more than just a quick day hike. A campsite located about a mile before the summit is a good spot to take a break and eat a picnic lunch among the breezy pines and sun-drenched mountain ridges.

El Capitan Trail

Beginning at Pine Springs Campground, this trail offers a compelling experience of desert savanna and a tremendous view of the dramatic El Capitan peak. The trail doesn't lead to the summit—the distinctive formation is sheer vertical rock wall—but it gradually climbs along its base. Hikers can choose to descend farther into the canyon after skirting the peak, but the hike is rigorous. Consider heading back to Pine Springs after experiencing the grandeur of El Capitan.

INFORMATION AND SERVICES

To get started on your journey, drop by the park's headquarters/visitors center at Pine Springs, accessible via U.S. Highway 62/180 (look for the signs on the highway—there isn't much else out here). Pick up a stack of maps and brochures, find out the current weather forecast, view an orientation slide show and interpretive exhibits, browse the bookstore, and talk to the knowledgeable and friendly park staff about your plans. Adjacent to the center is the Pinery Trail, a paved pathway with scenic views and educational panels providing information about the native plants. The short trail leads to the Butterfield Overland Mail stage station's historic ruins.

The visitors center is open daily 8am-4:30pm (Mountain Standard Time) in the winter and 8am-6pm in warmer months—generally April-October. Chat with the helpful park ranger, browse the impressive book selection, purchase a T-shirt, and check out the adequate exhibits dedicated to the park's history and natural assets. The entrance fee is $5 per person ages 16 and older, and the park pass you'll receive is valid for seven days. For more information, call the visitors center at 915/828-3251 or visit www.nps.gov/gumo.

GETTING THERE

For those heading straight to Guadalupe Mountains National Park, the closest airport is nearly 60 miles north in Carlsbad, New Mexico. Though service is provided only by Mesa Airlines from Albuquerque, it's an hour closer than El Paso. For Carlsbad flight information, contact **Cavern City Air Terminal** (505/887-1500).

For those driving to the park, the El Paso airport is approximately 110 miles west of the Guadalupe Mountains on U.S. Highway 62/180. For those arriving from the east, take either I-20 or I-10 to Van Horn, then head north for about an hour on Highway 54, one of the most scenic drives in the entire state.

Midland and Odessa

It may not be fair to lump these two distinctly different cities together, but they have more in common than they're willing to admit. Both cities can lay claim to the three p's: petroleum, pigskin, and presidents. Still, there's a fierce Midland vs. Odessa rivalry befitting of fiery West Texans, and like most neighboring communities in the rural United States, the competition between the two is hashed out on the football field. Unlike typical towns, however, the intensity of this gridiron action has been documented in the essential *Friday Night Lights* body of work (book, movie, and TV show).

The entire region is known as the Permian Basin, a reference to the vast Permian Sea that once covered much of the area nearly 300 million years ago. Native American tribes populated the region for much of the past 12,000 years before pioneer settlers arrived in the mid-1800s. The dry, dusty landscape appealed to only the hardiest of frontier settlers, who braved the conditions to (barely) make a living in ranching. In the late 1920s, oil was discovered deep beneath the sedimentary layers of the Permian Basin, forever altering the fate of Midland (population 142,344) and Odessa (120,568).

Thanks to the foresight of an entrepreneur named T. S. Hogan, who commissioned the construction of a stately 12-story office building in anticipation of the oil boom, Midland became the business center of the region. Though momentum slowed briefly during and after the Great Depression, exploration and drilling began again in haste in the 1950s, setting the big boom in motion. At one point, there were more than 600 oil companies, and the numerous multistoried corporate offices popping up downtown earned Midland the nickname "the tall city of the plains."

It was during this time that the two communities began taking on distinct identities. Midland became the white-collar town, with banks and businesses picking up where Hogan had left off by eagerly processing and capitalizing on the abundance of cash that flowed in conjunction with the precious black gold. Conversely, Odessa became the blue-collar city, where many of the roughnecks (oil workers) resided.

These able-bodied folks who handled the massive oil rigs and drilling equipment became parents to equally brawny teenage sons, who excelled on the gridiron. These hulkish kids—some topping out at six feet five, 300-plus pounds—became local heroes, playing college-caliber ball for crowds of 20,000 strong. The phenomenon was eloquently captured in H. G. "Buzz" Bissinger's captivating book *Friday Night Lights,* which eventually became an equally compelling movie and television show.

Another source of local pride is the Bush family presidential legacy. Though neither of the Georges were born in the Permian Basin, they spent formative years here, and both cities are eager to lay claim to the title of the Bushes' hometown. The family spent several years shuffling between Odessa and California before finally settling in Midland (and ultimately Houston). Their lives and times in West Texas are on display at Odessa's presidential museum and both cities' George W. Bush childhood homes.

Beginning in the early 2010s, the Midland-Odessa's Permian Basin Oilfield returned to its glory days, thanks primarily to fracking. As a result, it's a bit hectic, with many hotels maxed out by oil workers and crumbling roads due to the excessive number of trucks. At least until the next bust.

SIGHTS
★ The Petroleum Museum
You'll learn everything you ever needed (or wanted) to know about the industry that forever changed the lives of millions at the **Petroleum Museum** (1500 I-20 W., Midland, 432/683-4403, www.petroleummuseum.org, Mon.-Sat. 10am-5pm, Sun. 2pm-5pm, $12 adults, $8 seniors and students). This enormous, lofty-ceilinged structure contains information and exhibits related to every possible aspect of the oil industry, from prehistoric geological conditions and historic drilling equipment to current trends in oil recovery. Though the immense number of artifacts and technical information about the minutiae of the industry can be overwhelming at times, there are gems that offer fascinating insight. For example, there's a rotating drill bit in one exhibit room that dug a 5.6-mile-deep (!) well over the course of three years, requiring 166 replacements, including 21 diamond-infused bits. Other museum attractions include several galleries devoted to Western art and children's activities, and an area called "the oil patch" that features thousands of objects, from antique drilling equipment to modern machinery, in a 40-acre exhibit area behind the museum.

Presidential Museum and Leadership Library
The **Presidential Museum and Leadership Library** (4919 E. University Ave., Odessa, 432/363-7737, www.presidentialarchives.org, Mon.-Fri. 8am-5pm, free) was conceived well before both George Bushes ascended to the presidential throne. Originating after the 1963 assassination of John F. Kennedy, the museum was located in Odessa's main library before moving to fancy new digs in the early 2000s. Visitors first encounter a large rotunda area featuring a life-size replica of the presidential seal rug that lies in the real Oval Office, and then proceed through an intriguing exhibit area containing profound quotes from past commanders in chief, the presidents of the Republic of Texas (natch), and separate display cases devoted to each of the U.S. presidents in chronological order. The individual Plexiglas boxes contain fascinating artifacts and memorabilia,

Mojo Working

Odessa's Permian High School, the inspiration for *Friday Night Lights*

High school football is a religion in Texas, and in Odessa, the faithful worship at the shrine of Ratliff Stadium. This megasize monolith, with an astoundingly enormous capacity of 19,500, inspired the title of H. G. "Buzz" Bissinger's 1991 book *Friday Night Lights,* a fascinating story about the Permian High School (Odessa) football team's unforgettable 1988 season.

The book became a cultural phenomenon, spawning a successful movie and inspirational TV show chronicling the life of a football-crazed town dealing with typical issues in the rural United States: family relations, religion, and especially racism. Bissinger's account of Odessa was so detailed—his journalism background inspired him to intensively research and report his findings—it upset many locals, who objected to a seemingly unflattering portrayal of their community. Upon the release of his book, Bissinger became persona non grata in Odessa, despite the national attention Permian High School received for its football program.

GRIDIRON GIANTS

The Odessa/Midland area holds a unique distinction when it comes to producing gridiron giants. The kids here are exceptionally big, many spawning from brawny oil riggers and burly roughnecks who operate the heavy equipment in the nearby oil fields. It's common in these parts to see 300-pound teenagers towering over standard-size six-foot-tall mortal men. Step into a local burger joint at lunchtime on Friday, and you'll find tables full of hulking kids in letterman jackets devouring plates of gigantic burgers in just a few bites.

They're just as ravenous when they take the field. The Permian Panthers and cross-town archrivals the Midland Lee Rebels are two of Texas's most successful high school football programs. Their supersize students often play college-caliber ball, and their achievements are the stuff of legend among Texas's gridiron geeks. Permian claims two national championships (1972 and 1989) and six state championships (1965, 1972, 1980, 1984, 1989, and 1991), while Midland Lee boasts three consecutive state championships (1998-2000). The schools' most famous football alumni are former NFL stars Roy Williams (Permian) and Cedric Benson (Midland).

In the late 1960s, Permian fans began using the term "mojo" to describe the magic and emotion associated with their beloved Panthers' prowess, and the term quickly became an enthusiastic rallying cry representing the intensity of the ferocious players and fans. A testament to the power of the word permanently graces the high school's front facade, which boasts four enormous black letters requiring no explanation around here: MOJO.

including coins, printed mementos, and campaign buttons representing the past 230 years of American history. Perhaps most popular, however, is the plain little house behind the museum. This modest postwar structure was home to the Bush family (George H. W., Barbara, and George W.) in the late 1940s and was moved from its original location to the museum grounds in 2006. The museum proudly claims to have the only home to ever be occupied by two presidents and a first lady, which was painstakingly restored and decked out to its authentic 1948 appearance.

George W. Bush Childhood Home

Regardless of political leanings, it's quite compelling to learn personal details about a leader of the free world. Get a glimpse of this type of domesticity at the **George W. Bush Childhood Home** (1412 W. Ohio St., Midland, 432/685-1112, www.bushchildhoodhome.org, Tues.-Sat. 10am-5pm, Sun. 2pm-5pm, $5 adults, $3 seniors, $2 students). Built in 1939, the plain yet comfy home was the Bush family residence 1951-1955, when George W. was roughly 5-9 years old. Like the Odessa house, it's been redecorated based on photos and personal recollections to authentically represent the family's surroundings at the time. The highlight is little George's room, filled with 1950s memorabilia depicting the activities he was involved with at the time, namely Little League, Cub Scouts, and the Roy Rogers fan club. Other rooms replicate the homey feel of the kitchen and den, and the remaining spaces contain computer screens with '50s TV shows and commercials, as well as photos and informative panels putting the family's life and Midland history in context.

Odessa Meteor Crater

The **Odessa Meteor Crater** (five miles west of Odessa off I-20, exit 108, 432/381-0946, self-guided tours daily 9am-6pm) is an out-of-this-world experience. Billed as the second-largest crater in the United States (only the Arizona Crater is bigger), it was formed nearly 50,000 years ago when a shower of nickel-iron meteorites crashed into Earth, resulting in a 100-foot-deep, 550-foot-wide depression. Over time, accumulated sediments filled the crater to within six feet of the level of the surrounding plain, but visitors can still easily discern the recessed area on the flat West Texas prairie. In the 1940s, scientists dug a 165-foot-deep shaft in the center to try to find the big meteorite they assumed was still buried. They didn't find anything, supporting the subsequent theory that the 350-ton meteor was traveling so quickly, it exploded and vaporized upon contact with the ground. An interpretive center provides exhibits and a video related to the exploration of the Odessa Meteor Crater and related scientific facts.

Haley Library and History Center

Though it's set up for serious researchers of Western heritage, the **Haley Library and History Center** (1805 W. Indiana Ave., Midland, 432/682-5785, www.haleylibrary.com, Mon.-Fri. 10am-5pm, free) is worth dropping by for a quick visit. Named for overachieving rancher and writer J. Evetts Haley, who interviewed more than 700 Southwestern pioneers, the facility contains a modest yet impressive collection of Western artifacts and a tremendous archive of books and documents dedicated primarily to ranching culture. Visitors interested in Texana will delight in seeing the historic bell that once hung at the Alamo as well as the numerous saddles from regional pioneer families and the remarkable collection of silver spurs. The building also hosts occasional exhibits featuring the work of local and regional artists.

Museum of the Southwest

Housed in a sprawling 1937 mansion is the misleadingly grand-sounding **Museum of the Southwest** (1705 W. Missouri Ave., Midland, 432/683-2882, www.museumsw.org, Tues.-Sat. 10am-5pm, Sun. 2pm-5pm, $5 adults, $3 students). The magnificent home is

the main attraction here, offering a glimpse of a rich oil baron's homestead during Midland's boom years. Constructed on 12 contiguous lots, the 5,300-square-foot palace exudes opulence, with nearly a dozen fireplaces and ornamental architectural details. The art exhibits scattered throughout the rooms and added galleries aren't quite as impressive, featuring a smattering of Western paintings and pottery. The expansive complex also includes a decent yet small children's museum and one of the only planetariums open to the public in West Texas.

Ellen Noel Art Museum

For a blue-collar town, Odessa has a rather impressive cultural facility in the **Ellen Noel Art Museum** (4909 E. University, Odessa, 915/550-9696, www.noelartmuseum.org, Tues.-Sat. 10am-5pm, Sun. 2pm-5pm, free). The museum's three main galleries contain permanent and traveling exhibits typically showcasing modern art, historic paintings, and installation work. Even more intriguing is the outdoor portion of the museum, a "sculpture and sensory garden" designed with visually impaired children in mind. Everything in the garden is dedicated to senses other than sight—particularly touch, sound, and smell. A flowing fountain provides soothing sounds and cool tactile sensation, while various herbs offer fragrant and soft or scratchy leaves.

★ Monahans Sandhills State Park

For a true otherworldly experience, visit **Monahans Sandhills State Park** (exit 68 on I-20 W., Monahans, 432/943-2092, www.tpwd.state.tx.us, daily 8am-10pm, $5 ages 13 and older). Rising out of the West Texas desert scrub are miles of smooth, rotund, blindingly white sand dunes. These seemingly out-of-nowhere formations are a result of desert winds exposing ancient layers of sediment left behind by Pecos River erosion. Nowadays,

families flock to the park with their saucer sleds to "sandsurf," which is exactly what it sounds like—cruising down a steep hill with the help of a plastic contraption. It's kind of like snow sledding, just without the snow or subfreezing temperatures. Unfortunately, the idea of it is more fun than the reality—ice is much slicker by nature than sand. Traversing the dunes is an experience unto itself (wear sandals or shoes with some stable support), and it's especially fascinating to keep tabs on the myriad critter tracks, including snakes, birds, and lizards. Camping and picnic areas are available, and the park store offers sleds for sale or rent.

FOOD
Midland
AMERICAN

Midland's white-collar sensibilities are on full display at the ★ **Wall Street Bar and Grill** (115 E. Wall St., 432/684-8686, daily 11am-2:30pm and 5:30pm-10pm, $12-33). Located on the city's big-money street with all the tall buildings, this well-heeled and high-quality restaurant caters to the business crowd with copies of the *Wall Street Journal* in the bar area and a stock ticker running over the entryway. The food reflects the tony surroundings, with hearty flavorful steaks and succulent seafood dishes the menu items of choice.

Also notable is **Café at the Gardens** (3300 Fairgrounds Rd., 432/687-1478, www.alldredgegardens.com, lunch Mon.-Sat. 11am-2pm, dinner Thurs 5pm-10pm, $9-22), outside of town at Alldredge Gardens, one of Midland's premier greenhouse and nursery operations. Locals have long been taking root at the café for the tasty wraps and gourmet pizzas at lunch and the seafood entrées (snapper étouffée, crab cakes) for dinner.

MEXICAN AND TEX-MEX

One of the top choices for Mexican food in Midland is **La Bodega** (2700 N. Big Spring St., 432/684-5594, Sun.-Thurs. 11am-9pm, Fri.-Sat. 11am-10pm, $8-17). Known for its remarkable interior Mexican food, the

---

1: George W. Bush Childhood Home in Midland
2: Monahans Sandhills State Park

restaurant's specialty is its chiles rellenos, prepared with seasoned beef stuffed in a not-too-spicy chile, which is peppered with raisins and pine nuts. An added bonus: The margaritas here are some of the best in town. Note: Smoking is still allowed in the restaurant, so you may get a mouthful of smoke with your chips and salsa.

Another popular Mexican *restaurante* is the deceptively named **Caramba's Spanish Inn** (3116 W. Front St., 432/520-9724, Mon.-Fri. 11am-2pm and 5pm-9pm, Sat. 11am-9pm, $9-17). Despite the name, there are no Iberian specialties here, although many of the waitstaff speak the Spanish language. Caramba's specialties include traditional Mexican fare such as enchiladas (try the green chile chicken), tacos, burritos, and nachos.

Odessa

AMERICAN

Odessa doesn't have a reputation as a cuisine capital, but several restaurants in town do a respectable job with the basics, which around here means meat. One of the best representations of Odessa eats is the **Barn Door Steakhouse** (2140 Andrews Hwy., 432/580-7019, www.odessabarndoor.com, Mon.-Fri. 11am-9:30pm, Sat. 4pm-10:30pm, $11-24). There's something endearing about the hokey Western decor and theme, probably because it's the way things have been here for decades, offering the same kind of familiarity as the comfort food on the menu. Meals begin with a big block of cheese. Big. It's followed by a fresh loaf of bread, and there's more homey goodness to be found among the entrées—charbroiled steaks are the main draw here, but the chicken dishes and fried shrimp are popular, too.

Barbecue is a safe bet in a town like Odessa, and one of the best places to sample the local flavor is **Jack Jordan's Bar-B-Q** (1501 John Ben Shepperd Pkwy., 432/362-7890, Mon.-Sat. 11am-9pm, $9-17). West Texans are a fiery bunch, so it shouldn't come as a surprise that they like their barbecue spicy. The sauce here has a nice bite, orders come with jalapeños on

the side, and a big bottle of Tabasco sauce is on each table. Despite the fact it's housed in an uninspiring locale, people come here for the food, and in West Texas, that means beef. When they say ribs around here, they don't mean pork.

MEXICAN AND TEX-MEX

For a Texas town of nearly 100,000, there are surprisingly few options for quality Mexican food in Odessa. One of the consistently reliable choices is **La Bodega** (1024 E. 7th St., 432/333-4469, www.labodegamexicanrestaurant.com, daily 11am-10pm, $8-16). Operated by the same crew as the Midland outfit, La Bodega offers the same quality Mexican cuisine, including its famous chiles rellenos.

Another noteworthy spot is **Dos Amigos Bar & Grill** (4700 Golder Ave., www.dosamigos.com, Mon.-Sat. 11am-2am, $9-16). Housed in an old horse stable, Dos Amigos has become better known as a live music and bull-riding venue lately than as a restaurant, but the food remains decent, and it tastes even better when a band is accompanying the meal from the large stage across the large courtyard. You can't go wrong with the chicken enchiladas or anything else smothered in the New Mexico-style green chile sauce. Incidentally, the queso here is outstanding.

ACCOMMODATIONS
Midland

Travelers shouldn't have to spend a lot of money on a hotel room in the middle of nowhere, but many Midland accommodations don't adhere to this philosophy. Besides, there are oil companies paying for workers to fill the hotels. Fortunately, there are several worthy options in the semi-affordable range, including the **Plaza Inn** (4108 N. Big Spring St., 432/686-8733, www.plazainnmidland.com, $83 d). Though it caters largely to a business crowd, it's still a decent home away from home for a few nights. The Plaza offers Internet access and a free continental breakfast.

Another notable spot near downtown is **La**

Wrangling the World's First Rodeo

Attempting to lasso the legend of the world's first rodeo is almost as tough as roping an ornery steer in a dusty arena. Many western U.S. cities claim to have hosted the first rodeo-style event, but the West Texas town of Pecos appears to have the strongest case for this distinction.

Eyewitness accounts gathered in 1928 by a Pecos journalist detail the firsthand experiences of cowboys who participated in the 1883 event that's now referred to as the first rodeo. According to these reports, several men were hanging out at a local saloon when discussion turned to steer roping and bronco busting abilities. After some hemming and hawing, plans were made to host a July 4th competition to coincide with the crowds in town for a holiday picnic. What sets the Pecos event apart from other "first rodeo" claims is its distinction of being held in town for spectators and with prizes awarded to the winning cowboys.

By laying claim to hosting the world's first rodeo, Pecos has encountered its fair share of nay-sayers. Communities in other western states—Colorado, Arizona, and Oklahoma, to name a few—have disputed the title, but Pecos has fought diligently to prove its authenticity.

NO TRIVIAL MATTER

In an effort to make things official, an appeal was made to Encyclopedia Britannica in the 1930s by providing signed affidavits from Pecos residents who'd attended the rodeo event. Although encyclopedia researchers were eventually convinced about the authenticity of Pecos's claims, the official documents were lost in the process.

Another twist in this serious saga came in the mid-1980s, when the board game Trivial Pursuit included a question about a "rough-and-tumble Western sport" being first formalized in Arizona. Not surprisingly, the quiz card reference wasn't a trivial matter to Pecos residents, who reportedly threatened to sue the game company if the information wasn't changed. Ultimately, the wording wasn't changed since the game company decided the word formalized accurately applied to the Arizona event.

Regardless, Pecos maintains its claim to the title, and the community still hosts its annual West of the Pecos Rodeo each summer, drawing some of the sport's most accomplished athletes and thousands of spectators from across the country. The event has been held at its present location since 1936, and even though the memories of the first rodeo have long since faded into the vast, panoramic sky, the spirit of the 1883 competition endures in this proud West Texas community.

Quinta Inn (4130 W. Wall St., 432/697-9900, www.lq.com, $99 d), featuring free Wi-Fi and breakfast, as well as an outdoor pool.

For those looking to experience the upper echelon of Midland society, make reservations at the ★ Doubletree by Hilton Midland Plaza (117 W. Wall St., 432/683-6131, www.hilton.com, $117 d). Located in the heart of the downtown business district, the 250-room Hilton offers panoramic views of the wide-open plains and the city skyline. The Hilton's amenities include free Wi-Fi, a large fitness center and pool, and a swanky rooftop bar overlooking the city's Centennial Plaza.

Odessa

Odessa has more affordable rates than Midland, but most of the sub-$50 options are older hotels and motels badly in need of an upgrade. For a bit more money, travelers can lodge in comfort with all the necessary amenities. The best value in town (and virtually a required stay if you're traveling with children) is the ★ MCM Grande Hotel and Fun Dome (6201 E. I-20 Business, 432/362-2311, www.mcmgrande.com, $89 d). The Grande, also referred to as the "fundome," caters to families with its indoor atrium area containing a playscape, nine-hole mini-golf course, indoor/outdoor pool, and game tables. The rooms feature genuinely comfortable beds, and the free specials are equally impressive: hot breakfast, free Internet access, and complimentary drinks at happy hour.

Another option is **La Quinta** (5001 E. I-20 Business, 432/333-2820, www.lq.com, $139 d). About 10 miles west of the Midland airport, La Quinta offers free Wi-Fi, a complimentary continental breakfast, and an outdoor pool with a large sundeck.

Billing itself as West Texas's "only four-star hotel" is the **MCM Elegante** (200 E. University Blvd., 432/368-5885 or 866/368-5885, www.mcmelegante.com, $99 d). The Elegante prides itself on top-notch service not always found at run-of-the-mill establishments in town, with luxuries such as a bellhop, a spa and salon, and an extensive recreation area (jogging track, putting and chipping green, practice fields, horseshoe pits, and a playground), as well as free Wi-Fi and quality bedding.

INFORMATION AND SERVICES

Midland and Odessa each have a convention and visitors bureau promoting attractions and events in the community. To find out everything you need to know about Midland, including maps, brochures, and advice, contact the **Midland Convention & Visitors Bureau** (109 N. Main St., 432/683-3381 or 800/624-6435, www.visitmidlandtexas.com). For Odessa, get in touch with the **Odessa Convention and Visitors Bureau** (700 N. Grant, Ste. 200, 800/780-4678, www.odessacvb.com).

GETTING THERE AND AROUND

The **Midland International Airport** (9506 Laforce Blvd., 432/560-2200, www.flymaf.com) is exactly 10 miles between both cities and offers service to several major airlines. Although some hotels offer shuttle service, you'll be stuck there since public transportation systems are virtually nonexistent. Renting a car from the airport is the best option for getting around, especially since there are several interesting places worth visiting (Monahans Sandhills State Park, in particular) that require 20-plus miles of driving.

Big Bend Region

Everything about the Big Bend area is vast— the sky, the views, the mountains, the canyons, and especially the sense of wonder. It's a true getaway to a relatively untouched land, where the natural elements dominate the landscape and the visitors simply marvel at its beauty.

What sets this region apart from the rest of Texas is the presence of mountains. The relatively accessible Davis Mountains in Fort Davis are fairly impressive, featuring giant outcroppings of red rock rising thousands of feet into the West Texas sky, but the state's magnificent mighty peaks are in Big Bend's Chisos mountain range. A portion of Big Bend even evokes the Rocky Mountains in Colorado, with sheer vertical drops looming right outside the car window and tight switchbacks providing an element of suspense.

Big Bend National Park and Vicinity 401

Marfa and Vicinity 418

MARFA LIGHTS

THE MARFA LIGHTS, MYSTERIOUS AND UNEXPLAINED LIGHTS THAT HAVE BEEN REPORTED IN THE AREA FOR OVER ONE HUNDRED YEARS, HAVE BEEN THE SUBJECT OF MANY THEORIES. THE FIRST RECORDED SIGHTING OF THE LIGHTS WAS BY RANCHER ROBERT ELLISON IN 1883. VARIOUSLY EXPLAINED AS CAMPFIRES, PHOSPHORESCENT MINERALS, SWAMP GAS, STATIC ELECTRICITY, ST. ELMO'S FIRE, AND GHOST LIGHTS, THE LIGHTS REPORTEDLY CHANGE COLORS, MOVE ABOUT, AND CHANGE IN INTENSITY. SCHOLARS HAVE REPORTED OVER SEVENTY-FIVE LOCAL FOLK TALES DEALING WITH THE UNEXPLAINED PHENOMENON.

Highlights

Look for ★ to find recommended sights, activities, dining, and lodging.

★ **Descend into Santa Elena Canyon.** Its sheer 1,500-foot (460-m) cliffs along the Rio Grande are mesmerizing (page 406).

★ **Hike the Lost Mine Trail.** Combining moderate grades, extraordinary vantage points, and stupendous scenery, it's the ultimate Big Bend experience (page 407).

★ **Hike across the border,** trekking along the Rio Grande from Big Bend National Park to the tiny village of **Boquillas, Mexico** (page 408).

★ **Explore the Chihuahuan Desert.** A customized tour of **Big Bend Ranch State Park** offers genuine solitude amid 300,000 acres of remote wilderness (page 411).

★ **Visit the liveliest ghost town.** In addition to the spirits surrounding the historic cemetery, **Terlingua** offers quality restaurants and trendy lodging (page 411).

★ **Experience environmental art.** Housed in a former army camp, Marfa's world-renowned **Chinati Foundation** features some of the world's largest permanent installation artwork, created in harmony with the surrounding landscape (page 419).

★ **Investigate the mystery of the Marfa Lights.** The ethereal orbs bounce, split, appear, and disappear with no apparent source. Are they

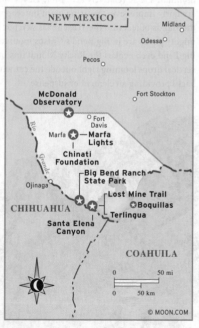

UFOs, Native American spirits, swamp gas, or something else? (page 421)

★ **Go stargazing.** Sitting 7,000 feet (2130 m) high atop the Davis Mountains, **McDonald Observatory** offers spectacular views of the heavens via massive telescopes (page 426).

Big Bend Region

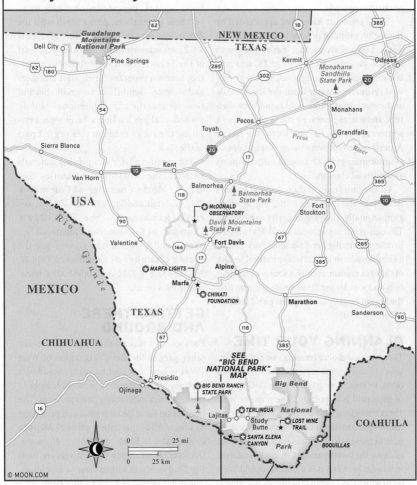

Though Marfa has landed on the radar of the international art community, the rest of the Big Bend area is desolate and unknown to most people outside the region. One look at a map reveals the lack of civilization, with vast areas of empty space dotted only by small towns with strange names like Study Butte, Balmorhea, and Van Horn.

It's this desolation, however, that makes the Big Bend region so appealing. The solitude and seclusion amid a gorgeous backdrop of rugged beauty are ultimately soul cleansing. You never realize how many utility poles, wires, and billboards surround you in everyday life until they're removed from your environment. Only then do you begin appreciating

Previous: hiking the Window Trail in Big Bend; the incredible Santa Elena Canyon on the Rio Grande; a historical marker for the Marfa Lights

the sight of milk-white clouds and fascinating native flora along with the endearing sound of chattering birds.

These elements have been appreciated by the region's inhabitants for more than 10,000 years. From early archaic native groups to Spanish colonists to Apache and Comanche tribes, people have sought out the area's natural resources—water from the Rio Grande and mountain streams, wild game, rock shelters, and native plants. By the time European settlers arrived in the late 1800s, the Native American groups were being displaced, and communities evolved around military posts and railroad stations.

Of the hundreds of thousands of visitors who make the long trek to the Big Bend region annually, the vast majority are Texans. Though you'll see an occasional Midwestern license plate in Big Bend National Park or hear a German accent in Marfa, the natural beauty of the area continues to be a source of fascination and wonder for Texas residents, who find the region equally as compelling and faraway as foreigners do.

PLANNING YOUR TIME

There's a good chance travelers won't find themselves in this remote region of the country too often, so maximizing time in this distinct part of the world is important. The popular West Texas triangle of Marfa-Alpine-Fort Davis is a natural place to start. Plan to spend two or three days in these towns, with at least half a day set aside for the incomparable Chinati Foundation in Marfa. Fort Davis is a charming Old West town with a day's worth of activities, but Alpine, despite its evocative name, only takes a morning or afternoon to appreciate.

Depending on your comfort level (tolerance for extreme topographical and climatic conditions), plan on spending 2-4 days in Big Bend National Park and its surroundings. Some visitors never leave the car, choosing instead to soak up the park's natural beauty on scenic drives, but hiking or camping is definitely the best way to appreciate this amazing topographical treasure.

INFORMATION AND SERVICES

For a regional perspective on where to go and how to get there, get in touch with the **Texas Mountain Trail Region** (432/294-4312, www.texasmountaintrail.com), part of the Texas Historical Commission's heritage tourism program. Their staff members and website—send them an email ahead of time for specific trip suggestions—will do a wonderful job lending a hand with navigating the rocky roads in this rugged part of the state.

For specific advice and printed materials related to the individual communities, contact the **Marfa Chamber of Commerce** (207 N. Highland St., 432/729-4942, www.marfachamber.org), the **Fort Davis Chamber of Commerce** (4 Memorial Sq., 432/426-3015, www.fortdavis.com), and the **Alpine Chamber of Commerce** (106 N. 3rd St., 432/837-2326 or 800/561-3735, www.alpinetexas.com).

GETTING THERE AND AROUND

For those not making the long haul from another part of the state, this region of West Texas is best accessed by plane. Southwest Airlines offers extremely reasonable rates to the area from most major cities in Texas. The best option for affordable rates and proximity to sites is **Midland International Airport** (9506 Laforce Blvd., 432/560-2200, www.flymaf.com), where you can rent a car and be in Big Bend or Marfa within three or four hours. The other option is **El Paso International Airport** (6701 Convair Rd., 915/780-4749, www.elpasointernationalairport.com), which offers a few more flights; unfortunately, it takes nearly five hours to get to Big Bend and about four hours to Marfa. There is no public transportation available to Big Bend or in the smaller surrounding communities, but the local chambers of commerce can suggest a private shuttle service to provide transportation within the region.

Big Bend National Park and V.

The namesake bend in the Rio Grande isn't the only enormous thing around here—this colossal park encompasses more than 800,000 acres of spectacular canyons, mesmerizing Chihuahuan Desert, awe-inspiring Chisos Mountains, and unexpectedly temperate woodlands. It's the kind of place that words can't quite describe, and photos can't even do it justice. Phrases like "majestic peaks" and "rugged beauty" barely begin to illustrate the Big Bend experience, but they at least offer a glimpse into this ultimate "must be seen to be believed" destination.

Big Bend is the kind of place where you feel compelled to pull your car over every half a mile to take a photo of the endless succession of stunning scenes. Avoid the temptation—you can return to the spots later once you've processed their context—and just soak up the natural beauty through your own eyes rather than a phone screen or camera viewfinder. Play some appropriate West Texas soundtrack music (Willie Nelson complements the scenery quite nicely) and marvel at the jagged peaks, desert cacti, and sweeping vistas. Just be sure to occasionally keep your eye on the road—the switchbacks on the way to Chisos Mountains Lodge are dramatic hairpin turns with a 10 mph speed limit.

Speaking of speed, other parts of the park are much more open, and it's easy to find yourself cruising at 70 mph en route to the hot springs or the dramatic Santa Elena Canyon. It's okay to slow down. One of the best things about being in Big Bend is leaving the city and daily routine behind you. If the old couple in front of you is plugging along at 40 mph, resist the temptation to pass them and pay attention instead to the javelina lurking in the desert brush or the volcanic rock formations. Unfortunately, just when you've tempered your commute-minded driving habits, you'll be headed back to rush hour traffic.

It may also be tempting to set an itinerary with goals of hikes or destinations to accomplish within a certain amount of time, but try not to get too caught up with an agenda. Some of the best experiences you'll have will be just sitting on a mountainside or relaxing at your campground. The absence of power lines, utility poles, billboard ads, and litter is cathartic, and the cleansing effect on your mind is equally therapeutic.

Sometimes it's necessary to get in touch with civilization (keeping up with the 'gram, your sports team, or office gossip doesn't count), and there are a few places in the park where this is possible. Wi-Fi is often accessible on the porch of the Chisos Mountains Lodge, and mobile phone service is slightly more reliable—just not in low-lying areas or around mountain peaks.

Aside from missing your email or favorite Netflix show, the only negative thing associated with Big Bend is its remote location—a blessing and a curse, since it's inconvenient to get to but wonderfully isolated and peaceful. Once you've experienced its many unique charms, you'll be able to justify the long drive for many future visits to this unrivaled natural masterpiece.

LAND AND CLIMATE

Several lengthy books are dedicated to the dynamic geography and climate of Big Bend, so summarizing the myriad scientific descriptions of this vast property is somewhat challenging. Geologists have referred to the diverse terrain as a paradise and a nightmare due to its complex collection of stratified rock, volcanic formations, and windblown sand dunes.

The park's topographical features run the gamut from mountains to canyons to the Rio Grande. However, it's the desert climate that

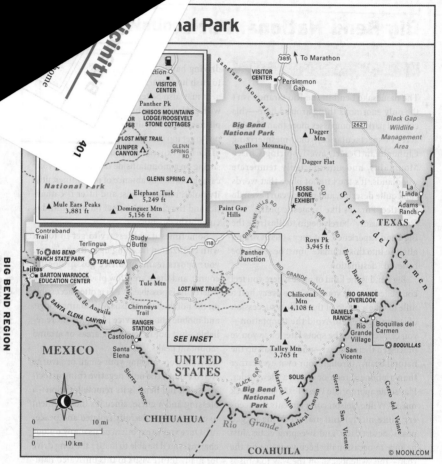

Big Bend National Park

dominates the landscape, with 98 percent of Big Bend classified as part of the Chihuahuan Desert. The key word associated with deserts is *contrast,* as in 50-degree daily temperature extremes, old and new natural erosion from water and wind, and dry stretches punctuated by violent flash flooding.

Though water and deserts aren't typically associated with each other, Big Bend is unique in its access to the Rio Grande and seasonal rains. Water affects all aspects of plant and animal life in the park, and the cycle of wet and dry periods makes Big Bend the fascinating natural landscape it's become, supporting intriguing and unfamiliar species ranging from cacti and agave plants to javelina and lizards.

The most obvious contrast in the park is elevation—the Chisos Mountains rise nearly 8,000 feet tall while the banks of the Rio Grande sit approximately 1,000 feet above sea level. An interesting fact: Air temperature changes by five degrees for every 1,000 feet of elevation, so temperatures in the upper reaches of the Chisos can be more than 20 degrees cooler than they are along the Rio Grande.

On paper, this variation in elevation and temperature makes Big Bend appear to be an ideal year-round park, but in reality, it's only comfortable about seven months a year (October-April). Summertime is ridiculously hot—this is the Chihuahuan Desert, after all—and despite the increased elevation and low humidity, triple-digit temperatures are still brutal. May and June are considered the hottest months since periodic rainstorms later in the summer help ease the intensity (and pain) of the heat. In fact, the park experiences a "rainy" season—typically less than a foot of moisture in the summer months. Because of the complete lack of water from the previous season, there's a mini growth spurt in early fall when colorful blossoms and grasses emerge among the dry landscape.

Some hearty souls aren't deterred by the park's harsh summer conditions, delighting in brisk morning hikes and nippy overnights in the mountains. Big Bend's rainy season even brings occasional heavy thunderstorms and flash flooding. Winter is the most volatile season in Big Bend, with generally mild temperatures, though extremes are possible, from 85°F scorchers to periods of light snow.

PLANTS AND ANIMALS

With its remarkably diverse geography and climate, it's not surprising Big Bend has a similarly varied collection of plants and animals. Containing more than 650 species of animals (plus 3,600 different kinds of bugs) and 1,000-plus species of plants, the park represents a fascinating laboratory of living things.

While hiking along any of the park's trails—from the short paved loops to the major mountain excursions—be sure to take a moment to physically stop and look around. Make a slow 360-degree turn and take in every detail—it's absolutely unbelievable how many little things you'll notice: bizarre bugs on cactus blossoms, exotic insects on a tree leaf, a round sherbet-orange flower peeking from behind a spiky agave plant. And that's just looking straight ahead. Look down and you'll see giant red ants clamoring into a hole. Look up and you'll find puffy cotton clouds mimicking the shape of the nearby mountain peak. Though it's tempting to forge ahead on

the trail and think about where you'll place your next step or how much farther you have to go, you'll truly benefit from a five-minute observation break.

Though Big Bend's animals can be elusive, particularly in the heat of the day, its plants are omnipresent and completely intriguing in their variety and just plain weirdness. The Chihuahuan Desert dominates the landscape, so the flora is largely of the scrub and cactus variety. Not surprisingly, Big Bend is home to more species of cacti (65) than any other national park. The tremendous diversity in landscape accounts for the enormous range of cacti, including the ubiquitous prickly pear, pitaya, and claret cup. Those visiting the park in spring or late summer will experience the bonus of seeing cacti in bloom, a colorful display of vivid yellow, red, and pink flowers.

Aside from cacti, one of the most eye-catching species in Big Bend is the century plant, an enormous agave with an equally gigantic distinction: It blooms only once in its 20- to 50-year life, but it makes the most of the situation by producing a colossal 15-foot-tall stalk with bright yellow flowers. Other agave in the park include the lechuguilla, unique to the Chihuahuan Desert, and the gracilipes. Incidentally, agave plants are the source of a natural ingredient found in most tequila.

Trees thrive in Big Bend's higher elevations, particularly oak and juniper. The cooler climate at these heights (upward of 7,000 feet) mimics the weather in northern states, so it's common to see Douglas fir, quaking aspen, and ponderosa pine, a rare treat for Texans accustomed to the limited varieties of trees associated with arid and subtropical climates.

Animals in Big Bend are a different story. They're equally as intriguing yet far more difficult to find. Two species in particular—mountain lion and black bear—draw the most attention due to their natural ferocity. Several dozen bears and a handful of mountain lions are reported each month, and some of the park's most popular trails (Lost Mine and Window) are hot spots for sightings of both creatures. Park officials advise hikers to ward off bears and mountain lions by intimidating them with loud noises, rock throwing, and plenty of arm waving (seriously).

It's far more fun to catch a glimpse of the javelina, a piglike creature with coarse black hair unique to the deserts of the American Southwest. Also known as the collared peccary, this fascinating fella is active in the cooler times of day, when it can be found munching mainly on prickly pear cactus and agave plants. They've also been known to invade campsites and investigate tents for food, so be sure to safely store everything edible in a vehicle or one of the many bear proof metal boxes located throughout the park.

Other interesting creatures roaming, scuttling, or flying throughout Big Bend include bats (representing the largest portion of the park's mammal species), 31 kinds of snakes, 22 types of lizards, roadrunners, tarantulas, owls, and myriad noisy insects.

RECREATION

There's no shortage of activities in Big Bend National Park, from extreme raft and canoe trips to low-key scenic drives to moderate day hikes. Without a phone or TV tethering you to the routines and clockwork of the real world, you can get away at your own pace and spend an entire day outside. It's practically the definition of *recreation*.

Driving in Big Bend

Some people may want to start out at full speed—the mountains can be so inspiring, it's tempting to turn your enthusiasm into energy by hiking or rafting. Others may want to take things slow and get their bearings. For unbelievably dramatic mountain scenery, it's imperative to make the drive to **Chisos Mountains Lodge.** Your ears will pop and your jaw will drop as you ascend the road into the mountain range, with the famous formations of **Casa Grande** and **Emory Peak** acting as a beacon to the basin. Be sure to keep an eye on the road as you navigate the tight turns amid the stunning surroundings.

An ideal introduction to the complex range of natural wonders at Big Bend is a jaunt along **Ross Maxwell Scenic Drive** in the western portion of the park. The vast vistas slowly transform to striking views of volcanic rock formations reminiscent of an otherworldly scene straight out of a *Star Trek* episode. Be sure to drop by the historic village of **Castolon** to see the small museum exhibits in the charming century-old military structures. This is a good place to grab a snack and a cold drink to soak up the views of the cliffs of Mexico across the river. Note: a wildfire severely damaged Castolon's historic general store in 2019. Efforts are underway to potentially restore the significant adobe structure; in the meantime, visitor services (including new restrooms), exhibits, and snacks are available in temporary and repurposed buildings.

A few miles down the road is the mustsee **Santa Elena Canyon.** If you're driving a high-clearance vehicle, tackle the nearby **Old Maverick Road** for the rare chance to experience the invigorating sensation of plowing through rugged terrain just like they do in SUV ads.

Not quite as dramatic yet certainly worth experiencing is the 20-mile drive to **Rio Grande Village.** The terrain slowly descends as you approach the river, and the charms of the Chihuahuan Desert are in full effect in the blooming cacti, gentle mesas, and the occasional javelina. For a little more excitement, take on the narrow road with a sharp vertical drop-off along the side to the hot springs.

A word of advice: If you're heading out for the evening (perhaps for dinner in Terlingua or Marathon), make an effort to get back to the park before sundown. Driving on park roads at night can be somewhat treacherous—especially when critters are out grazing on the roadside. Deer, javelina, and jackrabbits can jump out in front of your car at any time. Also, if you're staying in the basin, you'll

1: Santa Elena Canyon **2:** view at Big Bend National Park **3:** the beautiful River Road along the Rio Grande

have extra motivation to get back in time to catch the amazing view of the sunset through **The Window** formation near the lodge.

Navigating the Rio Grande

Once you've mastered the scenic drives and hiking trails in Big Bend, you may want to experience the park from a different perspective—by boat. Seeing the canyon walls from the source is imminently rewarding, and many options are available depending on your skill level and spirit of adventure, from Class IV rapids (on a I-V scale) to quiet canoe trips. For a comprehensive list of choices, consult Big Bend's website (www.nps.gov/bibe).

One of the most popular options is **Santa Elena Canyon** (downstream from Lajitas), a 13-mile adventure featuring easy desert paddling and severe rapid navigating. This stretch of the river is considered the most dramatic, with enormous 1,500-foot-tall cliffs towering overhead and the largest rapid, a Class IV run known as Rock Slide. For an easier day trip, consider the "boomerang" jaunt upstream and back to the canyon.

A portion of the park known as the **Rio Grande Wild & Scenic River** features several other trips appealing to beginner and intermediate boaters. The 10-mile-long Mariscal Canyon trek provides stunning scenery with 1,400-foot-tall limestone cliffs and some moderately exciting Class II-III rapids. For a longer excursion (2-3 days), consider the 33-mile-long trip through Boquillas Canyon, an ideal choice for beginners, since there aren't any rapids higher than Class II. Even longer (up to 10 days) is a trek through the lower canyons, where paddlers can experience true solitude in the wilderness since they often won't encounter another human being for days at a time.

To find out more about shuttles, equipment rental, and guided trips, contact **Big Bend River Tours** (800/545-4240, www.bigbendrivertours.com), **Desert Sports** (888/989-6900, www.desertsportstx.com), or **Far Flung Outdoor Center** (800/839-7238, www.bigbendfarflung.com).

HIKING AND BACKPACKING

Big Bend offers more than 200 miles of hiking trails ranging from short, easy nature walks to primitive mountain trails for experienced hikers. There's truly something for everyone here—families can take their time on moderate trails with printed interpretive brochures as a guide, while hard-core backpackers have the option of taking backcountry trails into the desolate wilderness for challenging treks at their own pace.

Day Hikes
★ SANTA ELENA CANYON

Talk about dramatic. You can see the massive walls of Santa Elena Canyon from miles away, but the effect of witnessing these sheer cliffs—more than 1,500 feet high on each side of the surprisingly narrow gap forged by the Rio Grande—is utterly mesmerizing up close. And it only gets better as the trail progresses.

It's a 1.6-mile trek, so plan about two hours to fully appreciate the experience. You'll be drawn to the wide swath of river flowing from the massive canyon walls, but the difficult-to-find trail entrance is off to your right. Look for the crude stone pathway across the shallow creekbed (your feet may get a bit wet), which leads to the trailhead. You'll encounter a series of tight switchbacks and concrete steps before ascending a rocky trail that eventually descends into the canyon. When you reach the end of the trail, you'll be surrounded by the stunning vertical cliff walls, which echo with the sounds of kids (even adults) playing in the water. This is one of the few places in the park where swimming is safe and generally tolerated. Santa Elena Canyon is truly a magical place where you can sit and absorb your surroundings for hours, so plan accordingly. Find a riverside rock and soak up the sounds and sights of the stunning canyon, from borderland birds soaring among the walls, to people on the riverbank tossing beer cans to passing paddlers. It's like no other place.

Note: In late summer/early fall (after the rainy season drops up to a foot of moisture on the park), there will be more water in the Rio Grande, which affects access to the Santa Elena Canyon trail. Instead of being able to walk across a stone pathway, you'll be faced with the not-very-recommended option of wading through several feet of murky water to get to the trail. Depending on the water level, you may be able to walk down the shoreline and cross around to the trailhead. Regardless, you can still get a sense of wonder just from being at the base of canyon, but you won't get the full experience of being within sheer cliff walls. There's always next time . . .

★ LOST MINE TRAIL

If you're staying at Chisos Mountains Lodge, this is an ideal trail for a nearby morning hike. But be sure to get there before 9am—the small parking lot at the trailhead fills up quickly. The cool temperatures on this trail are invigorating, and the scenery is stupendous. Considered one of the ultimate Big Bend hikes, Lost Mine Trail offers an ideal combination of moderate grades, a wide range of vegetation, extraordinary vantage points, and a handy interpretive brochure at the trailhead. The weather in this part of the park can be volatile, so prepare for anything. In April, you may encounter sunny short-sleeved weather while ascending the trail, then, after basking in the warmth and scenery, you may turn a corner while descending and encounter a wall of surreal snow flurries.

If you happen to be at the park in late summer or early fall (following the summertime rains), you'll get the bonus experience of seeing the Lost Mine Trail's environs in a mini growth spurt with plenty of subtle colors and emerging flora. Look for red, yellow, orange, and blue blossoms on bushes, trees, cacti, and stems around every bend. Be sure to take a few minutes to stop hiking and do a 360-degree turn, absorbing all the fresh-green growth of new leaves and blooming cactus. If you look (and listen) closely, you'll identify unfamiliar insects buzzing over new flowers, completely unaware of your presence.

The trail's 4.8-mile round-trip (roughly four hours) will get you back in time for a much-needed hearty lunch at the lodge's restaurant just a mile down the road. Those looking for a shorter venture are in luck: The most incredible view along the trail (and perhaps in the entire park) is about a mile into the trek—find a comfy rock to lean against and absorb the magnificent far-reaching view of Juniper Canyon. The untouched vista is absolutely mesmerizing—soak up the hundreds of miles of undulating terrain that's offered the same panoramic scene for fortunate viewers for thousands of years.

THE WINDOW TRAIL

Another classic Big Bend hike is the Window Trail. This is a great half-day hike (a circa 5-mile round-trip from the main lodge at Chisos Basin) with a lot of diverse scenery, fantastic views, and a one-of-a-kind destination. Start in the mid-morning and bring a lunch to enjoy the grand finale at the end of the trail: the namesake window formation. The hike is gently sloping before it intersects with a clear mountain stream (Oak Creek), providing a distinctive hiking accompaniment, with a waterfall (and semi-challenging footwork) along the trek. The window itself is a V-shaped intersection of vertical rocks with a pour-off in the crevice for Oak Creek. You can walk to the very edge of the dropoff for stunning views of the Chihuahuan desert, but be careful if the water is flowing quickly (or if you don't like heights) and beware of the slick rock. Bring plenty of water, since the hike back is uphill and can get pretty warm during the afternoon.

CHISOS BASIN LOOP TRAIL

This is an ideal starting trail if you're staying at the Chisos Basin Lodge or even if you're just visiting for the day and parked in the main lodge area. It's a 1.8-mile round-trip trek, offering moderate gradients and amazing views of the mountains and surrounding desert. You'll start at the parking lot and spend the first half-mile navigating through Mexican Pine and oak trees before ascending to a rocky elevation with stunning vistas. With Casa Grande behind you and the Chihuahuan Desert in front of you, it's easy to see why this is one of the ultimate Big Bend hiking experiences.

RIO GRANDE VILLAGE NATURE TRAIL

This short excursion will introduce you to just about everything you'll need to know about Big Bend. It's just under a mile round-trip, but set aside an hour to fully absorb the dramatic vistas and desert intricacies. The trail starts in a somewhat bizarre fashion, with a boardwalk crossing over a body of water originating from the wetland natural spring. It's a strange sight to see, especially since it's immediately followed by a hot and hardscrabble trek across rocky terrain among myriad cacti and desert scrub brushes (a handy sign at the trailhead provides interesting information about the different plants). The highlight is the view from the top of the moderately sloped hill, where you'll find sweeping vistas of the Rio Grande and Mexico. Look for the blocky bright white adobe buildings about a mile away in the Mexican village of Boquillas. The mighty Chisos Mountains loom in the background, presiding over a natural scene that is unlike any other you'll experience.

Backpacking Trails

Once visitors have experienced the awe-inspiring day hikes, they often feel compelled to take things to the next level. A popular follow-up excursion is to one of the backcountry campsites in the High Chisos Mountains along the trail system to the South Rim. These campsites, varying 1-8 miles each way, are accessible only by foot, and most involve an overnight trek. Be sure to bring plenty of water (at least a gallon per person daily), food, sturdy shoes, and sunscreen.

For these trips, an overnight backcountry permit is required ($10), available only in-person up to 24 hours in advance at all park visitors centers. Park staff can assist you with trip planning based on your needs and current trail conditions.

At 14 miles (22.5 km) round-trip, the **South Rim trek** takes at least eight hours to complete. Ascend to the South Rim via the **Laguna Meadows trail,** which traverses a dense forest popular with birders thanks to the abundant oak, maple, juniper, and piñon pine. This is a strenuous trek (with a 2,000-foot gain) but it's absolutely worth it for the stunning views from the South Rim.

An equally popular backpacking trip is to the **Emory Peak** campsite, 3.7 miles from the trailhead via the **Pinnacles Trail.** Since it's the highest elevation in the park and therefore a quest to be conquered, Emory Peak is a natural draw for many hikers. Not surprisingly, it's rocky and steep, but the payoff comes in astounding views of Boot Canyon and the back face and summit of Emory Peak. Note: the final stretch (a quarter mile or so) is super steep, and the very last part of the trek involves a slightly crazy dash up the exposed rock.

★ Boquillas, Mexico

One of the coolest experiences available at Big Bend is the rare opportunity to cross the Rio Grande and visit Mexico. Safely. The trek across the border to **Boquillas** is quick and easy; in fact, the hardest part is making sure you have a passport ahead of time. Otherwise, the journey is remarkably simple and fulfilling, while only taking about three or four hours total. Start at the Boquillas Crossing Port of Entry (Nov. 2–April 30, Wed.-Sun., 8am-5pm; May 1–Nov. 1, Fri.-Mon., 9am-6pm). Once you scan your passport and purchase a boat ticket ($5 round trip) at the tiny port station, you'll take a short walk down to the not-so-mighty Rio Grande, where someone will be waiting with a rowboat. The river crossing only takes three minutes, then you'll encounter a variety of transportation options on the Mexican border side. The pickup trucks, horses, and mules are a tempting option (feel free to try the experience), but be aware that there can be a catch involved:

namely, the owner's relatives often have a souvenir stand (or three) in Boquillas, and purchases are expected. Walking is quicker than a burro ride (it's about a 20-minute stroll on the sandy trail), and you're free to pursue the vendors on your own.

The village of Boquillas is tiny (population circa 300), but it's absolutely worth visiting. It's quiet and peaceful, a far cry from the unfortunate cartel-related violence and tension at most border towns. There are only two restaurants in town: Jose Falcon's and Boquillas Café. Both are equally good—Falcon's has more history, but Boquillas Café has a patio right on the border overlooking the Rio Grande. If you choose the café, be sure to order a hearty plate of chicken verde enchiladas with extra tortillas, accompanied by a cold Carta Blanca beer or bottle of Coke. The village is pretty sleepy, so there isn't much more to do than eat a meal, enjoy the scenery, and chat with the locals (a working knowledge of Spanish is needed). The souvenir stands are mainly handmade trinkets and T-shirts, offering a nice memento of your international trek and an important way to sustain the local economy.

FOOD

The only place to order a meal in Big Bend National Park is the **Chisos Mountains Lodge Restaurant** (432/477-2291, www.chisosmountainslodge.com, daily 7am-10am, 11am-4pm, and 5pm-8pm, $8-21). Fortunately, the food here is much better than expected for a remote national park, with a surprisingly varied menu offering regional fare (Tex-Mex, prickly pear cactus sauces, etc.), standard dishes (sandwiches, pastas), and hearty breakfasts to fuel a long morning trek. "Hikers lunches" are also available as to-go options. The views of the mountains (particularly The Window formation) are stunning through the floor-to-ceiling windows, and it's always nice to know a decent meal is available daily with enough variety (along with beer and wine) to make things interesting for several days' worth of eating.

NEARBY COMMUNITIES AND SIGHTS

The Big Bend region is rife with fascinating communities offering a unique perspective on the region's heritage (the silver mine ghost town of Terlingua) and culture (the desert

Jose Falcon's in Boquillas, Mexico

Adobe Walls

Fort Leaton State Historic Site in Presidio is a prime example of adobe architecture.

The Big Bend region qualifies as America's desert Southwest, so the abundance of adobe structures in the area should come as no surprise. But for many Texans and out-of-staters, their presence is beguiling and intriguing.

Considered one of the oldest building technologies, adobe is as natural as it gets—bricks comprised of earth, straw, and water are formed in wooden molds and dried in the sun for up to two weeks. A lime-based whitewall plaster is often applied to the walls to help deflect the sun and protect the bricks from the harsh desert elements. Unlike traditional oven-fired bricks, adobe is considered a low-strength product and therefore can only support minimal weight—most structures are no more than two stories tall.

The large bricks—typically between one and two feet thick—used in adobe structures provide ideal insulation against the extreme desert conditions of far West Texas. The roofs are typically flat, with tile or wooden *canales* (gutters) providing drainage off the sides of the building. Because the *vigas* (beams) supporting the roof tend to be restricted in length, the corresponding rooms are also narrow.

ANCIENT ARCHITECTURE

Archaeological evidence suggests adobe originated in the ancient Middle East, and it's typically associated in the United States with Native American tribes in present-day New Mexico and Arizona, particularly the impressive pueblos in Taos and Acoma. Spanish explorers brought a similar adobe tradition, resulting in now-iconic structures such as missions, presidios, and dwellings across the South and West Texas landscape.

Many of the region's adobe buildings are endangered due to erosion, but others remain in good shape thanks to dedicated restoration efforts and continual maintenance to repair crumbling bricks and deter moisture. The best examples of historic adobe architecture in the region include the Castolon historic district in Big Bend, the Sauceda Ranch in Big Bend Ranch State Park, Fort Leaton State Historic Site in Presidio, the Hudspeth County Courthouse in Sierra Blanca, and the Sacred Heart of Jesus Catholic Church in Ruidosa.

resort oasis in Lajitas). Consider planning an extra day or two for exploring these areas, or, if you're pressed for time, set aside an evening or afternoon for an excursion to these one-of-a-kind communities.

★ Big Bend Ranch State Park

West of Big Bend National Park is the awesome "little" cousin known as **Big Bend Ranch State Park** (1900 Sauceda Ranch Rd., 432/358-4444, www.tpwd.state.tx.us, $5 ages 13 and older). The park's east entrance is at Barton Warnock Environmental Education Center, one mile east of Lajitas on FM 170, and the west entrance is four miles southeast of Presidio at Fort Leaton State Historic Site on FM 170.

This enormous chunk of property—more than 300,000 acres of remote Chihuahuan Desert wilderness—is the largest state park in Texas and has become quite popular with those in search of a genuinely remote natural experience.

The best way to explore the park is via a daylong tour customized for individual interests. The tour is led by knowledgeable guides in air-conditioned four-wheel-drive vehicles equipped with emergency resources, allowing visitors to safely (and comfortably) explore whatever aspects of the park intrigue them, from photography and bird-watching to history and archeology. A highlight is the historic **Crawford-Smith Ranch**, which offers a step back in time to the region's prime ranching years (early 1900s) when the site was a thriving oasis with freshwater from a fruitful natural spring. These days, there are only ruins of the ranch buildings, sunbaked adobe walls, and scattered personal items, including a shriveled cowboy boot. Barbed wire is still entwined in hand-hewn fence posts that once encircled livestock pens.

The park is best known for its spectacular views, especially along **River Road** between Lajitas and Presidio, a nearly 20-mile stretch considered to be the most scenic drive in Texas. Be prepared to spend several hours oooh-ing and aaah-ing as you're greeted by magnificent mountain views around each turn and a compelling immediacy to the Rio Grande just a few feet away.

Containing some of the most isolated and rugged terrain in the state, Big Bend Ranch includes two mountain ranges formed by ancient volcanic activity and sheer-cliffed canyons. There are more than 100 miles of trails available for hiking and biking. Maps with updated routes are available on the park's website or at ranger stations. Other activities include birding, horseback riding, backpacking, and paddling; however, the park's remote and rugged nature should be taken into consideration.

If primitive backcountry camping and cooking don't sound appealing, the park provides access to civilization with food and lodging at its **Sauceda historic district.** Consider lodging the authentic/historic way, by staying in the nearby **Sauceda Bunk House** ($35 nightly). The facility is separated into two sides, one for men and the other for women, but a homey "big room" offers communal space for sitting by the fire or reading and playing games. Worth noting: The beds are in semi-private alcoves, which may not be for everyone, but certainly add to the unique experience. Contact the park in advance about meal availability, since you may have to bring your own food during the off-season (summer).

★ Terlingua

This is the liveliest ghost town you'll ever experience. Quality restaurants, trendy lodging, and funky gift shops are just a few of the things you'll encounter in the small community of Terlingua. Even the cemetery here is a major tourist attraction. The town was abandoned after its mercury mines closed in the 1940s (leading to its distinction as a ghost town), but it has since been revitalized as a tourist attraction with several hundred permanent residents.

Some of the souls laid to rest at the **Terlingua Cemetery** were workers at the Chisos Mining Co., a major quicksilver producer established in 1903. The liquid metal, eventually called mercury, was mined as cinnabar ore and recovered via a baking process to its metallic state. The mining company became one of the nation's leading producers of quicksilver, peaking during World War I when 40 percent of the mercury mined in the United States came from Terlingua.

By World War II, mining operations ceased, leaving Terlingua abandoned until the late 1960s, when the village became famous for its annual chili cook-off. In 1967, the Chili Appreciation Society named Terlingua the "Chili Capital of the World," and the event continues to draw thousands of people to this deserted desert community.

If you only have a short amount of time to spend here, be sure to visit the **Terlingua Trading Company** (100 Ivey St., 432/371-2234, 10am-8pm) and adjacent Starlight Theater. These two buildings perfectly capture the Terlingua vibe, with enough lively folk art, friendly locals, and spicy border-influenced food to rouse the spirits at the famed cemetery just down the road. You can easily spend a half hour in the Trading Company, browsing the impressive book collection featuring national, statewide, and regional titles (including the entertaining *Tales from the Terlingua Porch*), Mexican-themed artwork, local snacks, toys, and the requisite Viva Terlingua! stickers. And it's almost mandatory to grab a beer at the counter (they're sold by the bottle from a room in the back) and take it out to the porch, where you can enjoy stunning views of the Chisos Mountains while being regaled with colorful stories from the local characters who gather on the porch each evening to do just that (drink and talk).

Plan to have a meal at the adjacent **Starlight Theater** (432/371-2326, www.thestarlighttheatre.com, Sun.-Fri. 5pm-midnight, Sat. 5pm-1am, $9-33). This historic 1930s theater now serves as a restaurant featuring hearty American fare (you won't regret ordering the tasty brisket tacos), regional dishes (the chipotle-glazed pork medallions are a must), and some of the best margaritas

you'll ever experience (extra strong). Also, the filet mignon is well worth the $29, a pricey tag by West Texas standards. Order the grilled option with sautéed garlic and some of the tastiest mushrooms you'll ever experience. A troubadour often accompanies your meal with lonesome Western songs from a small stage in the main dining area.

For a true taste of Terlingua flavor and culture, check out **La Kiva Restaurant and Bar** (Hwy. 170, 432/371-2250, www.la-kiva.com, daily 5pm-midnight, $8-23). To enter the front of this loco local spot, you have to go into a mine-like opening and descend a short stairwell before finding the cavey bar and restaurant. The back portion of La Kiva overlooks Terlingua Creek, and there are plenty of windows and patio seats for those seeking to avoid the dark atmosphere. This rustic eatery is known for its barbecue, pizza and mediocre Mexican food—the best bet is the Terlingua Trio, a combo plate of smoked chicken, ribs, and brisket.

Unless you're visiting Terlingua during the raucous **chili festival** held the first week of November each year, you shouldn't have trouble finding a room. Surprisingly, there are several decent lodging options in and around this tiny village, but the best choice by far is **La Posada Milagro Guest House** (100 La Posada Ln., 432/371-3044, www.laposadamilagro.com, $185-$325 d). The historic stucco and stone facility offers luxury in the midst of the harsh desert climate via its four suites with large comfy beds, air-conditioning, sundecks, fire pits, hammocks, and Wi-Fi service. For those in search of a cheap place to rough it, consider the very low-key yet comfortable **Chisos Mining Company Motel** (23280 FM 170, 432/371-2254, www.motelsbigbend.com, $79 d). There's a rustic charm to the bare-bones, wood-paneled rooms, and don't be surprised

1: Sauceda Bunk House in Big Bend Ranch State Park **2:** the historic Terlingua Cemetery **3:** the Terlingua Trading Company's famous porch scene **4:** Terlingua's Starlight Theater

...e awoken in the night by the discon-
... sound of coyotes (seemingly) right
... your room.

...sidio

Approximately 60 miles west of Big Bend, Presidio (population 6,948) is known for its stunning scenery and incredibly hot weather.

Evidence of Native American tribes farming the fertile floodplains in the area dates to the 1200s, and the Spanish had a presence here beginning in the 1500s. As was the case in other areas of Texas, the Spaniards felt it was their mission to "civilize" the native groups, despite their proven ability to successfully cultivate crops, construct sturdy adobe homes, and practice their own religions.

The 1800s saw the arrival of Anglo settlers, including the controversial frontiersman Ben Leaton, who constructed a large fortress and ostracized locals. In recent decades, Presidio has gained a reputation as the end point of perhaps Texas's most scenic drive, the breathtaking **River Road** (FM 170), featuring dramatic canyon views and stunning topographic changes along the Rio Grande coming from Lajitas. Presidio's other claim to fame is not quite as enjoyable—its distinction as the hottest town in Texas. In June, temperature-gauge capacities are put to the test with astronomical highs *averaging* 103°F.

Presidio's only real tourist attraction is **Fort Leaton State Historic Site** (FM 170, 915/229-3613, www.tpwd.state.tx.us, daily 8am-4:30pm, $5 ages 13 and older), an enormous adobe home built by Leaton in 1848 on the site of a former Spanish settlement known as El Fortin de San Jose. Leaton is still considered a controversial figure by Mexican Americans. Originally employed by the Mexican government as a Native American scalp hunter, Leaton reportedly later encouraged Native American raids on Mexican villages by trading weapons and ammunition for stolen livestock. To this day, some locals of Mexican descent refuse to call the site Fort Leaton, opting instead to use its original name, "El Fortin."

Regardless, the impressive structure is still worth visiting, with more than half of its 40-plus original rooms featuring fully restored adobe walls and roofs with cottonwood beams and rails. It's easy to spend a few hours here just absorbing the fascinating adobe architecture—exposed walls reveal the sunbaked earthen bricks with straw and rocks, and stark wooden door and window frames. Outside, be sure to notice how the sun illuminates the soft corners of the plastered walls, casting evocative shadows and sunrays. Experience West Texas history through the informative exhibits and the region's vernacular architecture in the home's charming living and guest quarters, kitchen, dining room, and outbuildings.

Pretty much the only reliable place to eat in Presidio is the fortunately tasty **El Patio** (513 O'Reilly St., 432/229-4409, daily 6am-9pm, $7-18). It's an especially welcome meal after spending a few days in Big Bend subsisting on camping and lodge food. Be prepared to *hablar* some *espanol* at El Patio (or to point convincingly at a menu item) since most folks here don't speak English. It's actually a nice reminder that you're bordering another country while having the pleasure of sampling its authentic and flavorful food. Speaking of which, El Patio's chiles rellenos are perfectly prepared, with just the right amount of lightly crisped exterior breading covering a subtly spicy pepper filled with smooth white cheese. Be sure to order a few extra tortillas to sop up any remaining beans and sauce.

Lajitas

Ever fed a beer to the mayor and watched him try to eat the can afterward? It used to happen regularly in Lajitas (population circa 150), where the esteemed mayor—a goat known as the Honorable Clay Henry III—held court at the Lajitas Trading Post. Unfortunately, Clay Henry III is no longer with us, but that doesn't mean you can't still honor his legacy.

Located at the far southwestern edge of Big Bend National Park, the tiny village (pronounced La-HEE-tas) draws visitors for its rugged natural beauty and fancy

Mining for Mercury

Unlike most traditional burial sites, the barren and rocky Terlingua cemetery contains aboveground graves covered in shards of stone, with crude wooden crosses often serving as the only adornment. Most of these sites mark the final resting place of the region's quicksilver (mercury) miners, who largely fell victim to the region's harsh environment, mercury poisoning, and disease—all hazards of working for Terlingua's mining companies.

The largest operation by far was the Chisos Mining Co., which owned the town of Terlingua and was operated by mining magnate Howard Perry, a Chicago industrialist. Perry was respected among businesspeople but largely despised by the workers, many of them Mexicans who fled to Texas to escape cultural turmoil and their country's revolution. Miners were reportedly paid only $12 daily (or with coupons for Perry's company store) and often received only a bucket of water a day while having to carry 80-pound sacks of ore.

From its opening in 1903 until its bankruptcy in the mid-1940s, the Chisos Mining Co. produced nearly a third of the country's mercury supply. Initially mined as an ore called cinnabar, the silver liquid metal that became known as quicksilver (and eventually mercury) is ultimately recovered through a simple baking process completed on-site. The work was arduous—mercury poisoning could be fatal or have devastating side effects, including brain damage and tooth or hair loss.

DIGGING DEEPER

As demand for mercury escalated, Perry increased production by incorporating more industrialized methods, including a massive furnace and deeper exploration of the mountain ranges, resulting in the discovery of one of the richest veins of cinnabar ore in the Terlingua district. The discovery coincided with the outbreak of World War I, when the U.S. military demand for mercury was high, resulting in the Chisos Mining Co.'s most successful period.

Before vehicles arrived on the scene, the company used mules to deliver the mercury via wagon to the railroad in Alpine. Production declined in the late 1930s, and by 1942 the company had filed for bankruptcy. Several years later, the company's buildings and installations were demolished and sold for scrap. Its remaining legacy is represented by the mounds of rock and soil at the Terlingua Cemetery.

resort complex. Lajitas, Spanish for "little flat rocks," was inhabited by Native Americans for centuries before Anglo settlers arrived. Its namesake smooth-rock river bottom was considered one of the best crossings on the Rio Grande between Del Rio and El Paso. In 1916, Lajitas became a center of intense military activity when Gen. John J. Pershing's troops established a major cavalry post to protect the U.S. border against Pancho Villa and his bandits.

By the late 1970s, the town was virtually abandoned until entrepreneurs arrived to construct a luxury resort complex, drawing travelers from across the world who enjoyed a little pampering with their hiking and rafting. The resort has endured different owners and different approaches to dealing with locals and tourists, but it typically remains open,

even if it's in a limited capacity. The area has also been popular with movie producers who savor the incredibly untouched 360-degree vantage points.

One of the few activities available in Lajitas is the **Barton Warnock Environmental Education Center** (one mile east of town on FM 170, 432/424-3327, www.tpwd.state.tx.us, daily 8am-5pm, $5 ages 13 and older), showcasing the archaeology, history, and natural wonders of the Big Bend region. The center serves as the eastern gateway to Big Bend Ranch State Park and features exhibits and displays dedicated to 570 million years of geological history and the biological landscapes of the Chihuahuan Desert. A self-guided botanical garden is well worth visiting, offering a fascinating sample of the desert's characteristic flora.

Those looking for a bite to eat in town are in luck since the two restaurants within the Lajitas Resort and Spa feature high-quality regional fare. The **Candelilla Café** (daily 7am-9pm, $14-39) features contemporary Southwestern cuisine enhanced with local ingredients like prickly pear cactus, indigenous peppers, and homegrown herbs. At **Licha's Bakery** (daily 7:30-11am) you can get a homemade danish, muffin, or cinnamon roll with a welcoming decent mug of coffee.

For lodging, there's nothing else like the remarkable **Lajitas Golf Resort and Spa** (FM 170, 432/424-5000, www.lajitasgolfresort.com, $150-390). This 27,000-acre private estate boasts more than 100 rooms, ranging from modest hotel-size quarters with cowboy-chic decor to spacious and elegant hacienda cottages, all with coffeemakers, satellite television (a rarity out here), refrigerators, and luxurious amenities. Although the idea of a (partially) bright green golf course in the midst of a desert may seem off-putting to some, others embrace the opportunity to play a round in an unmatched natural environment. The resort offers myriad packages to choose from, combining lodging options with golfing packages, meals, activities, spa treatments, and day trips. There's also an equestrian center, an inviting pool, boardwalk shops (a couple, at least), and bird-watching tours. Check the website for available options.

Marathon

The rugged isolation of the Big Bend region lures adventure-minded visitors, but there are other travelers looking for activities involving less . . . adventure. These travelers may opt to make a run for Marathon, considered the "gateway" to Big Bend National Park since it's the last town on the last road to the park.

An ideal home base is the remarkable 1927 **Gage Hotel** (102 NW 1st St., 432/386-4205, www.gagehotel.com, $139-329). This welcoming oasis on the edge of the desert is teeming with authentic West Texas and Mexican-inspired decor, like handcrafted rustic doors and wrought-iron candelabra fixtures. Be sure to spend some time in the Gage's amazing White Buffalo Bar, an ideal place to chat with locals while sipping on a Big Bend Brewery ale under the watchful eye of the giant stuffed white buffalo on the adobe wall. Order some appetizers at the bar (the sliders are astounding), or walk a few steps over for dinner at the adjacent **12 Gage Restaurant** (daily 6-9pm, $13-40) where you can order a prickly pear margarita accompanied by tender steak, pork tenderloin, or wild boar.

The Gage also serves as a hub for the highly recommended heritage bike route, a five-mile ride to Post Park just south of Marathon (details at www.texasmountaintrail.com/bike). The scenic route offers a great escape for visitors in search of a moderate workout accompanied by fascinating history and unencumbered vistas. Stops include the historic Marathon Cemetery and Post Park, where Native Americans used to visit the natural springs nearly 7,000 years ago. Bicycle and equipment rental can be arranged by Gage staff.

If you're looking for something slightly more affordable, one of the only other options in town is the **Marathon Motel** (701 US-90, 432/386-4241, www.marathonmotel.com, $89-169). Things are pretty basic here, but the rooms are clean, the Wi-Fi is free, and there's a nice courtyard where you can enjoy a coffee.

ACCOMMODATIONS AND CAMPING

Many people travel to Big Bend for the amazing camping opportunities (more about those in a bit), but others just want to experience the great outdoors during the day with a reliable roof, walls, and bed frame surrounding them at night. Fortunately, the park offers the **Chisos Mountains Lodge** (432/477-2291, www.chisosmountainslodge.com, rooms average $139). Situated nearly a mile high in a cozy little basin surrounded by mountain peaks, the lodge offers a no-frills experience befitting of its remote and rugged location. The two-story lodge buildings are thankfully unremarkable in appearance and amenities, prompting guests to spend most of their time on hiking trails or on the sparse porches. In fact, one of the lodge's best amenities is its lack of a TV—you may have to read a book or (gulp) just talk to your fellow travelers while sipping on a tequila or glass of wine. The rooms include tile baths, tubs, and showers; hair dryers; coffeepots; refrigerators; microwaves; and housekeeping service, so you don't have to worry about being too far removed from the comforts of modern civilization.

If you plan far enough in advance (almost a year ahead of time), you can snag a coveted spot in the park's premier accommodations: the **Roosevelt Stone Cottages** (432/477-2291, www.chisosmountainslodge.com, $159). These five stone cottages are removed from the hub of activity at the main lodge, and each cabin features stone floors and three double beds, showers, hair dryers, coffeepots, refrigerators, microwaves, and ceiling fans (no air-conditioning is available, which isn't usually a problem at this elevation). The cabins are highly recommended, since it's likely you won't be out here very often and the appeal of staying in your own private quarters in this beautiful park is unparalleled. These historic (1940s) cottages are oozing with mountain

character, from the regional art and photos on the walls, to the welcoming porches, to the big windows that capture a nice gentle breeze. Keep them open at night for perfect sleeping weather—you won't even need to turn on the ceiling fan.

The park also offers three developed campgrounds—**Rio Grande Village, Chisos Basin,** and **Cottonwood Campground** (877/444-6777, www.recreation.gov, sites average $19 plus service fees)—for tent camping, trailers, and RVs. Rio Grande Village, on the far eastern edge of the park among trees (and insects) near the river, has the only available hookups for RVs. The campground has 100 sites, flush toilets, running water, and a dump station. The stunning Chisos Basin Campground is the most popular of the bunch and nearest to the full-service restaurant. It's rugged and hilly, and not recommended for RVs. This is the place to come if you want an unforgettable experience while tent camping—wake up in the morning and be immediately greeted by a scenic mountain sunrise, then close out the evening with a beverage while gazing at the moonlight on the Casa Grande rock formation. The campsites are intimately close, so you may hear everything your neighbors are saying. And doing.

camping at Chisos Basin in Big Bend National Park

On the west side of the park, Cottonwood Campground is in the lowlands of the Rio Grande. It's appealing for its namesake cottonwood trees and proximity to the historic Castolon village and Santa Elena Canyon. Big Bend also offers dozens of primitive camping sites (many are only accessible by high-clearance vehicle or four-wheel drive). These sites typically consist of only a flat gravel pad, and a backcountry permit is required from park headquarters.

INFORMATION AND SERVICES

Big Bend National Park includes several visitors centers offering maps and, most important, informed guides who help enhance visits by suggesting the perfect activities for travelers' particular comfort levels. The main center is at the park headquarters at **Panther Junction** (www.nps.gob/bibe), about 26 miles from the north entrance gate (arriving from Marathon) and 25 miles from the western gate. The renovated visitors center offers interpretive exhibits and scores of books, brochures, and maps. The park's other visitors centers—**Chisos Mountains, Castolon,** and **Rio Grande Village**—are slightly smaller and typically closed in the summer, but they're still packed with valuable information and helpful professionals.

A handy way to plan your trip to the Big Bend region is via the **Visit Big Bend** website (www.visitbigbend.com), offering interactive maps and handy resources for food, lodging, and activities. Another helpful option is the **Texas Mountain Trail Region** (432/294-4312, www.texasmountaintrail.com), part of the Texas Historical Commission's heritage tourism program.

Marfa and Vicinity

During the early 2000s, the small railroad stop of Marfa (population 1,772) became an unlikely cultural hotbed for artists and visitors from across the country and the world. When the Great Recession arrived a decade later, things slowed down somewhat, but the growth and international exposure left indelible marks on the community. Though it may seem like a positive thing—national exposure brings valued tourism dollars and puts a spotlight on the region's natural beauty and quirky charm—it generated concern among the independent-minded residents who weren't too keen on the higher property taxes and curious outsiders.

The town was established in 1883 as a railroad water stop and was reportedly named by a railroad executive's wife who made the suggestion based on a character from Fyodor Dostoyevsky's *The Brothers Karamazov,* which she was reading at the time. Two years later, a magnificent three-story Renaissance Revival courthouse was built downtown, providing a jarring contrast to the surrounding barren West Texas landscape. The courthouse remains a downtown focal point and one of the state's architectural gems.

In 1911, the U.S. military established a presence in Marfa in response to the nearby Mexican Revolution, and troops remained in the area for several decades with the establishment of the Marfa Army Air Field and Camp Albert (later renamed Camp Marfa, then Fort D. A. Russell, and now the home of the fascinating Chinati art foundation).

Another of Marfa's most compelling properties, the exquisite Hotel Paisano, served as the operations base for the epic 1956 film *Giant,* starring Rock Hudson, Elizabeth Taylor, and James Dean. With its sweeping vistas and spectacular sky, Marfa continues to draw filmmakers, most notably as the backdrop for many scenes in two Oscar-nominated movies: *No Country for Old Men* and *There Will Be Blood.*

Building 98

For those interested in Marfa's Chinati Foundation, there's another hidden gem housed inside former army barracks in this little West Texas town.

This one is known by its institutional-sounding military name, Building 98. What awaits inside, however, is anything but ordinary. In fact, the building's multifaceted art and history are an international phenomenon.

Constructed in 1920, the adobe structure was home to the officers' club and bachelor officers' quarters for the army's Fort D. A. Russell. But it's much better known for its occupants during World War II—the German prisoners of war (POWs) who painted colorful panoramic murals on many interior walls.

The widespread canvases represent the largest collection of POW art in the United States. The colorful and detailed murals are incredibly stunning, especially considering they were created with house paint by war prisoners. The POWs, inspired by their time in far West Texas, devoted most of their murals to capturing the surrounding wide-open landscapes, including scenes of cowboys cooking and the desert vegetation.

When the property was procured nearly a decade ago by representatives of the art-based International Woman's Foundation, the murals were in danger of disappearing—there were holes in the wall, and the rooms were filled with debris. Restoration artists and preservationists helped shore up the buildings and provide a stable environment for the paintings. Visitors and artists travel from all over the world to experience this unique aspect of art. And, perhaps most compelling, the descendants of the original artists were discovered and invited to Building 98 to experience the artwork. Appropriately, one is a well-known children's illustrator in Europe.

Those interested in seeing the artwork for themselves can schedule a tour of Building 98 by calling 432/386-3212.

With its lofty elevations and spectacular scenery, Marfa is also a popular spot for outdoor recreational activities, including the links at Marfa Municipal Golf Course, the highest golf course in Texas, and glider excursions, benefiting from the area's strong thermal updrafts and unparalleled views. When visitors aren't enjoying the cooler temperatures, they head to the trendy art galleries, boutiques, and coffee shops in the historic downtown area. Worth noting: Much of Marfa is closed on Monday and Tuesday, so be sure to check ahead with restaurants and attractions to make sure they're open before making plans for early in the week.

Marfa, Alpine, and Fort Davis form a nice West Texas triangle, each about 25 miles away from the other. To get there and around, take the lone highway to each and look for your destination—most are on the only/main highway in town.

SIGHTS

Despite being a tiny town in the absolute middle of nowhere, Marfa is packed with activities. The enormous sky is an attraction unto itself, but many visitors are captivated by the mysterious Marfa Lights and the Chinati Foundation, a worldwide destination containing avant-garde installation artwork housed in historic army barracks.

★ Chinati Foundation

There's nothing else in the world quite like the Chinati Foundation (1 Cavalry Row, 432/729-4362, www.chinati.org, tours Wed.-Sun., $10-25 adults, $5-10 students and seniors, ages 16 and under free). This unconventional art museum and artist compound is housed in nearly a dozen historic structures (barracks, artillery sheds, prisoner of war compounds) of the former Camp D. A. Russell army site. Based on the ideas of minimalist artist Donald Judd, Chinati features an

Marfa Was His Canvas

Far West Texas and New York City don't have much in common. In fact, they have nothing in common. When contemporary artist Donald Judd arrived in Marfa in the early 1970s, he saw two things that had been missing from his metropolitan environs: the sky and affordable land. He also saw the immense beauty of the West Texas terrain.

Judd set to work using the wide-open and rugged landscape as his canvas. He purchased several buildings in and around Marfa, most significantly the barracks, hangars, and gymnasium of Fort D. A. Russell, an abandoned army base. The hangars, which once held German prisoners during World War II, along with barrack buildings and artillery sheds, became galleries for modern art. The entire facility was ultimately developed as the Chinati Foundation, drawing art lovers and artists from around the world to experience the fascinating installation projects and educational seminars.

Judd spent much of the late 1970s and early 1980s developing and creating some of the world's largest permanent contemporary-art installations at Chinati. Most famous is *100 untitled works in mill aluminum,* installed in two former artillery sheds. The massive garage doors were replaced with windows, which disperse the omnipresent West Texas sunlight onto scores of metal boxes with the same outer dimensions yet completely different interior designs. The other large-scale piece, *15 untitled works in concrete,* was the first to be installed at the museum (1980-1984) and was cast and assembled on-site. The individual units have the same measurements—2.5 by 2.5 by 5 meters—and are made from 25-centimeter-thick concrete slabs.

Though his art was deemed puzzling by locals, Judd attempted to connect with Marfa residents by hosting an annual party with Mexican food and bagpipes (his favorite music). Despite the bizarre nature of the artwork, most Marfa residents welcomed Judd's peculiarities and especially the money Chinati brought to the community.

Judd died in 1994, leaving behind his foundation that would continue to attract international visitors intrigued by his vision for incorporating art with the environment. Though a few Marfa residents are complaining more loudly these days about the impact Chinati and its international spotlight has had on rising property values, they appreciate Judd's dedication to the incomparable charms of far West Texas.

amazing array of artwork, from Judd's large-scale pieces—most notably, a mammoth artillery shed containing stark metal boxes of varying size—to patterned fluorescent light sculptures, to sketches and paintings, to a large metal sculpture by famous Swedish-born artist Claes Oldenburg.

Judd's vision for the foundation was to blend art, architecture, and nature in an environment far different from traditional metropolitan art spaces. Artists and art lovers from across the world journey to this spectacular location to experience this fascinating confluence of elements, perhaps best represented by the compelling dichotomy presented in the barrack buildings: On one end of the room you'll find a bright pink fluorescent light sculpture, while the window on the opposite wall reveals the rugged beauty of the West Texas desert landscape.

Chinati offers one official tour Wednesday-Sunday, starting at 10am, featuring the foundation's permanent installations by Judd, John Chamberlain, Ilya Kabakov, Richard Long, and David Rabinowitch. After a noon-ish lunch break, the tour resumes at 2pm with a focus on permanent installations by Carl Andre, Dan Flavin, Roni Horn, Claes Oldenburg, and John Wesley, as well as the museum's current temporary exhibition. A separate self-guided tour, available Wednesday-Sunday noon-3pm, showcases Judd's permanent installation of *100 untitled works in mill aluminum.*

★ Marfa Lights

Drawing even more tourists than Chinati are the mysterious **Marfa Lights** (about 8 miles east of Marfa on U.S. Hwy. 90, 915/729-4942), typically visible just after dusk on clear evenings. These not-always-visible bouncing, splitting, and disappearing ethereal orbs have confounded people for more than a century (but mostly in the past six decades), and the viewing center just off the highway hosts thousands of curiosity seekers annually who flock to the site for a chance to see the mystifying white, yellow, and orange lights suspended in the air with no apparent source. Adding to the intrigue is their distance—at any given time they appear to be either 100 yards away or 10 miles away. There are many theories about the unexplained phenomenon, from Apache folklore to UFO sightings to vehicle headlights; however, a scientific explanation has yet to emerge.

First documented in 1883, explanations for the lights range from swamp gasses to bizarre bouts of electrostatic discharge to moonlight shining on shiny rocks in the Chinati Mountains. Scientists acknowledge their existence but take some of the fun out of the phenomenon by suggesting the lights are a mirage-like visual effect generated by the interaction of cold and warm layers of air, causing light to bend and move. Regardless, the absence of a valid and accepted explanation is ultimately the Marfa Lights' main draw. They defy explanation, and that's exactly why people continue to marvel at their mysteriousness.

Prada Marfa

Perhaps not surprisingly, one of the most popular attractions in the area is an enormous piece of art: *Prada Marfa* (about 37 miles west of Marfa on the south side of U.S. Hwy. 90). A permanent art installation mimicking a small Prada retail store, this adobe and plaster structure features display windows showcasing handbags and shoes with atmospheric interior lighting. Depending on who's doing the critiquing, the artwork is either mimicking the trendy visitors and artistes who descend on this remote landscape or is just "dumb," as vandals painted on the walls soon after its opening. Regardless, it's well worth the half-hour drive for the unique photo op (even Beyonce has done it) and to participate in the tradition of leaving behind a business card or shoe for the next round of pop-art aficionados to admire.

Chinati Foundation in Marfa

Presidio County Courthouse

Marfa's exquisite three-story **Presidio County Courthouse** (320 N. Highland St., 432/729-4670, www.co.presidio.tx.us) was built in 1886 and restored with the help of the Texas Historical Commission's Texas Historic Courthouse Preservation Program. The building is a remarkable example of Second Empire architecture, featuring a light pink exterior of stone and local brick along with the stylish detailing and mansard roofs fashionable in Europe at the time of its construction. If you're in town during weekday business hours, pop in for a look at the intricate interior woodwork and impressive attention to detail in the light fixtures and windows.

Hotel Paisano

Even if you're lodging elsewhere, it's worth dropping by the elegant **Hotel Paisano** (207 N. Highland Ave., 800/662-5517, www. hotelpaisano.com). Opened in 1930, the hotel was a gathering place for cattlemen and ranchers as well as a destination for railroad travelers between San Antonio and California. The Paisano's Spanish colonial-style architecture features colorful ceramic tile, ornate woodwork, and wrought iron. It became legendary in the 1950s when it served as headquarters for the classic movie *Giant,* starring Rock Hudson, Elizabeth Taylor, and James Dean. Several suites are named in their honor, and a display case in the lobby contains movie memorabilia. Visitors can enjoy a cocktail at the Paisano's courtyard patio, with its soothing fountain and pleasant atmosphere. The restaurant is also a major draw, featuring upscale dishes of contemporary and Southwestern fare.

Marfa Book Store Co.

A bookstore isn't typically a major tourist attraction, but most bookstores aren't like **Marfa Book Store Co.** (105 S. Highland Ave., 432/729-3700, www.marfabookco.com, daily 9am-8pm). The store is a magnet for the town's creative community, with an incredible selection of regional and intellectual-themed books, a small art gallery, and numerous readings and events. Its focus is on art and architecture, and you can get lost browsing through the sections devoted to photography, folk art, interior design, and other creative pursuits. The bookstore also showcases contemporary and regional writers and poets, and offers gifts, occasional coffees, and one of the few public Wi-Fi spaces in town.

FOOD

With the influx of out-of-towners and money, it's not surprising that Marfa's culinary scene is a bit more diverse than other Texas communities of its size. Fortunately, the new arrivals are respectful of local cuisine, and even if some of the prices are approaching Houston or Dallas levels, the atmosphere and variety of food are purely West Texan.

One of Marfa's "charms" is that its restaurants are open irregularly. Fortunately, hot meals are available throughout each day at Hotel Paisano's **Jett's Grill** (207 N. Highland Ave., 432/729-3838, www.hotelpaisano.com/ dining, daily 7:30am-10am and 2pm-9pm, $9-27). You don't have to be a hotel guest to enjoy Jett's tasty regional cuisine. For breakfast, grab a homemade egg-packed burrito with potatoes and a green chile sauce. Dinner is a highlight, particularly the chicken-fried steak with creamy gravy and a roasted jalapeño. Other top-notch options include the Angus burger and pistachio-crusted sirloin steak.

For an incredibly fresh, fancy, and full-flavored meal, be sure to stop by **Cochineal** (107 W. San Antonio St., 432/729-3300, www. cochinealmarfa.com, daily 5:30pm-10pm, $12-35). Located in the heart of downtown, Cochineal feels like it could be in Austin but doesn't seem out of place in Marfa. The space is open and contemporary, and the food is packed with flavor. The menu changes regularly, but past highlights include a super-tasty *chilaquiles* (a Mexican casserole with roast chicken, homemade tortilla chips, tomatillo sauce, and creamy cheese) and the rack of lamb with butternut squash.

The Most Treacherous Road in the State

If you have a sense of adventure (and a four-wheel-drive vehicle), be sure to set aside a morning or afternoon to experience **Pinto Canyon Road.** Traversing the rugged canyon land in the Chinati Mountains, this roughly 50-mile road stretches between Marfa and the border ghost town of Ruidosa.

If you're starting from Marfa, you'll sail smoothly on the first 32 miles of paved highway before encountering the treacherous/fun part. This stretch of rocky road is technically a county road, but it twists and turns through private ranch property and across purely untouched desert landscape.

The sights and sounds you'll encounter are fascinating, from colorful cacti to screeching birds to spiky ocotillo plants to leaping lizards. And those are just your immediate surroundings. Even more mesmerizing are the majestic mountains behind these objects, providing a scenic and solid backdrop to the entire panoramic vista.

Though it's tempting to keep your gaze on the peaks and natural wonders, it's important to pay attention to the rocky roadway before you. The route makes steep dips and unexpected turns, with massive gaps in the roadbed, random low-water crossings, and long-forgotten guardrails.

Rest assured, it's perfectly normal to be cruising along at a speedy clip of 10 mph. And be sure to make occasional stops to capture the astounding scenery on a camera or even just in your memory bank. It's not like you'll find yourself in the neighborhood again sometime soon. Just don't wander too far off the road, since private-property owners in this part of the country take their privacy and property very seriously.

LOST IN THE CHARM

Another occasionally disconcerting experience on the road is the overwhelming sense you've somehow drifted off the official roadway and onto a barely used ranch trail or historic driveway of some sort. Rest assured, it's just part of Pinto Canyon Road's charm. As soon as you round the next rocky elevation or ascend from a dry creekbed, you'll see signs of what passes for civilization out here—tire tracks from sometime in the past two days, a rusted sign, or a cattle guard.

By the time you get to the end of the road (plan about three hours for the entire trip), you'll be fairly exhausted yet exhilarated from the experience. You'll also be rewarded with a remarkable structure waiting in the ghost town of Ruidosa. The Sacred Heart of Jesus Catholic Church (circa 1914) is recognized as one of Texas's most significant adobe structures—its three major arches are considered the largest existing round-structural adobe arches in the state.

Though the church is in partial ruins, its architectural and historical importance has inspired people to organize several restoration efforts over the past decade. The Marfa-based Ruidosa Mission Project has helped stabilize the church by replacing its roof, fortifying the foundation, and grading the site for drainage. Regardless of its condition, the church is a divine ending (or beginning) to this treacherous trek through the desert.

BIG BEND REGION
MARFA AND VICINITY

Visitors can still order traditional small-town food in Marfa, too. A popular choice with locals and families is the **Pizza Foundation** (100 E. San Antonio St., 432/729-3377, Fri.-Sun. 1-8pm, $7-19). At the intersection of the only stoplight in town, this comfy eatery in a former gas station building is a welcome destination. The thin-sliced pie is perfectly prepared from scratch with a hearty tomato sauce and a fresh variety of toppings. The healthy salads and frozen limeade are necessary pairings with a slice or four of this tasty pizza—enjoy all of it inside or out on the small patio.

If eating outside is up your alley, head to the extremely popular mobile trailer called ★ **Food Shark** (usually located under the pavilion near the railroad tracks, 281/386-6540, Thurs.-Sat. noon-3pm, $6-10). Not surprisingly, the menu is somewhat limited at this restaurant-on-wheels, but the available options are creative and filling, skewing toward Mediterranean-style versions of West Texas favorites. A perfect example: the spicy, seasoned Marfalafel. Wash it all down with a sweet (as in real sugar) Mexican Coke in a bottle.

One of the only other downtown establishments within walking distance of the Thunderbird and Paisano hotels is the highly recommended **Marfa Burrito** (104 E. Waco St., 432/514-8675, Mon.-Sat. 6am-2pm, $6-13). Marfa Burrito serves up diner-style goodness with a Mexican twist. The eggs with green chiles are a perfect way to jump-start your day, the breakfast burritos are flavorfully wrapped in an astounding homemade tortilla, and the coffee is some of the best in town. Those same incredible tortillas wrap the lunch burritos, the best among them including picadillo beef and primo veggie.

ACCOMMODATIONS

Marfa's lodging options are limited but eclectic—there's something (except large chain hotels) for everyone. Visitors have the good fortune of choosing from the magnificent Hotel Paisano, the chic Thunderbird, or the standard Riata Inn. And don't forget the funky trailer park with outdoor showers.

For the ultimate West Texas lodging experience, book a room at the historic ★ **Hotel Paisano** (207 N. Highland Ave., 800/662-5517, www.hotelpaisano.com, $139-179 d). This charming and classy hotel lies just a block away from the majestic downtown courthouse and harkens back to the days of upscale accommodations for cross-country travelers and cattle traders. The Spanish colonial architecture adds a touch of regional elegance to the experience, and guests have a wide range of room options, from the smaller quarters in the original part of the hotel to larger suites with balconies, kitchens, and plasma TVs. Call well in advance to reserve the popular James Dean room, where the movie icon stayed during the filming of *Giant*.

Equally as extraordinary, for completely different reasons, is the trendy and sleek **Thunderbird Motel** (601 W. Hwy. 90/San Antonio St., 432/729-1984, www. thunderbirdmarfa.com, $179 d). Built in 1959 as a classic horseshoe-shaped roadside motel surrounding a swimming pool, the building has been tastefully remodeled with stylish stucco and accompanied by native flora. Rooms feature polished concrete floors, locally built pecan furniture, quality bedding, minibars with specialty beverages and organic and local snacks, Wi-Fi service, access to vintage Stack-O-Matic record players and a vinyl library, and a thermos of coffee in a cloth bag placed on the doorknob at 7am.

One of the funkiest and most popular lodging options in town is ★ **El Cosmico** (802 S. Highland Ave., 432/729-1950, www. elcosmico.com, $105 for safari tents, $165 for yurts, $190-299 for fully equipped trailers). This "campground hotel" consists of a cool collection of renovated vintage trailers, a tepee, a few eco-shack yurts, and several regular ol' campsites. The stylishly redecorated 1950s-era trailers include stoves, small fridges, fans, floor heating, and bathrooms with hot water. Bedding materials and cooking provisions are provided, and Wi-Fi access is available in the lobby lounge. Be aware that most trailers include an outdoor shower, which seems strange at first but is ultimately quite liberating without sacrificing privacy or comfort (strategically placed walls protect you from public view and the steady breeze).

El Cosmico is more than just a trendy/quirky place to spend the night, it's a concept—the goal is to build a sustainable community environment that "fosters and agitates artistic and intellectual exchange." Guests are encouraged to attain this by participating in the communal space (an elm grove filled with hammocks, an outdoor kitchen and dining spaces, and a community lounge and mercantile).

If these options offer too much character (or, more realistically, a strain on the wallet), the only "standard" choice in town is the commendable **Riata Inn** (1500 E. Hwy. 90, 432/729-3800, www.riatainnmarfa.com, $89-$109 d). The Riata features extra-large versions of typical hotel rooms, each offering

Buffalo Soldiers: Fighting for Survival

A Buffalo Soldier isn't just the name of a Bob Marley song. These fierce warriors were named by the Plains Indians who admired the bravery of the African American troops that served on the frontier in the post-Civil War army.

Buffalo Soldiers were stationed at several forts in western Texas, but they are perhaps best known for their service at **Fort Davis** (on Hwy. 17 in Fort Davis, 432/426-3224, www.nps.gov/foda), where they spent nearly 20 years (1867-1885) protecting settlers. Several infantries and cavalry units earned distinction for their work at the fort, despite the lack of high-profile battles or significant military incidents.

The primary mission of the Buffalo Soldier regiments was to protect the established mail and travel routes, control movements of area Native American tribes, and scout the terrain. One of the few military-related highlights occurred in 1879, when the army was waging a campaign against the Apaches who were attacking settlers in West Texas. Apache leader Victorio had fled to Mexico and was attempting to rejoin his tribe in the Fort Davis area when the Buffalo Soldier units were dispatched to prevent the regrouping. According to historians, several major confrontations occurred in the region, forcing Victorio to retreat to Mexico, where he was later killed by Mexican troops.

Otherwise, life for all the soldiers at Fort Davis was somewhat tedious. Routine duties and fatigue details occupied most of their time, with occasional excursions to patrol the frontier, guard water holes, and escort government survey crews, wagon trains, and mail coaches.

Internet access, flat-screen TVs with cable, and access to an outdoor pool.

INFORMATION AND SERVICES

The **Marfa Chamber of Commerce** (207 N. Highland Ave., 432/729-4942, www.marfacc.com) provides information about the community's limited yet interesting resources.

FORT DAVIS

Fort Davis (population 1,201) truly feels like the Old West. Nestled among the Davis Mountains—therefore dubbed "the highest town in Texas"—Fort Davis exhibits the charm of an authentic Western community, with wide windswept streets containing flat-faced and sun-faded buildings under an enormous sky.

Fort Davis was established in 1854 by Secretary of War Jefferson Davis as one of the key army posts in West Texas's development and defense. The fort was briefly abandoned during the Civil War, allowing Native Americans to strip much of the buildings' wood for fuel, but it was reoccupied in 1867

and by the mid-1880s was a major operation with more than 600 men and 60-plus adobe and stone structures.

During this time, Fort Davis was home to several regiments of Buffalo Soldiers, African Americans who earned distinction as brave fighters and served alongside Anglo soldiers, a rare case of desegregation in the late 1800s. As settlement increased in the area and native populations dispersed, the fort's original purpose became obsolete, and it was abandoned in 1891.

The town's remote and rugged location made it a difficult destination to reach, resulting in slow growth throughout the 1900s. These days, its mild climate and natural beauty draw thousands of visitors annually from Austin and other urban areas in search of a high-altitude respite from the grueling summer heat. Fort Davis's intrigue lies in its proximity to attractions like the fascinating McDonald Observatory and breathtaking Davis Mountains State Park, as well as its refreshingly unspoiled allure, particularly compared to the "discovered" towns of Marfa and Alpine.

Sights

FORT DAVIS NATIONAL HISTORIC SITE

Be sure to set aside an hour or two for **Fort Davis National Historic Site** (on Hwy. 17 in Fort Davis, 432/426-3224, www.nps. gov/foda, daily 8am-5pm, $10 ages 16 and older). Considered one of the country's best remaining examples of a 19th-century frontier military post, Fort Davis draws visitors from across the country. Families and history buffs can spend as much time as they like on the self-guided tour, showcasing the post's 20 buildings and more than 100 ruins. Of particular interest are the restored barrack buildings and officers' quarters with period furnishings and military equipment, offering a slice of life on a frontier base in the late 1800s. Opened in 1854, Fort Davis played a key role in the history of the Southwest by protecting settlers, mail coaches, and travelers on the San Antonio-El Paso Road. The fort is especially notable for serving as the base for several regiments of African American troops known as Buffalo Soldiers, who helped maintain peaceful settlement in the region.

★ MCDONALD OBSERVATORY

Sitting high atop 6,791-foot-tall Mount Locke, the remarkable **McDonald Observatory** (on Hwy. 118, 16 miles west of Fort Davis, 432/426-3640, www.mcdonaldobservatory. org, daily 10am-5:30pm, $9 adults, $8 children ages 6-12, additional charge for star parties) makes good use of its position approaching the heavens. Three large domes beckon visitors to the facility, which opened in 1939 with the world's second-largest telescope and has served astronomers and visitors ever since. The observatory's impressive equipment includes the massive Hobby-Eberly Telescope, with a 36-foot-wide mirror comprised of 91 laser-aligned segments, and two other telescopes to monitor the sun, stars, and planets. Visitors have the option of attending informative guided tours (11:30am and 2:30pm), solar viewings (30 minutes before the tours), and dramatic star parties (after dusk every Tues., Fri., and Sat.), but the spectacular views of the surrounding mountains and valleys are reason alone to make the journey.

OTHER SIGHTS

It's worth the 38-mile drive north of Fort Davis to experience the spectacular scenery and distinctive allure of ★ **Balmorhea**

Balmorhea's famous spring-fed pool

State Park (Hwy. 17, 432/375-2370, www. tpwd.state.tx.us, $7 ages 13 and older). If you have the time, book a night at the historic adobe motel, featuring spacious rooms with cable TV. Note: the motel was undergoing restoration in 2020, so check in advance about availability. The park's centerpiece is San Solomon Springs, gushing up to 26 million gallons of refreshingly cool water daily into a large artificial swimming pool. The deep artesian springs offer an ideal spot for scuba diving, so it's fairly common to see divers in the far corner of the pool exploring the unique aquatic life in the crystal-clear water. The springs also feed a fascinating desert wetland, providing a habitat and life source for scores of uncommon birds and plant life. The viewing areas—a large wooden overlook and subsurface water window—are especially intriguing.

Overlooking the Fort Davis area's signature red-hued outcroppings is **Davis Mountains State Park** (Hwy. 118, 432/426-3337, www. tpwd.state.tx.us, $6 ages 13 and older). The park boasts 1,000 feet of elevation change and is a popular destination for hikers and campers who relish the natural beauty and cooler temperatures. Considered one of Texas's most scenic areas, the park showcases its namesake mountains, the most extensive range in the state. The park draws mountain bikers and hikers from across the state who marvel at the incredible views of the park's picturesque canyon formed by Keesey Creek. Hard-core campers also appreciate the park's Limpia Canyon Primitive Area, with 10 miles of backcountry hiking trails and primitive tent campsites. Other popular activities include bird-watching, stargazing, and cruising Skyline Drive, a paved road with two spectacular overlooks showcasing the Chinati Mountains, located 75 miles to the southwest. The park is also home to the famous Indian Lodge, a historic adobe hotel still in operation.

Check out the mystique of the region's surroundings at the **Chihuahuan Desert Visitor Center** (43869 Hwy. 118, 432/364-2499, www.cdri.org, Mon.-Sat. 9am-5pm, $6.50 adults, children ages 12 and under free). Visitors can experience the wonders of the Chihuahuan Desert region firsthand by exploring the fairly strenuous Modesta Canyon Trail, a one-hour hike, and the scenic Clayton's Overlook hike, offering amazing views of the area's diverse topography. The center's succulent greenhouse features more than 200 species of Chihuahuan Desert cacti as well as other attractions, like the 20-acre botanical garden, an interpretive center with indoor and outdoor educational exhibits, and educational programs.

Food

A good place to kick off your limited Fort Davis culinary tour is the low-key and downhome **Fort Davis Drug Store** (113 N. State St., 432/426-3118, Mon.-Thurs. 11am-7:30pm, Fri.-Sat. 7:30am-8pm, Sun.7:30am-3pm, $9-18). This old-fashioned soda fountain and restaurant is known for its comfort food, namely, chicken-fried steak, thick burgers, and hearty breakfasts. Top your meal off with a root beer float and a souvenir from the attached old-fashioned drugstore.

The only place in town with a full Tex-Mex menu is the commendable **Cueva de Leon Cafe** (611 N. State St., 432/426-3801, Mon.-Fri. 11:30am-8:30pm, Sat. 11:30am-3pm, 5-8:30pm, $8-17). Located in the heart of the tiny downtown area, the restaurant is known for its spectacular chiles rellenos (perfectly breaded and not too spicy) and its flavorful chicken enchiladas with tangy green sauce.

The best place in town for a high-quality yet casual dinner is the **Hotel Limpia's Blue Mountain Bistro** (100 Main St., 432/426-3241, www.blue-mountain-bistro.com, daily 5pm-8pm, weekend tapas 3-5pm, $11-33). Opt for the gouda cheese fries or mushroom caps as a starter, and proceed to the recommended main course: a hearty char-grilled Angus steak. Or the stuffed pork chop. Or even the mountain trout. Be sure to save room for the homemade pies. Note: Blue Mountain Bistro proudly bills itself as "the only restaurant in

Civilian Conservation Corps

The Civilian Conservation Corps left an indelible mark across Texas, particularly in the Big Bend region. Step into one of the area's local, state, or national parks, and you're bound to encounter signage and literature chronicling the hard work CCC members contributed to the site's roads, drainage systems, and permanent facilities.

The CCC's origins were in President Franklin Roosevelt's New Deal legislation, which addressed the country's economic crises through myriad federal proposals providing relief and reform. In Texas, CCC projects helped develop the burgeoning state park system and with soil conservation and erosion control.

Much like other parts of the state, far West Texas's construction projects included buildings, bridges, dams, culverts, stone steps, and trails. The buildings and support systems were designed to tie in closely with their rustic sites by using natural materials such as native stone and timber. To this day, nearly half of the 56 state parks that incorporated CCC work in the 1930s remain in the state parks system.

Some of the most remarkable examples of the CCC legacy are in the Big Bend region. Most notable is Indian Lodge in Davis Mountains State Park in Fort Davis. The multilevel pueblo-style hotel remains a stunning work of architecture, with its stark whitewashed adobe walls encompassing rustic cedar woodwork offering a distinct Southwestern visceral experience.

Another significant CCC contribution is the remarkable adobe motor lodge and spring-fed swimming pool at Balmorhea State Park, where visitors can enjoy the spacious rooms and inviting water at the edge of the Chihuahuan Desert. In Big Bend National Park, the CCC projects have less of a visual impact but are just as important. The scenic road traversing through and winding among the Chisos Mountains was designed and constructed by corps members, along with several rustic stone cottages at the Chisos Mountains Lodge.

Fort Davis with a liquor license," so there's that.

Accommodations
HOTELS AND MOTELS

If you plan far enough in advance, you may have the good fortune of staying at the immensely popular ★ **Indian Lodge** (Park Rd. 3, 432/426-3254, www.tpwd.state.tx.us, $115 d). Built in the 1930s by the Civilian Conservation Corps, the multilevel pueblo-style hotel is nestled among the ridges of Davis Mountains State Park. The rustic cedar furnishings and woodwork coupled with the whitewash-covered 18-inch-thick adobe walls provide a distinctly Southwestern visceral experience. The lodge also features a full-service year-round restaurant (closed for renovations in 2020) and an outdoor swimming pool.

Another popular lodging option in Fort Davis is **Hotel Limpia** (100 Main St., 432/426-3241, www.hotellimpia.com, $99 and up), a beautifully restored 1912 hotel containing period furnishings, four buildings, and a cottage. The charming guest rooms and welcoming courtyard garden with rocking chairs and lush vegetation offer a pleasant respite from city life.

Those in search of a newer facility will find solace at the downtown **Harvard Hotel** (109 N. State St., 432/426-2500, www.harvardhotelandlodge.com, $99-129). This rustic-looking yet modern-feeling facility offers rooms with refrigerators, microwaves, and free Wi-Fi.

BED-AND-BREAKFASTS

With its quaint downtown and abundant natural beauty, Fort Davis is an ideal place to stay in a B&B. One of the best in town is **The Veranda** (210 Court Ave., 432/426-2233, www.theveranda.com, $115-145). Just a block away from the beautifully restored Jeff Davis County Courthouse, The Veranda's 13 antiques-bedecked suites feature 12-foot-tall ceilings, private baths, and free Wi-Fi service.

The inn also boasts walled gardens and quiet courtyards with rocking chairs and tables in the shadow of Sleeping Lion Mountain.

Just down the road are the cozy and comfortable **Butterfield Inn Cottages** (201 State St., 432/426-3252, www.butterfieldinn.com, $98-165). Each of these mini homes contains fireplaces, recliners, refrigerators, microwaves, and private baths with Jacuzzi tubs.

CAMPING

Aside from Big Bend, the best camping in the region is at **Davis Mountains State Park** (Hwy. 118, 432/426-3337, www.tpwd.state.tx.us). The park's northern section is the Limpia Canyon Primitive Area, a special-use district with 10 miles of backcountry hiking trails and primitive tent campsites. The park's developed facilities are south of Highway 118 and include restrooms with showers; campsites with water, electricity, sewer, and cable TV connection; and nine miles of hiking trails, some leading to Fort Davis National Historic Site.

Those traveling in RVs may want to hook up in downtown Fort Davis at the **Overland Trail Campground** (307 N. State St., 432/426-2250, www.texascamping.com), offering cable and Wi-Fi, a coin laundry, showers, tent areas with water and electric, fully equipped cabins, and a cyclists camping area with accessible facilities.

Information and Services

For a small town, Fort Davis has well-organized and extremely helpful visitor service. The best way to start planning your trip is via the handy website hosted by the **Fort Davis Chamber of Commerce** (4 Memorial Sq., 432/426-3015, www.fortdavis.com). Drop by the office for brochures, maps, and helpful advice.

ALPINE

Don't be fooled by the town's name. Alpine evokes images of snowcapped peaks and lofty magnificence. You won't find that here. Instead, you'll encounter plenty of West Texas charm and fantastic food along the extra-wide streets of this historic community that serves as the economic hub of the Big Bend region.

Alpine's (population 6,020) origins date to 1882 when laborers pitched their tents at the base of a mountain while working on the transcontinental railroad that traversed the region. The town slowly added residents until 1921, when the opening of Sul Ross State Normal College (now Sul Ross State University) resulted in a significant population increase. The university, railroad, and ranching industries solidified Alpine's status as the stable economic core of far West Texas.

Since Big Bend's opening in the 1940s, Alpine has become a destination for travelers who often schedule an extra day or two in town on their way to or from the park to enjoy the mild climate and cultural resources, including several noteworthy museums, restaurants, and year-round recreational activities. The Alpine visitors center offers a handy brochure with a map featuring a walking tour of historic downtown buildings. Popular annual events include the Texas Cowboy Poetry Gathering and Trappings of Texas in February, Cinco de Mayo celebration in May, and Big Bend Balloon Bash on Labor Day weekend.

Sights

Alpine's most significant cultural attraction is the **Museum of the Big Bend** (1000 E. Sul Ross Ave., 432/837-8730, www.sulross.edu/~museum, Tues.-Sat. 9am-5pm, Sun. 1pm-5pm, free). On the Sul Ross State University campus, the museum's impressive collections showcase the confluence of cultures in the region—Native American, Spanish, Mexican, and Anglo. Visitors learn about the cultures that have occupied the area for thousands of years via ancient tribal artifacts, historic frontier items, and life-size dioramas. Be sure to check out the fascinating Chihuahuan Desert Cactus Garden near the museum's entrance.

For some visitors—baseball fans, in particular—the city's cultural highlight is the amazing **Kokernot Field** (at the intersection of Hwy. 223 and N. 2nd St.). This beautiful historic ballpark is a baseball fan's dream, featuring unexpected details around every corner, such as the wrought-iron fencing with baseball-shaped patterns, the lamps with handmade stitched-baseball themes, and spectacular views of the mountains looming beyond the outfield. The park opened in 1947 when legendary rancher and philanthropist Herbert Kokernot used his fortune to bring semipro baseball to Alpine. Kokernot spared no expense, investing more than $1.5 million on the park—an exorbitant amount at the time—to make his dream a reality. The minor league Alpine Cowboys played at Kokernot Field from 1947 through 1958, drawing capacity crowds who appreciated the architectural gem and the quality of talent on the diamond. Since the ballpark is currently home to the Sul Ross State University Lobos, the field is typically closed to the public unless a game is scheduled (Feb.-Apr., check www.sulross.edu for game times).

It's a bit of a drive—everything out here is—but worth the effort to experience **Woodward Ranch** (18 miles south of Alpine on Hwy. 118, 432/364-2271, call for times and fees). The ranch offers several recreational activities, including hiking, scenic drives, bird-watching, and stargazing, but it's primarily known as a gemstone collecting destination. The 3,000-acre property contains more than 60 kinds of naturally occurring agates and gemstones that visitors can hunt and gather. Discover desirable (but not necessarily valuable) Texas agates such as red plume and pompom, as well as opal, jasper, and calcite. Upon returning to ranch headquarters, visitors can consult with staff about identifying and appraising their finds. Guide services are available, and a lapidary (stone) shop is on-site.

Food
AMERICAN
Alpine isn't known for its abundance of tourist attractions, but its quality restaurants are a major draw for visitors to the Big Bend region. One of the city's most famous eateries is the fantastic ★ **Reata Restaurant** (203 N. 5th St., 432/837-9232, www.reata.net, Mon.-Sat. 11:30am-2pm and 5pm-10pm, $13-45). Named for the iconic ranch depicted in the classic 1956 movie *Giant,* filmed in the area, this upscale cowboy cuisine with a West Texas flair even inspired a second location in Fort Worth. Start things off with a hot bowl of

Kokernot Field in Alpine

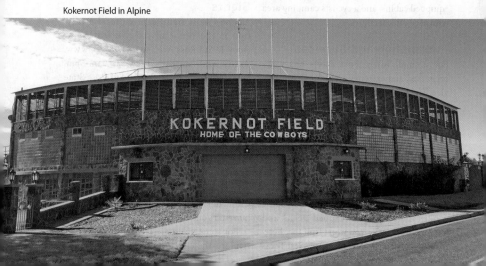

jalapeño cilantro soup, and proceed with any of the tantalizing menu items, from the renowned tenderloin tamales to the carne asada to the double pork chop stuffed with pears.

Not nearly as upscale is **Penny's Diner** (2407 E. Hwy. 90, 432/837-5711, open 24 hours, $7-17). Locals love the down-home diner atmosphere and the heapin' helpings of traditional favorites like chicken-fried steak, pork chops, and grilled chicken. The breakfasts here are hearty and flavorful, and you can order any time of the day or night.

For those seeking some beer and pub grub, head directly to **Harry's Tinaja** (412 E. Holland Ave., 432/837-5060, daily noon-2am, $5-14). Although Harry's is mainly a bar, it usually has a food trailer on-site (the Smokin' Cuban has some of the tastiest food in town). Harry's is known for its charming low-key atmosphere and extremely refreshing cold beer.

MEXICAN

The best Tex-Mex in town is in an unassuming little house on the other side of the railroad tracks. Aptly named **La Casita** (1104 E. Ave. H, 432/837-2842, Tues.-Sat. 11am-8:30pm, $8-17), this no-frills eatery focuses its efforts on flavorful food—hearty and spicy salsa, perfectly seasoned verde sauce on the chicken enchiladas, crispy jam-packed beef tacos, and satisfying chicken quesadillas.

A great way to start the day is with a huge breakfast taco at the tiny **Alicia's Mexican Restaurant** (708 E. Ave. G, 432/837-2802, Wed.-Sun. 8am-3pm, Mon., Wed. 9am-3pm, $5-9). Stuff it full of eggs, potatoes, cheese, bacon, and veggies before heading out for a hike or back to your room for a nap.

BREAKFAST

An ideal place to accompany the crisp mountain morning air is **Judy's Bread & Breakfast Bakery Cafe** (113 W. Holland Ave., 432/837-9424, www. judysbreadandbreakfast.com, Wed.-Mon. 7am-2pm, Sun. 8am-noon, $6-13). Not surprisingly, pastries and coffee are the main draws here, but they're extra tasty in a quaint

location like this. The most popular item by far is the cinnamon rolls, but it's worth saving some room for a fresh doughnut or three. If you're looking to fuel up for a long trip, dare to order a big ol' plate of biscuits and gravy; just be sure to grab a to-go coffee to get you through your most challenging endeavors.

Accommodations

For those in need of just the basics, the **Highland Inn** (1404 E. Hwy. 90, 432/837-5811, www.highlandinn.net, $79 d) offers simple and stark rooms with charmingly mismatched furniture. Directly across the road from Sul Ross State University, the Highland features a microwave and fridge in each room, along with free Wi-Fi access and an outdoor pool.

If rustic casual is your style, consider the **Antelope Lodge** (2310 W. Hwy. 90, 432/837-2451, www.antelopelodge.com, cabins $99 d). Built in the late 1940s as part of the national "motor lodge" trend, this decidedly unmodern lodge revels in its historic charm. Cottages and guest rooms contain kitchenettes with two-burner stoves, mini refrigerators, and available microwaves and utensils (call in advance). Each cottage has a stone porch with weathered chairs for enjoying the cool mountain air.

The best option in this price range, however, is the comfy and casual **Maverick Inn** (1200 E. Holland Ave., 432/837-0628, www. themaverickinn.com, $125 d). This former motor court received an extensive renovation with modern amenities like free Wi-Fi, flat-screen TVs, fancy linens, regional artwork, Saltillo-tiled floors, mini refrigerators, and microwaves.

For a truly memorable stay in Alpine, reserve a room or loft at the magnificent ★ **Holland Hotel** (209 W. Holland Ave., 432/837-3844, www.thehollandhoteltexas. com, $129-199). Built in 1912 for cattlemen and the occasional tourist, this impressive downtown hotel will charm you from the moment you enter the ornate front doors, where your room assignment awaits in an envelope (it's taped to the door). There aren't any standard rooms at the Holland—they range from tiny to sprawling—but you can get a sense of what's available by previewing options on the hotel's website. All rooms feature eclectic furnishings and colors, along with private bathrooms, refrigerators, and microwaves. Incidentally, free earplugs are available at the hotel office (open 8am-5pm) to help silence the trains that occasionally blast through town in the middle of the night.

Information and Services

For brochures, maps, and travel assistance, contact the **Alpine Chamber of Commerce** (106 N. 3rd St., 432/837-2326 or 800/561-3735, www.alpinetexas.com). To get a handle on what's going on in town, pick up a copy of the *Alpine Avalanche* at one of the rack boxes throughout town or drop by the downtown office (118 N. 5th Street) to grab your own personal copy of this commendable community newspaper.

Panhandle Plains

The Panhandle region of Texas is rather desolate, but the cities that sprang up among the windswept plains are distinctive in their identities—independent and hardy, with a flair for the artistic. Robust residents have forged a living off the land in this unforgiving climate for thousands of years, and despite the difficulties of dealing with snowy winters and 100°F summers, these proud Panhandlers are dedicated to maintaining their family ranches and agriculture-related businesses.

Historically, the Panhandle Plains have been home to these types of self-reliant people living off the land, from Native Americans to Spanish explorers to farmers and oilmen. Apaches ruled the region for several hundred years until the Comanches arrived in the 1700s.

Lubbock 438
Amarillo and Vicinity ... 446
Abilene 458
San Angelo 465

Highlights

Look for ★ to find recommended sights, activities, dining, and lodging.

★ **Pay tribute to a music legend.** A cultural hot spot in Lubbock, the **Buddy Holly Center** showcases this native son's brief life and significant contributions to rock music (page 438).

★ **Wander through windmills.** The 100-plus vintage windmills at the **American Wind Power Center** are unexpectedly compelling (page 439).

★ **Snap a pic at the Cadillac Ranch.** West of Amarillo, a bumper crop of 10 Cadillacs buried nose-down in a field is the best photo op in Texas (page 448).

★ **Bike through Palo Duro Canyon State Park.** With sheer cliffs and rock towers displaying stunning stratified reds, yellows, and oranges, it's a colorful ride (page 456).

★ **Talk to holograms.** Abilene's innovative history museum, **Frontier Texas!** uses interactive technology to showcase a slice of life in the Panhandle Plains in 1780-1880 (page 459).

★ **Relive the life of a soldier** in the late 1800s through the barracks, stables, and officers' quarters at **Fort Concho National Historic Landmark** (page 465).

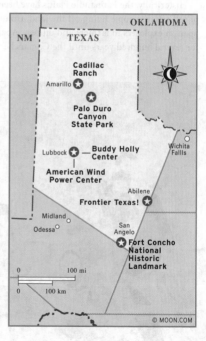

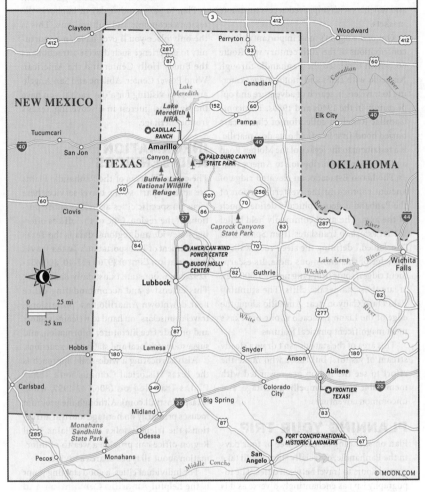

Panhandle Plains

Other tribes (Kiowa, Southern Cheyenne, and Arapaho), collectively known as the Southern Plains Indians, occupied portions of the region until 1874, when the U.S. Army launched a "successful" campaign to permanently move them onto the reservations in present-day Oklahoma. With Native Americans no longer in the area, Hispanic sheepherders from New Mexico known as *pastores* arrived on the scene. Livestock roamed the open ranges of the Panhandle until the 1870s, when barbed wire was introduced to the region.

Soon after, two other significant advances—the windmill and the railroad—forever altered life in the area by promoting its settlement. Windmills tapped

Previous: the famous Cadillac Ranch west of Amarillo; Palo Duro Canyon south of Amarillo; a reenactor at Fort Concho

into underground aquifers for water and irrigation, while railroads provided farmers and ranchers with improved access to remote markets.

One of the region's most important cultural contributions of the 20th century was Route 66, which traversed the Panhandle through Amarillo with cafés and motor lodges catering to travelers in search of adventure and opportunity in the 1940s and 1950s. The iconic Cadillac Ranch, a collection of classic cars buried hood-first in a field outside Amarillo, is a testament to the legacy of the Mother Road and a legendary contribution to Americana.

The Llano Estacado, an elevated ridge of ancient caprock in the western portion of the Panhandle, geographically defines much of the area. The most commonly held belief is that *estacado* translates from Spanish as "stockaded," defining the steep rock walls at the edge of this enormous mesa. Its escarpment ridges, some dropping nearly 1,000 feet, create those namesake cliffs. The stunning Palo Duro Canyon near Amarillo along the edge of the Llano Estacado is one of Texas's most magnificent physical features.

This area of the state doesn't draw a steady stream of visitors, but those who make the effort to see the region are rewarded with memorable vistas, compelling heritage, and uncommon adventures.

PLANNING YOUR TRIP

Plan on spending at least three or four days in the Panhandle, especially since it will take several hours to travel between cities. The topography isn't as enchantingly diverse as it is in far West Texas, so instead of enjoying/enduring the long drive from points east, some visitors choose to fly to Lubbock or Amarillo to begin their High Plains escapade.

To experience the best the Panhandle has to offer, set aside at least two days for Amarillo-area adventure. Plan a day of hiking or biking in beautiful Palo Duro Canyon and an overnight in the park's campground. Spend the next day or two exploring legendary Route 66 locales in nearby Amarillo and in the small towns east and west of the city just off I-40 (the Mother Road's soulless replacement).

Plan to pass another day in Lubbock, the region's economic and cultural hub. This is the only place you'll ever have an opportunity to experience such diverse attractions as the Buddy Holly Center and the American Wind Power Center. Abilene and San Angelo are worth visiting for a day each if you have the time and interest in discovering Texas's frontier heritage.

INFORMATION AND SERVICES

The occupied areas of the Panhandle Plains are spread apart, so the travel services here focus on specific cities as well as entire portions of the region. One of the offices offering statewide and regional data is the Texas Department of Transportation's **Texas Travel Information Center** (9700 E. I-40, 800/452-9292, www.dot.state.tx.us, daily 8am-5pm). This extensive and accommodating office near downtown Amarillo has "professional travel counselors" on hand to welcome visitors and provide free literature, information, and suggestions for local and statewide excursions.

Also advocating a wide-scale approach is the Texas Historical Commission's **Texas Plains Trail Region** (806/747-1997, www.texasplainstrail.com). Although the program focuses primarily on heritage tourism attractions, the friendly folks at the Plains Trail Region office can provide a wealth of information about all types of area activities.

For individual cities, a good starting point is the helpful **Amarillo Convention and Visitor Council** (1000 S. Polk St., 800/692-1338, www.visitamarillo.com, Mon.-Fri. 9am-6pm). Drop by for city maps, brochures about area attractions, and assistance with planning an excursion along old Route 66.

To find out everything you'd ever need or want to know about visiting the Lubbock area, go to the **Lubbock Convention & Visitors Bureau** (6th floor of the downtown Wells Fargo Center at 1500 Broadway St., 806/747-5232, www.visitlubbock.org). Likewise, you'll find travel literature and friendly folks in the restored historic train depot that now houses the **Abilene Convention and Visitors Bureau** (1101 N. 1st St., 325/676-2556, www.abilenevisitors.com, Mon.-Fri. 8:30am-5pm).

One of the state's most impressive travel service offices is the remarkable **San Angelo Chamber of Commerce Visitors Center** (418 W. Ave. B, 800/375-1206, www.sanangelo.org, Mon.-Fri. 8:30am-5pm, Sat. 9am-5pm, Sun. noon-4pm). Located in a facility on the banks of the scenic Concho River, the visitors center features enormous windows and cascading waterfalls along with helpful staff and bundles of brochures.

GETTING THERE AND AROUND

Driving to the Panhandle Plains from Dallas, Austin, or San Antonio isn't very exciting. Unlike the majestic mesas and mountains greeting travelers to far West Texas, the Panhandle Plains are about as inspiring as their flat-sounding name implies. The drive from San Antonio to Lubbock is more than seven hours, and it's almost two hours more from there to Amarillo. As a result, some travelers choose to take a cheap Southwest Airlines flight (around $100 each way from most major Texas cities) and rent a car to save time and gas money.

As the Panhandle's largest city and economic hub, Lubbock is a good place to start your visit, especially since most of the region's other major cities are only a few hours away. Book your flight to **Lubbock International Airport** (5401 N. Martin Luther King Blvd., 806/775-2035), northeast of the city, approximately 10 minutes from downtown. The airport offers service from American Eagle, United Express, and Southwest Airlines, and travelers can book reservations there with most of the major car rental companies if they're not taking an Uber. Lubbock's cab services include **City Cab** (806/765-7474) and **Yellow Cab** (806/370-3325).

Those focusing their travels exclusively on Amarillo and Palo Duro Canyon should use **Amarillo International Airport** (10801 Airport Blvd., 806/335-1671, www.ci.amarillo.tx.us). Situated seven miles east of downtown, the airport hosts arrivals and departures from American Eagle, United Express, and Southwest Airlines. If you're not using a ride share, there's car rental service through **Avis** (806/335-2313), **Enterprise** (806/335-9443), **Hertz** (806/335-2331), and **National** (806/335-2311) and cab companies like **Jack & Son Taxi Service** (806/626-5015) and **Yellow Checker Cab** (806/371-8294).

The region's smaller cities also provide airport and transportation service, even though connections are limited to Houston and Dallas. If you're Abilene bound, consider flying to **Abilene Regional Airport** (2933 Airport Blvd., 325/676-6367), offering flights with American Eagle and car rentals from Avis, Enterprise, and Hertz. Cab service is available via **Road Runner Taxi** (325/232-3295) and **Abilene Yellow Cab** (325/677-4334). For San Angelo travelers, there's **San Angelo Regional Airport** (8618 Terminal Cir., 325/659-6409, www.sanangelotexas.us), providing service from American Eagle and car rentals through Avis, Budget, and Hertz. The city's cab companies are **Red Ball Taxi & Shuttle** (325/942-8899) and **Checker Cab Co.** (325/655-3105).

Lubbock

Lubbock (population 255,885) is distractingly flat. In fact, the lack of topography is a bit disconcerting—there should be a hill or a creekbed or some geographical feature somewhere in the city; instead, you can just see miles and miles of Texas. There's nothing wrong with that; in fact, it's an engaging and defining characteristic of Lubbock's nature.

The ranching culture is ingrained in Lubbock residents, and they take pride in their hardworking, sensible heritage. Settlers began taking root here in the late 1800s but were occasionally displaced by the nasty, dust-storm-inducing winds. The hardy folks toughed it out.

Eventually a railroad arrived, and the city slowly emerged as the marketing center of the South Plains. By 1923, the Texas legislature authorized the establishment of Texas Technological College (now known as Texas Tech University), which went on to play a key role in establishing Lubbock's identity.

Another character-defining aspect of Lubbock's personality is its contribution to American popular music. Native son Buddy Holly helped revolutionize rock 'n' roll in the late 1950s, and other influential Lubbock-area country/rock artists include Roy Orbison, Waylon Jennings, Mac Davis, and Joe Ely.

Still, it's Texas Tech that makes locals the proudest, and their hometown academic institution brings worldly culture to the High Plains. Texas Tech has a healthy enrollment of nearly 33,000 students, and its agriculture and engineering programs continue to make a major impact on the economy and life of residents in the Panhandle and the entirety of West Texas.

SIGHTS

★ Buddy Holly Center

At one point, Buddy Holly was the single most influential creative force in early rock 'n' roll. Visitors will find a testament to this legacy at the fascinating **Buddy Holly Center** (1801 Crickets Ave., 806/767-2686, www.buddyhollycenter.org, Tues.-Sat. 10am-5pm, Sun. 1pm-5pm, $8 adults, $6 seniors ages 60 and older, $5 children ages 7-17). Holly's enormous impact on rock music is compounded by the fact that his professional career lasted merely 18 months. In that brief time, his distinct "Western bop" sound—a blend of country, blues, gospel, and bluegrass—had a major impact on rock legends, including the Beatles, the Rolling Stones, and Bruce Springsteen. Paul McCartney claims the Beatles meticulously studied Holly's work and used it as a basis for their first hit song, "Love Me Do," and Holly's 1958 tour of England was a watershed moment for future British Invaders.

Holly and his band, the Crickets, developed an influential sound evident on classic hit songs such as "That'll Be the Day," "Oh Boy!," "Peggy Sue," "Maybe Baby," and "Rave On." Holly's life came to a tragic end with other music legends Ritchie Valens and J. P. "Big Bopper" Richardson when their plane crashed in an Iowa cornfield on February 3, 1959, famously referred to as "the day the music died" by songwriter Don McLean.

These stories and more take center stage at the Buddy Holly Center, which showcases the Lubbock native's brief life and significant career through informative exhibits, an enlightening film, and distinctive memorabilia (the signature horn-rimmed glasses found at his death scene are at once nostalgic and chilling). Other items, including childhood artwork, handwritten notes, and personal knickknacks, provide additional insight into this influential Lubbock musician whose noteworthy life was cut tragically short.

Aside from having a major city street renamed in his honor, Holly's legacy is evident in several Lubbock locales. The Buddy Holly statue near the corner of Avenue Q and 8th

Lubbock

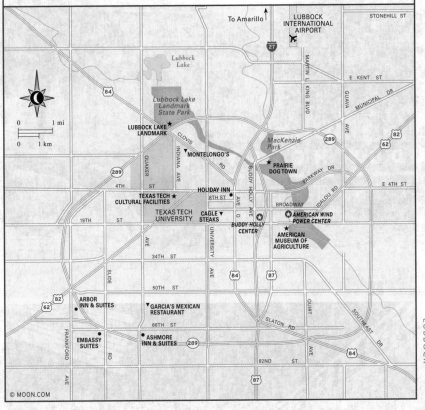

To Amarillo

LUBBOCK INTERNATIONAL AIRPORT

STONEHILL ST

27

E KENT ST

Lubbock Lake

84

MARTIN L KING BLVD

GUAVA AVE

MUNICIPAL DR

Lubbock Lake Landmark State Park

0   1 mi
0   1 km

LUBBOCK LAKE LANDMARK

CLOVIS RD

INDIANA AVE

QUAKER

MacKenzie Park

289

82

62

▼ MONTELONGO'S

BUDDY HOLLY AVE

289

4TH   ST

★ PRAIRIE DOG TOWN

PARKWAY DR

IDALOU RD

E 4TH ST

TEXAS TECH ★ CULTURAL FACILITIES

HOLIDAY INN ●

8TH ST

BROADWAY

✪ AMERICAN WIND POWER CENTER

TEXAS TECH UNIVERSITY

CAGLE ▼ STEAKS

19TH   ST

UNIVERSITY AVE

BUDDY HOLLY CENTER

★ AMERICAN MUSEUM OF AGRICULTURE

SLIDE

34TH   ST

AVE

50TH   ST

84

87

62

82

ARBOR INN & SUITES ●

▼ GARCIA'S MEXICAN RESTAURANT

QUIRT

SOUTHEAST DR

SLATON RD

84

66TH   ST

FRANKFORD AVE

EMBASSY SUITES ●

● ASHMORE INN & SUITES

289

RD

82ND   ST

AVE

87

© MOON.COM

Street (just past the entrance to the Lubbock Civic Center) is a lasting reminder of the city's celebrated native son, and its surrounding Walk of Fame pays homage to other famous Lubbock-area musicians, including Roy Orbison, Sonny Curtis (a member of the Crickets), Waylon Jennings, Mac Davis, and Joe Ely.

Holly's gravesite is also a popular attraction for die-hard fans. Just inside the entrance of the **Lubbock Cemetery** (at the east end of 31st Street), it contains admirers' mementos and the original spelling of his last name, "Holley"—the *e* was inadvertently omitted on his first recording contract, and the mistake was somehow never corrected.

★ American Wind Power Center

Who knew windmills could be so interesting? Apparently the owners of the unexpectedly compelling **American Wind Power Center** (1701 Canyon Lake Dr., 806/747-8734, www. windmill.com, Tues.-Sat. 10am-5pm and May-Sept. Sun. 2pm-5pm, adults $7.50, children 5-12 $5, under 5 free, $20 per family), who do a surprisingly good job of conveying the intrigue of many different kinds of wind-powered machines.

More than 100 historic and last-of-its-kind windmills from around the world reside in the center's giant barn, and dozens more punctuate the surrounding grounds. They range

Wind Power

Residents of the Panhandle Plains have been harvesting the wind for more than a century, using the natural element to power water-pumping windmills atop underground wells. These days, the ubiquitous wind currents on the High Plains can generate electricity via massive turbines on quaintly named wind farms.

Lubbock, a hotbed for wind harvesting, is home to the **American Wind Power Center** (1701 Canyon Lake Dr., 806/747-8734, www.windmill.com), a museum dedicated to windmills and related energy issues. The center showcases these fascinating machines, primarily from the mid-1800s to 1920, that represent the "ingenuity, hardship, success and failure of the early settlers as they applied a new technology to conditions in an environment with which they were barely familiar."

These self-governing windmills had an enormous impact on the development of Texas and the entire western two-thirds of the country. In their heyday, more than 700 companies manufactured tens of thousands of windmills to help westward-bound settlers tap into their subterranean groundwater supply for irrigation and home use. Incidentally, only two windmill companies remain, and one is in Texas (Aermotor Windmill Company in San Angelo).

According to the American Wind Energy Association, Texas has become the leader in wind power development in amount of electricity generated. The omnipresent winds of West Texas (and the Gulf Coast) have helped Texas surpass California by hosting some of the nation's largest wind farms, wind turbine supply companies, and utilities that use the most wind power for their customers.

To learn all you ever wanted to know about windmills and wind power, drop by Lubbock's compelling museum dedicated to these topics. The American Wind Power Center contains more than 100 historic and rare windmills inside a large barn and dozens more on the surrounding grounds, ranging from an enormous 25-foot-diameter model to inventive models used to power many Great Plains homes in the early 1900s.

from the enormous (25 feet in diameter) to the strange (two-pronged whirligigs) to the inventive (models used to power most Great Plains homes during the early 20th century). Dominating the entire scene is the massive 164-foot-tall Vestas Wind Turbine, a metal giant with three imposing rotating fins that generate electricity for the museum.

Adjacent to the center is the associated **American Museum of Agriculture,** offering hundreds of antique tractors, appliances, and equipment related to the region's ranching heritage. The back room contains hundreds of tiny model tractors and vintage riding tractor toys. Visitors with kids are in luck—instead of being taunted by untouchable artifacts, kids are allowed to ride the mini tractor toys to test their future farming abilities.

Texas Tech Cultural Facilities
MUSEUM OF TEXAS TECH UNIVERSITY

The enormous **Museum of Texas Tech University** (3301 4th St., 806/742-2490, www.depts.ttu.edu/museumttu, Tues.-Sat. 10am-5pm, Sun. 1pm-5pm, free) is far more remarkable than its name. In fact, while strolling through its multiple wings and impressive collections, it's easy to forget you're in a remote area of the Texas Panhandle.

Fascinating sculptures from Africa, colorful Latin American pottery, and rare pre-Columbian artwork transport visitors to other worlds. The museum's collections contain more than three million objects, and the thousands on display represent the upper echelon of the visual arts and natural sciences.

1: The Buddy Holly Center **2:** The American Wind Power Center in Lubbock

The Panhandle region and the entire southwestern United States are well represented by exhibits featuring ancient dinosaur fossils from the area and galleries showcasing historic Western art. The museum also encompasses a remodeled planetarium, a natural science research laboratory, a public auditorium, and a sculpture court. Just a note: If you prefer experiencing museums at a leisurely pace and in a distraction-free environment, consider visiting on the weekend, when large groups of local schoolchildren aren't set loose in the facility.

LUBBOCK LAKE LANDMARK

Though it's seemingly modest in comparison, **Lubbock Lake Landmark** (N. Loop 289 and U.S. Hwy. 84 on Landmark Ln., 806/742-1116, www.depts.ttu.edu/museumttu, Tues.-Sat. 9am-5pm, Sun. 1pm-5pm, free) showcases an aspect of history as significant as the artifact-rich Museum of Texas Tech by offering a window onto 12,000 years of the region's past.

The landmark's inspiring interpretive center puts the surrounding diverse geographic features—a rare sight in Lubbock—in full perspective. A spring-fed reservoir on the grounds has provided a source of life for plants, animals, and their associated human hunters for at least 12 millennia. The center walks visitors through the fascinating archaeological finds made during the past 75 years that document thousands of generations of humans, mammoth, bison, and even giant armadillo that habitually returned to the watering hole to sustain (and take) life.

A one-mile walking trail encircling the reservoir now known as Lubbock Lake provides context for this unique area. The lush green marshes and elevated river valley noticeably contrast with the surrounding High Plains' overwhelmingly flat topography.

NATIONAL RANCHING HERITAGE CENTER

The **National Ranching Heritage Center** (3121 4th St., 806/742-0498, www.nrhc.ttu.edu, Mon.-Sat. 10am-5pm, Sun. 1pm-5pm,

free) is a 16-acre mostly outdoor site featuring 36 authentic yet relocated ranching structures. Spanning 200 years, these American ranch-related buildings run the gamut from ramshackle barn to opulent home. Also included on the grounds are windmills and a locomotive, blacksmith shop, school, and bunkhouse. Visitors can't enter most structures, but several have open doors and gated windows offering views of period furnishings.

Prairie Dog Town and Mackenzie Park

The small area of parkland known as **Prairie Dog Town** (inside Mackenzie Park, entrance at 4th Street and I-27, 806/775-2687, open year-round sunrise-sunset) isn't as charming as it sounds. Don't get too excited about seeing scores of cute little fellas romping around and eating treats right out of your hand. They're definitely visible, and they are pretty cute, but aside from standing up on two legs and scanning the surrounding prairie, they don't do much. They pop out of holes relatively far away from the viewing area—you can get a better look at them if you have binoculars or a telephoto camera lens.

The prairie dogs remain in this part of Lubbock thanks to the efforts of one man, who spared their cute little lives in the 1930s when a push was made to eradicate their overpopulation. Incidentally, they get their canine-influenced name from the little dog-like barks they emit when danger—in this case, tourists—threaten on the prairie's horizon.

The surrounding **Mackenzie Park** is a welcome respite from Lubbock's flat environs, with hills and valleys offering an opportunity to experience actual topography. There is a disc golf course, a real golf course, an amphitheater, and a sculpture garden .Also on the park's grounds is a small amusement park dating to the 1940s called **Joyland** (806/763-2719, www.joylandpark.com, open weekends spring-fall, $20-23), a seemingly sketchy but totally legit place with a couple roller coasters and 30 rides.

ENTERTAINMENT AND EVENTS

Depot Entertainment District

Lubbock's downtown has seen better days, but the city's **Depot District** (just off I-27 and 19th St.) is a semi-lively collection of bars and clubs near the Buddy Holly Center that draws young professionals, Tech students, and even a few ranchers in search of rockabilly and 'ritas. The soul of the district is the venerable and beautifully restored 1930s Cactus Theater across from the historic Fort Worth to Denver Railroad Depot building, now serving as a portion of the Buddy Holly Center.

Make a point of dropping by the remarkable **Cactus Theater** (1812 Buddy Holly Ave., 806/762-3233, www.cactustheater.com). Ideally, you'll be able to catch a show—check the website for scheduled performances—from live country and western acts to soulful singer-songwriters to musicals and theatrical productions. The acoustics are amazing, and the wraparound caprock canyon mural is captivating. Next door is another noteworthy live music venue, the **Blue Light** (1808 Buddy Holly Ave., 806/749-5442, www.thebluelightlubbock.com), featuring Texas country and rock acts Tuesday-Saturday. Grab a frozen concoction or cold bottle of Lone Star at the adjoining **Tom's Daiquiri Place** and settle in for a fine evening of High Plains-style entertainment.

Those seeking a mellower scene should visit **La Diosa Cellars** (901 17th St., 806/744-3600, www.ladiosacellars.com, closed Sun.-Mon.), billing itself as the first and only winery inside the city limits. La Diosa ("the goddess") offers wines by the glass, bottle, or case and is known for its bistro menu of tasty tapas, its coffee bar, and its gourmet desserts. Of note: Lubbock is primarily a dry city, so this is one of the few places in town you can purchase alcohol to go.

Level (1928 Buddy Holly Ave., 806/762-4466) is a nice alternative to the typical twangy bars in the area. The kids can mingle and dance to hip-hop, techno, and house DJs.

Events

LUBBOCK ARTS FESTIVAL

Held each April at the civic center, the popular **Lubbock Arts Festival** (806/744-2787) is a feast for the senses. Stroll among booths of regional, national, and international artists offering everything from Southwestern jewelry to colorful murals to stone sculptures. Grab a tasty yet politically incorrect Indian taco (a corn tostada with beans and rice) from the food court, listen to a chamber music trio, and delight in Lubbock's arts scene.

NATIONAL COWBOY SYMPOSIUM AND CELEBRATION

One of the city's most highly anticipated and well-attended annual events is the **National Cowboy Symposium and Celebration** (806/798-7825, www.cowboy.org). Held at the civic center each September, this uniquely Texas event celebrates Old West cowboys through storytelling, poetry readings, music, art, and participation from honest-to-goodness cowboys. Attend readings, panel discussions, and performances by scholars and genuine cowpokes, along with a chuckwagon cook-off, horse parade, and trail ride.

SHOPPING

Western Wear

Lubbock is cowboy country, so the Western gear around here is genuine. A good starting point is the **Branding Iron Cowboy Outfitters** (3320 34th St., 866/312-0500, www.cowboy-outfitter.com), just south of the Texas Tech campus. This family-owned shop keeps things simple by focusing on quality Western brands and merchandise. Look for Stetson and Resistol hats (felt and straw), Justin and Tony Lama boots, and bunches of belt buckles. Another respected local Western shop is **Boot City Inc.** (6645 19th St., 806/797-8782, www.bootcity.com). West of town just outside the loop, Boot City specializes in boots (Tony Lama, Justin, Nocona, Anderson Bean, and Dan Post), cowboy hats, belts, buckles, and other Western apparel.

Antiques

Some may call it junk, but others delight in the bric-a-brac and Americana crammed into Lubbock's peerless **Antique Mall** (7907 W. 19th St., 806/796-2166, www.antiquemalloflubbock.com). Boasting 24,000 square feet of stuff, the Antique Mall peddles in nostalgia as much as (perhaps even more than) valuable objects. Texas Tech and Lubbock-related items offer a charming regional flair, and shoppers may find a treasure or two among the Depression-era glass and furniture, vintage drugstore/pharmacy collectibles, and historic advertising memorabilia.

FOOD
Mexican

Ask locals where to find the best Mexican food in town, and they're not likely to suggest the bright, busy eateries packed with ravenous students near Texas Tech University. More likely, you'll be directed to a satisfyingly authentic locale like ★ **Montelongo's** (3021 Clovis Rd., 806/762-3068, Thurs.-Tues 7am-8pm, closes at 5pm Sunday, $8-14), just northwest of downtown. The flavors at this unassuming family restaurant are *incredible,* particularly in the magnificent chicken mole, an exceptional dish featuring perhaps the best mole sauce in the Panhandle. Savor the rich yet delicate taste of the hearty sauce with its buttery nut base and accents of spicy pepper and bitter chocolate. The chicken is tender, and the rice and beans are elevated beyond mere side-item status. If you only eat one meal in Lubbock, make the effort to experience this exceptionally authentic item.

Not quite as satisfying yet still very tasty is **Garcia's Mexican Restaurant** (5604 Slide Rd., 806/792-0097, Mon.-Sat. 11am-9pm, Sun. 11am-2pm, $8-14). Located in a fairly new strip mall-esque building southwest of downtown, Garcia's serves fresh Tex-Mex that's consistently fulfilling. You can't go wrong with any of the standards here, from fajitas and enchiladas to tacos and quesadillas.

Although **Abuelo's** (4401 82nd St., 806/794-1762, www.abuelos.com, daily 11am-10pm, $8-21) is a Texas chain, it's well respected in these parts, and for good reason. The food here is far better than expected, and the atmosphere makes it even more recommendable. Abuelo's is always packed, especially for happy hour and dinner, when local bands play outside on the patio and margaritas flow freely. Be sure to sample the seafood dishes here, the grilled shrimp in particular. Other popular menu items include the jalapeño-stuffed shrimp, the bacon-wrapped beef tenderloin, and the delectable dulce de leche cheesecake.

Steak and Barbecue

There aren't many noteworthy restaurants in Lubbock's Depot Entertainment District, but one is worth experiencing. **Triple J Chophouse and Brew Co.** (1807 Buddy Holly Ave., 806/771-6555, www.triplejchophouseandbrewco.com, Sun.-Thurs. 11am-10pm, Fri.-Sat. 11am-midnight, $13-36) serves several hearty steaks to accompany the refreshing handcrafted beers. Filet mignon is the specialty here, but don't overlook the rib eye or prime rib. Alternate options include the smoked salmon or pork chop and grilled chicken.

Locals love **Cagle Steaks** (1212 Ave. K, 806/795-3879, www.caglesteaks.com, Mon.-Sat. 5:30pm-9pm, $11-39), a charmingly rustic spot with grade-A meat just west of town in an old house displaced by the railroad. Kick-start your meal with a "pasture pickle," a cheesy steak finger with jalapeños, and continue with a heaping helping of barbecue (the ribs are spectacular) or one of the tender and delicious rib eye steaks, offered by thickness of the cut, at three-quarters of an inch, one inch (just the right size at about 16 ounces), or one and a quarter inches.

Another popular place for Lubbockites in search of quality steaks and meat is **Las Brisas** (4701 112th St., 806/687-6050, www.lasbrisassouthweststeakhouse.com, Mon.-Sat. 4pm-10pm, Sun. 11am-9pm, $12-41), specializing in Southwestern specialties and prime cuts of beef including filet mignon, New York strip, pecan-crusted pork loin, blackened salmon, mesquite-smoked fajitas, chiles rellenos, grilled shrimp, and sea bass.

For barbecue, it doesn't get much better than **J&M Bar-B-Q** (3605 34th St., 806/796-1164, www.jandmbar-b-q.com, daily 11am-8pm, also J&M Express, 7924 Slide Rd., 806/798-2525, $11-25). J&M is known for its perfectly smoked and seasoned brisket, jalapeño sausage, and ribs topped with a tangy and spicy sauce. Be sure to save room for cobbler or banana pudding.

Lunch

On the heartier side is the **Crafthouse Gastropub** (3131 34th St., 806/687-1466, www.crafthousepub.com, Tues.-Sat. 11am-10pm, Sun. 10am-2pm, $8-20), where virtually every menu item is freshly made in-store daily. From breads to sauces to soups, pastas, chicken, sandwiches, and pork chops, Crafthouse is an ideal place to drop by for a satisfying and healthy lunch. The quality beer selection is known throughout Lubbock.

For a good ol' fashioned burger, head to **Buns Over Texas** (3402 73rd St., 806/793-0012, Mon.-Sat. 11am-9pm, $6-13). This traditional burger joint serves exactly what you'd expect—hot, juicy fresh-ground burgers on sweet hand-toasted buns accompanied by crispy onion rings or deliciously gooey cheese fries. Wash it all down with a thick chocolate shake.

ACCOMMODATIONS
$50-100

Affordable rooms abound in Lubbock, which tends to draw most of its out-of-towners for Texas Tech University-related activities (sporting events, alumni gatherings, commencement ceremonies, etc.). Those looking for a cheap and consistent place to stay near campus often go with the no-frills **Super 8** (501 Ave. Q, 806/762-8726, www.super8.com, $69 d), featuring a free continental breakfast, free Wi-Fi, and refrigerators in every room.

To get the most bang for your buck,

consider the popular and amenity-packed **Guesthouse Inn** (3815 21st St., 806/791-0433, $69 d), which strives for a homey atmosphere by offering suites with kitchenettes, living rooms with reading libraries, a free continental breakfast, and complimentary wireless, all just six blocks away from the Tech campus.

$100-150

If you're looking to stay downtown within walking distance of the many civic center activities, book your room at the **MCM Elegante** (801 Ave. Q, 806/763-1200, www.mcmelegantelubbock.com, $109 d). This regional chain offers rooms facing an open interior atrium featuring a large fountain in the center. The hotel rate includes free Wi-Fi and a fitness room, swimming pool, whirlpool, and sauna.

Farther outside of town is the independently owned and very recommendable ★ **Ashmore Inn & Suites** (4019 S. Loop 289, 806/785-0060, www.ashmoreinn.com, $109 d). Nothing here is over-the-top, but the service and amenities are better than expected, including spacious rooms with free Internet access, microwaves, and refrigerators, along with a free continental breakfast, an outdoor pool, and an exercise room and hot tub.

Consider spending a little extra money for one of the finest accommodations in town, **Arbor Inn & Suites** (5310 Englewood Ave., 806/744-1763, www.arborinnandsuites.com, $129 d). This memorable locale offers large rooms with full kitchens, free Wi-Fi, quality bedding, and free cold bottled water.

Just down the road is the commendable **Fairfield Inn** (4007 S. Loop 289, 806/795-1288, www.marriott.com, $139 d). Catering primarily to business travelers, the Fairfield features free Internet access as well as a spiffy indoor pool and spa and a free continental breakfast.

Farther south of town is the fancy **Embassy Suites** (5215 S. Loop 289, 806/771-7000, www.embassysuites.com, $169 d), featuring a Tuscan-style atrium with tropical plants and pathways meandering around a koi pond and miniature waterfalls. The hotel provides free Wi-Fi, complimentary nightly manager's receptions with drinks and food, a free hot breakfast, an exercise room, and a heated indoor pool.

Camping

Lubbockites love **Buffalo Springs Lake** (9999 High Meadow Rd., 806/747-3353, www. buffalospringslake.net, $12-25), a recreation area eight miles southeast of town with rare commodities—water, grass, and trees. The camping options here range from sites with paved pads and water access to spots with electric hookups to plain ol' tent sites. All the campgrounds have trees, and the tent area features grass along the water's edge. Other Buffalo Springs activities include a golf course, hike and bike trails, an amphitheater, a party house, and pavilions. The campground takes a limited number of reservations and requires a three-night minimum stay.

RVers return regularly to the popular **Lubbock RV Park** (4811 N. I-27, 806/747-2366, www.lubbockrvpark.com, $25), offering plenty of shade trees, an outdoor pool, laundry facilities, and showers.

INFORMATION AND SERVICES

To get a handle on all the travelers' services available in Lubbock, including brochures, maps, pamphlets, and other literature, drop by the **Lubbock Convention & Visitors Bureau,** on the 6th floor of the downtown Wells Fargo Center (1500 Broadway St., 806/747-5232, www.visitlubbock.org).

GETTING THERE AND AROUND

For those traveling to Lubbock by air, the **Lubbock International Airport** (5401 N. Martin Luther King Blvd., 806/775-2035) is about 10 minutes from downtown just northeast of the city. The airport offers service from American Eagle, Continental Express, and Southwest Airlines. Once there, ground transportation is available from most of the major car rental companies and Lubbock's cab services include **City Cab** (806/765-7474) and **Yellow Cab** (806/370-3325).

Amarillo and Vicinity

Amarillo (population 199,924) is the most compelling destination in the Panhandle because it offers two distinctly uncommon resources—Palo Duro Canyon and Route 66. Both involve some extra driving and exploring, but it's well worth the effort to experience these uniquely Texas attractions.

Amarillo's cultural heritage reflects a variety of influences: Native Americans, Spanish conquistadors, buffalo hunters, American settlers, cowboys, and the railroad. This combination of the Old and New West provides a captivating draw to this remote region of the state.

The city's name originates from a large nearby playa (seasonal lake) and creek referred to as *amarillo,* Spanish for yellow, by New Mexican traders and shepherds, describing the color of the soil. Though Native American tribes and Spanish explorers had traversed the area for thousands of years, the lack of a consistent water source prevented permanent settlements.

That changed in the late 1800s, when windmill-powered wells reached the deep water table, and particularly when the Fort Worth and Denver City Railway arrived in 1887, resulting in freight service to Amarillo and its subsequent status as a cattle-marketing center. Hundreds of herds from ranches in the Panhandle, South Plains, and eastern New Mexico were driven and corralled in holding pens near the railroad tracks for shipment to

Amarillo

meatpacking centers in the Midwest and the eastern United States.

In the late teens and early 1920s, Amarillo became a hotbed for the petrochemical industry when gas and oil were discovered in nearby fields, resulting in a mini boom of oil refineries and oil-shipping facilities. The discovery of the helium-rich Cliffside gas field in 1928 led to the establishment of the United States Helium Plant.

By the 1930s, cross-country automobile travel kicked into high gear thanks to the newly established transcontinental highways, most notably the famed Route 66. Amarillo represented the Mother Road's only urban outpost between Oklahoma City and Albuquerque, and the city's unique blend of fiery, friendly folks endeared many travelers to its rich pioneer spirit and independence. Gas stations, motor lodges, and dance halls

kept travelers served and entertained while passing through the Panhandle's largest city.

Throughout the remainder of the 20th century, Amarillo cemented its reputation as an economic hub for the petroleum, cattle, and agricultural industries (grain storage, processing, and feed). Though the city boasts several tourism-related attractions, including the iconic Cadillac Ranch just west of town, it's perhaps best known as the starting point for ventures beyond city limits to the alluringly desolate canyons and plains.

SIGHTS

Despite being hundreds of miles from nowhere, Amarillo has an artistic side that sets it apart from other cities in faraway areas of Texas and the United States. Cadillac Ranch and the Helium Monument are must-sees for pop culture enthusiasts, and the city's cowboy

Route 66: The Mother Road

Old Route 66 has a distinctive urban presence in Amarillo, with its art deco-themed streetscapes and awnings of Spanish tile offering an endearing nostalgic charm compared to today's bland strip centers. For a true sense of the Mother Road's legacy, however, venture to the smaller Panhandle communities, where you'll discover authentic diners providing a welcome respite from franchise restaurant chains, and motor courts' neon signs crackling vacancy notices without promoting free Wi-Fi or announcing corporate seminars.

You'll find most of the historic small-town Route 66 buildings east of Amarillo, just off the 100-mile stretch of I-40 to the Oklahoma border. An essential stop is the city of McLean, home of the Texas Old Route 66 and Devil's Rope Museums (100 Kingsley St., 806/779-2225, www.barbwiremuseum.com, Mar. 1-Nov. 1 Mon.-Sat. 9am-4pm, free). Though the barbed wire (aka "devil's rope") portion of the building is intriguing, the Texas Old Route 66 Museum offers a fascinating glimpse into the not-too-distant past, with vintage road signs, artwork from tourist traps—the enormous metal rattlesnake salvaged from the Regal Reptile Ranch is particularly amusing—and hundreds of mementos and souvenirs from the golden age of automobile travel. While in McLean, be sure to snap a few photos of the classic 1928 cottage-style Phillips 66 station on old Route 66 at the edge of town (westbound on Old Route 66, two blocks west of Main St.).

Just east of McLean is Shamrock, home of Texas's most impressive Route 66 building. The U-Drop Inn and Conoco Station (1242 N. Main St., 806/256-2516, Daily 10am-5pm) is a remarkable 1936 art deco landmark with a steeple-like spire that advertised food, gas, and lodging—three essential elements for Route 66 travelers. Refurbished to its original glory, this building, which inspired Ramone's detailing shop in Disney's animated *Cars* movie, now houses the Shamrock Chamber of Commerce.

West of Amarillo, the small town of Vega beckons travelers to the classic 1940s-era Vega Motel (1005 Vega Blvd., aka Old Route 66), which is no longer in operation but still welcomes curiosity seekers. The nearby Dot's Mini Museum (one block north of Old Route 66, 806/267-2828, free) isn't worth planning a trip around, but is worth a quick stop to see the "boot tree" and Route 66 artifacts (if it's open).

heritage is on full display at the American Quarter Horse Museum. Incidentally, while you're driving around town, keep an eye out for colorful fiberglass versions of this trusty steed. *Hoof Prints of the American Quarter Horse* is a city-wide public art display featuring more than 100 replicas of these horses, each painted or decorated by a local artist and displayed as a tribute to this animal integral to Amarillo's heritage and culture.

★ Cadillac Ranch

One of the premier photo ops in Texas, Cadillac Ranch (approx. 10 miles west of downtown Amarillo between exits 60 and 62—exit Arnot Rd. on the south side of I-40) is a permanent art installation of 10 Cadillacs buried nose-down in a field. This bumper crop was originally planted in 1974 but relocated farther west 23 years later due to encroaching development. The cars, representing the golden age of American automobiles (1949-1963) were positioned at the same angle as the pyramids in Egypt.

The 10 Cadillacs are covered with thick layers of paint and graffiti, a practice that's encouraged. At any given time, the cars may be painted in different colors or emblazoned with messages and signatures. To get there, park your car along the brim of the freeway and walk the well-worn path to the monument (open all hours). Be sure to bring a camera and/or a can of spray paint to document your visit.

American Quarter Horse Heritage Center & Museum

Horses are serious business in cowboy

Farther west on I-40 lies **Adrian,** another little town that time forgot. Its main Mother Road icon is the **MidPoint Café** (on the south side of Vega Blvd., 866/538-6380, Tues.-Fri. 8am-5pm, Sat. 8am-1pm, $8-14), named for its location on Route 66 midway between Chicago and Los Angeles (each 1,139 miles away). The Mid-Point Café is known for its delectable homemade pies (try the blueberry) and enormous hamburgers, but the best option on a chilly afternoon is a steaming bowl of hearty beef stew. Be sure to check out the Route 66-themed gift shop housed in the attached original café building, and don't forget to snap a photo in front of the famous Mid-Point sign across the street.

The end of the road for Route 66 in Texas is **Glenrio,** an abandoned community straddling the Texas-New Mexico border. You won't find empty saloons or bouncing tumbleweeds here, but it's a compelling place to get out of your car and explore. Check out the old gas station and post office buildings, and be sure to mosey by the vacant structure with a broken sign still announcing Last Motel in Texas on one side and First Motel in Texas on the other.

Shamrock's U-Drop Inn and Conoco Station

These communities are far removed from their heyday on Route 66, which once beckoned Americans with adventure and new beginnings around every bend of the highway. This sentiment was perhaps best captured by John Steinbeck in his classic 1939 novel *The Grapes of Wrath* in the passage, "They come into 66 from the tributary side roads, from the wagon tracks and the rutted country roads. 66 is the mother road, the road of flight."

country, and nowhere else is this more apparent than at the **American Quarter Horse Heritage Center & Museum** (2601 E. I-40, 806/376-5181, www.aqha.com, year-round Tues.-Sat. 9am-5pm, Memorial Day-Labor Day Sun. noon-5pm, $7 adults, $6 seniors, $3 children ages 6-18). This large and intriguing museum showcases the history and culture related to quarter horses, the country's most popular breed, revered for its skills on the ranch and its performance in rodeos. Museum visitors will learn everything they ever wanted to know about quarter horses through ranching and racing artifacts, interesting video clips, and interactive exhibits. More than 1,000 objects depict the breed's rise to prominence in racing and recreation throughout the Americas and Europe, while art and photo galleries highlight its exquisite

beauty. The museum's Grand Hall, an enormous area marked by an oversized medallion and hearty stone and timber columns, honors the people who shaped the quarter horse over the past several centuries. While at the museum, be sure to inquire about arena demonstrations featuring these exquisite equines in action.

Don Harrington Discovery Center

Families will love the delightful **Don Harrington Discovery Center** (1200 Streit Dr., 806/355-9547, www.discoverycenteramarillo.org, Tues.-Sat. 9:30am-4:30pm, Sun. noon-4:30pm, $14 adults, $9 ages 3-12). Science is the main attraction here, with dozens of fascinating exhibits and hands-on activities conveying the significance of biology, weather, and physics, to name a few. The center also features the region's only aquarium and planetarium, and an intriguing helium technology exhibit. Speaking of helium, the museum is home to the renowned **Helium Monument,** a four-pronged stainless-steel time column dedicated to the natural element found in great quantities near Amarillo. Three of the six-story-tall monument's columns form a tripod with four dangling spheres representing helium's molecular structure. Each column contains time capsules corresponding to natural resources to be opened 25, 50, 100, and 1,000 years from 1968, the year the monument was erected.

Amarillo Museum of Art

If you have a few hours to spare while in town, make a point of stopping by the **Amarillo Museum of Art** (2200 S. Van Buren St., 806/371-5050, www.amarilloart.org, Tues.-Fri. 10am-5pm, Sun. 1pm-5pm, free). On the campus of Amarillo College, the museum contains a worthy collection of paintings, photographs, prints, and sculptures representing a broad range of cultures and eras. The museum initially focused on early American Modernist paintings (four Georgia O'Keeffe watercolors represent this style), but it has since expanded to include centuries-old European paintings and an impressive collection of Asian art, including Buddhist and Hindu pieces from 200 BC to Khmer sculpture from the 1300s.

Amarillo Livestock Auction

If you're in town on a Tuesday, be sure to experience the **Amarillo Livestock Auction** (100 S. Manhattan St., 806/373-7464, www. amarillolivestockauction.com, auctions typically begin at 10am). This is the real deal—steers and heifers are corralled into the auction ring and bid on by genuine cowboys and ranch owners. There's a palpable excitement to the proceedings, as hundreds of cattle trade hands while prospective bidders gauge the scene. By the end of the year, more than

100,000 head of cattle will have been sold at the facility.

ENTERTAINMENT AND EVENTS
Bars and Clubs

Amarillo's nightlife scene is relatively generic, with the exception of a handful of venues west of downtown on 6th Avenue, formerly Route 66. This stretch of road has some vacant pockets, but the areas of activity, including more than 100 independently owned antiques shops, restaurants, and memorable bars, are housed in charming art deco buildings on quaint cobblestone sidewalks. The most famous of the bunch is the spectacular **Golden Light Cafe and Cantina** (2908 W. 6th Ave., 806/374-9237, www. goldenlightcafe.com). This unassuming spot, built in 1946 and featuring a modest sign over the door that appears to have inspired the Hard Rock Café logo, stages live country and blues acts every weekend in a laid-back, casual environment (not surprisingly, actor Matthew McConaughey has been spied here). Returning acts include Stoney LaRue, Macon Grayson, and Cooter Graw. Those might be the most Texas-worthy names ever. The cover charge is typically $5-10. Incidentally, the Golden Light runs a popular restaurant serving tasty down-home favorites like chicken-fried steak, burgers, and pork chops.

Another venerable venue on America's Main Street is the **Cattleman's Club** (3801 E. Amarillo Blvd., 806/383-9053, daily 11am-2am), a classic country and western bar featuring live music and cold beer. The lonesome sounds of twangy slide guitars provide an ideal accompaniment for the dark and low-key scene at Cattleman's, where you can kick back with a Lone Star and let your troubles mosey away.

Not quite as traditional yet equally intriguing is the newfangled **The 806** (2812 W. 6th Ave., 806/322-1806, www.the806.com), a roadside café for the current generation. Named for the Panhandle's area code, this coffeehouse is a hotbed for Amarillo's wireless laptop crowd, who tap away while sipping on strong java drinks and listening to open mic acts in the shadow of avant-garde artwork.

Events

TEXAS OUTDOOR MUSICAL

With the colorful cliff walls of Palo Duro Canyon State Park just south of the city serving as a picturesque backdrop, *Texas* (806/655-2181, www.texas-show.com, May-Aug. Tues.-Sun.) depicts the historical romance of the Old West and Texas's 19th-century settlement years. Fancy lights and sound effects, along with traditional costumes, dancing, and music, tell the popular story to rapt audiences each summer. A barbecue dinner is served 6pm-8pm before each show.

TRI-STATE FAIR

Drawing participants from Texas, New Mexico, and Oklahoma, the **Tri-State Fair** (www.tristatefair.com, 806/376-7767) offers late-summer fun (mid-Sept. in these parts) for area folks, with traditional activities such as rodeo and livestock shows, farming and ranching exhibits, and food and crafts booths.

NATIONAL SENIOR PRO RODEO

This popular event, held most years in November at the city's civic center, features the country's finals competition for rodeo cowboys over the age of 40. Despite the "old-timers" moniker, these dudes can still move quickly while riding and roping.

SHOPPING

Amarillo's shopping scene is particularly noteworthy for its kitschy antiques shops occupying charming historic retail stores along old Route 66. Since the city is entrenched in the agribusiness of the Old West, it's also a great place to find authentic boots, hats, and other Western gear.

Antiques

For a truly distinctive shopping experience, head on down to old Route 66 (now 6th Avenue, but referred to as 6th Street by locals) just west of downtown. Though some of the original charm has been "modernized," bulldozed, or abandoned, there are several pockets of America's Main Street offering a time warp to the road's busy heyday. The best stretch is between Georgia and Western Streets, where shoppers will encounter bright storefronts and cheery display windows in historic retail buildings, cafés, and service stations. One of the premier antiques stores in the area is **Texas Ivy Antiques** (3511 W. 6th Ave., 806/373-1427,Tues.-Sat. 11am-5pm), located in a quaint 1920s home. Specialties here include glassware, restaurant items, linens, toys, and retro furniture.

Antiques shops are by no means interchangeable, but the rotating nature of the stock makes it difficult to categorize them individually by content. The **Sixth Street Antique Mall** (2715 W. 6th Ave., 806/374-0459) has been in business for a considerable amount of time, rendering it recommendable.

Although most of its bustling antiques booths are gone, it's still worth dropping by the legendary **The Nat Antiques** (604 S. Georgia St., 806/236-6482, www.thenatroute66.com) for a glimpse of history and some vintage volumes at the bookstore. The building opened as a natatorium (indoor swimming pool) in 1922 and was soon after converted into a "dine and dance palace," with a maple dance floor constructed over the pool. The Nat now serves primarily as a special-event venue with a modest yet interesting collection of books for sale.

Boots and Western Wear

Amarillo is known for its quality Western wear stores, particularly its custom boot makers and abundance of cowboy hats and apparel. One of the legendary locales in town for exquisite custom-made boots is **Western Leather Craft Boot Co.** (1950 Civic Cir., 806/355-0174). Specializing in top-notch working and dress boots for nearly a century, Western Leather outfits locals and visitors

with work boots, art boots, wingtips, and flower inlays.

Other stores in town offer similar products (hats, leather goods, jeans, snap-button shirts, buckles, and other accessories) in less-inspiring environs. Look for this cowboy gear with lower prices at **Los Tres Vaqueros Western** (1105 S. Grand St., 806/374-0000), **Horse & Rider** (1805 S. Lakeside Dr., 806/352-5544, www.saddlediscounter.com), and **Cavender's Boot City** (7920 W. I-40, 806/358-1400).

FOOD
Mexican and Tex-Mex

If you're downtown (or even if you aren't) and craving a quality Mexican meal, head directly to ★ **Acapulco** (800 S. Polk St., 806/373-8889, www.acapulcomexicanrestaurant.net, Sun.-Thurs. 11am-10pm, Fri.-Sat. 11am-2am, $8-17). In a city far, far away from the Mexican border/Acapulco, this restaurant does it right, with flavorful combos in a lively and relaxed urban atmosphere. The margaritas and mojitos are tasty, and the Tex-Mex is far above average. If you're feeling adventurous, order a regional specialty like the barbacoa tacos or the West Texas-style chiles rellenos, with mild breaded peppers and creamy white cheese.

Locals satisfy their Tex-Mex cravings at the consistently reliable **Jorge's Tacos Garcia Mexican Cafe** (1100 S. Ross St., 806/371-0411, www.tacosgarcia.com, Mon.-Sat. 10:30am-10pm, Sun. 10:30am-3:30pm, $9-21). All the traditional favorites are here, from enchiladas to soft and crispy beef tacos to cheesy quesadillas. Jorge's margaritas and spicy salsa with chips are an ideal way to start your meal.

For a more traditional Mexican meal, head to **El Bracero** (3303 Bell St., 806/355-0889, daily 8am-9pm, $9-24). Meat is the main draw here, featured in exquisite dishes such as the tender *cabrito* (goat), tasty quail, and seasoned lamb chops. The seafood dishes are highly recommended, and be sure to save room for the velvety cinnamon-tinged flan.

Steaks and American

★ **The Big Texan** (7701 I-40 E., 800/657-7177, www.bigtexan.com, daily 7am-10:30pm, $12-40) is a must, even if you don't plan to eat the 72-ounce steak, free of charge if you can consume the entire placemat-size slab. It's a mighty challenge befitting of the restaurant's name, but before you tuck that napkin in your collar, be aware of a few minor details—you have to eat this mega meal, side dishes and all, in less than an hour. A few dozen hearty souls attempt the feat each month; of those, one or two earn the distinction of devouring 72 ounces of beef. The Big Texan's decor is perfectly kitschy—hokey cowboy themes and faux rustic timber—and the food is quite edible, uncommon for such a touristy place. Stick with the basics (a rib eye with baked potato or a big bowl of chili), and be sure to browse the enormous gift shop afterward.

Amarillo's other legendary steak house is the **Stockyard Cafe** (100 S. Manhattan St., 806/373-7999, Mon.-Fri. 6am-2pm, Sat.-Sun. 7am-2pm, $9-27). If you've ever considered ordering steak and eggs for breakfast, this is the place to do it. Located adjacent to the livestock auction warehouse (the beef *does* taste very fresh), the Stockyard Cafe's booths are packed most mornings with hungry workers, primarily farmers and truckers enjoying heaping helpings of bacon, huevos rancheros, flapjacks, and steaming mugs of bland coffee. The sirloin is a popular lunch item, and the banana pudding is a must.

Most locals will tell you the best barbecue in town is at **Tyler's Barbeque** (2014 Paramount Blvd., 806/331-2271, www.tylersbarbeque.com, Tues.-Fri. 11am-7:30pm, Sat. 11am-6pm, $10-24). This crowded home-grown establishment is best known for its spectacular brisket, but several other menu items are also worth sampling, including the pork ribs, cheeseburger, and sausage.

If you're staying downtown, it's well worth making the short walk to ★ **Crush Wine Bar and Grill** (701 S. Polk St., 806/ 418-2011, www.crushdeli.com, Mon.-Sat 11am-9pm, $9-19). Crush offers a refreshingly contemporary

1: Amarillo skyline **2:** The Big Texan in Amarillo

alternative to the many traditional steak houses and chicken shacks in Amarillo. The beer and wine options are diverse and local, and the cuisine is a notch above what you'd expect. The pork chop with accompanying poblano cream sauce and seasoned veggies is delicious, and the shepherd's pie is quite commendable.

ACCOMMODATIONS

Virtually all of Amarillo's decent hotels are chains located on I-40 that fall into the moderately affordable category. Unfortunately, most of the interesting historic hotels fell victim to the wrecking ball or are too run-down to recommend. The good news? The acceptable generic options are all within five minutes of the city's main attractions.

Hotels

If you don't mind a little wear and tear with your Texas kitsch, book a room at **The Big Texan Hotel** (7701 I-40 E., 806/372-5000, www.bigtexan.com/motel, $89 d). This is not a place for those seeking sleek, new amenities, but it's certainly a memorable experience, with its Old West-themed facades, Texas-shaped outdoor pool, faux cowhide bedspreads, and Texas flag shower curtains. It's Texas to the max.

Far less interesting yet cheaper and more modern is **Baymont Inn & Suites** (3411 I-40 W., 806/356-6800, www.baymontinns.com, $69 d), offering free breakfast, a fitness center, free Wi-Fi, and an outdoor pool. Another fine option is **Best Western** (4600 I-40 E, 806/372-1885, www.bestwestern.com, $99 d), featuring large rooms with free Wi-Fi, an indoor pool, and a fitness center and spa.

Also commendable is the independently owned **Ashmore Inn & Suites** (2301 I-40 E., 806/374-0033, www.ashmoresuites.com, $99 d). The Ashmore features a free continental breakfast, microwaves, refrigerators, free wireless, an indoor pool, a Jacuzzi, and a fitness center.

One of the newest additions to Amarillo's hotel scene—and the first located in the historic downtown business district—is the ★ **Courtyard Amarillo Downtown** (724 S. Polk St., 806/553-4500, www.marriott.com, $139 d). Occupying the historic 1927 Fisk Building, the hotel offers free Wi-Fi, a restaurant (breakfast is not included in the room rate), a bar, a free parking garage, a 24-hour business center, and even a concierge. The rooms are unexpectedly stylish with modern flairs around every corner, and the hotel is within walking distance from several top-notch restaurants.

Camping

There's really only one worthwhile place to camp in the Amarillo area (or even the Panhandle): **Palo Duro Canyon State Park** (11450 Park Rd. 5, 806/488-2227, www.tpwd.state.tx.us, $5 admission). About 15 miles south of Amarillo near the town of Canyon, Palo Duro is a true sight to behold. The park offers nearly 80 campsites ($12 nightly, $24 for sites with water and electric). If you plan ahead, you can snag a prized cabin—only seven are available, so they fill up quickly. Three of the cabins have two rooms ($100-125 nightly) and include two single beds and a queen bed, with linens and towels furnished. The park's four limited-service facilities ($60 nightly) contain two twin beds and a table and chairs, but no towels or linens.

For the RV crowd, the most popular option is **Amarillo Ranch RV Park** (1414 Sunrise Dr., 806/373-4962, www.amarillorvranch.com, $30), featuring an indoor heated pool, sauna, and hot tub, free limo service, coffee and doughnuts, and a private park.

INFORMATION AND SERVICES

The Texas Department of Transportation's **Texas Travel Information Center** (9700 E. I-40, 800/452-9292, www.dot.state.tx.us, daily 8am-5pm) near downtown Amarillo provides free literature, information, and suggestions for local and statewide excursions. For a more city-specific approach, head to the **Amarillo Convention and**

High and Dry

The Llano Estacado, a vast elevated mesa comprising the western portions of the Panhandle Plains region, literally translates as "staked plains" in modern Spanish, and the potential origins of this moniker vary wildly. Though some legends claim the words refer to wooden stakes jabbed into the ground to mark watering holes, or are an allusion to the area's spiky yucca leaves, most historians agree it's a reference to the sharp cliffs of the mesa's eastern edge that resemble the walls of a stockade (estacado).

This high tableland, with elevations ranging 3,000-5,000 feet above sea level, slopes at a rate of nearly 10 feet per mile toward the southeast. Considered one of the largest mesas on the continent, the Llano Estacado comprises 33 Texas counties (four in New Mexico) and covers approximately 32,000 square miles, larger than the entirety of New England.

Coronado's description of the land's geographical features in a 1541 letter to the king of Spain reveals not much has changed here over the past several centuries. He wrote, "I reached some plains so vast, that I did not find their limit anywhere . . . with no more land marks than if we had been swallowed up by the sea . . . there was not a stone, nor bit of rising ground, nor a tree, nor a shrub, nor anything to go by."

ISOLATED AND IMPENETRABLE

The composition of this enormous physical feature is somewhat difficult to comprehend, but an unofficial geological comparison would be to a colossal river delta comprised of aggraded materials deposited from the activity associated with the Rocky Mountains' formation. Evaporation created a hard caprock, leaving this arid area isolated and impenetrable.

Because of its elevation, geographic location, and solid ground material, the Llano Estacado is in a precipitous situation regarding water availability. Though not heavily populated, the area uses a considerable amount of water for irrigation, causing many residents in the region to fear the ramifications of depleting a potentially finite source of groundwater.

Nearly three-quarters of the Llano Estacado's residents live in cities, mainly Lubbock and Amarillo, though Midland and Odessa are considered to be on the southern edge. Over the course of a century (1880-1980), the population of this area increased from approximately 1,000 residents to more than 900,000. Now, the more than one million people who call the Llano Estacado home are hoping they don't soon find themselves literally high and dry.

Visitor Council (1000 S. Polk St., 800/692-1338, www.visitamarillotx.com, Mon.-Fri. 8am-5pm) for maps, brochures about area attractions, and assistance with planning an excursion on Route 66.

GETTING THERE AND AROUND

Amarillo International Airport (10801 Airport Blvd., 806/335-1671, www.ci.amarillo.tx.us) is seven miles east of downtown and offers flights on American Eagle and Southwest Airlines. Car rental service is available from **Avis** (806/335-2313), **Enterprise** (806/335-9443), **Hertz** (806/335-2331), and **National** (806/335-2311). Amarillo's cab companies include **Jack & Son Taxi Service** (806/626-5015) and **Yellow Checker Cab** (806/371-8294).

CANYON

Just 20 miles south of Amarillo, Canyon (population 14,887) is home to Palo Duro Canyon State Park, the most fascinating attraction in the Panhandle. The town's enormous historical museum is also notable, both for its impressive collection of Western art and artifacts and its striking art deco facility.

Colorful Canyon

Palo Duro Canyon

Aside from being the Panhandle's most stunning geographical feature, Palo Duro Canyon is the site of a significant battle (not necessarily in a good way) from the Red River War conflict between the U.S. Army and regional Native American tribes. In September 1874, U.S. colonel Ranald S. Mackenzie ordered a predawn attack on several Native American camps on the canyon floor. The surprise raid forced the tribe members to flee into the upper reaches of the canyon while army troops burned their villages and possessions.

While all this was happening, Mackenzie's partner in crime, Capt. Eugene Beaumont, rounded up more than 1,400 of the tribes' horses and mules, and drove them out of the canyon. He took all the animals to a nearby army camp, where nearly 1,000 of them were shot to death. With their provisions and means of mobility destroyed, the Native Americans' losses were catastrophic. Their will was ultimately broken, resulting in their surrender.

Employees at Palo Duro Canyon State Park have heard some fascinating legends about the battle and the tribes that lived in the area. One especially memorable tale was from an elder in the Kiowa tribe. The 80-year-old woman with reddish hair and light eyes talked about her great-grandfather being killed in the Battle of Palo Duro Canyon. He was a white man adopted by her ancestors after surviving a wagon attack as a child, and he was raised by the tribe to be a brave warrior.

The woman claimed he was a "dog soldier," the fiercest of fighters who would tether himself to a stake to defend his village and show loyalty by remaining there until released or even until death. Although records don't tell of the man's fate at the Palo Duro battle, the Kiowa elder took pride in her connection to the story of this brave warrior.

TOP EXPERIENCE

★ Palo Duro Canyon State Park

America's second-largest canyon is an absolute must. **Palo Duro Canyon State Park** (11450 Park Rd. 5, 806/488-2227, www.tpwd. state.tx.us, $5 ages 13 and older) offers colorful and topographical magnificence compared to the stark, level plains above. Though it's not quite as grand as its Arizona relative, Palo Duro (Spanish for "hard wood"; namely, the abundant mesquite and juniper trees) features a vast expanse of colorful soil and spectacular geographic formations. The stratified colors are particularly intriguing, with sheer cliffs, rock towers, and canyon walls displaying muted hues of red, yellow, and orange exposed by erosion from a tributary of the Red River and the ubiquitous High Plains winds.

Visitors can experience Palo Duro's topographic splendor by foot, bike, car, or horse year-round. The park's 18,000 acres offer a topographical getaway unlike any other in the Lone Star State. In addition to hiking and biking, Palo Duro visitors enjoy picnicking and camping, wagon rides, and campfire breakfasts, along with the park's souvenir shop, interpretive center, and amphitheater.

People have inhabited Palo Duro Canyon for nearly 12,000 years, including the Folsom and Clovis groups who hunted mammoth and giant bison. The area was later occupied by Apaches, Comanches, and Kiowas who sought out the water and animals that gathered at its watering holes.

Early Spanish explorers are credited with "discovering" the canyon and providing its name; however, it wasn't until 1852 that an American settler first set eyes on its colorful walls. Two decades later, the canyon was a battle site during the Red River War with Native American tribes. Private owners deeded the property to the state in 1933, and for several years afterward, the Civilian Conservation Corps developed it by building road access to the canyon floor, cabins, shelters, the visitors center, and the park headquarters.

The best place to start your Palo Duro adventure is the park's visitors center. Perched on the upper rim of the canyon, the building is one of several constructed by the CCC and contains an interesting museum with exhibits detailing the canyon's geographic and cultural history, as well as a store with books and gifts.

The real fun begins as soon as you descend from the flat upper environs to the otherworldly scene below the tabletop surface. A paved road offers an initial glimpse of the canyon's colorful rock formations and rugged beauty, but the real adventure awaits off the asphalt, where you can get up close views of bizarre and intriguing cacti, wildflowers, and wildlife (primarily lizards and snakes).

Hikers should make a point of taking the Lighthouse Trail (maps are available at the visitors center—the trailhead is marked on the main road). The three-mile-long route is perfect for a morning or afternoon hike, complete with interpretive panels and mesmerizing views, and culminating with a close-up look at the Lighthouse, the park's distinctive and oft-photographed rock tower. Plan to take a couple hours getting there through scenic surroundings along a rocky and sandy trail. Disregard the plastic strips at the end of the trail, and follow the dirt path upward to the lighthouse for spectacular panoramic views of the canyon and surrounding countryside. Be sure to carry a hydration pack or bring a gallon of water—it's always hotter in the canyon.

Mountain bikers have several worthy options to choose from, most notably the Capitol Peak Mountain Biking Trail (recommended) and the Givens, Spicer and Lowry Running Trail, a law firm-sounding yet immensely picturesque four-mile loop throughout the park. Both feature rugged terrain—plenty of loose rock, sand-filled holes, and narrow streambeds—so be sure to keep your eyes in front of you despite the irresistible urge to marvel at the spectacular natural surrounding scenery.

Many visitors choose to go old-school (in Palo Duro's case, Spanish explorers and cowboy settlers) by experiencing the canyon on horseback. The Old West Stables, located within the canyon, will take you on a guided tour to Timber Creek Canyon and the park's signature lighthouse tower. To make the required reservations, call 806/488-2180.

Panhandle-Plains Historical Museum

It's fitting that Texas's largest history museum is just a few miles down the road from the enormity of Palo Duro Canyon. The **Panhandle-Plains Historical Museum** (2503 4th Ave., 806/651-2244, www. panhandleplains.com, summer Mon.-Sat.

Native Naturalists

For thousands of years, many different tribes of Native Americans (most notably the Kiowa, Comanche, and Apache) called the Panhandle Plains and Palo Duro Canyon home. The steady flow of water from the Red River tributary on the canyon floor typically resulted in an associated supply of animals (bison, elk, and bear) and vegetation.

This vegetation, in particular, was an important source of many elements that helped the tribes sustain themselves in the often-harsh climate. They would grind roots, beans, berries, and plants to make breads and natural remedies. Tribe members would also use the abundant mesquite trees for medicinal purposes. They could chew the leaves to relieve stomachaches and make tea out of the bark and sap.

Visitors to Palo Duro Canyon can still see where tribe members ground the berries and plants in the small depressions (known as mortar holes) on the canyon-floor rocks. Exhibits and markers in the canyon tell the tales of the tribes' lifeways.

There are several well-known legends about the canyon, including references to discovering mythical items such as Coronado's Spanish armor and Casner's lost gold. One of the most popular stories tells of the "ghost horses of Palo Duro," which appear as clouds on the canyon rim at dusk. When groups of schoolchildren visit the park, they often claim they can see the horses or hear them whinny as their imaginations get caught up in the colorful tales of the canyon.

9am-6pm, Sun. 1pm-6pm, winter Mon.-Sat. 9am-5pm, Sun. 1pm-6pm, $12.50 adults, $10 seniors, $6 children ages 4-12) boasts "more than 500 million years of history across a 26,000 square mile expanse of the Panhandle-Plains." Indeed, the museum offers a far-reaching collection of diverse heritage-related exhibits, from dinosaurs to Native American culture to pioneers and petroleum. Science and art are also well represented, with displays focusing on archaeology, geology, and Southwestern art.

Particularly memorable exhibits include People of the Plains, showcasing ancient tribe members' use of the buffalo and an interactive pioneer home, a paleontology display featuring an impressive collection of 200-million-year-old fossils found in the Amarillo area (including a six-foot-long carnivorous amphibian), and an oil exhibit highlighting the importance of petroleum to the Panhandle.

Information and Services

To find out more about food and lodging options in Canyon, contact the **Canyon Chamber of Commerce** (1518 5th Ave., 800/999-9481, www.canyonchamber.org, Mon.-Fri. 9am-4:30pm).

Abilene

Abilene (population 122,999) is known for its frontier heritage and cattle drives. Its name, in fact, is an homage to the famous Kansas cattle town at the other end of the rail lines, and this midsize Panhandle-area city (some refer to this region of Texas as the Big Country) remains an important destination for ranchers and tourists.

Like other towns in this region, Abilene's origins are traced to railroads and ranching. Initially inhabited by nomadic Indians and occasional westward-bound frontier families, the city didn't make it onto most maps until the Texas & Pacific Railroad established it as a stock shipping station in 1881.

Agriculture has been Abilene's major economic force since its inception, with cattle and farming making up most of the city's product base. By the mid-1900s, oil became another contributing factor, along with a sizable population boom resulting from a significant amount of federal funding and infrastructure related to World War II training.

With the increase in people came an added emphasis on education and religion (typically combined). The city boasts several bastions of higher education, including Abilene Christian University, Hardin-Simmons University, and McMurry University. The fact that these three institutions are Christian based has prompted some to dub Abilene the "Buckle of the Bible Belt."

SIGHTS
★ Frontier Texas!

By nature, history museums aren't progressive places. That's why it's so refreshing to experience the innovative approach at **Frontier Texas!** (625 N. 1st St., 325/437-2800, www.frontiertexas.com, Mon.-Sat. 9am-6pm, Sun. 1pm-5pm, $10 adults, $7 seniors and military, $6 students, $5 children ages 3-12). For example: Comanche chief Esihabitu looks directly into your eyes as you hear his calm and measured voice tell a profound story about clashes with European settlers. In a flash he's gone, leaving an empty cave and vivid memories in the shadows. Esihabitu is one of the museum's "spirit guides," life-size spectral image movies (holograms) offering firsthand accounts of life in the Panhandle Plains from 1780 to 1880. These and other technology-based exhibits (intense 360-degree movies, educational computer games, and interactive displays) set Frontier Texas! apart.

Visitors take a chronological journey through the museum, beginning with Native American tribes, continuing to European expansion, and ending with Abilene's official founding in 1881. One exhibit that always draws visitors' attention is the roughly 15-foot-tall pile of buffalo skulls bathed in an ominous red light representing Abilene's late-1800s buffalo-bone business.

Not surprisingly, kids love the experience and come away with stories of shooting a replica buffalo-hunting gun and talking about the historical figures they "met," rather than breezing past glass-enclosed artifacts with accompanying explanatory plaques. It's almost worth making the trip to Abilene simply for the *Century of Adventure* movie, where viewers sit on benches surrounded by screens and special effects depicting life on the Texas frontier in intense fashion, complete with an Indian attack, buffalo stampede, violent thunderstorm, and firefly-filled evening.

National Center for Children's Illustrated Literature

Seemingly out of place in the remote city of Abilene is the **National Center for Children's Illustrated Literature** (102 Cedar St., 325/673-4586, www.nccil.org, Tues.-Sat. 10am-4pm, free). This contemporary urban-minded facility, housed in a former hotel parking garage, showcases the unheralded artists whose work is featured in children's storybooks. From *The Very Hungry Caterpillar* to *The Berenstain Bears,* the museum highlights the achievements of artists typically recognized only by youngsters and their parents. Fortunately, the museum's important work is appreciated beyond Abilene, since each exhibition travels to other institutions, public libraries, and galleries across the country. The museum also offers families the opportunity to meet visiting artists, free art activities every Saturday afternoon, an annual summer art camp, and the popular ArtWalk, featuring art exhibitions, live performances, movies, and interactive activities the second Thursday evening of each month.

Grace Museum

Across the street from the Children's Literature Center is Abilene's best-recognized downtown feature, the **Grace Museum** (102 Cypress St., 325/673-4587, www.thegracemuseum.org, Tues.-Sat. 10am-5pm, Thurs. until 8pm, $6 adults, $3 seniors and children ages 4-12). Housed in the magnificent four-story 1909 Grace Hotel, on the

National Register of Historic Places, the Grace contains three museums showcasing regional history, international artwork, and interactive children's exhibits. Relive the fancy days of Abilene's history in the Grace's luxurious marble-filled lobby and grand ballroom before proceeding to the exhibits. Highlights include a replicated hotel room from the Grace's early days, a cluttered yet fascinating re-created boot shop, and a hands-on musical art exhibit. An interesting historical fact: The hotel was briefly known as The Drake, allowing the budget-minded owner to replace only two letters on The Grace's gigantic rooftop sign.

Abilene Zoo

Billing itself as "one of the five largest zoos in Texas" is the popular and respectable **Abilene Zoo** (2070 Zoo Ln., Nelson Park, 325/676-6085, www.abilenezoo.org, daily 9am-5pm, Memorial Day-Labor Day until 9pm, $8 adults, $7 seniors, $5.50 children ages 3-12). The zoo contains more than 500 animals representing hundreds of species, including monkeys, rhinos, zebras, bison, and jaguars. Popular exhibits include the Creepy Crawler Center, Wetlands Boardwalk, butterfly gardens, and the giraffe area, where visitors can occasionally pet and feed the exotic creatures via a bridge crossing over their habitat. The zoo also offers educational programs, summer camps, and interactive tours.

Fort Phantom Hill

Rising out of the earth like eerie spirits of the past, the lonesome chimneys of **Fort Phantom Hill** (11 miles north of Abilene on FM 600, 325/677-1309) stand as a testament to the region's frontier heritage. A visitors kiosk provides historical information and a big brochure with a map and self-guided tour. The National Register-listed fort was one of the largest of its kind, with dozens of structures and hundreds of soldiers. The fort was built in 1851 to protect settlers from Native American raids but was abandoned three years later after a series of natural hardships. The Native American threat was largely unfounded, and the soldiers reportedly became so bored, they deserted in increasing numbers until it was completely forsaken. Soon after, most of the buildings were mysteriously burned, though it's suspected that lingering disaffected soldiers were to blame. What remains at the fort are the forlorn chimneys, foundations of buildings, and even a few stone structures (most notably a commissary and guardhouse). Interpretive panels tell the tale of this unique and oft-overlooked attraction. To get there, take the I-20 exit at FM 600 and go 11 miles north. The main portion of the fort is located on the east side of FM 600.

Buffalo Gap Historic Village

Fourteen miles south of Abilene is the charming **Buffalo Gap Historic Village** (133 N. William St., Buffalo Gap, 325/572-3365, Mon.-Sat. 10am-5pm, $7 adults, $6 seniors and military, $4 students). This quaint living-history museum showcases the region's frontier heritage with historic artifacts, maps, interpretive events, and a dozen relocated historic buildings. The village's courthouse museum contains an impressive collection of arrowheads and weapons, and car buffs (and kids) will enjoy the pair of Model T Fords on the museum's grounds.

Abilene State Park

One of the most popular places for area residents to enjoy the outdoors is **Abilene State Park** (150 Park Rd. 32, 325/572-3204, www.tpwd.state.tx.us, $5 ages 13 and older). Sixteen miles southwest of town, the 529-acre park is accented by rolling hills and sturdy rock structures constructed in the early 1930s by the Civilian Conservation Corps. Locals frequent the park for its sublime swimming pool and groves of shady pecan trees. Visitors drop by to catch a glimpse of the buffalo and the Official State of Texas Longhorn Herd (a portion of the group is on-site). Camping,

1: Grace Museum 2: Fort Phantom Hill 3: Perini Steakhouse near Abilene

hiking, fishing, and biking are other popular activities.

SHOPPING

Abilene has several well-known authentic Western wear shops specializing in custom-made leather goods. The city also has a surprisingly extensive collection of antiques stores, where visitors, particularly out-of-staters, will find plenty of Texas charm and maybe even a few treasures.

Boots and Western Wear

People travel hundreds of miles to experience the pleasure of ordering and purchasing boots from the legendary **James Leddy Boots** (1602 N. Treadaway Blvd., 325/677-7811, Mon.-Fri. 8am-5pm). Even if you don't order a pair of the perfectly designed and eminently comfortable cowboy boots, you can witness them being handcrafted in the store's workshop. Leddy family members are usually on hand to take visitors on personal tours, and the shop has a large section of boots available for immediate purchase if you find that perfect fit. Leddy's has outfitted the famous (George Jones, Jerry Lee Lewis, and Buck Owens) and the not so famous (local farmers and ranchers).

For a truly distinctive custom-made leather item, head to **5D Custom Hats and Leather** (517 Oak St., 325/673-9000, www.5dhats.com, Mon.-Sat. 9am-5:30pm). Hats are the main draw here—owner Damon Albus will create any style, shape, or color you desire—but don't pass up the opportunity to order something unique, like a personalized belt, purse, or phone holder.

Not quite as practical yet intriguing nevertheless is **Art Reed Custom Saddles** (361 E. South 11th St., 325/677-4572, Mon.-Fri. 9:30-11:30am, 2-5pm). The smell of leather is almost overwhelming (in a good way), and even if you're not in the market for a $2,000 saddle, you may find chaps or other cowboy gear to your liking.

Antiques

An Old West town like Abilene is a great place to buy old stuff. A popular shop with a kitschy twist is **Fabulous Finds** (715 Grape St., 325/677-5110, Thurs.-Sat. 10:30am-5:30pm or by appointment). You'll find plenty of antiques, glassware, and consignment items along with vintage costume jewelry and collectibles. Sift through the dated and elegant collection of furniture, lighting, home accessories, and pictures.

For an all-inclusive experience, head to the antiques mall at **Antique Station** (703 N. 3rd St., 325/675-6100, Tues.-Sat. 10am-5:30pm). Items at the dozens of vendor booths include furniture, china, home accessories, and advertising memorabilia.

FOOD

This is cowboy country, so most locals consider Abilene's best restaurants to be steak houses. As always, the Mexican food options are good; otherwise, fine dining is not one of Abilene's strong points.

Steaks

One of the best steaks you'll ever enjoy (in fact, it's the best steak this professional Texas travel writer has ever eaten) awaits at ★ **Perini Ranch Steakhouse** (3002 FM 89, Buffalo Gap, 325/572-3339, www.periniranch.com, Tues.-Thurs. 5pm-10pm, Fri.-Sun. 11am-10pm, $13-49). Tom Perini is a nationally respected expert on Texas cooking (he's cooked for former president George W. Bush and traveled to Russia at the request of Vladimir Putin), so it's a rare pleasure to be able to consume his exquisite creations at his charmingly rustic restaurant about 20 minutes southwest of Abilene. The key to Perini's sublime steaks is his chuckwagon-style of preparation—high-quality fresh steaks are prepared with a simple dry rub seasoning of light spices before being placed over intensely hot flames and mesquite coals. This unique Big Country method brings out the immense flavor of the prime beef (the bone-in rib eye is perhaps the best Texas-style meal you'll ever consume). What puts the experience over the top are the unique side dishes, particularly the restaurant's signature green chile hominy, an ideal blend of grits, chiles, cheese, and bacon. Save room for the delectable bread pudding or jalapeño cheesecake.

If you're in downtown Abilene and have a hankerin' for some pork or chicken, head directly to the **Beehive Restaurant and Saloon** (442 Cedar St., 325/675-0600, www. beehivesaloon.com, Tues.-Fri. 11am-1:30pm and 5pm-10pm, Sat. 5pm-10pm, $11-36). The Beehive, named for a former legendary outlaw saloon in nearby Albany, is known for its quality steaks with corn-fed beef (impressive in steak-lover circles). The bacon-wrapped pork chop is an indulgent yet delicious option, and the seafood dishes are surprisingly good.

Mexican and Tex-Mex

A bakery isn't the first place you expect to find amazing Mexican food, but that's exactly what's on the menu at **La Popular Bakery & Cafe** (1533 Pine St., 325/672-2670, daily 6am-9pm, $5-12), a hole-in-the-wall establishment near downtown. La Popular is a great place to go for brunch, since you can sample the tasty pastries (the gingerbread cookies and frosting-covered fruit Danishes are highly recommended) along with the lunch items. The burritos are legendary here, and you can't go wrong with anything made with its fresh tortillas—the beef tacos, in particular.

For a traditional Tex-Mex dinner, head to **TaMolly's Mexican Kitchen** (4400 Ridgemont Dr., 325/698-2000, www.tamollys. com, daily 11am-9pm, $8-18), a small regional chain. The personal mini bowl of salsa each diner receives is a nice touch, and the classic combo plates are pure comfort food—cheese enchiladas, chicken flautas, crispy tacos, and quesadillas. Top it all off with a strawberry crispito, consisting of fried tortilla strips smothered in fruit and whipped cream.

A couple other places in town also offer standard yet quality Tex-Mex fare. To get your fill of beef burritos, chicken enchiladas, carne asada, and loaded nachos, drop by **Alfredo's**

Mexican Food (2849 S. 14th St., 325/698-0104, daily 7am-10:30pm, $6-13).

American and Barbecue

It's a bit hokey, but you won't experience too many other places like the **Ball Ranch** (south of Abilene at 525 S. Hwy. 83-84, 800/365-6507, www.theballranch.com, Sat. nights Apr.-Dec., $12-21). You'll find a big ol' open barnlike structure with several trees growing inside and accented with Western-themed items (saddles, ranching equipment). Ball Ranch serves an authentic and better-than-average chuckwagon supper, featuring mesquite-smoked barbecue meat (the brisket is mighty tender) with potato salad, red beans, biscuits, and peach cobbler. After dinner, the Ball family takes the stage and treats the audience to Western swing and country classics. Call ahead for reservations.

On the complete opposite end of the spectrum is the fancy downtown **Cypress Street Station** (158 Cypress St., 325/676-3463, www. cypress-street.com, Tues.-Fri. 11am-1:30pm and 5pm-10pm, Sat. 11am-10pm, $10-33). Start your meal by selecting from one of the best wine lists in town, and continue with a tasty appetizer of almond-crusted baked brie with toast points, topped with a honey and balsamic reduction. For the main course, consider the pork chop with apple demi-glace, the filet mignon with stuffed crab and Boursin cheese, or the seafood risotto with roasted red peppers. You could also accompany your meal with a fine locally crafted brew.

An absolute must for fans of Texas barbecue is the legendary **Joe Allen's** (301 S. 11th St, 325/672-9948, Mon.-Sat. 11am-9pm, $10-21). The perfectly smoked meat is consistently flavorful—try the brisket, pork rib, and sausage combo—and the sides are way above average (the potato salad and homemade cornbread in particular). The sauce sometimes needs an extra kick, so add a dash of Tabasco to it before dunking your brisket in it. Even when they're not craving 'cue, locals line up for Joe Allen's delicious mesquite-grilled steak and trout.

ACCOMMODATIONS
Hotels and Motels

Chain hotels are the name of the game in Abilene, so travelers won't find many charming independent options. Another choice is **Best Western** (350 E. Overland Trail, 325/672-5501, www.bestwestern.com, $69 d), featuring free Wi-Fi, a complimentary hot breakfast, an outdoor pool, and an exercise room. Similar in price and amenities is **La Quinta** (3501 W. Lake Rd., 800/531-5900, www.lq.com, $69 d), offering rooms with free Internet access, a free continental breakfast, and an outdoor pool. **Courtyard Abilene** (4350 Ridgemont Dr., 325/695-9600, www.marriott.com, $101 d) is another option; amenities include free wireless Internet access, a 24-hour market, an indoor heated pool, a whirlpool, and a fitness center.

One of the newest and best in town is ★ **Residence Inn** (1641 Musgrave Blvd., 325/677-8700, www.residenceinn.com, $129 d), featuring contemporary suites with unexpectedly large kitchens, complimentary Internet access, a free hot breakfast, and free adult beverages and appetizers at happy hour. Also commendable is the **Holiday Inn Express** (1802 E. Overland Trail, 325/675-9800, www.ichotelsgroup.com, $129 d), offering free wireless, a free continental breakfast, an outdoor pool, and a fitness center. Occupying a former large chain hotel is the regionally operated and respected **MCM Elegante Suites** (4250 Ridgemont Dr., 325/698-1234, www.mcmelegantesuites.com, $159 d). The welcoming lobby area contains a large naturally lit atrium where a free breakfast is served each morning, and the rooms include two separate areas, with a wet bar, refrigerator, microwave, and free Wi-Fi.

Bed-and-Breakfasts

In a city overrun with chain hotels, it's nice to have the option of staying in an authentic environment—especially when it's just a few blocks from downtown. Many Abilene visitors opt to stay at the remarkable **Sparhawk** Bed & Breakfast (3695 S. 1st St., 325/437-3729, www.sparhawk.com, $75-105). This historic 1930s structure was once part of the historic Sunset Lodge. It's comfortable and spacious, with antiques-bedecked rooms offering free Internet access, cable TV, and private bathrooms.

Camping

The best place to pitch a tent (or rent a yurt) and enjoy a campfire in the Big Country is **Abilene State Park** (150 Park Rd. 32, 325/572-3204, www.tpwd.state.tx.us, $15-20, yurts $40). Campsites are available with water and electric hookups, and the park added three yurts (defined as "enhanced shelters") containing double/single bunk beds with mattresses, a fold-out sofa, and a microwave.

INFORMATION AND SERVICES

The **Abilene Convention and Visitors Bureau** and **Abilene Cultural Affairs Council** (1101 N. 1st St., 325/676-2556, www.abilenecac.org, Mon.-Fri. 8:30am-5pm) are worth visiting just to see the impressive facility they're both housed in—the beautifully restored Texas & Pacific Railroad Depot. Friendly staffers from both organizations will gladly offer assistance, suggestions, maps, and brochures.

GETTING THERE AND AROUND

The **Abilene Regional Airport** (2933 Airport Blvd., 325/676-6367, www.iflyabi.com) offers flights by American Eagle and car rentals from **Avis** (325/677-9240), **Budget** (325/677-7777), **Enterprise** (325/690-9338), and **Hertz** (325/673-6774). Cab service is available via **Road Runner Taxi** (325/232-3295) and **Abilene Yellow Cab** (325/677-4334). The city also offers bus service Monday-Saturday from the airport and throughout town via its **City Link** transit system (1189 S. 2nd St., 325/676-6287, www.abilenetx.com).

San Angelo

The mystique of West Texas and the Panhandle Plains begins to unfold just beyond the Hill Country in San Angelo (population 100,215), where rolling hills tumble into outstretched vistas of vast sky. The city has grown slowly yet steadily since its early days as an outpost for the adjacent Fort Concho, established in 1867 to protect westward-moving settlers against Native American raids.

Like other frontier forts in the region, Fort Concho was well manned yet rather monotonous due to the lack of attacks. Historians have described the fort's typical experience as being "long periods of tedium interspersed with short blasts of excitement." The only significant activity occurred when encroaching Native American tribes caused a stir, resulting in minor skirmishes.

The army's presence at Fort Concho, however, was directly responsible for San Angelo's early growth. With plenty of federal funding arriving regularly for supplies and salaries, soldiers took to the streets in search of personal supplies, construction materials, and even some illegal activity. Businesses soon popped up to take care of the soldiers' needs for goods and services along with women and whiskey. Bordellos and saloons were almost as numerous as merchandise outlets.

After Fort Concho closed in the late 1800s, the arrival of the railroad helped establish San Angelo as a major ranching center; to this day, it remains one of the country's leading producers of mohair and wool production. The city continues to boast one of the state's most diverse industrial bases, with more than 120 manufacturing companies producing products ranging from denim to metals to oil field equipment.

San Angelo's distinct heritage, burgeoning arts scene, and welcoming combo of small-town charm and big-city services make for a unique getaway. The impressive art museum and better-than-expected restaurant scene

allow tourists to enjoy impressive cultural amenities, while the wide downtown streets and charming historic buildings let them put a little West Texas swagger in their walk.

SIGHTS
★ Fort Concho National Historic Landmark

The time-transporting **Fort Concho National Historic Landmark** (630 S. Oakes St., 325/481-2646, www.fortconcho. com, Mon.-Sat. 9am-5pm, Sun. 1pm-5pm, $3 adults, $2 seniors, $1.50 students) is considered perhaps the best preserved of Texas's frontier forts. Relive the life of an army soldier in the late 1800s through nearly two dozen renovated and well-maintained facilities such as barracks, stables, and officers' quarters. Displays containing vintage artifacts and replica equipment effectively demonstrate the scene at Fort Concho, described as relatively active yet fairly mundane.

Constructed to protect settlers from Indian raids, the fort was much like a fire station: always poised for activity yet often encountering none. In fact, one of the more interesting aspects of Fort Concho is related to its soldiers rather than its enemies. An atypically diverse population (for Texas) emerged at the fort in the 1870s when Buffalo Soldiers, a colloquial name given to African American troops, joined the ranks. In its 22-year history as an active post, Fort Concho hosted almost as many African Americans as Caucasians. The exhibit dedicated to the Buffalo Soldiers is one of the highlights of a visit to Fort Concho.

San Angelo Museum of Fine Arts

Along with Fort Concho, the city's most significant cultural attraction is the **San Angelo Museum of Fine Arts** (1 Love St., 325/653-3333, www.samfa.org, Tues.-Sat. 10am-4pm, Sun. 1pm-4pm, $2 adults, $1 seniors and students). Boasting a hip physical address, this impressive museum showcases world-class exhibits and occasional regional shows. The building, with its dramatic saddle-shaped roof designed by an architectural firm known for its restoration work at Radio City Music Hall, is a masterpiece unto itself. The museum features three galleries focusing on contemporary work and U.S. ceramics, with a permanent collection of nearly 200 pieces, along with a research library, ceramics studio, and education wing. Visitors are allowed to view the artwork housed in storage, another unique opportunity at this one-of-a-kind facility.

Miss Hattie's Bordello Museum

Once home to "the most famous brothel in West Texas," this straight-out-of-a-Western scene on historic Concho Avenue is now **Miss Hattie's Bordello Museum** (18 E. Concho Ave., 325/653-0112, www.misshatties.com, Tues.-Sat. 10am-4pm, tours Thurs.-Sat. at the top of the hour 1pm-4pm, $6 adults). Cowpokes, business travelers, and especially soldiers from nearby Fort Concho were quite familiar with the 2nd floor of this downtown stone building, known simply as "Miss Hattie's." Vintage furniture and velvet drapes recall San Angelo's Wild West era, when patrons would drink whiskey and play cards in the downstairs saloon and parlor house, then complete their evening of entertainment upstairs. The museum's rooms, complete with original furnishings, lace curtains, and gilded pressed-tin ceilings, are named for the women who worked at the brothel.

Concho River Walk

It's a far cry from the famous San Antonio River Walk, but San Angelo's version of a riverside stroll, the **Concho River Walk** (915/653-1206), is much more relaxing and natural. Though the entire trail spans more than six miles, the most interesting and accessible portions run through downtown, where walkers can experience manicured gardens and landscaped parks, fountains, miniature

waterfalls, and stunning riverside homes. Watch out for the geese—they'll loudly demand a handout.

Railway Museum of San Angelo

Train buffs will be interested in the small **Railway Museum of San Angelo** (703 S. Chadbourne St., 325/486-2140, Sat. 10am-4pm). In the restored Santa Fe depot building just south of downtown, the museum features rotating displays of railroad-related artifacts, elaborate model-train exhibits (featuring a fascinating depiction of the city in 1928), and several railcars on permanent display. Unfortunately, the museum is only open on Saturday, so plan accordingly.

San Angelo State Park

Immediately west of town on the shores of Fisher Reservoir is **San Angelo State Park** (3900 Mercedes St., 325/949-4757, www.tpwd. state.tx.us, $5 ages 13 and older). This is where San Angeloans come to play, and there's plenty to enjoy; namely, 7,677 acres of mostly undeveloped property containing rolling hills, Native American pictographs, a portion of the Official State of Texas Longhorn Herd, and many recreational activities. Park visitors can enjoy camping, hiking, mountain biking, and horseback riding on the trails, and fishing and boating on the lake. Tours are available to the ancient Permian animal tracks and rock art. Contact the park for a tour schedule and fees.

SHOPPING

For a small city, San Angelo has an impressive range of shopping options. The city is particularly proud of its unique Concho Pearls cultivated in its own waterways.

Concho Pearls

Not many places can claim to be a source for jewelry, so San Angelo residents are rightfully proud of their homegrown, naturally produced Concho Pearl. This stunning lavender-colored pearl is present only in freshwater mussel shells found in area lakes, rivers, and streams. These distinctive beauties range in color from light pink to dark purple and vary in size and shape from spherical to baroque. The pearls have been coveted for more than 400 years, when Spanish explorers sought the colorful iridescent treasures in nearby waterways. Incidentally, the word *concho* is Spanish for shell.

The best place to shop for Concho Pearls is **Legend Jewelers** (18 E. Concho Ave., 325/653-0112, www.legendjewelers.com), in the heart of San Angelo's historic downtown commercial district. Legend's boasts the largest collection of Concho Pearls in the country, offering various designs and settings in rings, necklaces, and earrings. While there, check out Legend's interesting selection of horned toad jewelry, produced from rubber molds made from the actual toads in the 1970s.

Concho Avenue

Even guys won't mind browsing the charming shops along Concho Avenue in San Angelo's historic downtown commercial area. Consisting of a handful of shops in restored old buildings, this one-block area between Oakes and Chadbourne Streets is highlighted by **Eggemeyer's General Store** (35 E. Concho Ave., 325/655-1166), a genuine mercantile shop. Eggemeyer's offers a true blast from the past, with homemade candy and fudge (highly recommended); specialty coffees; bins filled with toys, knickknacks, and souvenirs; plenty of kitschy Texas-style home decor items; and an entire room filled with kitchen gadgets and recipe books.

Boots and Western Wear

Most West Texas cities have a legendary boot maker, and in San Angelo it's **J.L. Mercer & Sons Boot Co.** (224 S. Chadbourne St., 325/658-7634, www.jlmercerboots.com). Located in the downtown commercial district since 1923, the company has been consistently producing high-quality cowboy boots for generations of satisfied San Angeloans. Mercer's claims to have outfitted such luminaries as Lyndon B. Johnson and John Wayne, along with slightly less legendary folks like Charlie Daniels, Barry Corbin, and Tom Wopat. All of the boots are handmade on-site, from super ropers to cowboy boots with exotic skins and inlay work. Other popular Western wear shops in San Angelo offering boots, hats, cowboy apparel, and accessories include **Blair's Western Wear Inc.** (4230 Sherwood Way, 325/949-6287) and **M.L. Leddy's Boots & Saddlery** (222 S. Oakes St., 325/653-3397).

FOOD
Steaks

For an authentic West Texas steak house experience, go to the charmingly old-school **Western Sky Steak House** (2024 N. Chadbourne St., 325/655-3610, www. westernskysteakhouse.org, Mon.-Sat. 11am-9:30pm, Sun. 11am-3pm, $12-39). Located in a generic-looking stand-alone spot with a large hokey mural painted on one side, Western Sky proudly bills itself as the "home of San Angelo's biggest steak." Indeed, the 52-ounce sirloin is mighty in presence, and the hardy patrons (ranchers and cowboys from the area) who devour the megasize meat claim it's equally large in taste. Meanwhile, the mere mortals tend to opt for the tender T-bone and rib eye, or one of the restaurant's specialties, like the Spanish steak—a tasty rib eye topped with ranchero sauce and served with beans, french fries, salad, and several flour tortillas.

Tex-Mex

One of the best spots for Tex-Mex in town is **Fuentes Cafe** (101 S. Chadbourne St., 325/658-2430, Mon.-Sat. 11am-9:30pm, Sun. 11am-2pm, $8-18). Housed in a charming downtown building, Fuentes is highly regarded for its fajitas, enchiladas (try the spinach option), and particularly its *guiso,* a tantalizing dish featuring tender stew meat simmered in a richly seasoned sauce.

If you like Western Sky Steak House, you'll love its Mex-themed sister restaurant, **Franco's Café** (2218 Martin Luther King Blvd., 325/653-8010, www.francoscafe.org, daily 8am-10pm, $9-17). Like its *hermana,*

Franco's is uninspiring on the exterior and tremendously tasty on the plate. Popular items include the burritos and fajitas, but one of the best options on the menu is its unconventional approach to the chile relleno. Combining the approaches of the Rio Grande Valley and far West Texas, Franco's version offers an egg-fried Anaheim pepper filled with beef and topped with ranchero sauce.

Lunch

When you're in the historic downtown commercial district shopping for Concho Pearls, make sure to grab some lunch at **Miss Hattie's Restaurant** (26 E. Concho Ave., 325/653-0570, www.misshatties.com, daily 11am-10pm, $9-24). Once home to a notorious brothel, the building now offers tempting dishes of American fare. The restaurant still maintains the feel of an Old West saloon, with dark wood furnishings and Victorian-era paintings and details, and the food is similarly welcoming, especially the hearty chicken and dumplings and fancy gourmet sandwiches.

ACCOMMODATIONS

Chains dominate San Angelo's hotel landscape, with most commendable options located along U.S. Highway 87 northwest of downtown or on U.S. Highway 67 near San Angelo State University on the western edge of the city. Those looking for a unique lodging experience might want to take roost at the Inn at the Art Center, a former chicken farm turned B&B.

Hotels and Motels

One of the best deals in town, budget or otherwise, is **Quality Inn** (4613 S. Jackson, 325/658-6594, www.choicehotels.com, $74 d), featuring rooms with free Internet access, recliners, microwaves and refrigerators (upon request), an outdoor pool, and, most important, a coupon for free breakfast next door at Roxie's, a 1950s-style diner serving omelets, pancakes, biscuits, and mediocre coffee. On the northwestern edge of downtown is the **Inn of the Conchos** (2021 N. Bryant Blvd.,

325/658-2811, www.inn-of-the-conchos.com, $79 d). It's a bit rough around the edges, but the Concho is one of San Angelo's few independently operated hotels, as evidenced by its colorful slogan, "A darn good place to hang your hat." The hotel offers limited amenities but includes a large outdoor pool and free coffee in the lobby. Just down the road is **Ramada Limited** (2201 N. Bryant Blvd., 325/653-4482, www.ramada.com, $69 d), featuring rooms with free Wi-Fi, refrigerators, a free continental breakfast, and an outdoor pool.

Slightly more expensive is the **Comfort Suites** (4450 W. Houston Harte Expy., 325/944-8600, www.comfortsuites.com, $99 d), featuring free Internet access and a free hot breakfast. Also recommended is **Holiday Inn Express** (4613 Houston Harte Expy., 877/863-4780, www.ichotelsgroup.com, $111 d), offering free Wi-Fi, a fitness center, and an outdoor pool and spa near the San Angelo State University campus. Nearby is the fairly fancy **Fairfield Inn** (1459 Knickerbocker Rd., 325/482-8400, www.marriott.com, $112 d), providing a complimentary breakfast buffet, a fitness room, an outdoor pool and spa, and free wireless.

Bed-and-Breakfasts

Offering a true alternative to traditional corporate lodging is the fabulously funky ★ **Inn at the Art Center** (2503 Martin Luther King Blvd., 325/659-3836, www.chickenfarmartcenter.com, $85-112), near downtown. A former chicken farm, this 1970s-era compound contains a fascinating collection of artist studios, galleries, and a restaurant. The three rooms comprising the B&B portion of the art center are tastefully decorated with intriguing Western-themed works from the owner, and the whole place, with its colorful private gardens and meandering grapevines, has a Santa Fe via West Texas vibe. If you happen to be here on the first Saturday of the month, you'll be treated to live music performances and artists' demonstrations throughout the compound.

Camping

The best place to pitch a tent or park an RV is **San Angelo State Park** (3900 Mercedes St., 325/949-4757, www.tpwd.state.tx.us, $10-20), just west of town on the Fisher Reservoir. The park features six air-conditioned and heated mini cabins, sites with water and electricity, and tent sites with picnic tables and grills. Just southwest of town on Lake Nasworthy is the popular **Spring Creek Marina RV Park** (45 Fishermans Rd., 325/944-3850, www. springcreekmarina-rv.com, sites $25-38, cabins $50-70). The park contains 83 RV sites with full hookups, tent sites with water and electric hookups, and furnished cabins with air-conditioning, refrigerators, showers, and bathrooms.

INFORMATION AND SERVICES

The **San Angelo Convention and Visitors Bureau** stocks plenty of free brochures and maps at its impressive **visitors center** (418 W. Ave. B, 800/375-1206, www.sanangelo. org, Mon.-Fri. 9am-5pm, Sat. 10am-5pm, Sun. noon-4pm). This aesthetically pleasing facility, constructed with native materials—the limestone walls came from nearby quarries, and the floors and benches are made of local mesquite wood—is nestled along the Concho River, and its enormous windows and outdoor patio provide picturesque views of the river.

GETTING THERE AND AROUND

For San Angelo travelers, there's **San Angelo Regional Airport** (8618 Terminal Cir., 325/659-6409, www.sanangelotexas.us), providing service from American Eagle and car rentals through Avis, Budget, and Hertz. The city's cab companies are **Red Ball Taxi & Shuttle** (325/942-8899) and **Checker Cab Co.** (325/655-3105).

Background

The Landscape........470
Plants and Animals.....473
Climate................477
History 479
Government and
    Economy 482
People and Culture 484

The Landscape

Texas defies geographic categorization, yet another reason for its residents to beam with pride. Most states easily fit into a comfortably accepted natural compartment, such as plains, coasts, or mountains, but Texas has as many as 13 distinct geographic regions, including prairies, mountains, basins, and a valley. Together, these various geographical areas make up a land area of 261,914 square miles, roughly the size of New England, New York, Pennsylvania, Ohio, and North Carolina combined. Not surprisingly, Texas's geography contains enormous extremes. The highest point in the state is Guadalupe Peak, at

8,749 feet above sea level, and the lowest point is, well, sea level along the Gulf Coast. Texas occupies nearly 7 percent of the landmass of the United States and boasts the distinction of being larger than any European country.

GEOGRAPHY

Attempting to pin down a decisive and accepted approach to Texas's geographical regions is challenging. A variety of factors—natural, physical, cultural, even political—contribute to the complexity. For clarity's sake, a good way to tackle the subject is from a fairly unbiased standpoint: natural and physical features. However, even this supposedly simplified method reveals the intricate natural composition of the Lone Star State—its four main geographic regions (the Basin and Range Province, the Great Plains, the Interior Lowlands, and the Gulf Coastal Plains) contain more than 20 geographical subregions.

The Basin and Range Province

Texas's smallest geographic region is in far West Texas, bounded by New Mexico to the north, the Rio Grande to the south and west, and the Toyah Basin/Stockton Plateau to the east. Precipitation is very slight and erratic in this area—the average annual rainfall in El Paso is about eight minuscule inches—and most of the land is divided into large ranches.

The Basin and Range Province also contains a small portion of the Rocky Mountain system, though geologists continue to debate this claim. This entire area is also referred to as the mythic Trans-Pecos region, a rugged landscape that has captured the imagination of those who appreciate the beauty of nature in a panoramic and isolated setting.

This area is also home to the state's three main mountain ranges, the Guadalupe Mountains along the southern New Mexico border (home to the state's highest point, the 8,749-foot Guadalupe Peak), the Davis Mountains just north of Big Bend, and the Franklin Mountains in El Paso. Big Bend National Park, located along the biggest turning of the Rio Grande, contains the Chisos Mountains, where the highest elevation, Emory Peak, reaches a respectable 7,832 feet.

The basins of the region are noteworthy for not having a drainage outlet to the nearby Rio Grande. Instead, they channel the scant rainfall into "salt lakes." These areas are typically dry as a bone, and the exposed solid minerals in their beds were once a major source for commercial salt.

The Great Plains

In its entirety, this region extends all the way from Canada to Central Texas's Balcones Fault. It may seem like a stretch to connect these almost polar opposite regions of North America, but for the Panhandle residents who experience subfreezing temperatures when "blue northers" blow in, it's a chilling reality.

Because of its rocky surface composition, this region encompasses a variety of physical features, from the High Plains in the north to the Edwards Plateau in the south. The geologic structure of the Great Plains region also produces some of Texas's most breathtaking natural features. Palo Duro Canyon near Amarillo is a multicolored, otherworldly sight to behold, and the Hill Country's magnificent Enchanted Rock is a massive pink dome of solid granite that has beckoned people for centuries with its mystic aura.

This portion of the state is considered by many to be the most compelling and evocative region of Texas, especially in the southwestern area, which transitions into the fabled Trans-Pecos region. It's big sky country, where the surrounding natural beauty is astounding. Endless vistas, colorful rock formations, and the magnificent blue heavens are tourist attractions unto themselves, drawing visitors from around the globe who consider the wide-open spaces they have heard about to be merely a myth.

Previous: sunset over the Hill Country west of Austin

The western portion of the Panhandle is known as the Llano Estacado, or Staked Plains. According to legend, Spanish explorer Francisco Vasquez de Coronado marked his trek through the region with wooden stakes since the area was (and still is) virtually void of physical landmarks.

The lack of water—rainfall and rivers are scarce in the area—has been problematic throughout the history of the High Plains. Perhaps as a concession, the region inherited mineral wealth in the form of oil and natural gas deposits. These petroleum gold mines were discovered in the 1920s in the Panhandle and in the Permian Basin area near the cities of Midland and Odessa.

The southern portion of this region, the Edwards Plateau, is marked by the Balcones Escarpment, a geologic rift in the underlying layers of rock stretching roughly from Del Rio eastward to Austin. This area has a thin limestone-based soil and is primarily used for cattle, sheep, and goat ranching, resulting in its distinction as one of the major regions for wool and mohair production in the country.

The Interior Lowlands

Much like Texas's Great Plains, the Interior Lowlands extend from North Texas through the Midwest all the way to Canada. An abundance of rivers, hills, and cultivable land ties Texas's Interior Lowlands to its midcontinent neighbors, resulting in its largely agricultural use. Unlike the arid conditions of the Basin and Range Province, this region averages up to 30 inches of rain annually.

Within the Interior Lowlands are several subregions, including the North Central Plains, which comprise roughly two-thirds of the entire region. This area is marked by rolling hills and the West Texas Rolling Plains, which are just as their name implies—pleasant yet unimposing.

Other subregions reflect natural nomenclature—the Western and Eastern Cross Timbers and the Grand Prairie. These three areas stretch eastward to Fort Worth and are primarily home to cattle ranches and crops such

as wheat and cotton. The region's absence of a major water-producing aquifer necessitated the construction of several reservoirs for irrigation as well as strict conservation regulations. Two of Texas's major rivers, the Trinity and the Brazos, also traverse the area, allowing agricultural production of cotton and grain to continue.

The Gulf Coastal Plains

The last of Texas's geographic regions is its largest, comprising the southern and eastern third of the state. This area has the lowest elevation in Texas—less than 1,000 feet above sea level—and contains several bands of physical features and soil types formed by the weathering of underlying rock layers. As its name implies, the Gulf Coastal Plains include Texas's entire coastline and the mouths of most of the state's major rivers.

The Pine Belt comprises the eastern portion of this region along the Louisiana border. Pine trees, hay fields, and cattle pastures dominate the area, which is home to several national forests and the state's lumber industry. The region's natural features also include two major oil fields—Spindletop near Beaumont and the East Texas Oil Field.

West of the Pine Belt lie the Post Oak and Blackland Belts. These regions are known for their fertile soil and rolling prairies, and cotton remains the major crop. Settlers coveted the clear streams and quality soil in the Blackland Belt, which stretches east from Del Rio and northward through San Antonio, Austin, Waco, and Dallas. The prime agricultural conditions fueled Texas's growth, and the region retains some of the state's most densely populated areas.

Texas's southern tip is mostly comprised of the Rio Grande Plain, which includes the Lower Rio Grande Valley, known throughout the state simply as "the Valley." The Rio Grande Plain extends southward into Mexico for several hundred miles. Much of the area is covered with cacti, mesquite trees, and wild shrubs. Cattle production is also significant in the southern Rio Grande Plain, including on the famous King Ranch southwest of Corpus Christi. The Valley, meanwhile, thrives agriculturally, thanks to the rich delta soils and absence of freezing weather.

The region's Coastal Prairies stretch across the Gulf of Mexico coastline, reaching as far as 60 miles inland. The eastern portion of this region is thick with vegetation and supports crops ranging from rice to cotton. The southern portion contains grasslands and supports citrus fruits and vegetable farming.

ENVIRONMENTAL ISSUES

Texas probably isn't the first place that comes to mind when talk turns to environmental responsibility, but the state has its fair share of activists and defenders. One of Texas's chief environmental concerns is air pollution, particularly from vehicle emissions.

Since most of Texas's big cities sprawl into outlying wide-open spaces, cars are the preferred method of transportation. The state's steady increase in population has become problematic for environmentalists. Air pollution concerns in Texas's cosmopolitan areas have prompted ozone alerts, and Houston has been jockeying with Los Angeles for the coveted title of "smoggiest city."

Other troublesome issues for Texas environmental activists are water pollution and unsafe waste disposal. The Texas Commission on Environmental Quality, a state agency dedicated to protecting Texas's natural resources, oversees a multitude of monitoring efforts and public awareness campaigns designed to maintain control over potentially dangerous environmental hazards. The agency's air monitoring endeavors, water conservation districts, and efforts to keep tabs on industrial waste are commendable but don't always reach citizens at the local level.

That's where grassroots organizations like the Texas Campaign for the Environment come into play. The group's mission is to inform and mobilize Texans to maintain their quality of life and health. Their primary focus is improving trash and recycling policies to limit air, water, and soil pollution.

The indomitable Texas spirit is also represented in the environmental activism scene. PEER (Public Employees for Environmental Responsibility). The group's informative and entertaining website features information about wetlands, public health, and whistle blowers. The organization's goal is to educate the public about ways environmental hazards impact individual Texas residents.

Plants and Animals

The plant and animal kingdoms in Texas are a source of fascination. Thousands of plant varieties and more than 500 animal species call Texas home, and their compelling assortment is as diverse as the state's landscape. There's the expected (cacti, armadillos, and longhorn cattle) and the unexpected (pine forests, badgers, and cougars).

More than 750 miles separate the eastern and western portions of the state, and the northern and southern tips are nearly 800 miles apart; the resulting broad range of life throughout Texas is rather stunning. Texas's foliar variety mirrors its geographic regions,

with 10 corresponding vegetational areas ranging from gulf marshes to high plains. The state's wildlife is tied to its geography and climate. Most of Texas's mammals (aside from livestock) live in warmer, forested areas, and many exceptional birds and insects pass through the state on migratory routes.

TREES AND SHRUBS

Like most vegetation, the abundance and assortment of trees and shrubs in Texas are tied to the quality and quantity of soil and water. In West Texas, where annual average rainfall totals are often in single digits, only drought-resistant desert shrubs survive the arid conditions, and the main tree species—juniper and ponderosa pine—are found mostly in the higher elevations. As environmental conditions improve toward the east, tree species expand to include mesquite, live oak, and pecan, as well as colorfully named shrubs such as blackbrush, whitebrush, and greenbriar. The East Texas forests consist mainly of pine trees, with a healthy mix of oak, elm, and hickory.

GRASSES AND CACTI

Texas leads the United States in numbers of grasses, boasting more than 570 species, subspecies, and varieties. Cacti are not nearly as diversified (merely 106 species), yet they also represent a noteworthy aspect of Texas's ground-level vegetation. Found mainly in far West Texas, these spindly yet captivating plants—including the flowering prickly pear, agave, yucca, and even the hallucinogenic peyote—come in a fascinating variety of sizes, shapes, and colors.

Texas's grasses, meanwhile, are less viscerally intriguing and more botanically appealing. Although a fair number of native grasses have been lost to overgrazing, the several hundred remaining varieties endure in spite of Texas's variable weather and topography. Tolerant species such as sideoats grama (the official state grass), Texas grama, buffalo grass, and Indian grass still provide meals for livestock, while their hardiness also helps contain soil erosion.

WILDFLOWERS

Wildflowers in Texas are akin to fall foliage in New England. For most of March and April, nature puts on a brilliant display of iridescent blues, dazzling reds, and blinding yellows across fields and along highways throughout the state. The prime viewing area is the Hill Country, where landscapes are painted with bluebonnets, Indian paintbrushes, Mexican poppies, and black-eyed Susans.

Texas's wildflowers have been around for more than 130 million years, and the different species are greatly affected by the differences in the state's soils (azaleas thrive in acidic East Texas soil but struggle in the chalky Central Texas earth). Central Texans are fortunate since they're in the middle of several overlapping ecoregions. This biodiversity results in a plethora of springtime wildflowers—nearly 400 varieties in all—and a majority are native species.

The scenery is just as good in East Texas, home to blooming azaleas, yellow jasmine, dogwoods, and wisteria. Texas's arid and sandy regions don't offer quite the same visual spectacle, but daisies, cacti, and yucca in West Texas offer dashes of color to the monochromatic natural surroundings.

MAMMALS

Nearly 150 animal species traverse Texas's terrain, yet only two are emblematic of the Lone Star State. Texas's official small mammal is the armadillo (fun fact: female armadillos always have four pups, and all four are always the same sex), and the state's official large mammal is the Texas longhorn.

Though these iconic creatures can typically be seen from the road—in the armadillo's case, it's usually flat on the road—the animals lurking in forests and canyons are the most interesting. Cougars are still fairly common in the southwestern portions of the state, and Texas-worthy mammals like the javelina (a feral, tusked piglike creature officially known as the collared peccary), the kangaroo rat, and the antelope-ish pronghorn roam the prairies and brush country, especially in West Texas.

Also of interest is Texas's bat population, which includes 33 of the country's 43 known bat species. The world's largest bat colony lives in Bracken Cave near San Antonio, and each summer, more than one million Mexican free-tailed bats emerge from beneath Austin's Congress Avenue Bridge, much to the delight of tourists and townies. Texas's less distinctive yet still notable mammals include the white-tailed deer (estimated at nearly four million), black bear, coyote, and beaver.

BIRDS

Texas is a destination and crossing point for myriad bird species during migratory seasons. It's also home to hundreds of native varieties. More kinds of birds (approximately 600) are found in Texas than any other state—primarily due to its south-central location. Feathered pals from the eastern and western parts of the country occupy Texas's air space, and international travelers cross the Mexican border, drawing avid bird-watchers from across the United States.

Texas birds can be grouped into five major categories: permanent residents (mockingbirds, roadrunners, screech owls), migrants (snow geese, scarlet tanagers, various sandpipers), winter residents (common loons and terns, red-bellied woodpeckers), summer residents (purple martins, yellow-breasted chats, orchard orioles), and accidentals (greater flamingos, red-footed boobies, yellow-billed loons).

Spring is the prime time for bird-watching. Serious and amateur birders from across the country visit the Gulf Coast and Rio Grande Valley to catch a glimpse of migrating and native bird species. Pelicans, spoonbills, egrets, and herons are fairly easy to spot. Those looking for a unique birding experience can join a boat tour to spy whooping cranes, the massive white birds boasting a seven-foot-wide wingspan that were nearly extinct before efforts were made to revive the species. Now more than 100 spend their winters in the Aransas National Wildlife Refuge on the Gulf Coast.

Texas's other main endangered bird species is the golden-cheeked warbler, a migratory songbird that breeds only in Ashe juniper woodlands in Central Texas. Its habitat was reduced by about a quarter by encroaching development, but highly publicized campaigns to protect the species have helped secure its nesting grounds.

MARINE LIFE

An amazing variety of marine animals live in the Gulf of Mexico, home to thousands of fish and shellfish that depend on the coast's diverse habitats for food and shelter. These environs are typically categorized by five distinct water areas—salt marshes, coastal bays, jetties, nearshore waters, and the Gulf of Mexico.

Fish and shrimp enter salt marshes looking for food or for a place to lay their eggs. They're joined by several species of crabs (fiddler, hermit, and stone), snails, mussels, and worms. Coastal bays and beaches are home to two types of jellyfish, the Portuguese man-of-war

a tropical bird at Moody Gardens in Galveston

(stay away from this purplish baggy creature with the poisonous blue tentacles) and the relatively harmless cabbagehead, which looks like its namesake and is occasionally used by dolphins as toy balls.

The beach area also supports oysters, spotted sea trout, and several species of catfish. Jetties, which are used to prevent ship channels from piling up with sand and silt, consist of large stones providing shelter and food for a wide range of sealife, including sea anemones, urchins, crabs, grouper, and sea trout. Artificial reefs (stone rubble, old ships, oil rigs) open nearshore waters to mussels, shrimp, crabs, and a host of other animals, including the fish that feed on them (tarpon, kingfish, and others).

The Gulf of Mexico is home to some of Texas's heaviest hitters. Great barracuda and hammerhead, lemon, and bull sharks devour smaller varieties such as bluefish, striped bass, and tuna. When the currents and temperatures are just right, tropical species such as parrotfish, angelfish, and spiny lobsters also visit the gulf waters.

REPTILES

Snakes slither across much of Texas's surface, and the state's range of reptiles is rather impressive. Texas is home to 16 varieties of poisonous snakes (including 11 types of rattlesnakes), which can be extremely hazardous to hikers and campers. Other dangerous snakes include cottonmouth, copperheads, and Texas coral snakes.

Snakebites from these varieties require a few basic first-aid techniques if medical care is not immediately available. The American Red Cross suggests washing the bite with soap and water and keeping the bitten area immobilized and lower than the heart. Equally as important is avoiding popular remedy misconceptions: Do not apply hot or cold packs, do not attempt to suck the poison out, and do not drink any alcohol or use any medication.

Texas is also home to hundreds of nonvenomous snake species, some of which mimic their poisonous counterparts. The Texas bull snake realistically imitates a rattlesnake, all the way down to the rattling sound, and the milk snake and coral snake look disturbingly alike, with the same colors but in different orders. A time-honored Texas adage helps differentiate the two: Red and yellow, kill a fellow (the coral snake has red next to yellow stripes); red and black, friend of Jack (the milk snake has red next to black stripes).

Not to be overlooked are Texas's other distinctive reptiles. The official state reptile is the Texas horned lizard (charmingly referred to as the horny toad), which is primarily found in West Texas. The state's other noteworthy reptiles include alligators, sea turtles, geckos, and spinytail iguanas.

INSECTS AND BUTTERFLIES

Nearly 100,000 different kinds of pesky insects buzz around Americans' heads and ankles, and a third of those bugs have been found in Texas. The Lone Star State proudly claims to have more different kinds of insects than any other state.

Texas also has more butterfly species than any other state. Its 400 varieties number more than half the butterfly species in the United States and Canada. The recognizable monarch butterfly makes its annual migratory flight through Texas en route to its wintering grounds in Mexico. The southward flight in late summer and fall can be quite a spectacle, when monarchs fill the air and gather on trees by the thousands.

Texas's insects are just as numerous but not nearly as charming. Most of these winged and antennaed creatures are ecologically beneficial, but the two insects that creep immediately to most Texans' minds are the bothersome mosquito and the squirm-inducing cockroach.

AMPHIBIANS

Like most living things in Texas, amphibians are well represented due to the tremendous diversity in climate and temperature. Frogs, toads, and salamanders are common in all areas of the state, but the greatest abundance and diversity are in the relatively wet habitats of the eastern third of the state. Camping near lakes and streams in this area offers visitors an audio sampler of the various croaks and calls of Texas's native frog and toad species.

Perhaps the best-known Texas amphibian is the Barton Springs salamander, a tiny creature found only among the rocks of Austin's legendary spring-fed swimming pool. In 1997, the U.S. Fish and Wildlife Service added the Barton Springs salamander to the endangered and threatened wildlife list, and the city of Austin later caused a big stir when it adopted strict development guidelines to protect this pint-size creature.

Climate

A weather map in March or November tells the story of Texas's variable climate in a visually stunning way—the entire spectrum of colors is represented across the state. From icy 20°F blues in the Panhandle to balmy 90°F reds in the Valley, the rainbow of Texas's diverse climate is a revealing diagram.

When it comes to weather-related records, Texas's books are virtually off the chart. Consider these extreme extremes: The state's record temperatures range from -23°F (Seminole, in the southwestern Panhandle, 1933) to 120°F (Seymore, north of Abilene, 1936). Texas's greatest annual rainfall was 109 inches (Clarksville, in northeastern Texas, 1873), and the least was 1.8 inches (Wink, in far West Texas, 1956). Also of note, Texas's highest sustained wind velocity was 145 mph, when Hurricane Carla hit the Gulf Coast in 1961.

Otherwise, the state's average rainfall typically exceeds 56 inches annually in East Texas, while El Paso and other parts of West Texas typically receive less than 8 inches each year. The average annual precipitation in Dallas is nearly 35 inches, and Houston averages approximately 48 inches. One final note of interest: The Route 66 town of Vega in the Texas Panhandle receives an average of 23 inches of snow per year, while Brownsville at the mouth of the Rio Grande has no measurable snowfall on record.

Texas has two main seasons—a hot summer that lasts from approximately May through October, and a winter that starts in November and usually lasts until March. By the time summer is over, most of Texas's landscape is too crisp and dry for fall foliage. Some colors are visible in the East Texas forests, but most of the state settles into a brownish hue until rains bring life and greenery back in March.

CLIMATE REGIONS

When it comes to climate, meteorologists usually divide Texas into three areas—modified marine (aka subtropics), continental, and mountain. These climate types aren't set off by strict boundaries, but the vast majority of the state falls into the subtropics region (Central and East Texas), which can be further divided into four subcategories based on humidity. We'll just stick with the basics.

The subtropics region is primarily affected by tropical airflow from the Gulf of Mexico, and its four humidity-related subheadings delineate the moisture content of this northwest-moving air stream. The continental region is largely in the Panhandle and is similar to the U.S. plains states, with major temperature fluctuations, low relative humidity, and moderate amounts of randomly occurring rainfall. Cooler temperatures, low humidity, and arid conditions characterize the mountain climate in far West Texas.

Using these climate regions as a guide, it's safe to assume the following about Texas's weather: the eastern third of the state has a humid climate noted for its warm summers; the central region of Texas has a subhumid climate resulting in hot summers and dry winters; and most portions of West Texas tend to have semiarid to arid conditions, often with extreme differences in temperature throughout the year.

DANGEROUS WEATHER

Even the weather is extreme in Texas. Menacing hurricanes, treacherous tornadoes, and dangerous floods can strike at any time, and they wreak their havoc swiftly before clear skies and calm conditions return. Fortunately, Texans have learned from previous atrocities, resulting in evacuation plans and safety procedures. Though most of these events are seasonal, there's an unpredictable nature to Texas's nature, so visitors should be prepared for potential flash floods.

Historically, hurricanes have hit Texas's Gulf Coast about once every decade, usually in September or October. Most Gulf Coast communities have evacuation plans in place, along with reinforced buildings and homes to brace against the torrential winds. Many seaside structures are also raised on piers to prevent damage from the crashing waves during a tropical storm.

In the past decade, however, the hurricane activity in the gulf has been more frequent and severe. In addition to the devastation brought by Hurricanes Katrina and Rita, Hurricane Ike slammed into Galveston Island on September 13, 2008, leaving an enormous swath of destruction in its wake. Ike completely leveled several nearby communities, and its 110 mph winds ripped apart hotels, office buildings, and countless homes in Galveston, Houston, and the surrounding area. Of the nearly 7,000 documented historic buildings in Galveston, upward of 1,500 were seriously damaged. Devastation struck

again in 2017, when Hurricane Harvey walloped the city of Rockport near Corpus Christi with 130mph winds. The associated storms resulted in unprecedented flooding in Houston.

Things were quite different a century ago. Galveston experienced the most destructive storm in U.S. history (before Hurricanes Katrina, Rita, and Ike) in 1900, when a hurricane left at least 6,000 dead and leveled most of the city. A storm of equal intensity hit Galveston in 1915, but the city was prepared with its new seawall. The death toll was a comparatively low 275.

Texas also lies in the path of Tornado Alley, with its central corridor running from the Panhandle north through Kansas. The state's worst tornado on record struck downtown Waco in 1953, killing 114 people, injuring 597, and destroying or damaging more than 1,000 homes and buildings. In 1997, a mile-wide tornado (as in *one mile wide*) wreaked havoc on the Central Texas town of Jarrell, leaving only the concrete slabs of dozens of homes in its wake.

Floods have also taken their toll on Texas. Thunderstorms are a major event—they typically come barreling in from the west, spewing lightning and firing occasional hailstones everywhere in their path. Appearing as massive, intimidating red blobs on the radar screen, they furiously dump heavy sheets of rain on Texas's lands, leaving saturated fields and overflowing rivers and streams in their wake.

One of the most destructive rainstorms in Texas history occurred in 1921, when floods in Central Texas killed 215 people. San Antonio was sitting under nearly nine feet of water, and 36 inches of rain fell north of Austin in just 18 hours (a U.S. record).

History

No place has a sense of place quite like Texas, and that sentiment is indelibly tied to the state's fascinating past. Texans are proud of their history, and for good reason. The state was once its own country, and many modern-day residents would likely welcome a return to the idea of isolationism. Above all, there's something reverential about the pride Texans take in their heritage, from the Native American contribution of the word *tejas* (meaning friends), to the state's nearly 400-year-old Spanish mission buildings, to the aforementioned Republic of Texas, to the role Texas played in the Civil War, to its ranching and oil heritage.

Being proud of what a state represents is somewhat distinctive to Texas. Not to take away anything from other states' history, but a term like "Rhode Island pride" or the concept of a proud Idaho heritage just doesn't resonate the way Texas Pride does. It's a badge of honor, and the state's rough-and-tumble past makes it a deserved title.

Everyone knows about the Alamo, but those who set out to discover Texas's dynamic heritage will encounter fascinating stories, like the 4,000-year-old Native American pictographs in a rock shelter along the Rio Grande, the discovery of the 1686 Gulf Coast shipwreck of French explorer La Salle, the influence of Mexican *vaqueros* on Texas's cowboys, and life in an oil boomtown in the 1930s. And that's just scraping the surface.

PREHISTORIC ERA

Depending on the source, Texas's prehistoric past can be traced as far back as 13,000 years. That's 11,000 BC. Most archaeologists and historians divide the state's prehistoric era into three periods: Paleo-Indian, Archaic, and Late Prehistoric.

The Paleo-Indian period is significant for containing references to the earliest known inhabitants of the state (circa 9200 BC).

Archaeologists have discovered numerous distinctive Clovis fluted points (a type of arrowhead) from this era, which were sometimes used for hunting mammoth.

The longest span of Texas's prehistory falls under the Archaic period (circa 6000 BC–AD 700). It's noted for the changes in projectile points and tools, and the introduction of grinding implements for food preparation. A significant weapon used during the Archaic period was a spear-throwing device known as an atlatl.

The bow and arrow were introduced during Texas's Late Prehistoric period (AD 700 to historic times). Pottery is present during this period among the hunters and gatherers in Central, South, and coastal Texas. Bison hunting was also very important to people living in most regions of the state's present-day boundaries.

NATIVE AMERICANS

Historians have identified hundreds of Native American groups in Texas. The validity of their naming is problematic, however, because explorers used different languages (mainly Spanish, French, and English) to record what they heard of the newly "discovered" tribes they encountered.

Regardless, most historians agree that European diseases decimated Texas's native people. Anthropologist John C. Ewers identified at least 30 major epidemics (mostly smallpox and cholera) that wiped out as much as 95 percent of the state's Native Americans between 1528 and 1890. Until then, the four major tribes playing roles in Texas history were the Apache, Caddo, Comanche, and Kiowa.

The Apaches arrived in the area that would become Texas circa AD 1200. They were a nomadic tribe subsisting almost completely on buffalo, dressing in buffalo skins and living in tents made of tanned and greased hides. The Apaches were a powerful tribe that raided most groups they encountered. Eventually, their aggressive behavior turned their neighbors into enemies, and the Apaches had fled before the Comanches entered the region.

The Caddo were a collection of about 30 distinct groups, including the Tejas Indians, from whom Texas got its name, who had a similar language, political structure, and religious beliefs. Based in the current-day East Texas Piney Woods, the Caddo were mainly agricultural, living in permanent villages (as opposed to being nomadic). They weren't especially warlike, except for minor territorial conflicts they had with smaller nearby tribes over hunting grounds.

The Comanches were known as exceptional equestrians who played a prominent role in Texas frontier history in the 1700s and 1800s. They occupied much of what is now North, Central, and West Texas. Because of their trading skills, the Comanches controlled much of the region's commerce by bartering horses, buffalo products, and even captives for weapons and food. They lived in portable tepees constructed of tanned buffalo hide stretched over as many as 18 large poles.

The Kiowas acquired horses, slaves, and guns from the Spanish and eventually evolved a nomadic, warring lifestyle until they became one of the most feared tribes in the region that became Texas. By the late 1700s, the Kiowas had made a lasting peace with the Comanches and continued to live in the area until peacefully joining the Comanches with the Southern Cheyennes and Arapahos.

Before Texas became a state in 1845, most of the Native American groups were either eradicated by European settlers or moved to reservations in present-day Oklahoma. As a result, only three reservations currently exist in Texas today. They are the Alabama-Coushatta near Houston, the Tigua east of El Paso, and the Kickapoo along the Rio Grande between Del Rio and Laredo.

EUROPEAN EXPLORATION AND SETTLEMENT

The arrival (via shipwreck) of Spanish explorer Alvar Nunez Cabeza de Vaca in 1528 was one of Texas's first contacts with the Old World. His subsequent trek across the land that would become the Lone Star State offered Europeans some of the first clues about this newfound foreign region.

By 1685, the French were in on the action, dispatching explorer Robert Cavelier, Sieur de La Salle to find the mouth of the Mississippi River. He missed it by a long shot, ultimately wrecking his ship *La Belle* in a bay between present-day Houston and Corpus Christi. More than 200 years later, the Texas Historical Commission discovered the contents and remains of *La Belle*, which offered a rare glimpse at the material culture of a 17th-century New World colony in the form of glass trade beads, dinnerware, gunflints, and even a human skeleton.

By the early 1700s, the Spanish had solidified their presence in the region with several new mission buildings (the Alamo being one of them) used primarily to "civilize" the area's Native American tribes by converting them to Christianity. It didn't work as well as they'd hoped. By the early 19th century, European diseases had decimated most of the state's Native Americans, and many tribes had mixed in with other cultural groups, rendering the missions' objective obsolete.

Around this same time, the first wave of Germans arrived in Texas. Word spread quickly about Texas's bountiful land and ideal climate (perhaps they visited in springtime), prompting thousands of Germans to take root along rivers and streams in the state's fertile prairies and scenic hills.

THE REPUBLIC OF TEXAS AND STATEHOOD

An 1835 skirmish between colonists and Mexicans over ownership of a cannon is generally considered the opening battle of the Texas Revolution; subsequently, a provisional government was established in 1836 when delegates adopted the Texas Declaration of Independence on March 2 (which remains a state holiday). Texas's most famous battle occurred a week later with the 13-day siege of the Alamo. Mexican troops led by Gen. Antonio Lopez de Santa Anna eventually killed the remaining Texas defenders.

Later that month, about 350 Texan prisoners were executed by order of Santa Anna at Goliad. With these setbacks in mind, the Texans, led by Sam Houston, defeated Santa Anna's Mexican army on April 21 with rallying cries of "Remember the Alamo!" and "Remember Goliad!" Houston reported 630 Mexican troops killed, with only nine Texan lives lost. The revolution's end became official in May 1836 when both sides signed the Treaties of Velasco.

A year later, the United States, France, and England officially recognized the new Republic of Texas, and plots of land were soon sold in the republic's new capital, named for Stephen F. Austin, the state's preeminent colonist. In 1845, Texas became a U.S. state after Congress passed an annexing resolution, which was accepted by the republic's Texas Constitutional Convention and overwhelmingly supported by Texas voters.

From 1846 to 1848, Texas and Mexico engaged in a boundary battle known as the U.S.-Mexican War, which ultimately established the current international boundary. A decade later, the federal government moved Native American tribes in West and Central Texas to Indian Territory (now Oklahoma).

THE CIVIL WAR AND RECONSTRUCTION

Texas struggled with complexities during the Civil War. Some people supported the Union, including Governor Sam Houston, who refused to take an oath of allegiance to the Confederacy. It eventually cost him his office. For the most part, however, Texans identified with the rest of the southern United States, and in early 1861 that support became official when Texas seceded from the Union and became

the seventh state accepted by the provisional Confederate States of America government.

After four years of border skirmishes, Gulf Coast naval battles, and prisoner of war camps, Texas troops marked the true end of the Civil War with a battle near Brownsville, more than a month after the war officially ended (due to the time involved for the news to reach Texas). In June, it was announced that slavery had been abolished, an event still commemorated today during Juneteenth festivals in African American communities statewide.

Much of Texas's history during the late 1800s centers around the arrival of the railroads, which put towns on and off the map depending on their routes. Cattle rustling was an important part of Texas's commerce and identity before railroads took over the responsibility of moving cattle northward. Texas's development was made possible by the railroads, and they continued to sustain the local economy for decades since so many areas of the state still needed railroad service, including the lower Rio Grande Valley, the South Plains, the Panhandle, and West Texas.

THE 20TH CENTURY AND BEYOND

The 20th century kicked off with a boom—a 100-foot oil gusher blew in at Spindletop near Beaumont in 1901, boosting Texas into the petroleum age. Oil wells would be discovered for several decades, turning small communities into boomtowns with tens of thousands of wildcatters and roughnecks arriving overnight to work on the rigs.

The Wild West arrived in West Texas when the Mexican civil war (1911-1920) spilled across the border; as a result, supply raids and refugee harboring became common occurrences. The notorious Mexican general Pancho Villa was involved with some of these skirmishes.

By the 1950s and 1960s, Texas was gaining a reputation for its intellectual resources, resulting in the Dallas-based development of the integrated circuit (used in semiconductors and electronics) and the opening of the National Aeronautics and Space

Administration's Manned Spacecraft Center in Houston.

In one of the darker moments of Texas and U.S. history, President John F. Kennedy was assassinated in Dallas. It marked the end of the optimism of the nation under the Kennedy administration and ushered in a new president—Texan Lyndon B. Johnson. Johnson would go on to play a major role in advancing the country's civil rights movement. The final two decades of the 20th century were notable for two additional Texans being elected to the U.S. presidency: George H. W. Bush and his son George W. Bush.

Government and Economy

GOVERNMENT

Texas was annexed to the United States as the 28th state on December 29, 1845. From Reconstruction (the late 1800s) through the early 1960s, the Democratic Party dominated Texas politics. Keep in mind, the Democrats of those days differed considerably from the current political party. For almost a century, Texas Democrats consisted mainly of white conservatives, who prevailed in almost all statewide elections.

A Texas-worthy phrase was used during this era to describe the especially dedicated party members: "Yellow Dog Democrats" were the state's die-hard partisan loyalists who would vote for a yellow dog if it ran on the Democratic ticket. The phrase is now used to describe any Democratic loyalist, although the recent dominance of Republicans in Texas is rendering the term nearly obsolete.

Texas's bicameral legislature is comprised of 31 Senate members who serve for four years, and the House of Representatives, with 150 members elected for two-year terms. The legislature meets for its regular session in the spring of odd-numbered years, but the governor may convene a special session for the legislators to address particular issues. The governor of Texas is elected to a four-year term in November of even-numbered, non-presidential election years.

Texas is divided into a whopping 254 counties that average nearly 1,000 square miles in size. West Texas's Brewster County is especially enormous—at 6,169 square miles, it's roughly the size of Delaware and Rhode Island combined.

ECONOMY

Cotton, cattle, and crude (oil)—Texas's venerable "Three Cs" dominated the state's agricultural and economic development until the mid-20th century, and these land-based resources continue to support much of the state's wealth. Other factors contributing to Texas's economy are various industries not exclusive to the Lone Star State, such as retailing, wholesaling, banking, insurance, and construction.

Many national corporate headquarters have relocated to Texas (especially to the midcontinental location of Dallas), and petroleum companies continue to search for new sources of energy to provide fuel. In addition, Houston is home to many federal air installations and the NASA Space Center, while Austin is home to Dell Computers and other esteemed high-tech companies. Tourism has also become a major business, particularly in San Antonio, and Texas has become a leader in the areas of medicine and surgery.

Agriculture

Cattle and cotton remain staples of Texas's agricultural economy. The state's wide-open spaces allowed both commodities to spread freely when settlers arrived in the mid-1800s, and Texas's remaining abundance of available land continues to make it the most important cattle-raising state in the country.

Nearly all of the state's 254 counties derive

more revenue from cattle than any other agricultural commodity; those that don't almost always rank cattle second in importance. Cattle dominates Texas's livestock production, contributing approximately 70 percent of the state's livestock and products sales. And if those aren't enough agricultural accolades, consider this: Texas ranks first nationally in production of cattle, beef cattle, sheep, lamb, wool, goats, and mohair.

Cotton, meanwhile, became a prominent crop due to the immigration of settlers from the Deep South, who continued their plantation system of agriculture when they arrived in Texas. Cotton production grew steadily after 1900, and the crop became a major economic factor when suitable varieties were developed for the West Texas climate. Since that time, Texas has led all states in cotton production virtually every year, and it provides approximately one-quarter of the country's cotton supply.

In total value of farm crops, Texas has consistently ranked in the top five among the states since the mid-20th century and has been a leading producer of grain sorghums, peanuts (groundnuts), and rice. Incidentally, nearly all of the mohair produced in the United States comes from Texas's Angora goats.

Manufacturing and Industry

Texas's manufacturing roots lie with its agricultural processing—cotton gins, cottonseed mills, meatpacking plants, flour mills, oil field equipment, and canning plants. These days, the state's largest employment sector is categorized as the "trade, transportation, and utilities industry," which includes jobs in retail, wholesale, and finance.

Jobs in the petroleum, construction, and service industries are also typically steady across the state. Texas's top exported products are chemicals, petrochemicals, and transportation equipment. The state's remarkable number of exports is attributed to its proximity to Mexico, which receives nearly half of Texas's products. Texas is also responsible for a large number of U.S. exports to Mexico (approximately 50 percent).

Petroleum

Oil changed everything for Texas. It transformed the state from a backwoods frontier to an industrial giant. In January 1901, a gusher blew in at Spindletop near Beaumont, and the Texas oil boom erupted into the nation's consciousness. Thirty years later, an even more significant event occurred—the discovery of the enormous East Texas Oil Field. Within two years, 5,600 wells had been drilled near the cities of Kilgore and Longview, and 25,000 wells were in place by 1938.

Oil became the basis for Texas's mammoth petrochemical industry and provided the funding to develop the state's educational and highway systems. On the flip side, a massive drop in oil prices in the early 1980s resulted in a decline in Texas's economy.

Regardless, oil and natural gas remain the state's most valuable minerals, contributing nearly 20 percent of the country's oil production and 30 percent of its gas production in recent years. Texas leads all other states in oil and natural gas production. It also ranks first in oil-refining capacity. In 2017, Texas accounted for 37 percent of the country's crude oil production and 24 percent of the nation's marketed natural gas production.

Travel

The state's official travel slogan aptly captures its allure: "Texas, It's Like a Whole Other Country." More than 72 million people from out of state visit Texas annually. International travelers account for approximately 10 percent of Texas's total visitor spending.

The five countries with the highest visitation numbers are Mexico, Canada, the United Kingdom, Germany, and France. The top five destination cities for out-of-state visitors are Dallas-Fort Worth, Houston, various "rural Texas destinations," San Antonio, and Austin. Among the top tourist sites include the Alamo, the San Antonio River Walk, the Magnolia properties in Waco, The Texas State Capitol in Austin, and the Six Flags Over Texas amusement park near Dallas.

People and Culture

PEOPLE

The people of Texas equally reflect and defy all stereotypes associated with their dynamic nature. For every good ol' boy set in his ways, there's a progressive genius building her web-based empire. For every brash oilman making millions, there's a humble educator affecting lives. Intense football coaches coexist peacefully with environmental activists.

Like anywhere else, people in Texas have their differences, but there's one thing that transcends obstacles and is unique to this state—the common bond of being Texan. Not that it solves all problems, but most Texans look kindly upon their fellow citizens and genuinely display the spirit of Southern hospitality. It's infectious—"Y'all come back" becomes a true expression of kindness rather than a silly stereotype.

Transplants from the northern and eastern United States may initially be taken aback by random strangers in the grocery store commenting on their purchases, but they'll later find themselves doing the same thing. Offers of assistance are genuine rather than obligatory, and people make direct eye contact when they mutter a polite "Howdy."

There are many ways to categorize Texans—by age, ethnicity, religion, income level, etc.—but labels don't capture the soul of the state's residents, who aptly represent the character of the word *friend* in the origins of the word *Texas*.

Population

Texas's rate of population growth has exceeded the nation's in every decade since Texas became a state (1845), and recent population increases have been substantial. Population has more than doubled in the past 25 years, from roughly 11.2 million to nearly 29 million. Estimates based on recent growth rates suggest the state is surging by nearly 500,000 people annually.

Texas is the second most populous state in the U.S. and it's getting bigger, leading the nation in population growth. According to the most recent estimates by the U.S. Census Bureau, the population of Texas increased by nearly 2 million or 7.2 percent over roughly the past decade.

Interestingly enough, this growth has been anything but uniform, with some counties in West Texas losing population and others around Dallas and Austin growing by more than 60 percent. In fact, recent demographic reports associated reveal that nearly 85 percent of the state's population lives east of the I-35 corridor, which stretches north-south from Dallas to Laredo.

Ethnicity

Since the mid-1800s, most Texas residents have been of European descent, but for the first time in state history, their numbers are no longer the majority. Currently, about 41 percent of the population is of northern European ancestry; roughly 38 percent are Hispanic, and approximately 12 percent are African American.

The healthy pace of Texas's increased population is largely due to international immigration, which represented more than half of the state's population growth in recent years. Of note is the rapid growth of foreign-born residents in Texas's major metro areas compared to border metro cities.

According to recent reports, Hispanics accounted for two-thirds of Texas's growth over the past decade and now represent about 38 percent of the state's total population. Also of interest is the considerably younger age of the state's Hispanic population (approximately 25 years for the median age versus 38 for Anglos). The effect on Texas's population is a statewide median age of 34.

How to Speak Texan

Texas boasts several accents within its borders, from the slowly stretched-out East Texas drawl, to border-hopping Spanglish known as Tex-Mex, to the tight twang of the Panhandle and West Texas.

Even though Texans like to brag about their accomplishments, they can't take credit for the Southern accent that prevails below the Mason-Dixon Line. However, residents of Houston and the Gulf Coast region can claim some of the spice that makes the Southern dialect unique. For the most part, the following examples are found in rural areas of the state, though you'll occasionally hear a "yessir" or "fixin' to" in a downtown urban environment.

Let's start with the obvious: "Howdy, y'all." It's the quintessential Texas/Southern phrase, usually invoked by Northerners with a mocking twang. The truth is, Texans actually say these words often, but usually not together. "Howdy" is typically muttered as a polite greeting as opposed to a loud welcome, and its use as a friendly salutation is one of many cultural traditions taught at Texas A&M University. As for "y'all," it just makes sense—why refer to a group of people (women and children, in particular) as "you guys"? The common Texas phrase "all y'all" takes things to whole new level.

Rural Texans also use "sir" and "ma'am" regularly, just not in a formal or subservient way. It's common to hear men respond to each other with a simple "yessir" or "nosir," and it's just plain polite to express appreciation to someone—a police officer, fellow pedestrian, or store clerk—with a simple "thank you, ma'am." Up North, these terms take on military or old maid connotations, but in Texas it's just being cordial.

Like other Southerners, Texans of all ages refer to their parents as "mother" and "daddy." It's somewhat strange to hear a grown man talk about his "daddy's" influence, but it's charming, nevertheless.

Another Texas phrase that gets the Yankees giggling is "fixin' to." It's a handy term that's quintessentially Southern, indicating someone is getting ready to do something without fully committing to carrying out the task ("I'm fixin' to pay those bills soon"). Incidentally, the "fixin" also refers to food in Texas, garnishes in particular. If you order a burger or barbecue plate with all the fixins, you'll get onions, pickles, peppers, and any number of sides or sauces piled on the plate.

Speaking of food, occasional confusion arises when Texans refer to "dinner" and "supper." These are interchangeable in other parts of the country, but around here, "dinner" can mean lunch, while "supper" almost always refers to the evening meal.

Other examples of Lone Star speak are evident in the pronunciation of words. You can tell a Texan by the way they emphasize the first syllable in words like *umbrella* (UM-brella), *insurance* (IN-surance), and *display* (DIS-play). Others are subtler, like the tendency to flatten out the vowel sounds in words like *mail* (mell), *wheel* (well). Sometimes, entire letters disappear, like the L in "help" ("can I hep ya?").

Finally, you'll occasionally hear Texans using traditional rural sayings like "over yonder" (over there), "pitch a hissy fit" (a dramatic reaction), and even "gaddum" and its derivative "dadgum." Fortunately, Texans are such a friendly bunch, they won't pitch a hissy fit if you sound like a dadgum Yankee.

Religion

For the most part, Texas is a devoutly religious state, with Christianity dominating the spiritual scene. Although it mirrors national trends showing slightly declining congregation numbers, residents in the rural areas of the state remain committed churchgoers. In fact, a 15-county area in Texas's southeastern Panhandle is designated as a candidate for the "buckle of the Bible Belt," a wide band of the entire U.S. South where a majority of people identify themselves as Baptists.

The two primary religious groups in Texas are Baptist (approximately 22 percent) and Catholic (roughly 21 percent). The percentages are far lower for other religions—Muslim, Hindu, Buddhist, Jewish, and other faiths—which are mostly located in the state's urban areas. Texas's big cities also had the largest number of people claiming not to be affiliated with a religious group.

Language

English speakers in Texas account for 65 percent of the population, with Spanish running a distant, yet still notable second (29 percent). People speak Vietnamese and German in a few small pockets of the state, but for the most part, it's Spanish and English (and a few interesting varieties of the two).

A fair number of Hispanics in South Texas speak an unofficial language known as Tex-Mex, which combines Spanish and English words without any rigid guidelines determining when to use each. It's a distinctive regional practice, resulting from an impulsive tendency to toss in an English or Spanish word when the translation isn't immediately on the tip of the tongue, and it's most evident on Tejano radio stations in Corpus Christi and the Lower Rio Grande Valley, where rapid-fire DJs pepper their announcements in Spanish with random yet instantly recognizable English words.

Learning to speak Texan is an entirely different endeavor. Though the dialect sounds Southern on the surface, there are distinct variations in different parts of the state. In East Texas, vowels are more drawn out, and the slower cadence includes inflections of the Deep South. People in West Texas, meanwhile, speak with more of a tight twang. Pronunciation of the word *Texas* is an example—in East Texas, it can sound like "Tay-ux-us," and in West Texas it's often pronounced "Tix-is."

Just to make things interesting, young adults in the state's metropolitan areas tend to combine elements of their own Texas dialect with California's. Dallas-born actor Owen Wilson's accent is the quintessential example of this style of speech.

ARTS AND CULTURE

One of the specialty license plates available to Texans features a bold image of the state flag with the phrase "State of the Arts" at the bottom. This motto might not be the first attribute people associate with Texas (California and New York immediately jump to mind), but it's absolutely befitting of the Lone Star State.

Hundreds of world-renowned writers, artists, musicians, and actors call Texas home, and their influences and styles are as far-reaching as the stars in the West Texas sky.

a shrine in Port Arthur

Having 4 of the country's 10 largest cities also helps maximize exposure for artists and art aficionados. Premier exhibits and tours always include Texas on their schedule, and the dynamic magnetism of the state itself serves as an inspiration for a diverse mixture of creative endeavors. Anywhere that can claim Pulitzer Prize-winning (and Oscar-winning) writer Larry McMurtry and alternative rockers the Butthole Surfers is bound to be brimming with eclectic culture.

Literature

Larry McMurtry, famed author of the cattle-drive epic *Lonesome Dove* and drama *Terms of Endearment,* as well as screenplay writer for *The Last Picture Show* and *Brokeback Mountain,* is emblematic of the literary state of Texas. He approaches his craft with the sweeping majesty of one of his favorite subjects—the mythic Old West, with Texas as a focal point.

Another celebrated literary genre in Texas is folklore, and J. Frank Dobie (1888-1964) was and still is considered the foremost figure in the field. Dobie painted fascinating portraits of cowboys, cattlemen, hunters, and countless other Texas characters and critters. From an intellectual perspective, many Texans cite Pulitzer Prize-winning journalist, essayist, short story writer, and novelist Katherine Anne Porter (1890-1980) as the state's most accomplished writer. She is perhaps best known for her acute insight about complex subjects in her works *Pale Horse, Pale Rider* (1939) and *Ship of Fools* (1961).

An essential book about Texas by a non-Texan is H. G. Bissinger's *Friday Night Lights: A Town, A Team, A Dream* (1990), which accurately and compellingly chronicles the positive and negative aspects of Texas's passion for high school football. Texas journalist Molly Ivins (1944-2007) gained national fame as a sharp and scathing critic of the country's right-wing political movement in the early part of the 21st century. President George W. Bush was a frequent Ivins target, and her book *Bushwhacked: Life in George W. Bush's America,* was a success in liberal enclaves of the United States and especially her hometown of Austin. The latest legendary tome is 2013's The Son by Philipp Meyer. This incredible story, a finalist for the Pulitzer Prize in 2014, chronicles 200 years of Texas history through the fictional account of a powerful Texas family. Texas can even make a (partial) claim to acclaimed writer George Saunders, an Amarillo native, whose 2017 novel Lincoln in the Bardo is considered by many a modern-day classic.

Music

Texas has perhaps the most compelling music legacy in the country, and many of the state's artists have become influential figures in popular music history. Texans have contributed essential volumes to the world's music catalog by introducing and refining styles such as rhythm and blues, Western swing, Tejano, country, and rock. The state's musical giants are recognizable by a single name—Buddy, Janis, Willie, Selena, and Beyonce—and each have influenced generations of future musicians while getting plenty of boots scootin' and toes tappin' in the process.

Texas's documented musical history began with its initial wave of settlers in the late 1800s. A fascinating mix of cultures, including German, African American, Czechoslovakian, Mexican, and Anglo, resulted in an equally intriguing blend of musical styles. The best-known types of music in the U.S. South—blues and country—evolved into new and intriguing genres when accompanied by a Texas twist. Appalachian "fiddle music" migrated westward with pioneers and merged with distinctly Texan influences such as yodeling, accordions, and 12-string guitar, resulting in unique styles such as Western swing, conjunto, and rockabilly.

One of Texas's most influential musicians was Blind Lemon Jefferson, who introduced his signature country blues in the 1920s with his raw, potent track "Black Snake Moan." Borrowing the flamenco-influenced guitar work he heard from Mexican migrant

Texas in Song

Texas is immortalized in song perhaps more than any other state. Several sources list nearly 100 tunes with *Texas* (or *Lone Star* or Texas cities) in the title.

With all the options to choose from, it's unfortunate the official state song, "Texas, Our Texas," is unrecognizable by most people, including some Texans. Adopted by the legislature after being selected in a statewide competition, the song features inspirational (and poorly written) lyrics with simple rhymes like "all hail the mighty state" paired with "so wonderful, so great."

Our country's national anthem is rather difficult to sing due to its extremely wide tonal range and occasionally confusing lyrics, so Texas's official state song should be something recognizable and easy on the vocal chords. Some Texans have even proposed adopting an updated official tune to rouse the troops at athletic competitions and school or government events.

There are plenty to choose from, including iconic classics such as "Deep in the Heart of Texas," made famous by Gene Autry (and Pee Wee Herman); "The Yellow Rose of Texas," as performed by Bob Wills; Ernest Tubb's version of "Waltz Across Texas"; or even the fiddle-filled old-school dance craze "Cotton Eyed Joe." Collegiately patriotic Texans will insist their school fight songs are the most iconic Texas tunes, particularly "The Eyes of Texas" (University of Texas) and the "Aggie War Hymn" (Texas A&M University).

The 1970s were a golden time for Texas-themed songs, particularly in the country music scene. Though the following options haven't attained "official song" consideration status, they're known well enough in pop culture as ambassadors of Texas mystique. Highlights include Willie Nelson's adaptation of "San Antonio Rose," Marty Robbins's "(Out in the West Texas town of) El Paso," "Streets of Laredo" by Buck Owens, "Luckenbach, Texas (Back to The Basics of Love)" by Waylon Jennings, Glen Campbell's "Galveston," ZZ Top's "La Grange," and a couple of George Strait classics, "Amarillo by Morning" and "All My Exes Live in Texas." Unfortunately, there's also Alabama's hit, "If You're Gonna Play in Texas (You Gotta Have a Fiddle in the Band)."

The Texas-themed songs haven't been quite as prolific lately, but the state's music scene remains vital. Perhaps in the near future we'll see a remixed version of a Texas classic or a new Lone Star legend penned by one of Austin's indie rock sensations. Stay tuned.

---

workers, Jefferson's fast fingers and ear for melody inspired fellow Texas blues legends Huddy "Leadbelly" Ledbetter and Lightnin' Hopkins. Their work paved the way for generations of Texas blues heroes, including Albert Collins, Freddy King, Clarence "Gatemouth" Brown, and Buddy Guy. Legendary Austinite Stevie Ray Vaughan led a blues revival in the 1980s with his soulful guitar wizardry, scoring national hits with albums *Couldn't Stand the Weather* and *In Step* before he was tragically killed in a 1990 helicopter crash at the age of 35.

A wholly distinct sound from Texas is conjunto music (aka Tejano, Tex-Mex, norteno), which combines accordion and 12-string guitar to produce lively dance melodies with South Texas soul. The style originated with Texas and Mexican working-class musicians who adopted the accordion and the polka from 19th-century German settlers. Conjunto music was popular along the Rio Grande and throughout Latin America for decades before artists began reaching larger audiences in the late 1960s. The genre's best-known artist is Leonardo "Flaco" Jiménez, who has performed with renowned acts such as the Rolling Stones, Bob Dylan, Willie Nelson, Buck Owens, and Carlos Santana. An underappreciated Mexican-influenced style, dubbed "Chicano soul" or the "San Antonio West Side sound," emerged from the late-1950s influences of rhythm and blues and doo-wop. The instantly catchy sound represented an innovative blend of soulful Motown-style harmonies and melodies with Mexican-influenced accents from brass and reed instruments.

Although country music has its true origins in Anglo-based folk balladry, Texans took the style and made it their own. Several of country music's offshoots are Texas products, including Western swing, honky-tonk, and outlaw country. Bob Wills pioneered the jazz-based Western swing style of music in the 1920s, and Ernest Tubb's walking bass lines were a crucial component of 1940s honky-tonk country. In the late 1960s, Austin became the laid-back capital of outlaw country in response to the slick, produced material coming out of Nashville. A raw and loose version of country music emanated from the city's storied Armadillo World Headquarters, which regularly featured legendary outlaws like Willie Nelson, Waylon Jennings, and Jerry Jeff Walker. Overall, Texas's contributors to country music reads like a track listing from the style's greatest hits: Gene Autry, Buck Owens, George Jones, Kenny Rogers, Larry Gatlin, Barbara Mandrell, Townes Van Zandt, Kris Kristofferson, George Strait, Mark Chestnutt, Lyle Lovett, and Pat Green (and that's just volume one).

Rock 'n' roll also received a big ol' Texas brand on it during its formative years. Lubbock's Buddy Holly and the Crickets refined the country-blues style into a distinct rockabilly sound, which influenced the Beatles in ways far beyond their insect-inspired name. Another West Texan, Roy Orbison, made an impact in Memphis with a smoother approach to rockabilly. Port Arthur's Janis Joplin wowed Austin with her bluesy swagger in the late 1960s before moving to San Francisco, where she played a major role in solidifying the city's psychedelic sound. In the 1970s, Texas contributed to the future classic rock scene with artists such as the Steve Miller Band, ZZ Top, and Don Henley (of The Eagles).

During the past 20 years, Texans have continued to make their marks on myriad musical styles. Selena Quintanilla-Perez (1971-1995), known simply as Selena, led a surge in the Latino music scene's popularity in the early 1990s with her dancy pop tunes that drew thousands of converts to her spirited shows. The Dixie Chicks rose from relative obscurity to become one of the world's most popular country music acts with a sound inspired by traditional country, folk, and bluegrass. Their album *Wide Open Spaces* sold 12 million copies, becoming the best-selling album in country music history from a duo or group. Other significant Texas contributions to contemporary music in the early 21st century were Houston acts like Destiny's Child, Dallas songstress Kelly Clarkson, Fort Worth soulster Leon Bridges, northeast Texas native Kacey Musgraves, and artists from Austin such as Spoon, Explosions in the Sky, and Gary Clark Jr.

Film

More than 1,300 film projects have been made in Texas since 1910, including *Wings,* the first film to win an Academy Award for Best Picture (made in San Antonio in 1927). Film production in Texas has been a vital part of the state's economy for decades, bringing thousands of jobs and hundreds of millions of dollars to the state each year.

With mild winters and more than 267,000 square miles of diverse landscape to work with, Texas is an extremely versatile place to shoot movies, TV shows, music videos, commercials, and other independent film projects. Texas locations have doubled for the American Midwest; Mexico; Washington, D.C.; Vietnam; Afghanistan; Bolivia; Africa; Florida; and a host of other places throughout the world.

The Texas Film Commission, a division of the governor's office, lends filmmakers a hand by providing free information on locations, crews, talent, state and local contacts, weather, laws, sales tax exemptions, housing, and other film-related issues. The assistance certainly pays off, with the state receiving more than $2 billion in film-related expenditures during the past decade.

Filmmakers look kindly upon Texas because the state has experienced crew members, equipment vendors, and support services. On most features shot in Texas, 75 percent of the crew is hired locally, and the production company is exempt from state and local sales taxes on most of the services and items they rent or purchase. In addition, Texas has several regional film offices that court the major studios and provide production assistance.

Dozens of acclaimed and influential films have been shot on location in Texas (of the hundreds of projects completed), and several have become celluloid classics. Most notable are the 1956 movie *Giant,* starring Elizabeth Taylor, Rock Hudson, and James Dean, and John Wayne's 1960 film *The Alamo. Giant* was filmed in West Texas, and its legacy is still celebrated in Marfa, where the stately 1930 Hotel Paisano served as home base for the cast and crew. A glass case in the lobby displays movie-related magazine clippings and photos, and guests clamor to stay in James Dean's hotel room.

Other significant film projects shot in Texas include *The Last Picture Show* (1971, screenplay by Texan Larry McMurtry), *The Texas Chainsaw Massacre* (1973), *Urban Cowboy* (1979), *Terms of Endearment* (1983, based on McMurtry's novel), David Byrne's brilliant *True Stories* (1986), McMurtry's *Lonesome Dove* (1990), Austinite Richard Linklater's generation-defining *Slacker* (1990), David Lynch's *Wild at Heart* (1990), Austinite Robert Rodriguez's groundbreaking *El Mariachi* (1992), Linklater's classic *Dazed and Confused* (1992), Christopher Guest's hilarious *Waiting for Guffman* (1995), Dallas native Wes Anderson's masterpiece *Rushmore* (1997), Steven Soderbergh's *Traffic* (2000), Rodriguez's *Predators* (2010), Terence Malick's *The Tree of Life* (2011), *Texas Chainsaw 3D* (2012), *Transformers 4* (2013), and *Boyhood* (2014).

In addition to its mighty movie credits, Texas has hosted noteworthy television shows. Perhaps most significant of them all is *Dallas* (1978-1990, and again in 2013), which entranced audiences around the globe with its Texas-worthy dramatic storylines centered around oil magnate J. R. Ewing and his family. Equally as remarkable yet more artistically viable is PBS's venerable *Austin City Limits* (1975-present), showcasing top-notch country, roots, and alternative music across the United States and spawning its thriving annual music festival. In 2011, the program made a dramatic venue change, from the University of Texas's communications building to a swanky new theater on the ground floor of the upscale W hotel. Other notable Texas TV shows include Office Space (1999), NBC's critically acclaimed *Friday Night Lights* (2006-2011), HBO's *The Leftovers* (2014-2017), Netflix's documentary Cheer (2019), and finally, in the bizarro category, *Barney and Friends,* filmed in Dallas (1992-2010).

Visual Arts

The visual arts scene in Texas is particularly captivating, due in large part to available funding from the state's land and oil barons. World-class artwork is regularly exhibited throughout Texas in big cities and small towns, where philanthropists give generously to construct ornate museums and draw exceptional exhibits.

In addition, the Texas Commission on the Arts state agency funds education and cultural programs. Its grants help fund projects to educate Texas citizens about the importance of art, and the agency has been lauded for its work with at-risk youth and children with disabilities.

For the most part, Texas's fine arts opportunities are located in its metropolitan areas. Some of the country's best art museums are in Houston and Dallas-Fort Worth. Of particular note is Fort Worth's Kimbell Museum, where the facility housing the artwork is as impressive as the work it holds. Designed by architect Louis I. Kahn, its softly arching ceilings provide the perfect amount of natural light to complement the interior artwork by masters such as Picasso, Monet, Rembrandt, El Greco, Cézanne, and others in addition to its impressive collections of Asian and African art.

Other must-see art museums in Fort Worth are the Amon Carter Museum, showcasing high-quality Western art (Georgia O'Keeffe, Ansel Adams, Winslow Homer), and The Modern Art Museum of Fort Worth, a glass structure designed by famed Japanese architect Tadao Ando that seems to float in a surrounding shimmering pool. Inside are more than 26,000 works by renowned artists such as Picasso, Andy Warhol, and Jackson Pollock.

Dallas's premier art attraction, the Dallas Museum of Art, features an impressive $32 million two-acre sculpture garden showcasing the work of Miró, Rodin, Moore, de Kooning, and many others. The facility is also known for its Museum of the Americas, which showcases an impressive collection of historic art from North, Central, and South America.

Houston is the other main hub for Texas's fine arts, with nearly 20 major museums and galleries. The city's Museum of Fine Arts houses approximately 31,000 works of American, European, Latin American, Native American, and Asian art spanning 4,000 years. Its concentration is on the Renaissance and impressionism, but there are treasures hiding around every corner, especially the primitive Native American pieces.

Other worthy Houston museums are the Contemporary Arts Museum, which rotates exhibits every six weeks, offering visitors a fresh experience year-round, and the Menil Collection, which features rotating displays along with its permanent 10,000-piece collection including a stunning mix of styles, from African and Byzantine to surrealist and contemporary.

Essentials

Transportation.........492
Sports and Recreation..495
Food 498
Travel Tips 500
Health and Safety......501
Information and
    Services 502

Transportation

GETTING THERE

Texas is far removed from the transportation hubs on the East and West Coasts, but it's easily accessible by plane and relatively so by car.

Air

Texas is easy to get to by air because its two largest cities—Houston and Dallas—are primary hubs for major airlines (United and American, respectively). As a result, flights from all over the country wind up in the Lone Star State, often at affordable rates. Texas's other major

cities—Austin, San Antonio, and El Paso—have international airports, but the nonstop flights from points beyond aren't nearly as frequent (or cheap). Even Texas's smaller cities (populations of 100,000 or greater) have airports, but you'll have to go through Dallas or Houston to get there.

Car

The interstate highway system in Texas is pretty impressive for a state this huge. You can get from most major cities to the others (excluding El Paso) by noon. The roads tend to be in good shape since they don't often experience icy conditions, but as in most states, construction is a perpetual issue in Texas's metro areas. Increased truck traffic from Mexico has taken its toll on some of the freeways, and rural roads between smaller cities can get a bit rough, but that doesn't deter Texans from going 90 mph. The Texas Department of Transportation (www.txdot.gov) oversees all aspects of vehicular travel.

Train

Be forewarned: Traveling by train in Texas is not nearly as charming as it sounds. Trains stop frequently between destinations and for long periods of time. The trip from Austin to Fort Worth can take as long as nine hours—the same trek is about three hours by car. Unfortunately, the fares aren't usually low enough to make the extra time worthwhile. One of the few trips recommended by some train travelers is the scenic trek to far West Texas (Alpine and beyond to El Paso), even though it can take up to 24 hours to get there. For more information, contact Amtrak at www.amtrak.com or 800/872-7245.

Bus

For the most convenient scheduling system and affordable fares from other parts of the country, leave the driving to **Greyhound** (800/231-2222, www.greyhound.com). The venerable Dallas-based bus line has an easily navigable online reservation system (not always the case with bus companies) and hosts bus stops in cities across the country. Fares tend to run about half the price of a plane ticket, often a welcome option for travelers on a tight budget (and willing to make the trip in more time with less glamour). Greyhound can assist travelers with fares and schedules via email (ifsr@greyhound.com) and can serve Spanish-speaking travelers via phone (800/531-5332).

Boat

Texas's Gulf Coast has several major shipping ports, including Houston, Galveston, Corpus Christi, Beaumont, and Brownsville. Virtually all the activity is industrial, but cruise ships occasionally dock in Houston and Galveston. Contact the cruise lines (Carnival, Royal Caribbean, etc.) to see if they plan voyages to the Lone Star State.

GETTING AROUND

Texans love their cars—and trucks. In a state this big, a vehicle is virtually a necessity, despite some advances in metropolitan public transportation systems. To get anywhere in Texas's sprawling cities and widespread landscape, a vehicle is the most practical approach. In fact, the state is so spread out, travelers occasionally hop on planes to get from place to place. The drive from Lubbock to Corpus Christi would take about 13 hours by car but only 2 hours via plane. Other small cities with airports include Tyler, Waco, San Angelo, Amarillo, and Brownsville.

Car

Texas's major interstates are well maintained, and drivers are largely courteous, if a bit lead footed. The stretch of I-35 between Dallas and Austin is a racetrack, with cars and semi trucks regularly buzzing along at a 90 mph clip. That being said, some Texas drivers are notorious for hanging in the passing lane at 55 mph, forcing cars to line up behind them and pass on the right when there's a break in the "fast" lane. The true Lone Star autobahn experience is in far West Texas, where the posted speed limit is 80 mph, meaning drivers will go even faster since patrol cars are as abundant as trees out there. Incidentally, freeway ramps are unpredictable in Texas—some are only a few hundred yards short, while others seem to stretch for miles. Once you're off the interstate, be sure to keep an eye out for police, since some small Texas towns rely on speeding ticket fines to help fund their municipal budgets.

TOLL ROADS

Unlike other states with well-established turnpike and tollway systems, Texas is relatively new to the fees-for-freeways concept. Small stretches of highways in Dallas and Houston have charged tolls for decades, but only recently have other cities (Austin and Tyler) jumped on board.

For the most part, the tollways are welcome (unless they're placed or proposed on a previously public road) because they ease congestion on busy nearby interstates. Still, they rub some Texans the wrong way and can be underused due to perceived expense. The Texas Department of Transportation's system is surprisingly convenient and innovative (yet occasionally confusing), with electronic gates allowing drivers to cruise through the tolls and receive a bill in the mail several weeks later. Fees are reasonable: from 75 cents to several dollars, depending on the length of the toll road.

If you're renting a vehicle, be sure to ask the rental company if they have a toll tag or if you can purchase a prepaid tag. Otherwise, you may be unpleasantly surprised to later find you've been charged a $50 "convenience" fee for the company to handle the arrangements. If you don't have a tag, be sure to look for the highway signs letting you know if there's an option for paying an actual person at a toll gate; otherwise, you may want to take a more convenient route on a true freeway.

Bike

Texas has a considerable number of bicyclists, but its roadways aren't considered very bike-friendly. The best spots for riding are municipal and state parks, which contain well-designed and scenic hike and bike trails. The state's tremendous geographical diversity allows for a good variety of terrain, and several Texas locales—Palo Duro Canyon and the Hill Country, in particular—are major destinations for serious mountain bikers from across the country.

Bus

For those interested in traversing Texas by bus, it's worth contacting **Trailways** (319/753-2864, www.trailways.com). The company operates eight regional routes in Texas, offering passengers the option of making personalized trips using independently operated bus companies. This is an ideal option for travelers interested in exploring cities or smaller towns at their own pace without having to rely on a major bus tour operation with existing (and less-than-adventurous) itineraries. In addition, **Greyhound** (www.greyhound.com, 800/231-2222) has over 150 bus stations and stops throughout Texas.

Public Transportation

With so many "new" cities (less than 150 years old), Texas is known more for its sprawl than dense metropolitan environs. Unlike long-standing urban areas on the East Coast and in the Midwest with well-established subway and train-based transit lines, Texas's cities have traditionally used buses for public transportation. Light-rail can be a challenging system to incorporate on established traffic grids, but it's been successful in several cities, Dallas and Houston in particular. To find out more about public transportation options in Texas's major urban environments, visit the following websites: **Austin** (www.capmetro.org), **Corpus Christi** (www.ccrta.org), **Dallas** (www.dart.org), **El Paso** (www.elpasotexas. gov), **Fort Worth** (www.ridetrinitymetro. org), **Houston** (www.ridemetro.org), and **San Antonio** (www.viainfo.net).

Sports and Recreation

Texans spend a lot of time enjoying outdoor activities, despite the intolerably hot summers. For sports, football is the undisputed king, but baseball, basketball, and golf are also popular since they can be played year-round. The state's mild climate also allows nonprofessional (recreational) sporting activities to continue throughout the year. Campers, hikers, and mountain bikers flock to state and local parks year-round—in summer for the lower humidity and higher altitudes of far West Texas and in winter for the warm tropical climate of the Gulf Coast and Rio Grande Valley. The *Sports and Recreation* and *Camping* sections for specific cities in this guide provide detailed information about available resources.

Professional sports are a major attraction in Texas (the *Sports and Recreation* sections in the metropolitan areas contain detailed information). Most Texans are fans of the Dallas Cowboys (there are some Houston Texans supporters), but loyalties are divided by region when it comes to professional baseball (the Houston Astros or Arlington's Texas Rangers) and basketball (Dallas Mavericks, San Antonio Spurs, or Houston Rockets).

High school football is a religion in Texas (it's the inspiration for *Friday Night Lights* after all), but the most passionate fans in the state follow college sports. The University of Texas versus Texas A&M University rivalry is one of the fiercest in the nation, and Texas's sheer size allows for serious intrastate competition among several large schools (Texas Tech University, Baylor University, University of Texas at El Paso, Texas State University, etc.).

ECOTOURISM

One of the most popular ecotourism destinations in the country is emerging in South Texas, particularly the Lower Rio Grande Valley. The Valley's immense biodiversity and ecological complexity make it a natural crossing point for migratory birds, which traverse the region each fall and spring en route to and from their winter homes in the tropics.

Much like the birds that arrive in the Valley from the East Coast and Midwest, the birders who track and document their feathered friends flock from across the country in search of their favorite and rare species. The McAllen area is home to several acclaimed birding sites catering to the thousands of ecotourists who arrive annually, including the World Birding Center's **Quinta Mazatlan,** the highly regarded **Santa Ana National Wildlife Refuge,** and the **Bentsen-Rio Grande Valley State Park.** These parks retain the region's natural state by maintaining the distinctive woodlands, which draw species popular with the birding crowd, such as chacalacas, green jays, and broad-winged hawks.

STATE PARKS

The Texas Parks and Wildlife Department operates nearly 100 state parks (including natural areas and historic sites), which may sound like a lot at first but doesn't represent much of the state's geographic area. In fact, according to the state government, Texas has a total land area of 167.5 million acres, and the state parks' 586,501 total acres occupy one-third of 1 percent of that total.

Regardless, the state's enormous geographical diversity is aptly represented at the parks, from northern lakes to southern tropics and from western mountains to eastern forests. The largest park in the state's system is in the Panhandle region—the magnificent Palo Duro Canyon, at 26,275 acres (representing the country's second-largest canyon). The smallest is in West Texas—Balmorhea, at 46 acres (a spring-fed oasis near the Davis Mountains).

The most popular parks are in or near metropolitan areas. Recent figures show the state's most-visited parks were Cedar Hill State Park in Dallas County, San Jacinto Battleground in Harris County near Houston, and Goose Island State Park in Aransas County on the Gulf Coast. If you're planning to camp at these parks, it's highly recommended to make reservations several weeks in advance, since they're often fully booked and will turn away visitors at the gate. Incidentally, for those interested, the least-visited park was Devil's River State Natural Area in southwestern Texas.

Making Campground Reservations

As in many other states, funding for parks is scarce in Texas, but the Parks and Wildlife Department manages to run a decent operation with limited resources. For years, Texans complained mightily about the hassles of making campground reservations via antiquated systems such as phones. TPWD's online reservation system (http://texas.reserveworld.com), has provided added convenience.

Exploring Texas's Backcountry

For some, camping doesn't require a car or on-site gift shop. Backcountry camping is available across the state and, because of the varying geography, can be interpreted in different ways.

Traditionally, backcountry or primitive camping involves pitching a tent in an undeveloped, secluded area accessible only by foot without any amenities (except perhaps a fire pit). In Texas, this typically means an excursion in the western portions of the state (Bandera's Hill Country State Natural Area is a particularly popular destination), where campers can experience nature without the interference of adjacent campers and nearby highways. The definition of *backcountry* is expanded a bit in far West Texas, where campers can take a secluded mountain trail in Big Bend National Park, or even along the coasts, where the term encompasses beach camping in undeveloped areas.

For these types of excursions, most state parks require backcountry campers to register at the reservation desk to ensure their safety (if campers don't return by the expected date/time, park rangers can check on them). To find out more about a park's policies, visit www.tpwd.state.tx.us.

FISHING

Like other outdoor activities in Texas, fishing is a popular recreational endeavor due to the

paddling in the Texas Hill Country

mild year-round temperatures. The Lone Star State is also well known in angler circles for its freshwater reservoirs and streams packed with largemouth bass, smallmouth bass, crappie, panfish (bluegill, sunfish), and catfish, as well as the draw of the Gulf Coast's tarpon, amberjack, red drum, and spotted sea trout.

For recommendations about the best places to cast a line in Texas's fishing hot spots (along the Gulf Coast and in the reservoirs in East Texas's national forests), consult the appropriate regional sections in this guide. For detailed information about fishing reports, tides, and advisories, visit the Texas Park and Wildlife Department's comprehensive website (www.tpwd.texas.gov).

Since Texas is so big and fishing is so popular, there are nearly 1,700 locations to obtain a license (a requirement). Anglers can purchase a license at most bait and tackle shops, as well as local sporting goods stores, grocery stores, and even some department stores. Recreational licenses are available on a daily basis (fees vary by location, but usually cost around $7) or with an annual permit ($30 for freshwater, $35 saltwater, $40 "all-water"). These licenses can also be purchased in advance by phone (800/895-4248 Mon.-Fri. 8am-5pm) or via TPWD's website. In addition, the site offers a handy service that identifies the nearest local license vendor based on the city.

HUNTING

Hunting is huge in Texas, and the state's sheer size provides countless opportunities to grab a gun and wait patiently for your critter of choice. Deer hunting is one of the biggest draws, and deer season has a major cultural and economic impact on much of the state. Pick up a community newspaper during the winter, and you'll find plenty of photos of hunters, ranging in age from 8 to 88, in the back of their pickups proudly displaying the rack of the buck they just killed.

In general, Texas offers something for every kind of hunter, from waterfowl along the Gulf Coast to quail and pheasant in South Texas to feral hogs in East Texas to antelope in the Panhandle. The best place to find all the information you'll ever need about hunting in Texas—seasons, permits, regulations, restrictions, hunting lodges, and hunting leases—is the Texas Parks and Wildlife Department's website (www.tpwd.state.tx.us).

Like fishing licenses, Texas's hunting licenses are required and can be obtained at 1,700 locations across the state. Hunters can purchase a license at a local gun shop, sporting goods store, grocery store, or department store. Resident licenses are available for $25 (fees for out-of-staters are slightly higher) and allow hunting of "any legal bird or animal (terrestrial vertebrates)." The licenses can also be purchased in advance by phone (800/895-4248 Mon.-Fri. 8am-5pm) or via TPWD's website. As with the fishing licenses, the website offers a service that identifies local vendors based on the closest city.

Though most locals are well versed in the procedures associated with field dressing and transporting a deer after it's been killed, visitors may need a crash course on the state's requirements. To find out everything you need to know about appropriate tags, processing (four quarters and two backstraps), and keeping the deer in "edible condition," visit www.tpwd.texas.gov.

Food

Food lovers love Texas. Turn on the Food Network, and you'll probably soon be watching a feature about Texas barbecue, the many varieties of Mexican food in Texas, or recipes for the perfect Lone Star chili. The following types of cuisine are represented in the *Food* sections of virtually every city in this guide, but here's a quick overview of how they came to be culinary icons in Texas.

BARBECUE

The prime representation of Texas cuisine, barbecue is all about the meat—beef (brisket and ribs), pork (sausage, ribs, and chops), and turkey, chicken, mutton, goat, or anything else a Texan can put in a barbecue smoker. The tradition originated in the Caribbean as a method to cook meat over a pit on a framework of sticks known as a *barbacot*, and it eventually made its way across the southern United States, where it picked up various cultural influences on the way. Even in Texas there are several different methods for barbecuing meat, and there's plenty of debate about who does it the right way. Fortunately, everyone wins since all styles of Texas barbecue are exceptionally pleasing to the palate.

In general, the East Texas approach is aligned with delectable African American traditions of the South—the sauce is tomato based and somewhat sweet, and the sides (potato salad and coleslaw, in particular) are mayo based and sweet. Central Texas-style 'cue is considered the ideal representative of the Lone Star State, originating in the German and Czech communities in the Austin area. Based on traditions from European meat markets, the sausage and beef are smoked and served on waxed paper along with side items inspired by the former grocery store/butcher shops where they originated—bread slices, beans, tomatoes, cheese, and jalapeños. In West Texas, some restaurants and ranches still serve their meat "cowboy style," where an entire slab of beef is cooked over hot coals on open pits and basted with a "mop" of oil and vinegar.

Peel-and-eat shrimp is a classic Texas Gulf Coast seafood dish.

TEX-MEX

For most people, Mexican food means tacos, burritos, and nachos. In Texas, Mexican food can mean a variety of things—cuisine from the interior of Mexico with savory sauces and various meats, Southwestern-style Mexican food with green chiles and blue corn, or border-inspired Tex-Mex with gooey cheese, seasoned beef, and tortillas.

Though interior Mexican food is certainly worth sampling if you can find an authentic restaurant, it's Tex-Mex that prevails in Texas, and it's not hard to find a good representation of this regional comfort food in most cities across the state. In fact, mom-and-pop Tex-Mex restaurants are much like Italian eateries on the East Coast and in the Midwest—the best food is often in the most unassuming spot, like a strip mall or small house on a side street.

The main ingredients in Tex-Mex are ground beef, chicken, cheese, pinto beans, and tortillas. These items are combined differently for tasty variations, including a crispy or soft beef taco; a beef, cheese, or chicken enchilada; a bean chalupa; cheese quesadilla; or beef and chicken fajitas. Salsa, guacamole, lettuce, tomato, and sour cream are typically added as flavorful accompaniments.

SOUTHERN

Texas doesn't hold exclusive rights to this category, but Southern food is considered somewhat exotic to more than half the country, and, like just about everything else, Texas puts its own distinct spin on this style of down-home country cuisine.

It's unfair to generalize Southern cooking as being mostly fried, even though a good portion of it is encased in crispy goodness (just not always of the deep-fried variety). One of the best examples of Southern cookin' done right in Texas is chicken-fried steak, a thin cut of cube steak that's tenderized, breaded in egg batter or a seasoned flour mixture, pan fried in lard or vegetable oil, and served smothered in peppered cream gravy. The name likely refers to the similar process used in frying chicken. Other fried favorites include pork chops, catfish, okra, and chicken.

Another Southern cooking tendency is to include meat in veggie dishes (vegetarians should consider themselves warned). Beans, greens, and black-eyed peas are often spruced up with ham hock or bacon, and lard or bacon grease can add an extra dimension of flavor to just about any vegetable or bread recipe. Incidentally, if you order tea in a Texas restaurant, you'll get iced tea (occasionally sweetened), and you should never skip an opportunity to order a fruit cobbler or pecan pie for dessert.

CHILI

Texans take their chili seriously—maybe too seriously. But since Texans claim bragging rights to many things, it should be no surprise they profess to have the best chili, too. The main point of pride with the Texas variety is the absence of beans. It's meat and spices only. Beans are for wimps and Yankees.

There's no denying the results, however. A meat-based chili puts the emphasis where it belongs, on tender beef (occasionally venison) enhanced by a blend of fiery peppers and flavorful seasonings like garlic, onions, and oregano. Chili cook-offs are traditionally cultural celebrations in Texas towns, and winners become local celebrities. In fact, the granddaddy of all chili competitions, the Original Terlingua International Championship Chili Cook-Off, held near Big Bend each year, draws hundreds of renowned chili "chefs" by invitation only from across the country, much to the delight of the thousands of chili-heads in attendance.

Not surprisingly, Texans claim to have the original chili recipe, though food historians trace the dish to Incan, Aztec, and Mayan cultures. The Texas connection is tied to Canary Islanders, who arrived in San Antonio in the early 1700s with traditional meals of meat blended with herbs, garlic, wild onions, and other veggies, including pungent local peppers. These days, Texans typically opt to prepare their chili at home, since restaurants could never duplicate the perfect combination of ingredients passed down through the generations in family recipes.

Travel Tips

For the most part, traveling in Texas is similar to traveling in the rest of the United States, with the main exception being issues associated with crossing the Mexican border (which is avoided by most people these days). Otherwise, it's smooth sailing across state lines, with visitor information centers located on the Texas side of most major freeways entering the state.

BORDER CROSSING

Years ago, people were able to easily cross the Rio Grande sans passport or auto insurance, free to roam Mexican border towns. These days, people in border communities are wary of the violence across the border associated with warring drug cartels, even though they remain safe on the Texas side.

The violence and unrest in Mexico has been severe enough in recent years to warrant statewide warnings against visits to the neighboring country. Since this affects most tourists, it is advisable for travelers in Texas to remain in the state for safety's sake. Even longtime residents of Texas's border communities are reluctant to cross the border, unless a family or business emergency necessitates it.

If the volatile conditions in Mexico subside (as most border communities hope, since their tourism has historically been tied to border hops), visitors will once again return to Mexico's *restaurantes* and *tourista* areas. Meanwhile, many of these destinations (restaurants, in particular) have addressed the drop in business by opening new locations on the Texas side of the Rio Grande. It may not offer the same international flavor, but it provides visitors with something equally as palatable: safety.

INTERNATIONAL TRAVELERS

Since Texas shares an enormous border with another country, international travel has traditionally been commonplace in the Lone Star State. Not anymore. With the recent rise in violence associated with the warring drug cartels, visitors are advised against traveling to Mexico.

Overseas travel is a different story—recent numbers compiled by state government show Texas ranks seventh as a destination point among mainland U.S. states for overseas travelers, with New York, California, and Florida taking the top spots.

Before international travelers arrive in Texas, they're encouraged to address several issues that will make their experience more pleasant and convenient. Suggested action items include consulting their insurance companies to ensure their medical policy applies in the United States; making sure they have a signed, up-to-date passport and/or visa; leaving copies of their itinerary and contact info with friends or family for emergencies; and taking precautions to avoid being a target of crime (don't carry excessive amounts of money, don't leave luggage unattended, etc.).

SPECIAL CONSIDERATIONS
Travelers with Disabilities

Travelers with disabilities shouldn't have much trouble getting around in Texas; in fact, the only places that may not be wheelchair accessible are some outdated hotels and restaurants. Otherwise, parks, museums, and city attractions are compliant with the Americans with Disabilities Act, providing ramps, elevators, and accessible facilities for public-use areas.

Texas law requires cities to appoint one member to a transit board representing the interests of the "transportation disadvantaged," a group that can include people with disabilities. As a result, most cities have addressed accessibility issues in airports and public transportation services. For detailed information, contact the municipal offices in the city you're visiting or the Texas Department of Transportation's Public Transportation Division at 512/416-2810 or www.txdot.gov.

Other handy resources for disabled travelers en route to Texas are the **Handicapped Travel Club** (www.handicappedtravelclub.com), providing information about campgrounds with accessibility; and the **Society for Accessible Travel and Hospitality** (www.sath.org), containing a resources page with handy travel tips for anyone with physical limitations.

Senior Travelers

For seniors, it's always a good idea to mention in advance if you're a member of AARP or if you qualify for a senior discount (typically for ages 65 and older, but occasionally available for the 60 and older crowd). Most museums

in Texas offer a few dollars off admission fees for seniors, and many public transportation systems also provide discounts.

If you haven't done so already, inquire about travel options through **Road Scholar** (877/426-8056, www.roadscholar.org), an organization providing several dozen programs in Texas with seniors in mind. Excursions lasting 4-12 days are available, ranging from birding trails to heritage-based tours to art, nature, and fishing trips.

Gay and Lesbian Travelers

Texas's rural communities (and even some of its smaller cities) aren't quite as open-minded as its metropolitan areas. Houston, Dallas, and Austin have sizable gay communities, with bars, restaurants, and services catering exclusively to gay clientele.

To learn more about resources related to gay and lesbian travel in Texas, including accommodations, restaurants, and nightclubs, visit the following travel-related websites: www.gaytravel.com and the McKinney, Texas-based www.gayjourney.com. For additional information, contact the International Gay & Lesbian Travel Association (www.iglta.org).

Health and Safety

Texas isn't any more dangerous or any safer than other U.S. states, but there are several environment-related issues (weather, animals) that set it apart. Travelers with medical issues are encouraged to bring extra supplies of medications and copies of prescriptions—local visitors bureaus can recommend the best pharmacy or medical center, if needed.

CRIME

Although it's still often considered a Wild West state, Texas is similar to the rest of the nation regarding crime statistics and trends. According to a recent report by the Texas Department of Public Safety, criminal activity in Texas was separated into the following

categories: violent crimes (against people—robberies, assaults, etc.), which represented more than 10 percent of the reported offenses, and property crimes (burglary, car theft), representing the remaining circa 90 percent.

THE ELEMENTS

Texas's weather is as changeable as its landscape. Summers regularly reach triple digits, and winters are marked by vicious snowstorms in the Panhandle and northern plains. The biggest threat to travelers in winter is ice—bridges and overpasses become slick and are usually closed when a rare ice storm barrels through the state. Since Texans are unaccustomed to dealing with such slippery conditions, they often disregard the danger and plow across a patch of ice in their big, fancy trucks. The results are predictably disastrous.

Heat is by far the most serious threat to Texas travelers. From the sticky humidity of marshy East Texas to the dry desert conditions of the Big Bend region, the summer months (May-September in Texas) can be brutal. Hikers, bikers, and campers are encouraged to pack and carry plenty of water to remain hydrated.

WILDLIFE, INSECTS, AND PLANTS

Texas has some bizarre fauna and flora, which can occasionally pose a danger to travelers, particularly those who venture to the state's parks and natural areas. Of primary concern are snakes, which nestle among rocks and waterways throughout Texas (though rattlesnakes are largely found only in western portions of the state). Also of concern in the Big Bend region are black bears and mountain lions, which hikers and campers should intimidate with loud noises and rocks (seriously) to fend off their advances.

The most dangerous plant in Texas is cactus. There are many varieties in all regions of the state, and even though some appear harmless, they may contain barely visible needles that get embedded in your skin and cause major irritation. With cactus, the best approach is to look but don't touch.

Information and Services

The best way to find out about activities and services in the city you're visiting is through the local convention and visitors bureau, or in smaller communities, the chamber of commerce. Each destination in this guide includes contact information for visitor services, and even the most rural areas have discovered the value of promoting themselves online.

MONEY

It's always a good idea to have cash on hand for tips, valets, and parking lots, but you can get by in most Texas cities with a credit or debit card. Some smaller towns still don't accept them (old-fashioned restaurants in particular), but they're typically modern enough to have ATMs. Also available, yet not quite as accessible, are wire transfers and travelers checks. Call ahead for the bank's hours of operation since some institutions close at odd hours.

MAPS AND TOURIST INFO

Convention and visitors bureaus are the best resource for planning a trip to Texas. Call ahead to have maps and brochures sent before your trip, or check the town's website for walking tours and street maps. It's also a good idea to check these sites or call in advance to find out if the city you're visiting is randomly hosting its annual pecan days or biker festival at the same time. Depending on your outlook, this can enhance or hinder your excursion.

Resources

Suggested Reading

GENERAL INFORMATION

State Travel Guide. Each year, the Texas Department of Transportation publishes this magazine-size guide with maps and comprehensive listings of the significant attractions in virtually every town, including all the local history museums in Texas's tiny communities.

Texas Almanac. Published annually, this handy book includes virtually everything you'd ever need to know about Texas—current and historical information about politics, agriculture, transportation, geography, and culture, along with maps of each county (all 254 of 'em).

Texas Monthly. With a higher-end subscriber base, this monthly magazine features some of the best writers in the state offering insightful commentary and substantive feature articles about the state's politics, culture, history, and Texas-ness. It's available at most bookstores.

LITERATURE, FICTION, HISTORY

Bissinger, H.G. *Friday Night Lights.* Boston: Addison-Wesley, 1990. This book will tell you more about Texas than you could ever experience in a visit to the state. It's not just about football, but the passionate emotions involved with family, religion, and race in Odessa through the eyes of journalist Buzz Bissinger.

Dobie, J. Frank. *Tales of Old-Time Texas.* Austin: University of Texas press, 1955. Known as the Southwest's master storyteller, J. Frank Dobie depicts folk life in Texas unlike any other author, with 28 inspiring stories of characters (Jim Bowie) and culture (the legend of the Texas bluebonnet).

Fehrenbach, T.R. *Lone Star.* Cambridge, MA: Da Capo Press, 2000. Considered the definitive book on Texas history, this enormous book by the highly respected late historian covers Texas's lengthy and colorful heritage in fascinating and accurate detail.

Harrigan, Stephen. *The Gates of the Alamo.* London: Penguin Books, 2001. This is gripping historical fiction, with detailed history about the actual people and events associated with the Battle of the Alamo weaved with a dramatic narrative resulting in a completely compelling read.

Harrigan, Stephen. *Big Wonderful Thing: A History of Texas,* University of Texas Press, 2019. This 944-page book brings Texas' enormous legacy into the 21st century by acknowledging its multi-cultural past with thoughtful analysis and masterful storytelling.

McCarthy, Cormac. *All the Pretty Horses.* New York City: Alfred Knopf, 1992. Tracing a young man's journey to the regions of the unknown (though it technically takes place along the Texas-Mexico border), this novel depicts a classic quest with plenty of good, evil, and Texas mystique.

McMurtry, Larry. *Lonesome Dove*. New York City: Simon & Schuster, 1985. Beautifully written by Pulitzer Prize-winning novelist Larry McMurtry, this period piece (late 1800s) chronicles two ex-Texas Rangers on a cattle drive, leaving readers with a yearning for the compelling characters and the Texas of the past.

Meyer, Philipp. *The Son*. New York City: Harper Collins, 2013. This incredible story, a finalist for the Pulitzer Prize in 2014, chronicles 200 years of Texas history through the fictional account of a powerful Texas family. From tensions with Native Americans to border relations to oil barons, The Son captures Texas' complicated past in a fascinating novel.

MUSIC AND FOOD

Govenar, Alan. *Meeting the Blues: The Rise of the Texas Sound*. London: Penguin Books, 1994. This semi-obscure, thoroughly researched book provides fascinating insight about the development of the Texas blues through historical narrative, interviews, and photos.

Marshall, Wes. *The Wine Roads of Texas: An Essential Guide to Texas Wines and Wineries*. San Antonio: Maverick Books, 2002. Covering more than 400 Texas wines and the top wineries in Texas, this book offers a comprehensive sampling of wines from Big Bend to the bayous.

Porterfield, Bill. *The Greatest Honky Tonks of Texas*. Houston: Taylor Publishing Company, 1983. You'll likely have to do some searching to dig up a copy of this book, but it's worth it for the engaging text about the colorful culture associated with the state's iconic honky-tonks and historic dance halls.

Walsh, Robb. *Legends of Texas Barbecue*. San Francisco: Chronicle Books, 2002. This book is as fun to read as it is to use—learn about the fascinating history of the many different styles of Texas barbecue while trying out some of the state's best recipes and cooking methods.

Walsh, Robb. *The Tex-Mex Cookbook*. Emeryville, CA: Ten Speed Press, 2004. Well researched and comprehensive in approach, this informative book includes cultural information about classic and unknown Tex-Mex dishes and plenty of authentic recipes.

OUTDOORS

Tekiela, Stan. *Birds of Texas Field Guide*, 2004. Designed for amateur birders, this handy guide is color coded (corresponding to the birds' feathers) with helpful photos, maps, and descriptions.

Tennant, Alan. *A Field Guide to Texas Snakes*, 2002. This thorough guidebook provides essential information about understanding and appreciating Texas's venomous and nonvenomous snakes through identification keys and color photos.

Wauer, Roland. *Naturalist's Big Bend*, 2002. If you've ever wanted to know about the major and minor details of Big Bend's mammals, reptiles, insects, birds, trees, shrubs, cacti, and other living things, this is the place to find it.

Internet Resources

GENERAL TRAVEL INFORMATION

Office of the Governor, Economic Development and Tourism
www.traveltex.com
This indispensable site provides background and contact information for virtually every tourist attraction, major and minor, in the state.

Texas Department of Transportation
www.txdot.gov
Visit this site for information about road conditions and travel resources (maps, travel info center locations, etc.).

Texas Monthly
www.texasmonthly.com
The site of this award-winning magazine offers samples of feature articles and recommendations for quality dining and lodging options throughout the state.

HISTORIC PRESERVATION

Texas Historical Commission
www.thc.texas.gov
The official state agency for historic preservation, the THC provides helpful guidelines about its preservation programs and essential travel information about popular historic properties across the state.

Texas State Historical Association, *The Handbook of Texas* Online
www.tshaonline.org/handbook/online
The Handbook of Texas has long been considered the definitive source for accurate information about Texas's historical events, sites, and figures.

OUTDOORS

Texas Parks and Wildlife Department
www.tpwd.texas.gov
You can get lost (in a good way) exploring this site, with its comprehensive listings of state parks and detailed information about outdoors activities.

National Parks in Texas
www.nps.gov
Texas's national parks are astounding, and this site provides enough information to put these intriguing locales on your must-visit list.

Texas Campgrounds
www.texascampgrounds.com
Use this site to help find a commendable RV park or campground anywhere in the state.

Texas Outside
www.texasoutside.com
This site contains helpful info and links to outdoor activities in Texas such as hiking, biking, camping, fishing, hunting, and golfing.

Index

A

Abilene: 20, 458-464
Abilene State Park: 460
Abilene Zoo: 460
accents: 485
adobe: 410
Adrian: 449
African American history/sights: African
    American Museum 42; buffalo soldiers
    425; Buffalo Soldiers National Museum
    247; Ensemble Theatre 262; Gardere Martin
    Luther King Jr. Oratory Competition 262;
    George Washington Carver Museum and
    Cultural Center 108; Houston Juneteenth
    263; Juneteenth Celebration Fort Worth 81;
    National Multicultural Western Heritage
    Museum 77
agriculture: general discussion 482-483; Abilene
    458; American Museum of Agriculture 441;
    Brownsville 222; citrus industry 232
aircraft carriers: 330-332
Air Defense Artillery and Fort Bliss Museum: 369
air museums: 45-46
air travel: 492-493
Alabama-Coushatta reservation: 279
Alamo Drafthouse: 119
Alamo Heights: 175
Alamo Plaza: 175
The Alamo: 17, 18, 27, 175-178, 189
Aldridge Sawmill: 285
Alley Theatre: 262
Alpine: 20, 26, 429-432
Amarillo: 446-458
Amarillo Livestock Auction: 450
Amarillo Museum of Art: 450
American Museum of Agriculture: 441
American Quarter Horse Heritage Center &
    Museum: 448
American Wind Power Center: 439-441
Amistad National Recreation Area: 209
Amon Carter Museum: 73
amphibians: 476-477
amusement parks: Kemah Boardwalk 254;
    Pleasure Pier 308-310; Schlitterbahn
    Waterpark 310; Six Flags Fiesta Texas
    Amusement Park 183; Six Flags Hurricane
    Harbor 62; Six Flags Over Texas 60
Anderson Fair: 261
Andy Bowie Park: 355
Angelina National Forest: 285-286

animals: 473-477
Ann Richards Congress Avenue Bridge: 109
antiques: Abilene 462; Amarillo 451;
    Fredericksburg 154; Galveston 318; Gruene
    204; Houston 263; Lubbock 444; Lufkin 288
aquariums: Children's Aquarium at Fair Park 40;
    Dallas World Aquarium 45; Dolphin Research
    and Sea Life Nature Center 353; Houston
    Downtown Aquarium 248; Sea Center Texas
    327; Sea Turtle, Inc. 353; Texas State Aquarium
    330-332
arboretums: 45, 252
archaeological sights: 208-209, 374, 442
architecture: adobe 410; Asia Society Texas
    Center 247; Bass Performance Hall 78; Bayou
    Bend Collection 250; Ellis County Courthouse
    65; Grand 1894 Opera House 317; Hall of State
    40; Heritage Park 333; Hotel Paisano 422;
    House of the Seasons 300; Kokernot Field
    430; Magoffin Home State Historic Site 372;
    Majestic Theatre 48; McFaddin-Ward House
    275; mid-century modern 246; Museum of
    the Southwest 391-393; La Posada Hotel 215;
    Presidio County Courthouse 422; San Agustin
    Cathedral 215; San Fernando Cathedral 181;
    Spanish Governor's Palace 181; State Capitol
    102-104
Arlington: 28, 60
Armand Bayou Nature Center: 255
art events and sights: general discussion
    490-491; Blue Star Contemporary Art
    Center 185; Building 98 419; Cadillac Ranch
    448; Contemporary Austin 108; George
    Washington Carver Museum and Cultural
    Center 108; Houston Center for Photography
    247; Judd, Donald 420; Laredo Center for the
    Arts 215; Lubbock Arts Festival 443; Mayfest
    80; Nasher Sculpture Center 43; The Orange
    Show 253-254; Prada Marfa 421; Texas Folklife
    Festival 189; Uptown and Oak Lawn 38; see
    also cultural centers
Art Museum of South Texas: 334
art museums: Amarillo Museum of Art 450;
    Amon Carter Museum 73; Art Museum of
    South Texas 334; Blanton Museum of Art 104;
    Brownsville Museum of Fine Art 224; Chianti
    Foundation 419-420; Dallas Museum of Art 42;
    Ellen Noel Art Museum 393; El Paso Museum of
    Art 372; Houston 244, 249-250; International
    Museum of Art and Science 227; The Kimbell
    Art Museum 70-73; McNay Art Museum 180;

Meadows Museum 44; Mexic-Arte Museum 108; Modern Art Museum of Fort Worth 73; Museum of Fine Arts, Houston 244; Museum of Western Art 165; San Angelo Museum of Fine Arts 465-466; San Antonio Museum of Art 180; Sid Richardson Museum 77; Tyler Museum of Art 297; Wichita Falls Museum of Art at Midwestern State University 94

arts, the: 486-491

Ashton Villa: 312-314

AsiaFest: 262

Asian Cultures Museum: 333

Asia Society Texas Center: 247

AT&T Stadium: 60

The Atalanta: 300

Austin and the Hill Country 97-166; Austin 102-135; highlights 98; Hill Country 151-166; information and services 101; map 100; planning tips 18, 99; transportation 101; Waco 145-151

Austin City Limits: 116

Austin City Limits Music Festival: 116, 120

Austin's Bat Colony: 106, 109

Austin Spurs: 110

B

Babe Didrikson Zaharias Museum: 276

backpacking: general discussion 496; Big Bend National Park 408; Big Thicket National Preserve 281; Davis Mountains State Park 427

bald eagles: 136

ballet: Ballet Tyler 298; Houston 262; Wichita Falls 95

Balmorhea State Park: 426-427

Bandera: 24, 157-159

barbecue: 25, 124, 143-145, 498

Barton Creek Greenbelt: 111

Barton Springs Pool: 110

Barton Warnock Environmental Education Center: 415

baseball: Austin 110; Dallas 47; Houston 257; Kokernot Field 430; San Antonio 185

basin and range geography: 471

basketball: Austin 109; Dallas 47; Houston 257; San Antonio 185

Bass Concert Hall: 113

bat colony, Austin: 106, 109

Battle of the Alamo Commemoration: 189

Bayou Bend Collection: 250

Bayou City Cajun Fest: 262

Bayou Place: 261

beaches: Brazosport 328; Corpus Christi 334; Galveston 314; Mustang Island State Park 344; Padre Island National Seashore 343; San Jose Island 344; South Padre Island 352-353, 354-355

Beaumont: 275-277

Beaver Slide Trail: 281

Bentsen-Rio Grande Valley State Park: 228

best-of itinerary: 23-26

The Big Texan: 27, 453

Big Bend National Park: 11, 26, 401-418

Big Bend Ranch State Park: 411

Big Bend Region: 397-432; highlights 398; information and services 400; maps 399; Marfa 418-432; planning tips 20, 400; transportation 400

Big Thicket Loop: 281

Big Thicket National Preserve: 279-282

Big Thicket visitors center: 279

biking: Austin 111; Big Thicket National Preserve 281; Corpus Christi 336; Galveston Island State Park 316; Hotter 'n Hell One Hundred 95; Lufkin 290; Nacogdoches 294; River Legacy Living Science Center 63; San Antonio Missions Trail 176; South Padre Island 356; for transport 494; The Veloway 111

birds: 475

bird-watching: general discussion 495; Amistad National Recreation Area 209; bald eagles 136; Big Bend Ranch State Park 411; Big Thicket National Preserve 281; Brazoria National Wildlife Refuge 327; Brownsville 224; Galveston Island State Park 316; Laredo 215-217; McAllen 227; Pedernales Falls State Park 162; Sabine National Forest 287; Woodward Ranch 430

Bishop's Palace: 311-312

Black history/sights: *see* African American history/sights

Blackland Prairie: 18, 99

Black's Barbecue: 144

Blanton Museum of Art: 104

Blue Star Contemporary Art Center: 185

boating: Amistad National Recreation Area 209, 210; *Elissa* 310; Highland Lakes 135; Lady Bird Lake 111; Lake Arrowhead State Park 95; Lake Conroe 282; Lake o' the Pines 301; Lake Sam Rayburn 285; Lufkin 290; Meadows Center Glass-Bottom Boats 137; San Angelo State Park 466; for transport 493

Boquillas, Mexico: 408

border crossings: 216, 408, 500

Boulder Park: 47

bowling: 62, 63

Bowling Museum and Hall of Fame: 62, 63

Brackenridge Park: 186

Brackettville: 213

Brain Night for Kids: 262

Brazoria National Wildlife Refuge: 327

Brazosport: 326-330

Brazos River Trail Gulf Prairie Run: 328

508

INDEX

Brazos Valley Museum of Natural History: 142
breweries: Austin 130; Fredericksburg 154; Fredonia Brewery 292; Saint Arnold Brewing Company 248
Brinkley Mansion: 211
Brownsville: 18, 222-227
Brownsville Museum of Fine Art: 224
Bryan Beach: 328
Bryan-College Station: 140-143
The Bryan Museum: 310
Buddhist Temple, Buu Mon: 278
Buddy Holly Center: 438
Buffalo Gap Historic Village: 460
Buffalo Soldiers National Museum: 247
Building 98: 419
Bullock Texas State History Museum: 29, 106
Bush, George W.: 39, 141, 391
bus travel: 493, 494
butterflies: 227-228, 476
Buu Mon Buddhist Temple: 278

C

cacti: 474, 502
Caddo Lake: 301
Caddo Lake State Park: 301
Caddo Mounds State Historic Site: 292
Caddo people: 292
Cadillac Ranch: 27, 448
Cajun culture: 262
Caldwell Zoo: 297
Cameron Park Zoo: 148
Camp Bowie Boulevard: 69
camping: Abilene 464; Amarillo 454; Amistad National Recreation Area 211; Angelina National Forest 286; Big Bend National Park 417; Big Thicket National Preserve 279; Brazosport 330; Corpus Christi 342; Dallas 58-59; Davy Crockett National Forest 284; Del Rio 214; El Paso 383; Enchanted Rock State Natural Area 163; Frio and Sabinal Canyons 163; Galveston 324; Garner State Park 163; Guadalupe Mountains National Park 386; Highland Lakes 136; Hill Country State Natural Area 158; Houston 273; Lake Waco 151; Laredo 221; Lubbock 446; Lufkin 290; Marfa area 429; reservations 496; Sabine National Forest 287; Sam Houston National Forest 284; San Angelo 469; San Angelo State Park 466; San Antonio 202; South Padre Island 360; Wichita Falls 96
canoeing: *see* paddling
Canyon: 455-458
canyon communities, Hill Country: 164
Carter, Amon: 73
car travel: 493
Casa Grande: 404
Casa Navarro State Historic Site: 182-183

Casa Rio: 23, 192
Cathedrals/churches: Immaculate Conception Cathedral 224-225; La Lomita Chapel 227; missions, Spanish 177, 368; Presidio La Bahia 182; Rothko Chapel 250; San Agustin Cathedral 215; San Antonio Missions National Historical Park 176-178; San Fernando Cathedral 181
Castolon: 404
cattle ranching: 349-351
caves: Enchanted Rock State Natural Area 163; Natural Bridge Caverns 205-206; Wonder World 138
Centennial Museum: 373
The Center for the Arts & Sciences: 327
chicano soul music: 187
Chihuahua Desert Gardens: 373
Chihuahuan Desert Visitor Center: 427
Children's Aquarium at Fair Park: 40
Children's Health Holiday Parade: 50
Children's Museum of Houston: 29, 246
chili: 499
chili festival: 411
Chinati Foundation: 26, 419-420
Chisholm Trail BBQ: 145
Chisos Basin Loop Trail: 407
Chisos Mountains Lodge: 26, 404, 416
Christmas Bay Paddling Trail: 328
Cinco de Mayo: 49
citrus industry: 232
Civilian Conservation Corps: 428
Civil War history: 481
Civil War sights: 77, 278
classical music: Dallas 47-48; East Texas Symphony Orchestra 298; El Paso Symphony Orchestra 376; Houston Symphony 262; Van Cliburn International Piano Competition 81; Wichita Falls Symphony Orchestra 95
climate: 477-478
College Station: 141
colloquialisms: 485
Concho Avenue: 467
Concho Pearls: 466
Concho River Walk: 466
Congress Avenue: 28, 102
Contemporary Arts Museum of Houston: 244
Contemporary Austin: 108
Corps of Cadets: 141
Corpus Christi: 19, 25, 29, 330-343
Corpus Christi Beach: 334
Corpus Christi Botanical Gardens and Nature Center: 334
Corpus Christi Museum of Science and History: 332, 333
Cowan Center: 298
cowboys: *see* Western culture

Cowboys Stadium: 60
cowgirls: 74
Cowtown Coliseum: 70
crater, meteor: 391
Crawford-Smith Ranch: 411
crime: 501
cuisine: general discussion 498-499; barbecue 25, 124, 143-145, 498; Bayou City Cajun Fest 262; chili festival 411; Dr Pepper Museum 146, 147; Houston Vietnamese 249; Mexican 192-193; Southern cooking 283; Taste of Dallas 49; as a top experience 15, 25, 283; ZestFest 49
cultural centers: George Washington Carver Museum and Cultural Center 108; Institute of Texan Cultures 178; Latino Cultural Center, Dallas 45; Museum of the Big Bend 429; National Multicultural Western Heritage Museum 77; Tigua Indian Cultural Center 369-372
Cultural District: 68
culture: 486-491
currency, printing: 77

D

Dallas: 36-60
Dallas and Fort Worth: 24, 31-96; Dallas 36-60; Fort Worth 68-88; highlights 32; information and services 33; map 34; planning tips 18, 33; transportation 35; Wichita Falls 94-96
Dallas Arboretum: 45
Dallas County Historical Plaza: 42
Dallas Cowboys: 28, 46, 60
Dallas Heritage Village: 44
Dallas Mavericks: 47
Dallas Museum: 43-44
Dallas Museum of Art: 42
Dallas Opera: 48
Dallas Stars: 47
Dallas Symphony Orchestra: 48
Dallas World Aquarium: 45
Dallas Zoo: 45
dance: Dallas 49; Gruene Hall 204; Hill Country dance halls 153; San Antonio 188
Davis Mountains State Park: 427
Davy Crockett National Forest: 284-285
Day of the Dead: 189
Deco District: 175
Deep Ellum: 38, 48
Del Rio: 208-214
Denton: 89-92
Denton County Courthouse: 89
Denton County Courthouse-on-the-Square Museum: 89
Depot District: 443
deserts: Barton Warnock Environmental Education Center 415; Big Bend National Park

401; Chihuahuan Desert Visitor Center 427; Guadalupe Mountains National Park 385
Devil's Rope Museum: 448
Dewberry Plantation: 297
El Dia de Los Muertos: 189, 263
Dia de Los Muertos Festival: 263
Dickens on the Strand: 318
Dinosaur Valley State Park: 92
Discovery Science Place: 298
diving: 209, 355
Dixie Dude Ranch: 157
Dog Canyon: 387
Dolphin Research and Sea Life Nature Center: 353
dolphin-viewing: 356
The Domain: 121
Don Harrington Discovery Center: 449-450
The Doseum: 185
Dot's Mini Museum: 448
Downtown Aquarium: 29, 248
downtown Dallas: 38, 50
downtown Denton: 89
downtown Houston: 242, 247, 257
Downtown Tunnels: 248
driving: 493
Dr Pepper Museum: 146, 147
dude ranches: 157

E

East Austin: 117
East Beach: 314
East Texas: *see* Houston and East Texas
East Texas Fresh Farmer's Market: 298
East Texas Oil Museum: 296
East Texas Symphony Orchestra: 298
Los Ebanos Ferry: 227
economy: 482-483
El Camino Real de Tierra Adentro: 374
El Capitan: 385
El Capitan Trail: 387
Elissa: 27, 310
Ellen Noel Art Museum: 393
Ellen Trout Zoo: 288
Ellis County Courthouse: 65
Ellis County Museum: 65
El Paso and West Texas: 362-396; El Paso 367-384; Guadalupe Mountains National Park 384-388; highlights 363; information and services 366; maps 365; Midland and Odessa 388-396; planning tips 19, 364-366; transportation 366
El Paso Chihuahuas: 379
El Paso History Museum: 374
El Paso Museum of Archaeology: 374
El Paso Museum of Art: 372
El Paso Zoo: 372
Emma Long Metropolitan Park: 111
Emory Peak: 404, 408

Enchanted Rock State Natural Area: 163
Ensemble Theatre: 262
environmental issues: 337, 473
ethnicities: 484
European colonization: 480
Exotic Resort Zoo: 160

F
Fair Park: 24, 28, 39-40
fairs: Star of Texas Fair and Rodeo: 120; State Fair of Texas: 43, 49; Tri-State Fair: 451
fall color: 164
fall travel: 21
family activities: bat colony, Austin 106; Brain Night for Kids 262; Children's Aquarium at Fair Park 40; Children's Museum of Houston 246; Dallas World Aquarium 45; Discovery Science Place 298; Dolphin Research and Sea Life Nature Center 353; Don Harrington Discovery Center 449-450; Fort Worth Water Gardens 75; Fossil Rim Wildlife Center 92; Frontier Texas! 459; Health Museum 246; Hill Country Science Mill 160; Houston Downtown Aquarium 248; Houston Museum of Natural Science 243-244; itinerary for 28-29; Kemah Boardwalk 254; McKenna Children's Museum 205; National Center for Children's Illustrated Literature 459; Perot Museum of Nature and Science 40; Planetarium at UT Arlington 62; Pleasure Pier 308-310; River Legacy Living Science Center 62; San Antonio Children's Museum: The DoSeum 185; Schlitterbahn Waterpark 205; Sea Center Texas 327; Sea Turtle, Inc. 353; SeaWorld of Texas 181; Six Flags Fiesta Texas Amusement Park 183-184; Six Flags Hurricane Harbor 62; Six Flags Over Texas 60; Texas State Aquarium 330-332; Wonder World 138; see also zoos
farmers markets: 298
FC Austin: 110
FC Dallas: 47
Fiesta de las Flores: 377
Fiesta San Antonio: 189
Fiestas Patrias: 189
film: 489
Firehouse Gallery: 211
Fire Museum of Texas: 276
fishing: general discussion 496-497; Amistad National Recreation Area 209, 210; Brazosport 328; Bryan Beach 328; Galveston Island State Park 316; Garner State Park 163; Lake Arrowhead State Park 95; Lake Buchanan 136; Lake Conroe 282; Lake o' the Pines 301; Lake Sam Rayburn 285; Padre Island National Seashore 344; Pedernales Falls State Park 162; Port Aransas 346; Sabine National Forest 286;

San Angelo State Park 466; South Padre Island 355-356
floods: 478
folk art: 253-254
folk music: 165, 189
football: Alpine 430; Austin 109; Dallas 46-47; high school football 390; Houston 257
Ford Holiday River Parade: 189
forests: 279
Fort Bliss: 369
Fort Clark Springs: 213
Fort Concho National Historic Landmark: 465
Fort Davis: 20, 26, 425-429
Fort Davis National Historic Site: 426
Fort Leaton State Historic Site: 414
Fort McIntosh: 215-217
Fort Phantom Hill: 460
Fort Worth: 68-88; see also Dallas and Fort Worth
Fort Worth Botanic Garden: 75
Fort Worth Museum of Science and History: 73-74
Fort Worth Nature Center and Refuge: 75-76
Fort Worth Stock Show and Rodeo: 80
Fort Worth Stockyards National Historic District: 24, 28, 70
Fort Worth Water Gardens: 75
Fort Worth Zoo: 28, 74
Fossil Rim Wildlife Center: 92
fossils: Dinosaur Valley State Park 92; Guadalupe Mountains National Park 384; International Museum of Art and Science 227; Waco Mammoth National Monument 147; Witte Museum 183
Founders Plaza: 42
Four C National Recreation Trail: 284
Franklin Mountains State Park: 375
Fredericksburg: 152-157
Fredonia Brewery: 292
Friday Night Lights: 390
Frio and Sabinal Canyons: 163
Frio River: 24, 163
Frontiers of Flight Museum: 45-46
Frontier Texas!: 459
Frontier Times Museum: 158

G
Galleria: 263
Galveston: 25, 29, 308-325
The Galveston Naval Museum: 314
Galveston Island State Park: 29, 316
Galveston Tree Sculptures Tour: 312
gardens: Bayou Bend Collection 250; Buu Mon Buddhist Temple 278; Chihuahuan Desert Gardens 373; Corpus Christi Botanical Gardens and Nature Center 334; Dallas Arboretum 45; El Paso Museum of Archaeology 374; Fort Worth Botanic Garden 75; Houston

244; Lamar Vergara Environmental Science Center 215-217; Moody Gardens 312; Quinta Mazatlan 227; San Antonio Botanical Garden 186; Texas Discovery Gardens 40; Texas Home and Garden Show 262; Tyler Municipal Rose Garden and Museum 296-297; Zilker Botanical Gardens 111

Gardere Martin Luther King Jr. Oratory Competition: 262

Garner State Park: 163

gemstone collecting: 430

geography: 471-473

George Bush Presidential Library and Museum: 141

George Ranch Historical Park: 254-255

George Washington Carver Museum and Cultural Center: 108

George W. Bush Childhood Home: 391

George W. Bush Presidential Center: 39

German culture: 18, 152-154, 203

Ghost Tour: 263

Gingerbread Trail: 65

Gladys Porter Zoo: 225

Glenrio: 449

Glen Rose: 92-93

Globe Life Field: 60

golf: Houston 256; Lajitas 416; San Antonio 186

Gone with the Wind: 300-301

Goodman-LeGrand House Museum: 297

government: 482

Grace Museum: 459

Grand 1894 Opera House: 317

Granny Clare's Citrus at Rio Pride Orchards: 232

Grapevine: 204

Grapevine Vintage Railroad: 70

grass: 474

great plains region: 471

Greenville Avenue: 24, 38-39, 48

Gris: 206

The Grove: 300

Gruene General Store: 204

Gruene Hall: 204

Gruene Historic District: 203-204

Guadalupe Mountains National Park: 19, 384-388

Guadalupe Peak: 385

Guadalupe Peak Trail: 387

Guadalupe River: 205

Guenther House: 181

The Gulf Coast: 303-361; Brazosport 326-330; Corpus Christi 330-343; Galveston 308-325; geography 472; highlights 304; information and services 308; Kingsville 348-352; maps 306-307; Mustang Island 343-348; planning tips 19, 305; South Padre Island 352-361; transportation 307

Haley Library and History Center: 391

Hall of State: 40

Harlingen: 230-233

Harlingen Arts and Heritage Museum: 231

Harry Ransom Humanities Research Center: 106

health: 501-502

Health Museum: 246

Heard-Craig House Historic Center: 67

heatstroke: 502

The Heights: 243, 258

Heritage Park: 333

Heritage Society at Sam Houston Park: 248

Heritage Trails: 77

Hermann Park: 255

Highland Lakes: 135-137

high school football: 390

hiking: Austin 111; Big Bend National Park 406-408; Big Thicket National Preserve 281; Corpus Christi 336; Davis Mountains State Park 427; Davy Crockett National Forest 284; Enchanted Rock State Natural Area 163; Fort Worth Nature Center and Refuge 75-76; Galveston Island State Park 316; Garner State Park 163; Houston 255, 256; Lost Maples State Natural Area 164; Lufkin 290; Nacogdoches 294; Palo Duro Canyon State Park 457; River Legacy Living Science Center 63; Sam Houston National Forest 282; San Angelo State Park 466; Seminole Canyon State Park 208-209; South Padre Island 356; Woodward Ranch 430

Hill Country: 151-166; see also Austin and the Hill Country

Hill Country Flyer: 29, 108

Hill Country Science Mill: 160

Hill Country State Natural Area: 158

Historic Brownsville Museum: 222

Historic Courthouse Square: 67

historic sights: The Alamo 175-176; Aldridge Sawmill 285; Buffalo Gap Historic Village 460; Caddo Mounds State Historic Site 292; Casa Navarro State Historic Site 182-183; courthouses 76; Dallas 42, 44; Del Rio 211; El Paso mission trail 368; Fort Bliss 369; Fort Clark Springs 213; Fort Davis National Historic Site 426; Fort Leaton State Historic Site 414; Fort McIntosh 215-217; Fort Phantom Hill 460; Fort Worth 70, 75, 76, 77; Galveston 310, 311-312; George Ranch Historical Park 254-255; Gruene Historic District 203-204; Harlingen 231; The History Center 288; Houston 247, 248; Hueco Tanks State Historic Site 375; itinerary for visiting 27; Jefferson 300; King Ranch 349-351; King William Historic District 180-181; Laredo 215; of La Salle 332; La Villita Historic District 183; Lyndon B. Johnson National Historical

Park 160; Magoffin Home State Historic Site 372; McKinney 67; Nacogdoches 291; NASA Space Center 252-253; National Museum of the Pacific War 152; Palo Alto Battlefield National Historic Site 225; Palo Duro Canyon 456; Pioneer Museum Complex 152-154; plantation museums 297; Sabine Pass Battleground State Historic Site 278; San Angelo 465, 466; San Antonio Missions National Historical Park 176-178; San Jacinto Battleground State Historic Site 254; Sixth Floor Museum 38, 39; Spindletop-Gladys City Boomtown Museum 275; Texas Ranger Hall of Fame and Museum 148; of the Texas Revolution 182; as a top experience 13; Waxahachie 65; see also African American history/sights
history: general discussion 479-482; buffalo soldiers 425; mercury mining 415; Pancho Villa 377
The History Center: 288
hockey: 47
holiday events: 50
Holocaust Museum Houston: 247
horseback riding: Bandera 157-158; Corpus Christi 336; Davy Crockett National Forest 284; Hill Country State Natural Area 158; Palo Duro Canyon State Park 457; Sabine National Forest 286
horses, quarter: 448
horse shows: 81
Hotel Paisano: 422, 424
Hotter 'n Hell One Hundred: 95
House of the Seasons: 300
Houston and East Texas: 234-302; highlights 235; Houston 239-274; information and services 238; map 237; Piney Woods 279-302; planning tips 19, 236; transportation 238-239
Houston Arboretum & Nature Center: 252, 256
Houston Astros: 257
Houston Ballet: 262
Houston Center for Photography: 247
Houston Downtown Aquarium: 248
Houston Grand Opera: 261-262
Houston International Jazz Festival: 263
Houston Museum of Natural Science: 243-244
Houston Rockets: 257
Houston Symphony: 262
Houston Texans: 256
Houston Zoo: 29, 246
Hueco Tanks State Historic Site: 375
Hugh Ramsey Nature Park: 232
hunting: 286, 496-497
hurricanes: 311, 478

I
ice-skating: 318
Immaculate Conception Cathedral: 224-225
Indian Mounds Wilderness Area: 286
insects: 476, 502
Institute of Texan Cultures: 178
interior lowlands: 472
International Bowling Campus: 63
International Bowling Museum and Hall of Fame: 28, 62
International Museum of Art and Science: 227
international travelers: 501
International Woman's Foundation: 419
Internet resources: 505
Irish culture: 189
Isla Blanca Park: 354-355
itineraries: 23-30; Austin 104; Dallas 36; Houston 238; San Antonio 171
Iwo Jima Memorial and Museum: 231

J
Jackson Hill Park: 285
jazz: 261, 263
Jefferson: 299-302
Jefferson General Store: 300
jellyfish: 319
Jett Building: 75
John E. Conner Museum: 351
Johnson City: 159-162
Jones Center: 108
Judd, Donald: 420
Juneteenth: 81, 263

K
kayaking: see paddling
Kemah Boardwalk: 29, 254
Kenedy Ranch Museum of South Texas: 351
Kennedy, John F.: assassination 38; downtown Dallas sights 38; Kennedy Memorial Plaza 42; Sixth Floor Museum 39
Kennedy Memorial Plaza: 42
Kerrville: 165
Kerrville Folk Festival: 165
The Kimbell Art Museum: 24, 70-73
King Ranch: 27, 349-351
King Ranch Museum: 350
King Ranch Saddle Shop: 350
King Ranch Visitor Center: 350
Kingsville: 348-352
King William Historic District: 23, 175, 180-181
Kirby Nature Trail System: 281
kiteboarding: 355
kites: 358
Knights of Pythias Castle Hall: 75

Kokernot Field: 430
Kreuz Market: 144

L

Lady Bird Johnson Wildflower Center: 106-108, 113
Lady Bird Lake: 111
Laguna Gloria: 108
Laguna Meadows trail: 408
Lajitas: 414-416
Lake Amistad: 209
Lake Arrowhead State Park: 95
Lake Buchanan: 136
Lake Jackson: 327
Lake LBJ: 136
Lake o' the Pines: 301
Lake Sam Rayburn: 285, 287
Lake Tombigbee: 279
Lake Travis: 135
La Lomita Chapel: 227
Lamar Boulevard: 121
Lamar Vergara Environmental Science Center: 215-217
Land Title Building: 75
language: 486
Laredo: 18, 214-221
Laredo Center for the Arts: 215
Laredo Community College: 215-217
Laredo Independent School District: 215-217
La Salle: 332
Last Great Gunfight: 80
Latino Cultural Center: 45
Latinx culture: Cinco de Mayo 49; ethnic identifiers 184; Fiesta San Antonio 189; Mexic-Arte Museum 108; Selena Museum 334
La Villita: 190
La Villita Historic District: 183
L. B. Houston Nature Trail: 47
LGBTQ+ events and sights: Austin 117; Dallas 49; El Paso 377; travel tips 501
libraries: 106, 183
lighthouse: 354
literature: 487
livestock auctions: 450
Livestock Exchange Building: 70
living history museums: 44, 76, 254-255, 460
Llano Estacado: 455
Lockhart: 143-145
Log Cabin Village: 76
Lone Star Hiking Trail: 282
Long Barrack Museum: 176
Long Center for the Performing Arts: 113
Los Ebanos Preserve: 224
Lost Maples State Natural Area: 164
Lost Mine Trail: 407
Lower Pecos region: 209

Lubbock: 438-446
Lubbock Arts Festival: 443
Lubbock Cemetery: 439
Lubbock Lake Landmark: 442
Luckenbach: 153, 165-166
Lufkin: 287-291
lumber industry: general discussion 280; Aldridge Sawmill 285; Lufkin 287; Piney Woods 279; Texas Forestry Museum 288
Lyndon Baines Johnson Library and Museum: 106
Lyndon B. Johnson National Historical Park: 16, 24, 27, 160

M

Mackenzie Park: 442
Magee Beach: 334
Magnolia: 18, 149
Magnolia Market: 146
Magoffin Home State Historic Site: 372
Majestic Theatre: 48
mammals: 474
mammoth fossils: 147
manufacturing sector: 483
Marathon: 416
Mardi Gras: 317
Marfa: 20, 26, 418-432
Marfa Book Store Co.: 422
Marfa Lights: 26, 421
Marine Corps: 231
marine life: 475
Marine Science Institute: 344-346
Market Square: 190
Mayan Ranch: 157
Mayborn Museum Complex: 147-148
Mayfest: 80
McAllen: 227-230
McClendon House: 297
McDonald Observatory: 26, 426
McFaddin-Ward House: 275
McKenna Children's Museum: 205
McKinney: 67-68
McKinney Place Garage: 249
McKittrick Canyon Trail: 387
McLean: 448
McNay Art Museum: 180
Meadows Center Glass-Bottom Boats: 137
Meadows Museum: 44
Memorial Park: 255
Memorial Park Picnic Loop: 256
The Menil Collection: 249-250
mercury mining: 411, 415
Mesquite Championship Rodeo: 46
meteor crater: 391
Mexican Rodeo: 185
Mexic-Arte Museum: 108
Mexico-U.S. border crossings: 216, 408, 500

INDEX

mid-century modern architecture: 246
Midland and Odessa: 19, 388-396
Midpoint Cafe: 27, 449
midtown Houston: 242
midtown San Antonio: 175
Midwestern State University: 94
Miss Hattie's Bordello Museum: 466
missions, San Antonio: 176-178
missions, Spanish: 368
Mission San Juan Capistrano: 177
Missions National Historical Park: 23, 176-178
Mission Trail: 368
Modern Art Museum of Fort Worth: 24, 73
Monahans Sandhills State Park: 393
money: 502
Montrose-Kirby: 243, 249, 258
Moody Gardens: 29, 312
Moody Gardens Ice Land: 318
Moody Mansion: 312
mountain biking: Hill Country State Natural
    Area 158; Palo Duro Canyon State Park 457;
    Pedernales Falls State Park 162; Sabine
    National Forest 286; Sam Houston National
    Forest 282; San Angelo State Park 466
mountains: 385
Mount Cristo: 378
Mount Livermore: 385
movie sets: 119
murals: 67, 419
Museum District: 24, 242, 243
Museum of East Texas: 288
Museum of Fine Arts, Houston: 244
Museum of Natural Science: 29, 243
Museum of Texas Tech University: 441
Museum of the Big Bend: 26, 429
Museum of the Gulf Coast: 278
Museum of the Southwest: 391-393
Museum of Western Art: 165
music: 14; general discussion 487-489; Austin 112,
    116, 117-119, 120; Bayou City Cajun Fest 262;
    border radio stations 210; Buddy Holly Center
    438; Dallas 47-48; El Paso 376, 377; Fort Worth
    78; Hill Country dance halls 153; Houston
    257, 260-262, 263; Kerrville Folk Festival 165;
    Lubbock 443; Luckenbach 165-166; Museum
    of the Gulf Coast 278; San Antonio 187;
    Selena Museum 334; South by Southwest
    120; Texas Folklife Festival 189; Texas outdoor
    musical 451; Van Cliburn International Piano
    Competition 81; see also classical music
Mustang Island: 29, 343-348
Mustang Island State Park: 344
Mustang Island State Park Paddling Trail: 334

N

Nacogdoches: 291-295
NASA Space Center: 15, 19, 24, 29, 252-253
Nasher Sculpture Center: 43
National Butterfly Center: 227
National Center for Children's Illustrated
    Literature: 459
National Cowboy Symposium and Celebration:
    443
National Cowgirl Museum and Hall of Fame: 28,
    74
National Cutting Horse Association: 81
National Multicultural Western Heritage
    Museum: 77
National Museum of the Pacific War: 152
national parks/preserves: Angelina National
    Forest 285-286; Big Bend National Park 11, 401-
    418; Big Thicket National Preserve 279-282;
    Brazoria National Wildlife Refuge 327; Davy
    Crockett National Forest 284-285; Guadalupe
    Mountains National Park 19, 384-388; Padre
    Island National Seashore 12, 343; Sabine
    National Forest 286; Sam Houston National
    Forest 282-284; San Bernard National Wildlife
    Refuge 328
National Ranching Heritage Center: 442
National Senior Pro Rodeo: 451
Native American sights: Alabama-Coushatta
    reservation 279; ancient adobe buildings
    410; Caddo Mounds State Historic Site 292; El
    Paso Museum of Archaeology 374; Franklin
    Mountains State Park 375; Frontier Texas! 459;
    history 479-480; Hueco Tanks State Historic
    Site 375; Lower Pecos region 209; Museum
    of the Big Bend 429; Palo Duro Canyon 457,
    458; Panther Cave 209; San Angelo State Park
    466; Seminole Canyon State Park 208-209;
    Seminole Indian Scout Cemetery 213; Tigua
    Indian Cultural Center 369-372, 373
Natural Bridge Caverns: 205-206
Naval Museum: 314
Neiman Marcus: 24, 50
New Braunfels: 203-207
1904 Train Depot and Museum: 351
North Franklin Peak: 385
North Texas History Center: 67
Nuestra Señora de la Purísima Concepción: 177

O

Oak Lawn: 38, 53
observatories: 426
Ocean Star Offshore Drilling Rig and Museum:
    314
Odessa: 20, 388-396

Odessa Meteor Crater: 391
oil industry: general discussion 483; East Texas
    Oil Museum 296; Ocean Star Offshore Drilling
    Rig and Museum 314; Spindletop-Gladys
    City Boomtown Museum 275; Texas Energy
    Museum 276
Old Collin County Courthouse: 67
Old Fort Bliss Museum: 369
Old Maverick Road: 404
Old Red Museum of Dallas County History and
    Culture: 42
Old Stone Fort Museum: 291
opera: Dallas 48; El Paso Opera 376; Galveston
    317; Houston 261-262
The Orange Show: 25, 253-254
outlet stores, San Marcos: 138

P

paddling: Big Bend National Park 404; Big Thicket
    National Preserve 281; Brazosport 328; Corpus
    Christi 334, 335; Galveston Island State Park
    316; Rio Grande 406; South Padre Island 355
Padre Island National Seashore: 12, 343
Palo Alto Battlefield National Historic Site: 225
Palo Duro Canyon: 456
Palo Duro Canyon State Park: 16, 20, 456
Pan American Coastal Studies Laboratory: 354
Pancho Villa: 377
Panhandle Plains: 433-469; Abilene 458-464;
    Amarillo 446-458; highlights 434; information
    and services 436; Lubbock 438-446; map 435;
    planning tips 20, 436; San Angelo 465-469;
    transportation 437
Panhandle-Plains Historical Museum: 457
Panther Cave: 209
Park Cities: 39
parks, urban: Austin 110-111; Corpus Christi 333;
    Dallas 40, 47; Houston 252, 255; Lubbock 442;
    Lufkin 290; San Antonio 186
Paso del Indio Nature Trail: 215-217
Pawnee Bill's Wild West Show: 70
Pecos: 395
Pedernales Falls State Park: 160
performing arts: Austin 112-113; Chautauqua
    Auditorium 65; Corpus Christi 336; Dallas 47-
    48; El Paso 376; Fort Worth 78; Galveston 317;
    Houston 261-262; Lubbock 443; San Antonio
    186; Texas outdoor musical 451; Wichita Falls
    95
Permian Panthers: 390
Perot Museum of Nature and Science: 24, 28,
    39-40
The Petroleum Museum: 389
phrases, Texan: 485
piano competitions: 81
pictographs: 208-209, 375

pilgrimage, Mount Cristo: 378
Pine Springs: 387
Piney Creek Horse Trail: 284
Piney Woods: 279-302
Pinnacles Trail: 408
Pinto Canyon Road: 423
Pioneer Museum Complex: 152-154
Pitcher Plant Trail: 281
planetariums: 62, 89
planning tips: 18-20
plantation museums: 297, 327
plants: 473-477
plants, dangerous: 502
Pleasure Pier: 29, 308-310
politics: 482
population: 484-486
Port Aransas: 344
Port Arthur: 278-279
Port Isabel Lighthouse: 354
La Posada Hotel: 215
POW art: 419
Prada Marfa: 421
Prairie Dog Town: 442
preserves: Brownsville 224; Enchanted Rock State
    Natural Area 163; Fort Worth Nature Center
    and Refuge 75-76; Fossil Rim Wildlife Center
    92; Hill Country State Natural Area 158; Hugh
    Ramsey Nature Park 232; Lost Maples State
    Natural Area 164; McAllen 227-228; Quintana
    Beach County Park 328; River Bend Nature
    Center 95; see also national parks/preserves;
    state parks
presidential sights: George Bush Presidential
    Library and Museum 141; George W. Bush
    Childhood Home 391; George W. Bush
    Presidential Center 39-40; Lady Bird Johnson
    Wildflower Center 108; Lyndon Baines
    Johnson Library and Museum 106; Lyndon
    B. Johnson National Historical Park 160;
    Presidential Museum and Leadership Library
    389
Presidio: 414
Presidio County Courthouse: 422
Presidio La Bahia: 182
Pro Wrestling Hall of Fame and Museum: 94
public transportation: 494

QR

Quinta Mazatlan: 227
Quintana Beach County Park: 328
railroad sights: The Atalanta 300; Grapevine
    Vintage Railroad 70; Hill Country Flyer 108;
    1904 Train Depot and Museum 351; The
    Railroad Museum 314; Railway Museum of
    San Angelo 466; Texas State Railroad 291;
    Trains at NorthPark 49; Wichita Falls Railroad

Museum 94
Rainey Street: 113
ranching: American Quarter Horse Heritage
    Center & Museum 448-449; Crawford-Smith
    Ranch 411; Haley Library and History Center
    391; Kenedy Ranch Museum of South Texas
    351; King Ranch 349; National Ranching
    Heritage Center 442
Ratcliff Lake Recreation Area: 284
reading, suggested: 503-504
Reconstruction period: 481
recreation: 495-497
Red River Rodeo: 95
Red River Street: 117
Red Steagall Cowboy Gathering and Western
    Swing Festival: 81
religion: 485
religious events: 378
reptiles: 476
Republic of Texas: 480
Republic of the Rio Grande Museum: 215
Resaca de la Palma State Park: 224
Rice Student Center: 250
Rice University: 250
Rienzi: 250
Rio Grande: 406
Rio Grande Valley: 222-223
Rio Grande Village: 404, 417
Rio Grande Village Nature Trail: 408
Rio Pride Orchards: 232
River Bend Nature Center: 95
River Legacy Living Science Center: 62
River Road: 411, 414
River Walk: 23, 175, 178, 188
rock art, ancient: 209
rock climbing: 163
rodeos: Bandera 157; Dallas 46; Fort Worth Stock
    Show and Rodeo 80; Fort Worth Stockyards
    National Historic District 70; Mexican Rodeo
    185; National Senior Pro Rodeo 451; Red River
    Rodeo 95; San Antonio Stock Show and Rodeo
    189; Southwestern International Livestock
    Show and Rodeo 378; Star of Texas Fair and
    Rodeo 120; world's first 395
Rogers, Will: 74
roses: 295-297
Ross Maxwell Scenic Drive: 404
Rothko Chapel: 250
Round Rock Express: 110
Route 66: 20, 27, 448-449
Royal Road: 374

S
Sabal Palm Sanctuary: 224
Sabinal Canyon: 163
Sabine National Forest: 286-287

Sabine Pass Battleground State Historic Site: 278
Sacred Heart Church: 211
safety: 319, 501-502
Saint Arnold Brewing Company: 248
St. Patrick's Day River Parade: 189
Sam Houston National Forest: 282-284
Sam Houston Sanders Corps of Cadets Center:
    141
San Agustin Cathedral: 215
San Agustin Plaza: 215
San Angelo: 20, 465-469
San Angelo Museum of Fine Arts: 465-466
San Angelo State Park: 466
San Antonio and South Texas: 23, 167-233; Del
    Rio 208-214; highlights 168; information
    and services 170; Laredo 214-221; maps 169;
    planning tips 18, 170; Rio Grande Valley 222-
    223; San Antonio 172-207; transportation
    170-172
San Antonio Botanical Garden: 186
San Antonio Central Library: 183
San Antonio Charro Association: 185
San Antonio Children's Museum: The DoSeum:
    185
San Antonio Conservation Society: 180-181
San Antonio de la Espada: 177
San Antonio de Valero: 177
San Antonio Missions National Historical Park:
    27, 176-178
San Antonio Missions Trail: 176
San Antonio Museum of Art: 180
San Antonio River Walk: 178
San Antonio sound: 187
San Antonio Spurs: 185
San Antonio Zoo: 184
San Bernard National Wildlife Refuge: 328
sand castle competition: 318
sand dunes: 393
San Elizario: 368
San Felipe de Austin State Historic Site: 182
San Felipe Springs: 211-213
San Fernando Cathedral: 27, 181
San Jacinto Battleground State Historic Site: 13,
    27, 254
San Jacinto Museum of History: 254
San José: 177
San Jose Island: 344
San Marcos: 137-140
San Marcos River: 137
Santa Ana National Wildlife Refuge: 228
Santa Elena Canyon: 26, 406
Sauceda historic district: 411
Scarlett O'Hardy's Gone with the Wind Museum:
    300-301
scenic drives: best bets 30; Big Bend National
    Park 404; Big Bend Ranch State Park 411; Hill

Country canyon communities 164; Pinto Canyon Road 423; River Road 414; Route 66 448-449; South Padre Island 355; Woodward Ranch 430

Schlitterbahn Waterpark (Galveston): 29, 310

Schlitterbahn Waterpark (New Braunfels): 205

science museums: The Center for the Arts & Sciences 327; Corpus Christi Museum of Science and History 333; Discovery Science Place 298; Don Harrington Discovery Center 449-450; Fort Worth Museum of Science and History 73-74; Hill Country Science Mill 160; Houston Museum of Natural Science 243-244; Lamar Vergara Environmental Science Center 215-217; Marine Science Institute 344-346; Pan American Coastal Studies Laboratory 354; Perot Museum of Nature and Science 39-40; River Legacy Living Science Center 62; Witte Museum 183

sculpture: Galveston Tree Sculptures Tour 312; Laguna Gloria 108; Nasher Sculpture Center 43

Sea Center Texas: 327

season, travel tips by: 21

sea turtles: 337, 343, 353

Seawall Boulevard: 319, 322

SeaWorld of Texas: 28, 181

Selena Museum: 334

Seminole Canyon State Park: 208-209

senior travelers: 501

Seymour Lieberman Exercise Trail: 255

Shamrock: 448

shell collecting: 328

shrubs: 473-474

Sid Richardson Museum: 77

Silver Spur Guest Ranch: 157

Six Flags Fiesta Texas Amusement Park: 28, 183-184

Six Flags Hurricane Harbor: 28, 62

Six Flags Over Texas: 28, 60

6th Street: 113, 118, 121

Sixth Floor Museum: 24, 38, 39

Smitty's Market: 145

snorkeling: 355

soccer: 47, 110

Socorro: 368

Sophienburg Museum: 206

South Austin: 118

South by Southwest: 120

South Congress Avenue: 24, 120

South Dallas Cultural Center: 42

Southern cooking: 283, 499

Southfork Ranch: 43-44

South Padre Island: 19, 352-361

South Rim trek: 408

Southside District: 80

South Texas: see San Antonio and South Texas

Southwestern International Livestock Show and Rodeo: 378

Spanish Governor's Palace: 27, 181

spectator sports: Austin 109-110; Babe Didrikson Zaharias Museum 276; Dallas 46-47, 60; El Paso 379; Houston 256-257; Pro Wrestling Hall of Fame and Museum 94; San Antonio 185; Texas Sports Hall of Fame 149

SPI Kitefest: 358

Spindletop-Gladys City Boomtown Museum: 275

spring break: 354, 358

springs: Balmorhea State Park 427; Barton Springs Pool 110; Fort Clark Springs 213; Lubbock Lake Landmark 442; San Felipe 208, 211-213

spring travel: 21

stand-up paddleboarding: 355

stargazing: 163

Star of Texas Fair and Rodeo: 120

State Capitol: 24, 27, 29, 102-104

State Fair of Texas: 49

statehood: 480

state parks: general discussion 495-496; Abilene State Park 460; Balmorhea State Park 426-427; Bentsen-Rio Grande Valley State Park 228; Big Bend Ranch State Park 411; Caddo Lake State Park 301; Davis Mountains State Park 427; Dinosaur Valley State Park 92; Franklin Mountains State Park 375; Galveston Island State Park 316; Garner State Park 163; Lake Arrowhead State Park 95; Monahans Sandhills State Park 393; Mustang Island State Park 344; Palo Duro Canyon State Park 16, 456-457; Pedernales Falls State Park 160; Resaca de la Palma State Park 224; San Angelo State Park 466; Seminole Canyon State Park 208-209

stations, border radio: 210

Stephen F. Austin Experimental Forest: 294

Stephen F. Austin State University: 294

Sterne-Hoya House: 291

Steves Homestead: 181

Stewart Beach: 314

Stillman House Museum: 222

Stock Show and Rodeo: 189

Stockyards Championship Rodeo: 70

Stockyards' daily cattle drives: 70, 71

Stockyards District: 69, 70, 78, 81

Stockyards Museum: 70

Stockyards Visitor Center: 70

The Strand: 308, 318, 324

summer travel: 21

Sun Bowl Parade: 378

Sundance Square: 24, 69, 75, 80, 81

Sundew Trail: 281

surfing: Galveston 316; San Jose Island 344; South Padre Island 355; Texas State Surfing Championship 358

Surfside Beach: 328
suspension bridge, Waco: 148

T

Tarrant County Courthouse: 75
Taste of Dallas: 49
temperatures: 21, 477-478
Terlingua: 26, 411-414
Terlingua Cemetery: 411
Terlingua Trading Company: 412
Texas A&M University: 141
Texas Civil War Museum: 77
Texas Cowboy Hall of Fame: 77
Texas Discovery Gardens: 40
Texas Energy Museum: 276
Texas Folklife Festival: 189
Texas Forestry Museum: 288
Texas Home and Garden Show: 262
Texas Old Route 66 Museum: 27, 448
Texas outdoor musical: 451
Texas Ranger Hall of Fame and Museum: 148-149
Texas Rangers: 28, 47
Texas Revolution: 182, 254
Texas Seaport Museum: 310
Texas Sports Hall of Fame: 149
Texas Stars: 110
Texas State Aquarium: 25, 29, 330-332
Texas State Capitol: 102-104
Texas State Railroad: 291
Texas State Surfing Championship: 358
Tex-Mex cuisine: 499
Tigua Indian Cultural Center: 369-372, 373
toll roads: 494
top experiences: 10-17; The Alamo 17, 175; Big
     Bend National Park 401; cowboys 14, 70, 349;
     cuisine 15, 25, 283; Fort Worth Stockyards
     National Historic District 70; historic sights 13,
     254; King Ranch 349-351; music 14, 117; NASA
     Space Center 15, 252; Padre Island National
     Seashore 12, 343; Palo Duro Canyon State Park
     16, 455, 456-457; presidential sights 16, 39,
     160; Rio Grande 11, 401
tornadoes: 478
tourist industry: 483
tourist information: 502
Town Lake Metropolitan Park: 111
Trail Between the Lakes: 287
Trains at NorthPark: 49
train sights: *see* railroad sights
train travel: 493
transportation: 21-22, 492-494
travel tips: 500-501
trees: 473-474
Trinity River: 63
Tri-State Fair: 451
tubing: Guadalupe River 205; Pedernales Falls

State Park 162; San Marcos River 137
tunnels, Houston downtown: 248
Turkey Creek Trail: 281
twentieth century history: 481
Tyler: 295-299
Tyler Museum of Art: 297

UV

U-Drop Inn and Conoco Station: 27, 448
universities: Stephen F. Austin State University
     294; Texas A&M University 141; Texas Tech
     University 438, 441; University of North
     Texas 89; University of Texas at Arlington
     62; University of Texas at Austin 18, 104, 113;
     University of Texas at El Paso 379
University of Texas sports: 109
Uptown and Oak Lawn: 38
uptown Houston: 243, 258
U.S.-Mexican War: 225
USS *Lexington* Museum: 330-332
Val Verde County Courthouse: 211
Van Cliburn International Piano Competition: 81
vaqueros: 224
Varner-Hogg Plantation: 327
The Veloway: 111
Vereins Kirche Museum: 154
Vietnamese culture: 249
Villa Antigua Border Heritage Museum: 215
Volente Beach: 135

WXYZ

Waco: 145-151
Waco Mammoth National Monument: 147
Waco Suspension Bridge: 148
walking/biking trails: Concho River Walk 466;
     Dallas 47; Houston 255; Hugh Ramsey Nature
     Park 232; San Antonio River Walk 178
Warehouse District: 115, 118
Washington's Birthday Celebration Museum: 215
waterfalls: 94, 162
water parks: 62, 205, 310
Water Street Seafood Co.: 29, 338
Water Wall: 252
Waxahachie: 65-67
weather: 21, 477-478, 501
Wells Fargo Plaza: 249
West End District: 24, 33, 38
Western culture: Amarillo Livestock Auction 450;
     American Quarter Horse Heritage Center
     & Museum 448; Amon Carter Museum 73;
     Bandera 157; Fort Worth Stockyards National
     Historic District 70; Frontier Times Museum
     158; Haley Library and History Center 391;
     King Ranch 349-351; Last Great Gunfight 80;
     Museum of Western Art 165; National Cowboy

Symposium and Celebration 443; National Cowgirl Museum and Hall of Fame 74; Red Steagall Cowboy Gathering and Western Swing Festival 81; Sid Richardson Museum 77; Texas Cowboy Hall of Fame 77; Texas Ranger Hall of Fame and Museum 148-149; as a top experience 14; and vaqueros 224; Will Rogers Memorial Center 74; see also rodeos
Western Currency Facility Tour and Visitor Center: 77
Western wear: Abilene 462; Austin 122; Dallas 50; El Paso 378; Fort Worth 81; Lubbock 443; National Senior Pro Rodeo 451; San Angelo 467; San Antonio 191
West Texas: see El Paso and West Texas
West University: 243, 260
Whitehead Memorial Museum: 210, 211
White Rock Creek Greenbelt: 47
white-water rafting: 406
Wichita Falls: 94-96
Wichita Falls Museum of Art at Midwestern State University: 94
Wichita Falls Railroad Museum: 94
Wichita Falls Waterfall: 94

wildflowers: 106-108, 113, 474
wildlife viewing: dolphins 356; Fort Worth Nature Center and Refuge 75-76; Fossil Rim Wildlife Center 92; safety tips 502; sea turtles 343, 353, 357; see also bird-watching
Will Rogers Memorial Center: 74
wind power: 439-441
windsurfing: 344, 355
The Window: 406, 407
winter travel: 21
Witte Museum: 183
Wonder World: 138
Woodward Ranch: 430
World War II sights: 152, 231
wrestling: 94
Ysleta: 368
ZestFest: 49
Zilker Botanical Gardens: 111
Zilker Park: 111
zoos: Abilene Zoo 460; Caldwell Zoo 297; Cameron Park Zoo 148; Dallas Zoo 45; Ellen Trout Zoo 288; El Paso Zoo 372; Exotic Resort Zoo 160; Fort Worth Zoo 74; Gladys Porter Zoo 225; Houston Zoo 246; San Antonio Zoo 184

List of Maps

Front Map
Texas: 4–5

Discover Texas
chapter divisions map: 19

Dallas and Fort Worth
Dallas and Fort Worth: 34
Downtown Dallas: 37
Vicinity of Dallas and Fort Worth: 61
Fort Worth: 69

Austin and the Hill Country
Austin and the Hill Country: 100
Austin: 103
Downtown Austin: 105

San Antonio and South Texas
San Antonio and South Texas: 169
San Antonio: 173
Downtown San Antonio: 174
Laredo: 216
Brownsville: 223

Houston and East Texas
Houston and East Texas: 237
Houston: 240–241

The Gulf Coast
The Gulf Coast: 306–307
Galveston: 309
Downtown Galveston: 310
Corpus Christi: 331

El Paso and West Texas
El Paso and West Texas: 365
El Paso: 370–371

Big Bend Region
Big Bend Region: 399
Big Bend National Park: 402

Panhandle Plains
Panhandle Plains: 435
Lubbock: 439
Amarillo: 447

Photo Credits

ROAD TRIPS AND DRIVE & HIKE GUIDES

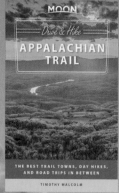

MOON

Drive & Hike

APPALACHIAN TRAIL

THE BEST TRAIL TOWNS, DAY HIKES,
AND ROAD TRIPS IN BETWEEN

TIMOTHY MALCOLM

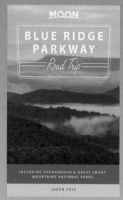

MOON

BLUE RIDGE PARKWAY

Road Trip

INCLUDING SHENANDOAH & GREAT SMOKY
MOUNTAINS NATIONAL PARKS

JASON FRYE

MOON

CALIFORNIA

Road Trip

SAN FRANCISCO, YOSEMITE, LAS VEGAS,
GRAND CANYON, LOS ANGELES,
& THE PACIFIC COAST HIGHWAY

STUART THORNTON

MOON

NASHVILLE TO NEW ORLEANS

Road Trip

NATCHEZ TRACE PARKWAY • MEMPHIS •
TUPELO • MISSISSIPPI BLUES TRAIL

MARGARET LITTMAN

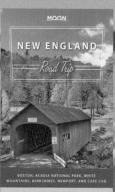

MOON

NEW ENGLAND

Road Trip

BOSTON, ACADIA NATIONAL PARK, WHITE
MOUNTAINS, BERKSHIRES, NEWPORT, AND CAPE COD

JEN ROSE SMITH

MOON

NORTHERN CALIFORNIA

Road Trips

DRIVES ALONG THE COAST, REDWOODS, AND MOUNTAINS
WITH THE BEST STOPS ALONG THE WAY

STUART THORNTON & KAYLA ANDERSON

MOON

OREGON TRAIL

Road Trip

HISTORIC SITES, SMALL TOWNS, AND
SCENIC LANDSCAPES ALONG THE LEGENDARY
WESTWARD ROUTE

KATRINA EMERY

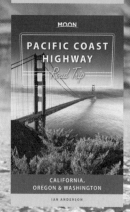

MOON

PACIFIC COAST HIGHWAY

Road Trip

CALIFORNIA,
OREGON & WASHINGTON

IAN ANDERSON

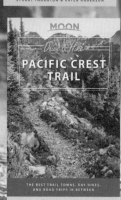

MOON

Drive & Hike

PACIFIC CREST TRAIL

THE BEST TRAIL TOWNS, DAY HIKES,
AND ROAD TRIPS IN BETWEEN

CAROLINE HINCHLIFF

MOON.COM | ROADTRIPUSA.COM

MOON

PACIFIC NORTHWEST
Road Trip

SEATTLE, VANCOUVER, VICTORIA,
THE OLYMPIC PENINSULA, PORTLAND,
THE OREGON COAST & MOUNT RAINIER

ALLISON WILLIAMS

MOON

ROUTE 66
Road Trip

JESSICA DUNHAM

MOON

SOUTH FLORIDA & THE KEYS
Road Trip

WITH MIAMI, WALT DISNEY WORLD, TAMPA &
THE EVERGLADES

JASON FERGUSON

MOON

SOUTHERN CALIFORNIA
Road Trips

DRIVES ALONG THE BEACHES, MOUNTAINS, AND DESERTS
WITH THE BEST STOPS ALONG THE WAY

IAN ANDERSON

MOON

SOUTHWEST
Road Trip

LAS VEGAS, ZION & BRYCE, MONUMENT VALLEY,
SANTA FE & TAOS, AND THE GRAND CANYON

TIM HULL

MOON

VANCOUVER & CANADIAN ROCKIES
Road Trip

VICTORIA, BANFF, JASPER, CALGARY,
THE OKANAGAN, WHISTLER &
THE SEA-TO-SKY HIGHWAY

CAROLYN B. HELLER

MOON

YELLOWSTONE TO GLACIER NATIONAL PARK
Road Trip

JACKSON HOLE, CODY, THE GRAND TETONS
& THE ROCKY MOUNTAIN FRONT

CARTER G. WALKER

MOON

the OPEN ROAD
50 BEST ROAD TRIPS in the USA

From Weekend Getaways
to Cross-Country Adventures

JESSICA DUNHAM

MOON

Road Trip USA
25TH ANNIVERSARY EDITION

CROSS-COUNTRY ADVENTURES ON
AMERICA'S TWO-LANE HIGHWAYS

Jamie Jensen

ACADIA
NATIONAL PARK

**ARCHES &
CANYONLANDS**
NATIONAL PARKS

BANFF
NATIONAL
PARK

**HIKE·CAMP
SEE WILDLIFE**

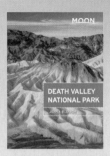

**DEATH VALLEY
NATIONAL PARK**

GLACIER
NATIONAL PARK

**HIKING · CAMPING
LAKES & PEAKS**

**GRAND
CANYON**

**HIKE·CAMP
RAFT THE
COLORADO RIVER**

**GREAT SMOKY
MOUNTAINS**
NATIONAL PARK

**HIKING · CAMPING
SCENIC DRIVES**

**JOSHUA TREE
& PALM SPRINGS**

**MOUNT RUSHMORE
& THE BLACK HILLS**

**ROCKY
MOUNTAIN**
NATIONAL PARK

**HIKE·CAMP
SEE WILDLIFE**

**SEQUOIA &
KINGS CANYON**

**HIKE·CAMP
SEE REDWOODS**

**YELLOWSTONE
& GRAND TETON**

**HIKE, CAMP,
SEE WILDLIFE**

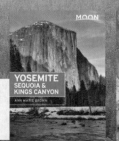

YOSEMITE
SEQUOIA &
KINGS CANYON

**ZION &
BRYCE**

In these books:

- Full coverage of gateway cities and towns
- Itineraries from one day to multiple weeks
- Advice on where to stay (or camp) in and around the parks

Get inspired for your next adventure

Follow **@moonguides** on Instagram or subscribe to our newsletter at **moon.com**

MAP SYMBOLS

═══════	Expressway	○	City/Town	ⓘ	Information Center	♠	Park
═══════	Primary Road	◉	State Capital	Ⓟ	Parking Area	⚲	Golf Course
═══════	Secondary Road	⊛	National Capital	⛪	Church	✛	Unique Feature
─ ─ ─ ─	Unpaved Road	✪	Highlight	☘	Winery/Vineyard	☟	Waterfall
··········	Trail	★	Point of Interest	TH	Trailhead	∧	Camping
··········	Ferry	•	Accommodation	Ⓡ	Train Station	▲	Mountain
┅┅┅┅┅	Railroad	▼	Restaurant/Bar	✈	Airport	⛷	Ski Area
▓▓▓▓	Pedestrian Walkway	■	Other Location	✗	Airfield	◎	Glacier
▭▭▭▭	Stairs						

CONVERSION TABLES

°C = (°F - 32) / 1.8
°F = (°C x 1.8) + 32
1 inch = 2.54 centimeters (cm)
1 foot = 0.304 meters (m)
1 yard = 0.914 meters
1 mile = 1.6093 kilometers (km)
1 km = 0.6214 miles
1 fathom = 1.8288 m
1 chain = 20.1168 m
1 furlong = 201.168 m
1 acre = 0.4047 hectares
1 sq km = 100 hectares
1 sq mile = 2.59 square km
1 ounce = 28.35 grams
1 pound = 0.4536 kilograms
1 short ton = 0.90718 metric ton
1 short ton = 2,000 pounds
1 long ton = 1.016 metric tons
1 long ton = 2,240 pounds
1 metric ton = 1,000 kilograms
1 quart = 0.94635 liters
1 US gallon = 3.7854 liters
1 Imperial gallon = 4.5459 liters
1 nautical mile = 1.852 km

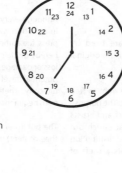

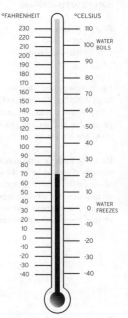

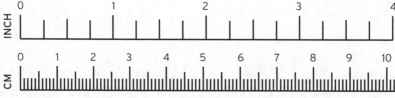

MOON TEXAS
Avalon Travel
Hachette Book Group
1700 Fourth Street
Berkeley, CA 94710, USA
www.moon.com

Editor: Rachael Sablik
Acquiring Editor: Nikki Ioakimedes
Series Manager: Kathryn Ettinger
Copy Editor: Christopher Church
Graphics and Production Coordinator:
    Suzanne Albertson
Cover Design: Faceout Studios, Charles Brock
Moon Logo: Tim McGrath
Map Editor: Albert Angulo
Cartographer: Andrew Dolan
Indexer: Rachel Kuhn

ISBN-13: 9781640499430

Printing History
1st Edition — 1990
10th Edition — January 2021
5 4 3 2 1

Front cover photo: Big Bend National Park
    © George H.H. Huey / Alamy Stock Photo
Back cover photo: The Texas Capitol
    © Andy Rhodes

Printed in China by RR Donnelley